USING INTERNATIONAL LAW IN DOMESTIC COURTS

Using International Law in Domestic Courts

SHAHEED FATIMA
LLB (Hons) (Glasgow), BCL (Oxon), LLM (Harvard)
Barrister, Blackstone Chambers
Lecturer in Law, Pembroke College, Oxford

•HART•
PUBLISHING
OXFORD AND PORTLAND, OREGON
2005

Published in North America (US and Canada) by
Hart Publishing
c/o International Specialized Book Services
920 NE 58th Avenue, Suite 300
Portland, OR 97213-3786
USA
Tel: +1 503 287 3093 or toll-free: (1) 800 944 6190
Fax: +1 503 280 8832
E-mail: orders@isbs.com
Web Site: www.isbs.com

Hart Publishing, Salters Boatyard, Folly Bridge, Abingdon Rd, Oxford, OX1 4LB
Telephone: +44 (0)1865 245533 Fax: +44 (0) 1865 794882
email: mail@hartpub.co.uk
WEBSITE: http//:www.hartpub.co.uk

British Library Cataloguing in Publication Data
Data Available

ISBN 1-84113-515-1 (hardback)

Typeset by Hope Services in Minion 10/12.5 pt
Printed and bound in Great Britain by
TJ International, Padstow, Cornwall

For Abu and Ami

Contents

PART II: USING INCORPORATING STATUTES AND INCORPORATED TREATIES

Foreword

In his presidential address to the Holdsworth Club of the University of Birmingham in 1972, the late Lord Hailsham observed that international law 'has always been a somewhat sickly patient.' He was no doubt referring to the well-known difficulty of enforcing the rules of international law against states which fail to comply with them, or are said to do so. There was indeed a time when international law was seen as the esoteric preserve of a handful of very distinguished professors and Foreign Office mandarins, but not something which impinged on the professional lives of ordinary practitioners and national courts.

Times have changed. To an extent almost unimaginable even thirty years ago, national courts in this and other countries are called upon to consider and resolve issues turning on the correct understanding and application of international law, not on an occasional basis, now and then, but routinely, and often in cases of great importance. This calls for special, and in many cases new, skills on the part of advocates who present cases and judges who decide them.

This book does not purport to be a textbook of international law. Such works exist, and are indispensable. This book does something different. It identifies the main sources of international law binding on the United Kingdom, and tells the searcher where to find them. It summarises the principles governing the interpretation of treaties. It shows, with a wealth of citations, mostly of recent, mostly of English, authority how our courts have up to now responded to the challenges which have come before them.

Armed with this interesting, timely and well-researched book, both Bar and Bench can move with greater confidence into what, for many, remains unfamiliar territory. Shaheed Fatima deserves the thanks of us all.

Tom Bingham.

Preface

> '[Their Lordships] remember the words of M. Portalis, one of Napoleon's commissioners, who said: "We have guarded against the dangerous ambition of wishing to regulate and to foresee everything . . . A new question springs up. Then how is it to be decided? To this question it is replied that the office of the law is to fix by enlarged rules, the general maxims of right and wrong, to establish firm principles fruitful in consequences, and not to descend to the detail of all questions which may arise upon each particular topic." (Quoted by Halsbury LC in Halsbury's Laws of England, Introduction, p.ccxi)'
>
> (*In Piracy Jure Gentium* [1934] AC 586 (PC), 600C–E (Viscount Sankey LC))

This is primarily a reference book for practitioners, setting out the key ways in which courts in the United Kingdom deal with the role and issues of international law in domestic law. Since the influence of international law is widely, and increasingly, felt, these issues cut across many areas of law. Practitioners are more than ever before likely to encounter questions such as: What is the status of an international treaty in domestic law? How may it form part of domestic law? What is the relevance and effect of its incorporation? How should international treaties be interpreted? What is the role of unincorporated treaties and rules of customary international law in domestic law and how can they be used?

Chapters 2–13 address these, and other, questions. Commentary has been kept to a minimum and the emphasis is on describing the law as it is. I have classified the material, in the hope that this will enable quick and easy reference of the key authorities (and illustrations) on a given point. Chapter 1 identifies, by subject matter, international instruments in diverse areas and provides information on, for example, where they can be found, the number of parties to the treaty and the date on which the United Kingdom ratified the treaty. Thus the presentation and form of the book has been largely driven by its purpose—to enable practitioners to use and apply international law within the framework of domestic law.

I have been fortunate in the support and guidance which I have had from friends and colleagues in preparing this book. In particular, from the inception of this book until its completion, I have had extraordinary encouragement, support, and mentorship from Michael Fordham. His has been the guiding hand and voice of reason at every single stage. Beyond gratitude, I am indebted to him. I am grateful also to Professor Christopher Greenwood QC, John Howell QC and Lord Lester of Herne Hill QC (for their helpful comments on drafts of the book); to Martin Smith, senior clerk (for supporting the project from the start and facilitating time away from practice); Scott Murphy, Daryl Hughes, James Clarke, Tom Winder and Rob Price, clerks (for their patient and efficient assistance in the collection of materials); Elaine Wintle, librarian and everyone else at Blackstone Chambers. Especial thanks go to my publisher, Richard Hart.

This preface would be entirely incomplete absent the name of Professor Peter Birks, my beloved mentor and friend, who died in July 2004. His remembrance will burn ever bright.

Most of all, to my family: my parents, to whom this book is dedicated with my love, my sisters (Hijab, Irum, Amber and Gulshan) and, especially, my husband, my anchor, Nomi: thank you—for everything.

London
30 June 2005

Table of Cases

European Court of Justice and Court of First Instance

ICSID Arbitration Tribunal

Inter-American Commission on Human Rights

International Court of Justice

United Nations Human Rights Committee

United States

Table of Statutes and Statutory Instruments

Anguilla

Australia

Bahamas

Table of International Treaties and Conventions

PART I

Sourcing International Law

1

International Law in Domestic Practice Areas

(1) Introduction

1.1. **The purpose of this Chapter is provide (a) an overview of the key sources of international law [§ 1.2–1.6]; and (b) illustrative examples of treaties and instruments (organised by subject-matter) by which the United Kingdom is bound on the international plane [§ 1.7–1.146].**

(2) Sources: Overview

1.2. **Key international law texts:**

- Brownlie, *Principles of Public International Law* (2003)
- Jennings and Watts (ed), *Oppenheim's International Law* (1996)
- Shaw, *International Law* (2003)

1.3. **Key international law journals:**

- AJIL – American Journal of International Law
- BYIL – British Yearbook of International Law
- ICLQ – International and Comparative Law Quarterly
- LMCLQ – Lloyd's Maritime and Comparative Law Quarterly

1.4. **Key international law reports:**

- ICJ Reports (International Court of Justice case law)
- ILR – International Law Reports

1.5. **Key treaty sources:**

- UNTS – the United Nations Treaty Series[1]
- ETS – the European Treaty Series (and, since 2004, the CETS – the Council of Europe Treaty Series)[2]
- UKTS – the United Kingdom Treaty Series[3]
- ILM – International Legal Materials
- CTS – Consolidated Treaty Series (for older treaties)
- BFSP – British and Foreign State Papers (for older treaties; up to 1968)
- Bowman and Harris, *Multilateral Treaties: Index and Current Status,* (1984; eleventh cumulative supplement 1994)

1.6. **Key websites:**

- United Nations Treaty Database: http://untreaty.un.org/ENGLISH/bible/englishinternetbible/bible.asp
- Electronic Information System for International Law: http://www.eisil.org/
- Fletcher-Ginn Multi-lateral Project: http://fletcher.tufts.edu/multilaterals.html
- International Committee of the Red Cross Database: http://www.icrc.org/web/eng/siteeng0.nsf/iwpList2/Info_resources:IHL_databases
- Council of Europe Treaties: http://conventions.coe.int/Treaty/Commun/ListeTraites.asp?CM=8&CL=ENG
- International Labour Organisation Treaties: http://www.ilo.org/ilolex/english/index.htm
- Maritime Treaties: http://www.comitemaritime.org/ratific/ratitle.html
- Environmental Law treaties: http://www.ecolex.org/ecolex/index.php

(3) International Law in Practice Areas

1.7. **[§§ 1.11–1.146] provides an illustrative list of international instruments in diverse practice areas. Each area has been ordered chronologically by the date on which the instrument was concluded. The United Kingdom is legally bound, in international law, by all of these instruments. Many of the instruments are directly**

[1] http://untreaty.un.org/.

[2] http://conventions.coe.int/treaty/EN/cadreprincipal.htm.

[3] http://www.fco.gov.uk/servlet/Front?pagename=OpenMarket/Xcelerate/ShowPage&c=Page&cid=1007029396014.

relevant in domestic law; having been incorporated into, or given effect in, domestic law. The information set out at [§§ 1.11–1.146] is intended to give a snapshot outline based on sources (many of them secondary) that I have been able to trace. Often this has meant reliance on two key sources: the Internet and Bowman and Harris, *Multilateral Treaties: Index and Current Status* (1984; updated to 1994) ('B&H'[4])[§ 1.5].

1.8. **The 'Parties' entry for the instruments at [§§ 1.11–1.146] shows the number of parties to the treaty as at either (a) the date to which the source indicates that it has been updated, or (b) the date of the last depositary action, ie the most recent signature/ratification/accession recorded by the depositary.**

1.9. **The 'UK' entry for the instruments at [§§ 1.11–1.146] represents the date on which the United Kingdom became legally bound as a matter of international law by the duties and obligations in the relevant instrument. This may have been by ratification ('R') or accession ('A') [§ 2.6]. In some instances the date on which the instrument entered into force for the United Kingdom has also been given.**

1.10. **Whilst I have included references to sources wherever possible, the status of multi-lateral treaties does not stand still. Thus, the information at [§§ 1.11–1.146] is no substitute for verifying the accuracy of the information in any individual case.**

A. Aviation Law

1.11. **International Convention for the Unification of Certain Rules Relating to International Carriage by Air (as amended) ('the Warsaw Convention'):**

- **Concluded/Entry into Force:** 12.10.29/13.2.33
- **Location:** Scheduled to the Carriage by Air Act 1961; UKTS 11 (1933), Cmd 4284; http://www.jus.uio.no/lm/air.carriage.warsaw.convention.1929/doc.html
- **Parties:** 151 (as at 30.6.03[5])
- **UK:** 14.2.33 (R; see fn 5)
- **Domestic status:** Given force of law by the Carriage by Air Act 1961
- **Reading:** Goldhirsch, *The Warsaw Convention annotated: a legal handbook*, (2000)

1.12. **Convention on International Civil Aviation (as amended) ('the Chicago Convention'):**

- **Concluded/ Entry into Force:** 7.12.44/4.4.47
- **Location**: UKTS 8 (1953), Cmd 8742; http://www.icao.int/icaonet/dcs/7300_8ed.pdf
- **Parties:** 188 (as at 21.5.02[6])

[4] These references are to the 1994 supplement unless otherwise stated.
[5] http://www.icao.int/icao/en/leb/wc-hp. htm.
[6] http://www.icao.int/icao/en/leb/chicago. htm.

- **UK:** 1.3.47 (R; see fn 6)
- **Domestic status:** Orders in Council which are "requisite or expedient" for carrying out the Chicago Convention may be made: Civil Aviation Act 1982, section 60.

1.13. **Convention on Offences and Certain Other Acts Committed on Board Aircraft ('the Tokyo Convention '):**
- **Concluded/Entry into Force:** 14.9.63/ 4.12.69
- **Location:** UKTS 126 (1969), Cmnd 4230; http://www.unodc.org/unodc/ terrorism_convention_aircraft.html
- **Parties:** 179 (as at 12.4.05[7])
- **UK:** 29.11.68 (R; see fn 7)
- **Domestic status:** Given effect by the Civil Aviation Act 1982

1.14. **Convention for the Suppression of Unlawful Seizure of Aircraft ('the Hague Convention'):**
- **Concluded/Entry into Force:** 16.12.70/ 4.10.71
- **Location:** UKTS 39 (1972), Cmnd 4956; http://www.unodc.org/unodc/en/terrorism_convention_aircraft_seizure.html
- **Parties:** 178 (as at 23.9.04[8])
- **UK:** 22.12.71 (R; see fn 8)
- **Domestic status:** Implemented by the Aviation Security Act 1982

1.15. **Convention for the Suppression of Unlawful Acts Against the Safety of Civil Aviation ('the Montreal Convention') (and Protocol):**
- **Concluded/Entry into Force:** 23.9.71/ 26.1.73
- **Location:** UKTS 10 (1974), Cmnd 5524 http://www.unodc.org/unodc/terrorism_convention_civil_aviation.html
- **Parties:** 180 (as at 19.4.04[9])
- **UK:** 25.10.73 (R; see fn 9)
- **Domestic status:** Implemented by the Aviation Security Act 1982

1.16. **Convention for the Unification of Certain Rules for International Carriage by Air ('the Montreal Convention'):**
- **Concluded/Entry into Force:** 28.5.99/ 4.11.03
- **Location:** UKTS 44 (2004), Cm 6369; http://www.fco.gov.uk/Files/kfile/990194_Cm%206369.pdf
- **Parties:** 65 (as at 1.6.05[10])
- **UK:** 29.4.04 (R; see fn 10)
- **Domestic status:** Given force of law by the Carriage by Air Act 1961.

B. Commercial Law and Intellectual Property Law

1.17. **Paris Convention for the Protection of Industrial Property:**
- **Concluded/ Entry into Force:** 20.3.1883 (as revised and amended)/6.7.1884
- **Location:** 161 CTS 409, 74 BFSP 44; http://www.wipo.int/treaties/en/ip/paris/trtdocs_wo020.html
- **Parties:** 169 (as at 3.1.05[11])
- **UK:** 7.7.1884 (entry into force; see fn 11)
- **Domestic status:** Certain provisions implemented by the Trade Marks Act 1994

1.18. **Berne Convention for the Protection of Literary and Artistic Works (as amended):**
- **Concluded/Entry into Force:** 9.9.1886/ 5.12.1887 (Revised most recently ('the Paris Act') on 24.7.71 and amended on 28.9.79)
- **Location:** 168 CTS 185, 77 BFSP 22; http://www.wipo.int/treaties/en/ip/berne/trtdocs_wo001.html (Paris Act: http://www.wipo.int/clea/docs_new/en/wo/wo001en.html)
- **Parties:** 159 (as at 19.1.05[12])
- **UK:** 5.12.1887 (entry into force; see fn 12) (Paris Act: 29.9.89; entry into force 2.1.90)
- **Domestic status:** Paris Act given effect by the Copyright, Designs and Patents Act 1988

[7] http://www.icao.int/icao/en/leb/Tokyo.htm.
[8] http://www.icao.int/icao/en/leb/Hague.htm.
[9] http://www.icao.int/icao/en/leb/Mtl71.htm.
[10] http://www.icao.int/icao/en/leb/mtl99.htm.
[11] http://www.wipo.int/treaties/en/ShowResults.jsp?lang=en&treaty_id=2.
[12] ttp://www.wipo.int/treaties/en/ShowResults.jsp?lang=en&treaty_id=15.

1.19. **International Convention for the Unification of Certain Rules of Law Relating to Bills of Lading ('the Hague Rules')(amended by the 1968 Protocol; 'the Hague-Visby Rules'):**
- **Concluded/Entry into Force**: 25.8.24/ 2.6.31; 23.3.68/23.6.77 (Hague-Visby Rules)
- **Location**: Hague Rules: UKTS 17 (1931), Cmnd 3806; http://www.admiraltylawguide.com/conven/haguerules1924.html. Hague-Visby Rules: Scheduled to the Carriage of Goods by Sea Act 1971; http://www.jus.uio.no/lm/sea.carriage.hague.visby.rules.1968/doc.html
- **Parties**: 76 (Hague Rules; as at 18.3.02[13]); 28 (Hague-Visby Rules, as at 29.4.99[14])
- **UK**: No long party to the Hague Rules – denounced on 13.6.77 (see fn 13); 1.10.76 (R; see fn 14)
- **Domestic status**: The Hague Rules were given the force of law by the Carriage of Goods by Sea Act 1924 (now repealed). The Hague-Visby Rules are given the force of law by the Carriage of Goods by Sea Act 1971, section 1(2).

1.20. **Convention on Road Traffic:**
- **Concluded/Entry into Force**: 19.9.49/ 26.3.52
- **Location**: UKTS 49 (1958), Cmnd 578; http://www.offshore-manual.com/ConventionTraffic.html
- **Parties:** 89 (as at 1994; B&H p 183)
- **UK:** 8.7.57 (R or entry into force; B&H (1984) pp 2–3, 183)
- **Domestic status:** Provides definition of 'vehicles' for the purposes of the Convention on the Contract for the International Carriage of Goods by Road (given force of law by Carriage of Goods by Road Act 1965; see Schedule, Article 2) [**§ 1.19**]

1.21. **Convention on the Contract for the International Carriage of Goods by Road ('CMR') (and the 1978 Protocol):**
- **Concluded/Entry into Force:** 19.5.56/ 2.7.61
- **Location:** Scheduled to the Carriage of Goods by Road Act 1965; UKTS 90 (1967), Cmnd 3455; http://www.jus.uio.no/lm/un.cmr.road.carriage.contract.convention.1956/doc.html
- **Parties:** 34 (as at 1994; B&H p 199)
- **UK:** 21.7.67 (Protocol: 5.10.79) (R or entry into force; B&H (1984) pp 2–3, 199)
- **Domestic status:** Given force of law by Carriage of Goods by Road Act 1965, section 1.
- **Reading:** Clarke, *International Carriage of Goods by Road: CMR*, (1997); Hill & Messent, *CMR: Contracts for the International Carriage of Goods by Road* (2000).

1.22. **Convention on the Recognition and Enforcement of Foreign Arbitral Awards ('the New York Convention'):**
- **Concluded/Entry into Force**: 10.6.58/ 7.6.59
- **Location**: Cmnd 6419; http://www.jurisint.org/pub/01/en/doc/152_1.htm
- **Parties**: 135 (as at 30.11.04[15])
- **UK**: 24.9.75 (A; see fn 15)
- **Domestic status**: New York Convention awards may be recognised and given effect (Arbitration Act 1996, sections 100-101)

1.23. **Convention on the Conflicts of Laws relating to the Form of Testamentary Dispositions**:
- **Concluded/Entry into Force**: 5.10.61/ 5.1.64
- **Location**: UKTS 5 (1964), Cmnd 2250 http://www.hcch.net/index_en.php?act=conventions.text&cid=40
- **Parties**: 37 (as at 28.2.05[16])
- **UK**: 6.11.63 (R; see fn 16)
- **Reading**: Explanatory Report by Henri Batiffol (http://www.hcch.net/index_en.php?act=publications.details&pid=2953&dtid=3)

1.24. **Convention relating to a Uniform Law on the International Sale of Goods**:
- **Concluded /Entry into Force**: 1.7.64/ 18.8.72
- **Location**: Annex to the Convention scheduled to the Uniform Law on International Sales Act 1967 (Schedule 1); UKTS 74 (1972), Cmnd 5029 http://www.unidroit.org/english/conventions/c-ulis.htm

[13] http://www.comitemaritime.org/ratific/brus/bru05.html.

[14] http://www.comitemaritime.org/ratific/brus/bru06.html 32.

[15] http://www.uncitral.org/uncitral/en/uncitral_texts/arbitration/NYConvention_status.html.

[16] ttp://www.hcch.net/index_en.php?act=conventions.status&cid=40.

- **Parties:** 6 (as at 1994; B&H p 225)
- **UK:** 31.8.67 (R or entry into force; B&H (1984) pp 2-3, 284)
- **Domestic status:** Annex to the Convention (the Uniform Law on Sales) given force of law by the Uniform Law on International Sales Act 1967, section 1(2).

1.25. **Convention relating to a Uniform Law on the Formation of Contracts for the International Sale of Goods:**
- **Concluded/Entry into Force**: 1.7.64/ 23.8.72
- **Location**: Annex to the Convention scheduled to the Uniform Law on International Sales Act 1967 (Schedule 2); UKTS 75 (1972), Cmnd 5030 http://www.unidroit.org/english/conventions/c-ulf.htm
- **Parties**: 6 (1994; B&H p 225)
- **UK**: 31.8.67 (R or entry into force; B&H (1984) pp 2–3, 284)
- **Domestic status:** Annex to the Convention (the Uniform Law on Formation) given the force of law by the Uniform Law on International Sales Act 1967, section 2(2).

1.26. **Convention on the Service Abroad of Judicial and Extrajudicial Documents in Civil or Commercial Matters**:
- **Concluded/Entry into Force**: 15.11.65/ 10.2.69
- **Location**: UKTS 50 (1969), Cmnd 3986 http://www.hcch.net/index_en.php?act=conventions.text&cid=17
- **Parties:** 52 (as at 21.6.05[17])
- **UK**: 17.11.67 (R; see fn 17)
- **Domestic status:** Article 15 (replacing Article 20 of the Brussels Convention on Jurisdiction and the Enforcement of Judgments in Schedule 1) given force of law by the Civil Jurisdiction and Judgments Act 1982, section 2.
- **Reading**: Explanatory Report by V. Taborda Ferreira (http://www.hcch.net/index_en.php?act=publications.details&pid=2942&dtid=3)

1.27. **International Convention Concerning the Carriage of Passengers and Luggage by Rail ('CIV')**:
- **Concluded/Entry into Force:** 7.2.70/ 1.1.75
- **Location:** UKTS 41 (1975), Cmnd 5898
- **Parties:** 33 (as at 1994; B&H (1984) p 335; no update for 1994)
- **UK:** 16.9.74 (R or entry into force; B&H (1984) pp 2–3, 335)

1.28. **International Convention Concerning the Carriage of Goods by Rail ('CIM'):**
- **Concluded/Entry into Force:** 7.2.70/ 1.1.75
- **Location:** UKTS 40 (1975), Cmnd 5897
- **Parties:** 33 (as at 1994; B&H (1984) p 335; no update for 1994)
- **UK:** 16.9.74 (R or entry into force; B&H (1984) pp 2–3, 335)

1.29. **Convention on the Taking of Evidence Abroad in Civil and Commercial Matters**:
- **Concluded/Entry into Force**: 18.3.70/ 7.10.72
- **Location**: UKTS 20 (1997), Cmnd 6727 http://www.hcch.net/index_en.php?act=conventions.text&cid=82
- **Parties**: 43 (as at 12.5.05[18])
- **UK**: 16.7.76 (R; see fn 18)
- **Reading**: Explanatory Report by Philip W. Amram (http://www.hcch.net/index_en.php?act=publications.details&pid=2968&dtid=3)

1.30. **Patent Co-operation Treaty**:
- **Concluded/Entry into Force**: 19.6.70 (as amended)/24.1.78
- **Location**: UKTS 78 (1978), Cmnd 7340 http://www.wipo.int/pct/en/texts/pdf/pct.pdf
- **Parties**: 127 (as at 15.6.05[19])
- **UK**: 24.1.78 (entry in force; see fn 19)
- **Domestic status**: Given effect by the Patents Act 1977 (see, for example, section 89B regarding international patent applications).

1.31. **Convention for the Protection of Producers of Phonograms against Unauthorized Duplication of their Phonograms**:
- **Concluded/Entry into Force**: 29.10.71/ 18.4.73
- **Location**: UKTS 41 (1973), Cmnd 5275; http://www.wipo.int/treaties/en/ip/pho

[17] http://www.hcch.net/index_en.php?act=conventions.status&cid=17.

[18] http://www.hcch.net/index_en.php?act=conventions.status&cid=82.

[19] http://www.wipo.int/treaties/en/ShowResults.jsp?lang=en&treaty_id=6.

nograms/trtdocs_wo023.html
- **Parties**: 74 (as at 6.4.05[20])
- **UK**: 5.12.72 (R) 18.4.73 (entry into force; see fn 20)

1.32. **Convention on the Law Applicable to Contractual Obligations ('the Rome Convention') (and three Accession Conventions regarding Greece (1984); Spain and Portugal (1992) and Austria, Finland and Sweden (1996))**
- **Concluded/Entry into Force**: 19.6.80 /1.1.88
- **Location**: UKTS 2 (1992), Cm 1794; http://www.rome-convention.org/instruments/i_conv_orig_en.htm
- **Parties**: 15 (9 as at 1994; B&H p 311 and six as a result of the three Accession Conventions)
- **UK**: 29.1.91 (R or entry into force; B&H (1984) pp 2–3, 456)
- **Domestic status**: Given force of law by the Contracts (Applicable Law) Act 1990, section 2.
- **Reading**: Giuliano and Lagarde Report (OJ C-282/1 of 31 October 1980) (http://www.rome-convention.org/instruments/i_rep_lagarde_en.htm); Plender and Wilderspin, *The European Contracts Convention* (2001);

1.33. **Convention on the Law Applicable to Trusts and on their Recognition**:
- **Concluded/Entry into Force**: 1.7.85/ 1.1.92
- **Location**: UKTS 14 (1992), Cm 1823 http://www.hcch.net/index_en.php?act=conventions.text&cid=59
- **Parties**: 10 (as at 20.5.05[21])
- **UK**: 17.11.89 (R; see fn 21)
- **Domestic status**: Parts of the Convention are given the force of law by the Recognition of Trusts Act 1971, section 1.
- **Reading**: Explanatory Report by Alfred E. von Overbeck (http://www.hcch.net/index_en.php?act=publications.details&pid=2949&dtid=3)

1.34. **Convention on Combating Bribery of Foreign Public Officials in International Business Transactions**:
- **Concluded/Entry into Force**: 17.12.97/ 15.2.99
- **Location**: http://www.oecd.org/document/21/0,2340,en_2649_34859_2017813_1_1_1_1,00.html#text
- **Parties**: 36 (as at 28.1.05[22])
- **UK**: 14.12.98 (R) 15.2.99 (entry into force; see fn 22)
- **Reading**: Commentaries on the Convention (http://www.oecd.org/document/1/0,2340,en_2649_34859_2048129_1_1_1_1,00.html)

C. Criminal Law

1.35. **Agreement for the Suppression of the Circulation of Obscene Publications (and 1949 Protocol):**
- **Concluded/Entry into Force:** 4.5.10/ 15.9.11
- **Location:** UKTS 11 (1911), Cd 5657; http://untreaty.un.org/English/CTC/CTC_04.asp; (Protocol is at UKTS 13 (1951), Cmd 8152);
- **Parties:** 42 (as at 28.6.05[23]) (and 60 colonies, dominions and protectorates)
- **UK:** 15.3.11

1.36. **International Convention for the Suppression of the Circulation of, and Traffic in, Obscene Publications (and 1947 Protocol)**:
- **Concluded/Entry into Force**: 12.9.23 (as amended 12.11.47)/7.8.24
- **Location**: UKTS 1 (1926), Cmd 2575; http://untreaty.un.org/English/CTC/CTC_04.asp
- (Protocol is at UKTS 2 (1952), Cmd 8438 and the URL above)
- **Parties**: 47 (as at 28.6.05[24]) (and colonies, dominions and protectorates)
- **UK**: 11.12.25 (R; see fn 24)

1.37. **Convention on the Prevention and Punishment of the Crime of Genocide**:
- **Concluded/Entry into Force**: 9.12.48/ 12.1.51
- **Location**: UKTS 58 (1970), Cmnd 4421 http://www.unhchr.ch/html/menu3/b/p_genoci.htm

[20] http://www.wipo.int/treaties/en/ShowResults.jsp?lang=en&treaty_id=18.
[21] http://www.hcch.net/index_en.php?act=conventions.status&cid=59.
[22] http://www.oecd.org/dataoecd/59/13/1898632.pdf.
[23] http://untreaty.un.org/ENGLISH/bible/englishinternetbible/partI/chapterVIII/treaty6.asp#participant.
[24] http://untreaty.un.org/ENGLISH/bible/englishinternetbible/partI/chapterVIII/treaty3.asp.

- **Parties**: 137 (as at 28.6.05[25])
- **UK**: 30.1.70 (A; see fn 25)
- **Domestic status**: Given effect by the International Criminal Court Act 2001 (section 51(1))
- **Reading**: Schabas, *Genocide in International Law: The Crime of Crimes* (2000)

1.38. **Single Convention on Narcotic Drugs (and 1972 Protocol):**
- **Concluded /Entry into Force**: 30.3.61/ 13.12.64 (25.3.72/8.8.75: Protocol)
- **Location**: UKTS 34 (1965), Cmnd 2631; http://www.unodc.org/pdf/convention_1961_en.pdf (Protocol is at UKTS 23 (1979) Cmnd 7466)
- **Parties**: 149 (as at 28.6.05[26]), 122 (Protocol; as at 29.6.05[27])
- **UK**: 2.9.64 (R; Convention; see fn 26) 20.6.78 (R; Protocol; see fn 27)
- **Domestic status:** Given effect, in part, by the Misuse of Drugs Act 1971.

1.39. **Convention on Psychotropic Substances:**
- **Concluded /Entry into Force**: 21.2.71/ 16.8.76
- **Location**: 10 ILM 261 http://www.unodc.org/pdf/convention_1971_en.pdf
- **Parties**: 176 (as at 29.6.05[28])
- **UK**: 24.3.86 (R; see fn 28)

1.40. **International Convention against the Taking of Hostages:**
- **Concluded/Entry into Force**: 17.12.79/ 3.6.83
- **Location**: UKTS 81 (1983), Cmnd 9100 http://www.unodc.org/unodc/terrorism_convention_hostages.html
- **Parties**: 148 (as at 28.6.05[29])
- **UK**: 22.12.82 (R; see fn 29)
- **Domestic status**: Implemented by the Taking of Hostages Act 1982.

1.41. **Council of Europe Convention on the Transfer of Sentenced Persons:**
- **Concluded/Entry into Force**: 21.3.83/ 1.7.85
- **Location**: UKTS 51 (1985) Cmnd 9617; http://conventions.coe.int/Treaty/en/Treaties/Html/112.htm
- **Parties**: 58 (as at 29.6.05[30])
- **UK**: 30.4.85 (see fn 30)
- **Reading**: Explanatory Report (http://conventions.coe.int/Treaty/en/Reports/Html/112.htm)

1.42. **UN Convention Against the Illicit Traffic in Narcotic Drugs and Psychotropic Substances:**
- **Concluded/Entry into Force**: 20.12.88/ 11.11.90
- **Location**: Misc 14 (1989), Cm 804 http://www.unodc.org/pdf/convention_1988_en.pdf
- **Parties**: 172 (as at 28.6.05[31])
- **UK**: 28.6.91 (R; see fn 31)

1.43. **Council of Europe Convention on Laundering, Search, Seizure and Confiscation of the Proceeds from Crime:**
- **Concluded/Entry into Force**: 8.11.90/ 1.9.93
- **Location**: UKTS 59 (1993), Cm 2337 http://conventions.coe.int/Treaty/en/Treaties/Html/141.htm
- **Parties**: 47 (as at 5.6.05[32])
- **UK**: 28.9.92 (R; see fn 32)
- **Reading**: Explanatory Report (http://conventions.coe.int/Treaty/en/Reports/Html/141.htm)

D. Employment and Industrial Relations Law

1.44. **Unemployment Convention (ILO 2):**
- **Concluded/Date of Entry**: 28.11.19/ 14.7.21

[25] http://untreaty.un.org/ENGLISH/bible/englishinternetbible/partI/chapterIV/treaty1.asp.

[26] http://untreaty.un.org/ENGLISH/bible/englishinternetbible/partI/chapterVI/treaty21.asp.

[27] http://untreaty.un.org/ENGLISH/bible/englishinternetbible/partI/chapterVI/treaty23.asp.

[28] http://untreaty.un.org/ENGLISH/bible/englishinternetbible/partI/chapterVI/treaty22.asp.

[29] http://untreaty.un.org/ENGLISH/bible/englishinternetbible/partI/chapterXVIII/treaty5.asp.

[30] http://conventions.coe.int/Treaty/Commun/ChercheSig.asp?NT=112&CM=8&DF=6/29/05&CL=ENG.

[31] http://untreaty.un.org/ENGLISH/bible/englishinternetbible/partI/chapterVI/treaty25.asp.

[32] http://conventions.coe.int/Treaty/Commun/ChercheSig.asp?NT=141&CM=8&DF=29/06/05&CL=ENG.

- **Location:** Cmd 627; http://www.ilo.org/ilolex/english/convdisp2.htm
- **Parties:** 55 (2005; see URL above)
- **UK:** 14.7.21 (R; see URL above)

1.45. **Freedom of Association and Protection of the Right to Organise Convention (ILO 87):**
- **Concluded/Entry into Force:** 9.7.48/4.7.50
- **Location:** Cmnd 7638; http://www.ilo.org/ilolex/cgi-lex/convde.pl?C087
- **Parties:** 144 (as at 2005[33])
- **UK:** 27.6.49 (R; see fn 33)

1.46. **Collective Bargaining Convention (ILO 98):**
- **Concluded/Entry into Force:** 1.7.49/18.7.51
- **Location:** Cmd 7852 http://www.ilo.org/ilolex/cgi-lex/convde.pl?C098
- **Parties:** 154 (as at 2005[34])
- **UK:** 30.6.50 (R; see fn 34)

1.47. **Equal Remuneration Convention (ILO 100):**
- **Concluded/Entry into Force:** 29.6.51/23.5.53
- **Location:** http://www.ilo.org/ilolex/english/convdisp2.htm
- **Parties:** 162 (as at 2005; see URL above)
- **UK:** 15.6.71 (R; see URL above)

1.48. **Discrimination (Occupation and Employment) Convention (ILO 111):**
- **Concluded/Entry into Force:** 25.6.58/15.6.60
- **Location:** Cmd 593; http://www.ilo.org/ilolex/cgi-lex/convde.pl?C111
- **Parties:** 162 (as at 2005[35])
- **UK:** 8.6.99 (R; see fn 35)

1.49. **Employment Policy Convention (ILO 100):**
- **Concluded/Entry into Force:** 9.7.64/15.7.66
- **Location:** UKTS 65 (1967), Cmnd 3360; http://www.ilo.org/ilolex/english/convdisp2.htm
- **Parties:** 95 (as at 2005; see URL above)
- **UK:** 27.6.66 (R; see URL above)

1.50. **Workers Representatives Convention (ILO 135):**
- **Concluded/Entry into Force:** 23.6.71/30.6.73
- **Location:** UKTS 30 (1974), Cmnd 5612; http://www.ilo.org/ilolex/english/convdisp2.htm
- **Parties:** 77 (as at 2005; see URL above)
- **UK:** 15.3.73 (R; see URL above)

E. Environmental Law

1.51. **Convention for the Protection of Plants and Plant Products:**
- **Concluded/Entry into Force:** 6.12.51/3.4.52
- **Location:** UKTS 16 (1954), Cmd 9077; http://www.fao.org/legal/treaties/004t-e.htm
- **Parties:** 137 (as at 21.6.05[36])
- **UK:** 7.9.53 (R; see fn 36)

1.52. **International Convention for the Protection of New Varieties of Plants:**
- **Concluded/Entry into Force:** 2.12.61 (as revised; most recently on 19.3.91)/10.8.68
- **Location:** UKTS 74 (1969), Cmnd 4081 http://www.upov.int/en/publications/conventions/1991/content.htm
- **Parties:** 58 (as at 9.11.04[37])
- **UK:** 17.9.65 (original version) 3.12.98 (1991 version[38])
- **Domestic status:** Given effect by the Plant Varieties Act 1997
- **Key Body:** International Union for the Protection of New Varieties of Plants (http://www.upov.int/index.html)

1.53. **European Convention for the Protection of Animals during International Transport:**
- **Concluded/Entry into Force:** 13.12.68/20.2.71

[33] http://www.ilo.org/ilolex/cgi-lex/ratifce.pl? C087.

[34] http://www.ilo.org/ilolex/cgi-lex/ratifce.pl?C098.

[35] http://www.ilo.org/ilolex/cgi-lex/ratifce.pl?C111.

[36] http://www.fao.org/legal/treaties/004s-e.htm.

[37] http://www.wipo.int/treaties/en/ShowResults.jsp?country_id=ALL&start_year=ANY&end_year=ANY&search_what=C&treaty_id=27.

[38] http://www.wipo.int/treaties/en/Remarks.jsp?cnty_id=1610C.

- **Location:** UKTS 31 (1974), Cmnd 5613 http://conventions.coe.int/Treaty/en/Treaties/Html/065.htm
- **Parties:** 24 (as at 30.6.05[39])
- **UK:** 9.1.74 (R; see fn 39)
- **Reading:** Explanatory Report (http://conventions.coe.int/Treaty/en/Reports/Html/065.htm)

1.54. **International Convention on Civil Liability for Oil Pollution Damage:**

- **Concluded/Entry into Force:** 29.11.69/19.6.75
- **Location:** UKTS 106 (1975), Cmnd 6183; http://www.admiraltylawguide.com/conven/civilpol1969.html
- **Parties:** 81 (as at 1994; B&H p 245)
- **UK:** 17.3.75 (R or entry into force; B&H (1984) pp 2-3, 333)
- **Domestic status:** Given effect by the Merchant Shipping Act 1995, Chapter III (see, for example, section 152)

1.55. **Convention on Wetlands of International Importance Especially as Waterfowl Habitat ('RAMSAR') (and 1982 Protocol):**

- **Concluded/Entry into Force:** 2.2.71/21.12.75
- **Location:** UKTS 34 (1976), Cmnd 6465 http://www.ramsar.org/key_conv_e.htm
- **Parties:** 146 (as at 2.6.05[40])
- **UK:** 5.1.76. (R; see fn 40)
- **Domestic status:** Given effect by the Wildlife and Countryside Act 1981, see, for example, section 37A. The following EU measures have been adopted regarding the Convention: Council Directive 79/409/EEC (the Birds Directive); Council Directive 92/43/EEC (the Species and Habitats Directive).
- **Key Bodies:** Conference of the Parties; RAMSAR Standing Committee (http://www.ramsar.org/about_stancomm.htm); Scientific and Technical Review Panel (http://www.ramsar.org/about_strp.htm/)

1.56. **Convention on the Prevention of Marine Pollution by Dumping of Wastes and Other Matter (and Protocol) ('the London Convention'):**

- **Concluded/Entry into Force:** 29.12.72/30.8.75
- **Location:** UKTS 43 (1976), Cmnd 6486; http://www.londonconvention.org/main.htm
- **Parties:** 82 (as at June 2005[41])
- **UK:** 17.11.75 (R or entry into force; B&H (1984) pp 2-3, 369)
- **Domestic status:** Implemented by the Food and Environment Protection Act 1985, Part II.

1.57. **International Convention on International Trade in Endangered Species of Wild Fauna and Flora ('CITES'):**

- **Concluded/Entry into Force:** 3.3.73 (as amended)/1.7.75
- **Location:** UKTS 101 (1976), Cmnd 6647 http://www.cites.org/eng/disc/text.shtml
- **Parties:** 167 (as at 9.11.04[42])
- **UK:** 2.8.76 (R; see fn 42)
- **Domestic case:** Key European measures adopted in relation to the Convention: EC Regulations 338/97 and 1808/01 (enforced within the UK by the Control of Trade in Endangered Species (Enforcement) Regulations 1997 (COTES)).
- **Key Bodies:** Conference of the Parties (http://www.cites.org/eng/disc/CoP.shtml); CITES UK Management Authority: Department for Environment, Food and Rural Affairs.
- **Reading:** The Cites Handbook (http://www.cites.org/eng/resources/publications.shtml)

1.58. **Convention on the Conservation of Migratory Species of Wild Animals ('CMS' or 'the Bonn Convention'):**

- **Concluded/Entry into Force:** 23.6.79/1.11.83
- **Location:** Misc 11 (1980), Cmnd 7888 http://www.cms.int/documents/convtxt/cms_convtxt.htm
- **Parties:** 89 (as at 1.2.05[43])
- **UK:** 1.10.85 (entry into force; see fn 43)
- **Domestic status:** Given effect by the Wildlife and Countryside Act 1981.

[39] http://conventions.coe.int/Treaty/Commun/ChercheSig.asp?NT=065&CM=8&DF=30/06/05&CL=ENG.

[40] http://erc.unesco.org/cp/convention.asp?KO=15398&language=E.

[41] http://www.londonconvention.org/main.htm.

[42] http://www.cites.org/eng/disc/parties/chronolo.shtml.

[43] http://www.cms.int/pdf/en/party_list/Partylist_eng.pdf.

- **Key Bodies**: Conference of the Parties (http://www.cms.int/bodies/cop_main page.htm); Standing Committee (http://www.cms.int/bodies/StC_main page.htm); Scientific Council (http:// www.cms.int/bodies/ScC_mainpage.ht m).
- **Reading**: CMS Brochure (http://www. cms.int/publications/cms_brochure.ht m)

1.59. **Convention on Long Range Transboundary Air Pollution (and eight Protocols)**:
- **Concluded/Entry into Force**: 13.11.79/ 16.3.83
- **Location**: UKTS 57 (1983), Cmnd 9037; http://www.unece.org/env/lrtap/full%2 0text/1979.CLRTAP.e.pdf (Protocols: http://www.unece.org/env/lrtap/sta tus/lrtap_s.htm)
- **Parties**: 49 (as at 28.6.05[44])
- **UK**: 15.7.82 (R; see fn 44)
- **Key Bodies**: Executive Body (http:// www.unece.org/env/eb/welcome.html) EMEP Steering Body (http://www. unece.org/env/emep/welcome.html)

1.60. **Convention on the Conservation of European Wildlife and Natural Habitats**:
- **Concluded/Entry into Force**: 19.9.79/ 1.6.82
- **Location**: http://conventions.coe.int/ treaty/en/Treaties/Html/104.htm
- **Parties**: 45 (as at 30.6.05[45])
- **UK**: 28.5.82 (R; see fn 45)
- **Domestic status**: Given effect by the Wildlife and Countryside Act 1981. Also given effect by the Council Directive 79/409/EEC (the Birds Directive); Council Directive 92/43/EEC (the Species and Habitats Directive).
- **Reading**: Explanatory Report (http:// conventions.coe.int/Treaty/en/Reports/ Html/104.htm)

1.61. **Convention on the Conservation of European Wildlife and Natural Habitats**:
- **Concluded/Entry into Force**: 19.9.79/ 1.6.82
- **Location**: UKTS 56 (1982), Cmnd 8738; http://conventions.coe.int/treaty/en/Tr eaties/Html/104.htm
- **Parties**: 45 (as at 29.6.05[46])
- **UK**: 28.5.82 (R; see fn 46)

1.62. **Convention for the Conservation of Salmon in the North Atlantic Area**:
- **Concluded/Entry into Force**: 2.3.82/ 1.10.83
- **Location**: Misc 7 (1983), Cmnd 8830 http://www.oceanlaw.net/texts/nasco.h tm
- **Parties**: 7 (as at 31.1.04[47])
- **UK**: Not directly a party to the Convention. The Convention entered into force for the EC on 14.12.82.
- **Key Body**: North Atlantic Salmon Conservation Organisation (http:// www.nasco.int/)

1.63. **World Charter for Nature**:
- **Concluded**: 28.10.82
- **Location**: http://www.un.org/docu ments/ga/res/37/a37r007.htm

1.64. **Vienna Convention for the Protection of the Ozone Layer (and Protocol on Substances that Deplete the Ozone Layer)**:
- **Concluded/Entry into Force**: 22.3.85/ 22.9.88 (Protocol: 16.9.87 (as amended)/1.1.89)
- **Location**: UKTS 1 (1990), Cm 910 http://www.unep.org/ozone/pdfs/vien-naconvention2002.pdf (Protocol: http://www.unep.org/ozone/pdfs/Mont real-Protocol2000.pdf)
- **Parties**: 190 (as of 28.6.05[48]) 188 189 (Protocol; as at 28.6.05[49])
- **UK**: 15.5.87 (R; Convention; see fn 48) 16.12.88 (R; Protocol; see fn 49)
- **Key Body**: Ozone Secretariat (http:// www.unep.org/ozone/About_the_Secre tariat/index.asp)

[44] http://untreaty.un.org/ENGLISH/bible/ englishinternetbible/partI/chapterXXVII/ treaty1.asp.

[45] http://conventions.coe.int/Treaty/Com mun/ChercheSig.asp?NT=104&CM=8&D F=30/06/05&CL=ENG.

[46] http://conventions.coe.int/Treaty/Com mun/ChercheSig.asp?NT=104&CM=8&D F=29/06/05&CL=ENG.

[47] http://www.oceanlaw.net/texts/sum maries/nasco.htm.

[48] http://untreaty.un.org/ENGLISH/bible/ englishinternetbible/partI/chapterXXVII/ treaty11.asp.

[49] http://untreaty.un.org/ENGLISH/bible/ englishinternetbible/partI/chapterXXVII/ treaty12.asp.

- **Reading**: Handbook for the International Treaties for the Protection of the Ozone Layer (6th edn, 2003)

1.65. **Convention on the Control of Transboundary Movement of Hazardous Wastes and their Disposal ('the Basel Convention')**:
- **Concluded/Entry into Force**: 22.3.89/5.5.92
- **Location**: Misc 4 (1990), Cm 984; http://www.basel.int/text/con-e-rev.pdf
- **Parties**: 165 (as at 8.4.05[50])
- **UK**: 7.2.94 (R; see fn 50)
- **Domestic status**: Implemented by the Transfrontier Shipment of Waste Regulations 1994 (SI 1994/1137)

1.66. **Convention on Environmental Impact Assessment in a Transboundary Context:**
- **Concluded/Entry into Force**: 25.2.91/10.9.97
- **Location**: http://www.unece.org/env/eia/documents/conventiontextenglish.pdf
- **Parties**: 40 (as at 24.6.05[51])
- **UK**: 10.10.97 (R; see fn 51)

1.67. **UN Framework Convention on Climate Change (and the Kyoto Protocol)**:
- **Concluded/Entry into Force**: 9.5.92/21.3.94 (Kyoto Protocol: 11.12.97/16.2.05)
- **Location**: Misc 6 (1993), Cm 2137 http://unfccc.int/resource/docs/convkp/conveng.pdf
- **Parties**: 189 (as at 28.6.05[52]); 150 (Kyoto Protocol; as at 28.6.05[53])
- **UK**: 8.12.93 (R; Convention; see fn 52) 31.5.02 (R; Protocol; see fn 53)
- **Decision-making Body**: Conference of the Parties (http://unfccc.int/documentation/decisions/items/2646.php)
- **Reading**: http://unfccc.int/2860.php

1.68. **Convention on Biological Diversity (and Cartagena Protocol on Biosafety)**:
- **Concluded/Entry into Force**: 5.6.92/29.12.93 (Protocol: 29.1.00/11.9.03)
- **Location**: Misc 3 (1993), Cm 2127; http://www.biodiv.org/convention/articles.asp (Protocol: http://www.biodiv. org/biosafety/protocol.asp
- **Parties**: 188 (Convention) 123 (Protocol) (as at 16.6.05[54])
- **UK**: 3.6.94 (Convention) 19.11.03 (Protocol) (see fn 54)
- **Key Bodies**: Conference of the Parties (http://www.biodiv.org/convention/cops.asp), the Subsidiary Body on Scientific, Technical and Technological Advice (SBSTTA) (http://www.biodiv.org/convention/sbstta.asp).

1.69. **Rio Declaration on Environment and Development:**
- Concluded: 14.6.92
- Location: http://www.un.org/documents/ga/conf151/aconf15126-1annex1.htm

F. European Treaties

1.70. **European Cultural Convention:**
- **Concluded/Entry into Force**: 19.12.54/5.5.55
- **Location**: UKTS 49 (1955), Cmd 9545 http://conventions.coe.int/Treaty/en/Treaties/Html/018.htm
- **Parties**: 48 (as at 30.6.05[55])
- **UK**: 5.5.55 (R; see fn 55)

1.71. **European Convention for the Peaceful Settlement of Disputes**:
- **Concluded/Entry into Force**: 29.4.57/30.4.58
- **Location**: UKTS 10 (1961), Cmnd 1298; http://conventions.coe.int/Treaty/en/Treaties/Html/023.htm
- **Parties**: 14 (as at 27.6.05[56])
- **UK**: 7.12.60 (R; see fn 56)

1.72. **European Convention on Extradition**:
- **Concluded/Entry into Force**: 13.12.57/18.4.60

[50] http://www.basel.int/ratif/frsetmain.php.

[51] http://www.unece.org/env/eia/convratif.html.

[52] http://untreaty.un.org/ENGLISH/bible/englishinternetbible/partI/chapterXXVII/treaty32.asp.

[53] http://untreaty.un.org/ENGLISH/bible/englishinternetbible/partI/chapterXXVII/treaty33.asp.

[54] http://www.biodiv.org/world/parties.asp.

[55] http://conventions.coe.int/Treaty/Commun/ChercheSig.asp?NT=018&CM=8&DF=30/06/05&CL=ENG.

[56] http://conventions.coe.int/Treaty/Commun/ChercheSig.asp?NT=023&CM=8&DF=27/06/05&CL=ENG.

- **Location**: 359 UNTS 276 http://conventions.coe.int/Treaty/en/Treaties/Html/024.htm
- **Parties**: 46 (as at 30.6.05[57])
- **UK**: 13.2.91 (R; see fn 57)
- **Reading**: Explanatory Report (http://conventions.coe.int/Treaty/en/Reports/Html/024.htm)

1.73. **European Social Charter**:
- **Concluded/Entry into Force:** 18.10.61/26.2.65
- **Location:** UKTS 38 (1965), Cmnd 2643; http://conventions.coe.int/Treaty/en/Treaties/Html/035.htm
- **Parties:** 27 (as at 30.6.05[58])
- **UK:** 11.7.62 (R; see fn 58)
- **Reading:** Gomein, Harris and Zwaak, *Law and Practice of the European Convention on Human Rights and the European Social Charter* (1996).

1.74. **European Agreement Relating to Persons Participating in Proceedings of the European Commission and Court of Human Rights**:
- **Concluded/Entry into Force:** 6.5.69/17.4.71
- **Location:** UKTS 44 (1971), Cmnd 4699; http://conventions.coe.int/Treaty/en/Treaties/Html/067.htm
- **Parties:** 26 (as at 27.6.05[59])
- **UK:** 24.2.71 (R; see fn 59)

1.75. **Convention on the Grant of European Patents ('European Patent Convention')**:
- **Concluded/Entry into Force:** 5.10.73/7.10.77
- **Location:** UKTS 20 (1978), Cmnd 7090; http://www.european-patent-office.org/legal/epc/e/ma1.html
- **Parties:** 30 (as at 22.3.05[60])
- **UK:** 7.10.77 (entry into force; B&H (1984) pp 2–3. 380)

1.76. **European Convention on the Suppression of Terrorism:**
- **Concluded/Entry into Force:** 27.1.77/4.8.78
- **Location:** UKTS 93 (1978), Cmnd 7340; http://conventions.coe.int/Treaty/en/Treaties/Html/090.htm
- **Parties:** 44 (as at 27.6.05[61])
- **UK:** 24.7.78 (R; see fn 61)
- **Reading:** Explanatory Report: http://conventions.coe.int/Treaty/en/Reports/Html/090.htm

1.77. **Convention for the Protection of the Architectural Heritage of Europe**:
- **Concluded/Entry into Force:** 3.10.85/1.12.87
- **Location:** UKTS 46 (1988), Cm 439; http://conventions.coe.int/Treaty/en/Treaties/Html/121.htm
- **Parties:** 36 (as at 27.6.05[62])
- **UK:** 13.11.87 (R; see fn 62)
- **Reading:** Explanatory Report: http://conventions.coe.int/Treaty/en/Reports/Html/121.htm

1.78. **European Convention for the Prevention of Torture and Inhuman or Degrading Treatment or Punishment**:
- **Concluded/Entry into Force**: 26.11.87/1.2.89
- **Location**: UKTS 5 (1991), Cm 1634 http://conventions.coe.int/Treaty/en/Treaties/Html/126.htm
- **Parties**: 45 (as at 30.6.05[63])
- **UK**: 24.6.88 (R; see fn 63)
- **Key Body:** European Committee for the Prevention of Torture and Inhuman or Degrading Treatment or Punishment: http://www.cpt.coe.int/en/about.htm. R Morgan and M Evans, *Combating Torture in Europe: The Work and Standards of the Committee for the Prevention of Torture* (2001)
- **Reading**: Explanatory Report (http://conventions.coe.int/Treaty/en/Reports/Html/126.htm).

57 http://conventions.coe.int/Treaty/Commun/ChercheSig.asp?NT=024&CM=8&DF=30/06/05&CL=ENG.
58 http://conventions.coe.int/Treaty/Commun/ChercheSig.asp?NT=035&CM=8&DF=30/06/05&CL=ENG.
59 http://conventions.coe.int/Treaty/Commun/ChercheSig.asp?NT=067&CM=8&DF=27/06/05&CL=ENG.
60 http://www.european-patent-office.org/epo/members.htm.
61 http://conventions.coe.int/Treaty/Commun/ChercheSig.asp?NT=090&CM=8&DF=27/06/05&CL=ENG.
62 http://conventions.coe.int/Treaty/Commun/ChercheSig.asp?NT=121&CM=8&DF=27/06/05&CL=ENG.
63 http://conventions.coe.int/Treaty/Commun/ChercheSig.asp?NT=126&CM=8&DF=30/06/05&CL=ENG.

1.79. **EU Charter on Human Rights and Fundamental Freedoms:**
- **Concluded:** 7.12.00
- **Location:** OJ C 364/01 http://www.europarl.eu.int/charter/pdf/text_en.pdf
- **Reading:** Peers and Ward, *The EU Charter of Fundamental Rights – Politics, Law and Policy* (2004)

1.80. **Treaty Establishing the European Community:**
- **Concluded/Entry into Force:** 24.12.02/1.2.03
- **Location:** http://europa.eu.int/abc/obj/treaties/en/entoc05.htm
- **UK:** 25.7.02
- **Reading:** [**§ 6.5**]

G. Family and Child Law

1.81. **Convention on the Recovery Abroad of Maintenance:**
- **Concluded/Entry into Force:** 20.6.56/25.5.57
- **Location:** UKTS 85 (1975), Cmnd 6084
- **Parties:** 60 (as at 28.6.05[64])
- **UK:** 13.3.75 (A; see fn 64)
- **Domestic status:** Given effect by Part II of the Maintenance Orders (Reciprocal Enforcement) Act 1972

1.82. **Convention on Consent to Marriage, Minimum Age for Marriage and Registration of Marriage:**
- **Concluded/Entry into Force:** 10.12.62/9.12.64
- **Location:** UKTS 102 (1970), Cmnd 4538 http://www.ohchr.org/english/law/convention.htm
- **Parties:** 42 (as at 1994; B&H p 220)
- **UK:** 9.7.70 (R or entry into force; B&H (1984) pp 2–3, 270)

1.83. **European Convention on the Adoption of Children:**
- **Concluded/Entry into Force:** 24.4.67/26.4.68
- **Location:** UKTS 51 (1968), Cmnd 3673 http://conventions.coe.int/Treaty/en/Treaties/Html/058.htm
- **Parties:** 18 (as at 29.6.05[65])
- **UK:** 21.12.67 (R; see fn 65)
- **Reading:** Explanatory Report (http://conventions.coe.int/Treaty/en/Reports/Html/058.htm)

1.84. **Hague Convention on the Recognition of Divorces and Legal Separations:**
- **Concluded/Entry into Force:** 1.6.70/24.8.75
- **Location:** UKTS 123 (1975), Cmnd 6248; http://hcch.e-vision.nl/index_en.php?act=conventions.text&cid=80
- **Parties:** 18 (as at 28.2.05[66])
- **UK:** 21.5.74 (R; see fn 66)
- **Reading:** Explanatory Report by P. Bellet and B. Goldman (http://www.hcch.net/index_en.php?act=publications.details&pid=2966&dtid=3)

1.85. **Hague Convention on the Recognition and Enforcement of Decisions relating to Maintenance Obligations:**
- **Concluded/Entry into Force:** 2.10.73/1.8.76
- **Location:** UKTS 49 (1980), Cmnd 7939 http://www.hcch.net/index_en.php?act=conventions.text&cid=85
- **Parties:** 21 (as at 28.2.05[67])
- **UK:** 21.12.79 (R; see fn 67)
- **Reading:** Explanatory Report by Michel Verwilghen (http://www.hcch.net/index_en.php?act=publications.details&pid=2946&dtid=3)

1.86. **European Convention on the Legal Status of Children Born Out of Wedlock:**
- **Concluded/Entry into Force:** 15.10.75/11.8.78
- **Location:** UKTS 43 (1981), Cmnd 8287 http://conventions.coe.int/Treaty/en/Treaties/Html/085.htm
- **Parties:** 21 (as at 29.6.05[68])
- **UK:** 24.2.81 (R; see fn 68)
- **Reading:** Explanatory Report (http://conventions.coe.int/Treaty/en/Reports/Html/085.htm)

64 http://untreaty.un.org/ENGLISH/bible/englishinternetbible/partI/chapterXX/treaty1.asp.

65 http://conventions.coe.int/Treaty/Commun/ChercheSig.asp?NT=058&CM=8&DF=29/06/05&CL=ENG.

66 http://hcch.e-vision.nl/index_en.php?act=conventions.status&cid=80.

67 http://www.hcch.net/index_en.php?act=conventions.status&cid=85.

68 http://conventions.coe.int/Treaty/Commun/ChercheSig.asp?NT=085&CM=8&DF=6/29/05&CL=ENG.

1.87. **European Convention on Recognition and Enforcement of Decisions Concerning the Custody of Children and on the Restoration of Custody of Children:**
- **Concluded/Entry into Force:** 20.5.80/1.9.83
- **Location:** UKTS 35 (1987), Cm 191 http://conventions.coe.int/Treaty/en/Treaties/Html/105.htm
- **Parties:** 34 (as at 29.6.05[69])
- **UK:** 21.4.86 (R; see fn 69)
- **Reading:** Explanatory Report (http://conventions.coe.int/Treaty/en/Reports/Html/105.htm)

1.88. **Hague Convention on the Civil Aspects of International Child Abduction:**
- **Concluded/Entry into Force:** 25.10.80/1.12.83
- **Location:** UKTS 66 (1986), Cm 33 http://www.hcch.net/index_en.php?act=conventions.text&cid=24
- **Parties:** 75 (as at 16.6.05[70])
- **UK:** 20.5.86 (R; see fn 70)
- **Domestic status:** Given the force of law by the Child Abduction and Custody Act 1985, section 1(2)
- **Reading:** Explanatory Report by Elisa Perez-Vera (http://www.hcch.net/index_en.php?act=publications.details&pid=2779&dtid=3).

1.89. **UN Declaration on Social and Legal Principles Relating to the Protection and Welfare of Children:**
- **Concluded:** 3.12.86
- **Location:** http://www.unhchr.ch/html/menu3/b/27.htm

1.90. **UN Convention on the Rights of the Child (and Protocols I (on the involvement of children in armed conflict) and II (on the sale of children, child prostitution and child pornography):**
- **Concluded/Entry into Force:** 20.11.89/2.9.90 (Protocol I: 25.5.00/12.2.02 Protocol II: 25.5.00/18.1.02)
- **Location:** UKTS 44 (1992), Cm 1976 http://www.unhchr.ch/html/menu3/b/k2crc.htm (Protocol I: http://www.unhchr.ch/html/menu2/6/protocolchild.htm) (Protocol 2: http://www.unhchr.ch/html/menu2/dopchild.htm)
- **Parties:** 192 (as at 28.6.05[71]) (Protocol I: 98[72]; Protocol II: 95[73])
- **UK:** 16.12.91 (R; Convention; see fn 71), 24.6.03 (R; Protocol I; see fn 72)
- **Key Body:** Committee on the Rights of the Child ('CRC'): http://www.ohchr.org/english/bodies/crc/index.htm. CRC documents can be accessed at http://www.unhchr.ch/tbs/doc.nsf.
- **Reading:** Van Beuren, *The International Law on the Rights of the Child* (1998).

1.91. **Hague Convention on the Protection of Children and Cooperation in Respect of Intercountry Adoption:**
- **Concluded/Entry into Force:** 29.5.93/1.5.95
- **Location:** 32 ILM 1134 http://www.hcch.net/index_en.php?act=conventions.text&cid=69
- **Parties:** 66 (as at 14.6.05[74])
- **UK:** 27.2.03 (R; see fn 74)
- **Reading:** Explanatory Report by G. Parra-Aranguren (http://www.hcch.net/index_en.php?act=publications.details&pid=2279&dtid=3)

H. Human Rights Law

1.92. **International Convention for the Suppression of Traffic in Women and Children (and 1947 Protocol):**
- **Concluded/Entry into Force:** 30.9.21/28.6.22
- **Location:** UKTS 26 (1923), Cmd 1986
- **Parties:** 73 (as at 28.6.05[75])
- **UK:** 28.6.22 (see fn 75)

[69] http://conventions.coe.int/Treaty/Commun/ChercheSig.asp?NT=105&CM=8&DF=6/29/05&CL=ENG.

[70] http://conventions.coe.int/Treaty/Commun/ChercheSig.asp?NT=105&CM=8&DF=6/29/05&CL=ENG.

[71] http://untreaty.un.org/ENGLISH/bible/englishinternetbible/partI/chapterIV/treaty19.asp.

[72] http://untreaty.un.org/ENGLISH/bible/englishinternetbible/partI/chapterIV/treaty21.asp.

[73] http://untreaty.un.org/ENGLISH/bible/englishinternetbible/partI/chapterIV/treaty22.asp.

[74] http://www.hcch.net/index_en.php?act=conventions.status&cid=69.

[75] http://untreaty.un.org/ENGLISH/bible/englishinternetbible/partI/chapterVII/treaty3.asp.

1.93. **Universal Declaration of Human Rights: Concluded:** 10.12.48
- **Location:** http://www.un.org/Overview/rights.html

1.94. **European Convention on Human Rights (and 14 Protocols):**
- **Concluded/Entry into Force:** 4.11.50/3.9.53
- **Location:** Scheduled in part to the Human Rights Act, 1998; UKTS 71 (1953), Cmd 8969; http://conventions.coe.int/Treaty/en/Treaties/Html/005.htm
- **Parties:** 45 (as at 30.6.05[76])
- **UK:** 8.3.51 (R; see fn 76)
- **Domestic status:** Given effect in part (Articles 2 to 12, 14; Articles 1 to 3 of the First Protocol and Articles 1 and 2 of the Sixth Protocol) by the Human Rights Acts 1998. Section 3 requires legislation to be read and give effect to, in so far as it is possible, in a way which is compatible with these parts of the Convention.
- **Reading:** [§ 7.5]

1.95. **Convention on the Political Rights of Women:**
- **Concluded/Entry into Force:** 20.12.52/7.7.54
- **Location:** UKTS 101 (1967), Cmnd 3449 http://www.unhchr.ch/html/menu3/b/22.htm
- **Parties:** 118 (as at 29.6.05[77])
- **UK:** 24.2.67 (A; see fn 77)

1.96. **Convention Against Discrimination in Education (and 1962 Protocol):**
- **Concluded/Entry into Force:** 14.12.60/22.5.62
- **Location:** UKTS 44 (1962), Cmnd 1760; http://www.unhchr.ch/html/menu3/b/d_c_educ.htm
- **Parties:** 90 (Convention: as at 2005[78])
- **UK:** 14.3.62 (R; Convention, see fn 78)

1.97. **International Convention on the Elimination of All Forms of Racial Discrimination:**
- **Concluded/Entry into Force:** 7.3.66/4.1.69
- **Location:** UKTS 77 (1969), Cmnd 4108 http://www.unhchr.ch/html/menu3/b/d_icerd.htm
- **Parties:** 170 (as at 29.6.05[79])
- **UK:** 7.3.69 (R; see fn 79)
- **Key Body:** Committee on the Elimination of Racial Discrimination (CERD): *http://www.unhchr. ch/html/menu2/6/cerd.htm*. CERD documents can be accessed at *http://www.unhchr.ch/tbs/doc.nsf*
- **Reading:** Lerner, *The United Nations Convention on the Elimination of All Forms of Racial Discrimination* (1980)

1.98. **International Covenant on Economic, Social and Cultural Rights:**
- **Concluded/Entry into Force:** 16.12.66/3.1.76
- **Location:** UKTS 6 (1977), Cmnd 6702 http://www.unhchr.ch/html/menu3/b/a_cescr.htm
- **Parties:** 151 (as at 29.6.05[80])
- **UK:** 20.5.76 (R; see fn 80)
- **Key Body:** Committee on Economic, Social and Cultural Rights ('CESCR') (*http://www.unhchr.ch/html/menu2/6/cescr.htm*). CESCR documents can be accessed at *http://www.unhchr.ch/tbs/doc.nsf*
- **Reading:** Craven, *The International Covenant on Economic, Social and Cultural Rights: A Perspective on its Development* (1995)

1.99. **International Covenant on Civil and Political Rights (and Optional Protocol and Second Optional Protocol on the abolition of the death penalty):**
- **Concluded/Entry into Force:** 16.12.66/23.3.76 (Covenant and Optional Protocol) 15.12.89/11.7.91 (Second Optional Protocol)
- **Location:** UKTS 6 (1977), Cmnd 6702 http://www.unhchr.ch/html/menu3/b/a_ccpr.htm (Optional Protocol: http://

[76] http://conventions.coe.int/Treaty/Commun/ChercheSig.asp?NT=005&CM=8&DF=30/06/05&CL=ENG.

[77] http://untreaty.un.org/ENGLISH/bible/englishinternetbible/partI/chapterXVI/treaty1.asp.

[78] http://portal.unesco.org/education/en/ev.php-URL_ID=27481&URL_DO=DO_TOPIC&URL_SECTION=201.html.

[79] http://untreaty.un.org/ENGLISH/bible/englishinternetbible/partI/chapterIV/treaty2.asp.

[80] http://untreaty.un.org/ENGLISH/bible/englishinternetbible/partI/chapterIV/treaty5.asp.

www.unhchr.ch/html/menu3/b/a_opt.htm)
- **Parties:** 154 (Covenant; as at 29.6.05[81]); 105 (Optional Protocol: as at 29.6.05[82]); 54 (Second Optional Protocol; as at 29.6.05[83])
- **UK:** 20.5.76 (R; Covenant; see fn 81), 10.12.99 (R; Second Optional Protocol; see fn 83)
- **Domestic status:** Given effect in part, for example, Criminal Justice Act 1988, section 133 giving effect to Article 14(6) (*R (Mullen) v Secretary of State for the Home Department* [2004] UKHL 18 [2005] 1 AC 1).
- **Key Body:** Human Rights Committee ('HRC'): D McGoldrick, *The Human Rights Committee: Its Role in the Development of the International Covenant on Civil and Political Rights* (1991); PR Ghandi, *Human Rights Committee and the Right of Individual Communication* (1998); *http://www.unhchr.ch/html/menu2/6/hrc.htm*. HRC documents can be accessed at *http://www.unhchr.ch/tbs/doc.nsf*.
- **Reading:** Joseph, Schultz and Castan, *The International Covenant on Civil and Political Rights and United Kingdom Law* (2001); M Nowak, *UN Covenant on Civil and Political Rights: CCPR Commentary* (1993).

1.100. **Declaration on the Rights of Mentally Retarded Persons:**
- **Concluded:** 20.12.71
- **Location:** http://www.ohchr.org/english/law/res2856.htm

1.101. **Declaration on the Rights of Disabled Persons:**
- **Concluded:** 9.12.75
- **Location:** http://www.ohchr.org/english/law/res3447.htm

1.102. **Convention on the Elimination of All Forms of Discrimination Against Women (and Optional Protocol):**
- **Concluded/Entry into Force:** 18.12.79/3.9.81 (Protocol: 6.10.99/22.12.00)
- **Location:** UKTS 2 (1989), Cm 643 *http://www.un.org/womenwatch/daw/cedaw/text/*
- *econvention.htm* (Protocol: *http://www.un.org/womenwatch/daw/cedaw/protocol/*)
- **Parties:** 180 (Convention; as at 29.6.05[84]), 71 (Protocol; as at 29.6.05[85])
- **UK:** 7.4.86 (R; Convention; see fn 84) 17.12.04 (R; Optional Protocol; see fn 85)
- **Key Body:** Committee on the Elimination of Discrimination Against Women ('CEDAW'): *http://www.un.org/womenwatch/daw/cedaw/committee.htm*. CEDAW documents can be accessed at *http://www.un.org/womenwatch/daw/cedaw/reporting.htm* and *http://www.unhchr.ch/tbs/doc.nsf*.

1.103. **Convention for the Protection of Individuals with Regard to Automatic Processing of Personal Data:**
- **Concluded/Entry into Force:** 28.1.81/1.10.85
- **Location:** UKTS 86 (1990), Cm 1329
- **Parties:** 33 (as at 27.6.05[86])
- **UK:** 26.8.87 (R; see fn 86)
- **Domestic status:** Given effect in part by the Data Protection Act 1998. For example see section 54, selecting the Information Commissioner as the designated authority for the purposes of the Convention.
- **Reading:** Explanatory Report: http://conventions.coe.int/Treaty/en/Reports/Html/108.htm

1.104. **Convention Against Torture and other Cruel, Inhuman or Degrading Treatment or Punishment (and Optional Protocol):**
- **Concluded/Entry into Force:** 10.12.84/ 26.6.87 (Optional Protocol: 18.12.02/ not yet in force)

81 http://untreaty.un.org/ENGLISH/bible/englishinternetbible/partI/chapterIV/treaty6.asp.

82 http://untreaty.un.org/ENGLISH/bible/englishinternetbible/partI/chapterIV/treaty7.asp.

83 http://untreaty.un.org/ENGLISH/bible/englishinternetbible/partI/chapterIV/treaty24.asp.

84 http://untreaty.un.org/ENGLISH/bible/englishinternetbible/partI/chapterIV/treaty10.asp.

85 http://untreaty.un.org/ENGLISH/bible/englishinternetbible/partI/chapterIV/treaty12.asp.

86 http://conventions.coe.int/Treaty/Commun/ChercheSig.asp?NT=108&CM=8&DF=27/06/05&CL=ENG.

- **Location:** UKTS 107 (1991), Cm 1775; *http://www.ohchr.org/english/law/cat.htm.* (Optional Protocol: *http://www.ohchr.org/english/law/cat-one.htm*)
- **Parties:** 139 (Convention; as at 29.6.05[87]); 10 (Optional Protocol; as at 29.6.05[88])
- **UK:** 8.12.88 (R; Convention; see fn 87); 10.12.03 (R; Protocol; see fn 88)
- **Domestic status:** Given effect in part. For example, by the Criminal Justice Act 1988, section 134 which provides that "A public official or person acting in an official capacity, whatever his nationality, commits the offence of torture if in the United Kingdom or elsewhere he intentionally inflicts severe pain or suffering on another in the performance or purported performance of his official duties."
- **Key Body:** Committee Against Torture ('CAT'): *http://www.ohchr.org/english/bodies/cat/.* CAT documents can be accessed at: *http://www.unhchr.ch/tbs/doc.nsf.*
- **Reading:** Burgers, Herman and Danelius, *The United Nations Convention Against Torture: A Handbook on the Convention Against Torture and Other Cruel, Inhuman and Degrading Treatment or Punishment* (1988).

1.105. **Declaration on the Elimination of all Forms of Intolerance and of Discrimination Based on Religion or Belief:**
- **Concluded:** 25.11.89
- **Location:** http://www.ohchr.org/english/law/religion.htm

1.106. **UN Principles for Older Persons:**
- **Concluded:** 16.12.91
- **Location:** http://www.ohchr.org/english/law/olderpersons.htm

1.107. **Declaration on the Elimination of Violence against Women:**
- **Concluded:** 20.12.93
- **Location:** http://www.ohchr.org/english/law/eliminationvaw.htm

1.108. **European Framework Convention for the Protection of National Minorities:**
- **Concluded/Entry into Force:** 1.2.95/1.2.98
- **Location:** http://conventions.coe.int/Treaty/EN/Treaties/Html/157.htm
- **Parties:** 37 (as at 306.05[89])
- **UK:** 15.1.98 (R; see fn 89)
- **Reading:** Explanatory Report (http://conventions.coe.int/Treaty/en/Reports/Html/157.htm)

1.109. **Universal Declaration on Cultural Diversity:**
- **Concluded:** 2.11.01
- **Location:** http://www.ohchr.org/english/law/diversity.htm

I. Immigration and Asylum Law

1.110. **Convention Relating to the Status of Refugees ('the Geneva Convention' or 'the Refugee Convention') (and 1967 Protocol):**
- **Concluded/Entry into Force:** 28.7.51/22.4.54 (Protocol: 31.1.67/4.10.67)
- **Location:** UKTS 39 (1954), Cmd 9171 http://www.unhchr.ch/html/menu3/b/o_c_ref.htm (Protocol: UKTS 15 (1969), Cmnd 3906 http://www.unhchr.ch/html/menu3/b/o_p_ref.htm)
- **Parties:** 142 (Convention; as at 24.6.05[90]), 142 (Protocol; as at 24.6.05[91])
- **UK:** 11.3.54 (R; Convention; see fn 90) 4.9.68 (A; Protocol; see fn 91)
- **Domestic status:** Given effect by the Asylum and Immigration Appeals Act 1993, section 2 ("Nothing in the immigration rules (within the meaning of the [Immigration Act 1971]) shall lay down any practice which would be contrary to the Convention.").
- **Key Body:** Office of the United Nations High Commissioner for Refugees: *http://www.unhcr.ch/cgi-bin/texis/vtx/home*

[87] http://untreaty.un.org/ENGLISH/bible/englishinternetbible/partI/chapterIV/treaty14.asp.

[88] http://untreaty.un.org/ENGLISH/bible/englishinternetbible/partI/chapterIV/treaty16.asp.

[89] http://conventions.coe.int/Treaty/Commun/ChercheSig.asp?NT=157&CM=8&DF=30/06/05&CL=ENG.

[90] http://untreaty.un.org/ENGLISH/bible/englishinternetbible/partI/chapterV/treaty2.asp#participant.

[91] http://untreaty.un.org/ENGLISH/bible/englishinternetbible/partI/chapterV/treaty5.asp.

- **Reading**: Goodwin-Gill, *The Refugee in International Law* (1996); Macdonald, *Immigration Law and Practice in the United Kingdom* (2001). UNHCR Hankbook on Procedures and Criteria for Determining Refugee Status (http://www.unhcr.ch/cgi-bin/texis/utx/publ/opendoc.pdf)tbl=publ&id=3d58e13b4).

1.111. **Convention Relating to the Status of Stateless Persons:**
- **Concluded/Entry into Force**: 28.9.54/6.6.60
- **Location**: UKTS 41 (1960), Cmnd 1098 http://www.unhchr.ch/html/menu3/b/o_c_sp.htm
- **Parties**: 57 (as at 24.6.05[92])
- **UK**: 16.4.59 (R; see fn 92)

1.112. **Convention for the Reduction of Statelessness:**
- **Done/Entry into Force**: 30.8.61/13.12.75
- **Location**: UKTS 158 (1975), Cmnd 6364 http://www.unhchr.ch/html/menu3/b/o_reduce.htm
- **Parties**: 29 (as at 24.6.05[93])
- **UK**: 29.3.66 (R; see fn 93)

1.113. **UN Declaration on the Human Rights of Individuals Who Are Not Nationals of the Country in Which They Live:**
- **Concluded**: 13.12.85
- **Location**: http://www.un.org/documents/ga/res/40/a40r144.htm

1.114. **Convention Determining the State Responsible for Examining Applications for Asylum Lodged in one of the Member States of the European Communities ('the Dublin Convention'):**
- **Concluded/Entry into Force:** 15.6.90/1.9.97
- **Location:** UKTS 72 (1997), Cmd 3806; EC 40 (1991), Cm 1623; http://www.unhcr.bg/euro_docs/en/_36_dublin_en.pdf
- **Parties:** 6 (as at 1994; B&H p 99)
- **UK:** 1.7.92 (R or entry into force; B&H p 99)
- **EU status:** Implemented by Council Regulation (EC) No 343/2003.

J. Immunities and Privileges

1.115. **Convention on the Privileges and Immunities of the United Nations:**
- **Concluded/Entry into Force**: 13.2.46/17.9.46
- **Location**: UKTS 10 (1950), Cmd 7891 http://www.uia.org/legal/app51.php
- **Parties**: 149 (as at 24.6.05[94])
- **UK**: 17.9.46 (A; see fn 94)

1.116. **Vienna Convention on Diplomatic Relations (and Optional Protocol concerning Acquisition of Nationality and Optional Protocol concerning the Compulsory Settlement of Disputes)**:
- **Concluded/Entry into Force**: 18.4.61/24.4.64 (Convention and the Optional Protocols)
- **Location**: Scheduled to the Diplomatic Privileges Act 1964; UKTS 19 (1965), Cmnd 2565 http://www.un.org/law/ilc/texts/diplomat.htm (Optional Protocol concerning Acquisition of Nationality http://www.un.org/law/ilc/texts/dipprona.htm) (Optional Protocol concerning the Compulsory Settlement of Disputes: http://www.un.org/law/ilc/texts/dipprodi.htm)
- **Parties**: 183 (Convention; as at 24.6.05[95]); 50 (Optional Protocol concerning Acquisition of Nationality; as at 24.6.05[96]) 62 (Optional Protocol concerning the Compulsory Settlement of Disputes; as at 24.6.05[97])
- **UK**: 1.9.64 (R; Convention and Optional Protocol concerning the Compulsory Settlement of Disputes; see fn 95 and 97)
- **Domestic status**: Given force of law by the Diplomatic Privileges Act 1964, section 2.

[92] http://untreaty.un.org/ENGLISH/bible/englishinternetbible/partI/chapterV/treaty3.asp.

[93] http://untreaty.un.org/ENGLISH/bible/englishinternetbible/partI/chapterV/treaty4.asp.

[94] http://untreaty.un.org/ENGLISH/bible/englishinternetbible/partI/chapterIII/treaty1.asp.

[95] http://untreaty.un.org/ENGLISH/bible/englishinternetbible/partI/chapterIII/treaty28.asp.

[96] http://untreaty.un.org/ENGLISH/bible/englishinternetbible/partI/chapterIII/treaty29.asp.

1.117. **Vienna Convention on Consular Relations (and Optional Protocol concerning Acquisition of Nationality and Optional Protocol concerning the Compulsory Settlement of Disputes)**:
- **Concluded/Entry into Force**: 24.4.63/ 19.3.67 (Convention and the Optional Protocols)
- **Location**: Scheduled to the Consular Relations Act 1964; UKTS 14 (1973), Cmnd 5219 http://www.un.org/law/ ilc/texts/consul.htm (Convention and the Optional Protocols)
- **Parties**: 167 (Convention; as at 24.6.05[98]), 39 (Optional Protocol concerning Acquisition of Nationality; as at 24.6.05[99]), 45 (Optional Protocol concerning the Compulsory Settlement of Disputes; as at 24.6.05[100]).
- **UK**: 9.5.72 (Convention and Optional Protocol concerning the Compulsory Settlement of Disputes; see fn 98 and 100)
- **Domestic status**: Given force of law by the Consular Relations Act 1968, section 1.

K. International Organisations

1.118. **Charter of the United Nations**:
- **Concluded/Entry into Force**: 26.6.45/ 24.10.45
- **Location**: UKTS 67 (1946) Cmd 7015 http://www.unhchr.ch/html/menu3/b/ ch-cont.htm
- **Members**: 191 (as at 24.6.05[101])
- **UK**: 20.10.45

[97] http://untreaty.un.org/ENGLISH/bible/englishinternetbible/partI/chapterIII/treaty30.asp.

[98] http://untreaty.un.org/ENGLISH/bible/englishinternetbible/partI/chapterIII/treaty31.asp.

[99] http://untreaty.un.org/ENGLISH/bible/englishinternetbible/partI/chapterIII/treaty32.asp.

[100] http://untreaty.un.org/ENGLISH/bible/englishinternetbible/partI/chapterIII/treaty33.asp.

[101] http://untreaty.un.org/ENGLISH/bible/englishinternetbible/partI/chapterI/treaty1.asp.

[102] http://untreaty.un.org/ENGLISH/bible/englishinternetbible/partI/chapterI/treaty3.asp.

1.119. **Statute of the International Court of Justice (Part of the Charter of the UN)**:
- **Concluded/Entry into Force**: 26.6.45/ 24.10.45
- **Location**: UKTS 67 (1946), Cmd 7015; http://www.icj-cij.org/icjwww/ibasicdocuments/Basetext/istatute.htm
- **Parties**: 191 (as at 24.6.05[102]). Parties making declarations under Article 36(2) of the Statute (recognising as compulsory the jurisdiction of the Court): 64 (as at 24.6.05[103]).
- **UK**: Declaration under Article 36(2) made on 1.1.69, as amended on 5.7.04.[104]
- **Key Body**: International Court of Justice: http://www.icj-cij.org/

1.120. **Constitution of the UN Educational, Scientific and Cultural Organisation ('UNESCO')**:
- **Concluded/Entry into Force**: 16.11.45/ 4.11.46
- **Location**: UKTS 50 (1946), Cmd 6963; http://unesdoc.unesco.org/images/0013/001337/133729e.pdf#page=7
- **Members**: 191 (as at 1.1.04[105])
- **UK**: 1.7.97

1.121. **Articles of Agreement for the International Monetary Fund ('IMF')**:
- **Concluded/Entry into Force**: 27.12.45/ 27.12.45
- **Location**: UKTS 21 (1946), Cmd 6885; http://www.imf.org/external/pubs/ft/aa/
- **Parties**: 184 (as at February 2005[106])
- **UK**: 27.12.45[107]

1.122. **Constitution of the World Health Organisation**:
- **Concluded/Entry into Force**: 22.7.46 (as amended)/7.4.48

[103] http://untreaty.un.org/ENGLISH/bible/englishinternetbible/partI/chapterI/treaty4.asp.

[104] http://untreaty.un.org/ENGLISH/bible/englishinternetbible/partI/chapterI/treaty4.asp.

[105] http://unesdoc.unesco.org/images/0013/001337/133729e.pdf#page=7 - See Section P.

[106] http://www.imf.org/external/np/exr/facts/glance.htm.

[107] http://www.imf.org/external/country/GBR/index.htm.

- **Location**: UKTS 43 (1948), Cmd 7458; http://w3.whosea.org/aboutsearo/const.htm
- **Parties**: 192 (as at 30.6.05[108])
- **UK**: 22.7.46 (Definitive Signature)

1.123. **Convention on the International Maritime Organisation**:
- **Concluded/Entry into Force**: 6.3.48 (as amended)/17.3.58
- **Location**: UKTS 54 (1958), Cmd 589 http://www.imo.org/home.asp?topic_id=161
- **Parties**: 165 (as at 29.6.05[109])
- **UK**: 14.2.49 (A; see fn 109)

1.124. **North Atlantic Treaty:**
- **Concluded/Entry into Force:** 4.4.49/24.8.49
- **Location:** UKTS 15 (1965), Cmnd 2566; http://www.nato.int/docu/basic-txt/treaty.htm
- **Member countries:** 26 (2005[110])
- **UK:** 7.6.49 (B&H (1984) pp 2-3, 147)

1.125. **Statute of the Council of Europe:**
- **Concluded/Entry into Force:** 5.5.49 (as amended)/3.8.49
- **Location:** UKTS 51 (1949), Cmd 7778; http://conventions.coe.int/Treaty/EN/CadreListeTraites.htm
- **Parties:** 46 (as at 30.6.05[111])
- **UK:** 26.7.49 (R; see fn 111)

1.126. **Statute of the Hague Conference on Private International Law:**
- **Concluded/Entry into Force:** 31.10.51/ 15.7.55
- **Location:** UKTS 65 (1955), Cmd 9582; http://hcch.e-vision.nl/index_en.php?act=conventions.text&cid=29
- **Parties:** 66 (as at 28.6.05[112])
- **UK:** 15.7.55 (entry into force; see fn 112)

1.127. **Convention Establishing the World Intellectual Property Organisation ('WIPO'):**
- **Concluded/Entry into Force:** 14.7.67/26.4.70
- **Location:** UKTS 52 (1970), Cmnd 4408; http://www.wipo.int/treaties/en/convention/trtdocs_wo029.html
- **Parties:** 182 (as at 3.1.05[113])
- **UK:** 26.2.69 (R; see fn 113)

1.128. **Rome Statute of the International Criminal Court**:
- **Concluded/Entry into Force**: 17.7.98/1.7.02
- **Location**: http://www.un.org/law/icc/statute/romefra.htm
- **Parties**: 99 (as at 29.6.05[114])
- **UK**: 4.10.01 (R; see fn 114)
- **Decision-making Body**: International Criminal Court (http://www.icc-cpi.int/)

L. Jurisdiction

1.129. **Brussels Convention on Jurisdiction and the Enforcement of Judgments in Civil and Commercial Matters**:
- **Concluded/Entry into Force:** 27.9.68/1.2.73. Since 1.3.02, Council Regulation 44/2001 on jurisdiction and the recognition and enforcement of judgments in civil and commercial matters (Brussels I Regulation) (22.12.00) has been in force
- **Location:** EC 46 (1978), Cmnd 7395; http://www.curia.eu.int/common/recdoc/convention/en/c-textes/_brux-textes.htm
- **Parties:** 12 (as at 1994; B&H p 239). Brussels I Regulation has entered into force in all EC Member States with the exception of Denmark: [2005] ILPr pp 413–414
- **UK:** 1.7.89 (entry into force for the Brussels Convention (see above re Brussels I Regulation); B&H p 239)
- **Domestic status:** Given the force of law by the Civil Jurisdiction and Judgments Act 1982, section 2. Brussels I Regulation given the force of law by

108 http://untreaty.un.org/ENGLISH/bible/englishinternetbible/partI/chapterIX/treaty1.asp.

109 http://untreaty.un.org/ENGLISH/bible/englishinternetbible/partI/chapterXII/treaty1.asp.

110 http://www.nato.int/structur/countries.htm.

111 http://conventions.coe.int/Treaty/EN/CadreListeTraites.htm.

112 http://hcch.e-vision.nl/index_en.php?act=conventions.status&cid=29.

113 http://www.wipo.int/treaties/en/ShowResults.jsp?lang=en&treaty_id=1.

114 http://untreaty.un.org/ENGLISH/bible/englishinternetbible/partI/chapterXVIII/treaty10.asp.

the Civil Jurisdiction and Judgments Order SI 2001/3929

1.130. **Lugano Convention on Jurisdiction and the Enforcement of Judgments in Civil and Commercial Matters:**
- **Concluded/Entry into Force:** 16.9.88/ 1.1.92
- **Location:** UKTS 53 (1992), Cm 2009; http://www.curia.eu.int/common/recdoc/convention/en/c-textes/_lug-textes.htm
- **Parties:** 15 EC countries and 3 EFTA countries (as at July 2005: [2005] ILPr p. 412).
- **UK:** 5.2.92 (B&H p 69)
- **Domestic status:** Given the force of law by the Civil Jurisdiction and Judgments Act 1982, section 3A.

M. Law of the Sea

1.131. **International Convention Relating to the Arrest of Sea-going Ships:**
- **Concluded/Entry into Force:** 10.5.52/ 24.2.56
- **Location:** UKTS 47 (1960), Cmnd 1128; http://www.admiraltylawguide.com/conven/arrest1952.html
- **Parties:** 84 (as at 2005[115])
- **UK:** 18.3.59 (R; see fn 115)

1.132. **Convention on the Continental Shelf:**
- **Concluded/Entry into Force:** 29.4.58/ 10.6.64
- **Location:** UKTS 39 (1964), Cmnd 2422 http://www.un.org/law/ilc/texts/contsh.htm
- **Parties:** 57 (as at 29.6.05[116])
- **UK:** 11.5.64 (R; see fn 116)

1.133. **Convention on Fishing and Conservation of Living Resources of the High Seas:**
- **Concluded/Entry into Force:** 29.4.58/ 20.3.66
- **Location:** UKTS 39 (1966), Cmnd 3028 http://www.un.org/law/ilc/texts/fish.htm
- **Parties:** 37 (as at 29.6.05[117])
- **UK:** 14.3.60 (R; see fn 117)

1.134. **Convention on the High Seas:**
- **Concluded/Entry into Force:** 29.4.58/ 30.9.62
- **Location:** UKTS 5 (1963), Cmd 1929 http://www.un.org/law/ilc/texts/hseas.htm
- **Parties:** 62 (as at 29.6.05[118])
- **UK:** 14.3.60 (R; see fn 118)

1.135. **Convention on the Territorial Sea and the Contiguous Zone:**
- **Concluded/Entry into Force:** 29.4.58/ 10.9.64
- **Location:** UKTS 3 (1965), Cmnd 2511 http://www.un.org/law/ilc/texts/terrsea.htm
- **Parties:** 51 (as 29.6.05[119])
- **UK:** 14.3.60 (R; see fn 119)

1.136. **International Convention for the Safety of Life at Sea ('SOLAS') (and Protocol):**
- **Concluded/Entry into Force:** 1.11.74/ 25.5.80
- **Location:** UKTS 46 (1980), Cmnd 7874; http://www.austlii.edu.au/au/other/dfat/treaties/1983/22.html
- **Parties:** 155 (as at 31.5.05[120])
- **UK:** 7.10.77 (R or entry into force; B&H (1984) pp 2-3, 392)

1.137. **UN Convention on the Law of the Sea:**
- **Concluded/Entry into Force:** 10.12.82/ 16.11.94
- **Location:** Misc 11 (1983), Cmnd 8941
- **Parties:** 148 (as at 29.6.05[121])
- **UK:** 25.7.97 (A; see fn 121)

[115] http://www.comitemaritime.org/ratific/brus/bru12.html.

[116] http://untreaty.un.org/ENGLISH/bible/englishinternetbible/partI/chapterXXI/treaty4.asp.

[117] http://untreaty.un.org/ENGLISH/bible/englishinternetbible/partI/chapterXXI/treaty3.asp.

[118] http://untreaty.un.org/ENGLISH/bible/englishinternetbible/partI/chapterXXI/treaty2.asp.

[119] http://untreaty.un.org/ENGLISH/bible/englishinternetbible/partI/chapterXXI/treaty1.asp.

[120] http://www.imo.org/home.asp?topic_id=161.

[121] http://untreaty.un.org/ENGLISH/bible/englishinternetbible/partI/chapterXXI/treaty6.asp.

N. Treaties

1.138. **Vienna Convention on the Law of Treaties:**
- **Concluded/Entry into Force:** 23.5.69/27.1.80
- **Location:** UKTS 58 (1980), Cmnd 7964 http://www.un.org/law/ilc/texts/treaties.htm
- **Parties:** 101 (as at 29.6.05[122])
- **UK:** 25.6.71 (R; see fn 122)

O. Warfare and Weapons Law

1.139. **International Convention with Respect to the Laws and Customs of War by Land ('Hague II'):**
- **Concluded/Entry into Force:** 28.7.1899/4.9.1900
- **Location:** UKTS 11 (1901), Cd 800; http://www.icrc.org/ihl.nsf/385ec082b509e76c41256739003e636d/81ef87b37f70d8fac125641e003513a1?OpenDocument
- **Parties:** 49 (as at 2005[123])
- **UK:** 4.9.1900 (R; see fn 123)

1.140. **International Convention with Respect to the Laws and Customs of War by Land ('Hague IV'):**
- **Concluded/Entry into Force:** 18.10.1907/26.10.1910
- **Location:** UKTS 9 (1910), Cd 5030; http://www.icrc.org/ihl.nsf/0/1d1726425f6955aec125641e0038bfd6?OpenDocument
- **Parties:** 35 (as at 2005[124])
- **UK:** 27.11.1909 (R; see fn 124)

1.141. **Geneva Conventions: (I) for the Amelioration of the Condition of the Wounded and Sick in Armed Forces in the Field; (II) for the Amelioration of the Condition of Wounded, Sick and Shipwrecked Members of Armed Forces at Sea; (III) Relative to the Treatment of Prisoners of War; (IV) Relative to the Protection of Civilian Persons in Time of War ('the Geneva Red Cross Conventions'):**
- **Concluded/Entry into Force:** 12.8.49/21.10.50
- **Location:** UKTS 39 (1958), Cmd 550; http://www.icrc.org/ihl.nsf/WebCONVFULL?OpenView
- **Parties:** 192 (as at 15.6.05[125])
- **UK:** 23.9.57 (R; see fn 125)

1.142. **Treaty on the Non-Proliferation of Nuclear Weapons:**
- **Concluded/Entry into Force:** 1.7.68/5.3.70
- **Location:** UKTS 88 (1970), Cmnd 4474; http://disarmament.un.org:8080/wmd/npt/npttext.html
- **Parties:** 189 (as at 5.3.03[126])
- **UK:** 29.11.68 (R; see fn 126)

1.143. **Convention on the Prohibition of the Development, Production and Stockpiling of Bacteriological (Biological) and Toxin Weapons and on their Destruction:**
- **Concluded/Entry into Force:** 10.4.72/26.3.75
- **Location:** UKTS 11 (1976), Cmnd 6397; http://disarmament.un.org:8080/wmd/bwc/BWCtext.htm
- **Parties:** 152 (as at 26.2.04[127])
- **UK:** 25.3.75 (R; see fn 127)

1.144. **Protocol I to the Geneva Conventions (Relating to the Protection of International Armed Conflicts):**
- **Concluded/Entry into Force:** 8.6.77/7.12.78
- **Location:** Misc 19 (1977), Cmnd 6927 http://www.ohchr.org/english/law/protocol1.htm
- **Parties:** 163 (as at 15.6.05[128])
- **UK:** 28.1.98 (R; see fn 128)

[122] http://untreaty.un.org/ENGLISH/bible/englishinternetbible/partI/chapterXXIII/treaty1.asp.

[123] http://www.icrc.org/ihl.nsf/WebNORM?OpenView&Start=1&Count=150&Expand=6.1#6.1.

[124] http://www.icrc.org/ihl.nsf/WebNORM?OpenView&Start=1&Count=150&Expand=15.1#15.1.

[125] http://www.icrc.org/Web/eng/siteeng0.nsf/htmlall/party_main_treaties/$File/IHL_and_other_related_Treaties.pdf.

[126] http://disarmament.un.org:8080/TreatyStatus.nsf.

[127] http://disarmament2.un.org/TreatyStatus.nsf.

[128] http://www.icrc.org/Web/eng/siteeng0.nsf/htmlall/party_main_treaties/$File/IHL_and_other_related_Treaties.pdf.

1.145. **Protocol II to the Geneva Conventions (Relating to the Protection of Non-International Armed Conflicts):**

- **Concluded/Entry into Force:** 8.6.77/7.12.78
- **Location:** Misc 19 (1977), Cmnd 6927 http://www.ohchr.org/english/law/protocol2.htm
- **Parties:** 159 (as at 15.6.05[129])
- **UK:** 28.1.98 (R; se fn 129)

1.146. **Convention on the Prohibition of the Development, Production, Stockpiling and Use of Chemical Weapons and on their Destruction:**

- **Concluded/Entry into Force:** 3.9.92/29.4.97
- **Location:** Misc 21 (1993), Cm 2331; http://www.un.org/Depts/dda/WMD/cwc/
- **Parties:** 169 (as at 29.6.05[130])
- **UK:** 13.5.96 (R; see fn 130)

[129] http://www.icrc.org/Web/eng/siteeng0.nsf/htmlall/party_main_treaties/$File/IHL_and_other_related_Treaties.pdf.

[130] http://untreaty.un.org/ENGLISH/bible/englishinternetbible/partI/chapterXXVI/treaty8.asp.

2

Sources of International Law

(1) Introduction

2.1. **Article 38(1) of the Statute of the International Court of Justice ('ICJ') authoritatively sets out the sources of international law:**

> 'The [ICJ], whose function it is to decide in accordance with international law such disputes as are submitted to it, shall apply: (a) international conventions, whether general or particular, establishing rules expressly recognised by the contesting states; (b) international custom, as evidence of a general practice accepted as law; (c) the general principles of law recognised by civilised nations; (d) subject to the provisions of Article 59, judicial decisions and the teachings of the most highly qualified publicists of the various nations, as subsidiary means for the determination of rules of law.'

2.2. **As between the parties to an 'international convention', that convention will take priority over 'international custom' and 'general principles of law', other than rules of customary international law which have the status of *jus cogens* [§ 2.16]. 'Judicial decisions' and 'teachings of highly qualified publicists' are ancillary sources of law.**

(2) Treaties

2.3. **Article 38 of the Statute of the ICJ [§ 2.1] identifies 'international conventions', or treaties, as a source of international law. A 'treaty' is defined in Article 2(1)(a) of the Vienna Convention on the Law of Treaties as:**

'An international agreement concluded between States in written form and governed by international law, whether embodied in a single instrument or in two or more related instruments and whatever its particular designation.'

2.4. **Treaties may also be known by other names, for example, conventions, covenants, declarations, statutes, charters or international agreements. Treaties may, contract-like, regulate the relationship between states (for example, bilateral extradition or investment treaties), they may make law by establishing new rules to guide the future conduct of states (for example, the Geneva Conventions on War Crimes [§ 1.141], the UN Convention on the Rights of the Child [§ 1.90]) or they may be declaratory of existing customary international law (for example, some parts of the Vienna Convention on the Law of Treaties [§ 1.138] or the Vienna Convention on Diplomatic Relations [§ 1.116]). Treaties may be bilateral, between a few states, regional (for example the European Convention on Human Rights [§ 1.94]) or international (for example, the International Covenant on Civil and Political Rights [§ 1.99]). Whether or not a particular agreement is to be regarded as a treaty and what document may form part of it involve mixed questions of law and fact. The UN Charter prevails over all other treaties.**

2.4.1. The superior status of the UN Charter:

- UN Charter, Article 103: 'In the event of a conflict between the obligations of the Members of the United Nations under the present Charter and their obligations under any other international agreement, their obligations under the present Charter shall prevail.'

2.4.2. Identifying whether a treaty exists:

Illustrations:

- *Republic of Italy v Hambros Bank Ltd* [1950] Ch 314, 325D–F (Vaisey J, considering whether a financial agreement made between the Governments of the United Kingdom and Italy was a treaty in international law 'and so outside my ken and purview.') [§ 8.5–8.7];
- *Lord Gray's Motion* [2002] 1 AC 124 (HL, Committee for Privileges), 136E–G (Lord Hope, describing the steps taken before the conclusion of the Union Agreement between England and Scotland in 1707. At 137F–138B, considering whether the Union Agreement is a binding agreement: 'Doubts have been expressed as to whether the Union Agreement ever had the status of a treaty in the sense in which that expression is used in inter-

national law and, if so, whether it can be said to have retained that status once the union took effect . . . In ["The Union of 1707 as Fundamental Law" [1957] PL 99 Professor Sir Thomas Smith QC] expressed the view that, although the articles of Union agreed between the commissioners could not be so regarded, the exchanged Acts of the two Parliaments did constitute a treaty jure gentium between Scotland and England. But, as the law of nations in international law is concerned only with states, and the states or kingdoms of Scotland and England ceased to exist on 1 May 1707, the treaty became an executed, or spent, treaty on that date as by the merger the obligants under the treaty had ceased to exist.'), 129E–G (Lord Slynn considering that there was an international treaty between England and Scotland but that since neither state existed as such in 1707 there is no party to the treaty which could enforce it).

2.4.3. **Identifying the different constituent parts of a treaty:**
Illustrations:

- *R v Secretary of State for Foreign and Commonwealth Affairs, Ex parte Rees-Mogg* [1994] QB 552 (DC), 564F–H (Lloyd LJ, construing section 1(2) of the European Communities (Amendment) Act 1993 (whether the Protocol on Social Policy was part of the Treaty on European Union): '[Counsel] drew our attention to Satow's Guide to Diplomatic Practice, 5th ed. (1979), pp.244–245, para. 29.27, where we find: "It is, however, correct to say that the protocol is now used principally as an instrument subsidiary to a treaty or convention, usually (but not necessarily) drawn up by the same negotiators, and dealing with ancillary or incidental matters such as interpretation or particular articles of the main treaty or any supplementary provision of a minor character. Ratification of the treaty or convention will normally ipso facto involve ratification of any supplementary or additional protocol of this nature." This bears out our view that the Protocols here are ancillary or incidental or supplementary to the provisions of the Treaty, and that ratification of the Treaty will automatically involve ratification of the Protocols.');
- *R v Secretary of State for the Home Department, Ex parte Manjit* Kaur 11 December 98 (DC) (unreported), [10] (Lightman J, considering that the Final Act on the accession of the United Kingdom to the European Communities, in 1972, was not in itself a treaty: 'The term "Final Act" is normally used to designate a document which constitutes a formal statement or summary of the proceedings of an international conference, enumerating the treaties or related treaty instruments drawn up as a result of its deliberations together with any resolutions or "voeux" (or wishes) adopted by the conference. It is a résumé of the work done by the conference and as such is signed by the parties present to affirm the authenticity of the record, but not to agree to be

bound by the treaties or other treaty instruments enumerated in it. Treaties and other treaty instruments require separate signature and (to the extent necessary) ratification. A Final Act does not constitute a treaty save in the most exceptional circumstances when in substance it is a treaty rather than a summary of the proceedings of the conference . . . As an alternative to a Final Act, the parties may instead (as an act of equivalent effect) issue an agreed communiqué.') (ECJ is at [2001] ECR I-1237).

2.4.4. **Distinguishing human rights treaties from other treaties:**

- *Matthew v of Trinidad and Tobago State* [2004] UKPC 33 [2005] 1 AC 433, [55] (Lord Bingham, Lord Nicholls, Lord Steyn and Lord Walker (dissenting) quoting from the Advisory Opinion of the Inter-American court of Human Rights *OC-2/82* of 24 September 1982 (Series A) No 2 (1982), [29]: ' "The court must emphasize, however, that modern human rights treaties in general, and the American Convention in particular, are not multilateral treaties of the traditional type concluded to accomplish the reciprocal exchange of rights for the mutual benefit of the contracting states. Their object and purpose is the protection of the basic rights of individual human beings irrespective of their nationality, both against the state of their nationality and all other contracting states. In concluding these human rights treaties, the states can be deemed to submit themselves to a legal order within which they, for the common good, assume various obligations, not in relation to other states, but towards all individuals within their jurisdiction. The distinct character of these treaties has been recognized, inter alia, by the European Commission on Human Rights, when it declared "that the obligations undertaken by the high contracting parties in the European Convention are essentially of an objective character, being designed rather to protect the fundamental rights of individual human beings from infringements by any of the high contracting parties than to create subjective and reciprocal rights for the high contracting parties themselves. (*Austria v Italy* (1961) 4 YB 116, 140)".');
- *Reservations to the Convention on the Prevention and Punishment of the Crime of Genocide* ICJ Reports 1951 p 15, 18 ILR 364 at 370 (ICJ on the Genocide Convention: 'In such a convention the contracting States do not have any interests of their own; they merely have, one and all, a common interest, namely the accomplishment of those high purposes which are the *raison d'être* of the convention. Consequently, in a convention of this type one cannot speak of individual advantages or disadvantages to states, or of the maintenance of a perfect contractual balance between rights and duties. The high ideals which inspired the Convention provide, by virtue of the common will of the parties, the foundation and measure of all its provisions.');

- *Case concerning Application of the Convention on the Prevention and Punishment of the Crime of Genocide (Bosnia and Herzegovina v Yugoslavia)* ICJ Reports 1996 p 595, 115 ILR 1 at 57 (Separate Opinion of Judge Weeramantry: 'Human rights and humanitarian treaties do not represent an exchange of interests and benefits between contracting States in the conventional sense, and in this respect may also be distinguished from the generality of multilateral treaties, many of which are concerned with the economic, security or other interests of states. Human rights and humanitarian treaties represent, rather, a commitment of the particular states to certain norms and values recognised by the international community.').

2.4.5. **Regional nature of certain treaties:**
Illustrations:
- *R (Al-Skeini) v Secretary of State for Defence* [2004] EWHC 2911 (Admin) [2005] 2 WLR 1401, [259] (Rix LJ referring to *Bankovic v Belgium* (2001) 11 BHRC 435 and, 'The significance of [the ECHR's] regional scope, of the European public order, of the legal space or *espace juridique*.');
- *Ashurst v Pollard* [2001] Ch 595 (CA), [34] (Jonathan Parker LJ stating that the words in Article 16(1) of the Brussels Convention on Jurisdiction and the Enforcement of Judgments have 'to be considered in the light of Community law and in a pan-European context.').

2.5. **All states possess the capacity to enter into and conclude treaties (Article 6, Vienna Convention on the Law of Treaties). Additionally, international organisations, for example the United Nations and the European Communities, possess the capacity to enter into and conclude treaties, as defined by their powers [§ 6.7.5].**

2.6. **A state may bind itself to a treaty by different routes and with varying effects. On the international plane a state establishes its consent to be bound by a treaty by ratification, acceptance, approval or accession. Mere signature alone is generally insufficient to create binding international obligations (unless the treaty provides otherwise: [§ 2.6.2]). Rather, signature traditionally constitutes the first stage of the dual signature-ratification process.**

2.6.1. **Different ways of expressing consent to be bound:**
- Article 11, 'Means of expressing consent to be bound by a treaty', Vienna Convention on the Law of Treaties: 'The consent of a State to be bound by a treaty may be expressed by signature, an

exchange of instruments constituting a treaty, ratification, acceptance, approval, accession, or by any other means if so agreed.'

2.6.2. **Signature:**

- Article 12, 'Consent to be bound by a treaty expressed by signature', Vienna Convention on the Law of Treaties: '(1) The consent of a State to be bound by a treaty is expressed by the signature of its representative when: (a) the treaty provides that signature shall have that effect; (b) it is otherwise established that the negotiating States were agreed that signature should have that effect; or (c) the intention of the State to give that effect to the signature appears from the full powers of its representative or was expressed during the negotiation. (2) For the purposes of paragraph 1: (a) the initialling of a text constitutes a signature of the treaty when it is established that the negotiating states so agreed; (b) the signature ad referendum of a treaty by a representative, if confirmed by his State, constitutes a full signature of the treaty.'

2.6.3. **Exchange of instruments constituting a treaty:**

- Article 13, 'Consent to be bound by a treaty expressed by an exchange of instruments constituting a treaty', Vienna Convention on the Law of Treaties: 'The consent of States to be bound by a treaty constituted by instruments exchanged between them is expressed by that exchange when: (a) the instruments provide that their exchange shall have that effect; or (b) it is otherwise established that those States were agreed that the exchange of instruments should have that effect.'

2.6.4. **Ratification, acceptance, approval:**

- Article 14, 'Consent to be bound by a treaty expressed by ratification, acceptance or approval', Vienna Convention on the Law of Treaties: '(1)The consent of a state to be bound by a treaty is expressed by ratification when: (a) the treaty provides for such consent to be expressed by means of ratification; (b) it is otherwise established that the negotiating States were agreed that ratification should be required; (c) the representative of the State has signed the treaty subject to ratification; or (d) the intention of the State to sign the treaty subject to ratification appears from the full powers of its representative or was expressed during the negotiation. (2) The consent of a State to be bound by a treaty is expressed by acceptance or approval under conditions similar to those which apply to ratification.'

2.6.5. **Accession:**

- Article 15, 'Consent to be bound by a treaty expressed by accession', Vienna Convention on the Law of Treaties: 'The consent of a State to be bound by a treaty is expressed by accession when: (a) the treaty provides that such consent may be expressed by that

State by means of accession; (b) it is otherwise established that the negotiating States were agreed that such consent may be expressed by that State by means of accessions; or (c) all the parties have subsequently agreed that such consent may be expressed by that State by means of accession.'

- Accession is used to skip over the stage of signature. For example, where a treaty has already been concluded by two or more states, a third state may become party to the treaty by acceding, without being required to sign first, or, in relation to multilateral treaties, a state may accede without being required to sign first where it participated in the negotiation and drafting of the treaty.
- *Molefi v Principal Legal Adviser* [1971] AC 182 (PC) (construing a letter from the Prime Minister of Lesotho to the Secretary General of the UN as constituting accession to the Refugee Convention).

2.6.6. **Exchanging or depositing instruments:**

- Article 16, 'Exchange or deposit of instruments of ratification, acceptance, approval or accession', Vienna Convention on the Law of Treaties: 'Unless the treaty otherwise provides, instruments of ratification, acceptance, approval or accession establish the consent of a State to be bound by a treaty upon: (a) their exchange between the contracting States; (b) their deposit with the depositary; or (c) their notification to the contracting States or to the depositary, if so agreed.'

2.7. **Where a treaty provision, of a fundamental norm-creating character, is supported by *opinio juris* [§ 2.15], of both contracting states and non-contracting states, it may constitute customary international law. The creation of customary international law by the treaty route does not usurp or replace a similar, independently existing, rule of customary international law.**

2.7.1. **Treaty provisions may constitute customary international law:**

- *North Sea Continental Shelf Cases (Federal Republic of Germany v Denmark; Federal Republic of Germany v The Netherlands)* ICJ Reports 1969 p 3, 41 ILR 29, [71] (ICJ in addressing the contention that a treaty provision had become a rule of customary international law: '[T]his contention . . . clearly involves treating that Article as a norm-creating provision which has constituted the foundation of, or has generated a rule which, while only conventional or contractual in its origin has since passed into the general *corpus* of international law, and is now accepted as such by the *opinio juris*, so as to have become binding even for countries which have never, and do not, become parties to the Convention. There is no doubt that this process is a perfectly possible one and does from time to time occur: it constitutes indeed one of the recognized methods by which new rules of customary international law may be formed. At the same time this result is not lightly to be regarded as having been attained.');

- *R (European Roma Rights Centre) v Immigration Officer at Prague Airport* [2004] UKHL 55 [2005] 2 WLR 1, [23] (Lord Bingham: 'The conditions to be satisfied before a rule may properly be recognised as one of customary international law have been somewhat differently expressed by different authorities, but are not in themselves problematical . . .[quoting from *North Sea Continental Shelf Cases (Federal Republic of Germany v Denmark; Federal Republic of Germany v Netherlands)* [1969] ICJ Rep 3, [70–71] (see above)] . . . The relevant law was, I think, accurately and succinctly summarised by the *American Law Institute Restatement of the Law, Foreign Relations Laws of the United States* 3d (1986), 102(2) and (3): "(2) Customary international law results from a general and consistent practice of states followed by them from a sense of legal obligation. (3) International agreements create law for the states parties thereto and may lead to the creation of customary international law when such agreements are intended for adherence by states generally and are in fact widely accepted." This was valuably supplemented by a comment to this effect: "c. Opinio juris. For a practice of states to become a rule of customary international law it must appear that states follow the practice from a sense of legal obligation (*opinio juris sive necessitatis*); a practice that is generally followed but which states feel legally free to disregard does not contribute to customary law. A practice initially followed by states as a matter of courtesy or habit may become law when states generally come to believe that they are under a legal obligation to comply with it. It is often difficult to determine when that transformation into law has taken place. Explicit evidence of a sense of legal obligation (e.g. by official statements) is not necessary; opinio juris may be inferred from acts or omissions."').

Illustrations:

- *Prosecutor v Furundžija* 121 ILR 123, [138] (International Criminal Tribunal for the Former Yugoslavia: 'That these treaty provisions [on the prohibition of torture] have ripened into customary international law is evinced by various factors. First, these treaties and in particular the Geneva Conventions have been ratified by practically all States of the world . . . [this] shows that all States accept . . . the prohibition of torture. In other words, this participation is highly indicative of the attitude of States to the prohibition of torture. Secondly, no State has ever claimed that it was authorized to practise torture in time of armed conflict, nor has any State shown or manifested opposition to the implementation of treaty provisions against torture . . . Thirdly, the International Court of Justice has authoritatively, albeit not with express reference to torture, confirmed this custom creating process: in the *Nicaragua* case it was held that common Article 3 of the 1949 Geneva Conventions . . . is now well-established as belonging to the corpus of customary international law.');

- *Case concerning Application of the Convention on the Prevention and Punishment of the Crime of Genocide (Bosnia and Herzegovina v Yugoslavia)* ICJ Reports 1996 p 595, 115 ILR 1 at 59 (Separate Opinion of Judge Weeramantry: 'The human rights and humanitarian principles contained in the Geneva Convention are principles of customary international law.');
- *I Congreso del Partido* [1983] 1 AC 244 (HL), 260E–H (Lord Wilberforce, considering whether various transactions were protected by sovereign immunity: 'Now there may be cases in which a multilateral convention may become part of general international law so as to bind states not parties (a proposition not uncontroversial) but at the least the convention must bear a legislative aspect and there must be a wide general acceptance of it as law-making, over a period, before this condition is satisfied. The Brussels Convention [on the Immunity of State Owned Ships 1926] does not nearly meet these requirements: it was a limited agreement between a limited number of states. At the very most it may, together with its progressive, though not numerous, ratifications and accessions, be evidence of the gradual seepage into international law of a doctrine of restrictive immunity.').

2.7.2. **Treaty provisions creating customary international law do not replace similar, independently existing, rules of customary international law:**

- *Case concerning Military and Paramilitary Activities in and against Nicaragua (Nicaragua v USA)* ICJ Reports 1986 p 3, 76 ILR 349, [177] (ICJ: '[E]ven if the customary norm and the treaty norm were to have exactly the same content, this would not be a reason for the Court to hold that the incorporation of the customary norm into treaty law must deprive the customary norm of its applicability as distinct from that of the treaty norm.' At [178–179] considering the reasons for the continued separate existence of treaty norms and customary international law norms, for example, because of the different methods of interpretation and application.)

2.8. Article 18 of the Vienna Convention on the Law of Treaties, obliges a state, in certain circumstances, to refrain from acts which would defeat the object and purpose of a treaty.

'A State is obliged to refrain from acts which would defeat the object and purpose of the treaty when: (a) it has signed the treaty or has exchanged instruments constituting the treaty subject to ratification, acceptance or approval, until it shall have made its intention clear not to become a party to the treaty; or (b) it has expressed its consent to be bound by the treaty, pending the entry into force of the treaty and provided that such entry into force is not unduly delayed.'

2.9. **In the United Kingdom, treaty-making is part of the royal prerogative and vests in the Crown, the executive. It is exercised on the advice of the Secretary of State for Foreign and Commonwealth Affairs. The Secretary of State will usually consult other government departments, as required and depending on the subject matter of the treaty, before exercising the treaty-making power. There is no constitutional obligation for parliamentary approval before a treaty is signed or ratified by the Secretary of State. However, since 1924, a general practice has developed: where there is an intention to ratify a treaty that treaty will be laid as a Command Paper, by the Secretary of State, before Parliament for 21 sitting days ('the Ponsonby Rule'). The treaty may be ratified on expiry of the 21-day period. The Ponsonby Rule arises from the statement made by Mr Arthur Ponsonby (Under-Secretary of State for Foreign Affairs) on 1 April 1924:**

> 'It is the intention of His Majesty's Government to lay on the table of both Houses of Parliament every treaty, when signed, for a period of 21 days, after which the treaty will be ratified and published and circulated in the Treaty Series. In the case of important treaties, the Government will, of course, take an opportunity of submitting them to the House for discussion within this period. But, as the Government cannot take upon itself to decide what may be considered important or unimportant, if there is a formal demand for discussion forwarded through the usual channels from the Opposition or any other party, time will be found for discussion of the Treaty in question . . . Resolutions expressing Parliamentary approval of every Treaty before ratification would be a very cumbersome form of procedure and would burden the House with a lot of unnecessary business. The absence of disapproval may be accepted as sanction, and publicity and opportunity for discussion and criticism are really material and valuable elements which henceforth will be introduced.' (HC Deb (1924) 171, c.1999–2005)

2.10. **The Ponsonby Rule only applies where a treaty has been signed by the United Kingdom and it is sought to ratify, accept, approve or accede to it. It is also applied to certain amendments: those relating to multilateral treaties which have been ratified and those which require legislation (as explained in the Response of July 1982 to the**

6th Report of the Joint Committee on Statutory Instruments (Session 1981–82)). There are, however, certain exceptions to the Ponsonby Rule.

Illustrations:

- Section 6 of the European Parliamentary Elections Act 1978 (as amended by section 3 of the European Communities (Amendment) Act 1986) provides: '(1) No treaty which provides for any increase in the powers of the European Parliament shall be ratified by the United Kingdom unless it has been approved by an Act of Parliament. (2) In this section "treaty" includes any international agreement, and any protocol or annex to a treaty or international agreement.'
- Bilateral double taxation agreements are excluded pursuant to the Lord Privy Seal's written answer to a parliamentary question in May 1981 (HC Deb. (1981) 4, WA 82): '[T]he purpose of the Ponsonby Rule is to afford Parliament the opportunity of considering commitments which the Government of the day are proposing to enter into. In the case of bilateral double taxation agreements, that purpose is already served by the statutory requirement that the draft of any Order in Council providing for double taxation relief shall be laid before the House of Commons for approval by affirmative resolution.'
- The Ponsonby Rule may be bypassed where there are other means of informing or consulting Parliament of the international commitments which the executive is proposing to ratify, for example, by answering a Parliamentary Question or passing a Bill.

2.11. **Once a treaty has entered into force for the United Kingdom it is published in the Treaty Series of Command Papers [§ 1.5]. Where a treaty is signed after 1 January 1997 it is accompanied by an Explanatory Memorandum, following a ministerial undertaking in 1996 (HC Deb (1996) 287, WA 94302, HL Deb (1996) 579, WA 101). These Memoranda give an overview of the treaty and the reasons why it should be ratified etc.**

2.12. **Reading:**

- Memorandum presented by the Foreign and Commonwealth Office to the House of Commons Select Committee on Procedure on 30 November 1998, (1998) BYIL 448–454
- Aust, *Modern Treaty Law and Practice* (2000)
- McNair, *The Law of Treaties* (1961)
- Sinclair, *The Vienna Convention on the Law of Treaties* (1984)

(3) Customary International Law

2.13. Customary international law, as defined in Article 38 of the Statute of the ICJ [§ 2.1], has two constituent elements: the actual widespread and consistent conduct of states ('state practice') and the belief that such conduct is required because a rule of law renders it obligatory ('*opinio juris*').

- *Case concerning the Continental Shelf, Libya/Malta*, ICJ Reports 1985 p13, 81 ILR 239, [27] (ICJ: 'It is of course axiomatic that the material of customary international law is to be looked for primarily in the actual practice and *opinio juris* of States, even though multilateral conventions may have an important role to play in recording and defining rules deriving from custom, or indeed in developing them.');
- *Legality of the Threat or Use of Nuclear Weapons* ICJ Reports 1996 p 226, 110 ILR 163, [64] (Citing the *Case Concerning the Continental Shelf, Libya/Malta* at [27] (see above));
- *Case concerning Military and Paramilitary Activities in and against Nicaragua (Nicaragua v USA)* ICJ Reports 1986 p 3, 76 ILR 349, [207] (ICJ: '[F]or a new customary rule to be formed, not only must the acts concerned "amount to a settled practice", but they must be accompanied by the *opinio juris sive necessitatis.* Either the States taking such action or other States in a position to react to it, must have behaved so that their conduct is "evidence of a belief that this practice is rendered obligatory by the existence of a rule of law requiring it. The need for such a belief, i.e. the existence of a subjective element, is implicit in the very notion of the *opinio juris sive necessitatis.*"' Quoting from the *North Sea Continental Shelf* cases, at [77]);
- *West Rand Central Gold Mining Co Ltd v The King* [1905] 2 KB 391 (DC), 406–407 (Lord Alverstone CJ: 'It is quite true that whatever has received the common consent of civilized nations must have received the assent of our country, and that to which we have assented along with other nations in general may properly be called international law, and as such will be acknowledged and applied by our municipal tribunals when legitimate occasion arises for those tribunals to decide questions to which doctrines of international law may be relevant. But any doctrine so invoked must be one really accepted as binding between nations, and the international law sought to be applied must, like anything else, be proved by satisfactory evidence, which must shew either that the particular proposition put forward has been recognised and acted upon by our own country, or that it is of such a nature, and has been so widely and generally accepted, that it can hardly be supposed that any civilised State would repudiate it. The mere

opinion of jurists, however eminent or learned, that it ought to be so recognised, are not in themselves sufficient. They must have received the express sanction of international agreement, or gradually have grown to be part of international law by their frequent practical recognition in dealings between various nations.').

Illustrations:

- *South West Africa Cases (Ethiopia v South Africa)(Liberia v South Africa) (Second Phase)* ICJ Reports 1966 p 4 at 293 (Judge Tanaka (dissenting): '[W]e consider that the norm of non-discrimination or non-separation on the basis of race has become a rule of customary international law.');
- *Prosecutor v Tadic (Appeal Against Conviction)* (Case IT-94-1-A) 38 ILM (1999) 1518, 124 ILR 63, [220] (International Criminal Tribunal for the Former Yugoslavia, Appeals Chamber: 'In sum, the Appeals Chamber holds the view that the notion of common design as a form of accomplice liability is firmly established in customary international law.');
- *Legality of the Threat or Use of Nuclear Weapons* ICJ Reports 1996 p 226, 110 ILR 163, [41] (ICJ: 'The submission of the exercise of the right of self-defence to the conditions of necessity and proportionality is a rule of customary international law. As the court stated in the case concerning *Military and Paramilitary Activities in and against Nicaragua (Nicaragua v USA)*: there is a "specific rule whereby self-defence would warrant only measures which are proportional to the armed attack and necessary to respond to it, a rule well established in customary international law." (ICJ Reports 1986, p 94, para.176).');
- *Prosecutor v Martić* (Rule 61) (Case IT-95-11-R61) 108 ILR 40, [17] (International Criminal Tribunal for the Former Yugoslavia: 'The rule which states that reprisals against the civilian population as such, or individual civilians, are prohibited in all circumstances, even when confronted by wrongful behaviour of the other party, is an integral part of customary international law and must be respected in armed conflict.');
- *Opel Austria v Council of the EU* [1997] ECR II-39, [90] ('The Court holds . . . that the principle of good faith is a rule of customary international law whose existence is recognised by the International Court of Justice (see the judgment of 25 May 1926, *German Interests in Polish Upper Silesia*, [PCIJ], Series A, No7, pp30 and 39) and is therefore binding on the Community.').

2.14. **To constitute state practice for the purpose of creating a rule of customary international law, the rule must have endured over time and achieved a wide level of consistency and acceptance. There is no specific time limit for which the practice must exist before it can be elevated into a rule of customary international law. Instead, this**

will depend on, for example, the subject matter of the rule, the nature of the state practice and the extent of its observance. The conduct must be evident in the behaviour of states. It must be practised extensively, uniformly and constantly. State practice may be evidenced by, for example, publications of government departments, resolutions and declarations of the UN General Assembly (including the ways in which states vote upon these and the explanations given by them on such occasions), case law [§ 2.21], treaties, the diplomatic and political interaction of states and historical records evidencing past conduct of states.

2.14.1. **Duration over time:**

- *North Sea Continental Shelf Cases (Federal Republic of Germany v Denmark; Federal Republic of Germany v The Netherlands)* ICJ Reports 1969 p 3, 41 ILR 29, [74] (ICJ: '[T]he passage of only a short period of time is not necessarily, or of itself, a bar to the formation of a new rule of customary international law on the basis of what was originally purely a conventional rule.').

2.14.2. **State practice must be constant, uniform and extensive:**

- *Asylum Case (Colombia/Peru)* ICJ Reports 1950 p 266, 17 ILR 280 at 284–285 (ICJ considering that the party claiming the existence of a particular rule of customary international law 'must prove that the rule invoked by it is in accordance with a constant and uniform usage practised by the States in question, and that this usage is the expression of a right appertaining to the State granting asylum and a duty incumbent on the territorial State.');
- *North Sea Continental Shelf Cases (Federal Republic of Germany v Denmark; Federal Republic of Germany v The Netherlands)* ICJ Reports 1969 p 3, 41 ILR 29, [74] (ICJ describing as an 'indispensable requirement' for the establishment of state practice, that it 'should have been both extensive and virtually uniform in the sense of the provision invoked; and should moreover have occurred in such a way as to show a general recognition that a rule of law or legal obligation is involved.');
- *Case concerning Military and Paramilitary Activities in and against Nicaragua (Nicaragua v USA)* ICJ Reports 1986 p 3, 76 ILR 349, [186] (ICJ: 'It is not to be expected that in the practice of States the application of the rules in question should have been perfect . . . The Court does not consider that, for a rule to be established as customary the corresponding practice must be in absolutely rigorous conformity with the rule. In order to deduce the existence of customary rules, the Court deems it sufficient that the conduct of States should, in general, be consistent with such rules, and that instances of State conduct inconsistent with a given rule should generally have been treated as breaches of that rule, not as indications of the recognition of a new rule.').

Illustration:

- *Mondev v United States* 42 ILM (2003) 85, 125 ILR 98, [125] (ICSID Arbitration Tribunal interpreting Article 1105(1), NAFTA ('Each Party shall accord to investments of investors of another party treatment in accordance with international law, including fair and equitable treatment and full protection and security.') by reference to prevailing international law: '[W]hose content is shaped by the conclusion of more than two thousand bilateral investment treaties and many treaties of friendship and commerce. Those treaties largely and concordantly provide for "fair and equitable" treatment of, and for "full protection and security" for, the foreign investor and his investments. Correspondingly the investments of investors under NAFTA are entitled, under the customary international law which NAFTA parties interpret Article 1105(1) to comprehend, to fair and equitable treatment and to full protection and security.').

2.14.3. **Consensus of nations as a legal fiction:**

- *Trendtex Trading Corp. v Central Bank of Nigeria* [1977] QB 529 (CA), 552–553 (Lord Denning: 'Like all rules of international law, this rule [regarding sovereign immunity] is said to arise out of the consensus of the civilised nations of the world. All nations agree upon it. So it is part of the law of nations. To my mind this notion of a consensus is a fiction. The nations are not in the least agreed upon the doctrine of sovereign immunity. The courts of every country differ in their application of it . . . Yet this does not mean that there is no rule of international law upon the subject. It only means that we differ as to what that rule is. Each country delimits for itself the bounds of sovereign immunity. Each creates for itself the exceptions from it.'), 567–568 (Stephenson LJ agreeing that the notion of universal consent is fictional).

2.14.4. **The importance of state practice may be limited regarding fundamental human rights:**

- *Sepet v Secretary of State for the Home Department* [2003] UKHL 15 [2003] 1 WLR 856, [41] (Lord Hoffmann: 'I do not think it is possible to apply the rules for the development of rules of international law concerning the relations of states with each other (for example, as to how boundaries should be drawn) to the fundamental human rights of citizens against the state. There are unhappily many fundamental human rights which would fail such a test of state practice and the Refugee Convention is itself a recognition of this fact. In my opinion a different approach is needed. Fundamental human rights are the minimum rights which a state ought to concede to its citizens. For the purpose of deciding what these minimum rights are, international instruments are important even if many state parties in practice disregard them. (The African Charter on Human and People's Rights, adopted in 1981, is perhaps a conspicuous example.) But the instruments show recognition that such rights ought to exist. The delinquent states do not normally deny this; they usually pretend that they comply. Equally, the fact that many states openly deny this existence of a human right is not necessarily a reason for saying that it does not exist. One may think, so much the worse for them. But state practice is nevertheless important because it is difficult to assert the existence of a universal fundamental human right disavowed by many states which take human rights seriously.')

2.14.5. **Treaties and international instruments may provide evidence of state practice:**

Illustrations:

- *R (European Roma Rights Centre) v Immigration Officer at Prague Airport* [2004] UKHL 55 [2005] 2 WLR 1, [24–28] (Lord Bingham, considering whether the Refugee Convention was supplemented by a more generous body of law by reference to, inter alia, the Bangkok Principles (formulated by the Asian-African Legal Consultative Committee, 1966), Resolution (67)14 of the Committee of Ministers of the Council of Europe, 1967 (adopted by the Committee of Ministers in 1984: Recommendation No R (84)1), Conclusion No. 6 (XXVIII, 1977) (Non Refoulement) and Conclusion No. 22 (XXXII, 1981) (Protection of Asylum Seekers in Situations of Large-Scale Influx) of the UNHCR Executive Committee, General Comment No 31 (The Nature of the General Legal Obligation Imposed on State Parties to the International Covenant on Civil and Political Rights) of the UN Human Rights Committee, adopted on 29 March 2004.);
- *Matthews v Ministry of Defence* [2003] UKHL 4 [2003] 1 AC 1163, [104] (Lord Millett: 'State immunity is a creature of customary international law; its existence was confirmed by the European Convention on State Immunity (1972) (Cmnd 5081).');
- *R (Abbasi) v Secretary of State for Foreign and Commonwealth Affairs* [2002] EWCA Civ 1598 [2003] UKHRR 76, [63–64] (Lord Phillips MR finding it 'enough' to cite Articles 9 and 2 of the International Covenant on Civil and Political Rights when recognising as a 'fundamental part of human rights law' the principle that every imprisonment is prima facie unlawful and requires to be justified as being a legal measure.)

2.15. ***Opinio juris* is the belief, by states, that the relevant conduct is required because a rule of law renders it obligatory.**

Illustrations:

- *Legality of the Threat or Use of Nuclear Weapons* ICJ Reports 1996 p226, 110 ILR 163, [70] (ICJ: '[General Assembly resolutions] can, in certain circumstances, provide evidence important for establishing the existence of a rule or the emergence of *opinio juris*. To establish whether this is true of a given General Assembly resolution, it is necessary to look at its content and the conditions of its adoption; it is also necessary to see whether an *opinio juris* exists as to its normative character. Or a series of resolutions may show the gradual evolution of the *opinio juris* required for the establishment of a new rule.' Concluding at [73]: 'The emergence, as *lex lata*, of a customary rule specifically prohibiting the use of nuclear weapons as such is hampered by the continuing tensions between the nascent *opinio juris* on the one hand, and the still strong adherence to the practice of deterrence on the other.');

- *Asylum Case (Colombia/Peru)* ICJ Reports 1950 p 266, 17 ILR 280 at 285 (ICJ noting that Colombia had not shown that the rule invoked by it was exercised by states 'as a right appertaining to them and respected by the territorial States as a duty incumbent on them and not merely for reasons of political expediency.').

2.16. **Within rules of customary international law, certain principles have the status of *jus cogens*. *Jus cogens*, or peremptory norms of customary international law, are principles of an acknowledged superiority: those which refer to the obligations of a state to the international community in general, rather than to one or a group of states, also known as obligations *erga omnes*. Examples of *jus cogens* include the prohibition of genocide, the prohibition of torture and the right to self-determination. Before a rule can become a peremptory norm it must be established as a general principle of international law and also accepted as part of *jus cogens*.**

2.16.1. **Defining peremptory norms of customary international law:**

- Article 53, 'Treaties conflicting with a peremptory norm of general international law (*jus cogens*)', Vienna Convention on the Law of Treaties: 'A treaty is void if, at the time of its conclusion, it conflicts with a peremptory norm of general international law. For the purposes of the present Convention, a peremptory norm of general international law is a norm accepted and recognized by the international community of States as a whole as a norm from which no derogation is permitted and which can be modified only by a subsequent norm of general international law having the same character.'
- *Case concerning the Barcelona Traction Light and Power Company Ltd (Belgium v Spain)* ICJ Reports 1970 p 3, 46 ILR 178, [33–34] (ICJ: '[A]n essential distinction should be drawn between the obligations of a State towards the international community as a whole, and those arising vis-à-vis other another State in the field of diplomatic protection. By their very nature the former are the concern of all States. In view of the importance of the rights

involved, all states can be held to have a legal interest in their protection, they are obligations *erga omnes*. Such obligations derive, for example, in contemporary international law, from the outlawing of acts or aggression, and of genocide, as also from the principles and rules concerning the basic rights of the human person, including protection from slavery and racial discrimination. Some of the corresponding rights of protection have entered into the body of general international law . . . others are conferred by international instruments of a universal or quasi-universal character.').

2.16.2. **Examples of peremptory norms of customary international law:**

- *Prosecutor v Furundžija* 121 ILR 213, [153] (International Criminal Tribunal for the Former Yugoslavia: '[T]his principle [the prohibition of torture] has evolved into a peremptory norm or *jus cogens*, that is, a norm that enjoys a higher rank in the international hierarchy than treaty law and even "ordinary" customary rules.');
- *R v Bow Street Magistrate, Ex parte Pinochet* [2000] 1 AC 147 (HL) (recognising torture as *jus cogens*, see for example: 198B (Lord Browne-Wilkinson), 261B (Lord Hutton), 277F–G and 278B (Lord Millett) and 290A (Lord Phillips));
- *Jones v The Ministry of the Interior Al-Mamlaka Al-Arabiya* [2004] EWCA Civ 1394 [2005] UKHRR 57, (recognising the prohibition of torture as *jus cogens*, see for example: [31] (Mance LJ) and [108] (Lord Phillips MR) [**§ 13.10.5**];
- *Al-Adsani v UK* (2002) 34 EHRR 11, [61] (ECtHR recognising the prohibition of torture as jus cogens) [**§ 7.13.2**];
- *Suresh v Canada* (2002) 208 DLR (4th) 1, 124 ILR 343 (Sup Ct, Canada), [65] ('Although this Court is not being asked to pronounce on the status of the prohibition on torture in international law, the fact that such a principle is included in numerous multi-lateral instruments, that it does not form a part of any known domestic administrative practice, and that it is considered by many academics to be an emerging, if not established peremptory norm, suggests that it cannot be easily derogated from.');
- *Case concerning Application of the Convention on the Prevention and Punishment of the Crime of Genocide (Bosnia and Herzegovina v Yugoslavia)* ICJ Reports 1996 p 595, 115 ILR 1, [31] (ICJ: '[T]he rights and obligations enshrined by the [Genocide] Convention are rights and obligations *erga omnes*.'), [101] (Dissenting Opinion of Judge Kreća: 'The norm prohibiting genocide, as a norm of *jus cogens*, establishes obligations of a State towards the international community as a whole community, hence by its very nature it is the concern of all States. As a norm of *jus cogens* it does not have nor could it possible have, a limited territorial application with the effect of excluding its application in any part

of the international community. In other words, the norm prohibiting genocide as a universal norm binds States in all parts of the world . . . The concrete norm is of universal application (a norm *erga omnes*), and hence "non-territoriality" as another pole of limited territorial application may be taken as an element of the very being of a cogent norm of genocide prohibition.');

- *Nulyarimma v Thompson* (1999) 165 ALR 621, 120 ILR 353 (Fed. Ct, Australia), [18] (Wilcox J: 'I accept that the prohibition of genocide is a peremptory norm of customary international law, giving rise to a non-derogatable obligation by each nation State to the entire international community. This is an obligation independent of the Convention on the Prevention and Punishment of the Crime of Genocide. It existed before the commencement of that Convention in January 1951, probably at least from the time of the United Nations General Assembly resolution in December 1946.');
- *Case concerning East Timor (Portugal v Australia)* ICJ Reports 1995 p 90, 105 ILR 227, [29] (ICJ: 'In the Court's view, [the] assertion that the right of peoples to self-determination, as it evolved from the [UN] Charter and from United Nations practice, has an *erga omnes* character, is irreproachable . . . it is one of the essential principles of contemporary international law.' At [31]: '[T]he Territory of East Timor remains a non self-governing territory and its people has the right to self-determination.');
- *Legality of the Threat or Use of Nuclear Weapons* ICJ Reports 1996, p 226, 110 ILR 163, [79] (ICJ: 'It is undoubtedly because a great many rules of humanitarian law applicable in armed conflict are so fundamental to the respect of the human person and "elementary considerations of humanity" as the Court put it in its Judgment of 9 April 1949 in the *Corfu Channel* Case (*ICJ Reports 1949*, p.22), that the Hague and Geneva Conventions have enjoyed a broad accession. Further these fundamental rules are to be observed by all States whether or not they have ratified the conventions that contain them, because they constitute intransgressible principles of international customary law.').

2.16.3. **A treaty is void if it conflicts with a peremptory norm of customary international law:**

- Article 53, 'Treaties conflicting with a peremptory norm of general international law (*jus cogens*)', Vienna Convention on the Law of Treaties: [§ **2.16.1**].

2.16.4. **General consequences of a rule becoming a peremptory norm:**

- *Prosecutor v Furundžija* 121 ILR 213, [153] (International Criminal Tribunal for the Former Yugoslavia: 'The most conspicuous consequence of this higher rank [of *jus cogens*] is that the principle at issue cannot be derogated from by States through international treaties or local or special customs or even general customary rules not endowed with the same normative force.' At [154–157]: 'Clearly the *jus cogens* nature of the prohibition against torture articulates the notion that the prohibition has now become one of the most fundamental standards of the international community. Furthermore, this prohibition is designed to produce a deterrent effect, in that it signals to all members of the international community and the individuals over whom they wield authority that the prohibition of torture is an absolute value from which nobody must deviate. The fact that torture is prohibited by a peremptory norm of international law has other effects at the inter-state and individual levels. At the inter-state level it serves to internationally de-legitimize any legislative, administrative or judicial act authorising torture . . . at the individual level . . . every State is entitled to investigate, prosecute and punish or extradite individuals accused of torture, who are present in a territory under its jurisdiction . . . other consequences include the fact that torture may not be covered by a statute of limitations, and must not be excluded from extradition under any political offence exemption.').

(4) General Principles of Law

2.17. **'General principles of law' is a source of international law (as identified by Article 38 of the Statute of the ICJ: [§ 2.1]) which provides courts with a reservoir of basic rules of law from which to deduce the applicable law where it does not already exist in either case law, statutes or treaties. General principles of law therefore provide a source of law which fills in any lacunae in international law. It is debatable whether this is a separate source of law or whether it is parasitic on treaty and customary law. It is, however, commonly accepted that whilst general principles may constitute a freestanding source of law it is a limited and restrictively applied category.**

- *North Sea Continental Shelf Cases (Federal Republic of Germany v Denmark; Federal Republic of Germany v The Netherlands)* ICJ Reports 1969 p 3, 41 ILR 29, [33] (Separate Opinion of Judge Ammoun: describing general principles of law as 'nothing other than the norms common to the different legislations of the world, united by the identity of legal reason therefor, or the *ratio legis*, transposed from the internal legal system to the international legal system.' At [35]: 'The general principles of law are indisputably factors which bring morality into the law of nations, inasmuch as they borrow from the law of nations principles of the moral order such as those of equality, responsibility and *faute*, *force majeure* and act of God, estoppel, non-misuse of right, due diligence, the interpretation of legal documents on the basis of spirit as well as the letter of the text and finally equity in the implementation of legal rules, from which derive the principles of unjust enrichment and *enrichissement sans cause*, as well as good faith "which is no more than a reflection of equity and which was born from equity." ').

Illustrations:

- *Chorzów Factory (Indemity) Case* PCIJ, Series A, No 17, p 29 at 47 ('The essential principle contained in the actual notion of an illegal act is that reparation must, as far as possible, wipe-out all the consequences of the illegal act and re-establish the situation which would, in all probability, have existed if that act had not been committed. Restitution in kind or, if this is not possible, payment of a sum corresponding to the value which restitution in kind would bear; the award, if need be, of damages for loss sustained which would not be covered by restitution in kind or payment in place of it—such are the principles which should serve to determine the amount of compensation for an act contrary to international law.' Described as 'still recognised as authoritative as a matter of general principle': *SD Myers v Canada* 121 ILR 73 (NAFTA Arbitration under the UNCITRAL Rules, 13 November 2000), at [311].);
- *North Sea Continental Shelf Cases (Federal Republic of Germany v Denmark; Federal Republic of Germany v The Netherlands)* ICJ Reports 1969 p 3, 41 ILR 29, [38–45] (Separate Opinion of Judge Ammoun: considering the role of equity, 'as a general principle of law', and the source of the 'equidistance-special circumstance rule.');
- *Administrative Tribunal Case* ICJ Reports 1954 p 47, 21 ILR 310 at 314 (ICJ describing *res judicata* as, 'a well established and generally recognized principle of law.');
- *AMCO v Republic of Indonesia* 89 ILR 366, [267] (ICSID Arbitration Tribunal declaring the full compensation of prejudice to be, 'a principle common to the main systems of municipal law, and therefore, a general principle of law which may be considered a source of international law.');
- *Nuclear Tests (Australia v France)* ICJ Reports 1974 p 253, 57 ILR 398, [46] (ICJ: 'One of the basic principles governing the creation and performance of legal obligations, whatever their source, is the principle of good faith. Trust and confidence are inherent in international co-operation, in particular in an age when this co-operation in many fields is becoming increasingly essential.' Cited in *Legality of the Threat or Use of Nuclear Weapons* ICJ Reports 1996 p226, 110 ILR 163, [102] and where, at [103], the ICJ concluded that good faith 'remains without any doubt an objective of vital importance to the whole of the international community today.');

- *M/V Saiga (No 2) (Saint Vincent and the Grenadines v Guinea)* 38 ILM (1999) 1323, 120 ILR 143 (International Tribunal for the Law of the Sea), [56] (Judge Warioba (dissenting) recognising 'as a cardinal principle of law' that a person should not be judged without being given an opportunity to be heard.);
- *Case concerning the Barcelona Traction Light and Power Company Ltd (Belgium v Spain)* ICJ Reports 1970 p 3, 46 ILR 178, [12] (Separate Opinion of Judge Gros describing Article 1, Protocol I, ECHR (right to the peaceful enjoyment of possessions) as 'the least that can be said is that here is a general principle of law which loses none of its binding force through being restated in the 1952 Protocol.');
- *Prosecutor v Erdemovic (Sentencing)* 108 ILR 180, [31] (International Criminal Tribunal for the Former Yugoslavia, Trial Chamber I noting that there is a general principle of law, 'common to all nations whereby the severest penalties apply for crimes against humanity in national legal systems.').

2.18. **The fact that it is broadly permissible to deduce and apply general principles of law, where there is no other applicable law, does not mean that it will always be possible to identify the relevant principle to be applied in a given case. For example, in the *Advisory Opinion on the Threat or Use of Nuclear Weapons* the ICJ was unable to state whether there was a generally applicable principle:**

> 'It follows from the above-mentioned requirements that the threat or use of nuclear weapons would generally be contrary to the rules of international law applicable in armed conflict, and in particular the principles and rules of humanitarian law; However in view of the current state of international law, and of the elements of fact at its disposal, the Court cannot conclude definitively whether the threat or use of nuclear weapons would be lawful or unlawful in an extreme circumstance of self-defence, in which the very survival of a State would be at stake.' ((1996) 110 ILR 163, 35 ILM (1996) 809, [105])

2.19. **'General principles of international law' is a term whose meaning varies with its use. It often refers to rules of customary international law, general principles of law or basic rules of both procedural and substantive international law:**

Illustrations:

- *Case concerning the Gabčikovo-Nagymaros Project (Hungary/Slovakia)* ICJ Reports 1997 p 7, 116 ILR 2 at 151 (Separate Opinion of Judge Koroma: 'Foremost among [the general principles of international law] is that of *pacta sunt servanda* which forms an integral part of international law.');

- *Legality of the Threat or Use of Nuclear Weapons* ICJ Reports 1996 p 226, 110 ILR 163, [29] (ICJ: 'The environment is not an abstraction but represents the living space, the quality of life and the very health of human beings, including generations unborn. The existence of the general obligation of States to ensure that activities within their jurisdiction and control respect the environment of other States or of areas beyond national control is now part of the corpus of international law relating to the environment.');
- *In the Matter of an International Arbitration under the UNCITRAL Rules between Sandline International Inc and the Independent State of Papua New Guinea* 117 ILR 552 (9 October 1998), [10.2] (Arbitration Tribunal: 'It is a clearly established principle of international law that acts of a State will be regarded as such even if they are ultra vires or unlawful under the internal law of the State.');
- *Salas v USA* (Case 10.573) 123 ILR 118, [9] (Inter-American Commission on Human Rights: 'The recognised principles of international law dictate that exhaustion [of remedies] is required only where adequate and effective remedies are available.');
- *Asian Agricultrual Products Ltd v Republic of Sri Lanka* 30 ILM (1991) 577, 106 ILR 416, [56] (ICSID Arbitration Tribunal recognising as a general principle of international law the rule that, as a matter of civil procedure, the burden of proof is on the claimant);
- *New Zealand Maori Council v Attorney General* [1987] 1 NZLR 641 (New Zealand High Court), 120 ILR 463 at 510–11 (Richardson J recognising the international law doctrine of good faith by reference to Article 2, UN Charter and Article 26, Vienna Convention on the Law of Treaties);
- *R (Al-Skeini) v Secretary of State for Defence* [2004] EWHC 2911 (Admin) [2005] 2 WLR 1401, [342] (Rix LJ: '[Counsel] was prepared to accept that there was a general principle of international law that a state which is responsible for a violation of a rule of international law has an obligation to make restitution.').

(5) Judicial Decisions and Academic Writings

2.20. **Judicial decisions and the writings of highly qualified publicists have a subsidiary role as sources of international law by virtue of Article 38 of the Statute of the ICJ [§ 2.1].**

2.21. **'Judicial decisions' refers to decisions of the Permanent Court of International Justice, the ICJ, national courts and international arbitral awards. Although the ICJ is not subject to a doctrine of precedent as understood in common law systems, the court does**

strive to maintain such consistency between its decisions as is possible. Decisions of national courts serve the dual purpose of providing authority as to the content of international law as well as constituting evidence of state practice in the development of rules of customary international law [§ 2.14].

2.22. **As a matter of historical fact, the status and use of writings of highly qualified publicists have declined considerably. Whilst such writings are still technically regarded as an ancillary source of international law, they are now more likely to provide structure, focus and analysis rather than a pure source of law.**

- *R v Keyn* (1876) 2 Ex D 63, 68–70 (Sir Robert Phillimore: 'In the memorable answer pronounced by Montesquieu to be réponse sans réplique, and framed by Lord Mansfield and Sir George Lee, of the British to the Prussian Government, "The law of nations is said to be founded upon justice, equity, convenience, and the reason of the thing, and confirmed by long usage" . . . With respect to "justice, equity, convenience and the reason of the thing," one particular class of authority has been much relied upon in the arguments of counsel, namely the treatises of learned writers on law . . . the value of these [digests] is affected by various circumstances; for instance, the period in which the particular work was written, the general reputation of the writer, the reception which his work has met with from the authorities of civilized states, are circumstances, which, though in no case rendering his opinion a substitute for reason, may enhance or derogate from the consideration due to it.'), 122 (Amphlett JA: 'To ascertain [international law] it is most important in this and all other cases to consult the published opinions of eminent jurists of different countries, for although, as has been justly said, those writers cannot make the law, still if there is found a practical unanimity or a great preponderance of opinion among them, it would afford weighty, and in many cases, conclusive evidence that their statement of the law had been received with the general consent of the civilized nations of the world.'), 202–203 (Cockburn CJ: 'For writers on international law, however valuable their labours may be in elucidating and ascertaining the principles and rules of law, cannot make the law. To be binding, the law must have received the assent of the nations who are to be bound by it.');
- *West Rand Central Gold Mining Co Ltd v The King* [1905] 2 KB 391 (DC), 406–407 (Lord Alverstone CJ) [**§ 2.13**].

Illustration:

- *R (European Roma Rights Centre) v Immigration Officer at Prague Airport* [2004] UKHL 55 [2005] 2 WLR 1, [27] (Lord Bingham, considering that notwithstanding the possibility of a consensus of academic opinion, there was insufficient state practice to support the creation of a rule of customary international law which provides that if a national of country A, wishing to travel to country B to claim asylum, applies in country A to officials of country B, he may not be denied leave to enter country B without appropriate enquiry into the merits of his asylum claim).

2.23. **Reading:**

- Brownlie, *Principles of Public International Law* (2003)
- Jennings and Watts (eds), *Oppenheim's International Law* (1996)
- Shaw, *International Law* (2003)

Part II

Using Incorporating Statutes and Incorporated Treaties

3

Incorporating Statutes

(1) Introduction

3.1. **There is a rising trend in the extent to which domestic legislation incorporates international treaties and makes them part of domestic United Kingdom law. It is no longer uncommon to find that Parliament has given the whole or parts of a treaty the direct force of law in the United Kingdom.**

3.2. **The terminology used to refer to treaties which have been made part of domestic law by statutes is variable. Treaties may be said to have become 'incorporated', 'transformed, 'domesticated', 'adopted' or 'patriated'. There is some debate on the most appropriate term.**

Illustrations:

- *Re McKerr* [2004] UKHL 12 [2004] 1 WLR 807, [63] (Lord Hoffmann considering that the terminology of 'incorporation' as applied to the ECHR 'is a misleading metaphor');
- Murray Hunt, *Using Human Rights Law in Domestic Courts* (1997) considering 'transformation' as apt to refer to treaty obligations and 'incorporation' as apt to refer to customary international law (p12, n 43).

3.3. **The terminology used in this book is one of 'incorporation' — both for treaties and customary international law. This is the terminology which is most commonly used in case law. However, it is simply convenient shorthand for denoting the formalised reception of international law into domestic law and it does not preclude the need for scrutiny in individual cases of the mode and degree of incorporation.**

3.4. Most incorporating statutes are self-contained transfusions of international law into domestic law. They have a clearly defined ambit and a restricted subject-matter. Other than their international dimension they are generally indistinguishable from purely domestic statutes. Two key exceptions to this rule, rooted in the recently developed common law distinction between constitutional and other statutes, are the European Communities Act 1972 and the Human Rights Act 1998 ('HRA') [chapters 6; 7].

> 'We should recognise a hierarchy of Acts of Parliament: as it were "ordinary" statutes and "constitutional" statutes. The two categories must be distinguished on a principled basis. In my opinion a constitutional statute is one which (a) conditions the relationship between the citizen and state in some general, overarching manner, or (b) enlarges or diminishes the scope of what we would now regard as fundamental constitutional rights. (a) and (b) are of necessity closely related: it is difficult to think of an instance of (a) that is not also an instance of (b). The special status of constitutional statutes follows the special status of constitutional rights. Examples are Magna Carta 1297 (25 Edw 1), the Bill of Rights 1689 (1 Will & Mary sess 2 c 2), the Union with Scotland Act 1706 (6 Anne c 11), the Reform Acts which distributed and enlarged the franchise (Representation of the People Act 1832 (2 & 3 Will 4 c 45), 1867 (30 & 31 Vict c 102) and 1884 (48 & 49 Vict c 3)), the Human Rights Act 1998, the Scotland Act 1998 and the Government of Wales Act 1998. The [European Communities Act 1972] clearly belongs in this family. It incorporated the whole corpus of substantive Community rights and obligations, and gave overriding domestic effect to the judicial and administrative machinery of Community law. It may be there has never been a statute having such profound effects on so many dimensions of our daily lives. The 1972 Act is, by force of the common law a constitutional statute.' (*Thoburn v Sunderland City Council* [2002] EWHC 195 (Admin) [2003] QB 151, [62–63] (Laws LJ))

(2) Routes to Incorporation

3.5. Parliament may incorporate treaties into domestic law as it sees fit. There is no rule specifying the precise mode of incorporation, as Lord Steyn noted when considering the incorporation of the Geneva Convention Relating to the Status of Refugees ('the Refugee Convention') by section 2 of the Asylum and Immigration Appeals Act 1993:

> 'It is true, of course, that a convention may be incorporated more formally by scheduling it to an instrument, eg the Carriage of Goods by Sea Act 1971 which enacted the Hague-Visby Rules, But there is no rule specifying the precise legislative method of incorporation. It is also possible to incorporate a treaty in part, eg the European Convention on Human Rights was incorporated into our law without article 13: see Human Rights Act 1998.' (*R (European Roma Rights Centre) v Immigration Officer at Prague Airport* [2004] UKHL 55 [2005] 2 WLR 1, [42])

3.6. **There are, however, a few recurring and readily identifiable modes of incorporation. A statute may expressly incorporate a treaty into domestic law by giving all or parts of it force of law. Commonly the relevant parts of such a treaty will be scheduled to the statute but there are instances where the statute merely refers to the treaty being incorporated. Once a treaty has been incorporated it is treated as a part of domestic law, for example it may be referred to in other legislation and will be subject to the effect of the HRA [§ 7.12.2]. A treaty, or parts of a treaty, may also be incorporated without being given express force of law (indirect incorporation), for example the Refugee Convention and the European Convention on Human Rights ('ECHR'). Treaty provisions may also, simply, be referred to in a statute as supplying a factual or legal definition. Finally, treaties may be incorporated into domestic law by virtue of Community law, for example the Dublin Convention was given effect by a Council Regulation [§ 6.7.6].**

3.7. **Treaties may be expressly incorporated into domestic law.**

3.7.1. **A treaty (or parts thereof) may be given force of law and scheduled to the relevant statute:**

Illustrations:

- Merchant Shipping Act 1995: sections 183(1), 185(1) and 224(1) give force of law to provisions of, respectively, the Convention relating to the Carriage of Passengers and their Luggage by Sea (in part I of schedule 6), the Convention on Limitation of Liability for Maritime Claims (in part I of schedule 7), and the Convention on Salvage 1989 (in Part I of Schedule 11).
- Contracts (Applicable Law) Act 1990: section 2(1) gives force of law to the Convention on the Law Applicable to Contractual Obligations (1980) (schedule 1), the Luxembourg Convention (schedule 2), and the Brussels Protocol (schedule 3).
- Recognition of Trusts Act 1987: section 1(1) gives force of law to the (scheduled) Hague Convention on the Law Applicable to Trusts and on their Recognition (1984).

- Child Abduction and Custody Act 1985: section 1(2) gives force of law to the provisions of the Hague Convention on the Civil Aspects of Child Abduction 1980 in schedule 1.
- Civil Jurisdiction and Judgments Act 1982: section 2 gives force of law to the Brussels Convention (schedule 1) and section 3A gives force of law to the Lugano Convention (schedule 3C) (as amended by and applied alongside Council Regulation (EC) No 44/2001 of 22 December 2000 on jurisdiction and the recognition and enforcement of judgments in civil and commercial matters given effect by the Civil Jurisdiction and Judgments Order SI 2001/3929).
- Carriage of Goods by Sea Act 1971: section 1(2) gives force of law to the Hague Rules (as amended by the Brussels Protocols; known as the Hague-Visby Rules), in the schedule attached.
- Consular Relations Act 1968: section 1 gives force of law to the provisions of the Vienna Convention on Consular Relations in schedule 1.
- Uniform Laws on International Sales Act 1967: section 1(2) gives force of law to the Uniform Law on Sales (schedule 1) and section 2(2) to the Uniform Law on Formation (schedule 2).
- Carriage of Goods of Road Act 1965: section 1 gives force of law to the provisions of the Convention on the Contract for the International Carriage of Goods by Road 1956 (scheduled).
- Diplomatic Privileges Act 1964: Section 2 gives force of law to articles of the Vienna Convention on Diplomatic Relations (1961) set out in Schedule 1.
- Carriage by Air Act 1961: section 1(1) gives force of law to the Warsaw Convention (1929) for the Unification of certain Rules relating to International Carriage by Air, as amended by the Hague Protocol (1955). Schedule 1 to the Act sets out the English and French texts of the Warsaw Convention (and has been amended by the Carriage of Goods by Air and Road Act 1979).
- Arbitration (International Investment Disputes) Act 1966: section 4 gives force of law to section 6, chapter 1 of the Convention on the Settlement of Investment Disputes between States and Nationals of Other States (scheduled).
- Geneva Conventions Act 1957: section 1 makes it an offence for anyone, whatever their nationality, and whether in or outside the United Kingdom, to commit, aid, abet or procure the commission by any other person of a grave breach of any of the scheduled conventions or the first protocol. Schedules 1 to 6 consist of, respectively, the Geneva Convention for the Amelioration of the Condition of the Wounded and Sick in Armed Forces in the Field, Geneva Convention for the Amelioration of the Condition of Wounded, Sick and Ship Wrecked Members of Armed Forces at Sea, Geneva Convention Relative to the Treatment of Prisoners of War, Geneva Convention Relative to the Protection of Civilian Persons in Time of War, Protocol I: Protocol Additional to the

Geneva Conventions of 12 August 1949, and Relating to the Protection of Victims of International Armed Conflict, Protocol II: Protocol Additional to the Geneva Convention of 12 August 1949, and Relating to the Protection of Victims of Non-International Armed Conflict.

- Fisheries Act 1891: section 1 gives the Declaration in Schedule 1 (Declaration Respecting the North Sea Fisheries made between the Government of the United Kingdom and the Government of Belgium) the 'same force as if they were enacted in the body of this Act.'

3.7.2. **A treaty (or parts thereof) may be given force of law without scheduling to the relevant statute:**
Illustrations:

- European Communities Act 1972: section 1(2) sets out the names of 'Treaties' and 'Community Treaties'. Section 2(1) provides: 'All such rights, powers, liabilities, obligations and restrictions from time to time created by or arising by or under the Treaties, and all such remedies and procedures from time to time provided for by or under the Treaties, as in accordance with the Treaties are without further enactment, to be given legal effect or used in the United Kingdom shall be recognised and available in law, and be enforced, allowed and followed accordingly' and section 2(4) provides, inter alia: 'any enactment passed or to be passed . . . shall be construed and have effect subject to the foregoing provisions of this section.' [**chapter 6**]
- International Transport Conventions Act 1983: section 1 gives the Convention concerning International Carriage by Rail 1980 force of law. Section 1(3) provides that the provisions which are given force of law are those in the Convention (as amended) and judicial notice is to be taken to those provisions as if they were contained in the Act.

3.7.3. **Incorporated treaty provisions may be referred to in domestic statutes, other than the incorporating statute:**
Illustrations:

- Crime (International Co-operation) Act 2003: section 52 (inserting sections 63A–63E into the Terrorism Act 2000) provides that a person is a protected person if they fall within Article 1(b) of the Vienna Convention on Diplomatic Relations (which is enacted, in relevant part, as a schedule to the Diplomatic Privileges Act 1964).
- Immigration and Asylum Act 1999: section 65 provides, inter alia: '(1) A person who alleges that an authority has, in taking any decision under the Immigration Acts relating to that person's entitlement to enter or remain in the United Kingdom, acted in breach of his human rights may appeal to an adjudicator against that decision unless he has grounds for bringing an appeal against the decision under the Special Immigration Appeals Commission Act

1997. (2) For the purposes of this Part, an authority acts in breach of a person's human rights if he acts, or fails to act, in relation to that other person in a way which is made unlawful by section 6(1) of the Human Rights Act 1998.'

- Scotland Act 1998: section 29(1) provides that an Act of the Scottish Parliament is not law in so far as any provision of the Act is outside the legislative competence of the Parliament. The limits of legislative competence are defined in section 29(2); subsection (d) provides that a provision is outside that competence if it is incompatible with any of the Convention rights. 'Convention rights' is defined in section 126(1) as having the same meaning as that in the Human Rights Act 1998. Furthermore, section 57(2) and (3) of the Scotland Act 1998 provide: '(2) A member of the Scottish Executive has no power to make any subordinate legislation, or to do any other act, so far as the legislation or act is incompatible with any of the Convention rights or with Community law. (3) Subsection (2) does not apply to an act of the Lord Advocate-(a) in prosecuting any offence, or (b) in his capacity as head of the systems of criminal prosecution and investigation of deaths in Scotland, which, because of subsection (2) of section 6 of the Human Rights Act 1998, is not unlawful under subsection (1) of that section.'
- Government of Wales Act 1998: sections 107 and 109 provide the same definition of human rights as in the HRA.
- Housing Act 1996: section 186 defines 'claim for asylum' by reference to the Refugee Convention and Protocol.
- County Courts Act 1984: section 27(1)(f) provides that the Admiralty county court has Admiralty jurisdiction over, inter alia, any claims under the Salvage Convention 1989 (ie the International Convention on Salvage 1989, as it has effect under the Merchant Shipping Act 1995, section 224) [§**3.7.1**].
- State Immunity Act 1978: section 20 confers personal immunity upon a head of state, family and servants by reference to the privileges and immunities given to the head of a diplomatic mission under the Vienna Convention on Diplomatic Relations 1961 (which was enacted, in relevant part, as a schedule to the Diplomatic Privileges Act 1964).

3.7.4. **Evidence of incorporation may be found in the long title of an incorporating statute:**

Illustrations:

- International Transport Conventions Act 1983, long title: 'An Act to give effect to the Convention concerning International Carriage by Rail signed on behalf of the United Kingdom on 9th May 1980; and to make further provision for the amendment of Acts giving effect to other international transport conventions so as to take account of revisions of the conventions to which they give effect.'

- Consular Relations Act 1968, long title: 'An Act to give effect to the Vienna Convention on Consular Relations.'
- Diplomatic Privileges Act 1964, long title: 'An Act to amend the law on diplomatic privileges and immunities by giving effect to the Vienna Convention on Diplomatic Relations and for purposes connected therewith.'
- Carriage by Air Act 1961, long title: 'An Act to give effect to the Convention concerning international travel by air known as "the Warsaw Convention as amended at the Hague, 1955", to enable the rules contained in that Convention to be applied, with or without notification, in other cases and, in particular, to non-international carriage by air; and for connected purposes.'
- Arbitration (International Investment Disputes) Act 1966, long title: 'An Act to implement an international convention on the settlement of investment disputes between States and nationals of other States.'
- Geneva Conventions Act 1957, long title: 'An Act to enable effect to be given to certain international conventions done at Geneva on the twelfth day of August, nineteen hundred and forty-nine, and for purposes connected therewith.'
- Fisheries Act 1891, long title: 'An Act to carry into effect an International Declaration respecting the North Sea Fisheries, and to amend the Law relating to Sea, Fisheries and Salmon and Freshwater Fisheries.'

3.8. **Treaties may be incorporated otherwise than by giving them express force of law. The partial incorporation of the Refugee Convention into domestic law provides a good example of how incorporation may occur in effect even where there is no express statutory provision giving force of law to the treaty.**

3.8.1. **Asylum and Immigration Appeals Act 1993:**

- Section 2: 'Nothing in the immigration rules (within the meaning of the [Immigration Act 1971]) shall lay down any practice which would be contrary to the Convention.'
- *R (European Roma Rights Centre) v Immigration Officer at Prague Airport* [2004] UKHL 55 [2005] 2 WLR 1, [40–42] (Lord Steyn: '[The Refugee Convention] is not a mere unincorporated treaty. Under rule 16 of the Statement of Changes in Immigration Rules (1983) (HC 169) it was formerly provided: "Where a person is a refugee full account is to be taken of the provisions of the Convention and Protocol relating to the Status of Refugees (Cmd 9171 and Cmnd 3906). Nothing in these rules is to be construed as requiring action contrary to the United Kingdom's obligations under these instruments" . . . The difficulty is, however, that Immigration Rules are not law but merely instructions to immigration officers. *By themselves* they cannot effect an

incorporation. Against this background, Parliament decided to make reference to the Refugee Convention in primary legislation. Parliament was informed that the new provision was to be "an additional safeguard": Hansard, Standing Committee A, 19 November 1992, col 151. Section 2 of the Asylum and Immigration Appeals Act 1993 provides: "Nothing in the immigration rules (within the meaning of the 1971 Act) shall lay down any practice which would be contrary to the Convention." It is necessarily implicit in section 2 that no administrative practice or procedure may be adopted which would be contrary to the Convention. After all, it would be bizarre to provide that formal immigration rules must be consistent with the Convention but that informally adopted practices need not be consistent with the Convention. The reach of section 2 of the 1993 Act is therefore comprehensive. Parliament must be taken to have been aware, in enacting the 1993 Act, that the courts had treated the references in the immigration rules to the Refugee Convention as "indirectly" or "for practical purposes" incorporating it into domestic law [as referred to in *R v Secretary of State for the Home Department, Ex parte Singh, The Times*, 8, June 1987 (DC) and *R v Secretary of State for the Home Department, Ex parte Sivakumaran* [1988] AC 958 (HL)] . . . In the context of the decisions of the Court of Appeal and the House of Lords in 1987 Parliament must have intended that the strengthened reference to the Refugee Convention in primary legislation would be treated by the courts as an incorporation of the Refugee Convention into domestic law. Moreover, the heading of section 2 is "Primacy of the Convention." This is a relevant and significant pointer to the overriding effect of the Convention in English law . . . In my view it is clear that the Refugee Convention has been incorporated into our domestic law.');

- *R (Pepushi) v CPS* [2004] EWHC 798 (Admin) [2004] All ER (D) 129 (May), [27] (Thomas LJ construing section 31 of the Immigration and Asylum Act 1999: '[T]he [Refugee] Convention has not been directly incorporated into the domestic law of the UK. When giving effect to the obligations of the UK under Article 31, Parliament did not incorporate the terms of the Article but chose to use the language set out in s. 31 which is narrower in scope than the meaning of Article 31 as declared by this Court in *Adimi*. The position under our domestic law in such circumstances, as established by decisions binding on us, is clear.');
- *R v Immigration Appeal Tribunal, Ex parte Shah* [1999] 2 AC 629 (HL), 647G–H (Lord Hoffmann: 'The United Kingdom is a party to [the Refugee Convention], which has been incorporated into domestic law by section 8 of the Asylum and Immigration Appeals Act 1993. Subsection (2) provides that a person who has limited leave to enter the United Kingdom may appeal to a special adjudicator against a refusal to vary leave "on the ground it

would be contrary to the United Kingdom's obligations under the Convention for him to be required to leave the United Kingdom after the time limited by the leave".');

- *R v Secretary of State for the Home Department, Ex parte Sivakumaran* [1988] AC 958 (HL), 990G–H (Lord Keith: 'The United Kingdom having acceded to the Convention and Protocol, their provisions have for all practical purposes been incorporated into United Kingdom law.');
- *T v Immigration Officer* [1996] AC 742 (HL), 759–760 (Lord Mustill: 'effect' is given to the Refugee Convention by the Asylum and Immigration Appeals Act 1993 and 'practical effect' is given to the Refugee Convention by the Immigration Rules).

3.8.2. **Human Rights Act 1998:**

- For relevant provisions of the HRA: [§ **7.6**]
- *Wilson v First County Trust Ltd (No 2)* [2003] UKHL 40 [2004] 1 AC 816, [126] (Lord Hobhouse: 'The [HRA] does not simply say, as do some comparable Acts (eg section 1(2) of the Carriage of Goods by Sea Act 1971), that the provisions of the European Convention "shall have the force of law". Its approach is more subtle. It has a limited definition of "Convention rights": section 1. It requires courts in determining a question in connection with a Convention right to "take into account" judgments of the European Court of Human Rights and other cognate material: section 2. It thus, at the outset, draws a distinction between the international obligations of the United Kingdom under the Convention and what are to be the municipal law obligations of the three organs of the state, the executive, the legislature and the judiciary.');
- *R v Lambert* [2001] UKHL 37 [2002] 2 AC 545, [135] (Lord Clyde: 'In approaching the problem of the retrospectivity of the [HRA] it is to be remembered at the outset that the Act did not incorporate the rights set out in the Convention into the domestic laws of the United Kingdom. The purpose of the Act, as set out in its long title, was "to give further effect to rights and freedoms" guaranteed under that Convention. The Convention rights have not become part of the constitution so as to obtain any superiority over the powers of Parliament or the validity of primary legislation.');
- *Re Mckerr* [2004] UKHL 12 [2004] 1 WLR 807, [25] (Lord Nicholls considering the distinction between the rights arising under the ECHR and those arising under the HRA by reference to the ECHR) [§ **3.12.3**];
- *R v Lyons* [2002] UKHL 44 [2003] 1 AC 976, [104] (Lord Millett considering that the ECHR has not been incorporated into domestic law so as to be directly enforceable by individuals) [§ **3.12.3**].

3.9. A statute may refer to the factual or legal definitions in a treaty.

Illustrations:

- International Criminal Court Act 2001: gives effect to the Statute of the International Criminal Court and makes it an offence against the law of England and Wales for a person to commit genocide, a crime against humanity or a war crime (section 51(1)), as defined by the Articles of the Statute of the International Criminal Courts, scheduled to the Act (schedule 8).
- Countryside and Rights of Way Act 2000: section 77 (inserting a new section 37A into the Wildlife and Countryside Act 1981) provides that English Nature and Countryside Council are to be notified where a wetland in Great Britain is designated for inclusion in the list of wetlands of international importance under Article 2(1) of the Ramsar Convention on Wetlands of International Importance especially as Waterfowl Habitat (signed on 2 February 1971), as amended by the Paris Protocol and the Regina Amendments.
- Data Protection Act 1998: section 54A defines 'the customs information system' by reference to the Convention on the Use of Information Technology for Customs Purposes (OJ 1995 C316/34), 'the Europol information system' by reference to the Convention on the Establishment of European Police Office (OJ 1995 C316/2 Cm 3050) and 'the Schengen information system' by reference to the Convention implementing the Schengen Agreement (OJ 2000 L239/19).
- Electricity Act 1989: section 36B(7) defines 'the use of recognised sea lanes essential to international navigation' by reference to Article 60(7) of the UN Convention on the Law of the Sea 1982 (Cmnd 8941).
- Harbours Act 1964: schedule 3, part I defines 'sensitive area' as including, inter alia, a property on the World Heritage List (under Article 11(2) of the UNESCO Convention for the Protection of the World Cultural and Natural Heritage 1972).
- Employment of Women, Young Persons, and Children Act 1920: section 4 defines 'industrial undertaking' by reference to the definition in the Convention fixing Minimum Age for Admission of Children to Industrial Employment 1919 (in part I of the schedule).

3.10. In addition to treaties which are directly and indirectly incorporated into domestic law, there are two hybrid categories: first, where a statute expressly provides, for example in the long title, that it gives effect to an unincorporated treaty but does not give the treaty force of law (the 'express reference' group) and secondly where, although a statute contains no express mention of a treaty, there is extrinsic evidence showing that the statute was intended to

give effect to the unincorporated treaty (the 'evidential nexus' group). These two hybrid categories are not treated as instances of incorporation. Rather, they are chiefly governed by the principles which apply to unincorporated treaties [§ 9.1].

(3) Interpreting Incorporating Statutes

3.11. **Incorporating statutes are portals through which treaties pass to be received into the corpus of domestic law. Whilst the terms of the treaty may be directly applied in domestic law, for example where they are given force of law and replicated in the incorporating statute, it is the statute and not the treaty which has primacy and which is the governing code in domestic law.**

3.11.1. Primacy of incorporating statutes:
Illustrations:

- *Rey v Government of Switzerland* [1999] 1 AC 54 (PC), 63B–E (Lord Steyn interpreting an extradition treaty entered into between the United Kingdom and Switzerland and partially incorporated into the Bahamian Extradition Act 1994:'The premise of the argument is that as between the Treaty and the Act of 1994 the former has primacy. That premise is wrong. Except in so far as the Act of 1994 incorporates by reference provisions of the Treaty into section 5(1)(b)(i) (list of offences) and section 10(4) (period for production of documents) of the Act of 1994, the Treaty is not part of the domestic law of The Bahamas. The Act of 1994 is the code governing extradition . . . The issues under consideration must therefore be decided not by reference to the Treaty but in the light of the provisions of the Act of 1994.');
- *R (Al-Skeini) v Secretary of State for Defence* [2004] EWHC 2911 (Admin) [2005] 2 WLR 1401, [301] (Rix LJ: 'We are in any event clear in our minds that the [ECHR] is only reached through the [HRA] and that it is the Act which we must apply in these courts.');
- *R (Al-Fawwaz) v Governor of Brixton Prison* [2001] UKHL 69 [2002] 1 AC 556, [146] (Lord Rodger: 'The terms of an extradition treaty cannot be used to construe the Act of Parliament under which the treaty is given effect in our domestic law. It is nevertheless worth noting that the language of article I of the 1972 treaty with the United States does not suggest that the parties were treating "territory" and "jurisdiction" as synonymous.');
- *R v Secretary of State for the Environment, Transport and the Regions, Ex parte International Air Transport Association* [2000] 1 Lloyd's Rep 242 (QBD), 244 (Jowitt J: 'The [Warsaw] Convention has been incorporated into our domestic law by s.1(1) of the

Carriage by Air Act, 1961 so that what I have to construe is in fact part of an English statute, albeit I must do so according to the canons of construction by which international treaties are construed.')

3.11.2. **Incorporated treaty provisions reflected in incorporating statute provisions:**
***Illustration*:**

- *Republic of India v Indian Steamship Co. (No 2)* [1998] AC 878 (HL), 910B–F (Lord Steyn, construing section 34 and schedule 1 (the Brussels Convention on Jurisdiction and the Enforcement of Judgments) to the Civil Jurisdiction and Judgments Act 1982: 'Counsel for the plaintiffs has emphasised that, unlike article 21, section 34 of the Act of 1982 is a provision of domestic origin designed to address a problem of domestic law. That is true. On the other hand, a comparison of article 21 and section 34 [reveals] a striking similarity in language. In drafting section 34 the draftsman must have taken article 21 as a model. In these circumstances it would be curious if one were to arrive at a decision "on the parties" in respect of section 34 which diverges from that which applies to section 21. This consideration reinforces the view that I take on the nature of an action in rem judged from the perspective of domestic English law.')

3.12. **The key step in construing legislation which refers to a treaty is to scrutinise the relationship between the legislation and the treaty, ie whether it incorporates the treaty (or uses the treaty less directly [§ 9.1]) and, if so, the precise mode and extent of incorporation. These considerations will dictate the nature of the statute and the scope and effect of the treaty in domestic law, for example whether it is necessary to interpret the treaty provisions [chapters 4; 5].**

3.12.1. **Differentiating between incorporating statutes, giving force of law (directly or indirectly) to all or part of a treaty, from statutes giving effect to all or part of a treaty (the express reference or evidential nexus groups: [§ 3.10; § 9.1]):**
Illustrations:

- *R (Lika) v Secretary of State for the Home Department* [2002] EWCA Civ 1855 [2002] All ER (D) 230 (Dec), [20] (Latham LJ, considering sections 2 and 3 of the Asylum and Immigration Act 1996 and concluding that: 'There is no doubt that the provisions of the Dublin Convention are not incorporated into domestic law.' Citing, as authority, *Ex parte Shefki Gashi; Ex parte Artan Gjoka* (15 June 2000) (unreported: CO/3559/1999 and CO/4506/1999), [11] (Collins J: 'I cannot accept that an individual can have any rights or expectations under the Dublin Convention since it is concerned not to confer benefits on the individual but to ascertain which state should be responsible for dealing with his claim. It may confer benefits on him indirectly in as much as he will not be passed from one state to another and back again.') and *Zeqiri v Secretary of State for the Home Department* [2002] Imm AR 42, [49] (Lord Phillips MR: 'The Dublin Convention does not form part of our domestic law and cannot govern the manner in which the 1996 Act operates.')) [**§ 9.1.2**];

- *R v Secretary of State for Transport, Ex parte Pegasus Holdings (London) Ltd* [1988] 1 WLR 990 (QBD), 1002F–1003A (Schiemann J construing section 60(2) of the Civil Aviation Act 1982 (providing that Orders in Council may include such provisions as are requisite or expedient for carrying out the Chicago Convention on International Civil Aviation): '[Counsel] says, and I accept, that it is not right to say that the Order is solely designed to incorporate the Convention into English law . . . however, as a matter of construction of section 60, Parliament did not authorise an Air Navigation Order containing provisions that conflict with the provisions of the Convention. The Order can go further than, but it cannot under the statute, in my judgment, run counter to, the Convention . . . An alternative way of approaching the problem is this: that the Order should, in my judgment be construed, if it is possible, in such a way that its powers are to be exercised in accordance with the country's obligations under the Convention.').

3.12.2. **Focus on the mode of incorporation used:**

- *Berkeley v Secretary of State for the Environment* [2001] 2 AC 603 (HL), 617D–H (Lord Hoffmann: 'In the present case the Directive [Council Directive (85/337/EEC)] had been transposed into domestic legislation [by the Town and Country Planning (Assessment of Environmental Effects) Regulations 1988 (SI 1988/1199)] and there was a failure to comply with the terms of that legislation. In my view, a court should not ordinarily be willing to validate such an act on the ground that a different form of transposing legislation (eg by allowing an environmental statement to take the composite form put forward in this case) might possibly also have satisfied the terms of the Directive.').

3.12.3. **Analysing the relationship between a treaty and a statute:**
Illustrations:

- *The Hollandia* [1982] QB 872 (CA), 885 (Sir Sebag Shaw stating, in the context of the Carriage of Goods by Sea Act 1971 and the Hague Visby Rules (the International Convention for the Unification of Certain Rules of Law Relating to Bills of Lading (as amended)), that where a convention is incorporated by giving it force of law and scheduling it to an Act the effect is to imbue it with the character of a statutory enactment). HL is at [1983] 1 AC

565, 572G–573A (Lord Diplock: 'The Hague-Visby Rules, or rather all of them that are included in the Schedule [to the Carriage of Goods by Sea Act 1971] are to have the force of law in the United Kingdom: they are to be treated as if they were part of directly enacted statute law.');

- *Re Mckerr* [2004] UKHL 12 [2004] 1 WLR 807, [25] (Lord Nicholls considering the distinction between rights arising under the ECHR and rights created by the HRA by reference to the ECHR: 'These two sets of rights now exist side by side. But there are significant differences between them. The former existed before the enactment of the 1998 Act and they continue to exist. They are not as such part of this country's law because the Convention does not form part of this country's law. That is still the position. These rights, arising under the Convention, are to be contrasted with rights created by the 1998 Act . . . They are part of this country's law. The extent of these rights, created as they were by the 1998 Act, depends upon the proper interpretation of that Act. It by no means follows that the continuing existence of a right arising under the Convention in respect of an act occurring before the 1998 Act came into force will be mirrored by a corresponding right created by the 1998 Act. Whether it finds reflection in this way in the 1998 Act depends upon the proper interpretation of the 1998 Act.');
- *Wilson v First County Trust Ltd (No 2)* [2003] UKHL 40 [2004] AC 816, [126] (Lord Hobhouse considering the mode of incorporation of the ECHR by the HRA) [§ **3.8.2**];
- *R v Lambert* [2001] UKHL 37 [2002] 2 AC 545, [135] (Lord Clyde noting that the HRA does not incorporate the ECHR directly into domestic law) [§ **3.8.2**];
- *R v Lyons* [2002] UKHL 44 [2003] 1 AC 976, [104] (Lord Millett considering that the ECHR has not been incorporated into domestic law by the HRA so as to be directly enforceable by individuals (see especially in relation to Article 46) whereas the Brussels Convention on Jurisdiction and Enforcement of Judgments is given the force of law in the United Kingdom by the Civil Jurisdiction and Judgments Act 1982 (section 2(1));
- *R (Al-Fawwaz) v Governor of Brixton Prison* [2001] UKHL 69 [2002] 1 AC 556, [102(5)] (Lord Millett: 'The Extradition Act [1989] is an enabling Act. It applies not only to existing treaties but also to future treaties yet to be entered into. These may, of course, place further restrictions on the powers of the English Courts to order extradition but they may not extend them beyond those conferred by the Act.').

3.12.4. **Considering the wider implications of incorporation:**

- For an overview of the effects of the European Communities Act 1972 [**chapter 6**];
- For an overview of the effects of the HRA [**chapter 7**];

Illustrations:

- *In re S (Children) (Child Abduction: Asylum Appeals)* [2003] EWCA Civ 843 [2002] 1 WLR 2548, [25] (Laws LJ considering how far the family court, acting under the Hague Convention on the Civil Aspects of International Child Abduction, or the wardship jurisdiction, is obliged to take account of or comply with Article 33 of the Refugee Convention seen as a freestanding instrument: 'That question raises issues as to the scope and the context of the incorporation of the 1951 Refugee Convention into our municipal law which are not without some sophistication. We are not required, and for my part I would not choose, to express anything like a concluded view on such issues. I would only go so far as this. Having regard to the rule as to the paramountcy of the child's interests arising under section 1 of the Children Act 1989, I would respectfully suppose that a family judge would at the least pay very careful attention to any credible suggestion that a child might be persecuted if he were returned to his country of origin or habitual residence before making any order that such a return should be effected.');
- *Republic of Haiti v Duvalier* [1990] 1 QB 202 (CA), 212 (Staughton LJ in deciding whether the plaintiffs could serve out of the jurisdiction without leave pursuant to RSC Ord 11 r 1(2), applied the principle of construction in *Garland v BR Engineering* [1983] 2 AC 751, 771 [§ **9.8.2**] to Ord.11 r.1(2) by construing it compatibly with Article 21 of the incorporated Brussels Convention on Jurisdiction and the Enforcement of Judgments);
- *The 'Herceg Novi' and 'Ming Galaxy'* [1998] 2 Lloyd's Rep 454 (CA), 460 (Sir Christopher Staughton considering the Convention Relating to the Limitation of the Liability of Owners of Sea-going Ships 1957 and the incorporated Convention on Limitation for Maritime Claims 1976 (by the Merchant Shipping Act 1995) in deciding whether an English action should be stayed on the basis that Singapore was a more appropriate forum and whether substantial justice would be available there given that the 1957 Convention was still part of Singaporean law. Concluding that: '(1) The 1976 Convention has not received universal acceptance or anything like it. It is *not* "an internationally sanctioned and objective view of where substantial justice is now viewed as lying" [*Caspian Basin Specialised Emergency Salvage Administration v Bouyges Offshore SA (No 4)* [1997] 2 Lloyd's Rep 507, 530 *per* Rix LJ]. It is simply the view of some 30 states. (2) The International Maritime Organisation is not a legislature. It may commend the 1976 Convention to the international community. But if by doing so it were found to have enacted an international consensus, that would be to deprive sovereign states to a large extent of their right to stay with some other regime . . . (3) . . . it is quite impossible to say that substantial justice is not

available in Singapore . . . neither Convention is objectively more just than the other.');

- *American Express v British Airways Board* [1983] 1 WLR 701 (QBD), 707E–708D (Lloyd J considering the submission that Article 18 of the Warsaw Convention on International Carriage by Air creates a statutory liability independently of any liability in tort or contract and, whilst being 'quite unwilling to enter the lists in this dispute' (708C) assuming 'that article 18 does create a statutory cause of action' (708D) in order to resolve the dispute);
- *In re P (A Minor) (Child Abduction: Non-Convention Country)* [1997] Fam 45 (CA) (the welfare of the child was the paramount and only relevant matter for the court to consider where a parent applied for the return of an abducted child to a non-Hague Convention country; that the judge had therefore misdirected himself in applying the test set out in Article 13 of the Hague Convention on the Civil Aspects of International Child Abduction in schedule 1 to the Child Abduction and Custody Act 1985).

3.13. **Incorporating statutes are generally subject to the same principles of statutory construction as other statutes, as illustrated by the following examples.**

3.13.1. **Principle of legal policy regarding international law applicable to both incorporating and other statutes [§ 8.1; § 9.5; § 10.1; § 13.16]: *Illustration:***

- *Saad, Diriye and Osorio v Secretary of State for the Home Department* [2001] EWCA Civ 2008 (2002) ACD 59, [15–16] (Lord Phillips MR, construing section 8 of the Immigration Appeals Act 1993: 'We approach this case on the basis set out in Bennion on "*Statutory Interpretation*" (3rd ed) p 630 that: "It is a principle of legal policy that the municipal law should conform to public international law. The court, when considering, in relation to the facts of the instant case, which of the opposing constructions of the enactment would give effect to the legislative intention, should presume that the legislator intended to observe this principle." It follows that, absent a clear Parliamentary indication to the contrary, we would expect our primary and delegated legislation to provide a system whereby claimants may have it determined whether they are refugees. It is only that determination which gives them access to Convention rights. We therefore approach questions of construction on that basis.' At [72(iv)–(v)]: 'It is to be inferred that the United Kingdom does not intend to act in breach of its international obligations, especially since. . .Lord Keith said in this context in *R v Secretary of State for the Home Department ex parte Sivakumaran* [1988] AC 958 at 990 that the provisions of the Convention "have for all practical purposes been incorporated into United Kingdom law." In these circumstances the 1993 Act should be construed, so far as possible, on the basis that the United Kingdom intended to comply with its international obligations under the Convention and thus to ensure that those who are refugees within the meaning of Article 1A are entitled to enjoy their Convention rights.').

3.13.2. **Principle of repeal by implication applied to incorporating statutes:**

Illustrations:

- *IRC v Collco Dealings Ltd* [1962] AC 1 (HL) (determining whether words in a 1955 taxing statute partly impliedly repealed provisions in an earlier statute giving continued effect to arrangements contained in a double taxation agreement between Ireland and the United Kingdom; held that earlier legislation which incorporates or replicates an international treaty is not immune from repeal by implication).
- *cf Thoburn v Sunderland City Council* [2002] EWHC 195 (Admin) [2003] QB 151, [613] (Laws LJ considering the HRA and the European Communities Act 1972 as constitutional statutes: 'Ordinary statutes may be impliedly repealed. Constitutional statutes may not. For the repeal of a constitutional Act or the abrogation of a fundamental right to be effected by statute, the court would apply this test: is it shown that the legislature's *actual*—not imputed, constructive or presumed—intention was to effect the repeal or the abrogation? I think the test could only be met by express words in the later statute, or by words so specific that the inference of an actual determination to effect the result contended for was irresistible. The ordinary rule of implied repeal does not satisfy this test. Accordingly, it has no application to constitutional statutes.').

3.13.3. **Incorporating statutes are always speaking** [**§ 4.6.1; § 5.11.6**]**:**

Illustration:

- *R (Al-Fawwaz) v Governor of Brixton Prison* [2001] UKHL 69 [2002] 1 AC 556, [37] (Lord Slynn construing both 'jurisdiction' in the definition of 'fugitive criminal' (in schedule 1 to the Extradition Act 1989) and 'jurisdiction' in the definition of 'extradition crime' (in section 26 of the Extradition Act 1870) as including the territorial and extraterritorial jurisdiction of the requesting state in the context of the Extradition Treaty between the United Kingdom and United States, given effect to and scheduled to the United States of America (Extradition) Order 1976 (SI 1976/2144): 'When the 1870 Act was passed crimes were no doubt largely committed in the territory of the state trying the alleged criminal but that fact does not, and should not, mean that the reference to the jurisdiction is to be so limited . . . It should not because in present conditions it would make it impossible to extradite for some of the most serious crimes now committed globally or at any rate across frontiers. Drug smuggling, money laundering, the abduction of children, acts of terrorism, would to a considerable extent be excluded from the extradition process. It is essential that that process should be available to them. To ignore modern methods of communication and travel as aids to criminal activities is unreal. It is no less unreal to ignore the fact that there are now many crimes where states assert extraterritorial jurisdiction, often as a result of international conventions.'), [64] (Lord Hutton considering extradition procedures in the context of 'the modern world of international terrorism and crime'), [102(4)] (Lord Millett considering the need to interpret extradition treaties in the context of 'today's global village where national borders are no impediment to international terrorists and other criminals.').

3.13.4. **Construction by reference to long title applied to incorporating statutes:**

Illustrations:

- *Holmes v Bangladesh Biman Corporation* [1989] AC 1112 (HL), 1151F–G (Lord Jauncey: 'It is clear from the long title of the [Carriage by Air Act 1961] that its primary purpose was to give effect in the law of the United Kingdom to the Hague Convention. An equally important purpose was to enable the Warsaw Convention to be reincorporated in the law of the United Kingdom on the repeal of the [Carriage by Air Act 1932]. These purposes are effected by section 1 and exercise of the powers conferred in section 10 of the Act of 1961.');
- *R v Lambert* [2001] UKHL 37 [2002] 2 AC 545 (HL), [135] (Lord Clyde, construing the HRA by reference to its long title; [**§ 3.8.2**]).

3.14. General principles of statutory interpretation may be modified to take into account the nature of the incorporated treaty.

Illustrations:

- *Holmes v Bangladesh Biman Corp* [1989] AC 1112 (HL), 1148E–G (Lord Jauncey construing the Carriage by Air Act 1961 and the Carriage by Air Acts (Application of Provisions) Order 1967 (SI 1967/480) and considering the presumption against extraterritorial legislation: '[T]he presumption proceeds upon the basis that Parliament is unlikely to seek to interfere and has no interest to interfere in matters which are properly the concern of the legislature of another state. In all these authorities the relevant legislation was unilateral in the sense that it did not seek to implement an international agreement. Where, however, Parliament incorporates into domestic legislation an international convention which necessarily gives to that domestic legislation extraterritorial effect in the broadest sense an entirely different situation arises. The extraterritorial effect of such legislation is not within the presumption at all since the basis for the presumption no longer exists. Even if the principle does apply to all legislation whether unilateral or not all the necessary conditions for its rebuttal would exist in the case of convention legislation.'), 1126G–1127A (Lord Bridge: 'In one sense all legislation enacted in the United Kingdom to give effect to international conventions, long familiar in the field of maritime law, is extraterritorial in effect. But it would be absurd to suggest that in legislating to embody the terms of such internationally agreed conventions in our municipal law Parliament is in any sense usurping an illegitimate authority over the subjects of foreign states.'), 1137G–1138B (Lord Griffiths considering the presumption against extraterritorial application of domestic statutes in the context of incorporating statutes);

- *R (Al-Skeini) v Secretary of State for Defence* [2004] EWHC 2911 (Admin) [2005] 2 WLR 1401, [269; 291] (DC, considering that the HRA mirrors the jurisdictional scope of the ECHR; that this scope is primarily territorial but that there is an exceptional and limited extraterritorial jurisdiction).

3.15. **Certain specific methods of interpretation apply to incorporating statutes. For example, an incorporating statute may be construed by reference to unincorporated parts of the incorporated treaty or by reference to other, analogous, incorporated treaties. Where the incorporating statute closely follows or replicates the incorporated treaty there will be, for all practical purposes, only one process of interpretation (even though there are two distinct analytical phases: construing the incorporating statute and then considering the incorporated treaty insofar as it is relevant and applicable). As part of this process it is permissible to take into account the wide-ranging supplementary material available when interpreting treaties [chapter 5].**

3.15.1. **Using unincorporated parts of an incorporated treaty to construe an incorporating statute (and to construe the incorporated parts of the treaty: [§ 5.19]):**

Illustrations:

- *A v Secretary of State for the Home Department* [2004] UKHL 56 [2005] 2 WLR 87, (considering unincorporated Article 15, ECHR, in construing the Human Rights Act 1998 (Designated Derogation) Order 2001 (SI 2001/3644) and part 4 of the Anti-Terrorism, Crime and Security Act 2001) [§ **5.19**];
- *R v Lambert* [2001] UKHL 37 [2002] 2 AC 545, [97] (Lord Hope noting that the omission of Article 13, ECHR from the HRA was

not accidental: 'the reason which was given for its omission from the articles set out in Schedule 1 to the Act was that sections 7 to 9 of the Act were intended to lay down an appropriate remedial structure for giving effect to the Convention rights as defined by section 1(1) of the Act. The state's obligations to provide an effective remedy before a national tribunal in the event of violation of the Convention rights is part of the background against which the provisions of subsections (2) to (4) of section 22 were enacted.');

- *R (Al-Skeini) v Secretary of State for Defence* [2004] EWHC 2911 (Admin) [2005] 2 WLR 1401, [291] (Rix LJ considering that, 'if possible, the [HRA] should be construed in conformity with the [ECHR]' including unincorporated article 1; 'we recognise that article 1 is not itself reproduced in Schedule 1 to the Act, but we do not favour [the] submission . . . that section 3 [of the HRA] is only concerned with the substance of the rights protected by the Convention and not with the jurisdictional scope of those rights.');
- *R v Kansal (No 2)* [2001] UKHL 62 [2002] 2 AC 69, [26] (Lord Steyn: 'We now know that "proceedings brought by or at the instigation of a public authority" in section 22(4) were singled out for special treatment in recognition of the United Kingdom's international obligations under the [ECHR].'), [55] (Lord Hope: 'These obligations [under articles 13 and 46, ECHR] have been binding on the United Kingdom in international law since ratification in 1951. Since 1966 the right of individual petition against the state under article 25 has been available. The purpose of sections 7 to 9 of the 1998 Act is to provide a structure within which effect can be given to these obligations in domestic law. The extent to which the 1998 Act gives retrospective effect to its provisions needs to be seen in that context.');
- *Brown v Stott* [2003] 1 AC 681 (HL), 715D–F (Lord Hope on why, although Article 13, ECHR, is not given effect by the HRA it has, nevertheless, not been overlooked since the scheme of the Act is to provide a remedial structure);
- *The Goring* [1988] AC 831 (HL), 850C–H and 852G–853C (Lord Brandon considering the history of the cause of action for salvage in determining whether there is under English law a cause of action for salvage regarding services rendered to a ship in a navigable non-tidal part of a river and by reference to the unincorporated parts of an incorporated treaty (the Brussels Convention for the Unification of Certain Rules relating to the Assistance and Salvage at Sea 1910; as partially incorporated by the Maritime Convention Act 1911);
- *In re S (A Minor) (Custody: Habitual Residence)* [1998] AC 750 (HL), 766C (Lord Slynn: 'The preamble to and article 1 of the Hague Convention [on the Civil Aspects of Child Abduction] are not set out in the Schedule to the Act but it is useful to recall them.').

3.15.2. **Using analogous incorporated treaties to construe incorporating statutes:**

Illustration:

- *Republic of India v Indian Steamship Co. (No 2)* [1998] AC 878 (HL), 912G–H (Lord Steyn, construing 'brought' in section 34 of the Civil Jurisdiction and Judgments Act 1982 (which incorporates the Brussels Convention on Jurisdiction and Enforcement of Judgments in Schedule 1): 'I am reinforced in this view by the fact that in an analogous context, viz. article 28 of the Warsaw Convention (1929) (Part B of Schedule 2 to the Carriage by Air Acts Act (Application of Provisions) Order 1967 (SI 1967 No.480), the Court of Appeal interpreted the word "brought" as embracing the initiation and pursuit of proceedings: *Milor Srl v British Airways Plc* [1996] QB 702.').

3.16. **Difficulties may arise when two or more incorporating statutes are framed by reference to the same treaty but have distinct, yet overlapping, spheres of operation.**

3.16.1. **Acts of the Scottish Lord Advocate:**

- *HM Advocate v R* [2002] UKPC D3 [2004] 1 AC 462, [117–118] (Lord Rodger, on the relationship between the HRA and the Scotland Act 1998: 'When prosecutions are mounted in his name, the Lord Advocate is a "public authority" for the purposes of section 6(1) of the Human Rights Act 1998: section 6(3)(b). The question whether an act or failure to act of the Lord Advocate is "incompatible with a Convention right" is therefore one that could arise on the wording of section 6(1) of the Human Rights Act 1998. Besides being a "public authority", the Lord Advocate is a member of the Scottish Executive: section 44(1)(c) of the Scotland Act 1998. So the question as to whether any act or failure to act of his "is incompatible with the Convention rights" may arise under section 100(1) of the Scotland Act 1998, while under section 57(2) of the same Act the court may have to consider whether any act of the Lord Advocate "is incompatible with any of the Convention rights". Each of these provisions uses slightly different wording . . . Despite the slight variations in language, what constitutes incompatibility with Convention rights must be the same under all the sections of the Scotland Act 1998 and the Human Rights Act 1998.' At [125], considering that 'act' in section 57(2) does not include failures to act. See also, on the same issue, [134–138]).

3.16.2. **Remedies under the Scotland Act 1998 and the HRA:**

- *HM Advocate v R* [2002] UKPC D3 [2004] 1 AC 462, [43] (Lord Hope, construing 'act' in section 57(2) of the Scotland Act 1998: 'The precise relationship between the remedies available under the Scotland Act 1998 and those which are available under the Human Rights Act 1998 is still in the course of being worked out.' At [51]: '[T]he prohibition from doing anything which is incompatible with the Convention rights and with Community law in section 57(2) has to be read with section 100, which seeks to ensure that Convention rights are protected by the Scotland Act 1998 in a manner which is consistent with the Human Rights Act 1998.'), [60] (considering whether, by reason of delay between charge and trial, the Lord Advocate had been deprived of the power to prosecute the appellant (under section 57(2) of the Scotland Act 1998) and whether the appellant was, therefore, entitled to have the charges dismissed: 'Section 8 of the Human Rights Act 1998 gives power to a court to grant such relief or remedy for a breach of a person's Convention rights as it considers appropriate. There is no equivalent provision in the Scotland Act 1998, so the power of the court to grant relief or to provide a remedy is left to common law principles.' At [66]: 'What section 57(2) of the Scotland Act 1998 does, in what I believe to be a unique provision not found anywhere else in the Commonwealth, is to declare that the Lord Advocate has "no power" to do any act which is incompatible with any of the Convention rights. If it would be incompatible with the Convention right for the Lord Advocate to prosecute the appellant because to do so would violate the right to a hearing within a reasonable time, the only answer which the court can give to the question if it is to comply with the provisions of the Scotland Act 1998 is to say that he has no power to proceed with the prosecution and that it must be stayed.' See also [69–71]), [89–90] (Lord Clyde considering the proper meaning of 'act' in section 57(2)), [122–124] and [151–156] (Lord Millett considering the proper remedy under section 57(2)), *cf* [9–15] and [157] (Lord Steyn and Lord Walker (dissenting));

- *cf Attorney-General's Reference (No 2 of 2001)* [2001] EWCA Crim 1568 [2001] 1 WLR 1869 (CA), [18–19] (Lord Woolf dismissing the submission that where the court has found there to be a contravention of the reasonable time requirement in Article 6(1) regarding legal proceedings it must stay those proceedings. At [23]: 'If there has been prejudice caused to the defendant which interferes with his right to a fair trial in a way which cannot otherwise be remedied, then of course a stay is the appropriate remedy. But in the absence of prejudice of that sort, there is normally no justification for granting a stay.'); *Dyer v Watson* [2002] UKPC D1 [2004] 1 AC 379, [111] (Lord Hope on the different remedies under the Scotland Act 1998 and the HRA).

3.17. Incorporating statutes may confer wider rights that those provided by treaty.

Illustrations:

- *R (Ullah) v Secretary of State for the Home Department* [2004] UKHL 26 [2004] 2 AC 323, [20] (Lord Bingham: 'It is of course open to member states to provide for rights more generous than those guaranteed by the [ECHR] but such provision should not be the product of interpretation of the Convention by national courts since the meaning of the Convention should be uniform throughout the states party to it.');
- *R (Mullen) v Secretary of State for the Home Department* [2004] UKHL 18 [2005] 1 AC 1, [35] (Lord Steyn in discussing the International Covenant on Civil and Political Rights: '[T]here is nothing to prevent Parliament when giving effect to the United Kingdom's international obligations from giving the citizen more rights that those obligations require that he be given.');
- *R (Williamson) v Secretary of State for Education and Employment* [2002] EWCA Civ 1926 [2003] QB 1300, [181] (Rix LJ: 'Compatibility with the [ECHR] does not necessarily prevent English law from enhancing or further entrenching a Convention right, unless in a particular case the effect of doing so would be to undermine another Convention right.') (HL is at [2005] UKHL 15 [2005] 2 WLR 590);
- *Runa Begum v Tower Hamlets LBC* [2003] UKHL 5 [2003] 2 AC 430, [69] (Lord Hoffmann) [§ **7.7.4**];
- *R (S) v Chief Constable of South Yorkshire Police* [2002] EWCA Civ 1275 [2002] 1 WLR 3223, [41] (Lord Woolf) [§ **7.7.4**].

4

Interpreting Treaties: General Principles

(1) Introduction

4.1. **A treaty which has been incorporated into domestic law [chapter 3], becomes subject to the interpretative jurisdiction of domestic courts in the same way as any other Act of Parliament.**

> 'Where, for instance, a treaty is directly incorporated into English law by Act of the legislature, its terms become subject to the interpretative jurisdiction of the court in the same way as any other Act of the legislature.'(*JH Rayner (Mincing Lane) Ltd v Department of Trade and Industry* [1990] 2 AC 418 (HL), 500D–E (Lord Oliver)).

4.2. **Accordingly, domestic courts have developed a body of case law on the principles of interpretation which apply to such treaties. These principles are generally applicable to both incorporated and unincorporated treaties. However, domestic case law focuses on the interpretation of incorporated treaties since domestic courts have less opportunity and scope to interpret unincorporated treaties (because of the restraints imposed by the principles of non-justiciability and no direct effect [chapter 8]). Whilst domestic case law provides a synthesis of the key principles of treaty interpretation, these may be supplemented, where necessary, by textbook commentary and case law of international courts and tribunals.**

- Reading: [§ 2.12]

4.3. **The framework for the interpretation of treaties is provided by the principles in the Vienna Convention on the Law of Treaties. The fundamental interpretative principles in the Vienna Convention on the Law of Treaties are embodied in Articles 31 and 32. It is**

generally accepted that these articles reflect customary international law [§§ 2.13–2.16]. Therefore, although the Vienna Convention entered into force on 27 January 1980 these articles apply equally when interpreting treaties passed before that date. The principles in the Vienna Convention have been applied and developed by domestic courts.

4.3.1. **Temporal scope of Vienna Convention on the Law of Treaties:**

- *El-Ali v Secretary of State for the Home Department* [2002] EWCA Civ 1103 [2003] 1 WLR 95, [18] (Laws LJ: 'The Vienna Convention strictly applies only to the construction of treaties concluded after its entry into force on 27 January 1980.');
- *R v Secretary of State for the Environment, Transport, and the Regions, Ex parte International Air Transport Association* [2000] 1 Lloyd's Rep 242 (QBD), 245 (Jowitt J: 'The Vienna Convention came into force on Jan. 27 1980 and strictly applies only to treaties which were concluded after that date.').

4.3.2. **Parts of the Vienna Convention on the Law of Treaties reflect customary international law:**

- *R (European Roma Rights Centre) v Immigration Officer at Prague Airport* [2004] UKHL 55 [2005] 2 WLR 1, [18] (Lord Bingham considering that Article 31 of the Vienna Convention on the Law of Treaties reflects customary international law) [§ **4.10.1**];
- *Revenko v Secretary of State for the Home Department* [2001] QB 601 (CA), 612A–B (Pill LJ: '[The Refugee Convention and the Convention on the Status of Stateless Persons 1954] preceded the Vienna Convention [on the Law of Treaties] but it is common ground that they [Articles 31 and 32 of the Vienna Convention] sufficiently reflect customary international law to provide a framework for construing the 1951 [Refugee] Convention.');
- *R v Secretary of State for the Environment, Transport, and the Regions, Ex parte International Air Transport Association* [2000] 1 Lloyd's Rep 242 (QBD), 245 (Jowitt J: 'The [Vienna Convention on the Law of Treaties] is regarded . . . as having codified existing public international law in relation to treaties.');
- *Fothergill v Monarch Airlines* [1981] AC 251 (HL), 282D (Lord Diplock: 'What [the Vienna Convention on the Law of Treaties] says in articles 31 and 32 about interpretation of treaties, in my view, does no more than codify already-existing public international law.');
- *R (Hoxha) v Special Adjudicator* [2002] EWCA Civ 1403 [2003] 1 WLR 241, [22] (Keene LJ: 'It is of course right that one is here dealing with an international convention [the Refugee Convention], in the interpretation of which the principles found in the Vienna Convention on the Law of Treaties (1980)(Cmnd

7964) articles 31 to 33 are applicable, because they reflect customary international law . . .') (HL is at [2005] UKHL 19 [2005] 1 WLR 1063);

- *Golder v United Kingdom* (1975) 1 EHRR 524 (ECtHR), [29] (ECtHR: 'The Court is prepared to consider . . . that it should be guided by Articles 31 to 33 of the Vienna Convention of 23 May 1969 on the Law of Treaties. That Convention has not yet entered into force and it specifies, at Article 4, that it will not be retroactive, but its Articles 31 to 33 enunciate in essence generally accepted principles of international law to which the Court has already referred on occasion.');
- *A v Minister for Immigration and Ethnic Affairs* (1997) 190 CLR 225, 277 (Gummow J explaining that the rules of interpretation which the Vienna Convention on the Law of Treaties sets out reflect customary international law);
- *cf R v Secretary of State for the Home Department, Ex parte Manjit Kaur*, 11 December 98 (DC) (unreported), [18(d)] (Lightman J: 'No authority or textbook has been cited to me which supports the proposition that Articles 31.2(b), 3 and 4 of the Vienna Convention represent international customary law.') (ECJ is at [2001] ECR I-1237).

4.3.3. **Vienna Convention on the Law of Treaties in domestic courts:**

- *Sepet v Secretary of State for the Home Department* [2003] UKHL 15 [2003] 1 WLR 856, (HL), [6] (Lord Bingham: 'In interpreting the [Refugee] Convention the House must respect articles 31 and 32 of the Vienna Convention on the Law of Treaties.');
- *Fothergill v Monarch Airlines* [1981] AC 251 (HL), 290C (Lord Scarman: 'Faced with an international treaty which has been incorporated into our law, British courts should now follow broadly the guidelines declared by the Vienna Convention on the Law of Treaties.');
- *R v Secretary of State for the Home Department, Ex parte Adan* [2001] 2 AC 477 (HL), 509F–G (Lord Slynn advocating the use of the Vienna Convention on the Law of Treaties whilst construing the Refugee Convention [§ **4.5.7**]), 516D–E (Lord Steyn), 530C (Lord Hobhouse) (both citing Lord Diplock in *Fothergill v Monarch Airlines* [1981] AC 251 (HL), 282D [§ **4.3.2**]);

Illustrations:

- *Canada Trust Co v Stolzenberg (No 2)* [2002] 1 AC 1 (HL), 8G (Lord Steyn using the principles in Article 31, Vienna Convention on the Law of Treaties: 'The answer to the central question [the meaning of "sued" in articles 2 and 6 of the Lugano Convention] must be found in the principal sources of treaty or convention interpretation, viz the text, its content and the object and purpose of the treaty or convention.');
- *R v Immigration Appeal Tribunal, Ex parte Shah* [1999] 2 AC 629 (HL), 643E–F (Lord Steyn: '[T]he restrictive interpretation [of

Article 1A(2) of the Refugee Convention] is at variance with the principle that a treaty ought to be construed in a purposive sense: see article 31 of the Vienna Convention on the Law of Treaties.');

- *El-Ali v Secretary of State for the Home Department* [2002] EWCA Civ 1103 [2003] 1 WLR 95, [18; 22; 40] (Laws LJ, using the Vienna Convention on the Law of Treaties to construe Article ID of the Refugee Convention);
- *Revenko v Secretary of State for the Home Department* [2001] QB 601 (CA), 611 (Pill LJ, using the Vienna Convention on the Law of Treaties to construe Article 1A(2) of the Refugee Convention);
- *R (Mullen) v Secretary of State for the Home Department* [2004] UKHL 18 [2005] 1 AC 1, [47–48] (Lord Steyn referring to Article 31, Vienna Convention on the Law of Treaties, in interpreting Article 14(6) of the International Covenant on Civil and Political Rights) **[§ 5.13.5; § 5.25.1]**.

4.3.4. **Vienna Convention on the Law of Treaties and European Community Treaties [§ 6.7]:**

- *Racke GmbH and Co v Hauptzollamt & Mainz* [1998] 3 CMLR 219 (ECJ), [24–27] (ECJ stating that the rules of customary international law and the principle of *pacta sunt servanda* (enshrined in Article 26, Vienna Convention on the Law of Treaties) are part of Community law);
- *R v Secretary of State for the Home Department, Ex parte Manjit Kaur* 11 December 1998 (DC) (unreported), [18(d)] (Lightman J: 'Undoubtedly the ECJ has on a number of occasions referred to provisions of the [Vienna Convention on the Law of Treaties] and treated them as applicable in cases involving the construction of treaties entered into by the European Community with third party states, but in no case has it yet treated the Vienna Convention as applicable in a case where questions arose as to the construction of the Community Treaties themselves or as to their scope. In the case of *Re Flynn* [1995] 3 CMLR 397, McCullough J read passages in the EEA Opinion as holding that the Vienna Convention applied to the construction of Community Treaties and he followed this holding. With respect, I must disagree: the passages in question in my reading of them treat the Vienna Convention as applicable in the construction of the EEA Treaty. In . . . *A. Racke GmbH & Co.* Case C-162/96 . . . The Opinion of Advocate General Jacobs (paras 29, 73, 76 and 83) and the Judgment of the ECJ (paras 24 and 53) . . . establish the proposition that the Vienna Convention does not bind the Community; that some of the provisions of the Vienna Convention do and some do not reflect customary international law; that the dividing line between those which do and those which do not is "largely uncharted waters" and fraught with uncertainty; and that only those which do (as an aspect of international law) can come into play in the construction of Community Treaties.') (ECJ is at [2001] ECR I-1237).

4.4. **The key provision of the Vienna Convention on the Law of Treaties, on interpretation, is Article 31, the general rule of interpretation:**

> '(1) A treaty shall be interpreted in good faith in accordance with the ordinary meaning to be given to the terms of the treaty in their context and in the light of its object and purpose. (2) The context for the purpose of the interpretation of a treaty shall comprise, in addition to the text, including its preamble and annexes: (a) any agreement relating to the treaty which was made between all the parties in connection with the conclusion of the treaty; (b) any instrument which was made by one or more parties in connection with the conclusion of the treaty and accepted by the other parties as an instrument related to the treaty. (3) There shall be taken into account, together with the context: (a) any subsequent agreement between the parties regarding the interpretation of the treaty or the application of its provisions; (b) any subsequent practice in the application of the treaty which establishes the agreement of the parties regarding its interpretation. (c) any relevant rules of international law applicable in the relations between the parties. (4) A special meaning shall be given to a term if it is established that the parties so intended.'

(2) Text

4.5. **The language of the treaty provides the starting point for construction. Particular regard must be had to, and reliance placed on, the ordinary meaning of the express terms in the treaty. These terms must be interpreted in good faith. The aim is to arrive at a common-sense interpretation, reading the treaty as a whole, considering the significance of, inter alia, reservations and derogations, and avoiding an over-sophisticated or over-linguistic construction (see Article 31(1), Vienna Convention on the Law of Treaties: [§ 4.4]).**

4.5.1. **Language as the starting point:**

- *R (Mullen) v Secretary of State for the Home Department* [2004] UKHL 18 [2005] 1 AC 1, [45] (Lord Steyn: 'The starting point [for interpretation] must, of course, be the language and the structure of article 14(6) [International Covenant on Civil and Political Rights] as enacted in United Kingdom law by section 133 [Criminal Justice Act 1988].');
- *Adan v Secretary of State for the Home Department* [1999] 1 AC 293 (HL), 305D (Lord Lloyd construing the Refugee Convention: 'the starting point must be the language itself');

- *Semco Salvage v Lancer Navigation* [1997] AC 455 (HL), 467D (Lord Mustill: '[A]lthough weight has rightly been given to the history of the Convention I prefer to begin with its words, read in the general context of the new regime.');
- *A v Minister for Immigration and Ethnic Affairs* (1997) 190 CLR 225, 255–6 (McHugh J, construing Article 1A(2) of the Refugee Convention: '[T]aking the text as the starting point is consistent with the basic principles of interpretation [in international law] that courts should focus their attention on the "four corners of the actual text" in discerning the meaning of that text. The text of the treaty, being the starting point in any investigation as to the meaning of the text, necessarily has primacy in the interpretation process. As the International Law Commission has noted [1966] 2 Yearbook of the International Law Commission 169, 220: "The article . . . is based on the view that the text must be presumed to be the authentic expression of the intentions of the parties; and that, in consequence, the starting point of interpretation is the elucidation of the meaning of the text, not an investigation ab initio into the intentions of the parties".');
- *R v Secretary of State for the Home Department, Ex parte Manjit Kaur* 11 December 1998 (DC) (unreported), [18(c)] (Lightman J: '[T]he order of priority in Article 31.1 of the Vienna Convention is terms of treaty, context and objectives and purpose; the order of priority in case of Community Treaties is spirit, the general scheme and wording.') (ECJ is at [2001] ECR I-1237).

4.5.2. **Importance of the express terms of the treaty:**

- *R (Hoxha) v Special Adjudicator* [2005] UKHL 19 [2005] 1 WLR 1063, [8] (Lord Hope construing Article 1C(5) of the Refugee Convention: 'A large and liberal spirit is called for when a court is asked to say what the Convention means. But there are limits to this approach. The court must recognise the fundamental fact that the Convention is an agreement between states. The extent of the agreement to which states committed themselves is to be found in the language which gives formal expression to their agreement.' At [9] referring to Article 31(1), Vienna Convention on the Law of Treaties: 'There is no warrant in this provision for reading into a treaty words that are not there. It is not open to a court, when it is performing its function, to expand the limits which the language of the treaty has set for it.'), [85] (Lord Brown: 'It is one thing to invite this House to construe the Convention as a living instrument generously and in the light of its underlying humanitarian purposes; quite another to urge your Lordships effectively to rewrite it . . . That would be to distort entirely the language and structure of the text and in my judgment do a serious disservice to the cause of human rights generally.');
- *Brown v Stott* [2003] 1 AC 681 (PC), 703E–F (Lord Bingham: '[It is] generally to be assumed that the parties have included the

terms which they wished to include or on which they were able to agree, omitting other terms which they did not wish to include and on which they were not able to agree.');

- *R (European Roma Rights Centre) v Immigration Officer at Prague Airport* [2004] UKHL 7 [2005] 2 WLR 1, [18] (Lord Bingham) [§ **4.10.1**];
- *R v Bow Street Magistrate, Ex parte Pinochet (No 3)* [2000] 1 AC 147 (HL), 218E–H (Lord Goff (dissenting) considering the nature of treaties, as products of international consensus, and the corresponding importance of express terms) [§ **4.8.1**];

Illustrations:

- *Morris v KLM Dutch Airlines* [2002] UKHL 7 [2002] 2 AC 628, [17] (Lord Steyn, construing 'bodily injury' in Article 17 of the Warsaw Convention on International Carriage by Air: 'In this context it is reasonable to expect that if it had been intended to cover mental injury or illness, it would have been provided for expressly. In the absence of such an express reference it is reasonable to interpret "bodily injury" and "lésion corporelle" as words of restriction, ie as referring to non fatal injury which is physical rather than mental: contrast the wide term in the Guatemala Protocol which never came into force.' At [26]: 'If cases of mental injuries and illnesses are to be brought within the Convention system, it must be done by amendment of the Convention system and not by judicial creativity.' At [28]: 'Courts of law must avoid the reproach that they are becoming the redrafters of the Convention'.), [147] (Lord Hobhouse: 'Whilst it is important to have regard to the international consensus upon the understanding of the provisions of international conventions and hence to what the courts in other jurisdictions have had to say about the provision in question, the relevant point for decision always remains: what do the actual words used mean?');
- *Horvath v Secretary of State for the Home Department* [2001] 1 AC 489 (HL), 505G (Lord Lloyd (dissenting), construing the Refugee Convention: 'To my mind it is most unlikely that the framers of the [Refugee] Convention had any such unusual case in mind, or that they intended to cover what the noble and learned Lord Clyde aptly refers to as "constructive" persecution by the state. If so then it is not for us to create a link between the activities of the thugs and discrimination by the state, so as to *extend* the scope of the Convention by judicial interpretation, any more than we should *limit* the meaning of persecution by introducing into the definition of persecution the concept of state protection.').

4.5.3. **Words should be given their natural and ordinary meaning:**

- *Stag Line Ltd v Foscolo, Mango & Co.* [1932] AC 328 (HL), 342–343 (Lord Atkin: 'I will repeat the well known words of Lord Herschell in the *Bank of England v Vagliano Brothers* [[1891] AC 107 at 144]. Dealing with the Bills of Exchange Act as a code he says: "I think the proper course is in the first instance to examine the language of the statute and to ask what is its natural meaning, uninfluenced by any considerations derived from the previous state of the law, and not to start inquiring with how the law previously stood . . ." He then proceeds to say that of course it would be legitimate to refer to the previous law where the provision of the code was of doubtful import, or where words had previously acquired a technical meaning or been used in a sense other than their ordinary one. But if this is the canon of construction in regard to a codifying Act, still more does it apply to an Act like the present [the Carriage of Goods by Sea Act 1924] which is not intended to codify the English law, but is the result (as expressed in the Act) of an international conference intended to unify certain rules relating to bills of lading. It will be remembered that the Act only applies to contracts of carriage of goods outwards from ports of the United Kingdom: and the rules will often have to be interpreted in the courts of the foreign consignees. For the purpose of uniformity it is, therefore, important that the Courts should apply themselves to the consideration only of the words used without any predilection for the former law, always preserving the right to say that words used in the English language which have already in the particular context received judicial interpretation may be presumed to be used in the sense already judicially imputed to them.');

- *Agnew v Länsförsäkringsbolagens AB* [2001] 1 AC 223 (HL), 240A–B (Lord Woolf MR, construing the Lugano Convention: 'Before turning to the guidance provided by the authorities it is useful to inquire whether there appears to be any reason of principle or policy which suggests that it would not be appropriate to give the language of the Convention what appears to be its ordinary meaning. I find no such policy or principle. On the contrary, it seems to me that both policy and principle are in favour in adopting the ordinary meaning of the language used.');
- *Morris v KLM Royal Dutch Airlines* [2002] UKHL 7 [2002] 2 AC 628, [76] (Lord Hope construing the Warsaw Convention on International Carriage by Air, scheduled to the Carriage by Air Act 1961: 'The ordinary and natural meaning of the words used in the English text in Part I of the Schedule provides the starting point. But these words must also be compared with their equivalents in the French text in Part II of the Schedule, as section 1(2) of the 1961 Act tells that if there is any inconsistency the text in French shall prevail.') [§ 5.22].

Illustrations:

- *In re H (Abduction: Acquiescence)* [1998] AC 72 (HL), 87G–H (Lord Browne-Wilkinson: 'What then does article 13 [of the Hague Convention on the Civil Aspects of International Child Abduction] mean by "acquiescence?" In my view, article 13 is looking to the subjective state of mind of the wronged parent. Has he in fact consented to the continued presence of the children in the jurisdiction to which they have been abducted? ... In my judgment [this approach] accords with the ordinary meaning of the word "acquiescence" in this context.');

- *Horvath v Secretary of State for the Home Department* [2001] 1 AC 489 (HL), 503A (Lord Lloyd (dissenting): '[I]t has been settled law since the decision of Nolan J in *R v Immigration Appeal Tribunal, Ex p Jonah* [1985] Imm AR 7, 13 that persecution should be given its ordinary dictionary meaning. So far as I know the correctness of that decision has not been challenged.');
- *Semco Salvage v Lancer Navigation* [1997] AC 455 (HL), 467D–E (Lord Mustill construing 'expenses' in Article 14(3) of the International Convention on Salvage 1989 by reference to its ordinary meaning);
- *In re J (A Minor)(Abduction: Custody Rights)* [1990] 2 AC 562 (HL), 578F–G (Lord Brandon construing 'habitually resident' in Article 3 of the Hague Convention on the Civil Aspects of International Child Abduction by reference to its ordinary and natural meaning);
- *Sandeman Coprimar SA v Transitos y Transportes Integrales SL* [2003] EWCA Civ 113 [2003] 2 WLR 1496, [35] (Lord Phillips MR considering the 'natural' reading of Article 23 of the Convention on the Contract for the International Carriage of Goods by Road (incorporated by the Carriage of Goods by Road Act 1965));
- *Milor Srl v British Airways Plc* [1996] QB 702 (CA), 706D–H (Phillips LJ construing 'brought' in Article 28 of the Warsaw Convention on International Carriage by Air by reference to its natural meaning);
- *El-Ali v Secretary of State for the Home Department* [2002] EWCA Civ 1103 [2003] 1 WLR 95 (CA), [58] (Lord Phillips construing Article 1D of the Refugee Convention by reference to its ordinary meaning);
- *Revenko v Secretary of State for the Home Department* [2001] QB 601 (CA), 621G (Pill LJ considering the ordinary meaning of Article 1A(2) of the Refugee Convention);
- *R v Secretary of State for the Environment, Transport and the Regions, Ex parte Channel Tunnel Group Ltd and France Manche SA* [2001] EWCA Civ 1185, [57] (Peter Gibson LJ interpreting provisions in a Concession Agreement, giving effect to a Treaty entered into between the United Kingdom and France, according to the ordinary and natural meaning of the words).

4.5.4. **Words should be given a common sense interpretation:**

- *Brown v Stott* [2003] 1 AC 681 (PC), 727F–G (Lord Hope: 'It is also to be remembered that [the ECHR] is dealing with the realities of life and it is not be applied in ways which run counter to reason and common sense . . . If the Convention was to be applied

by the courts in ways which would seem absurd to ordinary people then the courts would be doing a disservice to the aims and the purposes of the Convention and the result would simply be to prejudice public respect for an international treaty which seeks to express the basic rights and freedoms of a democratic society.');
- *Molefi v Principal Legal Adviser* [1971] AC 182 (PC), 196 (Lord Morris, considering the Refugee Convention: 'Their Lordships consider that the words in the definition of the term "refugee" must be applied with common sense while remembering that one event may often lead to another which in turn may lead to another or others. The words do not call for legalistic or philosophical examination. A mean can be found between too much stiffness of interpretation and too much easiness of application. When the facts of a situation are ascertained and known then in a fair-minded way those facts must be surveyed and an answer given to the straightforward question which is posed. If after a fair-minded approach an answer is readily and clearly given it may not be one that requires or permits of detailed elaboration.').

4.5.5. **Ambiguities in the treaty should be interpreted in the least onerous way:**
- *Marchiori v The Environment Agency* [2002] EWCA Civ 3 [2002] EuLR 225, [58] (Laws LJ: '[Counsel] referred . . . to the principle of Treaty interpretation summarised in the Latin phrase *in dubio mitius*: where a Treaty provision is ambiguous, the interpretation which is less onerous to the State owing the Treaty obligation is to be preferred.').

4.5.6. **The treaty should be interpreted in good faith:**
- Vienna Convention on the Law of Treaties, Article 26 ('*Pacta sunt servanda*'): 'Every treaty in force is binding upon the parties to it and must be performed by them in good faith.'
- UN Charter, Article 2: 'All Members . . . shall fulfil in good faith the obligations assumed by them in accordance with the present Charter.'
- *R (European Roma Rights Centre) v Immigration Officer at Prague Airport* [2004] UKHL 55 [2005] 2 WLR 1, [19] (Lord Bingham: 'Taken together, these rules [Articles 26 and 31(1) of the Vienna Convention on the Law of Treaties] call for good faith in the interpretation and performance of a treaty, and neither rule is open to question. But there is no want of good faith if a state interprets a treaty as meaning what it says and declines to do anything significantly greater than or different from what it agreed to do . . . While a state party must show good faith in interpreting and performing a treaty obligation, the International Court of Justice made plain in *In re Border and Transborder Armed Actions (Nicaragua and Honduras)* [1988] ICJ Rep 69, para 94, and repeated in *In re Land and Maritime Boundary between Cameroon*

and Nigeria (Cameroon v Nigeria) [1998] ICJ Rep 275, para 39, that "the principle of good faith is, as the Court has observed, 'one of the basic principles governing the creation and performance of legal obligations' . . . it is not in itself a source of obligation where none would otherwise exist."'), [62] (Lord Hope: 'In his review essay on La Bonne Foi en Droit International Public by Elisabeth Zoller (1977) Michel Virally criticises her conclusion that, as good faith is not an autonomous source of legal rights and duties, no general obligation to behave in good faith exists in public international law (1983) 77 AJIL 130, 131. The view which he takes, which I for my part would accept, is that good faith really is a principle of international law, that all the actors in the international legal order are subjected to it and that they must endure its consequences, since good faith will serve to determine both the legal effects of their declarations and behaviour and the extent of their duties: p 133. But he also accepts it as true that, in practice, this general principle of law has only marginal value as an autonomous source of rights and duties and that, on this point M Zoller's conclusions cannot be faulted. As he puts it, good faith is always related to specific behaviour or declarations. What it does is invest them with legal significance and legal effects: pp 133–4.').

4.5.7. **The treaty should be read as a whole:**

- *Fothergill v Monarch Airlines* [1981] AC 251 (HL), 279C (Lord Diplock: '[G]iving, as one must, a purposive construction to the Convention looked at as a whole.');
- *R (Mullen) v Secretary of State for the Home Department* [2004] UKHL 18 [2005] 1 AC 1, [38] (Lord Steyn: 'It is, of course, right that provisions of the [International Covenant on Civil and Political Rights] . . . must be read together as part and parcel of the scheme of the covenant.');
- *R (Ullah) v Special Adjudicator* [2004] UKHL 26 [2004] 2 AC 323, [36–7] (Lord Steyn, quoting from *Abdulaziz, Cabales and Balkandali v United Kingdom* (1985) 7 EHRR 471, [60]: '"*Above all*, the court recalls that the Convention and its Protocols must be read as a whole; consequently a matter dealt with mainly by one of their provisions may also, in some of its aspects, be subject to other provisions thereof".');
- *R v Secretary of State for the Home Department, Ex parte Adan* [2001] 2 AC 477 (HL), 509F–G (Lord Slynn: 'Just as the courts must seek to give a "Community" meaning to words in the Treaty of Rome (Cmd 5179-II) ("worker") so the Secretary of State and the courts must in the absence of a ruling by the International Court of Justice or uniform state practice arrive at their interpretation on the basis of the Convention as a whole read in the light of any relevant rules of international law, including the Vienna Convention on the law of Treaties (1980)(Cmd 7674).');

- *Horvath v Secretary of State for the Home Department* [2001] 1 AC 489 (HL), 479E–F (Lord Hope, considering that a holistic approach had to be taken to the definition of 'refugee' in the Refugee Convention).

Illustrations:

- *Marchiori v The Environment Agency* [2002] EWCA Civ 3 [2002] EuLR 225, [57] (Laws LJ construing the whole of the Euratom treaty to decide whether chapter III includes military installations).
- *Morris v KLM Royal Dutch Airlines* [2002] UKHL 7 [2002] 2 AC 628, [76] (Lord Hope: 'The [Warsaw Convention on International Carriage by Air] must be construed as a whole.' Citing *Grein v Imperial Airways Ltd* [1937] 1 KB 50 and *Fothergill v Monarch Airlines Ltd* [1981] AC 251);
- *Effort Shipping Co Ltd v Linden Management SA* [1998] AC 605 (HL), 627C (Lord Cooke considering that the Hague Rules (on bills of lading) 'have to be read as a whole');
- *Adan v Secretary of State for the Home Department* [1999] 1 AC 293 (HL), 305B–D (Lord Lloyd considering that a true construction of Article 1A(2) of the Refugee Convention could be arrived at only by 'seeking a meaning which makes sense in the light of the Convention as a whole.');
- *In re H (Minors) (Abduction: Custody Rights)* [1991] 2 AC 476 (HL), 498F (Lord Brandon stating that, in deciding between two meanings of the Hague Convention on the Civil Aspects of International Child Abduction 'it is necessary . . . to have regard to the context of the Convention as a whole.');
- *R v Secretary of State for the Environment, Transport and the Regions, Ex parte Channel Tunnel Group* QBD (Admin) (30 November 2000) (unreported), [29] (Dyson J construing Article 5(4) of a treaty between the United Kingdom and France and clause 3(2) of the Concession Agreement by reference to other terms of the instruments) (CA is at [2001] EWCA Civ 1185).

4.5.8. **Reading the treaty as a whole includes a consideration of relevant reservations and derogations:**

Illustrations:

- *R v Secretary of State for the Home Department, Ex parte Ahmed and Patel* [1999] Imm AR 22 (CA), 36 (Lord Woolf MR, pointing out that the appellants could not rely on the UN Convention on the Rights of the Child to establish a legitimate expectation because the United Kingdom had made a reservation to that Convention in the immigration context);
- *In re Westinghouse Uranium Contract* [1978] AC 547 (HL), 609D–F (Lord Wilberforce, whilst construing the Evidence (Proceedings in Other Jursidictions) Act 1975 noting that the Court of Appeal were misinformed about the existence of the United Kingdom's reservation under Article 23 of the Hague

Convention on the Taking of Evidence Abroad in Civil and Commercial Matters 1981);

- *Hinds v Attorney-General of Barbados* [2001] UKPC 56 [2002] 1 AC 854, [15] (Lord Bingham, after considering that the Constitution of Barbados was deliberately framed so as to omit a right to legal aid: 'Barbados has adhered to this position when acceding to international human rights instruments. On its accession to the International Covenant on Civil and Political Rights on 21 December 1972 the government of Barbados expressly reserved "the right not to apply in full, the guarantee of free legal assistance in accordance with paragraph 3(d) of article 14 of the Covenant, since, while accepting the principles contained in the same paragraph, the problems of implementation are such that full application cannot be guaranteed at present." Similarly, when ratifying the American Convention on Human Rights 1969, the government of Barbados with effect from 27 November 1982 made a reservation that "Barbadian law does not provide, as a minimum guarantee in criminal proceedings, any inalienable right to be assisted by counsel provided by the state. Legal aid is provided for certain scheduled offences such as homicide and rape".');
- *A v Secretary of State for the Home Department* [2004] UKHL 56 [2005] 2 WLR 87, [146–50] (Lord Scott) [§ **5.19**];
- *Gangadeen v Secretary of State for the Home Department* [1998] Imm AR 106 (CA), 116–117 (Hirst LJ, noting as an 'insuperable difficulty' to the appellants reliance on the UN Convention on the Rights of the Child, the United Kingdom's reservation regarding the immigration and citizenship context).

4.5.9. **An over-sophisticated interpretation of a treaty should be avoided:**

- *Sarrio SA v Kuwait Investment Authority* [1999] 1 AC 32 (HL), 41F (Lord Saville interpreting Article 22 of the Brussels Convention on Jurisdiction and the Enforcement of Judgments: 'I am of the view that there should be a broad commonsense approach to the question whether the actions in question are related, bearing in mind the objective of the article, applying the simple wide test set out in article 22 and refraining from an over-sophisticated analysis of the matter.');
- *Horvath v Secretary of State for the Home Department* [2001] 1 AC 489 (HL), 508F (Lord Clyde: 'The dangers of over-sophistication in the construction and application of the [Refugee] Convention are real and significant. Prolonged debate about the niceties of the language may readily lead to delay in the processing of what in the interests of everyone should be a relatively expeditious process. Of course there may often be difficult points of fact to be resolved and uncertainties in matters of fact which may not immediately be open to a clear answer. But it is obviously undesirable to heap onto the shoulders of the adjudicators and the members of the tribunals which already have a heavy burden of work an additional

complexity in the unravelling of legal issues on the precise construction of the particular words used in the Convention.');

- *Wilson v First County Trust Ltd (No 2)* [2003] UKHL 40 [2004] 1 AC 816, [35] (Lord Nicholls: 'Human Rights conventions are concerned with substance, not form, with practicalities and realities, not linguistic niceties.') **[§ 4.5.10]**;
- *Anton Durbeck GmbH v Den Norske Bank ASA* [2003] EWCA Civ 147 [2003] QB 1160, [39] (Lord Phillips MR rejecting counsel's submissions on the correct interpretation of Article 5 of the Lugano Convention on Jurisdiction and the Enforcement of Judgments as 'over-sophisticated and unsound'. At [46]: 'giving the words of article 5(5) their natural meaning.').

4.5.10. **An over-linguistic interpretation of a treaty should be avoided:**

- *Agnew v Länsförsäkringsbolagens AB* [2001] 1 AC 223 (HL), 246H–247A (Lord Cooke construing Article 5 of the Lugano Convention: 'Whether it is a term or condition "in" (or "under") the contract is the kind of question which schoolmen might debate, but that is a refinement of linguistics which, in my opinion, should be avoided if possible in interpreting a modern Convention intended to provide clear and broad rules as to the jurisdiction of the courts.');
- *Wilson v First County Trust Ltd (No 2)* [2003] UKHL 40 [2004] 1 AC 816, [35] (Lord Nicholls considering Article 6, ECHR: 'The distinction between the substantive content of a right and an unacceptable procedural bar to its enforcement by a court can give rise to difficulty in distinguishing the one from the other in a particular case. As a matter of drafting, a restriction on the scope of a right may be framed in several different ways. But the drafting technique chosen by the draftsman cannot be determinative of the issue. Human Rights conventions are concerned with substance, not form, with practicalities and realities, not linguistic niceties.');
- *R (Yogathas) v Secretary of State for the Home Department* [2002] UKHL 36 [2003] 1 AC 920, [9] (Lord Bingham, in the context of the Refugee Convention, the Dublin Convention (the Convention Determining the State Responsible for Examining Applications for Asylum Lodged in one of the Member States of the European Communities) and the ECHR: '[T]he judge and the Court of Appeal were in my opinion right to give weight, consistently with that fundamental principle [that where an administrative decision may put the applicant's life at risk, the basis for the decision must call for anxious scrutiny], to two important considerations. The first is that the Home Secretary and the courts should not readily infer that a friendly sovereign state which is party to the [Refugee] Convention will not perform the obligations it has solemnly undertaken . . . The second consideration is that the Convention is directed to a very important but

very simple and very practical end, preventing the return of applicants to places where they will or may suffer persecution. Legal niceties and refinements should not be allowed to obstruct that purpose. It can never, save in extreme circumstances, be appropriate to compare an applicant's living conditions in different countries if, in each of them, he will be safe from persecution or the risk of it.'), [58] (Lord Hope considering the need for anxious scrutiny in asylum cases);

- *Horvath v Secretary of State for the Home Department* [2001] 1 AC 489 (HL), 508D (Lord Clyde construing the Refugee Convention: 'We are concerned here with the construction of an international convention. The approach to be adopted must be appropriate to that situation. Regard must be given to the purpose of the Convention and the object which it seeks to serve. While the language of the article has to be respected, any pre-occupation with the precise words may fail to meet the broad intent of the Convention and any detailed analysis of its component elements may distract and divert attention from the essential purpose of what is sought to be achieved.');
- *The Hollandia* [1983] 1 AC 565 (HL), 572G–573A (Lord Diplock: '[The Hague-Visby Rules] should be given a purposive rather than a narrow literalistic construction, particularly whenever the adoption of a literalistic construction would enable the stated purpose of the convention . . . to be evaded by the use of colourable devices that, not being expressly referred to in the Rules, are not specifically prohibited.').

Illustrations:

- *Morris v KLM Royal Dutch Airlines* [2002] UKHL 7 [2002] 2 AC 628, [76] (Lord Hope on the need to give the Warsaw Convention on International Carriage by Air a purposive construction. Citing *Grein v Imperial Airways Ltd* [1937] 1 KB 50 and *Fothergill v Monarch Airlines Ltd* [1981] AC 251);
- *R (Alconbury Developments Ltd) v Secretary of State for the Environment, Transport and Regions* [2001] UKHL 23 [2003] 2 AC 295, [149] and [151] (Lord Clyde noting the need for a broad interpretation of article 6(1), ECHR.);
- *Adan v Secretary of State for the Home Department* [1999] 1 AC 293 (HL), 305B–D (Lord Lloyd exhorting a broad approach rather than a 'narrow linguistic approach' in construing the Refugee Convention) [§ **4.7.1**].

4.6. **Generally, treaties, like statutes, are always speaking. This reflects their status as living instruments [§ 4.7.2] and, together with the open-textured language typical of multilateral treaties, enables treaties to be applied to modern, changing conditions. Even where treaties use outdated concepts these may be brought up-to-date by applying them in accordance with current trends, as illustrated by**

other treaties. Exceptionally, the subject-matter of a treaty may require an interpretation located in a particular historical context.

4.6.1. **Treaties, like statutes, are always speaking [§ 3.13.3; § 5.11.6]:**

- *Morris v KLM Dutch Airlines* [2002] UKHL 7 [2002] 2 AC 628, [25] (Lord Steyn: 'Statutes are generally always speaking, and ought therefore to be interpreted in light of the contemporary social and scientific world. This is not a rule of law but a principle of construction, which may be displaced by a contrary intent revealed by a particular statutory context: *R v Ireland* [1998] AC 147, 158D–G. Given that the rationale of the principle is that statutes are generally intended to endure for a long time, one can readily accept that multilateral international trade conventions, which are by statute incorporated in our law, should be approached in a similar way. Indeed one may say that a fortiori they ought to be so interpreted.'), [149; 156] (Lord Hobhouse considering that it is 'mistaken to interpret a convention such as the Warsaw Convention . . . as if they were intended to be historical documents frozen in time.' ([149]) and that it is 'misconceived' to consider the meaning of the Convention in 1929 ([156]), [125] (Lord Hope: 'The search is for the meaning which the words were understood to have when the Convention was entered into [in 1929]. It would be wrong to regard article 17 as limited by the state of medical and scientific knowledge that was current in the 1920s. There is no reason to think that the contracting parties intended that no account should be taken of developments in medical science in determining the question whether a passenger had sustained a bodily injury . . . Whether or not there is such an injury will always depend on the evidence.' See also [82]: on whether the Warsaw Convention can be described as 'always speaking.');
- *R (Quintavalle) v Secretary of State for Health* [2003] UKHL 13 [2003] 2 AC 687, [9] (Lord Bingham: 'There is, I think, no inconsistency between the rule that statutory language retains the meaning it had when Parliament used it and the rule that a statute is always speaking.'), [22] (Lord Steyn: 'In the case law two contradictory approaches are to be found. It reminds one of the old saying that rules of interpretation "hunt in pairs": that for every rule there is a rule to the contrary effect: see *Burrows, Statute Law,* 3rd ed (2003), p 277 and chapter 12 generally. In the older cases the view often prevailed that a statute must be construed as if one were interpreting it on the day after it was passed: *The Longford* (1889) 14 PD 34, 36. . . . But even in older cases a different approach sometimes prevailed. It was the idea encapsulated by Lord Thring, the great Victorian draftsman, that statutes ought generally to be construed as "always speaking statutes".');
- *R v Ireland* [1998] AC 147 (HL), 158F (Lord Steyn: 'In cases where the problem arises it is a matter of interpretation whether

a court must search for the historical or original meaning of a statute or whether it is free to apply the current meaning of the statute to present day conditions. Statutes dealing with a particular grievance or problem may sometimes require to be historically interpreted. But the drafting technique of Lord Thring and his successors have brought about the situation that statutes will generally be found to be of the "always speaking" variety.');

- *McCartan Turkington Breen v Times Newspapers Ltd* [2001] 2 AC 277 (HL), 292A (Lord Bingham, construing 'public meeting' in the Defamation Act (Northern Ireland) 1955 by reference to modern conditions), 296A–F (Lord Steyn quoting from Cross, *Statutory Interpretation*, 3rd edn (1995), pp 51–2 and concluding that 'In other words, it is generally permissible and indeed necessary to take into account the place of the statutory provision in controversy in the broad context of the basic principles of the legal system as it has evolved.').

Illustrations:

- *Bellinger v Bellinger* [2003] UKHL 21 [2003] 2 AC 467, [20–21] (Lord Nicholls: 'This issue [regarding the sex of transsexual people] has been before the European Court of Human Rights on several occasions in the last 20 years. During this period the development of human rights law on this issue has been remarkably rapid. Until very recently the court consistently held that application of the *Corbett* [*Corbett v Corbett (orse Ashley)* [1971] P 83] criteria, and consequent non-recognition of change of gender by post-operative transsexual persons, did not constitute a violation of article 8 . . . or article 12 . . . In its most recent decision the court has taken the view that the sands of time have run out. The United Kingdom's margin of appreciation no longer extends to declining to give legal recognition to all cases of gender reassignment. This was the decision of the court, sitting as a grand chamber, in the case of *Goodwin v United Kingdom* (2002) 35 EHRR 447.' At [35]: '[I]n the more compassionate times in which we live, there is an international trend towards recognising gender reassignment and not condemning post-operative transsexual people to live in what was aptly described by the European Court of Human Rights in the *Goodwin* case . . . as an intermediate zone, not quite one gender nor the other.'), [74] (Lord Hobhouse considering 'new social attitudes to questions of sexuality' and the 'more specific changes in society and the law which should follow.');
- *R v Immigration Appeal Tribunal, Ex parte Shah* [1999] 2 AC 629 (HL), 657B–D (Lord Hope, interpreting 'particular social group' in Article 1A(2) of the Refugee Convention: 'I agree that the travaux préparatoires are uninformative. But it is more important to have regard to the evolutionary approach which must be taken to international agreements of this kind. This enables account to be taken of changes in society and of discriminatory

circumstances which may not have been obvious to the delegates when the Convention was being framed.') [§ **4.10.1**];

- *Card Protection Plan v Customs and Excise Commissioners* [1999] 2 AC 601 (ECJ), [27] (Advocate General Fennelly, quoting from *Commission of the European Communities v Kingdom of Spain* (Case C-35/90) [1991] ECR I-5073, 5086, para 9: '"in interpreting a provision of Community law it is necessary to take account of how the law stands at the date when the provision in question must be applied."');
- *Runa Begum v Tower Hamlets LBC* [2003] UKHL 5 [2003] 2 AC 430, [28–30] (Lord Hoffmann, construing Article 6, ECHR: '[T]he term "civil rights and obligations" was originally intended to mean those rights and obligations which, in continental European systems of law, were adjudicated upon by civil courts . . . [it] was not intended to cover administrative decisions which were conventionally subject to review (if at all) by administrative courts . . . In fact there has been no addition to the Convention to deal with administrative decisions and the Strasbourg court has been left to develop the law. It has done so in two ways. First, it has been concerned to ensure that state parties do not exploit the gap left in article 6 by changing their law so as to convert a question which would ordinarily be regarded as appropriate for civil adjudication into an administrative decision outside the reach of the article . . . The second development has been the doctrine, starting with *Ringeisen v Austria (No 1)* (1971) 1 EHRR 455, by which the Strasbourg court has extended article 6 to cover a wide range of administrative decision-making on the ground that the decision determines or decisively affects rights or obligations in private law.');
- *Phillips v Air New Zealand Ltd* [2002] 2 Lloyd's Rep 408, 414 (Morison J construing Article 17 of the Warsaw Convention on International Carriage by Air, given force of law by the Carriage by Air Act 1961, and the meaning of 'embarkation' in a way which 'makes good sense of the realities of modern air travel.').

4.6.2. **Open-textured language in a treaty can be adapted to current conditions:**

- *R (Pretty) v Director of Public Prosecutions (Secretary of State for the Home Department intervening)* [2001] UKHL 61 [2002] 1 AC 800, [56] (Lord Steyn: 'The language of the [ECHR] is often open textured. In 1950 the Lord Chancellor observed: "Vague and indefinite terms have been used just because they were vague and indefinite, so that all parties, hoping and expecting that these terms will be construed according to their separate points of view, could be induced to sign them." (Cabinet Office memorandum CAB 130/64) Sir Hartley Shawcross QC, the Attorney General, attributed lack of clarity in the drafting to a compromise to accommodate the different legal systems involved . . . The generality of the language permits adaptation of the European Convention to modern conditions. It is also, however, necessary to take into account that in the field of fundamental beliefs the European Court of Human Rights does not readily adopt a creative role contrary to a European consensus, or virtual consensus.');

- *Whaley v Lord Advocate* [2003] Scot CS 178 (CS), [45] (Lord Brodie: 'I do not accept that simply because an international treaty, for example, is not expressed with the precision and in the detail which is to be expected of an Act of Parliament, that it could not be a source of law or that it could not be understood by a Scottish court. . .In my opinion, that a text does not have the quality of precision that one looks for in a written statement of law, may be a pointer to its author or authors not intending it to have that status. It can be no more than that.').

4.6.3. **Outdated concepts in a treaty may be interpreted by reference to prevailing conditions:**

Illustration:

- *T v Immigration Officer* [1996] AC 742 (HL), 753B (Lord Mustill, on Article 1F of the Refugee Convention: 'These fundamental changes in method and perception [of violent crimes] have not been matched by changes in the parallel, although not identical, laws of extradition and asylum. These laws were conceived at a time when political struggles could be painted in clear primary colours largely inappropriate today . . . What I regard as the exceptional difficulty of this appeal is that the courts here, as in other legal systems, must struggle to apply a concept which is out of date.' At 755, 758, 762–3, considering that in such cases, it is permissible to interpret treaties by reference to modern trends, as manifested in, for example, other international conventions; interpreting 'serious non-political crime' in Article 1F(b) by reference to international conventions depoliticising crime, eg the European Convention on the Suppression of Terrorism (1977) and by reference to the revival of the doctrine *aut dedere aut punire* (in relation to certain types of offence, states are under an international obligation to punish criminals locally or return them to the place where the crime was committed)), 774 (Lord Slynn considering political asylum in the context of recent forms of terrorism).

4.7. **As products of international consensus, treaties are not drafted with the same precision as domestic legislation. This is particularly true of multilateral treaties. The principles of construction used to interpret domestic legislation should not, therefore, be applied to the interpretation of a treaty where this would defeat the purpose of the treaty and compromise its nature as a living**

instrument. Similarly domestic law concepts will have a minimal role to play in the process of treaty interpretation since treaties are applied across a range of different legal systems. Treaties should be interpreted flexibly, using 'broad principles of general acceptation' [§ 4.7.5]. The aim is to find the autonomous meaning of treaty provisions to encourage consistency throughout all contracting parties. However, where there are divergent interpretations of a treaty in different states then the United Kingdom will be required to form its own view.

4.7.1. **A treaty is the product of international consensus and must be interpreted against that background:**

- *R (Pretty) v Director of Public Prosecutions (Secretary of State for the Home Department intervening)* [2001] UKHL 61 [2002] 1 AC 800, [85] (Lord Hope: 'The [ECHR] . . . is the product of a broad consensus of international opinion about the core values which demand respect for human life and human dignity. It is against that background that we must answer the question [regarding assisted suicide], which is a question of law.');
- *MacWilliam v Mediterranean Shipping Co* [2005] UKHL 11 [2005] 2 WLR 554, [7] (Lord Bingham: '[A]rticle I(b) of the Hague-Visby Rules scheduled to the Carriage of Goods by Sea Act 1971 reproduces the language of article I(b) of the Hague Rules scheduled to the Carriage of Goods by Sea Act 1924, and the Hague Rules were the outcome of a series of international conferences, which were themselves a response to developments in a number of national jurisdictions. The Hague Rules thus represented an agreed international response to what were seen as common problems. Recognition of this important fact must govern the court's approach to interpretation of the Hague Rules and the Hague-Visby Rules, since effect must be given so far as possible to the international consensus expressed in the Rules and not to any divergent or inconsistent rules of domestic law.');
- *Adan v Secretary of State for the Home Department* [1999] 1 AC 293 (HL), 305B–D (Lord Lloyd: '[Counsel] points out that we are here concerned with the meaning of an international Convention. Inevitably the final text will have been the product of a long period of negotiation and compromise. One cannot expect to find the same precision of language as one does in an Act of Parliament drafted by parliamentary counsel. I agree. It follows that one is more likely to arrive at the true construction of article 1A(2) by seeking a meaning which makes sense in the light of the Convention as a whole, and the purposes which the framers of the Convention were seeking to achieve, rather than by concentrating exclusively on the language. A broad approach is what is needed, rather than a narrow linguistic approach. But having said that, the starting point must be the language itself.');

- *Chan Chi-Hung v The Queen* [1996] AC 442 (PC), 452G–H (Lord Mustill, construing Article 12(1) of the Hong Kong Bill of Rights (in the same terms as Article 15(1) of the International Covenant on Civil and Political Rights): 'Their Lordships have referred to the traditional common law methods of interpretation in acknowledgment that the Covenant springs from a consensus of nations, many of whose legal systems adopt a less linguistic and analytical approach to the interpretation of instruments than is taken for granted in countries whose systems originate in the common law. In the event, their Lordships doubt whether, once the problem is recognised, it makes any difference to the present case which philosophy of interpretation is chosen, but it is right as a precaution to adopt a broad approach by testing the apparent meaning of the words against the purpose which they are intended to fulfil.');
- *Horvath v Secretary of State for the Home Department* [2001] 1 AC 489 (HL), 508G (Lord Clyde: 'The [Refugee] Convention was worked out and agreed between states and it is at a state level that it has to be understood.'), 494H–495C (Lord Hope) [§ **4.7.3**]);
- *Re DVT and Air Travel Group Litigation* [2002] EWHC 2825 (QB) [2003] 1 All ER 935, [23] (Nelson J: 'The Warsaw Convention [on International Carriage by Air] was born of discussion and negotiation by delegates from many different states. The wording finally agreed upon was intended to apply in a uniform way across national and legal boundaries. Like all international conventions it is subject to rules of construction which recognise its international nature and these prima facie apply irrespective of the fact that the convention has been given the force of law with the text of the treaty scheduled to an Act of Parliament.') (CA is at [2003] EWCA Civ 1005 [2004] QB 234).

Illustration:

- *Dyer v Watson* [2002] UKPC D1 [2004] 1 AC 379, [49] (Lord Bingham: '[T]he standard of protection guaranteed [by the ECHR], if a minimum, was to be common. It could not be thought that suspects could be maltreated in country A because such maltreatment was known to be endemic in that country although unacceptable in other contracting states, or that state censorship of the media was acceptable in country B where it always existed although unacceptable to other contracting states. So to hold would be repugnant to and subversive to the whole notion of an international Convention to protect human rights and fundamental freedoms. If there were any room for doubt on this point, it would be resolved by the language of the Convention itself, which refers in article 7(2) to "the general principles of law recognised by civilised nations" and in articles 8, 9, 10 and 11 to limitation and restrictions "necessary in a democratic society". The Convention looks to an objective, common measure of protection.').

4.7.2. **A treaty is a living instrument and should be interpreted as such:**
Illustrations:

- *Brown v Stott* [2003] 1 AC 681, 727E–F (Lord Hope: 'The [ECHR] is plainly a living instrument.');
- *Dyer v Watson* [2002] UKPC D1 [2004] 1 AC 379, [49] (Lord Bingham: '[T]he [ECHR] is a living instrument, the standards guaranteed by the Convention are to be reinterpreted in accordance with changing perceptions of individual right.');
- *Sepet v Secretary of State for the Home Department* [2003] UKHL 15 [2003] 1 WLR 856, [6] (Lord Bingham, stating that the Refugee Convention must be seen as a living instrument 'in the sense that while its meaning does not change over time its application will.');
- *R v Secretary of State for the Home Department, Ex parte Adan* [2001] 2 AC 477 (CA and HL), 500G–H (Laws LJ in the CA: 'It is clear that the signatory states intended that the [Refugee] Convention should afford continuing protection for refugees in the changing circumstances of the present and future world . . . the [Refugee Convention] has to be regarded as a living instrument: just as, by the Strasbourg jurisprudence, the [ECHR] is so regarded.');
- *R v Uxbridge Magistrates' Court, Ex parte Adimi* [2001] QB 667 (DC), 688C–D (Newman J, construing Article 31(1) of the Refugee Convention: 'The Convention is a living instrument, changing and developing with the times so as to be relevant and to afford meaningful protection to refugees in the conditions in which they currently seek asylum.');
- *R v Immigration Appeal Tribunal, Ex parte Shah* [1997] Imm AR 145, 152 (Sedley J stating that unless the Refugee Convention is seen as a living instrument, 'adopted by civilised countries for a humanitarian end which is constant in motive but mutable in form, [it] will eventually become an anachronism.');
- *R (European Roma Rights Centre) v Immigration Officer at Prague Airport* [2004] UKHL 55 [2005] 2 WLR 1, [43] (Lord Steyn noting that the Refugee Convention is a 'living instrument and must be interpreted as such.');
- *Öcalan v Turkey* (2003) 37 EHRR 238, [193–194] (ECtHR reiterating that the ECHR is a living instrument which must be interpreted in the light of present day conditions).

4.7.3. **Distinguishing treaty interpretation from statutory interpretation:**

- *Horvath v Secretary of State for the Home Department* [2001] 1 AC 489 (HL), 494H–495C (Lord Hope: 'The point is commonly made in relation to the [Refugee] Convention that it is not right to construe its language with the same precision as one would if it had been an Act of Parliament. The Convention is an international instrument. So . . . its choice of wording must be taken to have been the product of the inevitable process of negotiation and compromise . . . And the general rule is that international treaties should, so far as possible, be construed uniformly by the national courts of all states. This point also suggests that the best guide to the meaning of the words used in the Convention is likely to be found by giving them a broad meaning in the light of the purposes which the Convention was designed to serve.');

- *Adan v Secretary of State for the Home Department* [1999] 1 AC 293 (HL), 305B–D (Lord Lloyd stating that the Refugee Convention cannot be expected to be as precise as domestic legislation and that a 'broad approach is what is needed, rather than a narrow linguistic approach.') [§ **4.7.1**];
- *James Buchanan & Co Ltd v Babco Forwarding & Shipping (UK) Ltd* [1978] AC 141 (HL), 157D–E (Viscount Dilhorne: 'In construing the terms of a convention it is proper and indeed right, in my opinion, to have regard to the fact that conventions are apt to be more loosely worded than Acts of Parliament. To construe a convention as strictly as an Act may indeed lead to a wrong interpretation being given to it. In construing a convention as in construing an Act where the language used is capable of two interpretations one must seek to give effect to the intentions of those who made it (Coke 4 Inst. 330).');
- *Canada Trust Co v Stolzenberg (No 2)* [2002] 1 AC 1 (HL), 10A (Lord Steyn: 'Given that the [Lugano Convention on Jurisdiction and the Enforcement of Judgments] was not drafted with the precision of a statute, this interpretation can readily be accommodated in the Convention system.');
- *R v Governor of Ashford Remand Centre, Ex parte Postlethwaite* [1988] AC 924 (HL), 947A–D (Lord Bridge after referring to *In re Arton (No 2)* [1896] QB 509, 517: '[T]he court should not, unless constrained by the language used, interpret any extradition treaty in a way which would "hinder the working and narrow the operation of most salutary international arrangements." The second principle is that an extradition treaty is "a contract between two sovereign states and has to be construed as such a contract. It would be a mistake to think that it had to be construed as though it were a domestic statute": *R v Governor of Ashford Remand Centre, Ex p Beese* [1973] 1 WLR 969, 973, per Lord Widgery CJ. In applying this second principle, closely related as it is to the first, it must be remembered that the reciprocal rights and obligations which the high contracting parties confer and accept are intended to serve the purpose of bringing to justice those who are guilty of grave crimes committed in either of the contracting states. To apply to extradition treaties the strict canons appropriate to the construction of domestic legislation would often tend to defeat rather than to serve this purpose.');
- *In re Burke* [2001] 1 AC 422 (HL), 428H–429B (Lord Hope considering that an extradition treaty 'is entitled to receive a liberal construction according to its own language, object and intent.'), see similarly 433D–E (Lord Hutton).

4.7.4. **Domestic law concepts should not generally be used in construing treaty provisions:**

- *Morris v KLM Royal Dutch Airlines* [2002] UKHL 7 [2002] 2 AC 628, [77] (Lord Hope construing the Warsaw Convention on International Carriage by Air: 'As the language was not chosen by English draftsmen and was not designed to be construed exclusively by English judges, it should not be interpreted according to the idiom of English law. What one is looking for is a meaning which can be taken to be consistent with the common intention of the states which were represented at the international conference. The exercise is not to be controlled by technical rules of English law or domestic precedent. It would not be right to search for the legal meaning of the words used, as the Convention was not based on the legal system of any of the contracting states. It was intended to be applicable in a uniform way across legal boundaries.' At [51]: 'It may be helpful, before embarking upon an examination of the words "any other bodily injury" in article 17 of the Convention, to examine the present state of our own jurisprudence as to how similar words in domestic legislation are to be interpreted. This is not to say that the approach which we take when we are construing our own legislation is the approach we should take when we are construing the Convention. The construction of an international convention proceeds upon different principles. But this exercise may help to put the problem in its current context.'), [26] (Lord Steyn, rejecting the interpretation of 'bodily injury' in Article 17 of the Warsaw Convention based on legal concepts from post-1929 English case law and, at [17], rejecting the approach of the Israeli Supreme Court, using domestic law in interpreting 'bodily injury'), [147] (Lord Hobhouse: 'It is not right to attempt to construe the words of the Convention by reference to the rules of any domestic law . . . Quite apart from defeating uniformity, such a course can only lead to the complication of simple issues, the inadequately informed investigation of the other legal systems and most importantly, to uncertainty.');
- *Agnew v Länsförsäkringsbolagens AB* [2001] 1 AC 223 (HL), 240D–F (Lord Woolf MR, considering the Lugano Convention on Jurisdiction and the Enforcement of Judgments: 'When interpreting a Convention which applies to a variety of jurisdictions, the less technical distinctions on the basis of domestic law which are adopted the better. They are inclined to produce the very uncertainty which the Convention was designed to remove. They result in satellite procedural litigation which is unproductive and expensive, both in monetary terms and in the delay to the legal proceedings which results. They make the language of the Convention incapable of being applied without resorting to an ever-increasing volume of authorities which will become progressively more difficult to reconcile.');

- *James Buchanan & Co Ltd v Babco Forwarding & Shipping (UK) Ltd* [1978] AC 141 (HL), 152C (Lord Wilberforce: 'I think that the correct approach is to interpret the English text . . . in a normal manner, appropriate for the interpretation of an international convention, unconstrained by technical rules of English law, or by English legal precedent.'), 158B (Viscount Dilhorne: '[I]t would not be right to seek to import common law doctrines into the Convention.');
- *Rey v Government of Switzerland* [1999] 1 AC 54 (PC), 62G–H (Lord Steyn, in interpreting an extradition treaty entered into between the United Kingdom and Switzerland and partially incorporated into the Bahamian Extradition Act 1994: '[T]he Treaty of 1880 must not be construed like a domestic statute. The Treaty was intended to serve the purpose of bringing to justice those who are guilty of grave crimes and it ought prima facie to be accorded a broad and generous construction so as to promote that objective.').

Illustrations:

- *Sarrio SA v Kuwait Investment Authority* [1999] 1 AC 32 (HL), 40E–G (Lord Saville determining whether 'irreconcilable judgments' in Article 22 of the Brussels Convention on Jurisdiction and the Enforcement of Judgments, should be given a limited meaning: '[I]t seems to me that to adopt the suggested limitation would in truth be to give the phrase "related actions" a special "English" meaning, which would be contrary to what the court decided in *The Maciej Rataj*, where it was pointed out . . . that since that phrase did not have the same meaning in all the member states, it was necessary to give it an independent interpretation . . . those who framed article 22 can hardly be suggested to have had in mind our English concepts of "cause of action" or "issue estoppel" when using the phrase "irreconcilable judgments" any more than courts in other Community countries faced with interpreting or applying article 22.');
- *In re H (Minors)(Abduction: Acquiescence)* [1998] AC 72 (HL), 87D–G (Lord Browne-Wilkinson, after reviewing recent English case law on the meaning of 'acquiescence' in Article 13 of the Hague Convention on the Civil Aspects of International Child Abduction: '[I]n English law acquiescence by one party normally depends upon his outward actions which must be known to the other party if the latter seeks to rely on them . . . It is this English concept of acquiescence which is reflected in references in the authorities on article 13 to the circumstances having to be viewed objectively and in the distinction between active and passive acquiescence. In my view these English law concepts have no direct application to the proper construction of article 13 of the Convention. An international Convention, expressed in different languages and intended to apply to a wide range of differing legal systems, cannot be construed differently in different jurisdictions.

The Convention must have the same meaning and effect under the laws of all contracting states. I would therefore reject any construction of article 13 which reflects purely English law rules as to the meaning of the word "acquiescence". I would also deplore attempts to introduce special rules of law applicable in England alone (such as the distinction between active and passive acquiescence) which are not to be found in the Convention itself or in the general law of all developed nations.');

- *Swiss Bank v Brink's MAT* [1986] QB 853, 860F–G (Bingham J, construing Articles 22 and 24 of the Warsaw Convention on International Carriage by Air: 'It does not seem to me that the English maritime practice [of excluding legal interest from the limits of liability which apply under the Hague Rules] is something which should be of very strong persuasive authority in the construction of this Convention in an entirely different field.');
- *In re A (Children)(Conjoined Twins: Surgical Separation)* [2001] Fam 147 (CA), 256 (Robert Walker LJ noting that the ECHR is 'to be construed as an autonomous text, without regard to any special rules of English law.');
- *R (Mullen) v Secretary of State for the Home Department* [2004] UKHL 18 [2005] 1 AC 1, [36] (Lord Steyn describing as erroneous the Court of Appeal's approach relying on 'the ordinary use of English' when construing Article 14(6), International Covenant on Civil and Political Rights);
- *In re S (Minors)(Abduction: Acquiescence)* [1994] 1 FLR 819 (CA), 832E–F (Hoffmann LJ construing Article 13 of the Hague Convention on the Civil Aspects of International Child Abduction: 'The term "acquiesce" is used in different languages in an international convention. It cannot be construed according to any technical doctrines of English law.');
- *Gatewhite Ltd and another v Iberia Lineas Aereas de Espana SA* [1990] 1 QB 326, 331F (Gatehouse J: 'In considering the construction of the [Warsaw Convention on International Carriage by Air] one needs to beware of adopting too parochial an approach. Representatives of many different countries took part in its drafting: not only from common law countries, but also from countries whose legal system was based upon the civil law and, it may well be, countries with systems of law even less familiar to English lawyers.');
- *Rothmans Ltd v Saudi Arabian Airlines Corp* [1981] QB 368, 385A–C (Roskill LJ after referring to Lord Wilberforce's warning in *James Buchanan* at 152 (see above) against construing the provisions of a Convention by reference to the 'technical rules of English law, or . . . English legal precedent': 'How much more, if I may say so, does the warning of Lord Wilberforce apply when one is dealing . . . not so much with technical rules of English substantive law but the technical rules of English procedure regarding service on foreign corporations which carry on business or

which can be said to reside within the jurisdiction because they have a place of business or an office of some kind here?').

4.7.5. **A treaty should be interpreted flexibly and using broad principles:**

- *Stag Line Ltd v Foscolo, Mango & Co* [1932] AC 328 (HL), 350D–F (Lord Macmillan construing the Carriage of Goods by Sea Act 1924 and the scheduled Hague Rules: 'As these rules must come under the consideration of foreign Courts it is desirable in the interests of uniformity that their interpretation should not be rigidly controlled by domestic precedents of antecedent date, but rather that the language of the rules should be construed on broad principles of general acceptation.');
- *James Buchanan & Co Ltd v Babco Forwarding and Shipping (UK) Ltd* [1978] AC 141 (HL), 152C (Lord Wilberforce, adopting the approach in *Stag Line Ltd v Foscolo, Mango & Co* [1932] AC 328 (HL), 350 (Lord Macmillan (see above));
- *Fothergill v Monarch Airlines* [1981] AC 251 (HL), 281G–282A (Lord Diplock construing the Warsaw Convention on International Carriage by Air: 'The language of that Convention that has been adopted at the international conference to express the common intention of the majority of the states represented there is meant to be understood in the same sense by the courts of all those states which ratify or accede to the Convention. Their national styles of legislative draftsmanship will vary considerably as between one another. So will the approach of their judiciaries to the interpretation of written laws and to the extent to which recourse may be had to travaux préparatoires, doctrine [the commentaries of learned authors] and jurisprudence [the decisions of foreign courts] as extraneous aids to the interpretation of the legislative text. The language of an international convention has not been chosen by an English parliamentary draftsman. It is neither couched in the conventional English legislative idiom nor designed to be construed exclusively by English judges. It is addressed to a much wider and more varied judicial audience than is an Act of Parliament that deals with purely domestic law.'), 285D (Lord Fraser referring to the approach in *Stag Line* (see above));
- *Brown v Stott* [2003] 1 AC 681 (PC), 704E–F (Lord Bingham: 'The general language of the [ECHR] could have led to the formulation of hard-edged and inflexible statements of principle from which no departure could be sanctioned whatever the background or the circumstances. But this approach has been consistently eschewed by the court throughout its history.');
- *Horvath v Secretary of State for the Home Department* [2001] 1 AC 489 (HL), 508D (Lord Clyde: 'We are concerned here with the construction of an international convention. The approach to be adopted must be appropriate to that situation. Regard must be given to the purpose of the Convention and the object which it

seeks to serve. While the language of the article has to be respected, any pre-occupation with the precise words may fail to meet the broad intent of the Convention and any detailed analysis of its component elements may distract and divert attention from the essential purpose of what is sought to be achieved.');

- *Morris v KLM Royal Dutch Airlines* [2002] UKHL 7 [2002] 2 AC 628, [78] (Lord Hope: 'In situations of this kind the language used should be construed on broad principles leading to a result that is generally acceptable . . . But this does not mean that a broad construction has to be given to words used in the Convention. As Lord Phillips of Worth Matravers MR said in Miss Morris's case [2002] QB 100, 125, para 90, it is not axiomatic that the broad principles of "general acceptation" described in these cases militates in favour of a broad rather than a narrow interpretation of the phrase "any other bodily injury" [in Article 17 of the Warsaw Convention on International Carriage by Air].');
- *Higham v Stena Sea Link Ltd* [1996] 2 Lloyd's Rep 26 (CA), 29 (Hirst LJ accepting as a general principle the need to give a broad interpretation to the Convention Relating to the Carriage of Passengers and their Luggage by Sea (given force of law by the Merchant Shipping Act 1995): 'but it does not follow that the intention of the makers was necessarily to relax the rules; it may just as likely have been to lay down, save in special cases, a strict and clear regime.').

Illustrations:

- *Mills v HM Advocate* [2002] UKPC D2 [2004] 1 AC 441, [10] (Lord Steyn, taking a broad, purposive approach to the construction of Article 6(1), ECHR);
- *Wilson v First County Trust Ltd (No 2)* [2003] UKHL 40 [2004] 1 AC 816, [181] (Lord Rodger: 'It is well recognised, however, that [ECHR] rights are to be seen as an expression of fundamental principles rather than as a set of mere rules. In applying the principles the courts must balance competing interests.');
- *Coppard v Customs and Excise Commissioners* [2003] EWCA Civ 511 [2003] 2 WLR 1618, [39] (Sedley LJ: 'We remind ourselves that the [ECHR] is not a United Kingdom statute, and that we should be concerned less with close analysis of the language than with the principles which animate it.');
- *In re Ismail* [1999] 1 AC 320 (HL) 326G–327C (Lord Steyn, interpreting section 1 of the Extradition Act 1989: '[T]here is the reality that one is concerned with the contextual meaning of "accused" in a statute intended to serve the purpose of bringing justice to those accused of serious crimes. There is a transnational interest in the achievement of this aim. Extradition treaties, and extradition statutes, ought, therefore to be accorded a broad and generous construction so far as the texts permits it in order to facilitate extradition.').

4.7.6. **Exceptions in treaties may require a restrictive interpretation:**
Illustrations:

- *R v Chief Constable of Sussex, Ex parte International Trader's Ferry Ltd* [1999] 2 AC 418 (HL), 436E (Lord Slynn, in the context of the EC Treaty: '[T]he exceptions to a fundamental rule of the Treaty like article 34 must not be liberally interpreted or applied.');
- *Agnew v Länsförsäkringsbolagens AB* [2001] 1 AC 223 (HL), 247F (Lord Cooke, construing Article 5 of the Lugano Convention on Jurisdiction and the Enforcement of Judgments: 'As to the general approach to the interpretation of the Lugano Convention, I accept that if there were real ambiguity the provisions of Section 2, being exceptions to the general rule of the defendant's domicile, should be interpreted restrictively. But Section 2 does provide quite an extensive range of exceptions, and I would not regard any grudging attitude to these as appropriate. The question must always be the fair meaning of the exception.'), 261G–H (Lord Millett: 'My Lords, it is a cardinal rule of construction of the Brussels and Lugano Conventions that the special rules of jurisdiction which derogate from the general principle enshrined in article 2 cannot be interpreted as going beyond the situations envisaged by the Convention.').

4.7.7. **Treaty provisions should, wherever possible, be given an autonomous meaning:**

- *R v Secretary of State for the Home Department, Ex parte Adan* [2001] 2 AC 477 (HL), 515G–516B (Lord Steyn: '[T]he inquiry must be into the meaning of the Refugee Convention approached as an international instrument created by the agreement of contracting states as opposed to regulatory regimes established by national institutions. It is necessary to determine the autonomous meaning of the relevant treaty provision. This principle is part of the very alphabet of customary international law . . . Closer to the context of the Refugee Convention are human rights conventions where the principle requiring an autonomous interpretation of convention concepts ensures that its guarantees are not undermined by unilateral state actions.' At 516G: '[T]he Refugee Convention must be given an independent meaning derivable from the sources mentioned in articles 31 and 32 [of the Vienna Convention on the Law of Treaties] and without taking colour from distinctive features of the legal system of any individual contracting state. In principle therefore there can only be one true interpretation of a treaty.');
- *Fothergill v Monarch Airlines* [1981] AC 251 (HL), 275F (Lord Wilberforce considering the international consensus on the interpretation of the Warsaw Convention on International Carriage by Air 'impressive');
- *In re H (Minors) (Abduction: Acquiescence)* [1998] AC 72 (HL), 87F (Lord Browne-Wilkinson: 'An international Convention,

expressed in different languages and intended to apply to a wide range of differing legal systems, cannot be construed differently in different jurisdictions. The Convention must have the same meaning under the laws of all contracting states.');

- *James Buchanan & Co Ltd v Babco Forwarding & Shipping (UK) Ltd* [1978] AC 141 (HL), 153C–G (Lord Wilberforce: '[T]he assumed and often repeated generalisation that English methods are narrow, technical and literal, whereas continental methods are broad, generous and sensible, seems to me insecure at least as regards interpretation of international conventions . . . This (CMR) Convention [on the Contract for the International Carriage of Goods by Road] has been accepted by more than 20 states some of them close to English ways of thought. I cannot credit them all, or some average of them, with recognisably superior, or even different, methods of interpretation. We should of course try to harmonise interpretation but . . . on this very Convention, courts in six member countries have produced 12 different interpretations of particular provisions—so uniformity is not to be reached by that road. To base our interpretation of this Convention on some assumed, and unproved, interpretation which other courts are to be supposed likely to adopt is speculative as well as masochistic.');
- *N v Secretary of State for the Home Department* [2005] UKHL 31 [2005] 2 WLR 1124, [21] (Lord Hope: 'The [ECHR] in keeping with so many other human rights instruments, is based on humanitarian principles. There is ample room, where the Convention allows, for the application of those principles. They may also be used to enlarge the scope of the Convention beyond its express terms. It is, of course, to be seen as a living instrument. But an enlargement of its scope in its application to one contracting state is an enlargement for them all. The question must always be whether the enlargement is one which the contracting states would have accepted and agreed to be bound by.').

Illustrations:

- *R (Mullen) v Secretary of State for the Home Department* [2004] UKHL 18 [2005] 1 AC 1, [36] (Lord Steyn: 'The concept of "miscarriage of justice" in article 14(6) [International Covenant on Civil and Political Rights] is an autonomous convention concept.');
- *R (S) v Chief Constable of South Yorkshire Police* [2004] UKHL 39 [2004] 1 WLR 2196, [27] (Lord Steyn: 'The question whether the retention of fingerprints and samples engages article 8(1) should receive a uniform interpretation throughout member states, unaffected by different cultural traditions.');
- *Matthews v Ministry of Defence* [2003] UKHL 4 [2003] 1 AC 1163, [3] (Lord Bingham noting that 'civil rights' in Article 6, ECHR, is autonomous and 'cannot be interpreted solely by reference to the domestic law of the member state.');

- *Sepet v Secretary of State for the Home Department* [2003] UKHL 15_[2003] 1 WLR 856, [6] (Lord Bingham stating that it is plain that the Refugee Convention has a single autonomous meaning, to which effect must be given by all states parties, regardless of where a decision falls to be made);
- *T v Immigration Officer* [1996] AC 742 (HL), 779B (Lord Lloyd interpreting the Refugee Convention by reference to American and Canadian case law: 'In cases concerning an international convention it is obviously desirable that decisions in different jurisdictions should, so far possible, be kept in line with each other');
- *Morris v KLM Dutch Airlines* [2002] UKHL 7 [2002] 2 AC 628, [16] (Lord Steyn: 'It follows from the scheme of the [Warsaw Convention on International Carriage by Air], and indeed from its very nature as an international trade law convention, that the basic concepts it employs to achieve its purpose are autonomous concepts. It is irrelevant what bodily injury means in other contexts in national legal systems. The correct inquiry is to determine the autonomous or independent meaning of "bodily injury" in the Convention.');
- *Jordan Grand Prix Ltd v Baltic Insurance Group* [1999] 2 AC 127 (HL), 134E–F (Lord Steyn: '[T]he concept of a counterclaim in article 11 [of the Brussels Convention on Jurisdiction and the Enforcement of Judgments] apparently derives from article 15 of the draft Belgian Judicial Code . . . And under article 15 of the Belgian Judicial Code a counterclaim was not permitted against new parties. For my part I would not place too much weight on this point because the primary search must be for an objective and independent interpretation capable of accommodating the needs of a diversity of national legal systems.');
- *Quantum Corp Inc v Plane Trucking* [2002] EWCA Civ 350 [2002] 1 WLR 2678, [38] (Mance LJ noting that the importance of a harmonised international interpretation: 'is underlined in the case of [the Convention on the Contract for the International Carriage of Goods by Road], when article 31 allows a claimant considerable scope for choosing between different forums.');
- *Raffeisen Zentralbank v Five Star Trading LLC* [2001] EWCA Civ 68 [2001] QB 825, [33] (Mance LJ: 'National courts must clearly strive to take a single, international or "autonomous" view of the concept of contractual obligation that is not blinkered by conceptions—such as perhaps consideration or even privity—that may be peculiar to their own countries. Further—and perhaps particularly so when the search is for an autonomous international view—the man-made concepts of contractual obligations and proprietary rights are neither so clear nor so inflexible that they may not receive shape from the subject-matter and wording of the Convention itself.');
- *Canada Trust Co v Stolzenberg (No 2)* [2002] 1 AC 1 (HL), 8D–F (Lord Steyn: 'The problem inherent in the application of the concepts of the [Lugano Convention on Jurisdiction and the

Enforcement of Judgments] in national legal systems requires a twofold classificatory inquiry. In the first place it is necessary to interpret a particular concept used in the Convention independently by reference to the language, structure, system and objectives of the Convention. Secondly, recognising that a concept of the Convention may have a different content in various national legal systems, it is necessary to apply it to the procedural regime of the particular legal system.'), 15G–H (Lord Hoffmann: 'The jurisprudence of the European Court distinguishes between those concepts in the Brussels Convention which have an autonomous or independent meaning, irrespective of their content in the law of any particular national system, and those which require the national court to give content to the Convention concept in accordance with its domestic law.');

- *Agnew v Länsförsäkringsbolagens AB* [2001] 1 AC 223 (HL), 256C–E (Lord Hope: 'The issue in the present case relates to the interpretation of one of the terms used in article 5(1) of the [Lugano Convention on Jurisdiction and the Enforcement of Judgments] . . . it should be given an autonomous interpretation as far as possible. This is to ensure its uniform application in all member states under article 293 of the EC Treaty (ex-article 220).'), 244B–C (Lord Woolf MR considering the inappropriateness of applying a legalistic distinction to a Convention 'which is seeking to lay down rules of jurisdiction of general application among a number of states.');
- *Riverstone Meat Co. Pty Ltd v Lancashire Shipping Co. Ltd* [1961] AC 807 (HL) 855E–F (Lord Merriman, construing 'due diligence to make the ship seaworthy' in Article IV, Rule 1, of the Hague Rules (on bills of lading): '[I]t is impossible, in my opinion, to ignore the desirability of preserving the uniformity of interpretation which has been given to these words in American, Canadian and New Zealand authorities, as well as in decisions of the courts of this country.'), 869D (Lord Keith considering the 'desirability of uniformity' in the construction of the Hague Rules as between different nations).

4.7.8. **Some differences of treaty interpretation between national courts are inevitable:**

Illustrations:

- *R v Secretary of State for the Home Department, Ex parte Adan* [2001] 2 AC 477 (HL), 518B–D (Lord Steyn construing Article 1A(2) of the Refugee Convention: 'Unanimity on all perplexing problems created by multilateral treaties is unachievable. National courts can only do their best to minimise the disagreements. But ultimately they have no choice but to apply what they consider to be the autonomous meaning.');
- *In re P (A Child) (Abduction: Custody Rights)* [2004] EWCA Civ 971 [2005] 2 WLR 201, [41] (Ward LJ noting that in an inter-

national convention on private law where there is no international tribunal which can give definitive rulings, 'there will inevitably be differences of approach to interpretation.');

- *Re DVT and Air Travel Group Litigation* [2002] EWHC 2825 (QB) [2003] 1 All ER 935, [140] (Nelson J interpreting the Warsaw Convention on International Carriage by Air: 'It is perhaps inevitable that there will be some difference of interpretation in different jurisdictions even of a uniform code.') (CA is at [2003] EWCA Civ 1005 [2004] QB 234);
- *Osman v Elasha* [2000] Fam 62 (CA), 69B (Thorpe LJ noting the commonality of values of signatories to the Hague Convention on the Civil Aspects of International Child Abduction: 'The member states by and large all derive their sense of law and justice from the Judaeo-Christian root. No state that settles civil and family disputes according to Islamic law has joined the club.' But then at 70 pointing out that 'It would be quite unrealistic to suppose that the concept of child welfare is equally understood and applied throughout the 57 member states.');
- *Ulster-Swift Ltd v Taunton Meat Haulage Ltd* [1977] 1 WLR 625 (CA), 631G–632E (Megaw LJ noting that 30 decisions of courts in Belgium, France, West Germany, the Netherlands, Italy and Austria had produced 12 different interpretations of Articles 17 and 18 of the Convention on the Contract for the International Carriage of Goods by Road).

4.7.9. **Need for uniform treaty interpretation displacing possibility of domestic law remedy:**

- *Sidhu v British Airways plc* [1997] AC 430 (HL), 454B (Lord Hope considering whether the Warsaw Convention on International Carriage by Air permits claims to be brought outside its terms, under the common law: 'The domestic courts are not free to provide a remedy according to their own law, because to do this would be to undermine the Convention. It would lead to the setting alongside the Convention of an entirely different set of rules which would distort the operation of the whole scheme.');
- *Western Digital Corp v British Airways plc* [2001] QB 733 (CA), [33] (Mance LJ referring to *Sidhu* (see above) as authority for the proposition: 'That the [Warsaw] Convention contains a code which supersedes common law rules relating to the nature and standard of liability is now clearly established.' But noting at [37] that: 'title to sue in respect of such a liability is a different matter . . . Under the Montreal Protocol No. 4 [which amended article 24 of the Warsaw Convention and is scheduled to the Carriage by Air and Road Act 1979], the intention seems clear to reserve a significant role to national law when it comes to determining by whom the claims allowed by articles 17 to 19 may be brought.').

4.7.10. **Where treaty provisions have been given diverging interpretations in different contracting states, a domestic view on the proper interpretation will need to be formed:**

Illustration:

- *R v Secretary of State for the Home Department Ex parte Adan* [2001] 2 AC 477 (HL), 512D (Lord Steyn: 'There is a divergence in state practice concerning the interpretation of the word "persecuted" in article 1A(2) [of the Refugee Convention]. The majority of contracting states, including the United Kingdom, do not limit persecution to conduct which can be attributed to a state. A minority of contracting states, including Germany and France, do so limit it.' See also 518B–D [§ **4.7.8**]), 510B (Lord Slynn interpreting section 2(2) of the Immigration and Asylum Act 1996: 'If some other states interpret the Convention differently in a way which [the Secretary of State] considers not to be in compliance with the Convention he must carry out his obligation in the way in which he is advised or is told by the courts is right. To do so is not in any way contrary to the comity of nations or offensive to other states who interpret it differently and it does not begin to suggest malafides on their part.').

4.8. **Terms may be implied into treaties where it is necessary or plainly right to do so and where they can be formulated with precision. The process of implication must be undertaken with caution and with recognition of the twin characteristics of a treaty as a product of carefully negotiated international consensus and as a living instrument [§ 4.7.1; § 4.7.2]. It may involve a consideration of the background to the treaty, its negotiating history, the travaux préparatoires [§§ 5.5–5.6] and any relevant explanatory reports or handbooks [§ 5.13].**

4.8.1. **The possibility of implication:**

- *Brown v Stott* [2003] 1 AC 681 (PC), 703F–G (Lord Bingham, considering that terms may be implied into the ECHR: '[T]he case law of the European court shows that the court has been willing to imply terms into the Convention when it was judged necessary or plainly right to do so. But the process of implication is one to be carried out with caution, if the risk is to be averted that the contracting parties may, by judicial interpretation, become bound by obligations which they did not expressly accept and might not have been willing to accept. As an important constitutional instrument the Convention is to be seen as a "living tree capable of growth and expansion within its natural limits" (*Edwards v Attorney General for Canada* [1930] AC 124, 136 per Lord Sankey LC) but those limits will often call for very careful consideration.');
- *R v Bow Street Magistrate, Ex parte Pinochet (No 3)* [2000] 1 AC 147 (HL), 218E–H (Lord Goff (dissenting) considering whether a

term could be implied into the Torture Convention: 'I recognise that a term may be implied into a treaty, if the circumstances are such that "the parties must have intended to contract on the basis of the inclusion in the treaty of a provision whose effect can be stated with reasonable precision;" see *Oppenheim's International Law*, vol I, pp. 1271–1272, n. 4. It would, however, be wrong to assume that a term may be implied into a treaty on the same basis as a term may be implied into an ordinary commercial contract, for example to give the contract business efficacy . . . This is because treaties are different in origin, and serve a different purpose. Treaties are the fruit of long negotiation, the purpose being to produce a draft which is acceptable in a number, often a substantial number, of state parties. The negotiation of a treaty may well take a long time, running into years . . . The agreed terms may well be the fruit of "horse-trading" in order to achieve general agreement, and proposed articles may be amended, or even omitted in whole or in part, to accommodate the wishes or anxieties of some of the negotiating parties. In circumstances such as these, it is the text of the treaty itself which provides the only safe guide to its terms, though reference may be made, where appropriate, to the travaux préparatoires. But implied terms cannot, except in the most obvious cases, be relied on as binding the state parties who ultimately sign the treaty, who will in all probability include those who were not involved in the preliminary negotiations.').

Illustrations:

- *Lord Gray's Motion* [2002] 1 AC 124 (HL, Committee for Privileges), 133F–G, 134D–E (Lord Nicholls, considering the possibility of an implied term in the Treaty of Union 1707 that British subjects in Scotland, as with those living in England and Wales, should be adequately represented in the Westminster Parliament);
- *In re Burke* [2001] 1 AC 422 (HL), 433B–D (Lord Hutton: 'Although the Treaty between this country and the United States does not use the term "unlawfully at large" in respect of a convicted person whose extradition is sought, the requirement that a convicted person should not be extradited unless he is "unlawfully at large" is contained in a number of provisions not related to the United States contained in extradition statutes (see, for example, section 1 of the Fugitive Offenders Act 1967 and sections 1(1)(b) and 9(8)(b) of the Extradition Act 1989) and I consider that the construction of article VII(4) contended for by the applicant is in conformity with the general intendment of an extradition statute or Treaty, namely that a convicted person should be extradited when he is unlawfully at large.').

4.8.2. **A range of source material may be used in determining whether a term may be implied into a treaty:**
Illustration:

- *R v Bow Street Magistrate, Ex parte Pinochet (No 3)* [2000] 1 AC 147 (HL), 219E–223A (Lord Goff (dissenting) considering the background, negotiating history, travaux préparatoires, and Handbook on the Torture Convention in determining whether a term could be implied into in the Torture Convention), 245F (Lord Hope considering whether the effect of the Torture Convention was to remove the former head of state immunity by necessary implication: 'The absence of any discussion on the issue [in the Reports of the Working Group on the Draft Convention] is not surprising, once it is appreciated that the purpose of the Convention was to put in place as widely as possible the machinery which was needed to make the struggle against torture more effective throughout the world.').

(3) Context

4.9. **The context and contemporary background of a treaty play an important role in the interpretation of treaty provisions. Context includes the negotiations leading up to the treaty, the preceding legal position and relevant rules of customary international law (see Article 31(2), Vienna Convention on the Law of Treaties: [§ 4.4]).**

4.9.1. **Importance of context and contemporary background:**

- *R (Mullen) v Secretary of State for the Home Department* [2004] UKHL 18 [2005] 1 AC 1, [36] (Lord Steyn construing Article 14(6), International Covenant on Civil and Political Rights: 'The Court of Appeal ought to have concentrated on the autonomous meaning of the concept in article 14(6) . . . On a broader basis I would add that generally in law the inquiry into what words mean is of no interest. The response of a court to such a generalised and unhelpful question must always be: "In what particular context?" And here the *only* relevant context is the international meaning of the words used in article 14(6) upon which section 133 [in the Criminal Justice Act 1988] is based.');
- *Riverstone Meat Co Pty Ltd v Lancashire Shipping Co Ltd* [1961] AC 807 (HL), 836D–G (Viscount Simonds, construing 'due diligence to make the ship seaworthy' in Article IV, Rule 1, of the Hague Rules (on bills of lading): 'To ascertain their meaning it is, in my opinion, necessary to pay particular regard to their history, origin and context, and, as I think the courts below have not paid sufficient regard to this aspect of the case, I must deal with it at

some length. The Hague Rules, as is well known, were the result of the Conference on Maritime Law held at Brussels in 1922 and 1923, Their aim was broadly to standardise within certain limits the rights of every holder of a bill of lading against the ship owner, prescribing an irreducible minimum for the responsibilities and liabilities to be undertaken by the latter. To guide them the framers of the rules had amongst other precedents the American Harter Act of 1893, the Australian Sea Carriage of Goods Act, 1904, the Canadian Water Carriage of Goods Act, 1910, and though they had no British Act as a model, they had decisions of the English courts in which the language of the Harter Act had fallen to be construed by virtue of its provisions being embodied in bills of lading. In all these Acts the relevant words, "exercise due diligence to make the ship sea worthy," are to be found. It was in all these circumstances that these were adopted in the Hague Rules.').

Illustrations:

- *Morris v KLM Dutch Airlines* [2002] UKHL 7 [2002] 2 AC 628, [17] (Lord Steyn, construing 'bodily injuries' in Article 17 of the Warsaw Convention on International Carriage by Air: 'The contextual scene is that in 1929 in legal systems generally there was compensation available for physical injuries. By contrast in 1929 the position was different in regard to mental injury and illness. The best view is that except in a few states mental injuries and illnesses were not compensatable or were a matter of controversy. In these circumstances one would have expected, if it was intended to cover mental injuries and illnesses by article 17, that it would have been debated in working sessions at Warsaw and expressly provided for . . . The importance of [this] is underlined if one takes into account that many untoward occurrences affecting aircraft may cause mental injury or illness alone but not physical injuries . . . The textually relevant circumstance is that in 1929 it would already have been appreciated that the imposition of strict liability for mental injury or illness would have opened the door to an avalanche of intangible claims, greatly in excess of the number of claims for physical injuries.' See also [26]), [146] (Lord Hobhouse considering the historical context of the Warsaw Convention);
- *R v Immigration Appeal Tribunal, Ex parte Shah* [1999] 2 AC 629 (HL), 652C–D (Lord Hoffmann: 'It may seem strange that sex (or gender) was not specifically enumerated in the [Refugee] Convention when it is mentioned in article 2 of the Universal Declaration of Human Rights. But the Convention was originally limited to persons who had become refugees as a result of events occurring before 1 January 1951. One can only suppose that the delegates could not think of cases before that date in which women had been persecuted because they were women.'), 660H (Lord Hutton: 'The inclusion of sex as a basis of discrimination in

the Universal Declaration and the failure to include it as a ground of persecution in the 1951 Convention is noteworthy. It may be due to the fact that, while sexual discrimination was widely practiced in 1951, and women are condemned to a subordinate and inferior status in many societies even today, it is difficult to imagine a society in which women are actually subjected to serious harm simply because they are women.');

- *El-Ali v Secretary of State for the Home Department* [2002] EWCA Civ 1103 [2003] 1 WLR 95, [9–17] (Laws LJ noting the 'unusually important' (at [9]) background when considering the history behind Article 1D in the Refugee Convention);
- *Matadeen v Pointu* [1999] 1 AC 98 (PC), 114B–F (Lord Hoffmann, in construing the effect of the Declaration of the Rights of Man on section 3 of the Constitution of Mauritius: 'The fact that [the Declaration of the Rights of Man] was adopted in Mauritius tells one nothing about which organ of government was intended to decide how its principles should be applied. The contemporary background suggests very strongly that the Assemblée Coloniale did not have any form of judicial review in mind. The adoption of the declaration took place at a time when France was ruled by the National Convention and its famous committees and representatives en mission. Elected by universal suffrage the Convention was considered the expression of the volonté générale to which article 4 referred. The notion that its decrees should be subject to review by a court of independent judges would have been greeted with incredulity.').

4.9.2. **Considering the negotiations preceding the conclusion of a treaty as part of the context:**

Illustration:

- *Agnew v Länsförsäkringsbolagens AB* [2001] 1 AC 223 (HL), 261D–E (Lord Millett: 'This [construction of section 3 of the Lugano Convention on Jurisdiction and the Enforcement of Judgments] is confirmed by the course of the negotiations which preceded the enactment of the Convention. The United Kingdom sought the exclusion of large risks from the scope of Section 3. Its request was viewed sympathetically as being consistent with the protective purpose of the Section, but it was rejected on the ground that it was impossible to devise a suitable line of demarcation which possessed a sufficient degree of certainty.').

4.9.3. **Considering the legal position preceding the conclusion of a treaty as part of the context:**

Illustration:

- *Effort Shipping Co Ltd v Linden Management SA* [1998] AC 605 (HL), 624F–G (Lord Steyn, considering the competing interpretations of the Hague Rules (on bills of lading), as between the United States and the United Kingdom: 'But there is a contextual consideration which must also be weighed in the balance. It is permissible to take into account the legal position in the United Kingdom and in the United States regarding the shipment of dangerous cargo before the Hague Rules were approved. It is relevant as part of the contextual scene of the Hague Rules.' At 625C–G: '[A]t the time of the drafting of the Hague Rules the dominant theory in a very large part of the world was that shippers were under an absolute liability not to ship dangerous goods. This circumstance must have been known to those who drafted and approved the Hague Rules. No doubt they also knew that there was an alternative theory namely that the shipper of dangerous goods ought to be liable only for want of due diligence in the shipment of dangerous goods. If this contextual scene is correctly described . . . one is entitled to pose the practical question: what would the framers of the Hague Rules have done if collectively they had been minded to adopt the step of reversing the dominant theory of shippers' liability for the shipment of dangerous goods? There is really only one realistic answer: they would have expressly provided that shippers are only liable in damages for the shipment of dangerous goods if they knew or ought to have known of the dangerousness of the goods . . . Moreover, if this idea had been put forward for discussion the travaux préparatoires would no doubt have reflected the observations of carriers on such a fundamental change to their rights. The idea was never put forward. The inference must be that the framers of the Hague Rules proceeded on what was at that time an unsurprising assumption that shippers would be absolutely liable for the shipment of dangerous cargo.').

4.9.4. **Considering customary international law as part of the context [§§ 2.13–2.16]:**

Illustrations:

- *R v Bow Street Magistrate, Ex parte Pinochet* [2000] 1 AC 61 (HL), 74G–H (Lord Slynn (dissenting): 'The provisions of the [State Immunity Act 1978] "fall to be construed against the background of those principles of public international law as are generally recognised by the family of nations": *Alcom Ltd v Republic of Colombia* [1984] AC 580, 597 *per* Lord Diplock. So also as I see it must the [Torture] Convention be interpreted.') [§ **13.16.3**];
- *R v Bow Street Magistrate, Ex parte Pinochet (No 3)* [2000] 1 AC 147 (HL), 243C (Lord Hope after describing the relevant customary international law relating to torture: 'This is the background against which I now turn to the Torture Convention.').

(4) Object and Purpose

4.10. **Treaties should be interpreted in the light of their spirit, object and purpose (see Article 31(1), Vienna Convention on the Law of Treaties: [§ 4.4]). These elements may be discerned from the text of the treaty, particularly the preamble or recitals. The process of treaty interpretation may be additionally facilitated by considering the object and purpose of individual treaty articles as part of the overall scheme of the treaty. This consideration is distinct from that of using one article as an aid in construing another article in the same treaty. Whether the latter course is permissible depends on the individual case.**

4.10.1. **Interpreting a treaty by considering its spirit, object and purpose:**

- *R (European Roma Rights Centre) v Immigration Officer at Prague Airport* [2004] UKHL 55 [2005] 2 WLR 1, [18] (Lord Bingham: '[Counsel] urged that the [Refugee] Convention should be given a generous and purposive interpretation, bearing in mind its humanitarian objects and purpose clearly stated in the Preamble . . . This is, in my opinion, a correct approach to interpretation of a Convention such as this and it gains support, if support be needed, from article 31(1) of the Vienna Convention on the Law of Treaties which, reflecting principles of customary international law, requires a treaty to be interpreted in the light of its object and purpose. But I would make an important caveat. However generous and purposive its approach to interpretation, the court's task remains one of interpreting the written document to which the contracting states have committed themselves. It must interpret what they have agreed. It has no warrant to give effect to what they might, or in an ideal world would, have agreed. This would violate the rule, also expressed in article 31(1) of the Vienna Convention, that a treaty should be interpreted in accordance with the ordinary meaning to be given to the terms of the treaty in their context.');
- *R (Hoxha) v Special Adjudicator* [2005] UKHL 19 [2005] 1 WLR 1063, [85] (Lord Brown) [**§ 4.5.2**];
- *Fothergill v Monarch Airlines* [1981] AC 251 (HL), 272G (Lord Wilberforce: 'Consideration of the purpose of an enactment is always a legitimate part of the process of interpretation'), 279C (Lord Diplock giving 'as one must, a purposive construction to the [Warsaw] Convention looked at as a whole'), 290H (Lord Scarman: 'It is the duty of the English courts to apply, if possible, an interpretation which meets the commercial purpose of the Convention.');
- *R v Bow Street Magistrate, Ex parte Pinochet (No 3)* [2000] 1 AC 147 (HL), 244B (Lord Hope: 'The preamble to the Torture

Convention explains its purpose.'), 260B (Lord Hutton considering the preamble to the Torture Convention);.

Illustrations:

- *R (Ullah) v Special Adjudicator* [2004] UKHL 26 [2004] 2 AC 323, [11] (Lord Bingham, quoting from *Soering v United Kingdom* (1989) 11 EHRR 439, paras 87–88, on the ECHR: ' "regard must be had to its special character as a treaty for the collective enforcement of human rights and fundamental freedoms. Thus, the object and purpose of the Convention as an instrument for the protection of individual human beings require that its provisions be interpreted and applied so as to make its safeguards practical and effective. In addition, any interpretation of the rights and freedoms guaranteed has to be consistent with 'the general spirit of the Convention, an instrument designed to maintain and promote the ideals and values of a democratic society'... It would hardly be compatible with the underlying values of the Convention, that the 'common heritage of political traditions, ideals freedom and the rule of law' to which the Preamble refers, were a contracting state knowingly to surrender a fugitive to another state where there were substantial grounds for believing that he would be in danger of being subjected to torture, however heinous the crime allegedly committed. Extradition in such circumstances, while not explicitly referred to in the brief and general wording of article 3, would plainly be contrary to the spirit and intendment of the article.');
- *Brown v Stott* [2003] 1 AC 681 (PC), 703A–C (Lord Bingham noting that the fundamental nature of the rights and freedoms in the ECHR is clear from the full title, contents and preamble), 707E–708D (Lord Steyn); 719B (Lord Hope) (both considering the preamble to the ECHR);
- *Matthews v Ministry of Defence* [2003] UKHL 4 [2003] 1 AC 1163, [49] (Lord Hope stating that Article 6(1), ECHR must be read in the light of the rule of law referred to in the preamble);
- *R v Immigration Appeal Tribunal, Ex parte Shah* [1999] 2 AC 629 (HL), 638G–639E (Lord Steyn: '[T]he preambles to the [Refugee] Convention are significant . . .The relevance of the preambles is twofold. First, they expressly show that a premise of the Convention was that all human beings shall enjoy fundamental rights and freedoms. Secondly, and more pertinently, they show that counteracting discrimination, which is referred to in the first preamble, was a fundamental purpose of the Convention. That is reinforced by the reference in the first preamble to the Universal Declaration of Human Rights of 1948 which proclaimed the principle of the equality of all human beings and specifically provided that the entitlement to equality means equality "without distinction of any kind, such as race, colour, sex, language, religion, political or other opinion, national or social origin, property, birth or other status".'), 650G–651D (Lord Hoffmann, referring

to the preamble to the Refugee Convention and the framers' intention), 656D–F (Lord Hope considering the preamble to the Refugee Convention);

- *Horvath v Secretary of State for the Home Department* [2001] 1 AC 489 (HL), 495C–D (Lord Hope: '[T]he best guide to the meaning of the words used in the [Refugee] Convention is likely to be found by giving them a broad meaning in the light of the purposes which the Convention was designed to serve . . . It seems to me that the Convention purpose which is of paramount importance for a solution of the problems raised by the present case is that which is to be found in the principle of surrogacy. The general purpose of the Convention is to enable the person who no longer has the benefit of protection against persecution for a Convention reason in his own country to turn for protection to the international community.'), 508G–509B (Lord Clyde, considering references, in the preamble to the Refugee Convention, to the Charter of the United Nations and the Universal Declaration on Human Rights);
- *In re H (A Minor) (Abduction: Rights of Custody)* [2000] 2 AC 291 (HL), 302D–E (Lord Mackay, giving a wide construction to Articles 8 and 5 of the Hague Convention: 'The objects of the [Hague Convention on the Civil Aspects of International Child Abduction] are (a) to secure the prompt return of children wrongfully removed to or retained in any contracting state; and (b) to ensure that rights of custody and of access under the law of one contracting state are effectively respected in the other contracting states. Since this is an international Convention to be applied under a variety of systems of law it is right that it should be given a purposive construction in order to make as effective as possible the machinery set up under it.');
- *R v Secretary of State for the Home Department, Ex parte Sivakumaran* [1988] 1 AC 958 (HL) (considering the general purpose of the Refugee Convention, in interpreting 'well-founded fear' in article 1A(2)), 992H–993A (Lord Keith: '[T]he general purpose of the Convention is surely to afford protection and fair treatment to those for whom neither is available in their own country.'), 1000E (Lord Goff: '[T]he true object of the Convention is not just to assuage fear, however reasonably and plausibly entertained, but to provide a safe haven for those unfortunate people whose fear of persecution is in reality well-founded.' See also 999A and 999H–1000A, considering the objects of the Refugee Convention.);
- *Adan v Secretary of State for the Home Department* [1999] 1 AC 293, 302E–F (Lord Slynn referring to the object and purpose of the Refugee Convention in interpreting Article 1A(2));
- *Morris v KLM Dutch Airlines* [2002] UKHL 7 [2002] 2 AC 628, [12] (Lord Steyn: 'It is important to understand the major objective of the Warsaw Convention . . . The purpose of the Warsaw

Convention, following the precedent of the earlier Hague Rules governing carriage by sea, was to bring some order to a fragmented system by a partial harmonisation of the applicable laws.' At [14]: 'The effect of the Convention was described by Lord Hope of Craighead in *Sidhu v British Airways plc* [1997] AC 430 . . . "The idea that an action of damages may be brought by a passenger against the carrier outside the Convention in the cases covered by article 17—which is the issue in the present case—seems to be entirely contrary to the system which these two articles were designed to create . . . In my opinion the answer to it is to be found not by an exact analysis of the particular words used but by a consideration of the whole purpose of the article. In its context the purpose seems to me to be to prescribe the circumstances—that is to say, the only circumstances— in which a carrier will be liable in damages to the passenger for claims arising out of his international carriage by air." . . . I respectfully adopt this analysis.');

- *R v Bow Street Magistrates, Ex parte Pinochet* [2000] 1 AC 61 (HL), 71G–72B (Lord Slynn (dissenting), considering the preamble in construing domestically incorporated parts of the Vienna Convention on Diplomatic Relations);
- *n re S (A Minor)(Custody: Habitual Residence)* [1998] AC 750 (HL), 766C–E (Lord Slynn considering the preamble and objects of the Hague Convention on the Civil Aspects of International Child Abduction. At 769H: 'As to the purpose of the [European Convention on Recognition and Enforcement of Decisions Concerning Custody of Children], the member states of the Council of Europe recited that "the making of arrangements to ensure that decisions concerning the custody of a child can be more widely recognised and enforced will provide greater protection of the welfare of children."');
- *Canada Trust Co v Stolzenberg (No 2)* [2002] 1 AC 1 (HL), 11F–H (Lord Steyn: 'It is also necessary to consider the rival arguments [on the interpretation of 'sued' in Articles 2 and 6 of the Lugano Convention] from the point of view of the attainment of the principal objectives of the Convention. The preamble of the Lugano Convention records the desire "to ensure as uniform an interpretation as possible of this instrument": see also articles 1 and 2 of Protocol No 2 on the Uniform Interpretation of the Convention, annexed to the Convention . . . The second major aim of the Convention is the achievement of predictability and certainty at all stages for all concerned.');
- *In re G (Children) (Foreign Order: Enforcement)* [2003] EWCA Civ 1607 [2004] 1 WLR 521, [27] (Thorpe LJ: 'Conventions for international enforcement of contact orders are prone to overreach themselves in their ambitions. Access orders can seldom be written on stone tablets. The orders are peculiarly vulnerable to change of circumstance, the maturation of children and the

dynamics within sometimes the old family and sometimes a newly constituted family. In consequence enforcement, not only after lapse of time but after relocation and in a foreign court is always likely to be problematic. These realities in my judgment demand a liberal construction of article 11(2) in order to achieve the overriding objectives of the European Convention [on Recognition and Enforcement of Decisions Concerning Custody of Children] one of which is to ensure that the act of relocation does not avoid the orders for contact made by the court that granted permission.').

4.10.2. **The object and purpose of individual articles or parts of a treaty may be considered in construing a treaty:**
Illustrations:

- *Jordan Grand Prix Ltd v Baltic Insurance Group* [1999] 2 AC 127 (HL), 134B (Lord Steyn: '[I]t must be borne in mind that in the words of the European Court of Justice the purpose of Section 3 [of the Brussels Convention on Jurisdiction and the Enforcement of Judgments in Civil and Commercial Matters] was "to protect the insured who is most frequently faced with a predetermined contract the clauses of which are no longer negotiable and who is a weaker economic position:" *Gerling Konzern Speziale Kreditversicherungs-AG v Amministrazione del Tesoro dello Stato* (*Case 201/82*) [1983] ECR 2503, 2516, para 17. This purpose must inform the approach to the interpretation of article 11');
- *Sarrio SA v Kuwait Investment Authority* [1999] 1 AC 32 (HL), 39F–H (Lord Saville, in construing Article 22 of the Brussels Convention on Jurisdiction and the Enforcement of Judgments: 'Both the Advocate General and the European Court [in *The Maciej Rataj* (Case C-406/92) [1995] 1 Lloyd's Rep 302; sub nom *The Tatry* [1994] ECR I-5439] were at pains to emphasise that the objective of article 22 is to improve co-ordination of the exercise of judicial functions within the Community and to avoid conflicting and contradictory decisions, thus facilitating the proper administration of justice in the Community . . . As the court pointed out . . . the objective of article 27(3) is different from the objective of article 22.');
- *Anton Durbeck GmbH v Den Norske Bank* [2003] EWCA Civ 147 [2003] QB 1160, [42–43] (Lord Phillips MR considering the purpose of Article 5(5) of the Lugano Convention).

4.10.3. **Articles should be considered as part of the overall scheme of the treaty** [§ **4.5.7**]:
Illustrations:

- *Jordan Grand Prix Ltd v Baltic Insurance Group* [1999] 2 AC 127 (HL), 132G–133E (Lord Steyn: 'Article 11 [of the Brussels Convention on Jurisdiction and the Enforcement of Judgments in Civil and Commercial Matters] must be construed in the scheme of the Convention. Article 2 contains the general principle that persons domiciled in a contracting state shall, whatever their nationality, be sued in the courts of that state. Section 2 provides for special jurisdiction in respect of various matters including contract, tort, delict or quasi-delict. Section 3 provides for special jurisdiction in regard to matters relating to insurance . . . This is the matrix in which article 11 is embedded. Before I can directly examine the interpretation of article 11 it is necessary to consider the status of Section 3 in the scheme of the Convention . . . The structure of the Convention, the language of Section 3, and in particular the express qualification contained in the words "without prejudice to the provisions of articles 4 and 5.5" in article 7, demonstrate that Section 3 is a self-contained and exclusive code governing insurance.' See also 134G–H considering the structure of the Brussels Convention);

- *R v Immigration Appeal Tribunal, Ex parte Shah* [1999] 2 AC 629 (HL), 638C–G (Lord Steyn considering Article 1A(2) in the scheme of the Refugee Convention);
- *Canada Trust Co v Stolzenberg (No 2)* [2002] 1 AC 1 (HL), 9F (Lord Steyn considering Articles 2 and 6 in the scheme of the Lugano Convention);
- *Sidhu v British Airways* [1997] AC 430 (HL) 438B–440E, 453C–D (Lord Hope considering Article 17 in the scheme of the Warsaw Convention on International Carriage by Air);
- *In re A (Minors) (Abduction: Custody Rights)* [1992] Fam 106 (CA), 115D–E (Balcombe LJ (dissenting) considering Article 13 in the scheme of Hague Convention on the Civil Aspects of Child Abduction);
- *Dresser UK Ltd v Falcongate Ltd* [1992] QB 502 (CA), 512D–E (Bingham LJ considering Articles 21–22 in the scheme of the Brussels Convention on Jurisdiction and the Enforcement of Judgments).

4.10.4. **Using one article as an aid in construing another article in the same treaty:**

Illustrations:

- *Revenko v Secretary of State for the Home Department* [2001] QB 601 (CA), 632F (Clarke LJ referring to *R v Secretary of State for the Home Department, Ex parte Sivakumaran* [1988] AC 958 as an example of the House of Lords using Article 33 of the Refugee Convention as an aid to construction of Article 1A(2). At 633B–C: 'However, I recognise that both in the Court of Appeal and in the House of Lords in *Adan's* case, it was said that article 33 cannot be used to construe article 1A(2): see [1997] 1 WLR 1107, 1116 and [1999] 1 AC 293, 306, apparently on the basis that the argument approaches the problem from the wrong end because it is article 1(2) which must govern the scope of article 33 and not vice versa . . . Nevertheless, it does seem to me that it must, in some cases at least, be permissible, when construing a particular article of a convention, to have regard to other provisions of it. Otherwise, it is difficult to see how the particular article can be considered in its context and, in the words of article 31.1 of the Vienna Convention, "in the light of its object and purpose." ');

- *R v Secretary of State for Employment, Ex parte Seymour-Smith* [1999] 2 AC 554 (ECJ), [70] (Advocate General Cosmas: 'In my opinion, in so far as the adoption of a longer or shorter qualifying period before there can be unfair dismissal constitutes a means of exercising government policy and is ultimately a political choice, it falls within the scope of articles 117 and 118 of the EC Treaty [now Articles 136 and 137]. Those articles, as the court has repeatedly held, are simply in the nature of a programme . . . (However those articles are not devoid of any legal effect but constitute an important aid for the interpretation of other provisions of the Treaty and of secondary Community law in social matters: see *Giménez Zaera* [*v Instituto Nacional de la Seguridad Social (Case 126/86)* [1987] ECR 3697, 3716], para. 14 and *Sloman Neptun* [*v Seebetriebsrat Bodo Ziesemer der Sloman Neptun Schiffahrts AG* (*Cases C-72 and 73/91*) [1993] ECR I-887], para. 26.').

(5) Subsequent Practice

4.11. **Subsequent state practice may provide evidence of an evolving treaty interpretation where it can be shown that there is widespread agreement regarding the interpretation amongst the parties (see Article 31(3)(c), Vienna Convention on the Law of Treaties: [§ 4.4]). This is distinct from actual subsequent agreements between the parties which relate to the interpretation of a treaty or the application of its provisions (Article 31(3)(b), Vienna Convention on the Law of Treaties). In relation to Article 31(3)(c) and subsequent state practice, lack of treaty amendment poses a considerable hurdle in showing such an evolving interpretation.**

4.11.1. **Establishing widespread agreement between contracting parties enables reliance on subsequent state practice in the process of construction:**

- *R (Hoxha) v Special Adjudicator* [2002] EWCA Civ 1403 [2003] 1 WLR 241, [43–44] (Keene LJ considering the contention that the restriction of the proviso of Article 1C(5) in the Refugee Convention to statutory refugees no longer has force, because state practice and the humanitarian purposes underlying the Convention should lead to a sufficiently wide interpretation so as to include all refugees: 'We readily accept that subsequent international practice in applying a treaty may indicate an agreement as to how that treaty should be interpreted [referring to Article 31 (3) of the Vienna Convention on the Law of Treaties] . . . It is to be observed that article 31(3)(b) requires the subsequent practice to establish the *agreement* of the parties regarding the interpretation . . . It is moreover easier to establish an interpretation by subsequent state practice where the treaty in question is a bilateral one rather than which has been agreed by a large number of countries.' Citing Sir Percy Spender in *Certain Expenses of the United Nations*, Judgment, ICJ Reports 1962, p 150, 191 (see below)). At [47]: 'Where one has clear and express language imposing a restriction upon the scope of a particular provision, as is the case with the proviso to article 1C(5), it must require very convincing evidence of a widespread and general practice of the international community to establish that that restriction is no longer to be applied as a matter of international law.' HL is at [2005] UKHL 19 [2005] 1 WLR 1063, [82] (Lord Brown considering that the Court of Appeal put the appellants' case too low but rejecting the submission that state practice had altered the scope of Article 1C(5));

- *Certain Expenses of the United Nations*, ICJ Reports 1962, p 150, 191 (Sir Percy Spender: 'In the case of multilateral treaties the admissibility and value as evidence of subsequent conduct of one or more parties thereto encounter particular difficulties. If all the parties to a multilateral treaty where the parties are fixed and constant, pursue a course of subsequent conduct in their attitude to the text of the treaty, and that course of conduct leads to an inference, and one inference only, as to their common intention and understanding at the time they entered into the treaty as to the meaning of its text, the probative value of their conduct again is manifest. If however only one or some but not all of them by subsequent conduct interpret the text in a certain manner, that conduct stands upon the same footing as the unilateral conduct of one party to a bilateral treaty. The conduct of such one or more could not of itself have any probative value or provide a criterion for judicial interpretation.');
- *Morris v KLM Royal Dutch Airlines* [2002] UKHL 7 [2002] 2 AC 628, [80] (Lord Hope: 'It is also legitimate to have regard to subsequent practice in the application of the Convention, if this shows that the contracting parties were in agreement as to its interpretation when it was entered into. General guidance to this effect is given, albeit only prospectively, in the Vienna Convention on the Law of Treaties (1980) (Cmnd 7964), articles 31(1) and 32.' At [98]: 'It would not be right to use subsequent practice to show that the meaning of ['bodily injury' in the Warsaw Convention on International Carriage by Air] has been changed. The proper way to change the meaning used in an international convention is by amending the convention.' Subsequent

practice considered by reference to the interpretation of the phrase in German-speaking countries, the work of the legal committee of the International Civil Aviation Organisation, and an international convention not yet in force (the Montreal Convention on Air Carrier Liability, signed on 28 May 1999)), [17] (Lord Steyn: '[U]ntil some 50 years after the Warsaw Convention no claims for mental injury or illness against carriers were ever brought to judgment anywhere in the world . . . The truth is that until the 1970s the view that such claims were not covered was the orthodox view throughout the commercial world. The Court of Appeal rightly attached importance to the fact that decades elapsed after 1929 before such claims were ever advanced against carriers.'), *cf* [148] (Lord Hobhouse) [**§ 5.5.4**].

Illustration:

- *R v Secretary of State for the Environment, Transport and the Regions, Ex parte Channel Tunnel Group Ltd and France Manche SA* [2001] EWCA Civ 1185, [48] (Peter Gibson LJ interpreting a Concession Agreement, giving effect to a Treaty entered into between the United Kingdom and France, finding it: 'impossible to say on the evidence that the [subsequent] practice of the two Governments establishes their agreement regarding its interpretation.').

4.11.2. **The lack of treaty amendment supports a static, rather than evolving, interpretation:**

Illustrations:

- *R (Hoxha) v Special Adjudicator* [2005] UKHL 19 [2005] 1 WLR 1063, [20] (Lord Hope construing Article 1C(5) of the Refugee Convention: 'The preamble to the [1967] Protocol indicates that there was a desire to bring those affected by refugee situations that had arisen since the Convention within its scope and that equal status should be enjoyed by all refugees covered by the definition in the Convention. But the preamble to article 1C(5) was left untouched. I think we must take it that, although they were aware that events had moved on since 1951, the states parties were still not willing to agree to a relaxation of a limitation that had been expressly written into the proviso.'), [69] (Lord Brown: 'The language of the proviso [in Article 1C(5)] is clear and unambiguous. The failure in 1967 to amend it . . . seems to me eloquent of the continuing intention of the contracting parties to confine the benefit of the proviso to the diminishing number of statutory refugees who would otherwise have remained vulnerable to the loss of their Convention rights under the cessation clause.') In the CA at [2002] EWCA Civ 1403 [2003] 1 WLR 241 (CA), [48] (Keene LJ: 'Moreover, it must be seen as significant that the international community did not take the opportunity at the time of the 1967 Protocol to amend the proviso to article 1C(5) when it was considering the temporal scope of the 1951 Convention.');

- *R (European Roma Rights Centre) v Immigration Officer at Prague Airport* [2004] UKHL 55 [2005] 2 WLR 1, [27] (Lord Bingham, considering whether the meaning of Article 33 of the Refugee Convention had changed: 'In considering whether the rule contended for has received the assent of the nations, it is pertinent to recall that the states parties to the 1951 Convention have not, despite much international discussion, agreed to revise its terms or extend its scope at any time since 1967 [the date of the Protocol].');
- *In re H (A Minor) (Abduction: Rights of Custody)* [2000] 2 AC 291 (HL), 304A–C (Lord Mackay construing the Hague Convention on the Civil Aspects of International Child Abduction: 'We have not been referred to any contrary decision and the report of the third Special Commission meeting to review the operation of the Hague Convention on the Civil Aspects of International Child Abduction which took place on 17 to 21 March 1997 reported in paragraph 15 the decision of the Supreme Court of Canada that the removal in *Thomson v Thomson* "breached the custody rights retained by the Scottish court." The absence from that report of any decision to the contrary strongly suggests that there was none, at least up to that time, and none since then has been brought to our attention.').

4.11.3. **UN General Assembly Resolutions do not constitute evidence of practice in the application of a treaty:**

- *El-Ali v Secretary of State for the Home Department* [2002] EWCA Civ 1103 [2003] 1 WLR 95, [40] (Laws LJ, construing Article 1D of the Refugee Convention: 'I think [it] is accepted on all hands, [that] resolutions of the General Assembly such as brought about the expansion of UNWRA's [UN Relief and Works Agency for Palestinian Refugees in the Near East] mandate are not legally capable of effecting an amendment to the Convention. But [counsel] argues . . . that these resolutions constitute "subsequent practice in the application of the treaty which establishes the agreement of the parties regarding its interpretation" within article 31(3) of the Vienna Convention [on the Law of Treaties], by force of which, therefore, they may be taken into account in the Refugee Convention's interpretation. However these resolutions are not in my judgment any evidence of "practice in the application of the treaty".').

4.11.4. **Explanatory Reports or Handbooks are capable of constituting evidence in the application of a treaty:**

Illustrations:

- *R v Secretary of State for the Home Department, Ex parte Adan* [2001] 1 AC 477, 500–501 [**§ 5.13.1**];
- *R v Secretary of State for the Home Department, Ex parte Robinson* [1998] QB 929 (CA), 938B–C (Lord Woolf) [**§ 5.13.1**];
- *R (Mullen) v Secretary of State for the Home Department* [2004] UKHL 18 [2005] 1 AC 1, [48] (Lord Steyn) [**§ 5.13.5**].

4.12. **Under Article 31(3)(c), Vienna Convention on the Law of Treaties [§ 4.4] any relevant rules of international law applicable in the relations between the parties may be taken into account in interpreting a treaty.**

Illustration:

- *Ali v The Public Prosecutor* [1969] 1 AC 430 (PC), 449G–450C (Viscount Dilhorne considering whether the appellants were entitled to the protection of the Geneva Convention Relative to the Treatment of Prisoners of War 1949: 'In neither the Hague Regulations nor in the Geneva Convention is it expressly stated that a member of the armed forces has to be wearing a uniform when captured to be entitled to be [treated as a prisoner of war]. In the case of certain militias and volunteer corps certain conditions have to be fulfilled in relation to those bodies for a member of them to be entitled to treatment as a prisoner of war. It is not, however, stated that such a member must at the time of his capture be wearing "a fixed distinctive sign recognisable at a distance". International law, however, recognises the necessity of distinguishing between belligerents and peaceful inhabitants . . . Although . . . the distinction has become blurred, it is still the case that each of the classes has distinct rights and duties. For the "fixed distinctive sign to be recognisable at a distance" to serve any useful purpose, it must be worn by members of the militias or volunteer corps.').

5

Interpreting Treaties: Supplementary Means

(1) Introduction

5.1. **In the process of treaty interpretation, the text of a treaty will always have primacy over other sources and aids to interpretations [§§ 4.5–4.8]. Unlike the words used in a treaty, supplementary means of interpretation are not an essential, or mandatory, part of the process of interpretation.**

> 'Aids are not a substitute for the terms of a convention: nor is their use mandatory. The court has a discretion.' (*Fothergill v Monarch Airlines* [1981] AC 251 (HL), 294F(Lord Scarman). See also 295C).

5.2. **The key provision of the Vienna Convention on the Law of Treaties, on supplementary means of interpretation is Article 32:**

> 'Recourse may be had to supplementary means of interpretation, including the preparatory work of the treaty and the circumstances of its conclusion, in order to confirm the meaning resulting from the application of article 31, or to determine the meaning when the interpretation according to article 31: (a) leaves the meaning ambiguous or obscure; or (b) leads to a result which is manifestly absurd or unreasonable.'

5.3. **Article 32 of the Vienna Convention on the Law of Treaties provides two examples of supplementary means of interpretation: preparatory work (travaux préparatoires) and the circumstances of a treaty's conclusion. Other examples include: case law (of international courts and tribunals, of other jurisdictions which are party to the same treaty and of jurisdictions with written constitutions, provisions of which are often analogous to those in human rights treaties); commentaries; explanatory memoranda; other treaties and international instruments. Additionally, where a treaty is expressed in different languages (or in an authentic language other than English), those languages may assist in interpreting the English language version or translation of the treaty.**

5.4. **On the domestic plane, the platform for interpreting incorporated treaties is the incorporating statute. It is the key to determining whether a treaty has been incorporated and, if so, in what way and to what extent [§§ 3.5–3.12]. However, once it is established that a treaty is incorporated into domestic law then the incorporating statute is likely to be of minimal relevance and assistance in interpreting the treaty. Exceptionally, where the relevant treaty is a bilateral or tripartite treaty some interpretative assistance may be derived from the incorporating statute.**

5.4.1. Limited and exceptional interpretative role of incorporating statute regarding bilateral/tripartite treaties:
Illustration:
- *R v Governor of Brixton Prison, Ex parte Minervini* [1959] 1 QB 155 (DC), 162H–163B (Lord Parker CJ: 'It is also relevant, I think, in this connexion [construing the Treaty of Extradition between the United Kingdom, Sweden and Norway of June 1873 pursuant to the Extradition Act 1870] to consider the terms of the Extradition Act 1870. [Counsel] says, quite rightly, that you cannot enlarge the scope of the Treaty by looking at the Act. With that I entirely agree, but in construing the words of the Treaty one is entitled to look at the Act itself. After all, the two contracting parties in 1873 must have had in mind the Act of 1870 and the fact that an Order in Council would be made referring to the Treaty and applying to it the provisions of the Act.').

5.4.2. No interpretative role of incorporating statute regarding multilateral treaties:
Illustration:
- *Sidhu v British Airways* [1997] AC 430 (HL), 441H–442C (Lord Hope: '[Counsel] took us through various provisions in the [Carriage by Air Act 1961] which he said could be relied on as

indicating that the intention was that the [Warsaw Convention on International Carriage by Air, as amended at The Hague, 1955] should provide the exclusive remedy. . . . For my part I do not think that the wording of the statute can assist us one way or the other. What we are concerned with in this case is the meaning to be given to the Convention. This must depend on the wording and structure of the Convention itself. All that need be taken from the Act for present purposes is that, in terms of section 1(1), the Convention as set out in Schedule 1 to the Act has the force of law in the United Kingdom in relation to any carriage by air to which the Convention applies.');

- *Re DVT and Air Travel Group Litigation* [2002] EWHC 2825 (QB) [2003] 1 All ER 935, [137] (Nelson J following Lord Hope in *Sidhu* (see above) that the wording of the Carriage by Air Act 1961 could not assist in interpreting the Warsaw Convention) (CA is at [2003] EWCA Civ 1005 [2004] QB 234);
- *In re S (Children) (Child Adbuction: Asylum Appeal)* [2002] EWCA Civ 843 [2002] 1 WLR 2548, [24] (Laws LJ rejecting the argument that the scope of section 15 of the Immigration and Asylum Act 1999 must be as wide as the scope of Article 33 of the Refugee Convention: 'The importance, or the generality, or the fundamental nature of article 33 cannot, in my judgment, afford a justification for a construction of section 15 of the 1999 Act which is wider than its terms or context will bear. There can be no suggestion that the scope of article 33 can be restricted or diminished by the scope of section 15 on the latter's true construction. Accordingly the proper scope of article 33 does not drive the construction of section 15.').

(2) Travaux Préparatoires

5.5. **Travaux préparatoires, the preparatory work leading to a treaty, may be used in construing an ambiguity or obscurity in a treaty or in confirming the meaning of a provision (see Article 32, Vienna Convention on the Law of Treaties: [§ 5.2]) provided that the material to be used is public and accessible and the travaux préparatoires clearly point to a definite legislative intention. It is unlikely that silence in the travaux on a given point can be taken as revealing a definite legislative intention. In all cases, travaux must be used cautiously to ensure that an accurate picture of the process of drafting and amendment is obtained.**

5.5.1. General preconditions for using travaux:

- *Fothergill v Monarch Airlines* [1981] AC 251 (HL), 276F–G, (Lord Wilberforce: 'When dealing with an international treaty or convention I think there is no doubt that international courts and tribunals . . . do in general make use of travaux préparatoires as an aid to interpretation . . . This practice is cautiously endorsed by the Vienna Convention on the Law of Treaties (1969) (Cmnd 4140), article 32.' At 278B–C: 'I think that it would be proper for us . . . to recognise that there may be cases where such travaux préparatoires can profitably be used. These cases should be rare, and only where two conditions are fulfilled, first, that the material involved is public and accessible, and secondly, that the travaux préparatoires clearly and indisputably point to a definite legislative intention . . . If the use of travaux préparatoires is limited in this way, that would largely overcome the two objections which may properly be made: first, that relating to later acceding states . . . and, secondly, the general objection that individuals ought not to be bound by discussions or negotiations of which they may never have heard.'), 283B (Lord Diplock stating that where the treaty text itself is ambiguous or obscure: '[A]n English court should have regard to any material which [the] delegates themselves had thought would be available to clear up any possible ambiguities or obscurities. Indeed, in the case of Acts of Parliament giving effect to international conventions concluded after the coming into force of the Vienna Convention on the Law of Treaties (Cmnd 4140) I think an English court might well be under a constitutional obligation to do so. By ratifying that Convention, Her Majesty's Government has undertaken an international obligation on behalf of the United Kingdom to interpret future treaties in this manner and since under our constitution the function of interpreting the written law is an exercise of judicial power and rests with the courts of justice that obligation assumed by the United Kingdom falls to be performed by those courts.'), 294D–H and 295A (Lord Scarman noting that aids to construction may also be used where a literal construction would conflict with the purpose of the convention and that it would be useful if international conferences could identify (possibly in the convention itself) documents to which reference may be made in interpreting the convention.);

- *Effort Shipping Co Ltd v Linden Management SA* [1998] AC 605 (HL), 623E–F (Lord Steyn: 'I would be quite prepared, in an appropriate case involving truly feasible alternative interpretations of a convention, to allow the evidence contained in the travaux préparatoires to be determinative of the question of construction . . . Only a bull's-eye counts. Nothing less will do.');
- *El-Ali v Secretary of State for the Home Department* [2002] EWCA Civ 1103 [2003] 1 WLR 95, [18] (Laws LJ: 'The relevance of the travaux préparatoires to the interpretation of the [Refugee Convention] . . . is not in doubt.');
- *R v Bow Street Magistrate, Ex parte Pinochet (No 3)* [2000] 1

AC 147 (HL), 218H (Lord Goff on the use of travaux préparatoires in interpreting a treaty);

- *Sidhu v British Airways* [1997] AC 430 (HL), 442E-G (Lord Hope considering the travaux préparatoires of the Warsaw Convention on International Carriage by Air).

5.5.2. **Using travaux where treaty is ambiguous or obscure:**

- *Black-Clawson International Ltd v Papierwerke Waldhof-Aschaffenburg AG* [1975] AC 591 (HL), 640G–H (Lord Diplock (dissenting), construing the Foreign Judgments (Reciprocal Enforcement) Act 1933: 'In construing a treaty recourse may be had, in public international law, to the travaux préparatoires for the purpose of resolving any ambiguity in the treaty; and it would appear from the history of the negotiations contained in the body of the report [Greer Report of the Foreign Judgments (Reciprocal Enforcement) Committee 1932, presented to Parliament before the passing of the 1933 Act] that the report itself might be regarded as forming part of the travaux préparatoires. If this were so, recourse to the report would in my view clearly lead to the conclusion that the high contracting parties in using the phrase "matter adjudicated upon" had undertaken to treat as conclusive the dispositive or operative part of the judgment.').

Illustrations:

- *R v Bow Street Magistrate, Ex parte Pinochet (No 3)* [2000] 1 AC 147 (HL), 200H (Lord Browne-Wilkinson referring to Reports of the Working Group on the Draft Convention in construing the Torture Convention), 245D, 247A (Lord Hope referring to Reports of the Secretary General to the United Nations in construing the Torture Convention);
- *Jones v The Ministry of the Interior Al-Mamlaka Al-Arabiya* [2004] EWCA Civ 1394 [2005] UKHRR 57, [18] (Mance LJ, construing an obscurity in Article 14(1) of the Torture Convention by reference to, inter alia, the United States' expressed position regarding the ambit of the article when ratifying the Convention);
- *Semco Salvage v Lancer Navigation* [1997] AC 455 (HL) 469B–F (Lord Mustill, construing Article 14(3) of the International Convention on Salvage 1989 by reference to a report by Professor Selvig (who chaired the sub-committee tasked with drafting the Convention) and a report by Mr Bent Nielsen, accompanying the final draft of the Convention);
- *Herd v Clyde Helicopters* [1997] AC 534 (HL), 552G (Lord Hope, construing schedule 1 to the Carriage by Air Acts (Application of Provisions) Order 1967 (SI 1967/480) by considering the minutes of the Second International Conference on Private Aeronautical Law, 4 to 12 October 1929 at Warsaw);
- *T v Immigration Officer* [1996] AC 742 (HL), 778E–F (Lord Lloyd: 'There is no English authority on the meaning of "non-political crime" in the Geneva Convention [on Refugees]. But it

was common ground that the words must bear the same meaning as they do in extradition law. Indeed, it appears from the travaux préparatoires that the framers of the Convention had extradition law in mind when drafting the Convention, and intended to make use of the same concept, although the application of the concept would, of course, be for a different purpose.');

- *El-Ali v Secretary of State for the Home Department* [2002] EWCA Civ 1103 [2003] 1 WLR 95, [18–21] (Laws LJ using travaux préparatoires regarding the introduction, discussion and amendment of Article 1D of the Refugee Convention), [69] (Lord Phillips MR considering that the ambiguity in Article 1D could be resolved by reference to the travaux and the objects of Article 1D);
- *R v Secretary of State for the Environment, Transport, and the Regions, Ex parte International Air Transport Association* [2000] 1 Lloyd's Rep 242 (QBD), 246 (Jowitt J using statements made by Sir Alfred Dennis on behalf of the British delegation at the 1929 Warsaw Conference in construing the Warsaw Convention on International Carriage by Air);
- *R v Secretary of State for the Home Department, Ex parte Sivakumaran* [1988] 1 AC 958 (HL) (travaux préparatoires (original proposals advanced by the United Kingdom, France and United States; report by the UN Ad Hoc Committee on Statelessness and Related Problems and that Committee's comments on the draft Convention and the Constitution of the International Refugee Organisation) used to interpret the Refugee Convention (see, eg 999C, 999H–1000H)).

5.5.3. **Using travaux to confirm treaty interpretation:**

- *Semco Salvage v Lancer Navigation* [1997] AC 455 (HL), 469A (Lord Mustill: '[Travaux] are a useful means of testing the tentative opinions already formed.').

Illustrations:

- *MacWilliam Co Inc v Mediterranean Shipping Co SA* [2003] EWCA Civ 556 [2004] QB 702, [56] (Rix LJ interpreting the Hague Rules (on bills of lading), by reference to travaux; noting that both counsel 'recognised that in this area "only a bull's eye counts".' At [59]: 'As often occurs, the travaux préparatoires are rich in ambiguity. I am not sure that either party has scored a bull's eye.' But concluding at [140] that the travaux, 'despite lacking unequivocal cogency, to my mind are not only consistent with the view I would prefer but go far to support it.') (HL is at [2005] UKHL 11 [2005] 2 WLR 554);
- *R v Secretary of State for the Home Department, Ex parte Read* [1989] AC 1014 (HL), 1052E–F (Lord Bridge: 'I reach this conclusion by giving to article 10 [of the Convention on the Transfer of Sentenced Persons], read in the context of article 9 and 11, the meaning which the language seems to me clearly intended to convey. But, if I felt any doubt, it would be resolved for me by the

text of the Explanatory Report on the Convention on the Transfer of Sentenced Persons (Council of Europe, Strasbourg, 1983) published with the text of the Convention by the committee by whom the Convention was drawn up within the Council of Europe under the authority of the European Committee on Crime Problems. The text of the explanatory report was prepared on the basis of the committee's discussions and submitted to the Committee of Ministers of the Council of Europe. Although it does not purport to be an authoritative interpretation of the Convention, it is available as an aid to construction as part of the "travaux préparatoires" and under article 31 of the Vienna Convention on the Law of Treaties 1969 (Cmnd. 4818).)';

- *Revenko v Secretary of State for the Home Department* [2001] QB 601 (CA), 606D (Pill LJ, referring to the 34th meeting of the Conference of Plenipotentiaries on 25 July 1951 in construing Article 1A(2) of the Refugee Convention);
- *Goldman v Thai Airways International Ltd* [1983] 1 WLR 1186 (CA), 1195B–G (Eveleigh LJ, construing Article 25 of the Warsaw Convention on International Carriage by Air, as amended at The Hague, 1955 by reference to travaux 'not in order to interpret article 25, but to check upon the interpretation which to me it seems to bear.').

5.5.4. **Silence in the travaux on a particular point is generally unlikely to reveal definite legislative intention:**

Illustrations:

- *Morris v KLM Dutch Airlines* [2002] UKHL 7 [2002] 2 AC 628, [17] (Lord Steyn, interpreting 'bodily injury' in Article 17 of the Warsaw Convention on International Carriage by Air: 'It is common ground that the travaux préparatoires reveal no discussion or mention of liability for mental injury or illness. Given the spectre of enormous exposure to liability for carriers if claims for mental illness or injury were held to be within article 17, the omission of a reference to such claims during working sessions is revealing. Undoubtedly, at Warsaw and before carriers, aircraft insurers and countries whose national systems did not recognise liability for mental injury or illness would have been likely to argue against including such claims. This is not a case of mere silence: if the idea of including claims for mental injury was under consideration it would have demanded discussion. This indicates clearly and convincingly that the idea of covering mental injury or illness was never contemplated: see *Fothergill v Monarch Airlines Ltd* [1981] AC 251, 278B–G, per Lord Wilberforce.'), [96] (Lord Hope: 'It seems reasonable to conclude from their silence that the delegates [at the Warsaw Convention] did not feel it necessary to discuss what was meant by the words "lésion corporelle"... This suggests that the meaning which they gave to the words was the simplest and least troublesome meaning that they would ordinarily bear.'), [148] (Lord Hobhouse: 'It is . . . a descent into unprincipled subjectivism to use, as do the Court of Appeal . . . the absence of travaux préparatoires as a tool of construction. Thus the Court of Appeal say . . . : "We consider that it is highly significant that no mention was made of liability for mental injury [sic] in the course of the negotiations that resulted in the Warsaw Convention." This is reasoning which speculates about the subjective intentions of the delegates and is not directed to the objective autonomous meaning of the words used. Likewise it is erroneous, in the absence of cogent travaux, to infer that a particular interpretation of a provision is intended from the fact that on a later occasion the Convention was amended without making any change to the provision in question. All that it shows is that on the later occasion the parties were content to leave the wording of the provision unaltered . . . Similarly, it is unprincipled to say as the Court of Appeal say . . . that it is "equally significant" that no claim was made for "mental injury" until the 1970s. One can only ask how it can be relevant to the question of the construction of the Convention.');

- *Re DVT and Air Travel Group Litigation* [2002] EWHC 2825 (QB) [2003] 1 All ER 935, [30] (Nelson J: '[Travaux] can only be considered with caution as the delegates may not have shared a common view, and an expression by one of them as to his own view is likely to be of little value if it was met simply by silence on the part of the other delegates.' At [32] on the opinions of Lord Steyn (at [17]) and Lord Hobhouse (at [148]) in *Morris* (see above): 'These passages do not differ in principle even if they differ in the application of such principles. Mere silence cannot point clearly and indisputably to a definite intention on the part of the delegates as to how an issue should be resolved.') (CA is at [2003] EWCA Civ 1005 [2004] QB 234);
- *Revenko v Secretary of State for the Home Department* [2001] QB 601 (CA), 635H (Bennet J: '[Counsel] was unable to point to any discussion in the travaux préparatoires relating directly or indirectly to the issue that he has raised before us. As Clarke LJ said in argument, such a lack of discussion could be said to be striking. I take that into account').

5.5.5. **Travaux préparatoires must be used with caution:**

- *Morris v KLM Royal Dutch Airlines* [2002] UKHL 7 [2002] 2 AC 628, [79] (Lord Hope: '[C]aution is needed in the use of [travaux préparatoires], as the delegates may not have shared a common view. An expression by one of them as to his own view is likely to be of little value if it was met simply by silence on the part of other delegates. It will only be helpful if, after proper analysis, the travaux clearly and indisputably point to a definite intention on the part of the delegates as to how the point at issue should be resolved.');

- *Semco Salvage v Lancer Navigation* [1997] AC 455 (HL), 469A (Lord Mustill: '[Travaux] are a useful means of testing the tentative opinions already formed. Some caution is however required. The documentary antecedents of the [International Convention on Salvage 1989] are incomplete, and there is nothing before the House to indicate the origins of the new safety-net provisions in L. O. F [Lloyd's Open Form] 1980.');
- *Sidhu v British Ariways plc* [1997] AC 430 (HL), 442E (Lord Hope: 'It is sufficient to say that cautious use may be made of [the travaux préparatoires of the Warsaw Convention on International Carriage by Air].');
- *Fothergill v Monarch Airlines Ltd* [1981] AC 251 (HL), 278B–C (Lord Wilberforce) [§ **5.5.1**].

Illustration:

- *R (Mullen) v Secretary of State for the Home Department* [2002] EWCA Civ 1882 [2003] QB 993, [14] (Schiemann LJ responding to counsel's use of the travaux préparatoires of Article 3, Seventh Protocol, ECHR, which is the same as the English version of Article 14(6), International Covenant on Civil and Political Rights and the provision to be construed: 'In general the travaux préparatoires of the instrument falling to be interpreted are more likely to be helpful than the travaux préparatoires of another instrument prepared later.') (HL is at [2004] UKHL 18 [2005] 1 AC 1).

5.6. **References to travaux will be unhelpful where the evidence is merely of a series of drafting amendments without more or where the evidence is neutral. To be helpful as aids to treaty interpretation travaux should be capable of disclosing, for example, why a particular amendment was made to a provision, at whose request, whether the amendment was debated, the degree of agreement concerning the amendment, whether it was subsequently re-amended (and why) or adopted, etc.**

Illustrations:

- *R (Mullen) v Secretary of State for the Home Department* [2004] UKHL 18 [2005] 1 AC 1, [9(2)] (Lord Bingham referring to the travaux of the negotiations which culminated in the adoption of the International Covenant on Civil and Political Rights: 'The travaux disclose no consensus of opinion on the meaning to be given to ['miscarriage of justice' in article 14(6) International Covenant on Civil and Political Rights and section 133, Criminal Justice Act 1988].'), [50–54] (Lord Steyn considering the travaux préparatoires of Article 14(6) but concluding: 'the travaux are neutral and do not assist in any way on the proper construction of article 14(6).' ([54]));

- *MacWilliam v Mediterranean Shipping Co* [2005] UKHL 11 [2005] 2 WLR 554, [19] (Lord Bingham considering the travaux préparatoires of the Hague Rules (on bills of lading): 'It must be remembered that in a protracted negotiation such as culminated in adoption of the Hague Rules there are many participants, with differing and often competing objects, interests and concerns. It is potentially misleading to attach weight to points made in the course of discussion, even if they appear at the time to be accepted. In the present case, I do not think that either party can point to such a clear, pertinent and consensual resolution of the issues before the House as would provide a sure ground of decision.'), [43] (Lord Steyn: 'The travaux préparatoires of the Hague Rules are plainly inconclusive and cannot be used to determine the intentions of the framers on the precise question before the House.');
- *Marchiori v The Environment Agency* [2002] EWCA Civ 3 [2002] EuLR 225, [56] (Laws LJ in response to the use of statements made on behalf of the French Government and by the European Commission regarding Euratom: 'I view with misgiving the citation of statements which form no part of the relevant *travaux preparatoires*, and are made by bodies or institutions whose word is not an authoritative source of the legislation's true construction. With very great respect, I do not find the Commission's statements to be of any assistance. And the French voice has not always been consistent.');
- *Adan v Secretary of State for the Home Department* [1999] 1 AC 293 (HL), 304G–305C (Lord Lloyd: '[Counsel] took us on a voyage of discovery through the early drafts of the [Refugee] Convention. He pointed out, for example, that in a draft prepared and circulated by the United Nations Economic and Social Council on 16 August 1950 (resolution 319 (XI) 8B) there appeared the words "who has had, or has, a well-founded fear of being the victim of persecution . . ." The words "has had, or has," dropped out in the draft circulated by the Third Committee on 12 December 1950 (UN Doc A/1682), and did not reappear in the final draft. While these changes are no doubt of interest to historians, from a lawyer's point of view they are inconclusive. For we do not know why the changes were made. All we know is that successive drafts (as one would expect) were subject to continual changes in the light of comments by governments and specialist agencies. It may be therefore that the changes in language were intended to reflect a change in substance. Or it may be that they were intended to reflect the same meaning in different words. We do not know.');
- *R v Immigration Appeal Tribunal, Ex parte Shah* [1999] 2 AC 629 (HL), 638G (Lord Steyn: 'In the search for the correct interpretation of the words "membership of a particular social group" the travaux préparatoires of the [Refugee] Convention are uninformative.'); 650G (Lord Hoffmann: 'The travaux préparatoires for

the Geneva Convention shed little light on the meaning of "particular social group". It appears to have been added to the draft at the suggestion of the Swedish delegate, who said that "experience had shown that certain refugees had been persecuted because they belonged to particular social groups".');

- *Sidhu v British Airways* [1997] AC 430 (HL), 448E–449B (Lord Hope considering the travaux préparatoires of the Warsaw Convention on International Carriage by Air: 'I do not think that it would be profitable for me to attempt to summarise this material. There are various passages in the minutes where the delegates are recorded as expressing views about the object of the Convention . . . But these are mere straws in the wind which emerged during several days of detailed discussion to which many delegates contributed. I do not find a sufficiently clear and consistent expression of views here about the objects of the Convention on the point which is at issue in this case to enable me to say that the answer to the problem is to be found in the minutes.');
- *Revenko v Secretary of State for the Home Department* [2001] QB 601 (CA), 635G–H (Bennett J: 'Such of the travaux préparatoires as were shown to us by counsel appeared in the various authorities. We were not shown any part of the travaux préparatoires which shed light on the point in issue in this case.');
- *Gatewhite Ltd v Iberia Lineas Aereas de Espana SA* [1990] 1 QB 326 (QBD), 331H (Gatehouse J after considering the travaux préparatoires preceding the amendments to the Warsaw Convention on International Carriage by Air in 1955: 'I have to say that I derived no assistance from this source.').

(3) Case Law

5.7. **Three categories of international case law may be relevant when construing treaties. First, case law from international courts or tribunals construing the same treaty (or analogous provisions in a similar instrument). Secondly, case law from other jurisdictions interpreting the treaty where they are party to the treaty ('comparative case law'). Finally, and in relation to human rights treaties, case law from jurisdictions with a written constitution where the constitution contains provisions analogous to that in the treaty to be construed ('constitutional case law').**

A. Case Law of International Courts or Tribunals

5.8. **Domestically, the two most important international courts, established under incorporated treaties, are the European Court of Justice ('ECJ') (under the EC Treaty) and the European Court of Human Rights ('ECtHR') (under the European Convention on Human Rights ('ECHR')). The role of these courts in the United Kingdom and their relationship with domestic courts is regulated by the provisions of the European Communities Act 1972 and the Human Rights Act 1998 ('HRA') respectively [§ 6.8; § 7.7]. The case law of these courts is of great importance when construing Community law or the ECHR. As a matter of principle, the case law of the ECJ and the ECtHR may also provide persuasive guidance when construing other (domestically incorporated) treaties.**

5.9. **Case law of international bodies in general, whether established under unincorporated treaties (for example, the UN Human Rights Committee under the auspices of the International Covenant on Civil and Political Rights) or international instruments (for example, the International Court of Justice under the Statute of the International Court of Justice), where it considers the same (or analogous) treaty provisions, may provide persuasive guidance, a comparative view or confirm the proper approach to treaty interpretation.**

Illustrations:

- *R (European Roma Rights Centre) v Immigration Officer at Prague Airport* [2004] UKHL 55 [2005] 2 WLR 1, [19] (Lord Bingham referring to case law of the ICJ: *In re Border and Transborder Armed Actions (Nicaragua and Honduras)* [1988] ICJ Rep 69 and *In re Land and Maritime Boundary between Cameroon and Nigeria (Cameroon v Nigeria)* [1998] ICJ Rep 275 in the context of considering good faith) [§ **4.5.6**];
- *R (Mullen) v Secretary of State for the Home Department* [2004] UKHL 18 [2005] 1 AC 1, [38] (Lord Steyn using, as confirmation of the interpretation of Article 14(6), International Covenant on Civil and Political Rights, case law of the UN Human Rights Committee);
- *R (Pretty) v Director of Public Prosecutions (Secretary of State for the Home Department intervening)* [2001] UKHL 61 [2002] 1 AC 802, [55] (Lord Steyn, considering the practice of other European states regarding assisted suicide, particularly Dutch measures relaxing the prohibition on euthanasia and assisted suicide: 'It is to be noted, however, that the UN Human Rights Committee in a report dated 27 August 2001 expressed serious

concerns about the operation of the system: CCPR/CO/72/NET, para. 5.');

- *R (Ullah v Special Adjudicator* [2004] UKHL 26 [2004] 2 AC 323, [23] (Lord Bingham: 'In resolving the issue expressed at the outset of this opinion, the primary source must be the Strasbourg jurisprudence. It is reassuring that the Human Rights Chamber for Bosnia and Herzegovina understood the effect of that jurisprudence much as I do: *Boudellaa v Bosnia and Herzegovina* (2002) 13 BHRC 297, para 259. A similar approach was adopted by the Human Rights Committee of the United Nations, interpreting the International Covenant of Civil and Political Rights in *ARJ v Australia* (Communication No 692/1996) 11 August 1997 (unreported).');
- *A v Secretary of State for the Home Department* [2004] EWCA Civ 1123 [2005] 1 WLR 414, [107–109; 113] (Pill LJ referring to case law of the International Tribunal for the Prosecution of Persons Responsible for Serious Violations of International Humanitarian Law Committed in the Territory of the Former Yugoslavia, the Committee against Torture (regarding the Convention against Torture) and the UN Human Rights Committee).

B. Comparative Case Law

5.10. **Comparative case law has persuasive force as an aid to construction, especially regarding multilateral treaties where there is no international tribunal (eg the Refugee Convention). Initially, and before focussing on the jurisprudence of individual states, it is important to assess whether there is international harmony between the contracting states on the proper interpretation of the treaty provision. Disharmony should discourage recourse to the case law of any one jurisdiction. Where there is international consensus and comparative case law is considered, the weight to be attached to it will depend on, inter alia, the reputation and status of the court, the extent to which it binds other courts in the same country and the extent of law reporting in that country.**

5.10.1. Statutory requirement to consider comparative case law:
Illustration:

- Section 3B (1), Civil Jurisdiction and Judgments Act 1982: 'In determining any question as to the meaning or effect of a provision of the Lugano Convention a court in the United Kingdom shall, in accordance with Protocol No.2 to that Convention, take account of any principles laid down in any relevant decision delivered by a court of any other Lugano Contracting State concerning provisions of the Convention.'

5.10.2. **Using comparative case law as an aid to construction:**

- *Fothergill v Monarch Airlines* [1981] AC 251 (HL), 284C (Lord Diplock: 'As respects decisions of foreign courts, the persuasive value of a particular court's decision must depend on its reputation and status, the extent to which its decisions are binding upon courts of co-ordinate and inferior jurisdiction in its own country and the coverage of the national law reporting system.'), 276H–278B (Lord Wilberforce considering the general practice of other contracting states to the Warsaw Convention on International Carriage by Air regarding the use of travaux), 294C–E (Lord Scarman: '[O]ur judges should be able to have recourse to the same aids to interpretation as their brother judges in other contracting states.');
- *Morris v KLM Dutch Airlines* [2002] UKHL 7 [2002] 2 AC 628, [81] (Lord Hope, referring to American, Israeli and Australian case law in interpreting 'bodily injury' in Article 17 of the Warsaw Convention on International Carriage by Air: 'In an ideal world the Convention should be accorded the same meaning by all those who are party to it. So case law provides a further potential source of evidence. Careful consideration needs to be given to the reasoning of courts of other jurisdictions which have been called upon to deal with the point at issue, particularly those which are of high standing. Considerable weight should be given to an interpretation which has received general acceptance in other jurisdictions. On the other hand a discriminating approach is required if the decisions conflict, or if there is no clear agreement between them.'), [160] (Lord Hobhouse noting the problems with overseas authorities: '[T]he decision may have been given on the basis of assumed facts, imprecisely defined, or without a clear statement in the report of the actual facts found.' At [178]: 'If your Lordships adopt the same view as I have of the effect of article 17, you will be promoting international uniformity rather than creating a risk that the law of the United Kingdom will be at odds with that elsewhere.');
- *Sidhu v British Airways* [1997] AC 430 (HL), 443C–E (Lord Hope considering decisions of foreign courts on the Warsaw Convention: 'Clearly much must depend upon the status of each court and of the extent to which the point of issue has been subjected to careful analysis. Material of this kind, where it is found to be of the appropriate standing and quality, may be of some help.');
- *Re DVT and Air Travel Group Litigation* [2003] EWCA Civ 1005 [2004] QB 234, [39] (Lord Phillips MR construing Article 17 of the Warsaw Convention: 'There is no English case law that bears directly on the issue before us. We are, however, dealing with an international Convention and decisions of courts of foreign jurisdictions in relation to that Convention can be of great assistance and deserve careful consideration.').

Illustrations:

- *In re H (A Minor) (Abduction: Rights of Custody)* [2000] 2 AC 291 (HL), 303–304 (Lord Mackay referring to case law from Canada and New Zealand in construing Articles 3, 5 and 8 of the Hague Convention on the Civil Aspects of International Child Abduction);
- *R v Immigration Appeal Tribunal, Ex parte Shah* [1999] 2 AC 629 (HL), 639H–643F (Lord Steyn construing 'membership of a particular social group' in Article 1A(2) of the Refugee Convention by reference to Australian, American and Canadian authorities);
- *In re H (Minors)(Abduction: Acquiescence)* [1998] AC 72 (HL), 88B–D (Lord Browne-Wilkinson, considering decisions of the French Cour de Cassation, the District of Massachusetts and the US Court of Appeals of the Sixth Circuit in determining that 'acquiescence' in Article 13 of the Hague Convention on the Civil Aspects of International Child Abduction was to be given its ordinary meaning: 'I am encouraged to find that this is also the view reflected in decisions in other jurisdictions.');
- *Quantum Corp Inc v Plane Trucking Ltd* [2002] EWCA Civ 350 [2002] 1 WLR 2678, [59] (Mance LJ after considering Belgian, Dutch and German case law: 'I have no real hesitation about adopting the conclusion which other European countries have reached' on the interpretation of Article 1 of the Convention on the Contract for the International Carriage of Goods by Road, scheduled to the Carriage of Goods by Road Act 1965);
- *Milor Srl v British Airways Plc* [1996] QB 702 (CA), 709F–710C (Phillips LJ referring to American and Singaporean case law in construing Article 28 of the Warsaw Convention on International Carriage by Air);
- *Karanakaran v Secretary of State for the Home Department* [2000] 3 All ER 449 (CA), 459–69 (Brooke LJ considering Canadian and Australian case law in interpreting the Refugee Convention), 478 (Sedley LJ: 'Like Brooke LJ, I find the Australian cases of the greatest assistance.');
- *MacWilliam Co Inc v Mediterranean Shipping Co SA* [2003] EWCA Civ 556 [2004] QB 702, (Rix LJ considering the application of the Hague-Visby Rules (on bills of lading) by reference to German law, and case law from Singapore [102], Holland [103], Hong Kong [107] and France [115]) (HL is at [2005] UKHL 11 [2005] 2 WLR 554);
- *Corocraft Ltd v Pan-American Airways Inc* [1969] 1 QB 616 (CA), 655F–G (Lord Denning MR, considering American case law on the Warsaw Convention on International Carriage by Air: 'The decisions of those courts are entitled to the highest respect. I find myself in entire agreement with them. Even if I disagreed, I would follow them in a matter which is of international concern. The courts of all the countries should interpret this Convention in the same way.').

5.10.3. **Lack of international harmony should discourage use of comparative case law:**

- *Effort Shipping Co Ltd v Linden Management SA* [1998] AC 605 (HL), 615A–C (Lord Lloyd, commenting on three authorities from the United States, in construing Article IV Rules 3 and 6 of the Hague Rules (on bills of lading): '[Counsel] pointed out how important it is that provisions of an international convention should, so far as possible, be given the same construction by the courts of different countries: see *Riverstone Meat Co Pty Ltd v Lancashire Shipping Co Ltd* [1961] AC 807, 840 *per* Viscount Simonds. This is an argument which would carry great weight with me, if there were what Viscount Simonds called "prevailing harmony" on the other side of the Atlantic. But such is not the case. There is no generally prevailing view on the precise point in issue, either in the US or in Canada.'), 623C–D (Lord Steyn, rather than considering the American decisions making use of a text (*Wilford, Coghlin and Kimball, Time Charters,* 4th edn (1995)), of which he noted: 'It is stated in this book that the courts in the United States have taken the view that article IV, r.3 qualifies article IV, r.6 . . . I am satisfied that this is the established position in the United States. That is a weighty factor against my initial view that article IV, r.6 contains a bundle of free-standing rights in favour of the owners. In the construction of an international convention an English court does not easily differ from a crystallised body of judicial opinion in the United States.');
- *James Buchanan & Co Ltd v Babco Forwarding & Shipping (UK) Ltd* [1978] AC 141 (HL), 161E–H (Lord Salmon, in construing the Convention on the Contract for the International Carriage of Goods by Road 1956: 'If a corpus of law had grown up overseas which laid down the meaning of article 23, our courts would no doubt follow it for the sake of uniformity which it is the object of the Convention to establish. But no such corpus exists . . . Far from there being any uniform corpus of law relating to the Convention, as Megaw LJ pointed out in *Ulster-Swift Ltd v Taunton Meat Haulage Ltd* [1977] 1 WLR 625 disharmony reigns, for 12 different interpretations have been produced by the courts of different member countries concerning the supposed meaning of various articles in the Convention. Our courts are therefore thrown back on their own resources.').

C. Constitutional Case Law

5.11. **Written constitutions often contain guarantees of fundamental human rights which are derived from those in human rights treaties (for example, the ECHR). Case law from jurisdictions with written constitutions, especially within the Commonwealth where the final court of appeal is the Privy Council, can therefore provide**

guidance, principally in two ways, when construing treaties such as the ECHR. First, the approach to constitutional interpretation, giving provisions a broad and purposive construction to ensure that they confer the full rights and freedoms which they enshrine, informs the approach to interpreting human rights treaties. Secondly, guidance on content may be extrapolated from constitutional provisions which are substantively similar to those in an incorporated treaty (see also the use of such case law regarding unincorporated treaties: [§ 9.19]).

5.11.1. **Using constitutional case law in domestic courts:**

- *R v DPP, Ex parte Kebilene* [2000] 2 AC 326 (HL), 375B–D (Lord Hope, after referring to Lord Woolf's approach to constitutional interpretation in *Attorney-General of Hong Kong v Lee Kwong-kut* [1993] AC 951, 966, Lord Wilberforce's observations in *Minister of Home Affairs v Fisher* [1980] AC 319, 328 and Lord Diplock's commentary in *Attorney-General of the Gambia v Momodou Jobe* [1984] AC 689, 700: 'The same approach will now have to be applied in this country when issues are raised under the [HRA] about the compatibility of domestic legislation and of acts of public authorities with the fundamental rights and freedoms which are enshrined in the Convention.');
- *Ghaidan v Godin-Mendoza* [2004] UKHL 30 [2004] 2 AC 557, [119–120] (Lord Rodger commenting on section 3 of the HRA: 'Your Lordships are also familiar with the exercise which has to be carried out under some Caribbean constitutions to bring existing laws into conformity with the rights guaranteed by the constitution. In *R v Lambert* [2002] 2 AC 545, 587, paras 85 and 86, Lord Hope cites two examples, *Vasquez v The Queen* [1994] 1 WLR 1304 and *Yearwood v The Queen* [2001] 5 LRC 247. Both of them show how far the Privy Council has been prepared to go in substituting very different words for the words of the relevant provision in order to bring it into conformity with the relevant rights guaranteed by the constitution. Such cases are instructive in suggesting that, where the court finds it possible to read a provision in a way which is compatible with Convention rights, such a reading may involve a considerable departure from the actual words. In other respects, however, the Privy Council decisions may not provide a sure guide to the approach to be adopted under section 3(1). They are all concerned with constitutions that are the supreme law, with which other laws must conform on pain of invalidity.').

5.11.2. **Interpreting constitutions: generous and purposive approach:**

- *Edwards v Attorney-General for Canada* [1930] AC 124 (PC), 136D (Lord Sankey, LC describing the constitution established by the British North America Act 1867 as a 'living tree capable of growth and expansion within its natural limits.' The provisions of the Act called for 'a large and liberal interpretation' and were not to be restricted 'by a narrow and technical construction.');

- *Minister of Home Affairs v Fisher* [1980] AC 319 (PC), 328F–H (Lord Wilberforce, construing the Constitution of Bermuda: 'It can be seen that this instrument has certain special characteristics. 1. It is, particularly in Chapter I, drafted in a broad and ample style which lays down principles of width and generality. 2. Chapter I is headed "Protection of Fundamental Rights and Freedoms of the Individual". It is known that this chapter, as similar portions of other constitutional instruments drafted in the post-colonial period, starting with the Constitution of Nigeria, and including the Constitutions of most Caribbean territories, was greatly influenced by the European Convention for the Protection of Human Rights and Fundamental Freedoms (1953) (Cmd. 8969). That Convention was signed and ratified by the United Kingdom and applied to dependent territories including Bermuda. It was in turn influenced by the United Nations' Universal Declaration of Human Rights of 1948. These antecedents, and the form of Chapter I itself, call for a generous interpretation avoiding what has been called "the austerity of tabulated legalism," suitable to give to individuals the full measure of the fundamental rights and freedoms referred to.' At 329C–F (on the proper method to be adopted in construing the Constitution): '[I]t would be to treat a constitutional instrument such as this as sui generis, calling for principles of interpretation of its own, suitable to its character as already described, without necessary acceptance of all the presumptions that are relevant to legislation of private law . . . This is in no way to say that there are no rules of law which should apply to the interpretation of a Constitution. A Constitution is a legal instrument giving rise, amongst other things, to individual rights capable of enforcement in a court of law. Respect must be paid to the language which has been used and to the traditions and usages which have given meaning to that language. It is quite consistent with this, and with the recognition that rules of interpretation may apply, to take as a point of departure for the process of interpretation a recognition of the character and origin of the instrument, and to be guided by the principle of giving full recognition and effect to those fundamental rights and freedoms with a statement of which the Constitution commences.');
- *Attorney-General v Momodou Jobe* [1984] AC 689 (PC), 700H (Lord Diplock, in construing the Constitution of the Gambia: 'A constitution, and in particular that part of it which protects and entrenches fundamental rights and freedoms to which all persons in the state are to be entitled, is to be given a generous and purposive construction.');
- *Pinder v The Queen* [2002] UKPC 46 [2003] 1 AC 620, [58–60] (Lord Nicholls and Lord Hope (dissenting), in response to an

argument supporting a wide interpretation of an exception (Article 17(2)) to the prohibition against torture or inhuman or degrading treatment (Article 17(1) in the Constitution of the Bahamas): 'The argument based on article 30 is that this article applies to article 17. If article 17(2) has no wider scope in relation to article 17(1) than article 30, article 17(2) is unnecessary because it adds nothing to the general saving provision of article 30. This type of legal logic routinely makes its appearance in cases involving the interpretation of statutes and documents. It appeals to the tidy legal mind. It has its place as an aid to interpretation, although redundancy arguments must always be handled with care. Redundancy arguments are based on the assumption that those who draft or approve documents carry out a meticulous comparison of the wording of each provision in the documents, often complex and obscure, and that they can be relied upon to weed out provisions which on careful analysis can be seen to be otiose. Often, perhaps usually, this assumption is at variance with what actually happens. The use, or more accurately, the misuse of this type of argument in the interpretation of constitutions led Lord Wilberforce famously to decry the "austerity of tabulated legalism": see *Minister of Home Affairs v Fisher* [1980] AC 319, 328. Never was there a more telling instance of this austerity than in the present case, where the constitutionality of inhuman punishment is said to depend, at least in part, on the inference to be drawn from the niceties of an argument based on redundancy of language. This approach, if adopted, would tragically impoverish the spirit of the Constitution of The Bahamas.');

- *Reyes v The Queen* [2002] UKPC 11 [2002] 2 AC 235, [26] (Lord Bingham: 'As in the case of any other instrument, the court must begin its task of constitutional interpretation by carefully considering the language used in the Constitution. But it does not treat the language of the Constitution as if it were found in a will or a deed or a charterparty. A generous and purposive interpretation is to be given to constitutional provisions protecting human rights. The court has no licence to read its own predilections and moral values into the Constitution.');
- *Société United Docks v Government of Mauritius* [1985] AC 585 (PC), 599H (Lord Templeman: 'A Constitution concerned to protect the fundamental rights and freedoms of the individual should not be narrowly construed in a manner which produces anomalies and inexplicable inconsistencies.');
- *Hinds v The Queen* [1977] AC 195 (PC), 211D (Lord Diplock: 'A written constitution, like any other written instrument affecting legal rights or obligations, falls to be construed in the light of its subject matter and of the surrounding circumstances with reference to which it was made.');
- *Huntley v Attorney-General for Jamaica* [1995] 2 AC 1 (PC), 12F–H (Lord Woolf, after citing *Minister of Home Affairs v Fisher*

[1980] AC 319 (see above): 'A person in the position of the appellant is therefore entitled to require the courts to adopt a non-rigid and generous approach to his rights which section 20 [of the Constitution of Jamaica] is designed to protect. However in doing this the court looks at the substance and reality of what was involved and should not be over-concerned with what are no more than technicalities. The approach is the same whether this is to his benefit or disadvantage.');

- *Hinds v Attorney-General of Barbados* [2001] UKPC 56 [2002] 1 AC 854, [15] (Lord Bingham: 'The Constitution [of Barbados] is to be read not as an immutable historical document but as a living instrument, reflecting the values of the people of Barbados as they gradually change over time.');
- *Boyce v The Queen* [2004] UKPC 32 [2005] 1 AC 400, [59] (Lord Hoffmann: 'The "living instrument" principle has its reasons, its logic and its limitations. It is not a magic ingredient which can be stirred into a jurisprudential pot together with "international obligations", "generous construction" and other such phrases, sprinkled with a cherished aphorism or two and brewed up into a potion which will make the Constitution [of Barbados] mean something which it obviously does not.').

Illustrations:

- *Benjamin v Minister of Information and Broadcasting* [2001] UKPC 8 [2001] 1 WLR 1040, [28–30] (giving a generous and purposive construction to section 11(1) of the Constitution of Anguilla (freedom of expression));
- *Attorney-General of Trinidad and Tobago v Whiteman* [1991] 2 AC 240 (PC), 247F (Lord Keith: 'The language of a Constitution falls to be construed, not in a narrow and legalistic way, but broadly and purposively, so as to give effect to its spirit, and this is particularly true of those provisions which are concerned with the protection of human rights.');
- *Greene Browne v The Queen* [2000] 1 AC 45 (PC) (section 3(1) of the Offences against the Person Act 1873 providing for juvenile convicted murderers to be 'detained during the Governor-General's pleasure' in lieu of sentence was unconstitutional under the Constitution of Saint Christopher and Nevis since the sentence was determined by a member of the executive and was therefore modified so as to make detention during the court's pleasure);
- *cf Matthew v State of Trinidad and Tobago* [2004] UKPC 33 [2005] 1 AC 433 (holding that although the mandatory death penalty in section 4 of the Offences Against the Person Act 1925 is cruel and unusual punishment and inconsistent with sections 4(a) and 5(2)(b) of the Constitution of Trinidad and Tobago, these constitutional provisions, pursuant to section 6 of the Constitution embodying a plain intention to preserve existing laws, cannot invalidate section 4 of the 1925 Act which was a pre-existing law when the Constitution was introduced).

5.11.3. **Using the constitutional preamble:**

- *Matthew v State of Trinidad and Tobago* [2004] UKPC 33 [2005] 1 AC 433, [46] (Lord Bingham, Lord Nicholls, Lord Steyn and Lord Walker (dissenting), using the preamble in the Constitution of Trinidad and Tobago: 'Of course the preamble to a statute cannot override the clear provisions of the statute. But it is legitimate to have regard to it when seeking to interpret those provisions . . . and any interpretation which conflicts with the preamble must be suspect.').

5.11.4. **Special place of entrenched human rights provisions:**

- *Attorney-General of Trinidad and Tobago v Whiteman* [1991] 2 AC 240 (PC), 247F (Lord Keith considering that the need to give a broad and purposive construction to the language of a constitution is particularly true regarding provisions protecting human rights) [§ **5.11.2**];
- *Matthew v State of Trinidad and Tobago* [2004] UKPC 33 [2005] 1 AC 433, [44] (Lord Bingham, Lord Nicholls, Lord Steyn and Lord Walker (dissenting): 'While entrenched human rights provisions expressed in a codified constitution are, like the other provisions of the constitution, a manifestation of the popular will, they none the less have a special place . . . Constitutional protection of human rights of course operates for the benefit of all the citizens of any state. But it is of particular importance to the weakest and most vulnerable members of society, who lack wealth and influence, among whom those subjected to admittedly cruel and unusual treatment or punishment must ordinarily be included.').

5.11.5. **Interpreting exceptions in constitutions restrictively:**

- *R v Hughes* [2002] UKPC 12 [2002] 2 AC 259, [35] (Lord Rodger: 'Since paragraph 10 [of schedule 2 to the Saint Lucia Constitution Order (SI 1978/1901)] introduces these exceptions to the rights and protection which people would otherwise have under the Constitution, it must be construed like any other derogation from constitutional guarantees. In *State v Petrus* [1985] LRC (Const) 699, 720D–F in the Court of Appeal of Botswana, Aguda JA referred to *Corey v Knight* (1957) 150 Cal App 2d 671 and observed that "it is another well known principle of construction that exceptions contained in Constitutions are ordinarily to be given strict and narrow, rather than broad, constructions." In case of doubt paragraph 10 should therefore be given a strict and narrow, rather than a broad, construction.');
- *Matthew v State of Trinidad and Tobago* [2004] UKPC 33 [2005] 1 AC 433, [45] (Lord Bingham, Lord Nicholls, Lord Steyn and Lord Walker (dissenting): 'In contrast with the broad and liberal construction to be given to constitutional provisions generally, and in particular those directed to the protection of human rights, the proper approach to the interpretation of savings clauses should be strict and narrow.').

Illustrations:

- *DPP of Jamaica v Mollison* [2003] UKPC 6 [2003] 2 AC 411, [19] (Lord Bingham: 'The thrust of section 2 of the [Jamaican] Constitution is to invalidate laws inconsistent with the Constitution. The rights guaranteed by the sections in Chapter III were intended to be enjoyed by the people of Jamaica. Provisions derogating from such rights should receive a strict and narrow rather than a broad construction.');
- *Pinder v The Queen* [2002] UKPC 46 [2003] 1 AC 620, [14] (Lord Millett interpreting the Constitution of the Bahamas: 'The appellant submitted that article 17(2) is a derogation from the constitutional guarantee contained in article 17(1), and that it must consequently be narrowly construed. Their Lordships agree . . . But it must not be pushed so far that narrow construction becomes misconstruction . . . If the court indulges itself by straining the language of the constitution to accord with its own subjective moral values then, as Holmes J said . . . [in *Otis v Parker* (1903) 187 US 606, 609] "a constitution, instead of embodying only relatively fundamental rules of right, as generally understood by all English-speaking communities, would become the partisan of a particular set of ethical or economical opinions".'), [58–61] (Lord Nicholls and Lord Hope (dissenting), in response to an argument supporting a wide interpretation of an exception (Article 17(2)) to the prohibition against torture or inhuman or degrading treatment (Article 17(1)). At [61]: 'It should never be forgotten that courts are the guardians of constitutional rights. A vitally important function of courts is to interpret constitutional provisions conferring rights with the fullness needed to ensure that citizens have the benefit these constitutional guarantees are intended to afford. Provisos derogating from the scope of guaranteed rights are to be read restrictively. In the ordinary course they are to be given "strict and narrow, rather than broad, constructions" . . . This must especially be so with the "torture proviso" which, to the extent of matters within its scope, permits the torture of citizens of The Bahamas and the infliction of inhuman and degrading punishment on them. Any exception which permits such conduct by the state calls for the most searching and critical scrutiny. An unambiguous literal interpretation should give way to a narrower purposive interpretation when it is sufficiently clear that this would accord better with the intended purpose of the exception.').

5.11.6. **Constitutions should be interpreted as always speaking [§ 3.13.3; § 4.6.1]:**

- *Boyce v The Queen* [2004] UKPC 32 [2005] 1 AC 400, [28] (Lord Hoffmann: '[T]he terms in which these provisions of the Constitution [of Barbados] are expressed necessarily co-opts future generations of judges to the enterprise of giving life to the abstract statements of fundamental rights. The judges are the mediators between the high generalities of the constitutional text and the messy detail of their application to concrete problems. And the judges in giving body and substance to fundamental rights, will naturally be guided by what are thought to be the requirements of a just society in their own time. In so doing, they are not performing a legislative function. They are not doing work of repair by bringing an obsolete text up to date. On the contrary, they are applying the language of these provisions of the Constitution according to their true meaning. The text is a "living instrument" when the terms in which it is expressed, in their constitutional context, invite and require periodic re-examination of its application to contemporary life.')

- *Matthew v State of Trinidad and Tobago* [2004] UKPC 33 [2005] 1 AC 433, [43] (Lord Bingham, Lord Nicholls, Lord Steyn and Lord Walker (dissenting): 'Section 10(1) of the Trinidad and Tobago Interpretation Act 1962 provides that "Every written law shall be construed as always speaking". This is a general principle of statutory interpretation, but it applies with particular force to constitutions. Their effect may change over time, and is not frozen at the historical moment of birth.' See further on the same point [66], [70–71] (Lord Nicholls));
- *DPP of Jamaica v Mollison* [2003] UKPC 6 [2003] 2 AC 411, [16] (Lord Bingham: '[I]t is now well established that constitutional provisions relating to human rights should be given a generous and purposive interpretation, bearing in mind that a constitution is not trapped in a time-warp but must evolve organically over time to reflect the developing needs of society.').

5.11.7. **Judicial modification of constitutional provisions:**

- *Ghaidan v Godin-Mendoza* [2004] UKHL 30 [2004] 2 AC 557, [119–120] (Lord Rodger) [§ **5.11.1**];

Illustrations:

- *Matthew v State of Trinidad and Tobago* [2004] UKPC 33 [2005] 1 AC 433, [54] (Lord Bingham, Lord Nicholls, Lord Steyn and Lord Walker (dissenting), considering that section 5(1) of the Constitution of Trinidad and Tobago required section 4 of the Offences Against the Person Act 1925 (mandatory death sentence for murder) to be modified to bring it into conformity with the Constitution: 'We find nothing strange in a provision which requires a court to construe an existing law with such modifications, adaptations, qualifications and exceptions as may be necessary to bring it into conformity with a human rights instrument but prohibits it from annulling the law. It is not dissimilar from the approach prescribed by . . . sections 3 and 4 of the United Kingdom Human Rights Act 1998. The initial stage of interpretation is close to what the Court of Justice of the European Communities had in mind in *Marleasing SA v La Comercial Internacional de Alimentación SA* (Case C-106/89) [1990] ECR I-4135 . . . [quoting para 8].') [§ **6.15.2**];

- *DPP v Mollison* [2003] UKPC 6 [2003] 2 AC 411 (modifying existing laws in Jamaica, providing for indefinite detention at the Governor-General's pleasure, to ensure that decisions on punishment should, absent a fixed statutory penalty, be made by the judiciary and not the executive);
- *Rojas v Berllaque* [2003] UKPC 76 [2004] 1 WLR 201 (fair trial provision in the Constitution of Gibraltar given effect by modifying a discriminatory existing law regarding the composition of juries);
- *Vasquez v The Queen* [1994] 1 WLR 1304 (PC) (section 116(a) of the Criminal Code of Belize which placed the burden of proof of provocation on the accused was in conflict with the presumption of innocence in section 6(3)(a) of the Constitution and was therefore modified so as to be compliant with the Constitution; see especially 1314);
- *Roodal v State of Trinidad and Tobago* [2003] UKPC 78 [2005] 1 AC 328 (modifying the law of Trinidad and Tobago so as to substitute a discretion to impose death sentences in place of the pre-existing mandatory death sentence. Considered to have been wrongly decided by the majority in *Matthew v State of Trinidad and Tabago* [2004] UKPC 33 [2005] 1 AC 433, [29] and the majority in *Boyce v The Queen* [2004] UKPC 32 [2005] 1 AC 400, [62]).

5.11.8. **Substantive use of constitutional case law:**

Illustrations:

- *Dyer v Watson* [2002] UKPC D1 [2004] 1 AC 379, [26–29] (Lord Bingham considering Privy Council cases on Commonwealth constitutions containing provisions similar to the reasonable time requirement in Article 6, ECHR), [86–94] (Lord Hope considering Commonwealth jurisprudence on the reasonable time requirement);
- *Mills v HM Advocate* [2002] UKPC D2 [2004] 1 AC 441, [4] (Lord Steyn comparing Article 6(1), ECHR to provisions in the Constitutions of Mauritius and Jamaica).

(4) Commentaries

5.12. **Commentaries published after a treaty has been concluded have persuasive force in the process of interpretation. In deciding whether, and to what extent, to rely on such commentaries, account should be taken of the eminence, experience and reputation of the writer. The travaux préparatoires [§§ 5.5–5.6] of a treaty are often only easily accessible by their inclusion or analysis in such commentaries.**

- *Fothergill v Monarch Airlines* [1981] AC 251 (HL), 284A–B (Lord Diplock: 'To a court interpreting [a] Convention subsequent commentaries can have persuasive value only . . . The persuasive effect of learned commentaries . . . will depend on the cogency of their reasoning.');
- *Adan v Secretary of State for the Home Department* [1999] 1 AC 293 (HL), 307B–C (Lord Lloyd: 'Of equal and perhaps of greater importance [than authorities] are the views of academic writers, since it is academic writers who provide the best hope of reaching international consensus on the meaning of the Convention.').

Illustrations:

- *R (R) v Durham Constabulary* [2005] UKHL 21 [2005] 1 WLR 1184, [40] (Baroness Hale considering the compatibility with Article 6, ECHR, of a warning given to a young offender under sections 66 and 68 of the Crime and Disorder Act 1998 by reference to the UN Convention on the Rights of the Child and the commentary in *The International Law on the Rights of the Child* by Professor Geraldine van Beuren (1998));
- *R (Mullen) v Secretary of State for the Home Department* [2004] UKHL 18 [2005] 1 AC 1, [9(5)] (Lord Bingham, considering the lack of academic opinion on Article 14(6), International Covenant on Civil and Political Rights (given effect in section 133, Criminal Justice Act 1988), referring to Stavros, *The Guarantees for Accused Persons under Article 6 of the European Convention on Human Rights* (1993) and van Dijk and van Hoof, *Theory and Practice of the European Convention on Human Rights* (1998, 3rd edn).);
- *R (Ullah) v Special Adjudicator* [2004] UKHL 26 [2004] 2 AC 323, [32] (Lord Steyn: 'In an illuminating analysis Professor Hathaway (*The Law of Refugee Status* (1991)) summarised the position as follows, at p 112: "In sum, persecution is most appropriately defined as the sustained or systemic failure of state protection in relation to one of the core entitlements which has been recognised by the international community." This view has already been approved by the House on two previous occasions: *Horvath v Secretary of State for the Home Department* [2001] 1 AC 489, 495, per Lord Hope of Craighead; *Sepet v Secretary of State for the Home Department* [2003] 1 WLR 856, 862, para 7, per Lord Bingham of Cornhill. I would respectfully also endorse it.');
- *Jones v The Ministry of the Interior Al-Mamlaka Al-Arabiya* [2004] EWCA Civ 1394 [2004] UKHRR 57, [18] (Mance LJ, referring to the 'full and helpful' discussion of Article 14(1) of the Torture Convention in A Byrne, 'Civil Remedies for Torture committed Abroad: An Obligation under the Convention against Torture', in *Torture as Tort* (Hart Publishing, 2001));
- *Quantum Corpn Inc v Plane Trucking* [2002] EWCA Civ 350 [2002] 1 WLR 2678, [63] (Mance LJ referring to the 'helpful' Clarke on *International Carriage of Goods by Road: CMR* (1997, 3rd edn));

- *R v Uxbridge Magistrates' Court, Ex parte Adimi* [2001] QB 667 (DC), 678D (Simon Brown LJ, construing Article 31 of the Refugee Convention: 'I am persuaded by the applicants' contrary submission, drawing as it does on the travaux prẻparatoires, various conclusions adopted by the UNHCR's executive committee (ExCom), and the writings of well respected academics and commentators (most notably Professor Guy Goodwin-Gill, Atle Grahl-Madsen, Professor James Hathaway and Dr Paul Weis.').
- *Kleinwort Benson Ltd v Glasgow City Council* [1999] 1 AC 153 (HL), 170F–G (Lord Goff referring to Gaudemet-Tallons, *Les Conventions de Bruxelles et de Lugano* (1996, 2nd edn) in the interpretation of Article 5, Brussels Convention on Jurisdiction and the Enforcement of Judgments);
- *Milor Srl v British Airways Plc* [1996] QB 702 (CA), 710C–D (Phillips LJ referring to Shawcross and Beaumont, *Air Law* (4th edn) in construing Article 28 of the Warsaw Convention on International Carriage by Air.);
- *Ulster-Swift Ltd v Taunton Meat Haulage Ltd* [1977] 1 WLR 625 (CA), 634F (Megaw LJ referring to the commentary by Professor R Loewe in construing the Convention on the Contract for the International Carriage of Goods by Road).

(5) Explanatory Reports

5.13. **Where available, explanatory reports and handbooks on treaties have persuasive force in the process of interpretation. They are not generally part of the treaty to which they relate. Rather, they are aids to construction and may provide evidence of state practice. One such handbook which is frequently used in domestic courts to interpret the Refugee Convention is the UNHCR Handbook on Procedures and Criteria for determining Refugee Status.**

5.13.1. Using the UNHCR Handbook on Procedures and Criteria for Determining Refugee Status (1979):

- *Revenko v Secretary of State for the Home Department* [2001] QB 601 (CA), 616G–H (Pill LJ: 'The Handbook has its origin in a request to the office of the High Commissioner "to consider the possibility of issuing—for the guidance of governments—a handbook relating to procedures and criteria for determining "refugee status". The first edition was issued in 1979. The 1988 edition purports to set out and explain the various components of the definition of "refugee" set out in the 1951 Convention and the 1967 Protocol. The explanations are said to be based on the knowledge accumulated by the High Commissioner's office over some 25 years since the entry into force of the 1951 Convention.');

- *R (Sivakumar) v Secretary of State for the Home Department* [2003] UKHL 14 [2003] 1 WLR 840, [7] (Lord Steyn describing the Handbook as 'important.');
- *Sepet v Secretary of State for the Home Department* [2003] UKHL 15 [2003] 1 WLR 865, [12] (Lord Bingham, describing the Handbook as an: 'important source of guidance on matters to which it relates.');
- *R v Secretary of State for the Home Department, Ex parte Adan* [2001] 2 AC 477 (HC), 520A–B (Lord Steyn: 'Under articles 35 and 36 of the Geneva Convention and under article II of the 1967 Protocol, the UNHCR plays a critical role in the application of the Refugee Convention . . . Contracting states are obliged to co-operate with UNHCR. It is not surprising therefore that the UNHCR Handbook, although not binding on states, has high persuasive authority, and is much relied on by domestic courts and tribunals.'), 525G (Lord Hutton quoting from the preamble to the European Union's Joint Position on the harmonised application of the definition of the term 'refugee' in article 1 of the Refugee Convention ([1996] OJ L263/2): '"the Handbook . . . is a valuable aid to member states in determining refugee status".'). The genesis of the Handbook is discussed by the CA at [2001] 2AC 477, 500–501 ('We have described the *Handbook's* genesis, to which we attach some importance. While the *Handbook* is not by any means itself a source of law, many signatory states have accepted the guidance which on their behalf the UNHCR was asked to provide, and in those circumstances it constitutes, in our judgement, good evidence of what has come to be international practice within article 31(3)(b) of the Vienna Convention.' (at 1296F–G)).
- *T v Immigration Officer* [1996] AC 742 (HL), 768B–C (Lord Mustill: '[T]he *Handbook*, which although without binding force in domestic or international law . . . is a useful recourse on doubtful questions'), 786B (Lord Lloyd describing the UNHCR Handbook as an 'important source of law (though it does not have the force of law itself).');

Illustrations:

- *R v Secretary of State for the Home Department, Ex parte Sivakumaran* [1988] 1 AC 958 (HL), (Handbook used to construe 'well-founded fear' in Article 1A(2) see eg Lord Goff at 1000A);
- *Horvath v Secretary of State for the Home Department* [2001] 1 AC 489 (HL) (Handbook used to construe 'persecution' in Article 1A(2); see 498H (Lord Hope), 506H (Lord Lloyd: 'In any event there is a danger in regarding the Handbook as if it had the same force as the Convention itself.'), 515A (Lord Clyde describing the Handbook as having 'the weight of accumulated practice behind it.');
- *Krotov v Secretary of State for the Home Department* [2004] EWCA Civ 69 [2004] 1 WLR 1825, [45] (Potter LJ: '[W]hile it must be

acknowledged that the Convention itself is silent as to conscientious objection and the norms of international law, I consider that the terms of the *Handbook* and court decisions have recognised a point at which punishment for objection to participation in a particular conflict on grounds of its legality may properly be regarded as established persecution for the purposes of the Convention.');

- *Revenko v Secretary of State for the Home Department* [2001] QB 601 (CA), 629G–630G (Clarke LJ noting especially the absence of any mention in the Handbook of a practice of treating stateless persons like refugees.);
- *R v Secretary of State for the Home Department, Ex parte Robinson* [1998] QB 929 (CA), 938B–C (Lord Woolf MR: 'There is no international court charged with the interpretation and implementation of the Convention, and for this reason [the UNHCR Handbook] is particularly helpful as a guide to what is the international understanding of the Convention obligations, as worked out in practice.').

5.13.2. **Using Explanatory Reports regarding the Brussels Convention on Jurisdiction and the Enforcement of Judgments:**

- Section 3(3), Civil Jurisdiction and Judgments Act 1982: '[T]he following reports (which are reproduced in the Official Journal of the Communities), namely—(a) the reports by Mr P Jenard on the 1968 Brussels Convention and the 1971 Protocol; and (b) the report by Professor Peter Schlosser on the Accession Convention; and (c) the report by Professor Demetrios I Evrigenis and Professor K D Kerameus on the 1982 Accession Convention; and (c) the report by Mr Martinho de Almeida Cruz, Mr Manuel Desantes Read and Mr P Jenard on the 1989 Accession Convention, may be considered in ascertaining the meaning or effect of any provision of the Brussels Conventions and shall be given such weight as is appropriate in the circumstances.'

Illustrations:

- *Kleinwort Benson Ltd v Glasgow City Council* [1999] 1 AC 153 (HL), 164D (Lord Goff using the Jenard Report to construe Article 5(1) in schedule 4 to the Civil Jurisdiction and Judgments Act 1982 (containing the modified version of the Brussels Convention regarding the allocation of jurisdiction within the United Kingdom);
- *Dresser UK Ltd v Falcongate Ltd* [1992] QB 502 (CA), 515D–G (Bingham LJ using the Schlosser Report in construing Articles 17 and 22 of the Brussels Convention);
- *QRS 1 ApS v Frandsen* [1999] 1 WLR 2169 (CA), 2174B–D (Simon Brown LJ using the Schlosser Report in construing Article 1 of the Brussels Convention (as amended by the Accession Convention)).

5.13.3. **Using Explanatory Reports on the Lugano Convention on Jurisdiction and the Enforcement of Judgments:**

- Section 3B (2), Civil Jurisdiction and Judgments Act 1982: '[T]he report on the Lugano Convention by Mr P Jenard and Mr G Möller (which is reproduced in the Official Journal of the Communities of 28th July 1990) may be considered in ascertaining the meaning or effect of any provision of the Convention and shall be given such weight as is appropriate in the circumstances.'

Illustrations:

- *Agnew v Länsförsäkringsbolagens AB* [2001] 1 AC 223 (HL), 237G–H (Lord Woolf MR referring to the permitted use of the Jenard and Möller Report on the Lugano Convention under the Civil Jurisdiction and Judgments Act 1982), 251E–H (Lord Hope, using the Jenard and Möller Report);
- *Anton Durbek GmbH v Den Norske Bank ASA* [2003] EWCA Civ 147 [2003] QB 1160, [12–15] (Lord Phillips MR using the Jenard and Möller Report on the Lugano Convention to construe article 5 of the Lugano Convention. See also, similarly, at [35–38]).

5.13.4. **Using Explanatory Reports on the Rome Convention on the Law Applicable to Contractual Obligations (and related Conventions):**

- Section 3(3), Contracts (Applicable Law) Act 1990: 'Without prejudice to any practice of the courts as to the matters which may be considered apart from this subsection—(a) the report on the Rome Convention by Professor Mario Giuliano and Professor Paul Lagarde which is reproduced in the Official Journal of the Communities of 31st October 1980 may be considered in ascertaining the meaning or effect of any provision of that Convention; and (b) any report on the Brussels Protocol which is reproduced in the Official Journal of the Communities may be considered in ascertaining the meaning or effect of any provision of that Protocol.').

Illustrations:

- *Raffeisen Zentralbank v Five Star Trading LLC* [2001] EWCA Civ 68 [2001] QB 825, [32] and [47] (Mance LJ using the Giuliano and Lagarde Report in considering Articles 1 and 12 of the Rome Convention);
- *Iss Machinery Services Ltd v Aelion Shipping SA (The 'Aelion')* [2001] EWCA Civ 1162 [2001] 2 Lloyd's Rep 641, 645 (Potter LJ using the Giuliano and Lagarde Report in construing Article 3(1) of the Rome Convention);
- *Welex AG v Rosa Maritime Ltd ('The 'Epsilon Rosa') (No 2)* [2002] EWHC 2035 (Comm) [2002] 2 Lloyd's Rep 701, 704 (David Steel J gaining 'some guidance' from the Giuliano and Lagarde Report on the Rome Convention).

5.13.5. **Using other handbooks and explanatory reports:**
Illustrations:

- *R (Mullen) v Secretary of State for the Home Department* [2004] UKHL 18 [2005] 1 AC 1, [48] (Lord Steyn using the Explanatory Report on the Seventh Protocol, ECHR: 'Inevitably, state practice will be based on the explanatory report, and in this way it becomes directly relevant to the interpretation of article 14(6) [International Covenant on Civil and Political Rights]: article 31(3)(b) of the Vienna Convention on the Law of Treaties.');
- *In re G (Children) (Foreign Contact Order: Enforcement)* [2003] EWCA Civ 1607 [2004] 1 WLR 521, [23] (Thorpe LJ using the Explanatory Report to the European Convention on Recognition and Enforcement of Decisions concerning Custody of Children and on Restoration of Custody of Children (incorporated by the Child Abduction and Custody Act 1985) to construe Article 10(1). At [39–47] using the Borrás Report on the proposed Brussels II Convention on Jurisdiction and the Recognition and Enforcement of Judgments in Matrimonial Matters);
- *R v Bow Street Magistrate, Ex parte Pinochet (No 3)* [2000] 1 AC 147 (HL), 199D and 200G (Lord Browne-Wilkinson), 212C (Lord Goff), 244H, 255H, 246D (Lord Hope), 260F, 261C (Lord Hutton), 276C, 277A (Lord Millett) (all using the Handbook on the Convention against Torture and Other Cruel, Inhuman or Degrading Treatment or Punishment (1988));
- *In re S (A Minor)(Custody: Habitual Residence)* [1998] AC 750 (HL), 766E (Lord Slynn: 'Your Lordships have been referred to a valuable Explanatory Report on the Hague Convention [on the Civil Aspects of International Child Abduction] by Professor Elisa Pérez-Vera, Reporter to the First Commission of the Hague Conference. It is not possible to set out long extracts from that report, helpful though they are, but I draw attention to a number of points which are made in it.');
- *R v Secretary of State for the Home Department, Ex parte Oshin* [2000] 1 WLR 2311 (QBD), 2315D–E (Tuckey LJ construing Article 9(3) of the Convention on the Transfer of Sentenced Persons 1983 by reference to its explanatory report);
- *R v R (Residence Order: Child Abduction)* [1995] Fam 209, 215G–H (Stuart-White J construing Article 16 of the Hague Convention on the Civil Aspects of Child Abduction by reference to the Explanatory Report by Professor Eliza Pérez-Vera: '[W]hilst no doubt the report is a permissible, useful and indeed authoritative aid to the construction of the Convention if the language of the Convention is unclear, on this point it seems to be that the language of the Convention is perfectly clear—indeed distinctively clearer than that of the report.').

(6) Treaties and International Instruments

5.14. **By virtue of both Article 31(3)(c) [§ 4.4] and Article 32 [§ 5.2] of the Vienna Convention on the Law of Treaties, a treaty may be construed by reference to other incorporated treaties, unincorporated treaties, international instruments, treaties which have never been enforced and treaties still to be enforced. In deciding which of these aids to use, and to what extent, context is everything. The status of these aids, ie whether or not they are incorporated in domestic law, is insignificant regarding the process of interpretation (the classification below being solely for ease of reference). The focus is on determining the autonomous meaning of the treaty provision in question [§ 4.7.7].**

A. *Incorporated Treaties*

5.15. **Incorporated treaties may be used as aids to interpretation when construing other incorporated treaties, as guiding the proper approach to interpretation, as points of comparison and as providing background and context. An incorporated treaty will be a helpful aid when interpreting another incorporated treaty where its purpose and objects, the subject-matter of its relevant provisions and, possibly, even its language, complement those of the treaty to be interpreted. Care must be taken to ensure that any analogies drawn are apt. It is also relevant to consider whether the same states are parties to both treaties to ensure that uniformity of interpretation is maintained.**

5.15.1. Using incorporated treaties as aids in construing other incorporated treaties:
Illustrations:
- *A v Secretary of State for the Home Department* [2004] UKHL 56 [2005] 2 WLR 87, [105] (Lord Hope, using the Refugee Convention to interpret the ECHR: 'What [the Secretary of State] was not entitled to do was to treat the right to liberty under article 5 of the [ECHR] of foreign nationals who happen to be in this country for whatever reason as different in any respect from that enjoyed by British nationals. How, one might ask, can such treatment be reconciled with article 33 of the United Nations Convention and Protocol relating to the Status of Refugees (1951) (Cmd 9171) and (1967) (Cmnd 3906)? Indefinite detention for reason of their nationality is one of the evils against which refugees who would otherwise be expelled are entitled to

protection under that article. A refugee who is faced with the prospect of that treatment abroad is protected, according to the principle set out in the preamble to the Convention that human beings shall enjoy fundamental rights and freedoms without discrimination. Why should that protection be any less complete while he remains here?');

- *R (Yogathas) v Secretary of State for the Home Department* [2002] UKHL 36 [2003] 1 AC 920, [61–62] (Lord Hutton, using the ECHR in construing the Refugee Convention: 'In considering these issues it is relevant to state at the outset four principles which are established by the decision of the European Court of Human Rights ("the European Court") in *TI v United Kingdom* [2000] INLR 211. Whilst the decision in *TI v United Kingdom* relates to alleged breaches of the European Convention I consider that these principles were also of relevance in considering alleged breaches of article 33(1) of the Geneva Convention, and as I state in paragraph 62 of this opinion I think that the obligations of the United Kingdom under article 33(1) of the Geneva Convention when considering the removal to another country of those claiming asylum are broadly similar to its obligations under article 3 of the European Convention . . . I consider that the decisions of this House in *R v Secretary of State for the Home Department, Ex p Bugdaycay* [1987] AC 514 and *R v Secretary of State for the Home Department, Ex p Adan* [2001] 2 AC 477 have established broadly similar principles in respect of the United Kingdom's obligations under article 33(1) of the Geneva Convention.'), [25] (Lord Hope, referring to ECtHR jurisprudence in construing the Refugee Convention);
- *In re H (A Minor) (Abduction: Rights of Custody)* [2000] 2 AC 291 (HL), 304D–G (Lord Mackay, considering the Hague Convention on the Civil Aspects of International Child Abduction by reference to the Brussels Convention on Jurisdiction and the Enforcement of Judgments: '[A] question arises as to the time at which the court acquires such right [of custody] . . . For the purposes of the Civil Jurisdiction and Judgments Act 1982, Schedule 1, article 21 and the 1968 Brussels Convention on Jurisdiction and the Enforcement of Judgments in Civil and Commercial Matters which is scheduled to that Act (Schedule 1) it has been held that an English court becomes definitively seized of proceedings for the purposes of that Convention on the date of service of the writ at which point it has jurisdiction over the merits of the dispute . . . In relation to the present Convention while in the wardship jurisdiction the issue of an application makes the child who was the subject of the application a ward of court I consider that generally speaking there is much force in using the service of the application as the time at which the court's jurisdiction is first invoked.');
- *C v C (Ancillary Relief: Nuptial Settlement)* [2004] EWHC 742 (Fam) [2004] Fam 141, [40] (Wilson J construing Article 15(b) of

the Hague Convention on the Law Applicable to Trusts and on their Recognition (incorporated by the Recognition of Trusts Act 1987) by reference to the Brussels Convention on Jurisdiction and the Enforcement of Judgments (as revised by Council Regulation (EC) 44/2001), and seeing 'no distinction between the meaning of "provisions . . . relating . . . to . . . the . . . proprietary effects of marriage" in article 15 of the Hague Convention and of "rights in property arising out of a matrimonial relationship" in article 1 of the Brussels I Convention.');

- *Agnew v Länsförsäkringsbolagens AB* [2001] 1 AC 223 (HL), 251E–G (Lord Hope, using the Lugano Convention to interpret the Brussels Convention: 'The relevant part of the special rule in article 5(1) [of the Lugano Convention] is in identical terms to the equivalent rule in the Brussels Convention. Having regard to Protocol No 2 to the Lugano Convention, On the Uniform Interpretation of the Convention, to chapter 1.1.2 of the Report on the Lugano Convention by Mr P Jenard and Mr G Möller (OJ 1990 C189, p 61) which refers to the various Reports on the Brussels Convention where the provisions of the Brussels and Lugano Conventions are identical and to the Declarations of EFTA and the European Union States dated 16 September 1988 (OJ 1988 L319, pp37, 40), it is plain that these provisions should receive a common interpretation and that where provisions in the Lugano Convention are in issue decisions of the European Court of Justice on identically worded provisions in the Brussels Convention should be applied.');
- *Western Digital Corp v British Airways* [2001] QB 733 (CA, 769 (Mance LJ construing Article 24(1) of the Warsaw Convention on International Carriage by Air by reference to a 'parallel convention in the same family as the Warsaw Convention—that is, the Convention on the Contract for the Carriage of Goods by Road.');
- *R v Governor of Pentonville Prison, Ex parte Sinclair* [1991] 2 AC 64 (HL), 92 (Lord Ackner, comparing the Extradition Treaty between the United Kingdom and United States (in Schedule 1 to the United States of America (Extradition) Order 1976 (SI 1976/2144)) with other bilateral extradition treaties, eg Treaty of 14 May 1872 between Germany and the United Kingdom (as amended), and the United Kingdom's treaties with Denmark, Argentine, Israel and Sweden as well as the older versions of the Treaty with the United States (ie of 1890 and 1935) to conclude that 'prosecution' in Article V(1)(b) meant only the initiation of criminal proceedings);
- *Ulster-Swift Ltd v Taunton Meat Haulage Ltd* [1977] 1 WLR 625 (CA), 636D–E (Megaw LJ considering the Convention on the Contract for the International Carriage of Goods by Road (given force of law by the Carriage of Goods by Road Act 1965) by analogy with the Hague Rules (scheduled to the Carriage of Goods by Sea Act 1971)).

5.15.2. **Incorporated treaties unhelpful as aids to construction regarding other incorporated treaties:**

Illustrations:

- *Milor Srl v British Airways Plc* [1996] QB 702 (CA), 709B–C (Phillips LJ: '[Counsel] has sought to support the judgment by urging an analogy between the effects of article 28 [of the Warsaw Convention on International Carriage by Air] and the provisions as to jurisdiction of the Brussels Convention on Jurisdiction and the Enforcement of Judgments in Civil and Commercial Matters (1968) (Cmnd 7395), which is scheduled to the Civil Jurisdiction and Judgments Act 1982. Having regard both to the difference in objects and the difference in language of the respective provisions, for myself I have not found that that analogy is either apt or helpful.');
- *Kleinwort Benson Ltd v Glasgow City Council* [1999] 1 AC 153 (HL), 168C–D (Lord Goff finding unhelpful a reference to the Rome Convention whilst interpreting the Brussels Convention and referring to the Court of Appeal judgment: 'Next Roch LJ . . . invoked article 10(1)(e) of the Convention on the Law Applicable to Contractual Obligations (1980) (Schedule 1 to the Contracts (Applicable Law) Act 1990) ("the Rome Convention") which expressly provides that the law applicable to a contract shall govern in particular "the consequences of nullity of the contract." However, the fact that such express provision is made in the Rome Convention in relation to the governing law provides no guidance on the scope of article 5(1) forming part of the Brussels Convention which is concerned with jurisdiction and which contains no such provision. It is for that purpose entirely neutral.');
- *Quantum Corp Inc v Plane Trucking Ltd* [2002] EWCA Civ 350 [2002] 1 WLR 2678, [19] and [28] (Mance LJ considering an interpretation of Article 1(1) of the Convention on the Contract for the International Carriage of Goods by Road by reference to the overlap between it and the Warsaw Convention on International Carriage by Air but pronouncing it 'too esoteric . . . to serve as any reliable guide to the scope of article 1(1)', at [28]);
- *In re S (A Minor)(Custody: Habitual Residence)* [1998] AC 750 (HL), 769G (Lord Slynn: 'The purpose and structure of the European Convention [on Recognition and Enforcement of Decisions concerning Custody of Children] is different from that of the Hague Convention [on the Civil Aspects of Child Abduction] and it does not follow, though it may be, that what constitutes, or does not constitute, an "unlawful removal" for the purposes of the Hague Convention is, or conversely is not, an "unlawful removal" for the purposes of the European Convention.');
- *Insured Financial Structures Ltd v Elektrocieplownia Tychy SA* [2003] EWCA Civ 110 [2003] QB 1260, [19] (Lord Woolf CJ: '[I]t

is not possible to obtain any benefit in directly construing article 17 of the Lugano Convention from Council Regulation (EC) No 44/2001 of 22 December 2000 on jurisdiction and the recognition of judgments in civil and commercial matters which has replaced the Brussels Convention.').

5.15.3. **Incorporated treaties guiding the proper approach to the interpretation of other incorporated treaties:**
Illustration:

- *Agnew v Länsförsäkringsbolagens AB* [2001] 1 AC 223 (HL), 256E–F (Lord Hope, using the approach to interpreting the Rome Convention as guidance in determining the approach to interpreting the Lugano Convention: '*Anton, Private International Law,* 2nd ed (1990) . . . observes, at p 319, that the question whether or not an obligation is to be considered a contractual one for the purposes of the EC Convention on the Law Applicable to Contractual Obligations (OJ 1980, L226, p 1) is likely to be regarded not as a matter of characterisation referable primarily to the court deciding the matter but as a matter going to the scope of the Convention. As such, it is properly to be decided by the Court of Justice as a matter of Community law. I would take the same view of the question as to the meaning of the word "obligation" in article 5(1) of the Lugano Convention. As this is a matter which goes to the scope of the special rule rather than its application to particular circumstances, it is a question which ought to be decided in the same way as if it had been raised as a matter of Community law under the Brussels Convention.').

5.15.4. **Incorporated treaties as points of comparison for other incorporated treaties:**
Illustration:

- *R (European Roma Rights Centre) v Immigration Officer at Prague Airport* [2004] UKHL 55 [2005] 2 WLR 1, [43–45] (Lord Steyn considering the weak non discrimination provision in Article 3 of the Refugee Convention by comparing it to the equally weak Article 14, ECHR and to the development of stronger, free-standing non-discrimination legal norms, pursuant to the Universal Declaration on Human Rights (1948) and the Charter of the United Nations (1945), as illustrated by the International Convention on the Elimination of All Forms of Racial Discrimination (1966) and the International Covenant on Civil and Political Rights (1966)).

5.15.5. **Incorporated treaties providing background and context for other incorporated treaties:**

Illustration:

- *In re Burke* [2001] 1 AC 422 (HL), 428D–G (Lord Hope, construing the Extradition Treaty between the United Kingdom and the United States, given force of law by the United States of America (Extradition) Order 1976 (SI 1976/2144) by reference to other extradition treaties: '[Counsel] pointed out that . . . [it] was not until comparatively recently that the Treaties had made express provision for a minimum custodial sentence part of which had not yet been carried out. But he said they were simply stating expressly what had hitherto been regarded as implied. The Treaty with Austria . . . was the first to include a provision to this effect . . . The first Treaty to include an express condition that a request for extradition relating to a convicted person shall not be granted unless there is evidence that he is unlawfully at large was the Treaty of Finland . . . The Treaty with the United States was concluded on 8 June 1972 when it was not the practice to include an express condition to this effect as it was regarded as implied. The inclusion of an express condition in the Treaty with Finland was not to be regarded as a radical departure from previous practice but as an organic development of what had always previously been understood as one of the requirements that had to be satisfied before a convicted person could be extradited.').

B. Unincorporated Treaties

5.16. **Unincorporated treaties may be used when construing incorporated treaties as aids to interpretation, as providing evidence of general international norms and as providing context. As with the use of incorporated treaties, it is important to select those treaties as aids which bear a degree of similarity of object and purpose, subject-matter and, possibly, even language with those of the treaty to be construed. An unincorporated treaty should be used with circumspection and after considering whether the same states are parties to it as are parties to the treaty being construed. This ensures that the meaning of treaty being interpreted is not distorted and that uniformity of interpretation across different contracting parties is maintained.**

5.16.1. Using unincorporated treaties as aids in construing Community law:

Illustrations:

- See the use of unincorporated treaties by the ECJ [§ **6.20**];
- *R v Secretary of State for Employment, Ex parte Seymour-Smith* [1999] 2 AC 554 (ECJ), [88] (Advocate General Cosmas, using

the ECHR (pre-HRA) in construing Community law: '[A]rticle 6 of the Directive [Council Directive (76/207/EEC) on the approximation of the laws of the member states relating to the application of the principle of equal pay] . . . constitutes the expression of a general principle of law underlying the constitutional traditions common to the member states which is also laid down by articles 6 and 13 of the Convention for the Protection of Human Rights and Fundamental Freedoms of 4 November 1950 (1953) (Cmd 8969). By virtue of article 6 of the Directive, interpreted in the light of that principle, all persons have the right to obtain an effective remedy in a competent court against measures which they consider to be contrary to the principle of equal treatment laid down in Directive 76/207.').

5.16.2. **Using unincorporated treaties as aids in construing the ECHR:** ***Illustrations:***

- See the use of unincorporated treaties by the ECtHR [**§ 7.13**];
- *R (Williamson) v Secretary of State for Education and Employment* [2005] UKHL 15 [2005] 2 WLR 590, [80] (Baroness Hale considering whether section 568 of the Education Act 1996 prevented a parent delegating to a teacher in an independent school the right to administer corporal punishment and whether any limits set by the state on corporal punishment could be justified under Article 9(2), ECHR: 'There can be no doubt that the ban on corporal punishment in school pursues the legitimate aim of protecting the rights and freedoms of children. It has long been held that these are not limited to their rights under the European Convention . . . Above all, the state is entitled to give children the protection they are given by an international instrument to which the United Kingdom is a party, the United Nations Convention on the Rights of the Child ("UNCRC").' Considering at [81–85] *inter alia* provisions of the UNCRC, Reports of the UN Committee on the Rights of the Child on the United Kingdom's compliance with the UNCRC and a Report of the UN Committee on Economic, Social and Cultural Rights. At [86]: 'With such an array of international and professional support, it is quite impossible to say that Parliament was not entitled to limit the practice of corporal punishment in all schools in order to protect the rights and freedom of all children . . . prohibiting only such punishment as would violate their rights under article 3 (or possibly article 8) would bring difficult problems of definition, demarcation and enforcement. It would not meet the authoritative international view of what the UNCRC requires.' In the CA, at [2002] EWCA Civ 1926 [2003] QB 1300, [243] (Arden LJ after noting, at [241], that the Secretary of State did not contend that the administration of correction necessarily involved an infringement of any of the rights of the child: 'On 4 October 2002 the Committee on the Rights of the Child established under that Convention

published a report in which it expressed the view that the defence of reasonable chastisement conferred on a parent under English law did not comply with the principles and provisions of that Convention. However, no reliance has been placed by the parties on the United Nations Convention on the Rights of the Child (1989) (Cm 1976), which has thus played no part in this case.');

- *R (R) v Durham Constabulary* [2005] UKHL 21 [2005] 1 WLR 1184, [26] (Baroness Hale considering whether a warning given to a young offender under sections 65 and 66 of the Crime and Disorder Act 1998 was incompatible with Article 6, ECHR, referring to the United Nations Standard Minimum Rules for the Administration of Juvenile Justice (the Beijing Rules) 1985: 'The Beijing Rules are not binding on member states, but the same principle is reflected in the United Nations Convention on the Rights of the Child 1989 ("UNCRC"), which has been ratified by all but two member states of the United Nations. This is not only binding in international law; it is reflected in the interpretation and application by the European Court of Human Rights of the rights guaranteed by the Convention: see, for example, *V v United Kingdom* (1999) 30 EHRR 121; to that extent, at least, therefore, it must be taken into account in the interpretation and application of those rights in our national law.' Also considering at [28] the United Nations Guidelines for the Prevention of Juvenile Delinquency (the Riyadh Guidelines) 1990);
- *Mills v HM Advocate* [2002] UKPC D2 [2004] 1 AC 441, [11] (Lord Steyn, construing Article 6, ECHR: 'It is interesting to compare the corresponding provision of the International Covenant on Civil and Political Rights (1966), which has been ratified by the United Kingdom but not incorporated into our law . . . [quoting Article 14] . . . There cannot even be a linguistic argument in favour of a construction that there is a single guarantee. Unquestionably, article 14(3) enshrines a separate and independent guarantee. It would be strange if article 6(1) of the European Convention, admittedly earlier in date, has on this point a different and more restrictive meaning.');
- *Dyer v Watson* [2002] UKPC D1 [2004] 1 AC 379, [104–106] (Lord Hope), [61] (Lord Bingham) [**§ 5.16.6**];
- *ID v Home Office* [2005] EWCA Civ 38 [2005] INLR 278, [36] (Brooke LJ using the UN Convention on the Rights of the Child (Article 37(b)) to assess the lawfulness of detention under Article 5, ECHR by reference to the 'duty to interpret the ECHR in the light of other obligations in international law, including treaty obligations: see *T and V v UK* (2000) 30 EHRR 121 at para. 76.');
- *A v Secretary of State for the Home Department* [2004] EWCA Civ 1123 [2005] 1 WLR 414, [266] (Laws LJ: 'Obligations arising under international law, including the terms of treaties other than the [ECHR] itself may inform and colour the interpretation of [the ECHR] provisions including article 6.' *cf* at [268]: 'Our

adherence to the [ECHR], and now our incorporation of its core provisions into our domestic law by the [HRA], does not carry on its back an acceptance that other international obligations should drive our administration of article 6.' At [270]: 'A general requirement to interpret article 6 in harmony with rules of international law does not make compliance with these other rules a condition of compliance with article 6. That proves too much; it makes for too exuberant a reading of the Convention.'), [467] (Neuberger LJ noting the need to bear: 'in mind that article 6(1) must be treated as informed by other international treaties, the general international determination to eliminate torture in all circumstances and the terms of article 15 of [the Convention Against Torture].');

- *Coppard v Customs and Excise Commissioners* [2003] EWCA Civ 511 [2003] QB 1428, [38] (Sedley LJ considering the doctrine of a judge-in-fact (where the acts of a judge may be held valid in law even though his appointment is invalid) in relation to Article 6, ECHR, by reference to Article 14(1), International Covenant on Civil and Political Rights, and the 'non-binding' EU Charter of Fundamental Rights (Article 47(2));
- *R (Spink) v Wandsworth BC* [2004] EWHC 2314 (Admin) [2005] 1 WLR 258, [60] (Richards J considering the UN Convention on the Rights of the Child in determining a local authority's duties to provide free assistance to disabled children and whether it could consider the financial resources of the child's parents. Concluding that his view: 'is supported by the provisions of the UN Convention on the Rights of the Child . . . They place a primary responsibility on the parents of a child and permit a parent's financial resources to be taken into account when determining whether free assistance is to be provided to a disabled child. The values embodied in the UN Convention may . . . represent only minimum standards, but they also help to inform the court's assessment of what is required under the [ECHR].');
- *R (Howard League for Penal Reform) v Secretary of State for the Home Department* [2002] EWHC 2497 (Admin) (2003) 1 FLR 484, [66–68] (Munby J reading Articles 3 and 8, ECHR 'in the light of' Articles 3 and 37, UN Convention on the Rights of the Child and Article 24, European Charter of Fundamental Rights of the EU ([66]) and by reference to the 'welfare principle' encapsulated in the UN Convention and the European Charter ([68]). At [51]: 'Neither the UN Convention nor the European Charter is at present legally binding in our domestic law and they are therefore not sources of law in the strict sense. But both can, in my judgment, properly be construed insofar as they proclaim, re-affirm or elucidate the content of those human rights that are generally recognised throughout the European family of nations, in particular the nature and scope of those fundamental rights that are guaranteed by the [ECHR].');

- *R (Kenny) v Leeds Magistrates Court* [2003] EWHC 2963 (Admin) [2004] 1 All ER 1333, [41] (Owen J describing Munby J in *Howard League* (see above) at [67] as providing a: 'persuasive analysis of the duty on public bodies to have regard to the principles embodied in the United Nations Convention on the Rights of the Child and the European Union Charter of Fundamental Rights.');
- *Singh v Entry Clearance Officer, New Delhi* [2004] EWCA Civ 1075 [2004] 3 FLR 72, [30] (Dyson LJ using the UN Convention on the Rights of the Child and the Hague Convention on the Protection of Children and Co-operation in respect of Inter-Country Adoption 1993 when considering Article 8, ECHR).

5.16.3. **Using unincorporated treaties as aids in construing the Refugee Convention:**

Illustrations:

- *R (European Roma Rights Centre) v Immigration Officer at Prague Airport* [2004] UKHL 55 [2005] 2 WLR 1, [13–17] (Lord Bingham, construing Article 33 of the Refugee Convention by reference to the Convention relating to the International Status of Refugees 1933; Article 14 of the Universal Declaration on Human Rights; the UNHCR Handbook on Procedures and Criteria for Determining Refugee Status (1992); UN Declaration on Territorial Asylum 1967 and the Draft UN Convention on Territorial Asylum.);
- *R (Hoxha) v Special Adjudicator* [2005] UKHL 19 [2005] 1 WLR 1063, [38] (Baroness Hale construing Article IC(5) of the Refugee Convention: '[T]he final question is whether the authorities would be able and willing to provide sufficient protection against their ill-treatment at the hands of their own communities . . . This has not been explored in evidence or argument. The most one can say is that it is not easy to protect against this sort of deep-seated prejudice but that in international law there is a clear duty to do so [quoting Article 5(a) of the Convention on the Elimination of All Forms of Discrimination Against Women].');
- *Revenko v Secretary of State for the Home Department* [2001] QB 601 (CA), 610B–E (Pill LJ, construing Article 1A(2) of the Refugee Convention: 'Though they may be related, the phenomenon of statelessness is distinct from that of persecution giving rise to a right of asylum. Under the [Convention Relating to the Status of Stateless Persons 1954], stateless persons are given protection similar to, though not identical with, the protection given to refugees under the 1951 Convention. In general, the 1954 Convention requires states to give to stateless persons the same rights of admission as they give to aliens. There is no doubt that some stateless persons came within the definition of "refugees" adopted in the 1951 Convention. The issue is whether stateless persons qualify as refugees and thereby for the protection of the 1951 Convention merely by establishing that they are unable to

return to the country of their former habitual residence. That there are many stateless persons who are not covered by the 1951 Convention is recorded in the preamble to the 1954 Convention ... Significant omissions from the 1954 Convention, as compared with the 1951 Convention, are articles equivalent to articles 31 and 33 of the 1951 Convention.');

- *El-Ali v Secretary of State for the Home Department* [2002] EWCA Civ 1103 [2003] 1 WLR 95, [38] (Laws LJ construing Article 1D of the Refugee Convention: 'Amongst alleged "bizarre results" is the suggestion, canvassed by [counsel] that this interpretation of "at present" [in Article 1D] which was adopted by the tribunal and which I consider to be correct sits ill with the application of other, near-contemporaneous international instruments, in particular the UNHCR Statute and the 1954 Convention relating to the Status of Stateless Persons (1960)(Cmnd 1098). The latter was adopted on 28 September 1954 and entered into force on 6 June 1960. It obliges the states parties to confer certain rights, comparable with many of the rights provided for in the Refugee Convention, upon stateless persons within their territory. Article 1(2)(i) is in the same terms as the first sentence of article 1D, with the addition at the end of the words "so long as they are receiving such protection or assistance". [Counsel's] point is that applying the same approach to the interpretation of the two measures gives the 28 July 1951 defining date for article 1D of the Refugee Convention and the 28 September 1954 defining date for article 1(2)(i) of the Stateless Persons Convention. But I do not think that is necessarily bizarre.');
- *T v Immigration Officer* [1996] AC 742 (HL), 786D (Lord Lloyd interpreting 'serious non-political crime' in Article 1F(b) of the Refugee Convention by considering the European Convention on the Suppression of Terrorism (1977) and its Explanatory Report and that although not directly relevant: 'it represents an attempt to limit by agreement among member states the availability of the political exception in extradition cases.').

5.16.4. **Using unincorporated treaties as aids in construing other incorporated treaties:**

Illustrations:

- *In re S (A Minor) (Abduction: Custody Rights)* [1993] 2 WLR 775 (CA), 783A–B (Balcombe LJ construing Article 13 of the Hague Convention on the Civil Aspects of International Child Abduction 1980 (scheduled to the Child Abduction and Custody Act 1985) and regarding as 'material' Article 12 of the UN Convention on the Rights of the Child);
- *Pearce v Ove Arup Partnership Ltd* [2000] Ch 403 (CA), 441–442 (Roch LJ considering whether provisions of the Brussels Convention on Jurisdiction and the Enforcement of Judgments are excluded from application to copyright infringement by Article 5(2) of the

Berne Convention for the Protection of Literary and Artistic Works 1886 (as revised in 1990) by comparing Article 5(2) of the Berne Convention with Article 64 of the European Patent Convention).

5.16.5. **Unincorporated treaties as evidence of general international norms:**

Illustration:

- *R v Immigration Appeal Tribunal, Ex parte Shah* [1999] 2 AC 629 (HL), 655D–E (Lord Hoffmann interpreting Article 1A(2) of the Refugee Convention: 'Although such discrimination [against women] is contrary not merely to western notions but to the constitution of Pakistan and a number of international human rights instruments, including the Convention on the Elimination of All Forms of Discrimination Against Women, which Pakistan ratified in 1996, it does not in itself found a claim under the [Refugee] Convention.').

5.16.6. **Unincorporated treaties as providing background and context for incorporated treaties:**

Illustration:

- *Dyer v Watson* [2002] UKPC D1 [2004] 1 AC 379, [104–106] (Lord Hope, interpreting the ECHR by reference to the UN Convention on the Rights of the Child: '[T]he Strasbourg court has taken into account the provisions of the following international instruments when considering the requirements imposed by the Convention in relation to proceedings involving juvenile offenders: *V v United Kingdom* (1999) 30 EHRR 121, 176, para 76. Article 1 of the United Nations Convention on the Rights of the Child 1989 defines a child as a human being under the age of 18 years. Article 40(2)(b) provides: "Every child alleged as or accused of having infringed the penal law has at least the following guarantees . . . (iii) To have the matter determined without delay . . ." Rule 20 of the United Nations Standard Minimum Rules for the Administration of Juvenile Justice 1985 ("the Beijing Rules") provides: "Each case shall from the outset be handled expeditiously, without any unnecessary delay." The United Nations Convention was ratified by the United Kingdom and came into effect on 15 January 1992 . . . Against this background I would hold that the delay in bringing this case to trial was so excessive as to give rise to a real concern that the respondent's Convention right [Article 6] has been violated.'), [61] (Lord Bingham: '[T]he reasonable time requirement [in Article 6 of the ECHR] must, when dealing with children, be read in the light of the UN Convention on the Rights of the Child and the Beijing Rules . . . both of which highlight the need for criminal proceedings, if brought at all, to be prosecuted with all due expedition.');
- *R v Secretary of State for the Home Department, Ex parte Chahal* [1995] 1 WLR 526 (CA), 533G–534B (Staughton LJ, pre-HRA,

considering whether Article 33 of the Refugee Convention required a balancing exercise between the threat to an individual's life or freedom if he were deported and the danger to the security of the United Kingdom if he was not: 'In support of the balancing exercise [counsel] referred us to three other international agreements, and what I think he described as international common law. The United Nations Convention Against Torture and Other Cruel, Inhuman or Degrading Treatment or Punishment (1985) (Cmnd 9593) deals in article 3 with expulsion or return of a person to a state where he would be in danger of torture. Article 7 of the International Covenant on Civil and Political Rights (1966) (Cmd 6702) prohibits torture; and article 13 contains provisions similar to article 32(2) of the Convention of 1951 [the Refugee Convention]. Similar provisions are also found in articles 3 and 13 of the European Convention for the Protection of Human Rights and Fundamental Freedoms (1953) (Cmd 8969). None of these instruments has been incorporated into English domestic law. Where their effect is the same as that of the Convention of 1951, incorporation is unnecessary. If their effect is different from that convention, incorporation might give rise to difficulty. For the present it is enough to say that the Convention of 1951 . . . is all that [counsel] needs to rely on.') (ECtHR is at (1996) 1 BHRC 405).

5.16.7. **Need to ensure that the same states are parties to the treaty to be construed and the treaty to be used as an aid to construction:**
Illustration:

- *Sidhu v British Airways* [1997] AC 430 (HL), 443F–H (Lord Hope: '[Counsel] submitted that it would be inconsistent with the obligations of the United Kingdom under various articles of the European Convention on Human Rights if a construction were to be placed on article 17 of the Warsaw Convention which excluded the claim which they were seeking to make in this case. Your Lordships had no hesitation in rejecting that argument. The provisions in the European Convention have no bearing on the interpretation of international conventions such as the Warsaw Convention on carriage by air—and there are many other examples—which are concerned with commerce between countries and which seek, by a process of compromise, to achieve uniformity across international frontiers in the application of trade law. It must also be observed that, while some parties to the Warsaw Convention are parties to the European Convention of Human Rights, some notably the United States of America—are not. We cannot assume that the principles expressed in the European Convention are common to all those countries who are parties to the Warsaw Convention. Thus we would risk introducing an element of distortion into the debate, in conflict with the broad aim of uniformity of interpretation between states, if we were to rely on the European Convention as an aid to the construction of the Warsaw Convention in the present case.').

C. International Instruments

5.17. **The designation 'international instrument' covers a plethora of material ranging from the Universal Declaration of Human Rights to Resolutions of the Parliamentary Assembly of the Council of Europe to statutes and charters establishing international tribunals. This material generally lacks binding legal force even on the international plane but has a useful, ancillary, role to play as an aid to interpretation. The flexible use of international instruments should not detract from the importance of the need to show their relevance and application to the treaty in question. International instruments have been used as aids in the interpretation of incorporated treaties, and as providing background and context.**

5.17.1. **Using international instruments as aids in interpreting incorporated treaties:**

Illustrations:

- *R (Hoxha) v Special Adjudicator* [2005] UKHL 19 [2005] 1 WLR 1063, [31] and [35] (Baroness Hale, construing Article IC(5) of the Refugee Convention, referring to the UN High Commission for Refugees *Guidelines on Gender-Related Persecution within the context of Article 1A(2) of the 1951 Convention and/or its 1967 Protocol relating to the Status of Refugees* (HCRR/GIP/02/02, 7 May 2002);
- *R (R) v Durham Constabulary* [2005] UKHL 21 [2005] 1 WLR 1184, [26] (Baroness Hale construing Article 6, ECHR, by reference to the Beijing Rules and the Riyadh Guidelines) [§ **5.16.2**];
- *R (Williamson) v Secretary of State for Education and Employment* [2005] UKHL 15 [2005] 2 WLR 590, [81–85] (Baroness Hale construing the ECHR, Article 9, by reference to Reports of the UN Committee on the Rights of the Child and the UN Committee on Economic, Social and Cultural Rights);
- *Dyer v Watson* [2002] UKPC D1 [2004] 1 AC 379, [1046] (Lord Hope), [61] (Lord Bingham) [§ **5.16.6**]
- *Coppard v Customs and Excise Commissioners* [2003] EWCA Civ 511 [2003] QB 1428, [38] (Sedley LJ) [§ **5.16.2**];
- *R v Lambert* [2001] UKHL 37 [2002] 2 AC 545, 569D–E (Lord Steyn interpreting Article 6(2), ECHR, by considering that it borrowed the language of Article 11(1), Universal Declaration on Human Rights, 'almost verbatim' and that Article 14(2), International Covenant on Civil and Political Rights, 'is to the same effect' as Article 6(2).);
- *R (Yogathas) v Secretary of State for the Home Department* [2002] UKHL 36 [2003] 1 AC 920, [35–36] (Lord Hope using the EU

Charter of Fundamental Rights in considering the ECHR and the Dublin Convention on Determining the State Responsible for Examining Applications for Asylum Lodged in one of the EC Member States);

- *R v Bow Street Magistrate, Ex parte Pinochet (No 3)* [2000] 1 AC 147 (HL), 244E–F, 246H–247B (Lord Hope), 261D–E (Lord Hutton) (both using the Rome Statute of the International Criminal Court, Statute of the International Tribunal for the Former Yugoslavia and Statute of the International Criminal Tribunal for Rwanda to construe the Torture Convention);
- *R v Bow Street Magistrate, Ex parte Pinochet* [2000] 1 AC 61 (HL), 109D–110A (Lord Nicholls, referring to the Charter of the Nuremberg International Military Tribunal (8 August 1945) and a UN General Assembly resolution in the context of the Torture and Hostage-Taking Conventions, determining the scope of head of state immunity and whether torture and hostage-taking can be regarded as functions of a head of state);
- *R (Pretty) v Director of Public Prosecutions (Secretary of State for the Home Department intervening)* [2001] UKHL 61 [2002] 1 AC 800, [19–23] (Lord Bingham referring to *Rodriguez v Attorney-General of Canada* [1994] 2 LRC 136 and the Canadian Charter of Rights and Freedoms in the context of assisted suicide and the ECHR and noting the differences between the ECHR and the Canadian Charter at [23]), [105] (Lord Hope: '[I]t is clear that the list of grounds for discrimination set out [in Article 14, ECHR] is not closed. This is made clear by the words "such as" which precede the list. I would hold that the article is capable of extending to discrimination in the enjoyment of the Convention rights on the grounds of physical or mental capacity. Section 15(1) of the Canadian Charter recognises that discrimination on these grounds is contrary to fundamental rights. I see no difficulty in recognising that article 14 of the European Convention has that effect too.'), see also [28] (Lord Bingham), [55] (Lord Steyn) and [109] (Lord Hobhouse) (all referring to the Council of Europe's Recommendation 1418 (1999) on the protection of the human rights and dignity of the terminally ill and dying in considering whether, if the claimant's rights under Article 8, ECHR, were infringed by the prohibition of assisted suicide in section 2 of the Suicide Act 1961, the infringement was justifiable under Article 8(2).);
- *R v Immigration Appeal Tribunal, Ex parte Shah* [1999] 2 AC 629 (HL), 653B–D (Lord Hoffmann interpreting Article 1A(2) of the Refugee Convention by reference to conclusion No 39 'Refugees, Women and International Protection' adopted by the Executive Committee of the United Nations High Commissioner for Refugees in 1985), 660E–661B (Lord Hutton construing Article 1A(2) of the Refugee Convention by 'deriving assistance' from the Universal Declaration on Human Rights);

- *Campbell v MGN Ltd* [2004] UKHL 22 [2004] 2 WLR 1232, [138] (Baroness Hale considering Articles 8 and 10, ECHR: '[N]either right takes precedence over the other. This is consistent with Resolution 1165 (1998) of the Parliamentary Assembly of the Council of Europe, para 11: "The Assembly reaffirms the importance of everyone's right to privacy, and of the right to freedom of expression, as fundamental to a democratic society. These rights are neither absolute nor in any hierarchical order, since they are of equal value."');
- *Horvath v Secretary of State for the Home Department* [2001] 1 AC 489 (HL), 509F and 515C (Lord Clyde referring to the Joint Position 96/196/JHA of the Council of Europe (on the harmonised application of the definition of 'refugee' in article 1 of the Refugee Convention [1996] OJ L63/2) for guidance in considering the definition of 'persecution' in Article 1A(2) of the Refugee Convention);
- *Agnew v Länsförsäkringsbolagens AB* [2001] 1 AC 223 (HL), 251E-G (Lord Hope considering the identical provisions in certain parts of the Brussels Convention and Lugano Convention by reference to the Declarations of EFTA and the European Union States [1988] OJ 1988 L319/37.);
- *R (Howard League for Penal Reform) v Secretary of State for the Home Department* [2002] EWHC 2497 (Admin) [2003] 1 FLR 484, [66–68] (Munby J) [**§ 5.16.2**];
- *R (Kenny) v Leeds Magistrates Court* [2003] EWHC 2963 (Admin) [2004] 1 All ER 1333, [41] (Owen J) [**§ 5.16.2**];
- *R v Secretary of State for the Home Department, Ex parte Robinson* [1998] QB 929 (CA), 938F (Lord Woolf MR construing 'is outside the country of his nationality' in Article 1A(2) of the Refugee Convention by reference to the UNHCR Handbook (para 91) and noting that: 'A similar concept is to be found in paragraph 8 of the joint position of 4 March 1996 (OJ 1996 L 63, p.2) defined by the Council of the European Union on the basis of article K3 of the Treaty on European Union (OJ 1992 C191) on the harmonised application of the definition of the term "refugee" in article 1 of the Geneva Convention.' At 940G: '[Counsel] accepted that it was appropriate to interpret this country's obligations under the Convention by reference to what is set out in paragraph 91 of the Handbook. This is scarcely surprising in the light of this country's recent adherence to the joint position of the Council of the European Union.' At 943B: 'In our judgment, the Secretary of State and the appellate authorities would do well in future to adopt the approach which is so conveniently set out in paragraph 8 of the European Union's Joint Position.');
- *R (A and B) v East Sussex CC* [2003] EWHC 167 (Admin) [2003] LGR 529, [93] (Munby J using the EU Charter of Fundamental Rights in considering the positive obligations of the state towards

the disabled alongside a consideration of Article 8, ECHR as incorporated by HRA).

5.17.2. **Using international instruments as background for incorporated treaties:**

Illustrations:

- *R (Pretty) v Director of Public Prosecutions (Secretary of State for the Home Department intervening)* [2001] UKHL 61 [2002] 1 AC 800, [56] (Lord Steyn: 'The human rights movement evolved to protect fundamental rights of individuals either universally or regionally. The theme of the [Universal] Declaration of 1948 was universal. It involved a common conception of human rights capable of commanding wide acceptance throughout the world despite huge differences between countries in culture, in religion and in political systems . . . Any proposal that the Universal Declaration should require states to guarantee a right to euthanasia or assisted suicide (as opposed to permitting states by democratic institutions so to provide) would have been doomed to failure. The aspirational text of the Universal Declaration was the point of departure and inspiration of the European Convention which opened for signature in 1950. It is to be noted, however, that the European Convention embodied in some respects a narrower view of human rights than the Universal Declaration. The framers of the European Convention required a shorter and uncontroversial text which would secure general acceptance among European nations. Thus the European Convention contains, unlike the Universal Declaration, no guarantees of economic, social and cultural rights. A further illustration relates to the guarantee of equality in the two texts. The guarantee in the Universal Declaration is free standing and comprehensive: see article 7. In the European Convention the provision is parasitic: it is linked with other Convention rights: article 14.');
- *Dyer v Watson* [2002] UKPC D1 [2004] 1 AC 379, [104–106] (Lord Hope), [61] (Lord Bingham) **[§ 5.16.6];**
- *A v Secretary of State for the Home Department* [2004] EWCA Civ 1123 [2005] 1 WLR 414, [113] (Pill LJ considering various sources as demonstrating the abhorrence with which the law regards torture including a Declaration of the UN General Assembly: 'General Assembly Declarations, of which there are many, do not impose legal obligations but act as guidelines for the world community.').

D. Other Sources of Soft Law

5.18. **Incorporated treaties may be construed by recourse to treaties which have never come into force as well as those which are not in force at the relevant time. It is likely that such treaties will provide marginal assistance as aids to interpretation.**

5.18.1. **Using treaties which have never come into force:**
Illustrations:

- *T v Immigration Officer* [1996] AC 742 (HL), 762–763 and 773 (Lord Mustill), 774 (Lord Slynn) (both interpreting 'serious non-political crime' in Article 1F(b) of the Refugee Convention by reference to the 'serviceable' definition of 'acts of terrorism' in the League of Nations Convention for the Prevention and Punishment of Terrorism (which never came into force));
- *Morris v KLM Dutch Airlines* [2002] UKHL 7 [2002] 2 AC 628, [17] (Lord Steyn, construing 'bodily injury' in Article 17 of the Warsaw Convention on International Carriage by Air: 'In this context it is reasonable to expect that if it had been intended to cover mental injury or illness, it would have been provided for expressly. In the absence of such an express reference it is reasonable to interpret "bodily injury" and "lésion corporelle" as words of restriction, ie as referring to non fatal injury which is physical rather than mental: contrast the wide term in the Guatemala Protocol which never came into force: see Protocol to amend the Convention for the unification of certain rules relating to International Carriage by Air, signed at Warsaw on 12 October 1929, as amended by the Protocol done at The Hague on 28 September 1955, signed at Guatemala City on 8 March 1971.').

5.18.2. **Using treaties still to be enforced:**
Illustrations:

- *Morris v KLM Dutch Airlines* [2002] UKHL 7 [2002] 2 AC 628, [31] (Lord Steyn referring to the Montreal Convention on Air Carrier Liability (signed on 28 May 1999) (which was not then in force) in interpreting 'bodily injury' in Article 17 of the Warsaw Convention on International Carriage by Air);
- *Re DVT and Air Travel Group Litigation* [2003] EWHC 2825 (QB) [2003] 1 All ER 935, [114] (Nelson J interpreting the Warsaw Convention by reference to the Montreal Convention on Air Carrier Liability (signed on 28 May 1999) 'which is not yet in force') (CA is at [2003] EWCA Civ 1005 [2004] QB 234);
- cf *R v Chief Constable of Sussex, Ex parte International Trader's Ferry Ltd* [1999] 2 AC 418 (HL), 450C–G (Lord Cooke considering that articles in the Consolidated Version of the Treaty on the European Union (not then in force) had no significant bearing in interpreting Articles 5, 34, 36 and 177 of the EC Treaty (now Articles 10, 29, 30 and 234 respectively)).

5.19. **When incorporating a treaty into domestic law, Parliament can pick and choose which parts to incorporate and which parts to omit [§ 3.5]. Domestic courts are bound by the principles of non-justiciability [§§ 8.5–8.7] and no direct effect [§§ 8.8–8.9] regarding the unincorporated parts and, therefore, have a limited**

jurisdiction to interpret these parts of the treaty. The unincorporated parts of an incorporated treaty may, nevertheless, be used as aids when construing the incorporated parts—particularly where the unincorporated sections illuminate the object and purpose of the treaty as a whole.

Illustrations:

- *R (Mullen) v Secretary of State for the Home Department* [2004] UKHL 18 [2005] 1 AC 1, [40] (Lord Steyn: 'The United Kingdom has not so far signed or ratified the Seventh Protocol [to the ECHR]. It is, however, relevant to an understanding of the European jurisprudence [relating to Article 6(2), ECHR].');
- *A v Secretary of State for the Home Department* [2004] UKHL 56 [2005] 2 WLR 87 (in determining the validity of the derogation, from Article 5, ECHR, in the Human Rights Act 1998 (Designated Derogation) Order 2001 (SI 2001/3644) and the compatibility of part 4 of the Anti-terrorism, Crime and Security Act 2001 with Article 5, ECHR detailed consideration was given by the HL to Article 15, ECHR, notwithstanding its unincorporated status), [146] (Lord Scott: 'Unlike the specified articles [in the HRA] article 15 did not, therefore, become part of our domestic law. It remained, and remains, no more than an article in a treaty to which the United Kingdom, by act of the executive, adheres.'), At [148–149]: 'So [by section 14] the Secretary of State may make an order declaring in advance that the United Kingdom is proposing to enact legislation that is inconsistent with a Convention right . . . It is noteworthy that section 14 makes no reference to article 15 of the ECHR.' At [152]: 'In the Preamble to the [Human Rights Act 1998 (Designated Derogation) Order 2001 (SI 2001/3644)] the Secretary of State purported to be exercising his section 14 powers but in the Schedule to the Order, in which the proposed notification of the derogation from article 5(1) is set out, the derogation is described as an exercise of "the right of derogation conferred by article 15(1) of the Convention." For the reasons I have indicated I have difficulty in understanding how the scope of the authority conferred by section 14 to make a designated derogation order can be regarded as limited by the terms of article 15 of the ECHR. But since the Attorney General was content to argue the case on the footing that the Order did have to be justified under article 15 I will set aside my doubts and consider the case on that footing.'), [164] (Lord Rodger: '[N]othing in [the HRA] would permit a domestic court to adjudicate on any alleged breach of [Article 15].'), [48] (Lord Bingham, assessing the scope of the ECHR by reference to article 1 whilst noting that it has not been expressly incorporated into domestic law);
- *A v Secretary of State for the Home Department* [2004] EWCA Civ 1123 [2005] 1 WLR 414, [482] (Neuberger LJ responding to the appellants' contention that the derogation effected by the Human

Rights Act 1998 (Designated Derogation) Order 2001 (SI 2001/3644) would be unlawful pursuant to the closing words in Article 15(1), ECHR: 'However, that Article is not incorporated into English law, because it is not identified as a Convention right under the 1998 Act. In those circumstances it appears to me that it may well not be open to an English court to conclude that a derogation effected by the UK government purportedly pursuant to article 15, and embodied in something which is plainly a "designated order", was ineffective because it does not comply with, or satisfy the requirements of, article 15.' At [484]: 'Even if the English courts cannot rule on the effectiveness of a derogation, I do not think that it would follow that it would not be open to an English court, when determining an issue, to take into account the fact that, if it is determined in one way, it would involve the UK infringing the Convention.');

- *In re H (Minors)(Abduction: Acquiescence)* [1998] AC 72 (HL), 81C–E (Lord Browne-Wilkinson: 'The recitals and article 1 of the [Hague Convention on the Civil Aspects of International Child Abduction] set out its underlying purpose. Although they are not specifically incorporated into the law of the United Kingdom, they are plainly relevant to the construction of an international treaty. The object of the Convention is to protect children from the harmful effects of their wrongful removal from the country of their habitual residence to another country or their wrongful retention in some country other than that of their habitual residence. This is to be achieved by establishing a procedure to ensure the prompt return of the child to the state of his habitual residence.');
- *R v Bow Street Magistrates, Ex parte Pinochet* [2000] 1 AC 61 (HL), 71G (Lord Slynn (dissenting): 'The Preamble to the Vienna Convention [on Diplomatic Relations] (which though not part of the Schedule [to the Diplomatic Privileges Act 1964] may in my view be looked at in the interpretation of the articles so scheduled).');
- *Quantum Corp Inc v Plane Trucking Ltd* [2002] EWCA Civ 350 [2002] 1 WLR 2678, [27] (Mance LJ considering counsel's submission that part of the Protocol to the Convention on the Contract for the International Carriage of Goods by Road, which was not part of the schedule to the Carriage of Goods by Road Act 1965, should, nevertheless, be used to construe Article 1 of the Convention).

(7) Different Languages

5.20. **The key provision of the Vienna Convention on the Law of Treaties, regarding the interpretation of treaties authenticated in two or more languages is Article 33, which provides that:**

> '(1) When a treaty has been authenticated in two or more languages, the text is equally authoritative in each language, unless the treaty provides or the parties agree that, in case of divergence, a particular text shall prevail. (2) A version of the treaty in a language other than one of those in which the text was authenticated shall be considered an authentic text only if the treaty so provides or the parties so agree. (3) The terms of the treaty are presumed to have the same meaning in each authentic text. (4) Except where a particular text prevails in accordance with paragraph 1, when a comparison of the authentic text discloses a difference of meaning which the application of articles 31 and 32 does not remove, the meaning which best reconciles the texts, having regard to the object and purpose of the treaty, shall be adopted.'

5.21. **The language in which an incorporated treaty is expressed, both on the international and domestic planes, is an important factor in its interpretation. A treaty may be incorporated into domestic law, vis-à-vis different language options, in a variety of ways. One example is where the authentic treaty text is in a language other than English it may be incorporated into domestic law by being scheduled to or written into a statute in a translated, English version. The statute may or may not indicate which text prevails in the event of conflict. Another example is where the authentic treaty text exists in two or more languages, one of which is English. The English text may be scheduled to or written into a statute. Again, the statute may or may not indicate which text prevails in the event of conflict.**

> 'Conventions, when made part of English law, may be expressed in language texts in various ways. There may be only an English statutory text which is based upon the convention, the convention itself not being incorporated into the statute. There may be an English convention text which is incorporated in the statute. There may be a French (or other language) convention text with an English translation adopted by the English statute; there may be convention texts in two languages with or without a provision that one shall prevail in cases of doubt (contrast this case with the Hague Convention of 1961 on Wills). Different principles of interpretation may apply in each of these cases.' (*James Buchanan & Co Ltd v Babco Forwarding & Shipping (UK) Ltd* [1978] AC 141 (HL), 152B–C (Lord Wilberforce))

5.22. **Where the incorporating statute includes both an English and another language version of the treaty and expressly provides that the other language version is to prevail if there is any inconsistency**

between the two texts then, generally, the proper approach is to interpret both the English text and the non-English text, separately and according to the principles relevant to construing treaties, and then compare the meanings.

- *Fothergill v Monarch Airlines* [1981] AC 251 (HL), 293E–294A (Lord Scarman: 'Being scheduled to [the Carriage by Air Act 1961, the French text of the Warsaw Convention] is part of our law. Further, in the event of inconsistency, it shall, as a matter of law, prevail over the English text. It is, therefore, the duty of the court to have regard to it. We may not take refuge in our adversarial process, paying regard only to the English text, unless and until one or other of the parties leads evidence to establish an inconsistency with the French. We are to take judicial notice of the French. We have to form a view as to its meaning . . . First, the court must have recourse to the English text. It is, after all, the meaning which Parliament believes the French to have. It is an enacted translation though not binding in law because Parliament has recognised the possibility of inconsistency and has laid down how that difficulty is to be resolved. Secondly, as with the English language, so also with the French, the court may have recourse to dictionaries in its search for a meaning. Thirdly, the court may receive expert evidence directed not to the questions of law which arise in interpreting the convention, but to the meaning, or possible meanings (for there will often be more than one), of the French. It will be for the court, not the expert, to choose the meaning which it considers should be given to the words in issue . . . At the end of the day, the court applying legal principles of interpretation, selects the meaning which it believes the law requires.'), 272D–F (Lord Wilberforce: '[I]n the present case the process of interpretation seems to involve: 1. Interpretation of the English text, according to the principles upon which international conventions are to be interpreted . . . 2. Interpretation of the French text according to the same principles but with additional linguistic problems. 3. Comparison of these meanings.'), 297D–299D (Lord Roskill, tracing the development of the construction of international conventions by reference to the French text.);

Illustrations:

- Section 1(8), Carriage by Air Act 1961: 'If there is any inconsistency between the text in English in Part I of Schedule 1 or 1A [the Warsaw Convention as amended by the Hague Protocol and the Warsaw Convention as amended by the Hague Protocol and Protocol No 4 of Montreal respectively] and the text in French in Part II of that Schedule, the French text shall prevail'.
- *Morris v KLM Royal Dutch Airlines* [2002] UKHL 7 [2002] 2 AC 628, [17] (Lord Steyn, interpreting 'lésion corporelle' (bodily injury) in Article 17 of the Warsaw Convention on International

Carriage by Air: '[T]he amendments to the French text of the parallel Convention concerning International Carriage by Rail are instructive. In 1952 the text of article 26, the liability provision corresponding to article 17, read "de la mort, les blessures et toute autre atteinte a l'integrite corporelle." However, in 1961 the text was amended to read "de la mort, les blessures et toute autre atteinte a l'integrite corporelle ou mentale". The expression in both the current text of 1980 and the revision of 1999 is "dommage resultant de la mort, des blessures ou toute autre atteinte a l'integrite physique or psychique du voyaguer". It follows that successive French drafters of the Convention over the last 50 years did not consider that, in the text of an international Convention, "corporelle" was wide enough to cover purely psychic injury.'), [74] and [76] (Lord Hope considering the relevant principles of interpretation, the natural meaning of the words in the English and French texts, travaux préparatoires and comparative jurisprudence [§ **4.5.3**]), [132] (Lord Hobhouse noting that no question of inconsistency arose since the word 'lésion' has a similar breadth of meaning as 'injury'.);

- *Milor Srl v British Airways Plc* [1996] QB 702 (CA), 707A–C (Phillips LJ, interpreting the Warsaw Convention on International Carriage by Air: 'It is of interest, though in the absence of ambiguity it is not a legitimate aid to interpretation, that in the French text the word that is the equivalent of "brought" in article 28 is "portée;" the word that is the equivalent of "brought" in article 29 is "intentée." It seems to me that the use of different words in each article is significant. "Intentée" conveys the narrow meaning that "brought" has in the context of article 29, namely "initiated." "Portée," in the context of article 28, naturally carries the meaning that I consider that "brought" has in that context, namely "commenced and pursued." ');
- *Goldman v Thai Airways International Ltd* [1983] 1 WLR 1186 (CA), 1194H–1195A (Eveleigh LJ, construing Article 25 of the Warsaw Convention: 'I had thought that I had found support for my reading of article 25 [ie assessing recklessness subjectively] when I looked at the French text and saw the words "avec conscience." I thought that phrase imported the meaning of awareness. In view of the decision of the French Cour de Cassation [adopting an objective approach], I hesitate to use the French text as a support of my interpretation of article 25.');
- *Rothmans Ltd v Saudi Arabian Airlines Corp* [1981] QB 368 (CA), 386D–388B (Roskill LJ interpreting Article 28(1) of the Warsaw Convention and warning of the dangers which may arise 'if one tries to apply the language of the text of other translations [here the American translation] to the English text of article 28 which is scheduled alongside the French text in our statute [the Carriage by Air Act 1961].' (at 388B)).

5.23. Where the incorporating statute gives force of law only to an English version of the treaty and where the treaty itself is authenticated in English and another language, then the other language version may be consulted where the English version is ambiguous, and possibly even absent any ambiguity.

Illustrations:

- *James Buchanan & Co Ltd v Babco Forwarding & Shipping (UK) Ltd* [1978] AC 141 (HL), 152C–152G (Lord Wilberforce: 'The [Convention on the Contract for the International Carriage of Goods by Road 1956] is in two languages, English and French, each text being equally authentic. The English text alone appears in the Schedule to [the Carriage of Goods by Road Act 1965] and is by that Act (section 1) given the force of law . . . It might therefore be arguable (though this was not in fact argued)—by distinction from a case where the authentic text is (for example) French and the enacted text an English translation—that only the English text ought to be looked at. In my opinion this would be too narrow a view to take, given the expressed objective of the Convention to produce uniformity in all contracting states. I think that the correct approach is to interpret the English text, which after all is likely to be used by many others than British businessman, in a normal manner, appropriate for the interpretation of an international convention . . . Moreover, it is perfectly legitimate in my opinion to look for assistance, if assistance is needed, to the French text. This is often put in the form that resort may be had to the foreign text if (and only if) the English text is ambiguous, but I think this states the rule too technically. As Lord Diplock recently said in this House the inherent flexibility of the English (and, one may add, any) language may make it necessary for the interpreter to have recourse to a variety of aids: *Carter v Bradbeer* [1975] 1 WLR 1204, 1206. There is no need to impose a preliminary test of ambiguity.'), 161B–C (Lord Salmon: 'If in a statute which is based on an international convention expressed in two different languages there is some doubt as to its meaning in one language, it is permissible to seek help from the way in which it is expressed in the other.'), 167C–D (Lord Edmund-Davies: 'I am not disposed to differ from the conclusion of my noble and learned friend, Lord Wilberforce, regarding the propriety of adverting to the French text of the 1965 Convention. But this is permissible only if the English version is ambiguous.'), *cf* 158E–F (Viscount Dilhorne: 'I have not found it necessary to refer to the French text of the Convention. I confess to some doubt as to the propriety of doing so when Parliament has only scheduled the English text to the Act and declared that it is to have force of law.');
- *Rothmans Ltd v Saudi Arabian Airlines Corporation* [1981] QB 368 (CA), 383D–384B (Roskill LJ adopting the approach of Lord

Wilberforce in *James Buchanan* at 152 and Lord Salmon at 160 (see above) in considering the right approach to the English text of the Warsaw Convention and observing: 'I do not find anything in the speeches of the other Law Lords to contrary effect.' (at 384B));

- *Ulster-Swift Ltd v Taunton Meat Haulage Ltd* [1977] 1 WLR 625 (CA), 632F–H (Megaw LJ construing the Convention on the Contract for the International Carriage of Goods by Road 1956, given force of law by the Carriage of Goods by Road Act 1965 (scheduling the English version of the Convention): 'We should willingly have looked at the text of the Convention in the French language to see whether it would provide any assistance on any doubtful questions as to the meaning of the Convention. But counsel, when the point was raised, did not invite the court to take that course . . . If we had [looked at the French text], and if we had thought that it did shed light on the matter, it would have been necessary despite the added delay and expense, to have given counsel the opportunity to make submissions relating to the court's provisional views, based on the French text.').

5.24. **There is authority suggesting that where the treaty itself is authenticated in a language other than English and the English statutory version is a translation from the authentic text, then in the event of any inconsistency between the two, the authentic text will prevail even though it is not part of domestic law.**

- *Corocraft Ltd v Pan-American Airways Inc* [1969] 1 QB 616 (CA), 652B–653A (Lord Denning MR: 'The Warsaw Convention is only law in England in so far as Parliament had made it so. But Parliament has made it part of our law. It passed the Carriage by Air Act, 1932, for the express purpose of *giving effect* to the Convention. But then in the very first section the Act says that: ". . . the provisions thereof (that is, of the Convention) *as set out in the First Schedule to this Act shall* . . . have the force of law in the United Kingdom . . ." Then if you turn to Schedule 1, you find the English text of the Convention: but it includes in article 36 the words: "*The Convention is drawn up in French in a single copy* which shall remain deposited in the archives of the Ministry of Foreign Affairs of Poland. . ." It was plainly the intention of all parties to the Convention that the French text should be the one official and authorised text; and it was plainly the intention of the English Parliament to give effect to that French text by making an exact translation of it into English. The English Parliament failed in their object. The translator whom they employed, by introducing the word "and", put his own gloss on the French text. He produced certainty where there was ambiguity: and clarity where there was obscurity. But this was a translator's gloss which he should not have inserted. In order to produce an exact translation, the translator should reproduce the French text faithfully, with all its defects, deficiencies, ambiguities and uncertainties . . . If there is any inconsistency between the English text and the French text, the text in French should prevail. I know that the Act of 1932 says that we are to give effect to the provisions of the Convention "*as set out* in the First Schedule". That description of the Convention is true enough so long as the translation is an exact translation. But as soon as any inconsistencies appear, the description is no longer a true description of the Convention but is a false description of it: and it should be rejected in accordance with the maxim "Falsa demonstration non nocet": see *Eastwood v Ashton* [[1915] AC 900] *per* Lord Parker of Waddington.' At 653E–G: 'I would also refer to the Carriage by Air Act, 1961, which gives effect to "the Warsaw Convention as amended at The Hague, 1955". That Act contains a similar provision to the Act of 1932, saying in section 1(1) that ". . . the provisions of the Convention . . . as set out in the First Schedule . . . shall . . . have the force of law . . ." But it goes on expressly in section 1(2) [now section 1(8): [§ **5.22**]] to say that: "If there is any inconsistency between the text in English . . . and the text in French . . . the text in French shall prevail." That makes explicit in the Act of 1961 what was implicit in the Act of 1932.').

5.25. **Different language versions of an incorporated treaty provision may be considered where this provides confirmation of the English language meaning. Equally, where only one word or phrase in a treaty provision is expressed in a language other than English, its original meaning may be considered:**

5.25.1. **Different languages providing confirmation of English language meaning of a treaty provision:**

Illustrations:

- *MacWilliam v Mediterranean Shipping Co* [2005] UKHL 11 [2005] 2 WLR 554, [44] (Lord Steyn construing Article I(b) of the Hague-Visby Rules (on bills of lading) and finding his view 'reinforced if one considers the French text of the 1924 Hague Rules.');
- *R (Mullen) v Secretary of State for the Home Deparment* [2004] UKHL 18 [2005] 1 AC 1, [47] (Lord Steyn regarding as 'relevant' the French text of Article 14(6), International Covenant on Civil and Political Rights, and as tending to 'reinforce the view at which I have arrived. In any event, the French dimension establishes state practice, which is relevant to treaty construction: article 31(3)(b) of the Vienna Convention on the Law of Treaties 1969 (Cmnd 4818).');
- *Agnew v Länsförsäkringsbolagens AB* [2001] 1 AC 223 (HL), 266E–F (Lord Millett, construing Article 5 of the Lugano Convention on Jurisdiction and the Enforcement of Judgments:

'"The place of performance of a contractual obligation" must surely mean the place where the contract stipulates that the obligation ought to be performed, not the place where it would have been performed in practice if it had been performed at all. This is reasonably clear in the English version of the Convention, but it is crystal clear in the German, French and Italian versions.');

- *R (McCann) v Manchester Crown Court* [2002] UKHL 39 [2003] 1 AC 787, [61] (Lord Hope, construing Article 6, ECHR: 'The words "criminal charge" themselves suggest that the proceedings which they have in mind are not just proceedings where a "charge" is made . . . This point emerges clearly from the French text of article 6(1), as Lord President Rodger pointed out in *S v Miller* 2001 SC 977, 988, para 21. It states that the matter which is to be determined must be either a dispute "sur ses droits et obligations de caractère civil" or an "accusation en matière pénale". The words "en matière pénale" indicate it is envisaged that there will be a penal element.');
- *R v Secretary of State for the Environment, Transport and the Regions, Ex parte Channel Tunnel Group Ltd and France Manche SA* [2001] EWCA Civ 1185, [44] (Peter Gibson LJ interpreting the English text of a Concession Agreement, giving effect to a Treaty entered into between the United Kingdom and France by using the 'equally authoritative' French text to reinforce the view he had formed of the English text), [57] (Laws LJ stating that the 'French texts offers significant support' for the favoured interpretation).

5.25.2. **Defining a non-English word or phrase in a treaty provision:**
Illustration:

- *R (European Roma Rights Centre) v Immigration Officer at Prague Airport* [2004] UKHL 55 [2005] 2 WLR 1, [69] (Lord Hope, consulting French dictionaries in construing 'refouler' in article 33 of the Refugee Convention).

5.26. **When considering the meaning of words in a language other than English, it is open to the court to use its own knowledge of the language and to refer to dictionaries, reference books, textbooks, and decided cases in construing both the English and non-English words. The court may also receive expert evidence on the possible meanings of the non-English language word.**

- *Fothergill v Monarch Airlines* [1981] AC 251 (HL), 293E–H (Lord Scarman: [§ **5.22**]), 273G–274A (Lord Wilberforce considering the means by which a foreign language should be considered: 'If a judge has some knowledge of the relevant language, there is no reason why he should not use it: this is particularly true of the French or Latin languages, so long languages of our courts. There is no reason why he should not consult a dictionary if the word is such that a dictionary can reveal its significance . . . [The parties] can supplement his resources with other material—other dictionaries, other books of reference, text-books and decided cases. They may call evidence of an interpreter, if the language is one unknown to the court, or of an expert if the word or expression is such as to require expert interpretation.');

- *James Buchanan & Co Ltd v Babco Forwarding & Shipping (UK) Ltd* [1978] AC 141 (HL), 152G–153C (Lord Wilberforce: 'I would not lay down rules as to the manner in which reference to the French text is to be made. It was complained—by reference to the use of the French text made [in the Court of Appeal]—that there was no evidence as to the meaning of the French text, and that the Lord Justices were not entitled to use their own knowledge of the language. There may certainly be cases when evidence is required to find the exact meaning of a word or phrase; there may be other cases when even an untutored eye can see the crucial point (cf. *Corocraft Ltd v Pan American Airways Inc.* [1969] QB 616 (insertion of "and" in the English text)). There may be cases again where a simple reference to a good dictionary will supply the key (see *per* Kerr J in *Fothergill v Monarch Airlines Ltd* [1978] QB 108, on "avarie"). In a case, such as I think the present is, when one is dealing with a nuanced expression, a dictionary will not assist and reference to an expert might also be unhelpful, for the expert would have to direct his evidence to a two-fold text situation rather than simply to the meaning of words in his own language, so that he would be in the same difficulty as the court. But I can see nothing illegitimate in the court looking at the two texts and reaching the conclusion that both are expressed in general or perhaps imprecise terms, so as to justify rejection of a narrow meaning.'), *cf* 158E–F (Viscount Dilhorne: 'I do not regard my knowledge of the nuances of the French language to be a reliable guide to the meaning to be given to these English words.').

6

The European Communities Act 1972: A Directly Incorporating Statute

(1) Introduction

6.1. **The European Communities Act 1972 is the premier example of a directly incorporating statute in domestic law. It incorporated the Community Treaties into domestic law and made binding principles in the judgments of the European Court of Justice ('ECJ') in domestic law. This is the largest single and most extraordinary incorporation of international law into domestic law. So effective has it been that Community law, which emanates from several European Community sources [§ 6.7], is now engrained as part of domestic law; to such an extent that it is almost artificial to analyse its use as one of international law. As Lord Denning MR noted, not long after the incorporation of Community law into domestic law:**

> '[T]he flowing tide of Community law is coming in fast. It has not stopped at high-water mark. It has broken the dykes and the banks. It has submerged the surrounding land. So much so that we have to learn to become amphibious if we wish to keep our heads above water.' (*Shields v Coomes* [1978] 1 WLR 1408 (CA), 1416B)

6.2. **This is not the place for detailed consideration of either Community law or the constitutional debates to which it has given rise. Rather, the overview given below concentrates on those parts** of Community law which distinguish the European Communities Act 1972 from other incorporating statutes, for example its constitutional impact (it is a 'constitutional statute' [§ 3.4]), and are relevant when considering the role of international law, especially unincorporated treaties, in domestic law.

6.3. The relationship between Community law and domestic law is important when analysing the role of unincorporated treaties in domestic law for two key reasons. First, the reception of Community law into domestic law challenges the traditional paradigm of parliamentary sovereignty. This is evident from the doctrine of the supremacy of Community law [§ 6.10], the direct effect of Community law [§§ 6.11–6.12] and the interpretative effect of Community law [§§ 6.13–6.16]. The dominant role of parliamentary sovereignty in the British constitution leads to its characterisation as a dualist system: one that considers international legal obligations, insofar as entered into by the executive, as separate from domestic law and unenforceable in domestic courts. Consequently, modifications of parliamentary sovereignty resulting from the European Communities Act 1972 may be relevant when considering the dualist rationale for the exclusion of unincorporated treaties from domestic law. Secondly, the reception of Community law into domestic law heralded the presence of an increasingly internationalist influence marked by the recognition of a supranational court as a source of binding legal principles. The spiralling use of unincorporated treaties and international instruments in domestic law tracks the same period as the domestic reception of Community law.

6.4. Thus, there are three key principles of Community law which are of especial significance in the present context, all of which are underpinned by the supremacy of Community law over domestic law: the direct effect of Community law (cf the principle of no direct effect of unincorporated treaties [§§ 8.8–8.9]), the interpretative effect (cf the interpretative command in section 3 of the Human Rights Act 1998 ('HRA') [§§ 7.9–7.10] and the rules of construction regarding unincorporated treaties, legislation [chapter 9] and the common law [chapter 10]) and effective protection of Community law [§ 6.17] (cf the general role of unincorporated treaties in domestic law). Community law has also had a wider impact on domestic law [§§ 6.18–6.20]. For example, principles of Community law have influenced the common law and sources of

law used by the ECJ have been influential in guiding domestic courts.

6.5. Reading:

- Anderson and Demetriou, *References to the European Court* (2002)
- Brealey and Hoskins, *Remedies in EC Law* (1998)
- Craig and De Burca, *EU Law: Text, Cases and Materials* (2002)

6.6. The key provisions of the European Communities Act 1972 are:

- Section 1(2): defining 'the Communities' and the 'the Community Treaties'.
- Section 2: '(1) All such rights, powers, liabilities, obligations and restrictions from time to time created or arising by or under the Treaties, and all such remedies and procedures from time to time provided for by or under the Treaties, as in accordance with the Treaties are without further enactment to be given legal effect or used in the United Kingdom shall be recognised and available in law, and be enforced, allowed and followed accordingly; and the expression "enforceable Community right" and similar expressions shall be read as referring to one which this subsection applies. (2) Subject to Schedule 2 to this Act, at any time after its passing Her Majesty may by Order in Council, and any designated minister or department may by regulations, make provision—(a) for the purpose of implementing any Community obligation of the United Kingdom, or of enabling any such obligation to be implemented, or of enabling any rights enjoyed or to be enjoyed by the United Kingdom under or by virtue of the Treaties to be exercised; or (b) for the purpose of dealing with matters arising out of or related to any such obligation or rights or the coming into force, or the operation from time to time, of subsection (1) above; and in the exercise of any statutory power or duty, including any power to give directions or to legislate by means of orders, rules, regulations or other subordinate instrument, the person entrusted with the power or duty may have regard to the objects of the Communities and to any such obligation or rights as aforesaid . . . (4) The provision that may be made under subsection (2) above includes, subject to Schedule 2 to this Act, any such provision (of any such extent) as might be made by Act of Parliament, and any enactment passed or to be passed, other than one contained in this Part of this Act, shall be construed and have effect subject to the foregoing provisions of this section; but, except as may be provided by any Act passed after this Act, Schedule 2 shall have effect in connection with the powers conferred by this and the following sections of this Act to make Orders in Council and regulations.'

- Section 3: '(1) For the purposes of all legal proceedings any questions as to the meaning or effect of any of the Treaties, or as to the validity, meaning or effect of any Community instrument, shall be treated as a question of law (and, if not referred to the European Court, be for determination as such in accordance with the principles laid down by and any relevant decision of the European Court or any court attached thereto. (2) Judicial notice shall be taken of the Treaties, of the Official Journal of the Communities and of any decision of, or expression of opinion by, the European Court or any court attached thereto on any such question as aforesaid; and the Official Journal shall be admissible as evidence of any instrument or other act thereby communicated of any of the Communities or of any Community institution.'
- Schedule 2: makes provisions for subordinate legislation under section 2(2).

6.7. **Community law is derived from several sources. Of particular interest in the present context are international agreements—those concluded between the Community and other states or international organisations. The provisions of such international agreements are capable of direct effect and therefore provide a source of rights upon which individuals may rely in domestic courts. Furthermore, where the EU is a party to an international agreement or treaty, the treaty may be given effect in Community law, for example by way of regulations or directives and thus become part of domestic law.**

6.7.1. **Treaties [§ 4.3.4]:**

- Treaty Establishing the European Community (Consolidated Version) [2002] OJ C325 ('EC Treaty').

6.7.2. **Regulations:**

- Article 249, EC Treaty: 'A regulation shall have general application. It shall be binding in its entirety and directly applicable in all Member States.'

6.7.3. **Directives:**

- Article 249, EC Treaty: 'A directive shall be binding, as to the result to be achieved, upon each Member State to which it is addressed, but shall leave to the national authorities the choice of form and methods.'

6.7.4. **Decisions:**

- Article 249, EC Treaty: 'A decision shall be binding in its entirety upon those to whom it is addressed.'

6.7.5. **International agreements [§ 4.3.4]:**

- Article 281, EC Treaty: 'The Community shall have legal personality.'
- Article 300, EC Treaty: '(1) Where this Treaty provides for the conclusion of Agreements between the Community and one or more states or international organisations, the Commission shall make recommendations to the Council, which shall authorise the Commission to open the necessary negotiations. The Commission shall conduct these negotiations in consultation with special committees appointed by the Council to assist it in this task and within the framework of such directives as the Council may issue to it . . . (3) The Council shall conclude agreements after consulting the European Parliament . . . (6) The European Parliament, the Council, the Commission or a Member State may obtain the opinion of the Court of Justice as to whether an agreement envisaged is compatible with the provisions of this Treaty . . . (7) Agreements concluded under the conditions set out in this Article shall be binding on the institutions of the Community and on Member States.'
- *Biret International SA v Council of the EU* Case C-93/02 P [2003] ECR I-10497, [32] (ECJ, citing from the judgment of the Court of First Instance (Case T-174/00 [2002] ECR II-17, [60]): '[T]he effects of [agreements concluded between the Community and a non-member state] must be determined in the light of the nature and purpose of the agreement in question. Thus in Case 104/81 *Kupferberg* [1982] ECR 3641, paragraph 17, the Court held that the effects within the Community of the provisions of an international agreement may not be determined without taking account of the international origins of the provisions in question and that in conformity with the principles of international law the contracting parties are free to agree what effect the provisions are to have in their internal legal order (see also Opinion of Advocate General Gulmann in Case C-280/93 *Germany v Council* [1994] ECR I-4973, at I-4980, paragraph 27).');
- *Demirel v Stadt Schwäbisch Gmünd* Case 12/86 [1987] ECR 3719, [7] (ECJ, commenting on the EEC-Turkey Association Agreement: '[A]s from its entry into force, the provisions of such an [international] agreement form an integral part of the Community legal system; within the framework of that system the Court has jurisdiction to give preliminary rulings concerning the interpretation of such an agreement.').

6.7.6. **International agreements given effect in Community law:**
Illustrations:

- Regulation (EC) No 343/2003 implementing the Convention Determining the State Responsible for Examining Applications for Asylum Lodged in one of the Member States of the European

Communities ('the Dublin Convention'). See, for example, *Omar v Secretary of State for the Home Department* [2005] EWCA Civ 285, [11] (Sir Swinton Thomas: 'It was and is common ground between the parties that until the coming into force of Council Regulation (EC) No.343/2003 of 18th February 2003 the Dublin Convention had not been incorporated into domestic law.').

- Regulation (EC) Nos 338/97 and 1808/01 implementing the Convention on International Trade in Endangered Species and Wild Flora and Fauna (given supplementary domestic effect by the Control of Trade in Endangered Species (Enforcement) Regulations 1997). See, for example, *R (Greenpeace Ltd) v Secretary of State for the Environment, Food and Rural Affairs* [2002] EWCA Civ 1036 [2002] 1 WLR 3304 (interpreting Regulation No. 338/97, Article 4(3)(a) by reference to the Convention on International Trade in Endangered Species of Wild Flora and Fauna);
- Directives 79/409/EEC (the Birds Directive) and 92/43/EEC (the Species and Habitats Directive) implementing the Convention on the Conservation of European Wildlife and Natural Habitats.

6.7.7. **Case law of the ECJ (including general principles of law, for example, proportionality [§ 6.19], legitimate expectation, fundamental rights [§ 6.20.2], non-discrimination etc):**

- Section 3, European Communities Act 1972: [§ **6.6**]
- Section 3, Civil Jurisdiction and Judgments Act 1982: '(1) Any question as to the meaning or effect of any provision of the Brussels Convention shall, if not referred to the European Court in accordance with the 1971 Protocol, be determined in accordance with the principles laid down by and any relevant decision of the European Court. (2) Judicial notice shall be taken of any decision of, or expression of opinion by, the European Court on any such question.'
- Section 3, Contracts (Applicable Law) Act 1990: '(1) Any question as to the meaning or effect of any provision of the Conventions [the Rome Convention on the Law Applicable to Contractual Obligations and related Conventions] shall, if not referred to the European Court in accordance with the Brussels Protocol, be determined in accordance with the principles laid down by, and any relevant decision of, the European Court. (2) Judicial notice shall be taken of any decision of, or expression of opinion by, the European Court on any such question.'

6.8. **Under section 3 of the European Communities Act 1972, any question as to the meaning or effect of Community law, as defined in section 3(1), must be determined in accordance with the principles laid down by the ECJ. The ECJ is also the authoritative source of**

guidance on the interpretation and effect of the Brussels Convention on Jurisdiction and the Enforcement of Judgments [§ 1.129] and the Rome Convention on the Law Applicable to Contractual Obligations [§ 1.32] (and related Conventions): [§ 6.7.7]. Additionally, questions of Community law may be referred to the ECJ by domestic courts under Article 234, EC Treaty. Initially the threshold considerations for making a reference were widely framed. These encouraged the making of a reference unless the domestic court could, with 'complete confidence resolve the issue itself'. Since then greater restraint, prompted by concerns about the ECJ's expanding case law, has been counselled.

6.8.1. **Preliminary rulings under the EC Treaty:**

- Article 234, EC Treaty: 'The Court of Justice shall have jurisdiction to give preliminary rulings concerning: (a) the interpretation of this Treaty; (b) the validity and interpretation of acts of the institutions of the Community and of the ECB; (c) the interpretation of the statutes of bodies established by an act of the Council, where those statutes so provide. Where such question is raised before any court or tribunal of a Member State, that court or tribunal may, if it considers that a decision on the question is necessary to enable it to give judgment, request the Court of Justice to give a ruling thereon. Where any such question is raised in a case pending before a court or tribunal of a Member State, against whose decisions there is no judicial remedy under national law, that court or tribunal shall bring the matter before the Court of Justice.'

6.8.2. **The criteria for making a reference: the encouraging approach:**

- *R v Stock Exchange, Ex parte Else Ltd* [1993] QB 534 (CA), 545E–F (Sir Thomas Bingham MR: 'I understand the correct approach in principle of a national court (other than a final court of appeal) to be quite clear: if the facts have been found and the Community law issue is critical to the court's final decision, the appropriate course is ordinarily to refer the issue to the Court of Justice unless the national court can with complete confidence resolve the issue itself. In considering whether it can with complete confidence resolve the issue itself the national court must be fully mindful of the differences between national and Community legislation, of the pitfalls which face a national court venturing into what may be an unfamiliar field, of the need for uniform interpretation throughout the Community and of the great advantages enjoyed by the Court of Justice in construing Community instruments. If the national court has any real doubt, it should ordinarily refer.');

- *R v Secretary of State for Defence, Ex parte Perkins* [1997] IRLR 297, [18] (Lightman J: 'The national court should only refuse a reference if the answer to the question of construction is so obvious as to leave no scope for reasonable doubt and should hesitate long before holding that there can be no reasonable doubt about the correct answer: see *BLP Group v CEC* [1994] STC 41 at 48 (CA) and *Conoco v CEC* [1995] STC 1022 at 1033.');
- *R v Secretary of State for the Home Department, Ex parte Hoverspeed* [1999] EuLR 595 (DC), 614G–H (Simon Brown LJ: 'I do feel that necessary degree of confidence which would justify our refusal to make a reference to the ECJ. Questions of public policy, justification, proportionality and necessity are largely dependent upon review and assessment of the relevant facts and are pre-eminently, therefore, questions for adjudication by the national courts. I cannot think that in these regards we need general guidance of the sort provided by the court.').

6.8.3. **The criteria for making a reference: the restraining approach:**

- *Wiener SI GmbH v Hauptzollamt Emmerich* Case C-338/95 [1997] ECR I-6495, [18] (Advocate General Jacobs after considering the difficulties imposed on the ECJ by increasing references for preliminary rulings: 'It seems to me that the only appropriate solution is a greater measure of self-restraint on the part of both national courts and this Court'. At [21]: 'In some areas of Community law, where there is already an established body of case-law, increasing refinement of the case-law is likely to lead to less legal certainty rather than to more.' At [60–61]: 'Community legislation has recently extended to many new fields; and the volume of legislation has greatly increased. Excessive resort to preliminary rulings seems therefore increasingly likely to prejudice the quality, the coherence, and even the accessibility, of the case-law, and may therefore be counter-productive to the ultimate aim of ensuring the uniform application of the law throughout the European Union . . . Experience has shown that [the ECJ's] case-law now provides sufficient guidance to enable national courts and tribunals . . . to decide many cases for themselves without the need for a reference.');
- *Trinity Mirror plc v Commissioners of Customs and Excise* [2001] EWCA Civ 65 [2001] 2 CMLR 33, [51–54] (Chadwick LJ citing *Else* [§ **6.8.2**], at [51]; considering it 'important to have in mind' the observations of Advocate General Jacobs in *Wiener* (see above), at [52–53], and concluding that there was no need for a reference to enable the court to give judgment, at [54]);
- *Professional Contractors Group v Commissioners of Inland Revenue* [2001] EWCA Civ 1945 (2002) STC 165, [91] (Robert Walker LJ: 'The principles stated by Sir Thomas Bingham MR in [*Else* at [§ **6.8.2**]] still hold good. But in applying them the court must also take account of the guidance given by the court (fol-

lowing European authority) in *Trinity Mirror* . . . [see above] The latter case has drawn attention both to the very heavy caseload of the Court of Justice and also to the greater familiarity with Community law which domestic courts now have. In this case as in many others, the real difficulty is not in ascertaining the relevant principles of Community law but in applying them to the facts; and that is a task for the national court.').

6.9. **Article 307 of the EC Treaty makes clear that it does not affect the duties of Member States owed to third countries under agreements preceding the EC Treaty. However, it makes equally clear the obligation on Member States, as a matter of Community law, to eliminate discrepancies between a pre-Community agreement and the EC Treaty.**

- Article 307, EC Treaty: 'The rights and obligations arising from agreements concluded before 1 January 1958 or, for acceding States, before the date of their accession, between one or more Member States on the one hand, and one or more third countries on the other, shall not be affected by the provisions of this Treaty. To the extent that such agreements are not compatible with this Treaty, the Member State or States concerned shall take all appropriate steps to eliminate the incompatibilities established. Member States shall, where necessary, assist each other to this end and shall, where appropriate, adopt a common attitude. In applying the agreements referred to in the first paragraph, Member States shall take into account the fact that the advantages accorded under this Treaty by each Member State form an integral part of the establishment of the Community and are thereby inseparably linked with the creation of common institutions, the conferring of powers upon them and the granting of the same advantages by all the other Member States.'
- *Advocate-General v Burgoa* Case 812/79 [1980] ECR 2787, [6] (ECJ considering that Article 234 (now Article 307) is of general scope and applies to any international agreement which is capable of affecting the application of the EC Treaty, irrespective of the subject-matter of the agreement);
- *T. Port GmbH & Co. KG v Council of the EU* Case T-2/99 [2001] ECR II-2093, [77] (Court of First Instance: '[F]or a Community provision to be deprived of effect as a result of an international agreement, two conditions must be fulfilled: the agreement must have been concluded before the entry into force of the EC Treaty and the third country concerned must derive from it rights which it can require the Member State concerned to respect.') (Appeal by T. Port to ECJ is at [2003] ECR I-4261 (dismissed));

- *Commission v Portuguese Republic* Case C-62/98 [2000] ECR I-5171, [49] (ECJ: '[A]lthough [under Article 307] . . . the Member States have a choice as to the appropriate steps to be taken, they are nevertheless under an obligation to eliminate any incompatibilities existing between a pre-Community convention and the EC Treaty. If a Member State encounters difficulties which make adjustment of an agreement impossible, an obligation to denounce that agreement cannot be excluded.' At [50] considering that Article 307 reflects a balance between the 'foreign-policy interests' and 'Community interests' of Member States. ECJ concluding that by failing to denounce or adjust the agreements concerning merchant shipping between the Portuguese Republic and non-EC Member States so as to provide for fair, free and non-discriminatory access by all Community nationals to cargo share due to the Portuguese Republic, as required by Council Regulation No 4055/86, the Portuguese Republic had failed to fulfil its obligations thereunder, at [52].);
- *Elide Gottardo v Istituto nazionale della previdenza sociale (INPS)* Case C-55/00 [2002] ECR I-413, [33] (ECJ: '[W]hen giving effect to commitments assumed under international agreements, be it an agreement between Member States or an agreement between a Member State and one or more non-member countries, Member States are required, subject to the provisions of Article 307 EC, to comply with the obligations that Community law imposes on them. The fact that non-member countries, for their part, are not obliged to comply with any Community-law obligation is of no relevance in this respect.');
- *Commission v Luxembourg* Case C-473/93 [1996] ECR I-3207, [40] (ECJ: '[I]t is settled case-law that, whilst the first paragraph of Article 234 [now Article 307] of the Treaty allows Member States to honour obligations owed to non-Member States under international agreements preceding the Treaty, it does not authorise them to exercise rights under such agreements in intra-Community relations.').

(2) Supremacy of Community Law

6.10. **The doctrine of the supremacy of Community law over domestic law has been developed by the ECJ. It is not based on a specific provision of the EC Treaty. Rather it is based on the unique nature of the Treaty: as having created a supranational legal order applying directly to Member States and to the individual citizens of those states. The supremacy of Community law means that it cannot be**

overridden by domestic law and that it prevails over any domestic laws inconsistent with it (even where these are embodied in primary legislation). Within the British constitution, the traditional, but by no means universally accepted, analysis is that the supremacy of Community law is a political construct rather a constitutional one. Thus, the European Communities Act 1972 is viewed as making Community law superior to the generality of domestic law but without detracting from the sovereignty of Parliament.

6.10.1. Community law is supreme over the domestic laws of Member States:

- *NV Algemene Transporten Expeditie Onderneming van Gend en Loos v Nederlandse Administratie der Belastingen* Case 26/62 [1963] ECR 1, 12 (ECJ: 'The objective of the EEC Treaty, which is to establish a Common Market, the functioning of which is of direct concern to interested parties in the Community, implies that this Treaty is more than an agreement which merely creates mutual obligations between the contracting states. This view is confirmed by the preamble to the Treaty which refers not only to governments but to peoples. It is also confirmed more specifically by the establishment of institutions endowed with sovereign rights, the exercise of which affects Member States and also their citizens. Furthermore, it must be noted that the nationals of the states brought together in the Community are called upon to cooperate in the functioning of the Community through the intermediary of the European Parliament and the Economic and Social Committee . . . The conclusion to be drawn from this is that the Community constitutes a new legal order of international law for the benefit of which the states have limited their sovereign rights, albeit within limited fields, and the subjects of which comprise not only Member States but also their nationals. Independently of the legislation of Member States, Community law therefore not only imposes obligations on individuals but is also intended to confer upon them rights which become part of their legal heritage. These rights arise not only where they are expressly granted by the Treaty, but also by reason of obligations which the Treaty imposes in a clearly defined way upon individuals as well as upon the Member States and upon the institutions of the Community.');
- *Flaminio Costa v ENEL* Case 6/64 [1964] ECR 585, 593 (ECJ: 'By contrast with ordinary international treaties, the EEC Treaty has created its own legal system which, on the entry into force of the Treaty, became an integral part of the legal systems of the Member States and which their courts are bound to apply. By creating a Community of unlimited duration, having its own institutions, its own personality, its own legal capacity and

capacity of representation on the international plane and, more particularly, real powers stemming from a limitation of sovereignty or a transfer of powers from the States to the Community, the Member States have limited their sovereign rights and have thus created a body of law which binds both their nationals and themselves.').

6.10.2. **Community law prevails over any inconsistent domestic law:**

- *A v Chief Constable of West Yorkshire (No 2)*[2004] UKHL 21 [2004] 2 WLR 1209, [9] (Lord Bingham: 'It is, of course, well established that the law of the Community prevails over any provision of domestic law inconsistent with it.');
- *Flaminio Costa v ENEL* Case 6/64 [1964] ECR 585, 593–594 (ECJ: 'The integration into the laws of each Member State of provisions which derive from the Community and more generally the terms and the spirit of the Treaty, make it impossible for the states, as a corollary, to accord precedence to a unilateral and subsequent measure over a legal system accepted by them on a basis of reciprocity. Such a measure cannot therefore be inconsistent with that legal system.').

6.10.3. **Community law cannot be overridden by domestic law:**

- *Flaminio Costa v ENEL* Case 6/64 [1964] ECR 585, 594 (ECJ: '[T]he law stemming from the Treaty, an independent source of law, could not, because of its special and original nature, be overridden by domestic legal provisions, however framed, without being deprived of its character as Community law and without the legal basis of the Community itself being called into question. The transfer by the states from their domestic legal system to the Community legal system of the rights and obligations arising under the Treaty carries with it a permanent limitation of their sovereign rights, against which a subsequent unilateral act incompatible with the concept of Community cannot prevail.');
- *Internationale Handelsgesellschaft mbH v Einfuhr- und Vorratsstelle für Getreide und Futtermittel* Case 11/70 [1970] ECR 1125, [3] (ECJ: 'Recourse to the legal rules or concepts of national law in order to judge the validity of measures adopted by the institutions of the Community would have an adverse effect on the uniformity and efficacy of Community law. The validity of such measures can only be judged in the light of Community law. In fact, the law stemming from the Treaty, an independent source of law, cannot because of its very nature be overridden by rules of national law, however framed, without being deprived of its character as Community law and without the legal basis of the Community itself being called into question. Therefore the validity of a Community measure or its effect within a Member State cannot be affected by allegations that it

runs counter to either fundamental rights as formulated by the constitution of that State or the principles of a national constitutional structure.').

6.10.4. **Traditional British constitutional theory describes Community law as supreme because it has been given that status by the European Communities Act 1972:**

- *R v Secretary of State for Transport, Ex parte Factortame (No 2)* [1991] 1 AC 603 (ECJ and HL), 659A–659C (Lord Bridge, post-ECJ reference judgment: '[W]hatever limitation of its sovereignty Parliament accepted when it enacted the European Communities Act 1972 was entirely voluntary. Under the terms of the Act of 1972 it has always been clear that it was the duty of a United Kingdom court, when delivering final judgment, to override any rule of national law found to be in conflict with any directly enforceable rule of Community law. Similarly, when decisions of the European Court of Justice have exposed areas of United Kingdom statute law which failed to implement Council directives, Parliament has always loyally accepted the obligation to make appropriate and prompt amendments. Thus there is nothing in any way novel in according supremacy to rules of Community law in those areas to which they apply and to insist that, in the protection of rights under Community law, national courts must not be inhibited by rules of national law from granting interim relief in appropriate cases is no more than a logical recognition of the supremacy.');
- *Thoburn v Sunderland City Council* [2002] EWHC 195 (Admin) [2003] QB 151, [69] (Laws LJ analysing the relationship between domestic and Community law: '(1) All the specific rights and obligations which EU law creates are by the 1972 Act incorporated into our domestic law and rank supreme: that is, anything in our substantive law inconsistent with any of these rights and obligations is abrogated or must be modified to avoid the inconsistency. This is true even where the inconsistent municipal provision is contained in primary legislation. (2) The 1972 Act is a constitutional statute . . . (3) The truth of (2) is derived, not from EU law, but purely from the law of England: the common law recognises a category of constitutional statutes. (4) The fundamental legal basis of the United Kingdom's relationship with the EU rests with the domestic, not the European, legal powers.' See also [58–59] rejecting the submission that the law of the EU entrenched its own supremacy and that the supremacy is part of British constitutional law.);
- *MacCarthys Ltd v Smith* [1979] ICR 785 (CA), 789E–F (Lord Denning MR (dissenting): 'If the time should come when our Parliament deliberately passes an Act—with the intention of repudiating the [EC] Treaty or any provision in it—and says so in express terms – then I should have thought that it would be

the duty of our courts to follow the statute of our Parliament . . . I do not however envisage any such situation.').

Illustration:

- *R v Secretary of State for Employment, Ex parte EOC* [1995] 1 AC 1 (HL), 27F–H (Lord Keith, considering whether judicial review was available for the purpose of securing a declaration that primary legislation was incompatible with European Community law: 'The *Factortame* case [see above] is thus a precedent in favour of the EOC's recourse to judicial review for the purpose of challenging as incompatible with European Community law the relevant provisions of the [Employment Protection (Consolidation) Act 1978]. . . This does not involve, as contended for the Secretary of State, any attempt by the EOC to enforce the international treaty obligations of the United Kingdom. The EOC is concerned simply to obtain a ruling which reflects the primacy of European Community law enshrined in section 2 of the [European Communities Act 1972] and determines whether the relevant United Kingdom law is compatible with the Equal Pay Directive and the Equal Treatment Directive.').

(3) Direct Effect of Community Law

6.11. **The direct effect of Community law into domestic law is achieved by section 2(1) of the European Communities Act 1972 [§ 6.6]. This is unlike other examples of provisions of incorporating statutes [chapter 3]. Here the international law being incorporated is not defined, as is generally the case, by reference to all or part of one treaty or a collection of treaties. Instead, the incorporation is ongoing and indefinite, referring to 'powers, liabilities, obligations and restrictions from time to time created by or arising by or under the Treaties, and all such remedies and procedures from time to time provided for by or under the Treaties'.**

6.12. **Where provisions of Community law have direct effect (or are 'directly applicable') they provide a direct source of rights for individuals before domestic courts which can be maintained against the state and emanations of the state ('vertical effect') or sometimes against other individuals ('horizontal effect'). Provisions of directives are only capable of vertical direct effect. Of the sources of Community law, only regulations are expressly endowed in the EC Treaty with direct effect. This concept, a fundamental principle of Community law, has been developed by the ECJ and applied to**

Treaty provisions, decisions, international agreements and directives. Provisions of these sources of Community law may have direct effect where they are clear, precise, negative, unconditional and do not require further implementing measures.

6.12.1. **Unique status of EC Treaty as foundation for direct effect:**

- *NV Algemene Transporten Expeditie Onderneming van Gend en Loos v Nederlandse Administratie der Belastingen* Case 26/62 [1963] ECR 1, 12 (ECJ, explaining the unique status of the EC Treaty and its creation of a new supranational order: 'Community law therefore not only imposes obligations on individuals but is also intended to confer upon them rights which become part of their legal heritage. These rights arise not only where they are expressly granted by the Treaty, but also by reason of obligations which the Treaty imposes in a clearly defined way upon individuals as well as upon Member States and upon the institutions of the Community.'). [§ **6.10.1**].

6.12.2. **Direct effect is a fundamental principle of Community law:**

- *R v Chief Constable of Sussex, Ex parte International Trader's Ferry Ltd* [1999] 2 AC 418 (HL), 446B (Lord Hoffmann: 'The concept of direct effect . . . is a fundamental principle of Community law.').

6.12.3. **Direct effect as part of domestic law:**

- Section 2(1), European Communities Act 1972: [§ **6.6**]
- *Shields v Coomes* [1978] 1 WLR 1408 (CA), 1414F (Lord Denning MR considering the meaning of 'directly applicable' provisions of Community law: 'This means that any citizen in a member state can bring proceedings in his own national courts to enforce the rights and obligations contained in this or that article of the [EEC] Treaty. He need not wait for his own Parliament to legislate. He can require his own courts to enforce his Treaty rights.');
- *R v Secretary of State for Transport, Ex parte Factortame* [1990] 2 AC 85 (HL), 140B–C (Lord Bridge: 'By virtue of section 2(4) of the [European Communities Act 1972] Part II of the [Merchant Shipping Act 1988] is to be construed and take effect subject to directly enforceable Community rights and those rights are, by section 2(1) of the Act of 1972, to be "recognised and available in law, and . . . enforced, allowed and followed accordingly;" . . . This has precisely the same effect as if a section were incorporated in Part II of the Act of 1988 which in terms enacted that the provisions with respect to registration of British fishing vessels were to be without prejudice to the directly enforceable Community rights of nationals of any member state of the EEC.');

- *Imperial Chemical Industries plc v Colmer (Inspector of Taxes) (No 2)* [1999] 1 WLR 2035 (HL), 2041C–F (Lord Nolan after quoting Lord Bridge in *Factortame* at 140 (see above): 'So, in the present case, the effect of section 2 of the [European Communities Act 1972] is the same as if a subsection were incorporated in section 258 of the [Income and Corporation Taxes Act 1970] which in terms enacted that the definition of "holding company" was to be without prejudice to the directly enforceable Community rights of companies established in the Community.').

6.12.4. **Consequences of direct effect:**

- *Amministrazione delle Finanze dello Stato v Simmenthal SpA* Case 106/77 [1978] ECR 629, [14–15] (ECJ: 'Direct applicability . . . means that rules of Community law must be fully and uniformly applied in all the Member States from the date of their entry into force and for so long as they continue in force. These provisions [which are directly applicable] are therefore a direct source of rights and duties for all those affected thereby, whether Member States or individuals, who are parties to legal relationships under Community law.' At [17]: 'Furthermore, in accordance with the principle of the precedence of Community law, the relationship between provisions of the Treaty and directly applicable measures of the institutions on the one hand and the national law of the Member States on the other is such that those provisions and measures not only by their entry into force render automatically inapplicable any conflicting provision of current national law but—in so far as they are an integral part of, and take precedence in, the legal order applicable in the territory of each of the Member States—also preclude the valid adoption of new national legislative measures to the extent to which they would be incompatible with Community provisions.').

Illustration:

- *Garden Cottage Foods Ltd v Milk Marketing Board* [1984] AC 130 (HL), 141C–D (Lord Diplock: '[Article 86] of the Treaty of Rome (the EEC Treaty) [now Article 82] was held by the European Court of Justice in *Belgische Radio en Televisie v SV SABAM* (Case 127/73) [1974] 1 ECR 51, 62, to produce direct effects in relations between individuals and to create direct rights in respect of the individuals concerned which the national courts must protect. This decision by the European Court of Justice as to the effect of article 86 is one which section 3(1) of the European Communities Act 1972 requires your Lordships to follow. The rights which the article confers upon citizens in the United Kingdom accordingly fall within section 2(1) of the Act. They are without further enactment to be given legal effect in the United Kingdom and enforced accordingly.').

6.12.5. **Key requirements for direct effect:**

- *NV Algemene Transporten Expeditie Onderneming van Gend en Loos v Nederlandse Administratie der Belastingen* Case 26/62 [1963] ECR 1, 13 (ECJ, construing Article 12 [now Article 25] of the EEC Treaty: 'The wording of Article 12 contains a clear and unconditional prohibition which is not a positive but a negative obligation. This obligation, moreover, is not qualified by any reservation on the part of states which would make its implementation conditional upon a positive legislative measure enacted under national law. The very nature of this prohibition makes it ideally adapted to produce direct effects in the legal relationship between Member States and their subjects. The implementation of Article 12 does not require any legislative intervention on the part of the states. The fact that under this Article it is the Member States who are made the subject of the negative obligation does not imply that their nationals cannot benefit from this obligation.');
- *R v Chief Constable of Sussex, Ex parte International Trader's Ferry Ltd* [1999] 2 AC 418 (HL), 446B–C (Lord Hoffmann: 'ITF are able to assert a Community right only if the article or articles which it alleges to have been infringed have *direct effect*, that is to say, they give rise to rights which are directly enforceable by citizens of member states against the state or against other citizens . . . Not all the provisions of the Treaty or subordinate legislation confer rights upon private persons such as ITF. Many will operate only at the level of international law, enforceable only by member states against each other or by the Commission in proceedings under article 169 [now Article 21].').

6.12.6. **Direct effect (except regarding directives) may be both horizontal and vertical:**

Illustrations:

- *Defrenne v Sabena* Case 43/75 [1976] ECR 455, [39] (ECJ: 'In fact, since Article 119 [now Article 141] is mandatory in nature, the prohibition on discrimination between men and women applies not only to the action of public authorities [vertical effect] but also extends to all agreements which are intended to regulate paid labour collectively, as well as to contracts between individuals [horizontal effect].');
- *Courage Ltd v Crehan* Case C-453/99 [2002] QB 507 (ECJ), [23] (Articles 85(1) and 86 (now Articles 81 and 82) produce direct effects in relations between two individuals).

6.12.7. **Regulations as directly applicable:**

- Article 249, EC Treaty [§ **6.7.2**]

Illustrations:

- *Commission v Italy* Case 39/72 [1973] ECR 101, [17] (ECJ considering the Italian Republic's failure properly to implement regulations relating to a system of premiums for slaughtering cows and for withholding milk and milk products from the market: 'According to the terms of Articles 189 and 191 of the Treaty [now Articles 249 and 254], Regulations are as such directly applicable in all Member States and come into force solely by virtue of their publication in the *Official Journal* of the Communities, as from the date specified in them, or in the absence thereof, as from the date provided in the Treaty. Consequently, all measures of implementation are contrary to the Treaty which would have the result of creating an obstacle to the direct effect of Community Regulations and of jeopardising their simultaneous and uniform application in the whole of the Community.' At [20]: 'Under the terms of Article 189 [now Article 249], the Regulation is binding "in its entirety" for Member States. In consequence it cannot be accepted that a Member State should apply in an incomplete or selective manner provisions of a Community Regulation so as to render abortive certain aspects of Community legislation which it has opposed or which it considers to be contrary to its national interests.');

- *In re G (Children) (Foreign Contact Order: Enforcement)* [2003] EWCA Civ 1607 [2004] 1 WLR 521, [34] (Thorpe LJ in proceedings concerning the European Convention on Recognition and Enforcement of Decisions Concerning Custody of Children noting that Article 37 of Brussels II (Council Regulation (EC) No. 1347/2000 on Jurisdiction and the Recognition and Enforcement of Judgments in Matrimonial Matters and in Matters of Parental Responsibility for Children of Both Spouses enforced on 1 March 2001) provides that: 'In relations between member states, this Regulation shall take precedence over the following Conventions . . . [including the European Convention].').

6.12.8. **Direct effect of Treaty provisions:**
Illustrations:

- *Flaminio Costa v ENEL* Case 6/64 [1964] ECR 585 (considering the direct effect of Article 37(2) (now Article 31(2)));
- *Defrenne v Société Anonyme Belge de Navigation Aérienne* Case 43/75 [1976] ER 455, [24] (considering the direct effect of Article 119 (now Article 141));
- *Zaera v Institutio Nacionale de la Seguridad Social* Case 126/86 [1987] ECR 3697, [18] (Article 2, addressing the promotion of an accelerated standard of living, does not have direct effect);
- *R v Human Fertilisation and Embryology Authority, Ex parte Blood* [1999] Fam 151 (CA) (considering the directly enforceable rights conferred by Articles 59 and 60 of the EC Treaty (now Articles 49 and 50) regarding medical treatment in another Member State);
- *Fitzgerald v Williams* [1996] QB 657 (CA), 674D (Sir Thomas Bingham MR following *Mund & Fester v Hatrex International*

Transport Case C-398/92 [1994] ECR I-467 by finding that Articles 6 and 220 of the EC Treaty (now Articles 12 and 293) confer directly enforceable rights in Member States following legislative implementation of the Convention).

6.12.9. **Direct effect of decisions:**

- *Franz Grad v Finanzamt Traunstein* Case 9/70 [1970] ECR 825, [5] (ECJ: 'It would be incompatible with the binding effect attributed to decisions by Article 189 [now Article 249] to exclude in principle the possibility that persons affected may invoke the obligations imposed by a decision, particularly in cases, where, for example, the community authorities by means of a decision have imposed an obligation on a Member State or all the Member States to act in a certain way, the effectiveness (*"l'effect utile")* of such a measure would be weakened if the nationals of that State could not invoke it in the courts and the national courts could not take it into consideration as part of Community law. Although the effects of a decision may not be identical with those of a provision contained in a regulation, this difference does not exclude the possibility that the end result, namely the right of the individual to invoke the measure before the courts, may be the same as that of a directly applicable provision of a regulation.').

6.12.10. **Direct effect of international agreements:**

- For direct effect of International Agreements given effect by Regulations or Directives, see [§ **6.7.6**];
- *Biret International SA v Council of the EU* Case C-93/02 P [2003] ECR I-10497 [32] (ECJ, citing from the judgment of the Court of First Instance (Case T-174/00 [2002] ECR II-17, [60]): 'In particular, in *Demirel* [Case 12/86 [1987] ECR 3719], the Court held, at paragraph 14 that a provision in an agreement concluded by the Community with non-member countries must be regarded as being directly applicable when, regard being had to its terms and the purpose and nature of the agreement itself, the provision contains a clear and precise obligation which is not subject, as regards its implementation or effects, to the adoption of any subsequent measure. The question whether such a stipulation is unconditional and sufficiently precise to have direct effect must be considered in the context of the agreement of which it forms part.');
- *Hauptzollant Mainz v Kupferberg* Case 104/81 [1982] ECR 3641, [17–27] (Article 21(1) of a free trade agreement between the EC and Portugal was sufficiently precise and unconditional to be directly effective. The ECJ noted the ability of the EC to make agreements with non-member countries and international organisations and that such agreements (under Article 228(2)) (now Article 300) are binding on Community institutions and Member States: [11]. The court explained that whether such

agreements have direct effect will depend on the facts of the particular case: [23]. At [17]: 'It is true that the effects within the Community of provisions of an agreement concluded by the Community with a non-member country may not be determined without taking account of the international origin of the provisions in question. In conformity with the principles of public international law Community institutions which have power to negotiate and conclude an agreement with a non-member country are free to agree with that country what effect the provisions of the agreement are to have in the international legal order of the contracting parties. Only if that question has not been settled by the agreement does it fall for decision by the courts having jurisdiction in the matter, and in particular by the Court of Justice within the framework of its jurisdiction under the Treaty, in the same manner as any question of interpretation relating to the application of the agreement in the Community.');

- *Amministrazione delle Finanze Stato v Chiquita Italia* Case C-469/93 [1995] ECR I-4533, [31–35] (ECJ considering that provisions of the Fourth ACP-EEC Lomé Convention, between the EC and the African, Caribbean and Pacific States could be directly effective notwithstanding the appreciable imbalance in the obligations of the contracting parties. At [25]: '[T]he Court has consistently held that the question of the direct effect of provisions contained in an agreement concluded by the Community with non-member countries invariably involves an examination of the spirit, general scheme and terms of the agreement.').

Illustrations:

- *Panayotova v Minister voor Vreemdelingenzaken en Integratie* Case C-327/02 (16 November 2004), [18] (Grand Chamber recognising the direct effect of provisions in the Communities-Bulgaria, Communities-Slovakia and Communities-Poland Agreements);
- *Parfums Christian Dior SA v Tuk Consultancy* Joined Cases C-300/98 and C-392/98 [2000] ECR I-11307, [42–49] (provisions of TRIPs (Trade-Related Aspects of Intellectual Property Rights) held not to be directly effective);
- *Portugal v Council* Case C-149/96 [1999] ECR I-8395, [47] (provisions of the WTO (World Trade Organisation) Agreement held not to be directly effective);
- *International Fruit Company v Produktschap voor Groenten en Fruit* Cases 21-24/72 [1972] ECR 1219, [7–8] (provisions of GATT (the General Agreement on Tariffs and Trade) considered insufficiently concrete and unconditional, and did not have direct effect (at [27]): 'Before the incompatibility of a Community measure with a provision of international law can affect the validity of that measure, the Community must first of all be bound by that provision. Before invalidity can be relied

upon before a national court, that provision of international law must also be capable of conferring rights on citizens of the Community which they can invoke before the courts.');

- *R (Abdulnasir Savas) v Secretary of State for the Home Department* Case C-37/98 [2000] ECR I-2927, [46–55] (ECJ acknowledging the direct effect of Article 41(1) of the Additional Protocol to the EEC-Turkey Association Agreement);
- *Hallouzi-Choho v Bestuur van de sociale Verekeringsbank* Case C-126/95 [1996] ECR I-4807, [19–20] (Article 41(1) of the EEC-Morocco Co-operation Agreement held to be directly effective);
- *Krid v CNAVTS* Case 103/94 [1995] ECR I-719, [21–24] (Article 39(1) of the EEC-Algeria Co-operation Agreement considered to be directly effective).

6.12.11. **Direct effect of directives:**

- *Van Duyn v Home Office* Case 41/74 [1974] ECR 1337, [12] (ECJ: 'It would be incompatible with the binding effect attributed to a directive by Article 189 [now Article 249] to exclude, in principle, the possibility that the obligation which it imposes may be invoked by those concerned. In particular, where the Community authorities have, by directive, imposed on Member States the obligation to pursue a particular course of conduct, the useful effect of such an act would be weakened if individuals were prevented from relying on it before their national courts and if the latter were prevented from taking it into consideration as an element of Community law.').

Illustrations:

- *Rieser Internationale Transporte GmbH v Autobahnen –und Schnellstraßen Finanzierungs AG* Case C-157/02 [2004] ECR I-1477, [22] (ECJ affirming that where a directive is not implemented into national law within the specified period and where its provisions are unconditional and sufficiently precise it may 'be relied upon as against any national provision which is incompatible with the directive or in so far as the provisions define rights which individuals are able to assert against the State.' Similarly: [34]. At [42]: Article 7(4) of Directive 93/89 and Article 7(9) of Directive 1999/62 considered not to be directly effective.);
- *Bernhard Pfeiffer v Deutsches Rotes Kreuz, Kreisvenband Waldshut eV* Joined Cases C-397/01 to C-403/01 (5 October 2004), [104] (Grand Chamber concluding that Article 6(2) of Directive 93/104 has direct effect since it is unconditional and sufficiently precise).

6.12.12. **Directives are capable of vertical direct effect only:**

- *Marshall v Southampton and South-West Hampshire Area Health Authority* Case 152/84 [1986] QB 401, [48] (ECJ: 'With regard to the argument that a directive may not be relied upon against an individual, it must be emphasised that according to article 189 of the EEC Treaty [now Article 249], the binding nature of a directive, which constitutes the basis for the possibility of relying on the directive before a national court, exists only in relation to "each Member State to which it is addressed." It follows that a directive may not of itself impose obligations on an individual and that a provision of a directive may not be relied upon as such against such a person.' At [49]: '[W]here a person involved in legal proceedings is able to rely on a directive as against the state he may do so regardless of the capacity in which the latter is acting, whether employer or public authority.');

- *Marleasing SA v La Comercial Internacional de Alimentación SA* Case C-106/89 [1990] ECR I-4135, [6] (ECJ: '[W]ith regard to the question whether an individual may rely on the directive against a national law, it should be observed that, as the Court has consistently held, a directive may not of itself impose obligations on an individual and, consequently, a provision of a directive may not be relied upon as such against a person.' Citing Case 152/84 *Marshall v Southampton and South-West Hampshire Area Health Authority* [1986] ECR 723 (see above));
- *Bernhard Pfeiffer v Deutsches Rotes Kreuz, Kreisvenband Waldshut eV* Joined Cases C-397/01 to C-403/01 (5 October 2004), [108–109] (ECJ Grand Chamber: '[T]he Court has consistently held that a directive cannot of itself impose obligations on an individual and cannot, therefore, be relied upon as such against an individual . . . It follows that even a clear, precise and unconditional provision of a directive seeking to confer rights or impose obligations on individuals cannot of itself apply in proceedings exclusively between private parties.');
- *cf CIA Security International SA v Signalson SA and Securitel SPRL* Case C-194/94 [1996] ECR I-2201, [42] and [55] (In a case between private parties, Belgian security firms, Articles 8 and 9 of Directive 83/189/EEC were considered to be directly effective and could be relied upon by individuals in national courts. The effect of such reliance before a national court would be to compel the court to decline to apply a national technical regulation which was not notified in accordance with the directive).

6.12.13. **Directives may only be invoked against the state and emanations of the state:**

- *Marshall v Southampton and South-West Hampshire Area Health Authority* Case 152/84 [1986] QB 401, [49] [§ **6.12.12**];
- *Fratelli Costanzo SpA v Comune di Milano* Case 103/88 [1989] ECR 1839, [31] (ECJ: 'It follows that when the conditions under which the Court has held that individuals may rely on the provisions of a directive before the national courts are met, all organs of the administration, including decentralised authorities such as municipalities, are obliged to apply those provisions.');

- *Foster v British Gas plc* Case C-188/89 [1991] QB 405, [20] (ECJ: 'It follows from the foregoing that a body, whatever its legal form, which has been made responsible, pursuant to a measure adopted by the state, for providing a public service under the control of the state and has for that purpose special powers beyond those which result from the normal rules applicable in relations between individuals is included among the bodies against which the provisions of a Directive capable of having direct effect may be relied upon.' Applied in the HL to British Gas, at [1991] 2 AC 306 (HL).);
- *NUT v Governing Body of St Mary's Church of England (Aided) Junior School* [1997] 3 CMLR 360 (CA), [45] (Schiemann LJ considering governors of a voluntary-aided school to be an emanation of the state);
- *Griffin v South-West Water Services Ltd* [1995] IRLR 15, 16 (considering South-West Water Services, a privatised water company, to be an emanation of the state in accordance with the conditions in *Foster v British Gas* (see above)).

(4) Interpretative Effect of Community Law

6.13. **The supremacy of Community law over domestic law dictates that full effect must be given to Community law. This means that domestic laws cannot prevail over Community law, and that Community law will override any inconsistent provisions of domestic law [§ 6.10]. Thus all domestic laws must be read compatibly with Community law, regardless of whether or not they were enacted to give effect to Community obligations.**

6.13.1. **Domestic law must give full effect to Community law:**

- *Amministrazione delle Finanze dello Stato v Simmenthal SpA* Case 106/77 [1978] ECR 629, [21] (ECJ: '[E]very national court must, in a case within its jurisdiction, apply Community law in its entirety and protect rights which the latter confers on individuals and must accordingly set aside any provision of national law which may conflict with it, whether prior or subsequent to the Community rule.' At [24]: '[A] national court . . . is under a duty to give full effect to [provisions of Community law], if necessary refusing of its own motion to apply any conflicting provision of national legislation, even if adopted subsequently, and it is not necessary for the [domestic] court to request or await the prior setting aside of such provision by legislative or other constitutional means.') [§ **6.12.4**];
- *Garland v BR Engineering Ltd* [1983] 2 AC 751 (HL), 771A–C (Lord Diplock: 'My Lords, even if the obligation to observe the

provisions of article 119 [now Article 141] were an obligation assumed by the United Kingdom under an ordinary international treaty or convention and there were no question of the treaty obligation being directly applicable as part of the law to be applied by the courts in this country without need for any further enactment, it is a principle of construction of United Kingdom statutes, now too well established to call for further citation of authority, that the words of a statute passed after the Treaty has been signed and dealing with the subject matter of the international obligation of the United Kingdom, are to be construed, if they are reasonably capable of bearing such a meaning, as intended to carry out the obligation, and not to be inconsistent with it. A fortiori is this the case where the Treaty obligation arises under one of the Community treaties to which section 2 of the European Communities Act 1972 applies.') [§§ **9.8.2; 9.14**];

- *Shields v Coomes* [1978] 1 WLR 1408, (CA), 1415A–B (Lord Denning MR where, on the facts, there was no actual conflict between national law and Community law considering that: '[W]henever there is a conflict or inconsistency between the law contained in an article of the [EEC] Treaty and the law contained in the internal law of one of the member states, whether passed before or after joining the Community' then the supremacy of Community law requires 'that in any such event the law of the Community shall prevail over that of the internal law of the member state.');
- *Macarthys v Smith* [1979] ICR 785 (CA), 789D (Lord Denning MR (dissenting) where a conflict arose between section 1 of the Equal Pay Act 1970 and Article 119 of the EC Treaty considering that: '[w]e are entitled to look at the Treaty as an aid to construction: and even more, not only as an aid but as an overriding force').

Illustrations:

- *Commission v Luxembourg* Case C-473/93 [1996] ECR I-3207, [38] (ECJ, responding to an argument from the Grand Duchy of Luxembourg that the nationality requirement said to be a breach of various treaty and regulation provisions was a supreme rule of Luxembourg law: '[I]t is sufficient to refer to the Court's settled case-law according to which recourse to the provisions of the domestic legal systems to restrict the scope of the provisions of Community law would have the effect of impairing the unity and efficacy of that law and consequently cannot be accepted.' Citing Case 11/70 *Internationale Handelsgesellschaft* [1970] ECR 1125, [3] [§ **6.10.3**]);
- *R v Secretary of State for Transport, Ex parte Factortame (No 2)* [1991] 1 AC 603 (ECJ and HL), [20–21] (ECJ, after referring to *Amministrazione delle Finanze dello Stato v Simmenthal SpA* Case 106/77 [1978] ECR 629 (see above): 'It must be added that the full effectiveness of Community law would be just as much

impaired if a rule of national law could prevent a court seised of a dispute governed by Community law from granting interim relief in order to ensure the full effectiveness of the judgment to be given on the existence of the rights claimed under Community law. It follows that a court which in those circumstances would grant interim relief, if it were not for a rule of national law, is obliged to set aside that rule.'), (HL: applied the judgment of the ECJ and awarded interim relief);

- *R v Secretary of State for Employment, Ex parte EOC* [1995] 1 AC 1 (HL), 25B–C (Lord Keith: 'If the discriminatory measures in the [Employment Protection (Consolidation) Act 1978] are not objectively justified, Mrs Day has a good claim for redundancy pay against her employers, the Hertfordshire Area Health Authority, under article 119, which by virtue of section 2(1) of the [European Communities Act 1972] prevails over the discriminatory provisions of the Act of 1978. She would also have a good claim under the Equal Pay Directive and the Equal Treatment Directive, which are directly applicable against her employers as being an emanation of the state.').

6.13.2. **The interpretative effect encompasses all Community law:**

- *Van Munster v Rijksdienst voor Pensionen* Case C-165/91 [1994] ECR I-4661, [34] (ECJ: 'When applying domestic law, the national court must, as far as is at all possible, interpret it in a way which accords with the requirements of Community law.' Citing Case 157/86 *Murphy v Bord Telecom Eireann* [1988] ECR 673, [11], Case C-106/89 *Marleasing* [1990] ECR I-4135, [8] [**§ 6.15.2**] and Case C-91/92 *Faccini Dori* [1994] ECR I-3325, [26]).

6.14. **The extent of the interpretative effect of Community law is clearly seen in cases where domestic courts have implied words into statutory provisions in order to make them compatible with Community law. Alongside the doctrine of direct effect, it demonstrates the extent to which the sanctity of legislation (and hence of parliamentary sovereignty) has been modified by Community law:**

Illustrations:

- *Pickstone v Freemans plc* [1989] AC 66 (HL), 120H–121A (Lord Templeman, construing section 1(2)(c) of the Equal Pay Act 1970: 'In my opinion there must be implied in paragraph (c) after the word "applies" the words "as between the woman and the man with whom she claims equality." This construction is consistent with Community law.'), 125G–126D (Lord Oliver considering that the construction of an ambiguous statutory provision which 'involves not so much doing violence to the language of the section as filling a gap by an implication which arises . . . from the manifest purpose of the Act and the mischief it was intended to remedy' must be recognised as 'a departure from a number of well-established rules of construction . . . The fact that a statute is passed to give effect to an international treaty does not, of itself, enable the treaty to be referred to in order to construe the words used other than in their plain and unambiguous sense . . . I think, however, that it has also to be recognised that a statute which is passed in order to give effect to the United Kingdom's obligations under the EEC Treaty falls into a special category and it does so because, unlike other treaty obligations, those obligations have, in effect, been incorporated into English law by the European Communities Act 1972'. Described as 'a case which illustrates the lengths our courts will go in construing Acts of Parliament to uphold the supremacy of substantive Community rights.': *Thoburn v Sunderland City Council* [2003] QB 151 (DC), [67] (Laws LJ));

- *Litster v Forth Dry Dock & Engineering Co Ltd* [1990] 1 AC 546 (HL), 554G–H (Lord Keith construing regulation 5(3) of the Transfer of Undertakings (Protection of Employment) Regulations 1981: '[I]t is the duty of the court to give to regulation 5 a construction which accords with the decision of the European Court upon the corresponding provisions of the Directive to which the regulation was intended by Parliament to give effect. The precedent established by *Pickstone v Freemans plc* [[1989] AC 66 (see above)] indicates that this is to be done by implying the words necessary to achieve that result. So there must be implied in regulation 5(3) words indicating that where a person has been unfairly dismissed in the circumstances described in regulation 8(1) he is to be deemed to have been employed in the undertaking immediately before the transfer or any of a series of transactions whereby it was effected.'). See similarly: 558E–G (Lord Templeman), 559D–F, 576F–577C (Lord Oliver). Described as an illustration of 'how far [the *Marleasing*] principle can be taken': *Commissioners of Customs and Excise v First Choice Holidays plc* [2004] EWCA Civ 1044 (2004) STC 1407, [23] (Rix LJ). On the *Marleasing* principle see [**§ 6.15.2**].

6.15. **The interpretative effect of Community law is commonly seen in relation to directives. It requires domestic legislation to be interpreted compatibly with directives both where the legislation implements the directive but also, more generally, where it does not and regardless of whether the legislation was enacted before or after the directive (the *Marleasing* principle). The *Marleasing* principle, like the interpretative effect of Community law in general, may require words to be read into legislation to make it compatible with Community law. Whilst this gives courts plenty of scope for creative statutory interpretation the line will be drawn to**

preclude an interpretation which distorts statutory language or exceeds reasonable limits. The interpretative effect has especial importance regarding directives because they are only capable of vertical direct effect (which limits the application of directives as compared to Treaty provisions, regulations, decisions and international agreements [§§ 6.12.11–6.12.13]).

6.15.1. **Domestic legislation adopted to implement directives must be interpreted compatibly with the directive:**

- *Von Colson and Kamann v Land Nordrhein-Westfalen* Case 14/83 [1984] ECR 1891, [26] (ECJ determining whether individuals might rely on a directive in national courts where the directive has not been transposed into domestic law within the specified periods: '[T]he Member States' obligation arising from a directive to achieve the result envisaged by the directive and their duty under Article 5 [now Article 10] of the Treaty to take all appropriate measures, whether general or particular, to ensure the fulfilment of that obligation, is binding on all the authorities of Member States including, for matters within their jurisdiction, the courts. It follows that, in applying the national law and in particular the provisions of a national law specifically introduced in order to implement Directive No 76/207, national courts are required to interpret their national law in the light of the wording and the purpose of the Directive in order to achieve the result referred to in the third paragraph of Article 189.' At [28]: 'It is for the national court to interpret and apply the legislation adopted for the implementation of the directive in conformity with the requirements of Community law, in so far as it is given discretion to do so under national law.').

Illustrations:

- *Campbell v MGN Ltd* [2002] EWCA Civ 1373 [2003] QB 633, [96] (Lord Phillips MR: 'The [Data Protection Act 1998] should, if possible, be interpreted in a manner that is consistent with the Directive.') (HL is at [2004] UKHL 22 [2004] WLR 1232);
- *Wilson v St Helens Borough Council* [1999] 2 AC 52 (HL), 69E–H (Lord Slynn considering the obligation on member states under Article 5 of the EC Treaty (now Article 10) to interpret national laws compatibly with directives);
- *Coote v Granada Hospitality Ltd* Case C-185/97 [1999] ICR 100, [18] (ECJ: '[I]n applying national law, in particular legislative provisions which, as in the present case, were specially introduced in order to implement the Directive, the national court is required to interpret its national law, so far as possible, in the light of the wording and the purpose of the Directive in order to achieve the result pursued by the third paragraph of article 189 [now Article 249] of the EC Treaty.').

6.15.2. **All domestic legislation must be interpreted compatibly with directives (the *Marleasing* principle):**

- *Marleasing SA v La Comercial Internacional de Alimentación SA* Case C-106/89 [1990] ECR I-4135, [8] (ECJ: '[I]n applying national law, whether the provisions in question were adopted before or after the directive, the national court called upon to interpret it is required to do so, as far as possible, in the light of the wording and the purpose of the directive in order to achieve the result pursued by the latter and thereby comply with the third paragraph of Article 189 [now Article 249] of the Treaty.'), [7–8] (Advocate General Van Gerven explaining that the interpretative effect as applied to directives 'does not mean that a provision in a directive has direct effect in any way as between individuals. On the contrary, it is the national provisions themselves which, interpreted in a manner consistent with the directive, have direct effect.');
- *Bernhard Pfeiffer v Deutsches Rotes Kreuz, Kreisvenband Waldshut eV* Joined Cases C-397/01 to C-403/01 (5 October 2004), [115] (Grand Chamber: 'Although the principle that national law must be interpreted in conformity with Community law concerns chiefly domestic provisions enacted in order to implement the directive in question, it does not entail an interpretation merely of those provisions but requires the national courts to consider national law as a whole in order to assess to what extent it may be applied so as not to produce a result contrary to that sought by the directive.')

Illustrations of ECJ case law:

- *Björnekulla Fruktindustrier v Procordia Food AB* Case C-371/02 [2004] ECR I-5791 [13] (ECJ applying the *Marleasing* principle in interpreting Article 12(2)(a) of Directive 89/104/EEC regarding trade marks);
- *Rechnungshof v Östrreichischer Rundfunk* Joined Cases C-465/00, C-138/01 and C-139/01 [2003] ECR I-4989, [93] (ECJ applying the *Marleasing* principle to Article 6(1)(c), 7(c) and (e) of Directive 95/46/EEC on the protection of individuals with regard to the processing of personal data);
- *Mau v Bundesanstalt für Arbeit* Case C-160/01 [2003] ECR I-4791, [36] (ECJ applying the *Marleasing* principle to the interpretation of Articles 3 and 4 of Directive 80/987 relating to the protection of employees in the event of their employer's insolvency).

Illustrations of domestic case law:

- *Webb v EMO Air Cargo (UK) Ltd (No 2)* [1995] 1 WLR 1454 (HL), 1459–1460 (Lord Keith, construing the Sex Discrimination Act 1975 so as to comply with the ECJ's interpretation of the Equal Treatment Directive. Before the reference to the ECJ, the HL had considered that *Marleasing* did not oblige domestic courts to 'distort' the meaning of the statute: *Webb v*

EMO Air Cargo (UK) Ltd [1993] ICR 175 (HL), 186D–F, 187F–G (Lord Keith) [§ **6.15.4**]);

- *Commissioners of Customs and Excise v First Choice Holidays plc* [2004] EWCA Civ 1044 (2004) STC 1407, [43] (Rix LJ interpreting section 53 of the VAT Act 1994, implementing Article 26 of the Sixth Council Directive 77/388/EEC of 19 July 1977 by 'adopting the same purposive construction . . . as the European Court of Justice applied to the Sixth Directive, and with the added advantage of the ruling of that Court [to which a reference had been made in the same case] and, still further, in the light of the *Marleasing* obligation to interpret domestic legislation, so far as possible, in line with EU legislation.');
- *R v Johnstone* [2003] UKHL 28 [2003] 1 WLR 1736, [17] (Lord Nicholls construing section 10 of the Trade Marks Act 1994 in accordance with the Trade Marks Directive 89/104 following *Marleasing*), see similarly [63] (Lord Walker);
- *R (IDT Card Services Ireland Ltd) v HM Customs & Excise* [2004] EWHC 3188 (Admin) (2005) STC 314, [35–36] (Moses J noting that before applying the *Marleasing* principle it must be possible to identify the Community legislation or the ruling of the ECJ in accordance with which domestic legislation is to be construed);
- *R v Secretary of State for Health, Ex parte Imperial Tobacco Ltd* [2001] 1 WLR 127 (HL), 139A–139C (Lord Hoffmann considering that the basis for the *Marleasing* principle is: '[T]hat the duty of a member state to give effect to a Directive applies not only to its legislature or executive, which would, under the national constitution, ordinarily have the power to take the necessary measures, but also to its judiciary.');
- *Berkeley v Secretary of State for the Environment* [2001] 2 AC 603 (HL), 614H–615B (Lord Hoffmann applying *Marleasing* to the construction of the Town and Country Planning (Assessment of Environmental Effects) Regulations 1988 (SI 1988/119));
- *Institute of Chartered Accountants in England and Wales v Customs and Excise Commissioners* [1999] 1 WLR 701 (HL), 705A–B (Lord Slynn considering that there was no difficulty in construing the Value Added Tax Act 1994 compatibly with Council Directive 77/388/EEC in accordance with the *Marleasing* principle);
- *Blackland Park Exploration Ltd v Environment Agency* [2003] EWCA Civ 1795 (2004) Env LR 33, [3] (Scott Baker LJ considering that it was 'trite law' that the Landfill (England and Wales) Regulations 2002 SI 2002/1559 (implementing Council Directive 1999/31/EC on the landfill of waste) should be interpreted in accordance with the *Marleasing* principle);
- *R (Friends of the Earth) v Environment Agency and Able UK Ltd* [2003] EWHC 3193 (Admin) (2004) Env LR 31, [57] (Sullivan J construing regulation 3(4) of the Conservations (Natural Habitats) Regulations 1994 in accordance with the

Habitats Directive 92/43/EEC by reference to the *Marleasing* principle);
- *R (Jones) v Mansfield District Council* [2003] EWCA Civ 1408 (2004) Env LR 21, [19] (Dyson LJ considering that there was no conflict between the Town and Country Planning (Assessment of Environmental Effects) Regulations 1988 implementing Council Directive 85/337/EEC which required resolution by reference to the *Marleasing* principle);
- *R (Friends of the Earth and Greenpeace) v Secretary of State for the Environment, Food and Rural Affairs and Secretary of State for Health* [2001] EWCA Civ 1847 (2002) Env LR 24, [12] (Simon Brown LJ applying *Marleasing* to construe the Radioactive Substances Act 1993, in accordance with Council Directive 96/29/Euratom: 'This may mean reading words into legislation or applying it through conforming administrative action. Here it involved the Secretaries of State reaching a view on justification under Article 6 when deciding how to exercise their powers under sec.23 of the 1993 Act to give directions to the [Environment Agency] with regard to authorising MOX [a mixture of plutonium oxide and uranium oxide] production.').

6.15.3. **Importance of interpretative effect for directives:**
- *Relaxion Group Plc v Rhys-Harper* [2003] UKHL 33 [2003] ICR 867, [104] (Lord Hope, after noting that the relevant Directive did not have direct effect: 'So a directive works its way into our domestic system by means of the legislation which is designed to give effect to it. It is then for the courts to interpret that legislation, as far as possible, in a way that gives effect to the country's obligations under the treaty.').

6.15.4. **Limits of the interpretative effect as applied to directives:**
- *Webb v EMO Air Cargo (UK) Ltd* [1993] ICR 175 (HL), 186D–F (Lord Keith: 'The Directive (76/207/EEC) does not have direct effect upon the relationship between a worker and an employer who is not a state or an emanation of the state, but nevertheless it is for a United Kingdom court to construe domestic legislation in any field covered by a Community Directive so as to accord with the interpretation of the Directive as laid down by the European Court of Justice, if that can be done without distorting the meaning of the domestic legislation.' At 187D–E, after referring to *Marleasing*: 'As the European Court of Justice said, a national court must construe a domestic law to accord with the terms of a Directive in the same field only if it is possible to do so. That means that the domestic law must be open to an interpretation consistent with the Directive whether or not it is also open to an interpretation inconsistent with it.');

- *Clarke v General Accident Fire and Life Insurance Corporation plc* [1998] 1 WLR 1647 (HL), 1656A–C (Lord Clyde: 'The adoption of a construction which departs boldly from the ordinary meaning of the language of the statute is, however, particularly appropriate where the validity of legislation has to be tested against the provisions of European Law. In that context it is proper to strain to give effect to the design and purpose behind the legislation, and to give weight to the spirit rather than the letter. In this way the court may implement the requirement formulated by the European Court of Justice in *Marleasing*. . . [quoting para 8 of *Marleasing* [§ **6.15.2**]] But even in this context the exercise must still be one of construction and it should not exceed the limits of what is reasonable.');
- *White v White* [2001] UKHL 9 [2001] 1 WLR 481, [22] (Lord Nicholls, considering that the *Marleasing* principle did not apply to the Motor Insurers' Bureau (Compensation of Victims of Uninsured Drivers) Agreement 1988, made between the Secretary of State for the Environment, Transport and Regions and the Motor Insurers' Bureau because it 'cannot be stretched to the length of requiring contracts to be interpreted in a manner that would impose on one or other of the parties obligations which, *Marleasing* apart, the contract did not impose. This is so even in the case of a contract where one of the parties is an emanation of government, here the Secretary of State. The citizen's obligations are those to which he agreed, as construed in accordance with normal principles of interpretation.');
- *Criminal Proceedings Against Luciano Arcaro* Case C-168/95 [1996] ECR I-4705, [42] (ECJ: 'However, that obligation of the national court to refer to the content of the directive when interpreting the relevant rules of its own national law reaches a limit where such an interpretation leads to the imposition on an individual of an obligation laid down by a directive which has not been transposed, or, more especially, where it has the effect of determining or aggravating, on the basis of the directive and in the absence of a law enacted for its implementation, the liability in criminal law of persons who act in contravention of that directive's provisions.');
- *Criminal Proceedings against X* Case C-60/02, [59–64] (ECJ noting the qualification to the *Marleasing* principle of compatible interpretation in relation to criminal matters; at [61]: 'However, a particular problem arises where the principle of compatible interpretation is applied to criminal matters. As the Court has also held, that principle finds its limits in the general principles of law which form part of the Community legal system, and, in particular, in the principle of legal certainty and non-retroactivity. In that regard, the Court has held on several occasions that a directive cannot, of itself and independently of a national law adopted by a Member State for its implementation,

have the effect of determining or aggravating the liability in criminal law of persons who act in contravention of the provisions of that directive.');

- Pre-*Marleasing: Duke v GEC Reliance Ltd* [1988] AC 618 (HL), 638C–639B and 641F–G (Lord Templeman stating that the construction of an Act of Parliament passed after the European Communities Act 1972, will be based on the language of the legislation considered in the light of circumstances prevailing at the date of enactment, therefore the Sex Discrimination Act 1975 (enacted on 12 November 1975) was not intended to give effect to the Equal Treatment Directive (dated 9 February 1976) as construed by the ECJ in *Marshall v Southampton and South-West Hampshire Area Health Authority (Teaching)* [1986] QB 401 (published on 20 February 1986), [§ **6.12.12**]. At 630F–H, 639G–640A and 641F–G noting that section 2(4) of the European Communities Act 1972 does not empower or require an English court to distort the meaning of a domestic statute in order to enforce against an individual an EC directive which has no direct effect between individuals; it applies only where EC provisions are directly applicable);
- *Finnegan v Clowney Youth Training* [1990] 2 AC 407 (HL), 415F–416A (Lord Bridge upholding *Duke* (see above): '[T]he enactment applicable to the present employer's claim is indistinguishable from the enactment which fell to be applied in *Duke* . . . it would appear, therefore, to dictate the inevitable result that the appeal must fail'.);
- *Thoburn v Sunderland City Council* [2002] EWHC 195 (Admin) [2003] QB 151, [72] (Laws LJ, commenting on *Duke* (see above)).

6.16. **The interpretative effect of Community law is analogous to section 3, HRA [§§ 7.9–7.10] and to the interpretation of constitutional provisions [§ 5.11]. In all these cases the emphasis is on creative interpretation (not legislation) to ensure the compliance of statutory (or constitutional) provisions with a broader scheme, be it Community law or human rights law.**

- *Ghaidan v Godin-Mendoza* [2004] UKHL 30 [2004] 2 AC 557 (consideration of *Marleasing* [§ **6.15**] in the context of construing section 3, HRA), [44–45] (Lord Steyn) [**§ 7.9.2**];
- *Matthew v State of Trinidad and Tobago* [2004] UKPC 33 [2005] 1 AC 433, [54] (Lord Bingham, Lord Nicholls, Lord Steyn and Lord Walker (dissenting) considering the similarity between constitutional interpretation and the *Marleasing* principle) [§ **5.11.7**].

(5) Effective Protection of Community Law

6.17. **Unlike the principles of direct effect and interpretative effect, the principle of effective protection (or 'effectiveness'), is rooted in the text of the EC Treaty (Article 10). It requires Member States to abstain from rendering practically impossible or excessively difficult the exercise of rights conferred by Community law. This contrasts with the narrow dualist approach, which, by virtue of a strict application of the principles of non-justiciability [§§ 8.5–8.7] and no direct effect [§§ 8.8–8.9], treats the infringement of international (unincorporated) treaty obligations as being of no domestic significance.**

6.17.1. Source of the principle of effectiveness:

- Article 10, EC Treaty: 'Member States shall take all appropriate measures, whether general or particular, to ensure fulfilment of the obligations arising out of this Treaty or resulting from actions taken by the institutions of the Community. They shall facilitate the achievement of the Community's tasks. They shall abstain from any measure which could jeopardise the attainment of the objectives of this Treaty.'

6.17.2. The principle of effectiveness as a fundamental principle of Community law:

- *R v Secretary of State for the Home Department, Ex parte Gallagher* [1996] 2 CMLR 951, [10] (Lord Bingham CJ: 'It is a cardinal principle of Community law that the laws of Member States should provide effective and adequate redress for violations of Community law by Member States where these result in infringement of specific individual rights conferred by the law of the Community.').

6.17.3. The principle of effectiveness:

- *Safalero Srl v Prefetto di Genova* Case C-13/01 [2003] ECR I-8679, [49] (ECJ: '[I]n the absence of Community rules governing the matter, it is for the domestic legal system of each Member State to designate the courts and tribunals having jurisdiction and to lay down the detailed procedural rules governing actions for safeguarding rights which individuals derive directly from Community law, provided that such rules are not less favourable than those governing similar domestic actions (principle of equivalence) and that they do not render practically impossible or excessively difficult the exercise of rights conferred by Community law (principle of effectiveness).');

- *Rewe-Zentral Finanz v Landwirtschaftskammer für das Saarland* Case 33/76 [1976] ECR 1989, [5] (ECJ: 'Applying the principle of co-operation laid down in Article 5 of the Treaty [now Article 10], it is the national courts which are entrusted with ensuring the legal protection which citizens derive from the direct effect of the provisions of Community law. Accordingly in the absence of Community rules on this subject [the prohibition on charges having an equivalent effect to customs duties], it is for the domestic legal system of each Member State to designate the courts having jurisdiction and to determine the procedural conditions governing actions at law intended to ensure the protection of the rights which citizens have from the direct effect of Community law, it being understood that such conditions cannot be less favourable than those relating to similar actions of a domestic nature.');
- *Preston v Wolverhampton Healthcare NHS Trust (No 2)* [2001] UKHL 5 [2001] 2 AC 455, [3–4] (Lord Slynn citing *Rewe-Zentral Finanz* (see above) before noting: 'However, where reliance is placed on the performance of domestic procedural conditions, those conditions must not be such as to make the enforcement of Community law rights impossible in practice and they must not be less favourable than those applying to a similar claim of a domestic nature.' Concluding at [12] that the rules in section 2(5) of the Equal Pay Act 1970 and in regulation 12 of the Occupational Pension Schemes (Equal Access to Membership) Regulations 1976 (SI 1976/142) were incompatible with, and 'precluded' by, Community law);
- *Autologic Holdings Plc v IRC* [2004] EWCA Civ 680 [2005] 1 WLR 52, [25] (Peter Gibson LJ: 'The importance of the principle of effectiveness in Community law cannot be overstated. Any provision of national law which makes the exercise of a right conferred by Community law practically impossible or excessively difficult cannot prevail.');
- *Phillip Bros. v The Republic of Sierra Leone and the Commission of the EC* [1995] 1 Lloyd's Rep 289 (CA), 296 (Hoffmann LJ: 'It is well settled that this article [regarding the principle of effectiveness] does not require the Courts of a Member State to give direct effect in its own law to a part of the treaty or subordinate legislation which was not intended to have direct effect.').

(6) Wider Effect of Community Law

6.18. **In addition to its incorporation of substantive law, Community law has had a wider effect on domestic law. For example, principles of Community law, such as proportionality, legitimate expecta-**

tion, non-discrimination and fundamental rights have influenced the common law. Another example is the powerful effect of the ECJ's use of treaties, unincorporated in domestic law, and international instruments, non-binding even on the international plane, in developing and defining Community law. The use of these sources by the ECJ has guided and influenced domestic courts when interpreting Community law.

A. *Community Law and the Common Law*

6.19. **One illustration of a general principle of Community law which has been influential in domestic law is the principle of proportionality. This is a fundamental part of Community law. It requires legislative measures to be appropriate and necessary in order to achieve their objectives. Apart from applying to Community law issues, the principle of proportionality has been used as part of the artillery of judicial review concepts stimulated by the incorporation of the ECHR in the HRA. Thus, it will often be necessary to ask whether the principle of proportionality is satisfied when analysing whether acts of public authorities are Convention-compliant. Despite these developments, however, it is questionable whether proportionality exists as a wholly independent ground of review, displacing the traditional *Wednesbury* test, in cases where neither Community law not ECHR issues are engaged.**

6.19.1. The principle of proportionality as part of Community law:

- *R (Omega Air Ltd) v Secretary of State for the Environment, Transport and the Regions* Joined Cases C-27/00 and C-122/00 [2002] ECR I-2569 [62] (ECJ applying the principle of proportionality in considering the validity of Article 2(2) of Regulation No 925/1999: '[I]t should be remembered that it is settled case-law that the principle of proportionality, which is one of the general principles of Community Law, requires that measures adopted by Community institutions should not exceed the limits of what is appropriate and necessary in order to attain the objectives pursued by the legislation in question, and where there is a choice between several appropriate measures, recourse must be had to the least onerous and the disadvantages caused must not be disproportionate to the aims pursued.');
- *Garage Molenheide BVBA v Belgium State* Joined Cases C-286/94, C-340/95, C-401/95 and C-47/96 [1997] ECR I-7281, [46–49] (ECJ describing the requirements of the principle of proportionality in Community law);
- *R v Goldstein* [1983] 1 WLR 151 (HL), 155B (Lord Diplock referring to 'the concept in Community law (derived principally

from German law) called "proportionality." In plain English it means "You must not use a steam hammer to crack a nut, if a nutcracker would do".').

6.19.2. **The principle of proportionality applied to ECHR issues in domestic law:**

- *De Freitas v Permanent Secretary of Ministry of Agriculture, Fisheries, Lands and Housing* [1999] 1 AC 69 (PC), 80G (Lord Clyde, in determining whether a limitation on a Convention right is arbitrary or excessive a court should ask itself whether (as formulated by Gubbay CJ in Zimbabwean case law): '"(i) the legislative objective is sufficiently important to justify limiting a fundamental right; (ii) the measures designed to meet the legislative objective are rationally connected to it; and (iii) the means used to impair the right or freedom are no more than is necessary to accomplish the objective".').

Illustrations:

- *R v Shayler* [2002] UKHL 11 [2003] 1 AC 247, [57] (Lord Hope: 'The word "necessary" in article 10(2) [ECHR] introduces the principle of proportionality, although the word as such does not appear anywhere in the Convention.' At [60–61]: 'The European Court has not identified a consistent or uniform set of principles when considering the doctrine of proportionality . . . But there is a general international understanding as to the matters which should be considered where a question is raised as to whether an interference with a fundamental human right is proportionate.');
- *A v Secretary of State for the Home Department* [2004] UKHL 56 [2005] 2 WLR 87, [44] (Lord Bingham, considering an appeal where the court at first instance was SIAC: 'The European Court does not approach questions of proportionality as questions of pure fact: see, for example, *Smith and Grady v United Kingdom* [(1999) 29 EHRR 493] . . . Nor should domestic courts do so. The greater intensity of review now required in determining questions of proportionality, and the duty of the courts to protect Convention rights, would in my view be emasculated if a judgment at first instance on such a question were conclusively to preclude any further review.' See also [30] considering proportionality in the context of article 15, ECHR);
- *R v A (No 2)* [2001] UKHL 25 [2002] 1 AC 45, [37–38] (Lord Steyn), [58] (Lord Hope) (both applying proportionality as part of domestic law under the HRA).

6.19.3. **The principle of proportionality as part of domestic law:**

- *R (Daly) v Secretary of State for the Home Department* [2001] UKHL 26 [2001] 2 AC 532, [26–28] (Lord Steyn: 'There is a material difference between the *Wednesbury* and *Smith* grounds of review and the approach of proportionality applicable in respect of review where Convention rights are at stake . . . What is the difference for the disposal of concrete cases? . . . The starting point is that there is an overlap between the traditional grounds of review and the approach of proportionality. Most cases would be decided in the same way whichever approach is adopted. Making due allowance for important structural differences between various convention rights, which I do not propose to discuss, a few generalisations are perhaps permissible. I would mention three concrete differences without suggesting that my statement is exhaustive. First, the doctrine of proportionality may require the reviewing court to assess the balance which the decision-maker has struck, not merely whether it is within the range of rational or reasonable decisions. Secondly, the proportionality test may go further than the traditional grounds of review inasmuch as it may require attention to be directed to the relative weight accorded to interests and considerations. Thirdly, even the heightened scrutiny test developed in *R v Ministry of Defence, Ex p Smith* [1996] QB 517, 554 is not necessarily appropriate to the protection of human rights. . . . The differences in approach between the traditional grounds of review and the proportionality approach may therefore sometimes yield different results. It is therefore important that cases involving Convention rights must be analysed in the correct way.'); (cited in *R v Shayler* [2002] UKHL 11 [2003] 1 AC 247, [33] (Lord Bingham), [75–77] (Lord Hope));

- *R (Alconbury Developments Ltd) v Secretary of State for the Environment, Transport and the Regions* [2001] UKHL 23 [2003] 2 AC 295, [51] (Lord Slynn: 'There is a difference between [the principle of proportionality] and the approach of the English courts in *Associated Provincial Picture Houses Ltd v Wednesbury Corpn* [1948] 1 KB 223. But the difference in practice is not as great as is sometimes supposed. The cautious approach of the European Court of Justice in applying the principle is shown inter alia by the margin of appreciation it accords to the institutions of the Community in making economic assessments. I consider that even without reference to the Human Rights Act 1998 the time has come to recognise that this principle is part of English administrative law, not only when judges are dealing with Community acts but also when they are dealing with acts subject to domestic law. Trying to keep the *Wednesbury* principle and proportionality in separate compartments seems to me to be unnecessary and confusing. Reference to the Human Rights Act 1998 however makes it necessary that the court should ask whether what is done is compatible with Convention rights. That will often require that the question should be asked whether the principle of proportionality has been satisfied.');
- *R (Association of British Civilian Internees) v Secretary of State for Defence* [2003] EWCA Civ 473 [2003] QB 1397, [32] (Dyson LJ: 'A preliminary question that arises is whether proportionality

exists as a separate ground of review in a case which does not concern European Community law or human rights protected by the European Convention for the Protection for Human Rights and Fundamental Freedoms, as scheduled to the Human Rights Act 1998.' At [34–37]: 'Support for the recognition of proportionality as part of English domestic law in cases which do not involve Community law or the Convention is to be found in para 51 of the speech of Lord Slynn of Hadley in *R (Alconbury Developments Ltd) v Secretary of State for the Environment, Transport and the Regions* [2003] 2 AC 295, 320–321; and in the speech of Lord Cooke of Thorndon in *R (Daly) v Secretary of State for the Home Department* [2001] 2 AC 532, 548–549, para 32. See also *de Smith, Woolf & Jowell, Judicial Review of Administrative Action*, 5th ed (1995), p. 606. It seems to us that the case for this is indeed a strong one . . .. But we consider that it is not for this court to perform its burial rites. The continuing existence of the *Wednesbury* test has been acknowledged by the House of Lords on more than one occasion . . .. The suggestion that it is open to this court to hold that the *Wednesbury* test is no longer part of English domestic law is entirely at odds with the approach of the House of Lords in [*R v Secretary of State for the Home Department, Ex parte Brind* [1991] 1 AC 696] and in [*R v Chief Constable of Sussex, Ex parte International Trader's Ferry Ltd* [1999] 2 AC 418]. Finally, the passages in the speeches of Lord Slynn in *R (Alconbury Developments Ltd) v Secretary of State for the Environment, Transport and the Regions* [2003] 2 AC 295, 320–321 and Lord Cooke in the *Daly* case [2001] 2 AC 532, 548–549 . . . themselves imply a recognition that the *Wednesbury* test survives, although their Lordships' clearly expressed view is that it should be laid to rest. It seems to us that this is a step which can only be taken by the House of Lords. We therefore approach the issues in the present appeal on the footing that the *Wednesbury* test does survive, and that this is the correct test to apply in a case such as the present which does not involve Community law and does not engage any question of rights under the Convention. ').

Illustrations:

- *South Bucks DC v Porter* [2003] UKHL 26 [2003] 2 AC 558, [58] (Lord Steyn, considering the original and discretionary jurisdiction to grant injunctive relief, conferred on the court by section 187B of the Town and Country Planning Act 1990: 'Even if it had previously been possible to ignore great or marked hardship in the exercise of discretion under section 187B—a hypothesis which I do not accept—such an approach is no longer possible. Sometimes, perhaps more often than not, the interference with a Convention right may be justified on public interest grounds. But effective protection of a Convention [ECHR] right requires the court to approach the matter in a structured fashion in accordance with the principle of proportionality. What in the context of the present case is required was explained by Simon Brown LJ in terms on which I cannot improve. He said . . . : "Proportionality requires not only that the injunction be appropriate and necessary for the attainment of the public interest objective sought—here the safeguarding of the environment—but also that it does not impose an excessive burden on the individual whose private interests—here the gipsy's private life and home and the retention of his ethnic identity—are at stake".');

- *R (P) v Secretary of State for the Home Department* [2001] EWCA Civ 1151 [2001] 1 WLR 2002, [64] (Lord Phillips MR: 'On the new *Daly* approach we have to determine in these appeals whether the interference proposed by the Prison Service in the application of its policy in each of these cases is really proportionate to the legitimate aim, sanctioned by article 8(2) of the [ECHR], which it seeks to pursue. In making this judgment we must be careful to show appropriate deference to the fact that the Prison Service is the expert body appointed to carry out this sensitive public function.');
- *R v Chief Constable of Sussex, Ex parte International Trader's Ferry Ltd* [1999] 2 AC 418 (HL), 439F (Lord Slynn considering proportionality as applied by the ECJ), 452B (Lord Cooke considering that on the facts the 'European concepts of proportionality and margin of appreciation produce the same result as what are commonly called *Wednesbury* principles. Indeed in many cases this is likely to be so.');
- *A v Secretary of State for the Home Department* [2004] UKHL 56 [2005] 2 WLR 87, [40] (Lord Bingham considering the margin of discretion accorded by the ECtHR to national courts and the requirements of proportionality).

B. *Sources of Law Used by the ECJ*

6.20. **In defining and interpreting Community law, the ECJ uses treaties, including those which are unincorporated in domestic law. The ECJ also uses international instruments which often lack binding force, even on the international plane. The way in which such treaties and international instruments are used by the ECJ as sources of soft law provides a precedent which domestic courts may, by virtue of section 3, European Communities Act 1972 [§ 6.6], follow when interpreting and applying Community law. This domestic use of unincorporated treaties and international instruments is in addition to the other ways in which they are used by domestic courts [chapters 9–11].**

6.20.1. Domestic law to be informed by sources of law used by the ECJ:

- *A v Chief Constable of West Yorkshire (No 2)* [2004] UKHL 21

[2004] 2 WLR 1209, [13] (Lord Bingham after considering the 'important judgment' of the ECJ in *P v S* Case C-13/94 [1996] ICR 795: 'The importance of the [ECHR] in this appeal derives not from the decision in *Goodwin* [*v United Kingdom* (2002) 35 EHRR 447] but from the part which the Convention has played in shaping the current European understanding of what fundamental human rights mean and require.');

- *R v Hertfordshire CC, Ex parte Green Environmental Industries Ltd* [2000] 2 AC 412 (HL), 422B (Lord Hoffman: '[S]ince the [Environmental Protection Act 1990] gives effect to a Directive it must be interpreted according to principles of Community law, including its doctrines of fundamental human rights. For this purpose Community law looks to analogous principles in national laws of member states and the international conventions and covenants to which they are parties. In particular it has regard to the [ECHR].');
- *R v Secretary of State for the Home Department, Ex parte McQuillan* [1995] 4 All ER 400 (QBD), 421 (Sedley J, pre-HRA: 'Through the jurisprudence of the Court of Justice the principles, though not the text, of the [ECHR] now inform the law of the European Union. If, as the United Kingdom government accepted in *Vilvarajah v UK* (1991) 14 EHRR 248, an irrationality challenge can be mounted where a real risk of infringement of art 3 can be shown to have been ignored, and if on the wider scale it is for the courts of the United Kingdom to apply principles of European law wherever appropriate, the principles and standards set out in the convention can certainly be said to be a matter of which the law of this country now takes notice in setting its own standards . . . Once it is accepted that the standards articulated in the convention are standards which both march with those of the common law and inform the jurisprudence of the European Union, it becomes unreal and potentially unjust to continue to develop English public law without reference to them.') [**§ 10.4.4; § 11.6**].

6.20.2. **ECJ using fundamental rights as embodied in the ECHR, pre-HRA, to interpret Community law:**
Illustrations:

- Lord Browne-Wilkinson writing extra-judicially: 'The European Court [of Justice], although not tying itself to the ECHR as the only source of the law on fundamental human rights, in practice tests such cases by reference to the Convention. There is no case in which the European Court has upheld the validity of actions which conflicted with the ECHR. It seems therefore, that in those areas affected by the EEC Treaties, the ECHR is already indirectly incorporated into English domestic law. The principles of the Convention form an integral part of EEC law and English domestic law is subject to EEC law. United Kingdom legislation must comply with directly applicable EEC legislation, which itself falls to be construed so as to give effect to the ECHR. Although [in *Brind v Secretary of State for the Home Department* [1991] AC 696, the House of Lords] refused to give effect to the ECHR "by the back door" so long as Parliament by failing to incorporate it had not admitted it by the front door, in one area Parliament has left the back door open. In that area we already enjoy a full Bill of Rights: the Convention is directly enforceable in our courts.' 'The Infiltration of a Bill of Rights' [1992] PL 397, 401.

- *Johnston v Chief Constable of the Royal Ulster Constabulary* [1987] QB 129 Case 222/84 [18] (ECJ: 'The requirement of judicial control stipulated by [Article 6 of Council Directive 76/207/EEC on the principle of equal treatment for men and women as regards access to employment] reflects a general principle of law which underlies the constitutional traditions common to the member states. That principle is also laid down in articles 6 and 13 of the European Convention for the Protection of Human Rights and Fundamental Freedoms of 4 November 1950 (1953) (Cmd. 8969). As the European Parliament, Council and Commission recognised in their joint declaration of 5 April 1977 (Official Journal 1977 No. C 103, p.1) and as the court has recognised in its decisions, the principles on which that Convention is based must be taken into consideration in Community law.');
- *Elliniki Radiophonia Tiléorassi-AE v Dimotiki Etairia Pliroforissis* C-260/89 [1991] ECR I-2925, [41] (ECJ: '[A]s the Court has consistently held, fundamental rights form an integral part of the general principles of law, the observance of which it ensures. For that purpose the Court draws inspiration from the constitutional traditions common to the Member States and from the guidelines supplied by international treaties for the protection of human rights on which the Member States have collaborated or of which they are signatories. . . The European Convention on Human Rights has special significance in that respect.' At [45]: 'The reply to the national court [of Greece] must therefore be that the limitation imposed on the power of the Member States to apply the provisions referred to in Articles 66 and 56 [now Articles 55 and 46 respectively] of the Treaty on grounds of public policy, public security and public health must be appraised in the light of the general principle of freedom of expression embodied in Article 10 of the European Convention on Human Rights.');
- *Rutili v Minister for the Interior* Case 36/75 [1975] ECR 1219, [32] (ECJ: 'Taken as a whole, these limitations placed on the powers of Member States in respect of control of aliens are a specific manifestation of the more general principle, enshrined in Articles 8, 9, 10 and 11 of the Convention for the Protection of Human Rights and Fundamental Freedoms . . . and in Article 2

of Protocol No 4 of the same Convention . . . which provide, in identical terms, that no restrictions in the interests of national security or public safety shall be placed on the rights secured by the above-quoted articles other than such as are necessary for the protection of those interests "in a democratic society".');

- *Limburgse Vinyl Maatschappij NV v Commission* Joined Cases T-305/94 and others [1999] ECR II-931, [120] (Court of First Instance, after considering the role of fundamental rights in Community law: 'For that purpose, the Court of Justice and the Court of First Instance rely on the constitutional traditions common to the Member States and the guidelines supported by international treaties and conventions on the protection of human rights on which the Member States have collaborated or to which they were signatories. The European Convention on Human Rights has special significance in that respect.');
- *R v Secretary of State for Employment, Ex parte Seymour-Smith* Case C-167/97 [1999] 2 AC 554, [88] (Advocate General Cosmas, using the ECHR (pre-HRA) in construing Community law: '[A]rticle 6 of the Directive [Council Directive (76/207/EEC) on the approximation of the laws of the member states relating to the application of the principle of equal pay] . . . constitutes the expression of a general principle of law . . . which is also laid down by articles 6 and 13 of the Convention for the Protection of Human Rights and Fundamental Freedoms . . . By virtue of article 6 of the Directive, interpreted in the light of that principle, all persons have the right to obtain an effective remedy in a competent court against measures which they consider to be contrary to the principle of equal treatment laid down in Directive 76/207.');
- *Bamberski v Krombach* Case C-7/98 [2001] QB 709, [25] (ECJ noting that the court draws inspiration from the constitutional traditions common to the Member States and from the guidelines supplied by international treaties for the protection of human rights which Member States have collaborated on, or of which they are signatories, especially the ECHR).

6.20.3. **ECJ using treaties unincorporated into domestic law and international instruments in construing and applying Community law: *Illustrations:***

- *Grant v South West Trains* Case C-249/96 [1998] ICR 449, [44–45] (ECJ: 'The [International Covenant on Civil and Political Rights] is one of the international instruments relating to the protection of human rights which the Court takes into account in applying the principles of Community law (see, for example, Case 374/87 *Orkem v Commission* [1989] ECR 3283, paragraph 31, and Joined Cases C-247/88 and C-197/89 *Dzodzi v Belgian State* [1990] ECR I-3763 paragraph 68). However, although respect for the fundamental rights which form an integral part of those general principles of law is a condition of the legality of Community acts, those rights cannot in themselves have the effect of extending the scope of the EC Treaty provisions beyond the competences of the Community.');

- *Carlo Garcia Avello v Belgian State* Case C-148/02 [2003] ECR I-11613, [36] (Advocate General Jacobs referring to the UN Convention on the Rights of the Child and, at [29], to the International Commission on Civil Status Convention on the law applicable to surnames and forenames 1980 in construing Articles 17 and 18, EC Treaty);
- *R (Broadcasting, Entertainment, Cinematographic and Theatre Union) v Secretary of State for Trade and Industry* Case C-173/99 [2001] All ER (EC) 647, [27–28] (Advocate General Tizzano: '[T]he Charter of Fundamental Rights of the European Union has not been regarded as having genuine legislative scope in the strict sense . . . the fact remains that it includes statements which appear in large measure to reaffirm rights which are enshrined in other instruments . . . I think, therefore, that, in proceedings concerned with the nature and scope of a fundamental right, the relevant statements of the Charter cannot be ignored; in particular, we cannot ignore its clear purpose of serving, where its provisions so allow, as a substantive point of reference for all those involved—member states, institutions, natural and legal persons—in the Community context. Accordingly, I consider that the Charter provides us with the most reliable and definitive confirmation of the fact that the right to paid annual leave constitutes a fundamental right.');
- *Council of the EU v Heidi Hautala* Case C-353/99 P [2001] ECR I-9565, [67] (Advocate General Léger: 'The Court of Justice ensures compliance with fundamental rights. It contributes to their recognition and participates in the definition of their content. The general principles of Community law, of which fundamental rights are an integral part, are often derived from international instruments such as the European Human Rights Convention or the [International Covenant on Civil and Political Rights].');
- *Z v European Parliament* Case C-270/99 P, [2001] ECR I-9197, [40] (Advocate General Jacobs: '[T]he Charter of Fundamental Rights of the European Union, while itself not legally binding, proclaims a generally recognised principle in stating in Article 41(1) that "Every person has the right to have his or her affairs handled impartially, fairly and within a reasonable time by the institutions and bodies of the Union".').

7

The Human Rights Act 1998: An Indirectly Incorporating Statute

(1) Introduction

7.1. The Human Rights Act 1998 ('HRA') is the premier example of an indirectly incorporating statute in domestic law. It indirectly incorporates certain rights in the European Convention on Human Rights ('ECHR') into domestic law. Unlike the European Communities Act 1972 [chapter 6], the HRA does not confer the force of law on the ECHR. Instead it defines 'Convention rights' by reference to the ECHR, requires courts to apply and enforce these rights by statutory interpretation where possible and renders unlawful (with limited exceptions) any conduct of public authorities, including courts, which violates Convention rights, for which conduct they become civilly liable [§ 3.8.2]. The HRA also makes judgments of the European Court of Human Rights ('ECtHR') a relevant, but not a binding, source of law for these purposes [§ 7.7].

7.2. This is not the place for detailed consideration of Convention rights or the constitutional debates to which the HRA has given rise. Instead, as with Community law, the overview given below concentrates on those parts of the HRA which distinguish it from other incorporating statutes, for example its constitutional effect [§ 7.8], and are relevant when considering the role of international law, especially unincorporated treaties, in domestic law.

7.3. **Two key factors which distinguish the HRA from other incorporating statutes are the interpretative command in section 3 [§§ 7.9–7.10] which requires legislation to be interpreted compatibly with Convention rights, so far as possible, and section 4 which enables courts to make declarations of incompatibility where legislation cannot be read compatibly with Convention rights [§ 7.11].**

7.4. **The indirect incorporation of the ECHR into domestic law has also had a wider effect. It has affected the common law and has been applied to other incorporated treaty rights (to ensure that such rights are Convention-compliant). Further, the sources of law used by the ECtHR, for example treaties unincorporated in domestic law and international instruments, provide persuasive authority and instructive examples of how these sources may be used in domestic law when interpreting Convention rights [§§ 7.12–7.13].**

7.5. **Reading:**

- Clayton and Tomlinson, *The Law of Human Rights* (2001)
- Grosz, Beatson and Duffy, *Human Rights: The 1998 Act and the European Convention* (2000)
- Harris, O'Boyle and Warbrick, *Law of the European Convention on Human Rights* (2005)
- Lester and Pannick (eds), *Human Rights Law and Practice* (2004)

7.6. **The key provisions of the Human Rights Act 1998 are:**

- Section 1, 'The Convention Rights': '(1) In this Act "the Convention rights" means the rights and fundamental freedoms set out in—(a) Articles 2 to 12 and 14 of the Convention, (b) Articles 1 to 3 of the First Protocol, and (c) Article 1 of the Thirteenth Protocol, as read with Articles 16 to 18 of the Convention.'
- Section 2, 'Interpretation of Convention rights': '(1) A court or tribunal determining a question which has arisen in connection with a Convention right must take into account any—(a) judgment, decision, declaration or advisory opinion of the European Court of Human Rights, (b) opinion of the Commission given in a report adopted under Article 31 of the Convention, (c) decision of the Commission in connection with Article 26 or 27(2) of the Convention, or (d) decision of the Committee of Ministers taken under Article 46 of the Convention, whenever made or given, so far as, in the opinion of the court or tribunal, it is relevant to the proceedings in which that question has arisen.'
- Section 3, 'Interpretation of legislation': '(1) So far as is possible to do so, primary legislation and subordinate legislation must be

read and given effect in a way which is compatible with Convention rights. (2) This section—(a) applies to primary legislation and subordinate legislation whenever enacted; (b) does not affect the validity, continuing operation or enforcement of any incompatible primary legislation; and (c) does not affect the validity, continuing operation or enforcement of any incompatible subordinate legislation if (disregarding any possibility of revocation) primary legislation prevents removal of the incompatibility.'

- Section 4, 'Declaration of incompatibility': (1) Subsection (2) applies in any proceedings in which a court determines whether a provision of primary legislation is compatible with a Convention right. (2) If the court is satisfied that the provision is incompatible with a Convention right, it may make a declaration of that incompatibility. (3) Subsection (4) applies in any proceedings in which a court determines whether a provision of subordinate legislation, made in the exercise of a power conferred by primary legislation, is compatible with a Convention right. (4) If the court is satisfied—(a) that the provision is incompatible with a Convention right, and (b) that (disregarding any possibility of revocation) the primary legislation concerned prevents removal of the incompatibility, it may make a declaration of that incompatibility. (5) In this section "court" means—(a) the House of Lords; (b) the Judicial Committee of the Privy Council; (c) the Courts-Martial Appeal Court; (d) in Scotland, the High Court of Justiciary sitting otherwise than as a trial court or the Court of Session; (e) in England and Wales or Northern Ireland, the High Court or the Court of Appeal. (6) A declaration under this section ("a declaration of incompatibility")—(a) does not affect the validity, continuing operation or enforcement of the provision in respect of which it is given; and (b) is not binding on the parties to the proceedings to which it is made.'
- Section 6, 'Acts of public authorities': '(1) It is unlawful for a public authority to act in a way which is incompatible with a Convention right. (2) Subsection (1) does not apply to an act if—(a) as the result of one or more provisions or primary legislation, the authority could not have acted differently; or (b) in the case of one or more provisions of, or made under, primary legislation which cannot be read or given effect in a way which is compatible with the Convention rights, the authority was acting so as to give effect to or enforce those provisions. (3) In this section "public authority" includes—(a) a court or tribunal, and (b) any person certain of whose functions are functions of a public nature but does not include either House of Parliament or a person exercising functions in connection with proceedings in Parliament. (4) In subsection (3) "Parliament" does not include the House of Lords in its judicial capacity. (5) In relation to a particular act, a person is not a public authority by virtue only of subsection

(3)(b) if the nature of the act is private. (6) "An act" includes a failure to act but does not include a failure to—(a) introduce in, or lay before, Parliament a proposal for legislation; or (b) make any primary legislation or remedial order.'

- Section 7: '(1) A person who claims that a public authority has acted (or proposes to act) in a way which is made unlawful by section 6(1) may—(a) bring proceedings against the authority under this Act in the appropriate court or tribunal, or (b) rely on the Convention right or rights concerned in any legal proceedings, but only if he is (or would be) a victim of the unlawful act. (6) In subsection 1(b) "legal proceedings" includes—(a) proceedings brought by or at the instigation of a public authority; and (b) an appeal against the decision of a court or tribunal.'
- Schedule 1 sets out the Convention rights.

(2) The ECtHR and Domestic Courts

7.7. **Under section 2 [§ 7.6] of the HRA, domestic courts must take into account any relevant case law of the ECtHR. The role of the ECtHR in domestic law is supervisory, according domestic courts a margin of appreciation based, inter alia, on the recognition that it is domestic, rather than supranational, courts which are best able to gauge the application of law in the local context. Domestic courts should keep pace with the clear and constant jurisprudence of the ECtHR in all but exceptional cases. Once domestic remedies in the United Kingdom have been exhausted, the right of individual petition permits recourse to the ECtHR directly (Article 34, ECHR).**

7.7.1. **Supervisory role of ECtHR:**

- *R v DPP, Ex parte Kebilene* [2000] 2 AC 326 (HL), 380G (Lord Hope, noting that the margin of appreciation is: 'an integral part of the supervisory jurisdiction which is exercised over state conduct by the [ECtHR].').

7.7.2. **Distinguishing between the United Kingdom's international relationship and domestic courts' statutorily-defined relationship with the ECtHR:**

- *Re McKerr* [2004] UKHL 12 [2004] 1 WLR 807, [64] (Lord Hoffmann: 'Under the Convention, the United Kingdom is bound to accept a judgment of the Strasbourg court as binding: article 46(1). But a court adjudicating in litigation in the United Kingdom about a domestic "Convention right" is not bound by a decision of the Strasbourg court. It must take it into account.' At [68]: 'In the Court of Appeal [in *R (Khan) v Secretary of State for Health*] [2003] 3 FCR 341, Brooke LJ, giving the judgment of the court . . . said, at p 364, para 82: "we do not believe the court at Strasbourg would look at the matter in this way." I daresay it would not. But that is because the court would be concerned with the international obligations of the United Kingdom and not with the extent to which the 1998 Act was retrospective.').

7.7.3. **Domestic courts should keep pace with the clear and constant jurisprudence of the ECtHR:**

- *R (Ullah) v Special Adjudicator* [2004] UKHL 26 [2004] 2 AC 323, [20] (Lord Bingham: 'While such [ECtHR] case law is not strictly binding it has been held that courts should, in the absence of some special circumstances, follow any clear and constant jurisprudence of the Strasbourg court . . . This reflects the fact that the Convention is an international instrument, the correct interpretation of which can be authoritatively expounded only by the Strasbourg court. From this it follows that a national court subject to a duty such as that imposed by section 2 should not without strong reason dilute or weaken the effect of the Strasbourg case law . . . the meaning of the Convention should be uniform throughout the states party to it. The duty of national courts is to keep pace with the Strasbourg jurisprudence as it evolves over time: no more, but certainly no less.' Endorsed in *N v Secretary of State for the Home Department* [2005] UKHL 31 [2005] 2 WLR 1124, [24] (Lord Hope));
- *R (Alconbury Developments Ltd) v Secretary of State for the Environment, Transport and Regions* [2001] UKHL 23 [2003] 2 AC 295, [26] (Lord Slynn: 'In the absence of some special circumstances it seems to me that the court should follow any clear and constant jurisprudence of the European Court of Human Rights. If it does not do so there is at least a possibility that the case will go to that court, which is likely in the ordinary case to follow its own constant jurisprudence.'), [63] (Lord Nolan considering decisions of domestic courts as a contribution to the growth of Convention jurisprudence);
- *R v Lyons* [2002] UKHL 44 [2003] 1 AC 976, [46] (Lord Hoffmann: 'It is obviously highly desirable that there should be no divergence between domestic and ECHR jurisprudence . . . If . . . an English court considers that the ECHR has misunderstood or been misinformed about some aspect of English law, it may wish to give a judgment which invites the ECHR to reconsider the question . . . There is room for dialogue on such matters.');
- *R (Pretty) v DPP (Secretary of State for the Home Department intervening)* [2001] UKHL 61 [2002] 1 AC 800, [7] (Lord Bingham considering that where there is no direct Strasbourg authority on a given point, it may be relied upon, more generally, to confirm the proper approach to be taken. At [9], considering that the interpretation of ECHR rights may be undertaken by reference to entrenched principles of English law where such principles are not inconsistent with Strasbourg jurisprudence);

- *R (Anderson) v Secretary of State for the Home Department* [2002] UKHL 46 [2003] 1 AC 837, [18] (Lord Bingham, after referring to section 2(1)(a) of the HRA: '[T]he House will not without good reason depart from the principles laid down in a carefully considered judgment of the [ECtHR] sitting as a Grand Chamber'.);
- *Han v Customs and Excise Commissioners* [2001] EWCA Civ 1040 [2001] 1 WLR 2253, [100] (Sir Martin Nourse: 'We are required to take into account the decisions of the Strasbourg court. We cannot make our own decision without doing so and, in taking them into account, we must give them due weight, even though the doctrine of stare decisis does not apply. But it is important to emphasise that that doctrine is inapplicable, not only between decisions of the Strasbourg court and those of our own courts, but also between decisions of the Strasbourg court themselves.').

7.7.4. **Domestic courts may go beyond ECtHR jurisprudence [§ 3.17]:**
Illustrations:

- *Runa Begum v Tower Hamlets LBC* [2003] UKHL 5 [2003] 2 AC 430, [69] (Lord Hoffmann: 'I think that to apply the *Salesi* doctrine [*Salesi v Italy* (1993) 26 EHRR 187] to the provision of benefits in kind, involving the amount of discretion which is inevitably needed in such cases, is to go further than the Strasbourg court has so far gone. This would not matter—domestic courts are perfectly entitled to accord greater rights than those guaranteed by the Convention—provided that it was acceptable that the scope of judicial review should be limited in the way it is by section 204 [of the Housing Act 1996].');
- *R (S) v Chief Constable of South Yorkshire* [2002] EWCA Civ 1275 [2002] 1 WLR 3223, [41] (Lord Woolf MR noting as a result of the court's application of Article 8, ECHR: '[I]n this jurisdiction article 8(1) may have a longer reach than is strictly required by the [ECHR] as applied by Strasbourg.') (HL is at [2004] UKHL 39 [2004] 1 WLR 2196);
- *cf N v Secretary of State for the Home Department* [2005] UKHL 31 [2005] 2 WLR 1124, [25] (Lord Hope: 'It is for the Strasbourg court, not for us, to decide whether its case law is out of touch with modern conditions and to determine what further extensions, if any, are needed to the rights guaranteed by the Convention. We must take its case law as we find it, not as we would like it to be.'), [76] (Lord Brown: 'It would not be appropriate for this House to interpret the scope of Convention protection in this sort of case significantly more generously that does the European Court of Human Rights itself.').

7.7.5. **Increased desirability of following ECtHR judgments involving domestic cases:**
Illustrations:

- *Jones v The Ministry of the Interior Al-Mamlaka Al-Arabiya* [2004] EWCA Civ 1394 [2005] UKHRR 57, [15] (Mance LJ, in response to the submission that judgments of the ECtHR are not binding on domestic courts: 'However, the European Court of Human Rights [in *Al-Adsani*] was considering a judgment of the English Court of Appeal which is itself binding on us. The European Court concluded that this judgment was in conformity with international legal principles of immunity and as a result in accordance with the Convention. We would, if we were to accept [counsel's] submission, be departing without justification both from a previous decision of this court and from strongly expressed reasoning of a majority of the European Court of Human Rights regarding international legal principles of state immunity.').

7.7.6. **Domestic courts may diverge from the ECtHR in exceptional cases:**

- *R (Alconbury Developments Ltd) v Secretary of State for the Environment, Transport and Regions* [2001] UKHL 23 [2003] 2 AC 295, [76] (Lord Hoffmann: 'The House is not bound by the decisions of the [ECtHR] and, if I thought that the Divisional Court was right to hold that they compelled a conclusion fundamentally at odds with the distribution of powers under the British constitution, I would have considerable doubt as to whether they should be followed.');
- *R (Williamson) v Secretary of State for Education and Employment* [2002] EWCA Civ 1926 [2003] QB 1300, [37] (Buxton LJ accepting that section 2, Human Rights Act 1998, does not require English courts to treat the jurisprudence of the Convention organs 'just as if it were binding domestic authority. At the same time, however, the court must tread very carefully even where it thinks that rulings by the court or Commission may eventually prove to have been mistaken . . . I am certainly not prepared to ignore, and much less to hold to have been wrong, a reasoned decision of the Commission.') (HL is at [2005] UKHL 15 [2005] 2 WLR 590);

Illustrations:

- *Barrett v Enfield LBC* [2001] 2 AC 550 (HL), 558C–560D (Lord Browne-Wilkinson, considering that the problems in applying the reasoning of the ECtHR in *Osman v United Kingdom* (*The Times*, 5 November 1998) to the English law of negligence 'are many and various'.);
- *R (Al-Skeini) v Secretary of State for Home Department* [2004] EWHC 2911 (Admin) [2005] 2 WLR 1401, [265] (Rix LJ on the difficulties of following a judgment of the ECtHR which conflicted with earlier, Strasbourg, case law).

7.7.7. **A margin of appreciation is accorded by the ECtHR to national courts:**

- *R v DPP, Ex parte Kebilene* [2000] 2 AC 326 (HL), 380E–381C (Lord Hope: 'The doctrine of the "margin of appreciation" is a familiar part of the jurisprudence of the European Court of Human Rights. The European Court has acknowledged that, by reason of their direct and continuous contact with the vital forces of their countries, the national authorities are in principle better placed to evaluate local needs and conditions than an international court: *Buckley v United Kingdom* (1996) 23 EHRR 101, 129, paras.74–75. Although this means that, as the European Court explained in *Handyside v United Kingdom* (1976) 1 EHRR 737, 753, para. 48, "the machinery of protection established by the Convention is subsidiary to the national systems safeguarding human rights," it goes hand in hand with a European supervision. The extent of this supervision will vary according to such factors as the nature of the Convention right in issue, the importance of that right for the individual and the nature of the activities involved in the case. This doctrine is an integral part of the supervisory jurisdiction which is exercised over state conduct by the international court. By conceding a margin of appreciation to each national system, the court has recognised that the Convention, as a living system, does not need to be applied uniformly by all states but may vary in its application according to local needs and conditions.') Cited in *Brown v Stott* [2003] 1 AC 681 (PC), 711A (Lord Steyn);

- *Runa Begum v Tower Hamlets LBC* [2003] UKHL 5 [2003] 2 AC 430, [57] (Lord Hoffmann: 'National traditions as to which matters are suitable for administrative decisions and which require to be decided by the judicial branch of government may differ. To that extent, the Strasbourg court will no doubt allow a margin of appreciation to contracting states.').

7.7.8. **The right of individual petition:**

- Article 34, ECHR: 'The Court may receive applications from any person, non-governmental organisation or group of individuals claiming to be the victim of a violation by one of the High Contracting Parties of the rights set forth in the Convention or the protocols thereto. The High Contracting Parties undertake not to hinder in any way the effective exercise of this right.'

(3) Constitutional Effect of the HRA

7.8. **Unlike the generality of incorporating statutes, the HRA is a 'constitutional statute' [§ 3.4]. Whilst it preserves parliamentary sovereignty it has had a significant impact on the constitutional role of the courts: the HRA creates a new hierarchy of constitutional (Convention) rights and gives courts new powers and responsibilities: the powerful command to interpret (section 3) and discretion**

to make declarations of incompatibility (section 4). These powers are, however, conferred within set parameters. The interpretative command in section 3 requires judicial interpretation, not legislation. Similarly, the declaration of incompatibility is not a tool which affects the legal validity of legislation; it simply provides courts with a mechanism with which to convey the incompatibility of the impugned legislation to Parliament.

7.8.1. Recognising the HRA as a catalyst for change before commencement:

- *R v DPP, Ex parte Kebilene* [2000] 2 AC 326 (HL), 374H–375A (Lord Hope: 'It is now plain that the incorporation of the European Convention on Human Rights into our domestic law will subject the entire legal system to a fundamental process of review and, where necessary, reform by the judiciary.' At 378D–E: '[I]t is clear that until now, under the doctrine of sovereignty, the only check on Parliament's freedom to legislate in this area has been political. All that will now change with the coming into force of the Human Rights Act 1998. But the change will affect the past as well as the future. Unlike the constitutions of many of the countries within the Commonwealth which protect pre-existing legislation from challenge under their human rights provisions, the Act of 1998 will apply to all legislation, whatever its date, in the past as well as the future.');
- *R v North and East Devon Health Authority, Ex parte Coughlan* [2001] QB 213 (CA), [90] (Lord Woolf MR considering that in the period between the enactment and coming into force of the Human Rights Act 1998, the courts should pay 'particular attention' to the values in the ECHR, in this context, Article 8.);
- *Redmond-Bate v DPP* (DC) (2000) HRLR 249, [10] (Sedley LJ: 'Parliament has now enacted the Human Rights Act 1998, requiring every public authority, including the police and the courts, to give effect to the scheduled Convention rights unless statutory provision makes it impossible to do so. The bulk of the Act is not yet in force . . . But in this interregnum it is far from immaterial. Not only is it now accepted that the common law should seek compatibility with the values of the Convention insofar as it does not already share them; executive action which breaches the Convention already runs the risk, if uncorrected by law, of putting the United Kingdom in breach of the Convention and rendering it liable to proceedings before the European Court of Human Rights. There is, therefore, and has been for a long time, good reason for policing and law in this field to respect the Convention.').

7.8.2. The HRA should be recognised and interpreted as a constitutional measure:

- *McCartan Turkington Breen v Times Newspapers Ltd* [2001] 2 AC 277 (HL), 297G (Lord Steyn: 'The Convention fulfils the function of a Bill of Rights in our legal system. There is general agreement that the Human Rights Act 1998 is a constitutional measure.');
- *R v Offen* [2001] 1 WLR 253 (CA), [92] (Lord Woolf CJ: '[I]t is important to recognise that the 1998 Act is a constitutional instrument introducing into domestic law the relevant articles of the Convention.');
- *Thoburn v Sunderland City Council* [2002] EWHC 195 (Admin) [2003] QB 151, [62–63] (Laws LJ) [§ **3.4**].

7.8.3. **The constitutional effects of the Scotland Act 1998, the Government of Wales Act 1998 and the Northern Ireland Act 1998 are analogous to that of the HRA:**

- *HM Advocate v R* [2002] UKPC D3 [2004] 1 AC 462, [121] (Lord Rodger: 'The Scotland Act 1998 is a major constitutional measure which altered the government of the United Kingdom. This is reflected in the fact that, apart from section 25, the whole Act applies throughout the United Kingdom: section 131.'*);*
- *Brown v Stott* [2003] 1 AC 681 (PC), 715E–G (Lord Hope: 'The structure of the devolved system of government which is set out in the Scotland Act 1998 takes account of the state's obligations under the [ECHR] in the same way that it takes account of its obligations in Community law. In both respects Parliament has chosen to legislate in a way which ensures that those obligations are respected both by the Scottish Parliament and the Scottish Executive by limiting their competence. It has also chosen to ensure that questions which arise as to whether the Parliament or the Executive have acted or are proposing to act in a way that is incompatible with any of the Convention rights or with Community law may be resolved, as devolution issues, under the system laid down in Schedule 6. The same system has been adopted for the determination of devolution issues under the Government of Wales Act 1998 and the Northern Ireland Act 1998. These systems seek to achieve uniformity in the determination of these issues throughout all parts of the United Kingdom by reserving to the Judicial Committee of the Privy Council the power of final decision in all these matters.' See also 715H–716F);
- *Montgomery v HM Advocate* [2003] 1 AC 641 (PC), 659–662 (Lord Hope considering the aims and functions of the Scotland Act 1998);
- *R v DPP, Ex parte Kebilene* [2000] 2 AC 326 (HL), 376F (Lord Hope considering the impact of the Scotland Act 1998 on the Scottish Parliament and the Scottish Executive).

7.8.4. **The HRA preserves Parliamentary sovereignty:**

- *R (Hooper) v Secretary of State for Work and Pensions* [2005] UKHL 29 [2005] 1 WLR 1681, [105] (Lord Brown referring to 'the sovereignty of Parliament' as 'the cardinal principle enshrined in the [HRA].'). See, similarly, [70] and [78] (Lord Hope).

- *R v DPP, Ex parte Kebilene* [2000] 2 AC 326 (HL), 367A–B (Lord Steyn: 'It is crystal clear that the carefully and subtly drafted Human Rights Act 1998 preserves the principle of parliamentary sovereignty. In a case of incompatibility, which cannot be avoided by interpretation under section 3(1), the courts may not disapply the legislation. The court may merely issue a declaration of incompatibility which then gives rise to a power to take remedial action.');
- *R v Lyons* [2002] UKHL 44 [2003] 1 AC 976, [14] (Lord Bingham: '[A] Convention duty, even if found to exist, cannot override an express and applicable provision of domestic statutory law.'), [58] (Lord Hutton: 'Leaving aside any question as to the primacy of European Community law which does not arise in this case, Parliament is the supreme law-making body for the United Kingdom and a statute enacted by Parliament which cannot be read under section 3(1) of the Human Rights Act 1998 in a way which is compatible with the Convention prevails over any provision of the Convention or any judgment of the European Court whether the statute was passed before or after the coming into operation on 2 October 2000 of the 1998 Act.');
- *Wilson v First County Trust Ltd (No 2)* [2003] UKHL 40 [2004] 1 AC 816, [127–131] (Lord Hobhouse considering the preservation of Parliamentary sovereignty by the HRA).

7.8.5. **Potency of new constitutional (Convention) rights:**

- *Wilson v First County Trust Ltd (No 2)* [2003] UKHL 40 [2004] 1 AC 816, [180] (Lord Rodger: 'Although the Act is not entrenched, the Convention rights that it confers have a peculiar potency. Enforcing them may require a court to modify the common law. So far as possible, a court must read and give effect to statutory provisions in a way that is compatible with them. Rights that can produce such results are clearly of a higher order than the rights which people enjoy at common law or under most other statutes.');
- *International Transport Roth GmbH v Secretary of State for the Home Department* [2002] EWCA Civ 158 [2003] QB 728, [71] (Laws LJ: 'In its present state of evolution, the British system may be said to stand at an intermediate stage between parliamentary supremacy and constitutional supremacy . . . Parliament remains the sovereign legislature; there is no superior text to which it must defer (I leave aside the refinements flowing from our membership of the European Union); there is no statute which by law it cannot make. But at the same time, the common law has come to recognise and endorse the notion of constitutional, or fundamental rights. These are broadly the rights given expression in

the Convention for the Protection of Human Rights and Fundamental Freedoms.').

7.8.6. **Under the HRA, courts are guardians of human rights:**

- *International Transport Roth GmbH v Secretary of State for the Home Department* [2002] EWCA Civ 158 [2003] QB 728, [27] (Simon Brown LJ: '[T]he court's role under the 1998 Act is as the guardian of human rights. It cannot abdicate this responsibility.' At [54]: '[J]udges nowadays have no alternative but to apply the Human Rights Act 1998. Constitutional dangers exist no less in too little judicial activism as in too much. There are limits to the legitimacy of executive or legislative decision-making, just as there are to the decision-making by the courts.');
- *A v Secretary of State for the Home Department* [2004] UKHL 56 [2005] 2 WLR 87, [42] (Lord Bingham: 'It is of course true that the judges in this country are not elected and are not answerable to Parliament. It is also of course true . . . that Parliament, the executive and the courts have different functions. But the function of independent judges charged to interpret and apply the law is universally recognised as a cardinal feature of the modern democratic state, a cornerstone of the rule of law itself. The Attorney General is fully entitled to insist on the proper limits of judicial authority, but he is wrong to stigmatise judicial decision-making as in some way undemocratic. It is particularly inappropriate in a case such as the present in which Parliament has expressly legislated in section 6 of the 1998 Act to render unlawful any act of a public authority, including a court, incompatible with a Convention right, has required courts (in section 2) to take account of relevant Strasbourg jurisprudence, has (in section 3) required courts, so far as possible, to give effect to Convention rights and has conferred a right of appeal on derogation issues. The effect is not, of course, to override the sovereign legislature authority of the Queen in Parliament, since if primary legislation is declared to be incompatible the validity of the legislation is unaffected (section 4(6)) and the remedy lies with the appropriate minister (section 10), who is answerable to Parliament. The 1998 Act gives the courts a very specific, wholly democratic, mandate.');
- *Wilson v First County Trust Ltd (No 2)* [2003] UKHL 40 [2004] 1 AC 816, [61] (Lord Nicholls: 'The Human Rights Act 1998 requires the court to exercise a new role in respect of primary legislation. This new role is fundamentally different from interpreting and applying legislation. The courts are now required to evaluate the effect of primary legislation in terms of Convention rights and, where appropriate, make a formal declaration of incompatibility.').

7.8.7. **The HRA is not retrospective** [§ 7.9.5]:

- *R v Lambert* [2001] UKHL 39 [2002] 2 AC 545 (subject to the limited exception in section 22(4), an accused whose trial took place before 2 October 2000 could not rely, after that date, in the course of an appeal, on a breach of his Convention rights by the trial court), *cf* 567F–H (Lord Steyn dissenting on the basis that section 6(1) binds the HL; its effect is to provide that it is unlawful for the HL to act in a way which is incompatible with a Convention right, therefore it would be unlawful for the HL to uphold a conviction obtained in breach of a Convention right);
- *R v Kansal (No 2)* [2001] UKHL 62 [2002] 2 AC 69 (the reasoning in *R v Lambert*, excluding appeals from section 22(4), was mistaken but there was no compelling reason requiring the HL to depart from that decision), *cf* [50–77] (Lord Hope dissenting);
- *Re McKerr* [2004] UKHL 12 [2004] 1 WLR 807 (section 6(1), HRA, applied to an alleged violation of Article 2 where the killing occurred after 2 October 2000. Where the alleged violation of Article 2 is a failure to carry out a proper investigation into a killing and where the killing occurred before 2 October 2000, then section 6(1) does not apply);
- *R v Rezvi* [2002] UKHL 1 [2003] 1 AC 1099, [5] (Lord Steyn assuming that the Human Rights Act 1998 applied to the appeal even though the relevant events occurred before 2 October 2000; '[G]iven the fact that the Court of Appeal dealt with the Convention issues and bearing in mind the importance of the points, it would be sensible to give consideration to the potential impact of the Convention on the [Criminal Justice Act 1988].'), [26–27] (Lord Hope considering that the reasoning in *Lambert* and *Kansal (No 2)* (see above) applied to the present case even though those cases concerned appeals against conviction whereas the present case was an appeal against sentence but agreeing with Lord Steyn that: '[I]t would be sensible for your Lordships to take the opportunity of considering the potential impact of the Convention on confiscation proceedings under Part VI of the [Criminal Justice Act 1988].');
- *cf R v DPP, Ex parte Kebilene* [2000] 2 AC 326 (HL and DC), 341A–B (Lord Bingham (DC): 'If, at the time of the appeal hearing, the central provisions of the [HRA] had been brought into force, the applicants would on appeal be entitled to rely on sections 7(1)(b) and 22(4) of the Act.'), 368 B–C (Lord Steyn (HL): 'On appeal to the House, but not in the Divisional Court, [counsel] argued that section 22(4), read with section 7(1)(b), is apt only to extend to trial. It was an argument of some technicality. The language of the statute does not compel its adoption and a construction which treats the trial and the appeal as parts of one process are more in keeping with the purpose of the Convention and the Act of 1998.');

- *R (McCann) v Manchester Crown Court* [2002] UKHL 39 [2003] 1 AC 787 (on whether proceedings regarding the making of anti-social behaviour orders under section 1 of the Crime and Disorder Act 1998, are criminal in nature under domestic law and involve 'a criminal charge' under Article 6), [3] (Lord Steyn: 'In both cases [the proceedings being before 2 October 2000] the Human Rights Act 1998 is not directly applicable: *R v Kansal (No 2)* [2002] 2 AC 69. The House has, however, been invited by all counsel to deal with the appeals as if the Human Rights Act 1998 is applicable. My understanding is that your Lordships are willing to do so.');
- *Porter v Magill* [2001] UKHL 67 [2002] 2 AC 357, [82] (Lord Hope: 'One of the points which I made in my dissenting judgment [in *R v Kansal (No 2)*(see above)] was that I did not see how it was possible to confine the decision in that case to criminal cases only: see para 48 of my judgment. But this point has yet to be decided in a civil appeal, and it is perhaps still open to argument. As your Lordships did not hear any argument on it, I would prefer to approach the respondents' submissions as to fairness on the assumption that they are entitled to rely on their Convention rights in this appeal irrespective of the fact that all the acts in question took place before 2 October 2000.').

7.8.8. **Section 7, HRA, and retrospectivity:**

- *Wilson v First County Trust Ltd (No 2)* [2003] UKHL 40 [2004] 1 AC 816, [90] (Lord Hope: 'I do not think that there is any mystery as to why this provision [section 22(4)] was included in the 1998 Act, although the consequences that flow from it are much less certain. The explanation lies in the fact that the purpose of sections 6 to 9 of the Act is to provide a remedial structure in domestic law for the rights guaranteed by the Convention. As article 13 of the Convention makes clear, it is the obligation of states which have ratified the Convention to provide everyone within their jurisdiction with an effective remedy if the rights or freedoms which it protects are violated. The scheme of the Act is to give effect in domestic law to the obligation which is set out in article 13. If that scheme was to be followed through, victims had to be given an effective remedy in domestic law for a violation by the state of their Convention rights. The principle upon which the Act proceeds is that actions by public authorities are unlawful if they are in breach of Convention rights: section 6(1). Effect is given to that principle in section 7. But it was appreciated that victims of a violation by the state of their Convention rights were already entitled to obtain a remedy in the European Court of Human Rights under article 41 of the Convention. In that context it made sense for the provisions of section 6(1) to be made available for use defensively where proceedings are brought against the victim by or at the instigation of a public authority, whenever the violation took place. That is what section 22(4) achieves by enabling section 7(1)(b) to be given effect retrospectively.').

(4) Interpretative Effect of the HRA

A. *Section 3: The Interpretative Command*

7.9. **Section 3 of the HRA is of mandatory application when construing legislation. It commands courts to both interpret all legislation, and to give effect to it, in a Convention-compliant manner, if possible, regardless of whether it reveals any ambiguities or obscurities. Section 3 is, therefore, an express statutory enactment of the principle of legality [§§ 9.15–9.17]. It applies to all legislation in force, whenever enacted, but only applies to events occurring or causes of action accruing on or after 2 October 2000. Compatibility is assessed by reference to the date when the issue arises for determination, which will generally be when the alleged infringement occurred, not when the legislation was actually enacted or when its operation commenced.**

7.9.1. **Section 3 contains an interpretative command:**

- Section 3: [**§ 7.6**]
- *R v DPP, Ex parte Kebilene* [2000] 2 AC 326 (HL), 366B (Lord Steyn: 'Section 3(1) enacts a strong interpretative obligation.'), 373F (Lord Cooke: '[The new canon of interpretation in section 3(1)] is a strong adjuration.');
- *Ghaidan v Godin-Mendoza* [2004] UKHL 30 [2004] 2 AC 557, [44–45] (Lord Steyn) [**§ 7.9.2**], [59] (Lord Millett, on Lord Cooke's description in *Kebilene* (see above): 'With respect, it is more than this. It is a command. Legislation "*must*" be read and given effect to in a way which is compatible with Convention rights. There is no residual discretion to disobey the obligation which the section imposes.').

Illustrations:

- *R v Lambert* [2001] UKHL 37 [2002] 2 AC 545 (reading down section 28(2) and (3) of the Misuse of Drugs Act 1971 to make them compliant with Article 6(2), so as to impose an evidential and not a legal burden of proof on the defendant);
- *R (Sim) v Parole Board* [2003] EWHC 152 (Admin) [2003] 2 WLR 1374 (QBD) (reading section 44A(4) of the Criminal Justice Act 1991 compatibly with Article 5 by requiring the Parole Board to direct the release of a prisoner recalled during his licence period unless the Board was positively satisfied that public interest considerations compelled continued confinement) (CA, upholding

construction of section 44A(4) is at [2003] EWCA Civ 1845 [2004] 2 WLR 1170);

- *R v Carass* [2001] EWCA Civ 2845 [2002] 1 WLR 1714 (reading down the defence provided by section 206(4) of the Insolvency Act 1986 to make it compliant with Article 6(2), so as to impose an evidential and not a legal burden on an individual accused of concealing the debts of a company in anticipation of its winding up);
- *Goode v Martin* [2001] EWCA Civ 1899 [2002] 1 WLR 1828 (construing CPR 17.4(2) so as to be compliant with Article 6);
- *Sheldrake v DPP* [2003] EWHC 273 (Admin) [2004] QB 487 (reading down section 5(2) of the Road Traffic Act 1988 so as to be compliant with Article 6);
- *Ghaidan v Godin-Mendoza* [2004] UKHL 30 [2004] 2 AC 557, (further examples in the appendix to the opinion of Lord Steyn).

7.9.2. **Section 3 applies even where legislation is not ambiguous:**

- *Ghaidan v Godin-Mendoza* [2004] UKHL 30 [2004] 2 AC 557, [44–45] (Lord Steyn: 'It is necessary to state what section 3(1), and in particular the word "possible", does not mean. First, section 3(1) applies even if there is no ambiguity in the language in the sense of it being capable of bearing two *possible* meanings. The word "possible" in section 3(1) is used in a different and much stronger sense. Secondly, section 3(1) imposes a stronger and more radical obligation than to adopt a purposive interpretation in the light of the ECHR. Thirdly, the draftsman of the Act had before him the model of the New Zealand Bill of Rights Act which imposes a requirement that the interpretation to be adopted must be reasonable. Parliament specifically rejected the legislative model of requiring a reasonable interpretation. Instead the draftsman had resort to the analogy of the obligation under the EEC Treaty on national courts, as far as possible, to interpret national legislation in the light of the wording and purpose of Directives. In *Marleasing SA v La Comercial Internacional de Alimentación SA (Case C-106/89)* [1990] ECR I-4135, 4159, the European Court of Justice defined this obligation . . . Given the undoubted strength of this interpretative obligation under EEC law, this is a significant signpost to the meaning of section 3(1) in the 1998 Act.'[**§ 6.15.2**]), [29] (Lord Nicholls: 'It is now generally accepted that the application of section 3 does not depend upon the presence of ambiguity in the legislation being interpreted.');
- *R v A (No 2)* [2001] UKHL 25 [2002] 1 AC 45, [44] (Lord Steyn: 'The White Paper made clear that the obligation [in section 3] goes far beyond the rule which enabled the courts to take the Convention into account in resolving any ambiguity in a legislative provision: see Rights Brought Home: The Human Rights Bill (1997) (Cm 3782), para 2.7 . . . Under ordinary methods of interpretation a court may depart from the language of the statute to

avoid absurd consequences: section 3 goes much further. Undoubtedly, a court must always look for a contextual and purposive interpretation: section 3 is more radical in its effect. It is a general principle of the interpretation of legal instruments that the text is the primary source of interpretation: other sources are subordinate to it: compare, for example, articles 31 to 33 of the Vienna Convention on the Law of Treaties (1980) (Cmnd 7964). Section 3 qualifies this general principle because it requires a court to find an interpretation compatible with Convention rights if it is possible to do so.'), [108] (Lord Hope: 'The rule of construction which section 3 lays down is quite unlike any previous rule of statutory interpretation. There is no need to identify an ambiguity or absurdity. Compatibility with Convention rights is the sole guiding principle. That is the paramount object which the rule seeks to achieve.').

Illustrations:

- *Ghaidan v Godin-Mendoza* [2004] UKHL 30 [2004] 2 AC 557 (unambiguous legislation interpreted as Convention-compliant: Schedule 1, paragraph 2 to the Rent Act 1977, referring to: 'a person living with the original tenant as his or her wife or husband' applied to the survivor of homosexual couples living in a close and stable relationship);
- *R v A (No 2)* [2001] UKHL 25 [2002] 1 AC 45 (words read into section 41 of the Youth Justice and Criminal Evidence Act 1999 so as to make section 41 compliant with an accused's right to a fair trial under Article 6).

7.9.3. **Section 3 expressly enacts the common law principle of legality [§§ 9.15–9.17]:**

- *R v Secretary of State for the Home Department, Ex parte Simms* [2000] 2 AC 115 (HL), 131G–132B (Lord Hoffmann, after describing the protection afforded by the common law to human rights (the principle of legality): 'The Human Rights Act 1998 will make three changes to this scheme of things. First, the principles of fundamental human rights which exist at common law will be supplemented by a specific text, namely the European Convention on Human Rights and Fundamental Freedoms. But much of the Convention reflects the common law: see *Derbyshire County Council v. Times Newspapers Ltd.* [1993] AC 534, 551. That is why the United Kingdom government felt able in 1950 to accede to the Convention without domestic legislative change. So the adoption of the text as part of domestic law is unlikely to involve radical change in our notions of fundamental human rights. Secondly, the principle of legality will be expressly enacted as a rule of construction in section 3 and will gain further support from the obligation of the minister in charge of a Bill to make a statement of compatibility under section 19. Thirdly, in those unusual cases in which the legislative infringement of fundamental human rights is so clearly expressed as not to yield to the principle of legality, the courts will be able to draw this to the attention of Parliament by making a declaration of incompatibility. It will then be for the sovereign Parliament to decide whether or not to remove the incompatibility.');

- *A v Secretary of State for the Home Department* [2004] EWCA Civ 1123 [2005] 1 WLR 414, [233] (Laws LJ: 'The construction of statutes is hardly ever a value-free exercise. Where a statute on its ordinary construction infringes a constitutional right the courts will look to see whether it may after all be construed so as to avoid or at least diminish such an infringement. This is not merely a function of the Human Rights Act 1998 section 3(1). It is a function also of the common law, which gives special protection to constitutional fundamentals, albeit that section 3(1) is an interpretative tool of particular force in the context of [ECHR] rights.');
- *International Transport Roth GmbH v Secretary of State for the Home Department* [2002] EWCA Civ 158 [2003] QB 728, [73–75] (Laws LJ describing the principle of legality) **[§ 9.15.4].**

7.9.4. **There are two obligations in section 3: construing legislation to be Convention-compliant and giving effect to such legislation in a Convention-compliant way:**

- *Ghaidan v Godin-Mendoza* [2004] UKHL 30 [2004] 2 AC 557, [107] (Lord Rodger: 'The use of the two expressions, "read" and "given effect", is not to be glossed over as an example of the kind of cautious tautologous drafting that used to be typical of much of the statute book. That would be to ignore the lean elegance which characterises the style of the draftsman of the 1998 Act. Rather, section 3(1) contains not one, but two, obligations: legislation is to be read in a way which is compatible with Convention rights, but it is also to be given effect in a way which is compatible with those rights. Although the obligations are complementary, they are distinct. So there may be a breach of one but not of the other.').

7.9.5. **Section 3 and retrospectivity:**

- *Wilson v First County Trust Ltd (No 2)* [2003] UKHL 40 [2004] 1 AC 816, [17] (Lord Nicholls: 'Section 3 is retrospective in the sense that, expressly, it applies to legislation whenever enacted. Thus section 3 may have the effect of changing the interpretation and effect of legislation already in force.' At [20]: 'I agree with Mummery LJ in *Wainwright v Home Office* [2002] QB 1334, 1352, para 61, that in general the principle of interpretation set out in section 3(1) does not apply to causes of action accruing before the section came into force.'), [99] (Lord Hope: '[The] purpose [of section 3] is to ensure that legislation is read and given effect in a way that is compatible with Convention rights, so far as it is possible to do so, whenever the legislation was enacted. To restrict the application of the interpretative obligation, without exception, to "events" that happened or "transactions" entered into on or after 2 October 2000 would be to introduce a restriction which is not stated expressly anywhere in the 1998 Act. A restriction in such absolute and all-embracing terms would seem to be contrary to the intention of the legislation and incapable of being read into it by necessary implication.');

- *Wainwright v Home Office* [2001] EWCA Civ 2081 [2002] QB 1334, [27] (Lord Woolf considering that section 3, HRA, could not be applied to rule 86 of the Prison Rules 1964, made pursuant to the Prison Act 1952, when that rule was to be applied retrospectively to events when the HRA was not in force), [61] (Mummery LJ: 'I was wrong in the remarks made by me obiter in *JA Pye (Oxford) Ltd v Graham* [2001] Ch 804, 823, para 48 on the applicability of the principle of interpretation in section 3(1) to causes of action arising before the action came into force. Section 3(1) does not apply retrospectively to the cause of action in this case, which arose in 1997.').

Illustration:

- *Bellinger v Bellinger* [2003] UKHL 21 [2003] 2 AC 467, [65] (Lord Hope: interpretative obligation in section 3(1) of the Human Rights Act 1998 not available in relation to a marriage ceremony before 2 October 2000).

7.9.6. **Date for assessing compatibility under section 3:**

- *Ghaidan v Godin-Mendoza* [2004] UKHL 30 [2004] 2 AC 557, [23] (Lord Nicholls: 'Under the Human Rights Act 1998 the compatibility of legislation with the Convention rights falls to be assessed with when the issue arises for determination, not as at the date when the legislation was enacted or came into force.').

7.9.7. **Misunderstanding section 3:**

- *Ghaidan v Godin-Mendoza* [2004] UKHL 30 [2004] 2 AC 557, [39–41] (Lord Steyn, attaching an appendix to his opinion of statistics regarding the use of sections 3 and 4 of the HRA as an illustration of the misunderstandings about the remedial scheme of the Act).

7.9.8. **Application of section 3 to HRA itself:**

- *R v Lambert* [2001] UKHL 37 [2002] 2 AC 545, [110] (Lord Hope: '[Counsel] said that the interpretative obligation in section 3(1) applies to the provisions the 1998 Act in exactly the same way as it applies to any other statute. I agree.'), *cf* [142] (Lord Clyde: 'It is suggested that the 1998 Act should itself be subject to the interpretative regime contained in section 3. But I am not persuaded that there is any "Convention right" which requires appeals to be determined in that way. It is to be remembered that article 13 of the Convention is not included within the "Convention rights" for the purposes of the 1998 Act.').

7.10. **Where legislation is not Convention-compliant the precise source of incompatibility, the particular word or phrase, must be identified. The incompatibility should be construed to conform with Convention rights by, for example, giving the words a non-literal construction, reading down the words and giving them a restricted meaning or by reading additional words into the statute. Identifying the source of incompatibility is important for maintaining analytical rigour but also for ensuring that judicial interpretation does not trespass into legislation. This would be to exceed the limits of section 3. Therefore, where compatibility can only be achieved by rendering the legislation unworkable, the answer is to make a declaration of incompatibility and leave the matter to Parliament.**

7.10.1. **Section 3 requires precise identification of the word or phrase which is the source of incompatibility:**

- *R v Lambert* [2001] UKHL 37 [2002] 2 AC 545, [80] (Lord Hope: '[G]reat care must be taken, in cases where a different meaning has to be given to the legislation from the ordinary meaning of the words used by the legislator, to identify precisely the word or phrase which, if given its ordinary meaning, would otherwise be incompatible.');
- *In re S (Minors) (Care Order: Implementation of Care Plan)* [2002] UKHL 10 [2002] 2 AC 291, [41] (Lord Nicholls, considering section 3 in the context of the Court of Appeal's introduction of a 'starring system' under the Children Act 1989: 'When a court, called upon to construe legislation, ascribes a meaning and effect to the legislation pursuant to its obligation under section 3, it is important the court should identify clearly the particular statutory provision or provisions whose interpretation leads to that result. Apart from all else, this should assist in ensuring the court does not inadvertently stray outside its interpretation jurisdiction.');
- *Anderson v Scottish Ministers* [2001] UKPC D5 [2003] 2 AC 602, [36] (Lord Hope, applying his observations in *R v Lambert* [2002] AC 545, [78–81] (see above) to the equivalent interpretative obligation in the Scotland Act 1998, section 101).

7.10.2. **Parliament's discretionary area of judgment:**

- *Ghaidan v Godin-Mendoza* [2004] UKHL 30 [2004] 2 AC 557, [23] (Lord Nicholls: 'In the present case the House is concerned with the interpretation and application of domestic legislation. In this context the domestic counterpart of a state's margin of appreciation is the discretionary area of judgment the court accords Parliament when reviewing legislation pursuant to its obligations under the [HRA].');

- *R v DPP, Ex parte Kebilene* [2000] 2 AC 326 (HL), 381B–E (Lord Hope: 'In some circumstances it will be appropriate for the courts to recognise that there is an area of judgment within which the judiciary will defer, on democratic grounds, to the considered opinion of the elected body or person whose act or decision is said to be incompatible with the Convention . . . the area in which these choices may arise is conveniently and appropriately described [in Lester and Pannick (eds), *Human Rights Law and Practice* (1999) p 74, para 3.21] as the "discretionary area of judgment". It will be easier for such an area of judgment to be recognised where the Convention itself requires a balance to be struck, much less so where the right is stated in terms which are unqualified. It will be easier for it to be recognised where the issues involve questions of social or economic policy, much less so where the rights are of high constitutional importance or are of a kind where the courts are especially well placed to assess the need for protection.');
- *Brown v Stott* [2003] 1 AC 681 (HL), 703C–E (Lord Bingham: 'While a national court does not accord the margin of appreciation recognised by the European court as a supra-national court, it will give weight to the decisions of a representative legislature and a democratic government within the discretionary area of judgment accorded to those bodies.'), 711A (Lord Steyn: '[N]ational courts may accord to the decisions of national legislatures some deference *where the context justifies* it.');
- *R (Prolife Alliance) v BBC* [2003] UKHL 23 [2004] 1 AC 185, [75] (Lord Hoffmann: 'My Lords, although the word "deference" is now very popular in describing the relationship between the judicial and other branches of government, I do not think that its overtones of servility, or perhaps gracious concession, are appropriate to describe what is happening. In a society based upon the rule of law and the separation of powers, it is necessary to decide which branch of government has in any particular instance the decision-making power and what the legal limits of that power are. That is a question of law and must therefore be decided by the courts.'), [137–139], [143] and [144] (Lord Walker: '[T]he scope and reach of the 1998 Act is so extensive that there is no alternative [to a complex and contextually sensitive approach]. It might be a mistake, at this stage in the bedding-down of the 1998 Act, for your Lordships' House to go too far in attempting any comprehensive statement of principle. But it is clear that any simple "one size fits all" formulation of the test would be impossible', at [144]).

Illustrations:

- *Secretary of State for the Home Department v Rehman* [2001] UKHL 47 [2003] 1 AC 153, [31] (Lord Steyn construing 'conducive to the public good' and 'national security' in sections 3(5)(b) and 15(3) of the Immigration Act 1971 respectively: 'It is

Woolf MR stating that unless the legislation in question would otherwise be in breach of the ECHR, section 3, HRA, can be ignored).

7.10.4. **Techniques which may be used under section 3:**

- *R v A (No 2)* [2001] UKHL 25 [2002] 1 AC 45, [45] (Lord Steyn: '[S]ection 3 requires the court to subordinate the niceties of the language of [the statute] . . . to broader considerations of relevance judged by logical common sense criteria of time and circumstances.');
- *R v Lambert* [2001] UKHL 39 [2002] 2 AC 545, [80] (Lord Hope: '[C]are must . . . be taken to say how the word or phrase is to be construed if it is to be made compatible . . . It ought to be possible for any words that need to be substituted to be fitted in to the statute as if they had been inserted there by amendment. If this cannot be done without doing such violence to the statute as to make it unintelligible or unworkable, the use of this technique will not be possible. It will then be necessary to leave it to Parliament to amend the statute and to resort instead to the making of a declaration of incompatibility.' At [81], considering that courts are not bound by previous authority as to what a statute means; a strained or non-literal construction may be adopted, additional words may be read in, words may be 'read down' to give them a narrower construction than they would ordinarily bear, the words used may be expressed in different language to explain how they are to be read in a way that is compatible or it may be enough to say what the effect of the provision is without altering the ordinary meaning of the words used);
- *Ghaidan v Godin-Mendoza* [2004] UKHL 30 [2004] 2 AC 557, [32] (Lord Nicholls: '[Section 3] is also apt to require a court to read in words which change the meaning of the enacted legislation, so as to make it Convention-compliant.'), [119] (Lord Rodger: '[W]here the court finds it possible to read a provision in a way which is compatible with Convention rights, such a reading may involve a considerable departure from the actual words.'), [44–45] (Lord Steyn, using the *Marleasing* approach to inform interpretation of the Human Rights Act 1998) [**§ 7.9.2**].

7.10.5. **Distinguishing ordinary statutory construction from section 3:** ***Illustrations:***

- *R v J* [2004] UKHL 42 [2004] 3 WLR 1019, [15] Lord Bingham, construing section 14(1) of the Sexual Offences Act 1956: 'It is the duty of the court to give full and fair effect to the meaning of a statute. In a purely domestic context such as this, it cannot construe the statute by reference to any extraneous legal instrument. It must seek to give effect to all the provisions of a statute. It cannot pick and choose, giving effect to some and discounting others. It has no warrant, in a case such as this where no Convention right is engaged, to resort to the unique interpretative technique required by section 3 of the Human Rights Act 1998. If a statutory provision is clear and unambiguous, the court may not decline to give effect to it on the ground that its rationale is anachronistic, or discredited or unconvincing.');

- *R (Quintavalle) v Secretary of State for Health* [2003] UKHL 13 [2003] 2 AC 687, [21] (Lord Steyn: 'In reaching a conclusion that cell nuclear replacement is a process covered by section 1(1) of the Human Fertilisation and Embryology Act 1990, the Court of Appeal adopted a purposive approach: p 639, para 27. . . The Court of Appeal found the basis for such an approach in the fact that the Human Rights Act 1998 extended "the boundaries of purposive interpretation . . . where needs must". Given that the 1998 Act is not applicable in the present case I would accept the submission of counsel for the appellant that this approach is not appropriate. On the other hand, the adoption of a purposive approach to construction of statutes generally, and the 1990 Act in particular, is amply justified on wider grounds.').

7.10.6. **Section 3 requires courts to interpret not legislate:**

- *R (Wilkinson) v Commissioners of Inland Revenue* [2005] UKHL 30 [2005] 1 WLR 1718, [17] (Lord Hoffmann: 'I do not believe that section 3 of the 1998 Act was intended to have the effect of requiring the courts to give the language of statutes acontextual meanings. That would be playing games with words. The important change in the process of interpretation which was made by section 3 was to deem the Convention to form a significant part of the background against which all statutes, whether passed before or after the 1998 Act came into force, had to be interpreted. Just as the "principle of legality" meant that statutes were construed against the background of human rights subsisting at common law (see *R v Home Secretary, Ex p Simms* [2000] AC 115), so now, section 3 requires them to be construed against the background of Convention rights. There is a strong presumption, arising from the fundamental nature of Convention rights, that Parliament did not intend a statute to mean something which would be incompatible with those rights . . . But, with the addition of the Convention as background, the question is still one of *interpretation*, ie the ascertainment of what, taking into account the presumption created by section 3, Parliament would reasonably be understood to have meant by using the actual language of the statute.');
- *In re S (Minors) (Care Order: Implementation of Care Plan)* [2002] UKHL 10 [2002] 2 AC 291, [40–41] (Lord Nicholls, considering section 3, HRA, in the context of the Court of Appeal's introduction of a 'starring system' under the Children Act 1989: '[A] meaning which departs substantially from a fundamental feature of an Act of Parliament is likely to have crossed the boundary

between interpretation and amendment. This is especially so where the departure has important practical repercussions which the court is not equipped to evaluate. In such a case the overall contextual setting may leave no scope for rendering the statutory provision Convention compliant by legitimate use of the process of interpretation. The boundary line may be crossed even though a limitation on Convention rights is not stated in express terms.');

- *R v A (No 2)* [2002] UKHL 11 [2002] 1 AC 45, [108] (Lord Hope: '[T]he rule [in section 3] is only a rule of interpretation. It does not entitle the judges to act as legislators . . . The compatibility is to be achieved only so far as this is possible.');
- *R v Shayler* [2002] UKHL 11 [2003] 1 AC 247, [52] (Lord Hope: 'The obligation [in section 3], powerful as it is, is not to be performed without regard to its limitations . . . The techniques of judicial interpretation on the one hand and of legislation on the other are different, and this fact must be respected.').

Illustration:

- *R (Anderson) v Secretary of State for the Home Department* [2002] UKHL 46 [2003] 1 AC 837, [30] (Lord Bingham: 'Since, therefore, [section 29 of the Crime (Sentences) Act 1997] leaves it to the Home Secretary to decide whether or when to refer a case to the [Parole] board, and he is free to ignore its recommendation if it is favourable to the prisoner, the decision on how long the convicted murderer should remain in prison for punitive purposes is his alone . . . To read section 29 as precluding participation by the Home Secretary, if it were possible to do so, would not be judicial interpretation but judicial vandalism: it would give the section an effect quite different from that which Parliament intended and would go well beyond any interpretative process sanctioned by section 3 of the 1998 Act.').

7.10.7. **Overlap between sections 3 and 4: leaving it to Parliament:**

- *R v Shayler* [2002] UKHL 11 [2003] 1 AC 247, [52] (Lord Hope: 'If compatibility cannot be achieved without overruling decisions which have already been taken on the very point at issue by the legislator, or if to do so would make the statute unintelligible or unworkable, it will be necessary to leave it to Parliament to amend the statute. The only option left to the court will be to make a declaration of incompatibility under section 4(2) of the Act.');
- *R v A (No 2)* [2001] UKHL 25 [2002] 1 AC 45, [108] (Lord Hope: 'Plainly [compatibility] will not be possible if the legislation contains provisions which expressly contradict the meaning which the enactment would have to be given to make it compatible. It seems to me that the same result must follow if they do so by necessary implication, as this too is a means of identifying the plain intention of Parliament');
- *R v Lambert* [2001] UKHL 37 [2002] 2 AC 545, [80] (Lord Hope) [**§ 7.10.4**];

- *Bellinger v Bellinger* [2003] UKHL 21 [2003] 2 AC 467, [67] (Lord Hope), [78] (Lord Hobhouse) (both considering the overlap between sections 3 and 4).

B. *Section 4: Declarations of Incompatibility*

7.11. **Section 4 provides courts with discretion to make declarations of incompatibility [§ 7.6]. A declaration of incompatibility is a measure of last resort. It is only to be used when it is not possible to read legislation in a Convention-compliant manner under section 3 and where the legislation is incompatible with Convention rights. A declaration of incompatibility does not affect the legal validity of the legislation concerned. Instead it enables the government to make a political choice about whether to maintain the offending legislation on the statute book and triggers ministerial powers to amend the legislation. A declaration of incompatibility has separate utility as a formal record of incompatibility. Therefore, it may be made even where ministerial powers to amend have already been triggered.**

7.11.1. Declarations of incompatibility trigger ministerial power to amend:

- Section 10, HRA, 'Power to take remedial action': '(1) This section applies if—(a) a provision of legislation has been declared under section 4 to be incompatible with a Convention right . . . (b) it appears to a Minister of the Crown or Her Majesty in Council that, having regard to a finding of the European Court of Human Rights made after the coming into force of this section in proceedings against the United Kingdom, a provision of legislation is incompatible with an obligation of the United Kingdom arising from the Convention. (2) If a Minister of the Crown considers that there are compelling reasons for proceedings under this section, he may by order make such amendments to the legislation as he considers necessary to remove the incompatibility. (3) If, in the case of subordinate legislation, a Minister of the Crown considers—(a) that it is necessary to amend the primary legislation under which the subordinate legislation in question was made, in order to enable the incompatibility to be removed, and (b) that there are compelling reasons for proceeding under this section, he may by order make such amendments to the primary legislation as he considers necessary.'
- Schedule 2, HRA, makes provision for remedial orders.

7.11.2. **Declarations of incompatibility as measures of last resort:**

- *R v A (No 2)* [2001] UKHL 25 [2002] 1 AC 45, [44] (Lord Steyn: 'A declaration of incompatibility is a measure of last resort. It must be avoided unless it is plainly impossible to do so. If a *clear* limitation on Convention rights is stated *in terms*, such an impossibility will arise.'), [108] (Lord Hope) [§ **7.10.7**];
- *In re S (Minors) (Care Order: Implementation of Care Plan)* [2002] UKHL 10 [2002] 2 AC 291, [40–41] (Lord Nicholls: 'Lord Steyn's observations in *R v A (No 2)* [2002] 1 AC 45, 68D–E, para 44 [see above] are not to be read as meaning that a clear limitation on Convention rights in terms is the only circumstance in which an interpretation incompatible with Convention rights may arise.');
- *Bellinger v Bellinger* [2003] UKHL 21 [2003] 2 AC 467, [67] (Lord Hope referring to declarations of incompatibility as measures of last resort);
- *Ghaidan v Godin-Mendoza* [2004] UKHL 30 [2004] 2 AC 557, [50] (Lord Steyn: '[R]esort to section 4 must always be an exceptional course').

Illustrations:

- *R (Anderson) v Secretary of State for the Home Department* [2002] UKHL 46 [2003] 1 AC 837 (declaration of incompatibility made regarding section 29 of the Crime (Sentences) Act 1997 on the basis that the Home Secretary was not competent, under Article 6, to decide the tariff to be served by mandatory life sentence prisoners);
- *Bellinger v Bellinger* [2003] UKHL 21 [2003] 2 AC 467 (making a declaration of incompatibility where section 11(c) of the Matrimonial Causes Act 1973 could not be interpreted as extending to transsexuals);
- *International Transport Roth GmbH v Secretary of State for the Home Department* [2002] EWCA Civ 158 [2003] QB 728 (incompatibility of carriers fixed penalty scheme under section 32 of the Immigration and Asylum Act 1999 with Article 6 could not be rendered Convention-compliant by using section 3);
- *R (H) v London North and East Region Mental Health Review Tribunal* [2001] EWCA Civ 415 [2002] QB 1 (section 73 of the Mental Health Act 1983 declared incompatible with Article 5);
- *Ghaidan v Godin-Mendoza* [2004] UKHL 30 [2004] 2 AC 557, (further examples in the appendix to the opinion of Lord Steyn).

7.11.3. **Declarations of incompatibility have political effect:**

- *A v Secretary of State for the Home Department* [2004] UKHL 56 [2005] 2 WLR 87, [142] (Lord Scott: 'Whether the terms of the [Anti-terrorism, Crime and Security Act 2001] are consistent with the terms of the [ECHR] is, so far as the courts of this country are concerned, relevant only to the question whether a declaration of incompatibility under section 4 of the Human Rights

Act 1998 should be made. The making of such a declaration will not, however, affect in the least the validity under domestic law of the impugned statutory provision. The import of such a declaration is political not legal.').

7.11.4. **Declarations of incompatibility as formal records of incompatibility:**

- *Bellinger v Bellinger* [2003] UKHL 21 [2003] 2 AC 467, [54–55] (Lord Nicholls: '[Counsel] submitted that a declaration of incompatibility would serve no useful purpose . . . [because] the minister's powers have already been triggered in the present case under section 10(1)(b), by reason of the decisions of the European Court of Human Rights in [*Goodwin v United Kingdom* (2002) 35 EHRR 447] and the associated case of *I v United Kingdom* (Application No 25680/94)(unreported) 11 July 2002. Further, the Government has already announced its intention to bring forward primary legislation on this subject . . . I am not persuaded by these submissions. If a provision of primary legislation is shown to be incompatible with a Convention right the court, in the exercise of its discretion, may make a declaration of incompatibility under section 4 of the Human Rights Act 1998 . . . when proceedings are already before the House, it is desirable that in a case of such sensitivity this House, as the court of final appeal in this country, should formally record that the present state of statute law is incompatible with the Convention. I would therefore make a declaration of incompatibility as sought.');
- *A v Secretary of State for the Home Department* [2004] UKHL 56 [2005] 2 WLR 87, [90] (Lord Hoffmann: 'Under the 1998 Act, the courts still cannot say that an Act of Parliament is invalid. But they can declare that it is incompatible with the human rights of persons in this country. Parliament may then choose whether to maintain the law or not. The declaration of the court enables Parliament to choose with full knowledge that the law does not accord with our constitutional traditions.').

7.11.5. **Hansard may be used for background information when considering whether to make a declaration of incompatibility:**

- *Wilson v First County Trust Ltd (No 2)* [2003] UKHL 40 [2004] 1 AC 816, [63–66] (Lord Nicholls considering that when deciding whether to make a declaration of incompatibility: '[S]ometimes the court may need additional background information . . . This additional background information may be found in published documents, such as a government white paper. If relevant information is provided by a minister or, indeed, any other member of either House in the course of a debate on a Bill, the courts must also be able to take this into account. The courts, similarly, must be able to have regard to information contained in explanatory notes prepared by the relevant government department and published with a Bill . . . I expect that occasions when resort to Hansard is necessary as part of the statutory "compatibility" exercise will seldom arise. . .. Should such an occasion arise the courts must be careful not to treat the ministerial or other statement as indicative of the objective intention of Parliament. Nor should the courts give a ministerial statement, whether made inside or outside Parliament, determinative weight.'), [118] (Lord Hope: 'Resort to information of this kind [about Parliamentary proceedings] may cast light on what Parliament's aim was when it passed the provision in question or it may not. If it does not this cannot, and must not, be a ground for criticism. But if it does the court would be unduly inhibited if it were to be disabled from obtaining and using this information for the strictly limited purpose of considering whether legislation is compatible with Convention rights.').

(5) Wider Effect of the ECHR via the HRA

A. *Convention Rights as Part of Domestic Law*

7.12. **The indirect incorporation of the ECHR through the HRA has had a wide impact on domestic law. This is partly because courts, defined as public authorities under the HRA, section 6(3) [§ 7.6], are required not to act in a way which is incompatible with Convention rights. Convention rights, which were already reflected to a large extent in the common law [§ 9.17; §§ 10.7–10.8] and in the exercise of judicial discretion [§ 11.12] pre-HRA, have transfused the common law. Furthermore, where treaties have been incorporated (or partially incorporated) into domestic law it follows that they will be subject to the effect of the HRA just like any other domestic statutes.**

7.12.1. **The ECHR and the common law [§ 9.17; § 10.8]:**

- *R (Smith) v Parole Board* [2005] UKHL 1 [2005] 1 WLR 350, [74] (Lord Slynn: 'But the Convention can and does inform the common law, and the common law informs the Convention.');
- *Campbell v MGN Ltd* [2004] UKHL 22 [2004] 2 WLR 1232, [17] (Lord Nicholls: 'The time has come to recognise that the values enshrined in articles 8 and 10 are now part of the cause of action for breach of confidence . . . The values embodied in articles 8 and 10 are as much applicable in disputes between individuals or between an individual and a non-governmental body such as a newspaper as they are in disputes between individuals and a public authority.'), [46] (Lord Hoffmann, considering develop-

ments in the law of confidence: '[One development] has been the acceptance, under the influence of human rights instruments such as article 8 of the European Convention, of the privacy of personal information as something worthy of protection in its own right.' At [49–50], considering the same development further), [86] (Lord Hope commenting on the 'new breadth and strength' given to the cause of action for breach of confidence by the ECHR), [132] (Baroness Hale noting the '1998 Act does not create any new cause of action between private persons. But if there is a relevant cause of action applicable, the court as a public authority must act compatibly with both parties' Convention rights.');

- *A v B plc* [2002] EWCA Civ 337 [2003] QB 195, [4] (Lord Woolf CJ: '[Articles 8 and 10] have provided new parameters within which the court will decide, in an action for breach of confidence, whether a person is entitled to have his privacy protected by the court or whether the restriction of freedom of expression which such protection involves cannot be justified. The court's approach to the issues which the applications raise has been modified because, under section 6 of the 1998 Act, the court, as a public authority, is required not to act "in a way which is incompatible with a Convention right." The court is able to achieve this by absorbing the rights which articles 8 and 10 protect into the long-established action for breach of confidence. This involves giving a new strength and breadth to the action so that it accommodates the requirements of these articles.');
- *Coppard v Customs and Excise Commissioners* [2003] EWCA Civ 511 [2003] QB 1428, [28] (Sedley LJ considering the concept of a judge in fact (de facto)(where the acts of a judge may be held valid in law even though his appointment is invalid): 'The true ambit of the de facto doctrine cannot be logically determined by the requirements of article 6: to do this would be to adjust the common law defensively, not to declare it objectively. It is one thing to bring the substantive doctrines of the common law into harmony with the Convention in the manner described by this court in *A v B plc* [2003] QB 195, 202, para. 4 [see above]. It is another for a legal system to hold itself to be Convention compliant by ratifying what would otherwise be non-compliant.');
- *In re S (A Child) (Identification: Restrictions on Publication)* [2003] EWCA Civ 963 [2004] Fam 43, [47–48] (Hale LJ (dissenting, but whose detailed analysis of the law was accepted by the other members of the court) rejecting counsel's submission that the court can only strike a balance between the countervailing rights of individuals under article 8 and of the media under article 10 in an action for breach of confidence: 'An action for breach of confidence cannot be the only context in which the courts have to strike a fair balance between the rights of the individual under article 8 and article 10. While the court cannot invent a new cause of

action between private persons, the same issues arise whenever it has jurisdiction to restrain publications.');

- *Jones v The Ministry of the Interior Al-Mamlaka Al-Arabiya* [2004] EWCA Civ 1394 [2005] UKHRR 57, [91] (Mance LJ interpreting the State Immunity Act 1978: '[I]n so far as the present case is concerned with underlying or residual principles, these are themselves sufficiently open and flexible to respond to the inspriration of the European Convention.');
- *ID v Home Office* [2005] EWCA Civ 38 [2005] INLR 278, [82] (Brooke LJ in response to the use of *W v The Home Office* [1997] Imm AR 302 by counsel as authority for the proposition that English law provides no cause of action for an invalid administrative action of wrongful detention ([77–81]): 'But it must be observed that [the case] preceded the coming into force of the 1998 Act and the rigorous observations made by the House of Lords in recent years about the importance of the right to liberty.' At [100], considering the effect of the HRA on the remedy for invalid administrative acts, noting that *R v Governor of Brockhill Prison, Ex parte Evans (No 2)* [2001] AC 19 'shows how ECHR Article 5 not only made compensation for its violation mandatory but was also to add two further important ingredients into our law if the executive is to succeed in a defence of lawful justification: the law must be accessible and it must be proportionate.' At [113] viewing English law, 'through the prism of the ECHR.').

7.12.2. **Convention rights applied to incorporated treaties:**
Illustrations:

- *Re DVT and Air Travel Group Litigation* [2002] EWHC 2825 (QB) [2003] 1 All ER 935, [161] (Nelson J considering that the HRA applies to the Warsaw Convention on International Carriage by Air, as incorporated by the Carriage by Air Act 1961: 'The fact that a treaty so incorporated into our law retains its international character for the purposes of interpretation does not determine whether or not it amounts to primary legislation under the [HRA].' At [163]: 'Even where, as here, there is an indirect enactment of a treaty, the presence of that treaty in a schedule of the Act makes it part of that Act and hence itself primary legislation. It matters not that primary legislation is not defined in the 1998 Act so as to specifically include international treaties. Nor is pre-1998 Act authority relevant to whether or not the legislation is primary.' At [168]: 'If the international convention is enacted in such a way that it is primary legislation under s 3(1) of the 1998 Act its compatibility with the [ECHR] is relevant and must be considered.' Concluding, at [196], that Articles 7 and 24 of the Warsaw Convention are compatible with Articles 6(1) and 8, ECHR) (CA is at [2003] EWCA Civ 1005 [2004] QB 234);
- *S v B and Y* [2005] EWHC 733 (Fam), [35] (Sir Mark Potter P noting counsel's submission that 'the Hague Convention [on

International Child Abduction] as introduced into English Law by the [Child Abduction and Custody Act 1985] now requires to be interpreted as ECHR compliant'; after construing Article 13 of the Hague Convention and the 1985 Act: 'Nor do I consider that my obligation to construe the 1985 Act in a Convention-compliant manner and to have regard to Y's ECHR rights leads to any different result.' (at [52]).

B. *Sources of Law Used by the ECtHR*

7.13. **The ECtHR uses a wide range of international material in interpreting the ECHR to inform its analysis. This includes treaties which are unincorporated as a matter of the relevant state's national law and instruments which lack binding force even on the international plane (for example, the Universal Declaration on Human Rights [§ 1.93] and the EU Charter on Fundamental Freedoms [§ 1.79]). Since domestic courts are required to take into account ECtHR jurisprudence (HRA, section 2 [§ 7.6]), the use of such material by the ECtHR (as with the ECJ: [§ 6.20]) provides an indirect influence on domestic law (in addition to the other ways in which such sources are used by domestic courts: [chapters 9–11] and persuasive guidance on how it might be used in interpreting the ECHR.**

7.13.1. ECtHR influencing sources of law used by domestic courts:
Illustrations:

- *R (R) v Durham Constabulary* [2005] UKHL 21 [2005] 1 WLR 1184, [26] (Baroness Hale) [**§ 5.16.2; § 8.7.2**];
- *Dyer v Watson* [2002] UKPC D1 [2004] 1 AC 379, [104–106] (Lord Hope, interpreting the ECHR by reference to the UN Convention on the Rights of the Child and the United Nations Standard Minimum Rules for the Administration of Juvenile Justice 1985 ('the Beijing Rules') on the basis that: '[T]he Strasbourg court has taken into account the provisions of the following international instruments when considering the requirements imposed by the Convention in relation to proceedings involving juvenile offenders: *V v United Kingdom* (1999) 30 EHRR 121, 176, para 76.' (at [104])) [61] (Lord Bingham also interpreting Article 6, ECHR, by reference to the UN Convention on the Rights of the Child and the Beijing Rules.);
- *ID v Home Office* [2005] EWCA Civ 38 [2005] INLR 278, [36] (Brooke LJ using the UN Convention on the Rights of the Child to assess the lawfulness of detention under Article 5, ECHR by reference to the 'duty to interpret the ECHR in the light of other obligations in international law, including treaty obligations: see *T and V v UK* (2000) 30 EHRR 121 at para. 76 [**§ 7.13.2**].').

7.13.2. **International law, unincorporated treaties and international instruments used by the ECtHR as aids to construction:**
Illustrations:

- *Bankovic v Belgium* (2001) 11 BHRC 435, [57] (ECtHR: '[T]he principles underlying the [ECHR] cannot be interpreted and applied in a vacuum. The court must also take into account any relevant rules of international law when examining questions concerning its jurisdiction and, consequently, determine state responsibility in conformity with the governing principles of international law, although it must remain mindful of the convention's special character as a human rights treaty . . . The convention should be interpreted as far as possible in harmony with other principles of international law of which it forms a part.');
- *Al-Adsani v United Kingdom* (2002) 34 EHRR 11 (in determining whether the United Kingdom had failed to secure the applicant's right not to be tortured under Article 3, ECHR the ECtHR considered the prohibition against torture in Article 5, Universal Declaration of Human Rights [26]; Article 7, International Covenant on Civil and Political Rights [27]; Article 3, UN Declaration on the Protection of All Persons from Being Subjected to Cruel, Inhuman or Degrading Treatment or Punishment [28]; articles of the UN Convention Against Torture and Other Cruel, Inhuman and Degrading Treatment or Punishment [29]; and case law of the ICJ [30]. These were used to conclude that: 'Other areas of public international law bear witness to a growing recognition of the overriding importance of the prohibition of torture.' [60]. The Court accepted 'on the basis of these authorities, that the prohibition of torture has achieved the status of a peremptory norm in international law.' [61]) [**§ 2.16.2**];
- *T and V v United Kingdom* (1999) 30 EHRR 121, [76–77] (in considering the right to privacy of juvenile offenders, the ECtHR used the UN Convention on the Rights of the Child ('binding in international law on the UK', at [77]) and the United Nations Standard Minimum Rules for the Administration of Juvenile Justice 1985 ('the Bejing Rules') see [73]);
- *Muller v Switzerland* (1988) 13 EHRR 212, [27] (ECtHR referring to Article 19(2), International Covenant on Civil and Political Rights in construing Article 10, ECHR as providing 'confirmation that the concept of freedom of expression is such as to include artistic expression.');
- *Groppera Radio AG v Switzerland* (1990) 12 EHRR 321 (ECtHR construing Article 10(1), ECHR, by reference to Article 19, International Covenant on Civil and Political Rights, and its travaux; for example, noting that the absence of a provision in Article 19, International Covenant on Civil and Political Rights corresponds to the third sentence of Article 10(1));

- *Glasenapp v Germans* (1986) 9 EHRR 25, [48] (ECtHR comparing the provisions of article 21(2), Universal Declaration on Human Rights and Article 25, International Covenant on Civil and Political Rights on the right of equal access to public services with the absence of such a right in the ECHR and its Protocols).

7.13.3. **Unincorporated treaties and international instruments used by the ECtHR as background to the process of construction:**
Illustrations:

- *Sahin v Germany* (2003) 15 BHRC 84, [39–41] (Grand Chamber considering, as relevant international law, the UN Convention on the Rights of the Child, described as setting out: 'The human rights of children and the standard to which all governments must aspire in realising these rights for all children.' (at [39]));
- *Bladet Tromso and Stensaas v Norway* (1999) 29 EHRR 125, [65] (ECtHR noting that the protection of honour and reputation is internationally recognised by Article 17, International Covenant on Civil and Political Rights);
- *Melynchenko v Ukraine* [2004] ECHR 17707/02, [27–28] (ECtHR considering, as relevant international law, Article 25, International Covenant on Civil and Political Rights and the UN Human Rights Committee General Comment No 25 (1996));
- *Burghartz v Switzerland* (1994) 18 EHRR 101, [24] (ECtHR comparing Article 8, ECHR and the absence of explicit provisions on names to Article 24(2), International Covenant on Civil and Political Rights, Articles 7 and 8, UN Convention on the Rights of the Child and Article 18, American Convention on Human Rights);
- *Streletz, Kessler and Krenz v Germany* (2001) 33 EHRR 31, [93–94] (referring to the convergence of Article 3, Universal Declaration on Human Rights, Article 6, International Covenant on Civil and Political Rights and Article 2(1), ECHR as 'significant: it indicates that the right to life is an inalienable attribute of human beings and forms the supreme value in the hierarchy of human rights.');
- *Makaratzis v Greece* [2004] ECHR 50385/99, [28–29] (ECtHR Grand Chamber noting, as relevant international law, Article 6(1), International Covenant on Civil and Political Rights and the UN Human Rights Committee General Comment No 6).

PART III

Using Unincorporated Treaties

8

Unincorporated Treaties

(1) Introduction

8.1. Two overlapping principles have traditionally determined the role of unincorporated treaties in the domestic context. First, that domestic courts have no jurisdiction to construe or apply such treaties (the principle of non-justiciability) [§§ 8.5–8.7]. Secondly, that unincorporated treaties are not part of domestic law and cannot create directly enforceable rights in domestic law nor deprive individuals of existing domestic law rights (the principle of no direct effect) [§§ 8.8–8.9]. Despite these restricting principles, unincorporated treaties have an important role to play in relation to both statutory and common law. It is a principle of legal policy that domestic law should conform to international law. This principle has informed the development of presumptions of compatibility that both statutory and the common law should be interpreted in a way which does not place the United Kingdom in breach of (a) its international, unincorporated treaty, obligations [chapters 9; 10] nor (b) rules of international law [chapter 13].

8.2. The principles of non-justiciability and no direct effect are rooted in British constitutional orthodoxy: parliamentary sovereignty, the separation of powers and the constitutional role of the Crown prerogative [§ 2.9]. Treaties are made by the Crown, exercising its prerogative power. As such, the validity of treaties cannot be challenged in domestic law. The principle of non-justiciability is, therefore, strongly connected to the general non-justiciability of any exercise of the Crown's prerogative. Further, unincorporated treaties do not form part of domestic law. As agreements

concluded on the international plane, between international legal persons (whether states or international organisations), they fall outside the purview of domestic legal process.

- *JH Rayner (Mincing Lane) Ltd v Department of Trade and Industry* [1990] 2 AC 418 (HL), 499F–500C (Lord Oliver: 'It is axiomatic that municipal courts have not and cannot have the competence to adjudicate upon or to enforce the rights arising out of the transactions entered into by independent sovereign states between themselves on the plane of international law . . . On the domestic plane, the power of the Crown to conclude treaties with other sovereign states is an exercise of the Royal Prerogative, the validity of which cannot be challenged in municipal law . . . That is the first of the underlying principles. The second is that, as a matter of the constitutional law of the United Kingdom, the Royal Prerogative, whilst it embraces the making of treaties does not extend to altering the law or conferring rights upon individuals or depriving individuals of rights which they enjoy in domestic law without the intervention of Parliament. Treaties, as it is sometimes expressed, are not self-executing. Quite simply a treaty is not part of English law unless and until it has been incorporated into the law by legislation.'), 476F–477A (Lord Templeman discussing the inability of unincorporated treaties to alter domestic laws);
- *Higgs v Minister of National Security* [2000] 2 AC 228 (PC), 241A–242A (Lord Hoffmann considering two consequences of the Crown's unrestricted treaty-making power: first, treaties form no part of domestic law unless enacted by the legislature and, secondly, that unincorporated treaties have no effect upon the rights and duties of citizens in common or statute law);
- *British Airways v Laker Airways* [1984] QB 142 (CA), 192D–E (Sir John Donaldson MR, in the context of two bilateral treaties between the United Kingdom and the United States: '[A]s a matter of English law, a treaty is an agreement between sovereign states which does not of itself give rise to either rights or obligations in private individuals. Consistently with this approach this court has no jurisdiction to determine the meaning or effect of any treaty to which the Government of the United Kingdom is a party and indeed is not equipped to do so, that being a matter of public international law. This court is, however, concerned to be informed of the views of Her Majesty's Government concerning any treaty which forms part of the background to a dispute between private persons.' At 191A–C considering that treaties are not part of domestic law and can only be honoured or breached by states) (HL is at [1985] AC 58).

8.3. **The application of these traditional principles to human rights treaties has been criticised. Whilst the significance of such**

criticism may have declined post-HRA, it continues to stimulate the debate regarding future doctrinal development. The key criticisms have been noted by Lord Steyn:

> 'Since the *International Tin Council* decision is regularly cited in our courts, a brief reference to its reception in subsequent jurisprudential analysis may not be out of place . . . [D]istinguished commentators have criticised what has been called the narrowness of the decision in the House of Lords: see the criticism of Sir Robert Jennings in his 1989 F A Mann lecture: "An International Lawyer Takes Stock" (1990) 39 ICLQ 513, 524–526; and of Dame Rosalyn Higgins, "The Relationship between International and Regional Human Rights Norms and Domestic Law", in *Developing Human Rights Jurisprudence* (1993), vol 5, pp 16–23. The latter writer observed, at p 20: "international law is part of the law of the land. Some rights contained in international human rights treaties are not the produce of inter-State contract, but antedate any such multi-lateral agreement. The treaty is merely the instrument in which a rule of general international law is repeated. It bears repetition in an international instrument, partly because relatively 'new' rights may also be included, and partly because the treaty may involve procedural undertakings for the states parties. But none of that changes the character of a given right as an obligation of general international law. Freedom from torture, freedom of religion, free speech, the prohibition of arbitrary detention, should all fall in that category. As such—and even were these rights not already secure through a separate domestic historic provenance—they would be part of the common law by virtue of being rules of general international law." There is also growing support for the view that human rights treaties enjoy a special status: *Murray Hunt, Using Human Rights Law in English Courts* (1998), pp 26–28. Commenting on *Lewis v Attorney General of Jamaica* [2001] 2 AC 50 Lawrence Collins J commented that "it may be a sign that one day the courts will come to the view that it will not infringe the constitutional principle to create an estoppel against the Crown in favour of individuals in human rights cases": "Foreign Relations and the Judiciary" (2002) 51 ICLQ 485, 496. That is not to say that the actual decision in the *International Tin Council* case is wrong. On the contrary, the critics would accept the principled analysis of Kerr LJ in the Court of Appeal that the issue of the liability of member states under international law is justiciable in the national court, and that under international law the member states were not liable for the debts of the international organisation . . . The rationale of the dualist theory, which underpins the *International Tin Council* case, is that any inroad on it would risk abuses by the executive to the detriment of citizens. It is, however, difficult to see what relevance this has to international human rights treaties which create

fundamental rights for individuals against the state and its agencies. A critical re-examination of this branch of the law may become necessary in the future.' (*Re McKerr* [2004] UKHL 12 [2004] 1 WLR 807, [49–50])

8.4. **Arguably, therefore, human rights treaties should be treated as an exception to the principles of non-justiciability and no direct effect.**

- *Lewis v Attorney-General of Jamaica* [2001] 2 AC 50 (PC), 84H (Lord Slynn: 'It is of course well established that a ratified but unincorporated treaty, though it creates obligations for the state under international law, does not in the ordinary way create rights for individuals enforceable in domestic courts . . . But even assuming that that applies to international treaties dealing with human rights, that is not the end of the matter.');
- *R (Lika) v Secretary of State for the Home Department* [2002] EWCA Civ 1855 [2002] All ER (D) 230 (Dec), [31] (Lawrence Collins J commenting on Lord Hope's opinion in *R v Secretary of State for the Home Department, Ex parte Launder* [1997] 1 WLR 839, 867 (considering that executive decisions could be reviewed for rationality or legality where they took into account a potential breach of the, then unincorporated, ECHR): 'Like the cases on legitimate expectation, what he said represents a development in the relaxation of the basic rule of United Kingdom constitutional law that an unincorporated treaty cannot confer rights or impose duties in domestic law. Indeed it may be that those developments may yet lead to the creation of an estoppel against the Crown in favour of individuals in the case of unincorporated treaties dealing with human rights which are plainly intended to benefit individuals.') [§§ **11.10–11.11**];
- *R (Pepushi) v CPS* [2004] EWHC 798 (Admin) [2004] All ER (D) 129 (May), [29] (Thomas LJ referring to Lord Steyn's observations in *Re McKerr* [§ **8.3**] and noting: 'The cogent arguments advanced that, in the field of human rights treaties, there may be a limitation, whether by estoppel or otherwise, on the ability of the Executive to act against an individual where that action is in breach of the obligations undertaken by the Executive under international human rights treaties.');
- *Thomas v Baptiste* [2000] 2 AC 1 (PC), 23C (Lord Millett after noting that unincorporated treaties cannot alter domestic law: 'It is sometimes argued that human rights treaties form an exception to this principle. It is also sometimes argued that a principle which is intended to afford the subject constitutional protection against the exercise of executive power cannot be invoked by the executive itself to escape from obligations which it has entered into for his protection.');

- *cf R (Abbasi) v Secretary of State for Foreign and Commonwealth Affairs* [2002] EWHC 651 (Admin), [11] (Richards J referring to *R v Secretary of State for the Home Department, Ex p Brind* [1991] 1 AC 696 (HL) [§ **9.8.2**; § **9.8.4**] as 'a good illustration of the fact that so far as concerns the status of international treaties [in domestic law] no distinction is to be drawn for these purposes between international human rights treaties and other international treaties.') (CA is at [2002] EWCA Civ 1598 (2003) UKHRR 76).

(2) Non-Justiciability of Unincorporated Treaties

8.5. **The principle of non-justiciability regarding unincorporated treaties gives effect to the general non-justiciability of exercises of the Crown's prerogative powers [§ 8.2]. It is no longer the case that courts will refuse, in principle, to review exercises of the prerogative power since the source of executive power is no longer purely determinative of its amenability to judicial review. It is now well established that it is the subject-matter of executive power, rather than its source, which justifies review by courts. However, treaty-making has not been reviewed, since it is still regarded as a non-justiciable part of the prerogative power and a matter for the Crown in its conduct of foreign relations [§ 12.2].**

8.5.1. Treaty-making has not been subjected to judicial review and remains part of the traditional non-justiciable Crown prerogative [§ 12.3.7]:

- *Lewis v Attorney-General of Jamaica* [2001] 2 AC 50 (PC), 77B (Lord Slynn: 'Although in some areas the exercise of the prerogative may be beyond review, such as treaty-making and declaring war, there are many areas in which the exercise of the prerogative is subject to judicial review.');
- *Attorney-General v Nissan* [1970] AC 179 (HL), 216F–G (Lord Morris: 'The making of a treaty is an act of prerogative and both its making and its perfecting will be beyond the domain of municipal law.');
- *Blackburn v Attorney-General* [1971] 1 WLR 1037 (CA), 1040B (Lord Denning MR, considering a challenge to the Treaty of Rome: 'When [Her Majesty's] Ministers negotiate and sign a treaty . . . they act on behalf of the country as a whole. They exercise the prerogative of the Crown. Their action in so doing cannot be challenged or exercised in these courts.');
- *Ex parte Molyneaux* [1986] 1 WLR 331 (QBD), 335H–336B (Taylor J: 'As its name indicates, the Intergovernmental

Conference between the Government of the United Kingdom and that of another sovereign state would be of an international nature. The agreement itself is in the field of international relations. It is akin to a treaty. It concerns relations between the United Kingdom and another sovereign state and it is not the function of this court to inquire into the exercise of the prerogative in entering into such an agreement or by way of anticipation to decide whether the method proposed of implementing the agreement is appropriate.');

- *Lonrho Exports Ltd v Export Credits Guarantee Department* [1999] Ch 158, 179D–E (Lightman J: 'The interpretation of treaties not by statute incorporated into municipal law and the decision whether or not they have been complied with are matters exclusively for the Crown in its conduct of foreign relations.') [§ **12.2.3**];
- *Council of Civil Service Unions v Minister for the Civil Service* [1985] AC 374 (HL), 398 (Lord Fraser), 407 (Lord Scarman), 411 (Lord Diplock) [§ **8.5.2**].

8.5.2. **The potential reviewability of exercises of the Crown prerogative:**

- *Council of Civil Service Unions v Minister for the Civil Service* [1985] AC 374 (HL), 398 (Lord Fraser), 407 (Lord Scarman), 411 (Lord Diplock) (all considering that the justiciability of executive actions depends, not on the source of the power but on the subject matter), 418B–C (Lord Roskill: 'Many examples were given during the argument of prerogative powers which as at present advised I do not think could properly be made the subject of judicial review. Prerogative powers such as those relating to the making of treaties, the defence of the realm, the prerogative of mercy, the grant of honours, the dissolution of Parliament and the appointment of ministers as well as others are not, I think susceptible to judicial review because their nature and subject-matter are such as not to be amenable to the judicial process.');
- *R (Abbasi) v Secretary of State for Foreign and Commonwealth Affairs* [2002] EWCA Civ 1598 (2003) UKHRR 76, [106 (i)] (Lord Phillips: 'It is not an answer to a claim for judicial review to say that the source of the power of the Foreign Office is the prerogative. It is the subject-matter that is determinative.').

8.6. **The non-justiciability of the treaty-making power is, however, simply one element of the non-justiciability of unincorporated treaties. Another key element is that unincorporated treaties do not form part of English law. Domestic courts therefore lack jurisdiction to interpret them and are unable to adjudicate upon the issues arising from them. An undiscriminating application of this aspect of non-justiciability would render domestic courts unable to consider, for example, whether a party to an unincorporated**

treaty was in breach of its international law obligations and unable to consider the effects, in domestic law, of breaches of international law obligations. Domestic courts have, therefore, adopted a modified approach to non-justiciability [§ 8.7].

8.6.1. **Domestic courts have no jurisdiction to interpret unincorporated treaties since they are not part of domestic law:**

- *R v Lyons* [2002] UKHL 44 [2003] 1 AC 976, [27] (Lord Hoffmann, citing *JH Rayner (Mincing Lane) Ltd v Department of Trade and Industry* [1990] 2 AC 418 (see below and [§ **8.2**]) for the proposition that 'international treaties do not form part of English law and . . . English courts have no jurisdiction to interpret or apply them . . . Parliament may pass a law which mirrors the terms of the treaty and in that sense incorporates the treaty into English law. But even then, the metaphor of incorporation may be misleading. It is not the treaty but the statute which forms part of English law. And English courts will not (unless the statute expressly so provides) be bound to give effect to interpretations of the treaty by an international court, even though the United Kingdom is bound by international law to do so.');
- *A v Secretary of State for the Home Department* [2004] EWCA Civ 1123 [2005] 1 WLR 414, [434] (Neuberger LJ noting that it is 'well established' that international treaties do not form part of domestic law and that English courts have no jurisdiction to apply them directly as domestic law until they are incorporated);
- *JH Rayner (Mincing Lane) Ltd v Department of Trade and Industry* [1990] 2 AC 418 (HL), 515C–D (Lord Oliver considering that it would infringe the principle of non-justiciability for courts to embark upon the exercise of interpreting the terms of treaty and ascertaining, on the basis of that interpretation, the rights of the parties in international law and the consequences in municipal law of the rights so determined);
- *British Airways v Laker Airways* [1985] AC 58 (HL), 85H (Lord Diplock: 'The interpretation of treaties to which the United Kingdom is a party but the terms of which have not either expressly or by reference been incorporated in English domestic law by legislation is not a matter which falls within the interpretative jurisdiction of an English court of law.');
- *cf Rustomjee v The Queen* (1876–7) 2 QBD 69 (CA), 73 (Lord Coleridge CJ, dismissing the claim partly on the basis of the construction of Article 5 of the treaty between the Queen and the Emperor of China 'and upon the true construction of the language of the treaty, quite apart from higher and wider considerations.').

Illustrations:

- *JH Rayner (Mincing Lane) Ltd v Department of Trade and Industry* [1990] 2 AC 418 (HL), 510F–511H (Lord Oliver concluding that an express reference to the Sixth International Tin Agreement, an international treaty, in a 1972 Order in Council creating the legal persona of the International Tin Council 'imposes no necessary or mandatory requirements to jettison the general rule of non-justiciability of an unincorporated treaty and to consider the nature of the ITC in international law' (511G). Rather he considered the reference to be merely a formal declaration doing 'no more than [recognising] that there is an international organisation, created by treaty, of which the United Kingdom is a member . . . It cannot be deduced from this that Parliament was opening the door for the reception into English law of all the terms of the treaty and the creation, sub silentio, of rights and duties not grounded upon domestic law but created solely by the treaty provisions.' (511H));

- *cf JH Rayner (Mincing Lane) Ltd v Department of Trade and Industry* [1989] Ch 72 (CA), 180C (Kerr LJ: '[T]he claims of the doctrine of non-justiciability are particularly weak in cases such as the present, since the Order in Council of 1972 refers expressly to the Headquarters Agreement and [the Sixth International Tin Agreement] . . . That appears to be an unprecedented hybrid situation between an unincorporated and wholly incorporated treaty. In this novel situation I do not think that the doctrine of non-justiciability should properly preclude consideration of the [Sixth International Tin Agreement] and of its effect in international law.' See generally 177F–180D);
- *cf* also *Arab Monetary Fund v Hashim* [1991] 2 AC 114 (HL), 165C–E (Lord Templeman: 'The *Tin Council* case reaffirmed that the English courts can only identify and allow actions by individuals, sovereign states and corporate bodies. The *Tin Council* case reaffirmed that the English courts cannot identify and allow actions by international organisations which sovereign states by treaty agree to bring into existence. The *Tin Council* case decided, however, that the international organisation called the ITC had been created a body corporate by the English Order in Council . . . In the present case the English courts cannot identify and accept the right to sue of an international organisation which sovereign states by the AMF agreement agreed to create. But the English courts can identify and accept the right to sue of a corporate body created by a sovereign state pursuant to the obligations accepted by that state in the agreement.');
- *Briggs v Baptiste* [2000] 2 AC 40 (PC), 53D–E (Lord Millet: '[Their Lordships] are sitting as the final Court of Appeal for Trinidad and Tobago, i.e. the state concerned. They are concerned to apply the domestic law of Trinidad and Tobago. They have no jurisdiction to pronounce on the interpretation and effect of the [American Convention on Human Rights 1969] or the meaning of the Inter-American Court's orders.');
- *British Airways v Laker Airways* [1985] AC 58 (HL), 83D–F (Lord Diplock, considering that since a bilateral treaty with the United

States formed no part of domestic law it could not be interpreted by domestic courts);

- *Kingdom of Spain v Christie, Manson & Woods* [1986] 1 WLR 1120 (ChD), 1124E–F (Sir Nicholas Browne-Wilkinson V-C after referring to the International Convention relating to the exporting of works of art 'by way of background' (1123G) in determining whether the Kingdom of Spain could obtain a declaration to protect its property stating: 'It is no part of my function to construe that Convention. It is sufficient to say that it apparently only provides for the return of goods which have been stolen from museums and other public places.').

8.6.2. **Domestic courts have no jurisdiction to adjudicate on unincorporated treaties since they are not part of domestic law:**

- *R v Khan* [1997] AC 558 (HL), 581H–582C (Lord Nolan, after considering that breaches of Article 8, ECHR might be relevant to the exercise of power under section 78 of the Police and Criminal Evidence Act 1984: 'This does not mean that the trial judge is obliged to decide whether or not there has been a breach of the Convention . . . That is not his function, and it would be inappropriate for him to do so.');
- *JH Rayner (Mincing Lane) Ltd v Department of Trade and Industry* [1990] 2 AC 418 (HL), 499F–G (Lord Oliver: 'It is axiomatic that municipal courts have not and cannot have the competence to adjudicate upon or to enforce the rights arising out of transactions entered into by independent sovereign states between themselves on the plane of international law.' Citing *Cook v Sprigg* [1899] AC 572 and *Secretary of State in Council of India v Kamachee Boye Sahaba* (1859) 13 Moo. PCC 25);
- *R (CND) v The Prime Minister* [2002] EWHC 2777 (Admin) [2002] All ER (D) 245 (Dec), [36] (Simon Brown LJ: 'Laws LJ's dictum in paragraph 40 of his judgment in [*Marchiori v The Environment Agency* [2002] EWCA Civ 03] . . . that "democracy itself requires that all public power be lawfully conferred and exercised, and of this the courts are the surety". . . is not in point here: the domestic courts are the surety for the lawful exercise of public power only with regard to domestic law; they are not charged with policing the United Kingdom's conduct on the international plane.' At [37], differentiating between the consideration of an international treaty by reference to the facts of an individual case and general pronouncements upon the true interpretation and effect of a treaty: 'There is no distinction between the position of the United Kingdom and that of all other States to whom Resolution 1441 applies. Why should the English courts presume to give an authoritative ruling on its meaning? Plainly such a meaning would not bind other States. How could our assumption of jurisdiction here be regarded around the world as anything other than an exorbitant arrogation of adjudicative power?');

- *West Rand Central Gold Mining Co Ltd v The King* [1905] 2 KB 391 (DC), 408–409 (Lord Alverstone CJ: '[T]here is a series of authorities from the year 1793 down to the present time holding that matters which fall properly to be determined by the Crown by treaty or as an act of State are not subject to the jurisdiction of the municipal Courts, and that rights supposed to be acquired thereunder cannot be enforced by such Courts . . . It is a well-established principle of law that the transactions of independent States between each other are governed by other laws than those which municipal Courts administer.');
- *Cook v Sprigg* [1899] AC 572 (JC), 578 (Lord Chancellor: 'It is a well-established principle of law that the transactions of independent States between each other are governed by laws other than those which municipal courts administer.');
- *Uppal v Home Office The Times*, 21 October, 1978 (Sir Robert Megarry V-C: 'Obligations in international law which are not enforceable as part of English law cannot, in my judgment, be the subject of declaratory judgments or orders');
- *Attorney-General for Canada v Attorney-General for Ontario* [1937] AC 326 (PC), 347 (Lord Atkin stating that the stipulations in a ratified treaty, as acts of the executive, have no force of law).

Illustrations:

- *A v Secretary of State for the Home Department* [2004] UKHL 56 [2005] 2 WLR 87, [145] (Lord Scott: 'It is not, normally, the function of the courts to entertain proceedings the purpose of which is to obtain a ruling as to whether an Act of Parliament is compatible with an international treaty obligation entered into by the executive. The executive cannot make laws for the United Kingdom otherwise than pursuant to and within the constraints imposed by an enabling Act of Parliament. The executive has extensive and varied prerogative powers that it can exercise in the name of the Crown but none that permit lawmaking. In being asked, therefore, to perform the function to which I have referred, the courts are, it seems to me, being asked to perform a function the consequences of which will be essentially political in character rather than legal.');
- *R v Ministry of Defence, Ex parte Smith* [1996] QB 517 (CA), 558H (Sir Thomas Bingham MR: '[Questions relating to the future liability of the UK under the ECHR are not questions] to which answers may be properly or usefully proffered by this court.'), 564D–F (Henry J considering that courts do not entertain hypothetical questions on the effect of unincorporated treaties because, inter alia, Parliament has not given judges primary jurisdiction over the issues contained in the unincorporated treaty and domestic courts should refrain from speculation on international obligations.);
- *Ex parte Molyneaux* [1986] 1 WLR 331 (QBD), 335H–336B (Taylor J) [§ **8.5.1**];

- *Malone v Metropolitan Police Commissioner* [1979] Ch 344, 352A–354E (Sir Robert Megarry V-C considering that a declaration regarding international obligations could not be made under RSC Ord 15, r 16 since the ECHR was an unincorporated treaty and 'not justiciable in this way' (354C). At 355D: 'Even if I have jurisdiction to make them . . . I do not think the court should make useless declarations, especially when the object in seeking them seems to be to support some contention under a treaty over which the court has no jurisdiction.');
- *Republic of Italy v Hambros Bank Ltd* [1950] Ch 314, 329 (Vaisey J refusing a declaration regarding a financial agreement between the United Kingdom and Italy because the agreement was 'not cognisable or justiciable in this court.');
- *Westland Helicopters v AOI* [1995] QB 282, 294C (Colman J considering that it would be 'quite contrary to the principle of non-justiciability' to adjudicate on whether there has been a breach of treaty obligations by foreign states).

8.7. **The consequences of the principle of non-justiciability have been ameliorated in two ways. First, domestic courts interpret unincorporated treaties where this is relevant for determining the rights and obligations of parties in domestic law. Such instances are most likely to arise where domestic courts construe statutory provisions or the common law in the light of unincorporated treaty obligations [chapters 9–11]. Secondly, domestic courts have interpreted unincorporated treaties as part of the process of finding the United Kingdom to be in breach of its international law obligations. Where unincorporated treaties are considered by domestic courts they are interpreted according to the same principles as incorporated treaties: [chapters 4; 5].**

8.7.1. **Domestic courts have an interpretative jurisdiction over unincorporated treaties where this is relevant in determining rights and obligations in domestic law:**

- *JH Rayner (Mincing Lane) Ltd v Department of Trade and Industry* [1989] Ch 72 (CA), 164B–D (Kerr LJ discussing the principle of non-justiciability: 'But that is as far as the doctrine goes. It does not preclude the decision of justiciable issues which arise against the background of an unincorporated treaty in a way which renders it necessary or convenient to refer to, and consider, the contents of the treaty. Indeed, any contest as to whether or not an issue connected with an unincorporated treaty is justiciable will usually require some reference to the treaty. Apart from this, a court must be free to inform itself fully of the contents of a treaty whenever these are relevant to the decision of any issue which is not in itself a non-justiciable issue.');

- *R (CND) v The Prime Minister* [2002] EWHC 2777 (Admin) [2002] All ER (D) 245 (Dec), [36] (Simon Brown LJ: 'Should the court determine the meaning of an interntional instrument operating purely on the plane of international law? In my judgment the answer is plainly no. All of the cases relied upon by the applicants in which the court has pronounced upon some issue of international law are cases where it has been necessary to do so in order to determine rights or obligations under domestic law [referring to *Adan* [2001] 2 AC 477, *Oppenheimer v Cattermole* [1976] AC 249, *Abbasi* [2002] EWCA Civ 1598, *Launder* [1997] 1 WLR 839 and *Kebilene* [2000] 2 AC 326] . . . As [counsel] points out, there is in the present case no point of reference in domestic law to which the international law issue can be said to go; there is nothing here susceptible of challenge in the way of the determination of rights, interests or duties under domestic law to draw the court into the field of international law.'), [61] (Richards J summarising the situations in which unincorporated treaties may be considered in domestic law);
- *Coverdale v Tony Blair PM* [2003] EWCA Civ 436, [7] (Buxton LJ pointing out two 'insuperable difficulties' in claims that a war or invasion of Iraq by military force would be illegal and that the activities of the United Kingdom and United States in the 'No Fly Zones' in Iraq were illegal: 'First, the foreign relations of this country, and in particular decisions about the waging of war, are an act of the prerogative of a kind the courts have never interfered with and do not see themselves as having jurisdiction to address. Secondly, ours courts will not interpret or give rulings under instruments of international law unless there is a question of domestic law directly involved.' Citing as authority, at [9], *R (CND) v The Prime Minister* [2002] EWHC 2777 (Admin) at [36] (see above));
- *R v Secretary of State for Foreign and Commonwealth Affairs, Ex parte Rees-Mogg* [1994] QB 552 (DC) 67–68 (Lloyd LJ considering an exception to the principle of non-justiciability, viz., section 6 of the European Parliamentary Elections Act 1978 (as amended by section 3 of the European Communities (Amendment) Act 1986), which requires domestic courts to consider whether any treaty which the government proposed to ratify involved an increase in the powers of the European Parliament (and therefore required approval by Act of Parliament).

Illustrations:

- See generally [**chapters 9–11**];
- *The Republic of Ecuador v Occidental Exploration and Production Company* [2005] EWHC 774 (Comm) (the doctrine of non-justiciability did not prevent an English court from entertaining Ecuador's application to challenge the substantial jurisdiction of the Tribunal (of three arbitrators; the arbitration arising out of a Bilateral Investment Treaty concluded between the United States and Ecuadaor) under section 67 of the Arbitration Act 1996);

- *Saad, Diriye and Osorio v Secretary of State for the Home Department* [2001] EWCA Civ 2008 (2002) ACD 59, [11] (Lord Phillips MR: 'The concept of an individual having rights bestowed upon him by a treaty is not without jurisprudential difficulty. But any jurisprudential difficulties are of no immediate concern and it is convenient to refer to refugees in respect of whom Contracting States have duties under the [Refugee] Convention as having Convention rights. Public international law requires that signatories to the Convention must implement it in a manner which is reasonably efficacious. There is no doubt that this country is under an obligation under international law to enable those who are in truth refugees to exercise their Convention rights.');
- *Ex parte Molyneaux* [1986] 1 WLR 331 (QBD), 335F (Taylor J considering the text of the inter-governmental conference between the United Kingdom Government and the Government of the Republic of Ireland in November 1985 and concluding that it did not contravene any statute, rule of common law or any constitutional convention);
- *Pan-American World Airways Inc v Department of Trade* [1976] 1 Lloyd's Rep 257 (CA), 260 (Lord Denning MR, stating that a bilateral agreement (the Bermuda Agreement) between the United Kingdom and United States did not form part of the municipal law of the United Kingdom but, nevertheless, commenting on the proper interpretation to be given to it), *cf* 262 (Scarman LJ: 'I wish to reserve my opinion and indeed I do not think my opinion ought ever to be asked as to the meaning of annex II to the Bermuda Agreement.');
- *Attorney-General for Canada v Attorney-General for Ontario* [1937] AC 326 (PC) (Canadian legislation passed in performance of treaty obligations could not be justified under section 132 of the British North America Act 1867 because the obligations under the ratified conventions were not the obligations of Canada as part of the British Empire but of Canada in her status as an international person).

8.7.2. **Domestic courts adjudicating on international obligations under unincorporated treaties:**

Illustrations:

- *A v Secretary of State for the Home Department* [2004] UKHL 56 [2005] 2 WLR 87, [68] (Lord Bingham, in determining the validity of the derogation under Article 15, ECHR from Article 5, ECHR, in the Human Rights Act 1998 (Designated Derogation) Order 2001 (SI 2001/3644) and the compatibility of part 4 of the Anti-terrorism, Crime and Security Act 2001 with Article 5, ECHR: 'What cannot be justified here is the decision to detain one group of suspected international terrorists, defined by nationality or immigration status, and not another. To do so was a violation of article 14 [ECHR]. It was also a violation of article 26 of the [International Covenant on Civil and Political Rights] and so inconsistent with the United Kingdom's other obligations under international law within the meaning of article 15 of the European Convention.'), *cf* [145] (Lord Scott) [§ **8.6.2**]);

- *R (European Roma Rights Centre) v Immigration Officer at Prague Airport* [2004] UKHL 55 [2005] 2 WLR 1, [44–46] (Lord Steyn, finding that by operating a pre-clearance immigration system at Prague Airport the United Kingdom was in breach of its international obligations under Article 2, International Convention for the Elimination of All Forms of Discrimination, Article 26, International Covenant on Civil and Political Rights and the rule of customary international law of non-discrimination), [98–103] (Baroness Hale stating that the pre-clearance operation 'was not only unlawful in domestic law but also contrary to our obligations under customary international law and under international treaties to which the United Kingdom is a party', [98], referring to Article 26, International Covenant on Civil and Political Rights, [99], and Article 2, Convention on the Elimination of All Forms of Racial Discrimination, [100]);
- *R (R) v Durham Constabulary* [2005] UKHL 21 [2005] 1 WLR 1184, [19] (Lord Bingham considering that a warning given to a young offender under sections 65 and 66 of the Crime and Disorder Act 1998 to which neither he not his stepfather, as the appropriate adult, consented, was not incompatible with Article 6, ECHR, because his fair trial rights were not engaged and that there was no breach of the 'spirit or the letter' of the UN Convention on the Rights of the Child), [39–40] (Baroness Hale commenting on the inconsistency between provisions of the 1998 Act with rule 11 of the Beijing Rules (the UN Standard Minimum Rules for the Administration of Juvenile Justice) and Article 40(3)(b) of the UN Convention on the Rights of the Child and concluding, at [42]: 'I have grave doubts about whether the statutory scheme is consistent with the child's rights under the international instruments dealing with children's rights.' At [44]: 'But that does not mean that it was in breach of the child's rights under the European Convention on Human Rights, These are less extensive than his rights under the UNCRC, although the European court would undoubtedly take those rights into account when interpreting and applying articles 6 and 8.').

8.7.3. **Unincorporated treaties are construed using the same principles as are applied to incorporated treaties:**

- [**chapters 4; 5**].

(3) No Direct Effect of Unincorporated Treaties

8.8. **The starting point for the principle of 'no direct effect' is that unincorporated treaties are not part of domestic law. This underpins the consequences which flow from the principle, for example: unincorporated treaties cannot confer rights directly on individuals in domestic law, they cannot deprive individuals of rights which they have as a matter of domestic law, they are not contracts capable of enforcement in domestic courts, they cannot prevail over statutes, and the infringement of international, unincorporated treaty, obligations has no domestic significance (even when declared by international tribunals).**

8.8.1. **Unincorporated treaties are not part of domestic law:**

- *Thomas v Baptiste* [2000] 2 AC 1 (PC), 23B (Lord Millett stating that unincorporated treaties are not part of domestic law and cannot alter domestic law) [§ **8.8.3**];
- *Mortensen v Peters* (1905–6) F (JC) 93, 100–101 (Lord Dunedin: 'For us an Act of Parliament duly passed by Lords and Commons and assented to by the King, is supreme, and we are bound to give effect to its terms . . . It is a trite observation that there is no such thing as a standard of international law extraneous to the domestic law of a kingdom, to which appeal may be made.').

Illustrations:

- *Pan-American World Airways Inc. v Department of Trade* [1976] 1 Lloyd's Rep 257 (CA), 260 (Lord Denning MR, construing the Civil Aviation Act 1949 (enacted to give effect to the Chicago Convention on International Civil Aviation 1944): 'But now Pan-Am rely on the "Bermuda agreement" of 1946 [a bilateral agreement between the United Kingdom and the United States of America] . . . Now I would like to say at the outset that in my judgment this Bermuda agreement forms no part of the municipal law of this country . . . [The Bermuda Agreement] is a useful illustration as to what the Governments have agreed between themselves, but it seems to me it cannot restrict, as far as the Courts are concerned, any powers of the Secretary of State.'), 261 (Scarman LJ citing *Blackburn v Attorney-General* [1971] 1 WLR 1037 and *Rustomjee v The Queen* (1876) 2 QBD 69. At 262, considering that the Bermuda Agreement was 'at best' an arrangement between governments and therefore: 'It cannot possibly be that in the municipal field the Chicago Convention should be construed, or limited, in the light of that bilateral agreement.');
- *In re M and H (Minors)(Local Authority: Parental Rights)* [1990] 1 AC 686 (HL), 721F–H (Lord Brandon explaining that under section 9 of the Guardianship of Minors Act 1971, courts had no

jurisdiction to conduct a merits review of local authorities' decisions about children in their care and there was no ground for departing from this where the denial of a merits review breached rights under the (then unincorporated) ECHR).

8.8.2. **The general principle of no direct effect:**

- *The Parlement Belge* (1879) 4 PD 129, 150 (Sir Robert Phillimore pointing out that there exist: 'Treaties the provisions of which were inoperative without the confirmation of the legislature; while there are were others which operated without such confirmation.' Concluding, at 154–155, that the terms of a treaty conferring immunity were ineffective in English law unless confirmed by the enactment of Parliament.) (CA is at (1880) 5 PD 157);
- *Walker v Baird* [1892] AC 491 (JC) 496–497 (Lord Herschell noting that reliance on a treaty as justifying interference with private rights affords no defence in municipal law);
- *JH Rayner (Mincing Lane) Ltd v Department of Trade and Industry* [1990] 2 AC 418 (HL), 500B–D (Lord Oliver: '[T]he Royal Prerogative, whilst it embraces the making of treaties, does not extend to altering the law or conferring rights upon individuals or depriving individuals of rights which they enjoy in domestic law without the intervention of Parliament . . . So far as individuals are concerned [an unincorporated treaty] is res inter alios acta from which they cannot derive rights and by which they cannot be deprived of rights or subjected to obligations; and it is outside the purview of the court not only because it is made in the conduct of foreign relations, which are a prerogative of the Crown, but also because, as a source of rights and obligations it is irrelevant.').

8.8.3. **Unincorporated treaties cannot confer directly enforceable rights on individuals in domestic law nor deprive them of their pre-existing domestic law rights:**

- *JH Rayner (Mincing Lane) Ltd v Department of Trade and Industry* [1990] 2 AC 418 (HL), 500B–D (Lord Oliver stating that treaties are not self-executing, therefore they cannot confer rights on individuals nor deprive them of pre-existing domestic law rights) [§ **8.8.2**];
- *R v Lyons* [2002] UKHL 44 [2003] 1 AC 976, [13] (Lord Bingham: 'It is true . . . that rules of international law not incorporated into national law confer no rights on individuals directly enforceable in national courts.'), [40] (Lord Hoffmann) [§ **8.9**];
- *Thomas v Baptiste* [2000] 2 AC 1 (PC), 23B (Lord Millett: 'The making of a treaty, in Trinidad and Tobago as in England, is an act of the executive government . . . It follows that the terms of a treaty cannot effect any alteration to domestic law or deprive the subject of existing legal rights unless and until enacted into domestic law by or under the authority of the legislature. When

so enacted, the courts give effect to the domestic legislation not to the terms of the treaty.'), 32E–33C (Lord Goff and Lord Hobhouse (dissenting) interpreting 'due process of law' as synonymous with 'law of the land' in the Constitution of Trinidad and Tobago. At 31E construing references to 'law' in the Constitution as references to municipal law therefore excluding the unincorporated International Covenant on Civil and Political Rights and the American Convention on Human Rights. At 33D–E, rejecting an interpretation of 'due process of law' in the Constitution to take account of unincorporated treaty rights: 'This conclusion will disappoint those who contend for the application of unincorporated international human rights conventions in municipal legal proceedings so that such rights will be *directly* enforced in national courts as if they were rights existing in municipal law. The widest possible adoption of humane standards is undoubtedly to be aspired to. But it is not properly to be achieved by subverting the Constitutions of states nor by a clear misuse of legal concepts and terminology; indeed, the furthering of human rights depends upon confirming and upholding the rule of law.') [§ **8.8.1**];

- *In re M and H (Minors) (Local Authority: Parental Rights)* [1990] 1 AC 686 (HL), 721G (Lord Brandon: 'Although the United Kingdom is a party to the [ECHR], Parliament has not so far seen fit to make it part of our country's domestic law. This means that English courts are under no duty to apply its provisions.').

Illustrations:

- *R v Uxbridge Magistrates' Court, Ex parte Adimi* [2001] QB 667 (DC), 692H–693A (Newman J: 'I am unable to follow how an individual asylum seeker who has committed an offence within the jurisdiction can assert any private rights to have the law applied to him in a way which differs from other offenders by relying upon the terms of an international convention.' Citing *JH Rayner per* Lord Oliver at 499–500 (see above));
- *Philip Bros v The Republic of Sierra Leone and the Commission of the EC* [1995] 1 Lloyd's Rep 289 (CA), 295 (Hoffmann LJ considering the Lomé Convention entered into between the EC, Member States of the EC and certain African, Caribbean and Pacific States: 'The courts of the United Kingdom have no power to enforce at the behest of any sovereign state or at the behest of any individual citizen of any sovereign state rights granted or treaty obligations imposed in respect of a treaty by international law.');
- *Winfat v Attorney-General* [1985] 1 AC 733 (PC) (land developers in the New Territories failed in their claim that the Crown Lands Resumption Ordinance, which permitted the potential development value of land to be disregarded when calculating compensation for compulsory acquisition, was ultra vires a bilateral treaty between the United Kingdom and the Emperor of

China, the Peking Convention, which provided that any expropriation of land had to be bought at a fair price. The Board held that the Peking Convention did not give rise to rights enforceable in municipal courts and no municipal court had authority to enforce an obligation of the British Government entered into as an act of state—see especially 746A–H, 747H–748A (Lord Diplock));

- *Rustomjee v The Queen* (1876) 1 QBD 487, 497 (Lush J, considering that no rights could arise in individuals, enforceable against the Crown, by reason of an unincorporated treaty); in the CA at (1876) 2 QBD 69, 74 (Lord Coleridge: '[The Queen] acted throughout the making of the treaty in relation to each and every of its stipulations in her sovereign character, and by her own inherent authority; and, as in making the treaty, so in performing the treaty, she is beyond the control of municipal law, and her acts are not to be examined in her own Courts.');
- *Blackburn v Attorney-General* [1971] 1 WLR 1037, 1039G–H (Lord Denning MR relying on *Rustomjee* (see above) for the conclusion that domestic courts take 'no notice of treaties until they are embodied in laws enacted by Parliament.');
- *Littrell v United States of America (No 2)* [1995] 1 WLR 82 (CA), 88G–H (Rose LJ, considering the Visiting Forces Act 1952 which enacted various provisions to enable the government to ratify SOFA (the Status of Forces Agreement), albeit making no reference to SOFA, in the context of a US serviceman serving in England bringing an action against the US Government for personal injury: 'SOFA has no relevance to this plaintiffs claim').

8.8.4. **Unincorporated treaties are not domestically enforceable contracts:**

- *JH Rayner (Mincing Lane) Ltd v Department of Trade and Industry* [1989] Ch 72 (CA), 164B (Kerr LJ: 'Although treaties are agreements intended to be binding upon the parties to them, they are not contracts which our courts can enforce.');
- *Hoani Te Heuheu Tukino v Aotea District Maori Land Board* [1941] AC 308 (JC), 324D–325D (Viscount Simon LC: 'It is well settled that any rights purporting to be conferred by such a treaty of cession cannot be enforced in the courts, except in so far as they have been incorporated in the municipal law . . . So far as the appellant invokes the assistance of the court, it is clear that he cannot rest his claim on the Treaty of Waitangi, and that he must refer the court to some statutory recognition of the right claimed by him.').

8.8.5. **Unincorporated treaties cannot prevail over domestic statutes:**

- *R v DPP, Ex parte Kebilene* [2000] 2 AC 326 (HL and DC) (unincorporated treaties cannot prevail over domestic statutes even where there is an incorporating statute which has been enacted but which has not yet commenced), 340C–E (Lord Bingham, in the Divisional Court, explaining the inappropriateness of simply treating sections 16A and 16B of the Prevention of Terrorism (Temporary Provisions) Act 1989 as a 'dead letter' because: 'The [ECHR], despite its recent advance towards incorporation, has not crossed the Rubicon which separates prospective law from binding law. Prospective law cannot override binding law.');

- *R v Lyons* [2002] UKHL 44 [2003] 1 AC 976 [§ **8.8.7**];
- *R v Staines* [1997] 2 Cr App R 426 [§ **8.8.7**].

8.8.6. **Infringements of unincorporated treaties have no direct domestic law significance:**

- *R v Secretary of State for the Home Department, Ex parte Brind* [1991] 1 AC 696 (HL), 747H (Lord Bridge: 'It is accepted, of course, by the applicants that, like any other treaty obligations which have not been embodied in the law by statute, the [ECHR] is not part of the domestic law, that the courts accordingly have no power to enforce Convention rights directly and that, if domestic legislation conflicts with the Convention, the courts must nevertheless enforce it.');
- *Whaley v Lord Advocate* [2003] Scot CS 178 (CS), [44] (Lord Brodie: '[I]t would be without any legal consequence (and, indeed, meaningless) for the court to declare that [a statute] is incompatible with or non-compliant with or not in conformity with [unincorporated treaties and other international instruments].');
- *Derbyshire CC v Times Newspapers* [1992] QB 770 (CA), 818E–F (Ralph Gibson LJ pre-HRA: 'If by established principles of English law it is clear that Derbyshire County Council has the right to sue for libel then this court must say so and let the action proceed. It would not matter that the consequence of so holding might be that the defendants, if they should lose the action, would satisfy the European Court of Human Rights that any verdict against them would constitute a breach of article 10 the European Convention for the Protection of Human Rights and Fundamental Freedoms. Article 10, as with any other provision of the Convention, is not a rule of law of this country.');
- *R v Secretary of State for the Home Department, Ex parte Bugdaycay* [1987] 1 AC 514 (HL), 524G–525B (Lord Bridge considering that it would be 'plainly untenable' to require the Secretary of State's decision-making powers in determining refugee status to conform to recommendations in the UNHCR Handbook on Procedures and Criteria for Determining Refugee Status where this would have the effect of overriding statutory express terms.).

8.8.7. **Judgments of international courts declaring the United Kingdom to be in breach of its international obligations are of no direct effect in domestic law:**

- *R v Lyons* [2002] UKHL 44 [2003] 1 AC 976 (HL) (holding that section 434(5) of the Companies Act 1985 prevailed over any provisions of the (then unincorporated) ECHR or any judgment of the ECtHR), [44] (Lord Hoffmann distinguishing the application of judicial comity (requiring that judgments of international tribunals should be followed in a case between the same parties) on the present facts and regarding a judgment of the ECtHR where it was dealing with international law issues whereas the domestic court was required to deal with domestic law issues);
- *R v Staines* [1997] 2 Cr App R 426 (CA), 442–444 (Lord Bingham CJ, addressing the submission that section 78 of the Police and Criminal Evidence Act 1984 should be interpreted in accordance with a judgment of the ECtHR rather than with statutory provisions conflicting with the judgment: 'That would amount to a repeal, or a substantial repeal, of an English statutory provision which remains in force in deference to a ruling which does not have direct effect and which, as a matter of strict law, is irrelevant.' Quoting from *Saunders* [1996] 1 Cr App R 463, 477G (Lord Taylor CJ) '. . . But our duty at present is to apply our domestic law which is unambiguous . . . It cannot be right for a judge to exercise his discretion to exclude evidence of interviews simply on the ground that Parliament ought not to have countenanced the possibility of self-incrimination.').

8.9. **One way in which unincorporated treaty obligations could be given effect is to invoke the duty of courts, as one of the three organs of the state, to uphold the United Kingdom's international obligations. This argument has, however, been summarily dismissed by Lord Hoffmann:**

> 'The argument that the courts are an organ of the state and therefore obliged to give effect to the state's international obligations is . . . a fallacy. If the proposition were true, it would completely undermine the principle that the courts apply domestic law and not international treaties . . .[I]n the present context, to describe the courts as an organ of the state is significant only in international law. International law does not normally take account of the internal distribution of powers within a state. It is the duty of the state to comply with international law, whatever may be the organs which have the power to do so. And likewise, a treaty may be infringed by the actions of the Crown, Parliament or the courts. From the point of view of international law, it ordinarily does not matter. In domestic law, however, the position is very different. The domestic constitution is based upon the separation of powers. In domestic law, the courts are obliged to give effect to the law as enacted by Parliament. This obligation is entirely unaffected by international law.' (*R v Lyons* [2002] UKHL 44 [2003] 1 AC 976, [40]).

(4) An Exception

8.10. **An exception to the principles of non-justiciability [§§ 8.5–8.7] and no direct effect [§§ 8.8–8.9] is where the royal prerogative is independently effective in creating law, for example, an exercise of the royal prerogative can independently extend or contract the jurisdiction without the need for legislation. Treaties entered into in such areas are justiciable and have direct effect in domestic law.**

- *JH Rayner (Mincing Lane) Ltd v Department of Trade and Industry* [1990] 2 AC 418 (HL), 500H (Lord Oliver referring to 'the very rare case in which the exercise of the Royal Prerogative directly effects an extension or contraction of the jurisdiction without the constitutional need for internal legislation' in his list of examples where domestic courts might be required to adjudicate upon unincorporated treaties).

Illustrations:

- *Post Office v Estuary Radio Ltd* [1968] 2 QB 740 (CA), 753E–F (Diplock LJ: 'It still lies within the prerogative power of the Crown to extend its sovereignty and jurisdiction to areas of land or sea over which it has not previously claimed or exercised sovereignty or jurisdiction. For such an extension the authority of Parliament is not required. The Queen's courts . . . must give effect to it and are bound by it.' At 756F–757A: 'No question, therefore, arises as to the Crown's right to abandon sovereignty without the authority of Parliament; and the Convention [on the Territorial Sea and the Contiguous Zone], of which this court must take judicial notice, thus constituted a declaration by the Crown of an extension to the area over which it would claim to exercise territorial sovereignty as internal waters of the United Kingdom when the Convention came into force, as it did, on September 10, 1964—a matter which lies within the sole prerogative power of the Crown without any constitutional need for the consent of Parliament.');
- *The Parlement Belge* (1879) 4 PD 129, 150 (Sir Robert Phillimore giving an example of treaties which were operative without the confirmation of the legislature: 'The strongest instance . . . is the Declaration of Paris in 1856, by which the Crown in the exercise of its prerogative deprived this country of belligerent rights, which very high authorities in the state and in the law had considered to be of vital importance to it. But this declaration did not affect the private rights of the subject.') (CA is at (1880) 5 PD 197).

(5) Evidential Use of Unincorporated Treaties

8.11. **The principles of non-justiciability [§§ 8.5–8.7] and no direct effect [§§ 8.8–8.9] do not prohibit domestic courts from considering or construing unincorporated treaties in all cases. It has already been noted that domestic courts interpret unincorporated treaties where this is relevant for determining the rights and obligations of parties under domestic law and have adjudicated upon the United Kingdom's obligations in unincorporated treaties [§ 8.7]. Further, unincorporated treaties also have indirect effect in relation to legislation, common law, and exercises of executive and judicial discretion [chapters 9–11]. There are also other ways in which unincorporated treaties may be used. For example, treaties may be referred to where they provide evidence of factual propositions: the conclusion of a treaty and its terms are matters of fact. Additionally, where parties have entered into a contract in which they have chosen to incorporate the terms of a treaty, domestic courts may interpret the treaty to determine the rights and obligations of the parties under the contract.**

8.11.1. Using unincorporated treaties to resolve questions of fact:

- *JH Rayner (Mincing Lane) Ltd v Department of Trade and Industry* [1990] 2 AC 418 (HL), 500H–501B (Lord Oliver: 'It must be borne in mind, furthermore, that the conclusion of an international treaty and its terms are as much matters of fact as any other fact. That a treaty may be referred to where it is necessary to do so as part of the factual background against which a particular issue arises may seem a statement of the obvious. But it is, I think, necessary to stress that the purpose for which such reference can legitimately be made is purely an evidential one.' At 487C, considering the terms of the treaty as part of the 'essential background.');
- *Littrell v United States of America (No 2)* [1995] 1 WLR 82 (CA), 93H–94B (Hoffmann LJ: 'No doubt the courts may look at a treaty to see whether the foreign forces are here by invitation. This would not offend against the rule that treaties are not justiciable . . . [citing Lord Oliver in *JH Rayner (Mincing Lane) Ltd v Department of Trade and Industry* [1990] 2 AC 418 (see above)] This, I think, is the element of truth in [counsel's] assertion that the courts may take account of treaties of peace. The termination of a state of war has consequences in private law and the court may therefore examine the treaty to see whether peace has been concluded.' See also 92G–93C);
- *Zoernsch v Waldock* [1964] 1 WLR 675 (CA), 682D–E (Willmer LJ construing the International Organisations (Immunities and

Privileges) Act 1950 and the Council of Europe (Immunities and Privileges) Order 1960 (SI 1960/442): 'Whether or not the commission is an organ of the council seems to me to be a question of fact, to be resolved by a consideration of the provisions of the [ECHR], whereby it was set up.').

8.11.2. **Using unincorporated treaties as part of a contract:**

- *JH Rayner (Mincing Lane) Ltd v Department of Trade and Industry* [1990] 2 AC 418 (HL), 500F (Lord Oliver: 'Clearly, also, where parties have entered into a domestic contract in which they have chosen to incorporate the terms of the treaty, the court may be called upon to interpret the treaty for the purposes of ascertaining the rights and obligations of the parties under their contract.').

Illustrations:

- *R v Secretary of State for the Environment, Transport and the Regions, Ex parte Channel Tunnel Group Ltd and France Manche SA* [2001] EWCA Civ 1185 (Peter Gibson LJ interpreting a Treaty between the United Kingdom and France regarding the Channel Tunnel where a Concession Agreement entered into between the two countries had the 'legal status of a contract' ([8]) and provided that the relationship between the parties is to be governed by the Treaty, as given effect to in the Concession Agreement ([12]) and where domestic legislation implemented but did not incorporate the Treaty and Concession Agreement: Channel Tunnel Act 1987, section 1(1) ([16]));
- *Semco Salvage v Lancer Navigation* [1997] AC 455 (HL) 462B–C (Lord Mustill, considering the relevance of the International Convention on Salvage 1989 in a claim based on Lloyd's Open Form 1990 (LOF 1990), where the Convention was incorporated by reference into LOF 1990. At 464A: noting the preamble to the Convention: 'which although not directly incorporated in LOF 1990 is plainly relevant to a proper understanding [of the Convention and LOF 1990].');
- *Westland Helicopters Ltd v Arab Organisation for Industrialisation* [1995] QB 282, 308C–F (Colman J: 'I have no doubt whatever that the proper law governing the existence, constitution and authority of its officers to represent the AOI is public international law. In arriving at this conclusion I have referred to the terms of the treaty and the basic statute. That has been a permissible course, without transgressing the frontiers between justiciability and non-justiciability.');
- *Phillipson v Imperial Airways Ltd* [1939] AC 332 (HL) (whether a carriage of goods by air was international carriage (between High Contracting Parties) was to be determined by reference to the Warsaw Convention 1929 rather than by reference to the contract itself), 346F–G (Lord Atkin: 'To ascertain what the contract between the parties means by High Contracting Parties to the

Convention the correct course must in my opinion be to look at the Convention itself. The phrase is one of diplomatic usage, and its use in these general conditions, based as they expressly are on the Convention, must, I think, depend on the meaning in the Convention.');

- *Marc Rich & Co v Bishop Rock Ltd* [1996] AC 211 (HL), 222B–223D (Lord Lloyd considering that where a voyage charterparty provided that bills of lading issued under the charterparty should incorporate the Hague Rules, the Hague Rules were irrelevant in considering whether a classification society owed a duty of care to cargo owners laden on vessel), 240B–C (Lord Steyn: 'The result of a recognition of a duty in this case will be to enable cargo owners, or rather their insurers, to disturb the balance created by the Hague Rules and Hague-Visby Rules as well as by tonnage limitation provisions, by enabling cargo owners to recover in tort against a peripheral party to the prejudice of the protection of shipowners under the existing system.').

9

Unincorporated Treaties and Legislation

(1) Introduction

9.1. **Unincorporated treaties relate to domestic legislation in three key ways ('the three levels of engagement'). First, and at the level closest to that of an incorporated treaty, a statute may expressly provide that it gives effect to an unincorporated treaty (for example in the long title) or that it requires statutory conferrals of executive power to be exercised in accordance with treaty obligations (collectively the 'express reference' group). Secondly, even where a statute does not expressly refer to an unincorporated treaty it may be clear from extrinsic evidence that it was intended to give effect to the treaty (the 'evidential nexus' group). Finally, an unincorporated treaty may be of general relevance to domestic statutes by addressing the same underlying issues or principles (the 'general relevance' group). This last group covers treaties which are purely unincorporated. The other two groups are hybrids—there is a connection between the legislation and the unincorporated treaty but it is insufficiently close to give those treaties the status of incorporation. Although, for the purposes of general classification, these hybrids are treated similarly to purely unincorporated treaties in the general relevance group, as a matter of practice it is easier to invoke unincorporated treaties when construing and applying hybrid statutes in the express reference or the evidential nexus groups.**

9.1.1. The express reference group:
Illustrations:

- Suppression of Terrorism Act 1978, long title: 'An Act to give effect to the European Convention on the Suppression of Terrorism'. The Convention is not given force of law.

- Civil Aviation Act 1982, section 60(2) enables Orders in Council to contain provisions which are requisite or expedient for carrying out the Chicago Convention (the Convention on International Civil Aviation 1944).
- Prevention of Pollution Act 1971, section 1(2) provides that it shall apply to regulations made by the Secretary of State 'having regard to the provisions of any Convention accepted by Her Majesty's Government in the United Kingdom in so far as it relates to the prevention of pollution of the sea by oil, or having regard to the persistent character of oil of that description and the likelihood that it would cause pollution if discharged from a ship into any part of the sea outside the territorial waters of the United Kingdom.'
- Railways and Transport Safety Act 2003, section 103(1) provides that the Secretary of State may make regulations for the purpose of giving effect to the Convention concerning International Carriage by Rail 1980.

9.1.2. **The evidential nexus group:**
Illustrations:

- Criminal Justice Act 1988, section 133 gives effect to Article 14(6), International Covenant on Civil and Political Rights (see, for example: *R (Mullen) v Secretary of State for the Home Department* [2004] UKHL 18 [2005] 1 AC 1) [§ **9.14.1**] ;
- Asylum and Immigration Act 1996, sections 2 and 3 give effect to the Dublin Convention on the State Responsible for Examining Applications for Asylum Lodged in one of the Member States of the European Communities (see, for example: *R (Lika) v Secretary of State for the Home Department* [2002] EWCA Civ 1855 [2002] All ER (D) 230 (Dec), [20] (Latham LJ) [§ **3.12.1**]);
- Children Act 1989, part III reflects the obligation in Article 18(2) of the UN Convention on the Rights of the Child (see, for example, *R (G) v Barnet LBC* [2003] UKHL 57 [2004] 2 AC 208, [68] (Lord Hope));
- Criminal Justice Act 1988, section 134(1) gives effect to Article 1(1), of the UN Convention Against Torture and Other Cruel, Inhuman and Degrading Treatment or Punishment 1984 (see, for example, *R v Bow Street Magistrate, Ex parte Pinochet* [2000] 1 AC 147 (HL), 200B (Lord Browne-Wilkinson [§ **9.14.1**]));
- Evidence (Proceedings in Other Jurisdictions) Act 1975 was passed to give effect to the principles of the Hague Convention on the Taking of Evidence Abroad in Civil and Commercial Matters of 1970 (see, for example: *In re Westinghouse Uranium Contract* [1978] AC 547 (HL), 608B–C (Lord Wilberforce).

9.2. **Although the principles of non-justiciability [§§ 8.5–8.7] and no direct effect [§§ 8.8–8.9] have limited the formal role of unincor-**

porated treaties in domestic law they have not impeded the steady, and continuing, use of such treaties as a source of (soft) law when construing statutory provisions. The nucleus of the relationship between unincorporated treaties and legislation is represented by two canons of interpretation: the presumption of compatibility [§§ 9.7–9.14] and the principle of legality [§§ 9.15–9.17]. The presumption of compatibility is used to construe ambiguities and obscurities in legislation compatibly with the United Kingdom's international obligations in unincorporated treaties. The principle of legality is used to construe general words in legislation in accordance with fundamental human rights.

> '[T]here are two well known canons of statutory interpretation which [are relevant] when the courts are concerned with the interpretation of a statute in a field where this country has bound itself by international treaty obligations: ". . . Parliament does not intend to deprive the subject of his or her common-law rights except where this is made clear by express words or necessary implication:" see *de Smith, Woolf and Jowell, Judicial Review of Administrative Action*, 5th ed. (1995), p.326, para. 6-054; see also *Bennion, Statutory Interpretation*, 2nd ed. (1992), pp.561–564: "it is a principle of construction of United Kingdom statutes . . . that the words of a statute passed after the Treaty has been signed and dealing with the subject matter of the international obligation of the United Kingdom, are to be construed, if they are reasonably capable of bearing such a meaning, as intended to carry out the obligation and not to be inconsistent with it": *Garland v British Rail Engineering Ltd* [1983] 2 AC 751, 771, *per* Lord Diplock.') (*R v Radio Authority, Ex parter Bull* [1998] QB 294 (CA), 315B–D (Brooke LJ))

9.3. **The traditional trigger for the application of the presumption of compatibility is statutory ambiguity or obscurity. There is some authority, however, which suggests that the presumption of compatibility may be of wider application so that even general words in statutes should be construed compatibly with the United Kingdom's unincorporated treaty obligations. Whether this suggestion crystallises into a more widely accepted part of the presumption of compatibility remains to be seen [§ 9.14].**

9.4. **Around this nucleus is a hazily defined—and ever expanding—penumbra where unincorporated treaties are used freely and creatively subject to the restraining effect of the principles of non-justiciability [§§ 8.5–8.7] and no direct effect [§§ 8.8–8.9]. For**

example, unincorporated treaties are used as aids in construing legislation (even where the requirements for the presumption of compatibility and the principle of legality are not met), as providing background and context for legislation and as points of comparison and analogy [§ 9.18].

9.5. **The presumption of compatibility and the principle of legality are anchored in the recognition that unincorporated treaties have no direct domestic legal force [§§ 8.8–8.9]. Rather, these canons of interpretation insinuate unincorporated treaties into domestic law as a matter of legal policy, ie they are based on the premise that Parliament cannot have intended to enact laws contrary to either unincorporated treaty obligations or fundamental rights. This is part of the broader notion of legal policy, that domestic law should conform with international law, where possible. The legal policy fuelling these canons of interpretation has been acknowledged even by strict adherents of dualism such as Dicey:**

> '[J]udges, when attempting to ascertain what is the meaning to be affixed to an Act of Parliament, will presume that Parliament did not intend to violate . . . the principles of international law, and will therefore, wherever possible, give such an interpretation to a statutory enactment as may be consistent with the doctrines of international morality.' (AV Dicey, *An Introduction to the Study of the Law of the Constitution*, 10th ed (Macmillan, 1959) at pp 62–63).

9.6. **Unlike the principle of legality, the application of the presumption of compatibility is not confined to fundamental rights in human rights treaties. However, this has been the principal area in which the presumption has been shaped and applied due, no doubt, to the normative force of such rights, and their wide-ranging and diverse application.**

(2) The Presumption of Compatibility

9.7. **The presumption of compatibility is a canon of interpretation. The premise underlying the presumption is that Parliament cannot have intended to legislate contrary to its unincorporated treaty obligations. The presumption of compatibility applies to ambiguous or obscure provisions in primary or subordinate legislation [§§ 9.8–9.10] and enables recourse to unincorporated treaties for**

the resolution of the ambiguity or obscurity in a way that is compatible with the United Kingdom's international law obligations [§ 9.11]. The presumption is displaced and has no application where an express statutory provision makes clear the parliamentary intention to legislate contrary to the United Kingdom's international obligations [§ 9.12].

9.8. **The presumption has traditionally been applied to legislation enacted after the ratification of the unincorporated treaty (on the basis that Parliament is presumed to have legislated in accordance with its existing international obligations) but is not precluded from applying even to legislation previously enacted (on the bases that statutes are always speaking [§ 4.6.1] and courts, as one of the branches of government, are bound to uphold the United Kingdom's treaty obligations; *cf* [§ 8.9]). The presumption applies regardless of the level of engagement between the legislation and the unincorporated treaty [§ 9.1]. Thus, it may apply to legislation whether or not it was intended to give effect to the unincorporated treaty and whether or not extrinsic evidence reveals a connection between the legislation and the treaty.**

9.8.1. Applying the presumption of compatibility to legislation pre-dating the ratification (or signature) of the unincorporated treaty:

- *Boyce v The Queen* [2004] UKPC 32 [2005] 1 AC 400, [25–26] (Lord Hoffmann: '[I]nternational law can have a significant influence upon the interpretation of the Constitution [of Barbados] because of the well established principle that the courts will so far as possible construe domestic law so as to avoid creating a breach of the State's international obligations. "So far as possible" means that if the legislation is ambiguous ("in the sense that it is capable of a meaning which either conforms to or conflicts with the [treaty]": see Lord Bridge of Harwich in *R v Secretary of State for the Home Department Ex p Brind* [1991] 1 AC 696, 747) the court will, other things being equal, choose the meaning which accords with the obligations imposed by the treaty. This principle is obviously at its strongest when it appears that the domestic law was passed to give effect to an international obligation or may otherwise be assumed to have been drafted with the treaty in mind. Its application to laws which existed before the treaty is more difficult to justify as an exercise in construction but their Lordships are willing to proceed on the hypothesis that the principle requires one to construe the Constitution and other contemporary legislation in the light of treaties which the government afterwards concluded.');

- *Matthew v State of Trinidad and Tobago* [2004] UKPC 33 [2005] 1 AC 433, [55] (Lord Bingham, Lord Nicholls, Lord Steyn and Lord Walker (dissenting) interpreting the Constitution of Trinidad and Tobago and considering that the presumption of compatibility applied even where international obligations were undertaken after the date of the Constitution) [§ **9.19.1**].

Illustration:

- *Ahmad v ILEA* [1978] QB 36 (CA), 48C–F (Scarman LJ (dissenting) construing section 30 of the Education Act 1944 in the light of the then unincorporated ECHR) [§ **9.14.2**]

9.8.1. **Applying the presumption of compatibility to legislation post-dating the ratification (or signature) of the unincorporated treaty:**

- *R v Brown* [1994] 1 AC 212 (HL), 256E–F (Lord Lowry, in response to submissions relying on the ECHR, pre-HRA: '[A]rticle 8 is not part of our law. Secondly, there has been no legislation which, being post-Convention and ambiguous, falls to be construed so as to confirm with the Convention rather than contradict it.');
- *Garland v British Rail* [1983] 2 AC 751 (HL), 771A–C (Lord Diplock, in the context of unincorporated treaties generally: '[I]t is a principle of construction of United Kingdom statutes, now too well established to call for citation of authority, that the words of a statute passed after the Treaty has been signed and dealing with the subject matter of the international obligation of the United Kingdom, are to be construed, if they are reasonably capable of bearing such a meaning, as intended to carry out the obligation, and not to be inconsistent with it.');
- *R v Secretary of State for the Home Department, Ex parte Brind* [1991] 1 AC 696 (HL), 760D–G (Lord Ackner interpreting the dicta of Lord Diplock in *Garland* (see above) [§ **9.9.2**].

9.8.2. **Applying the presumption of compatibility where there is a link between the legislation and the unincorporated treaty:**

Illustrations:

- *Salomon v Commissioners of Customs and Excise* [1967] 2 QB 116 (CA), 144B–F (Diplock LJ: 'It has been argued that the terms of an international convention cannot be consulted to resolve ambiguities or obscurities in a statute unless the statute itself contains either in the enacting part or in the preamble an express reference to the international convention which it is the purpose of the statute to implement . . . I can see no reason in comity or common sense for imposing such a limitation upon the right and duty of the court to consult an international convention to resolve ambiguities and obscurities in a statutory enactment. If from extrinsic evidence it is plain that the enactment was intended to fulfil Her Majesty's Government's obligations under a particular convention, it matters not that there is no express reference to the convention in the statute. One must not presume that Parliament intends to break an international convention merely because it does not say expressly that it is intending to observe it. Of course the court must not merely guess that the statute was intended to give effect to a particular international convention. The extrinsic evidence of the connection must be cogent.');

- *Hogg v Toye & Co Ltd* [1935] Ch 497, 520 (Maugham J regarding as unnecessary that there should be express reference to the convention in the statute itself if it was apparent from a comparison of the subject-matter of the statutory provision and the convention that the former was enacted to carry out obligations in international law under the convention);
- *Quazi v Quazi* [1980] AC 744 (HL), 808 (Lord Diplock) [§ **9.11**];
- *Black-Clawson International Ltd v Papierwerke Waldhof-Aschaffenburg AG* [1975] AC 591 (HL), 640H–641B (Lord Diplock) [§ **9.11**];
- *Coldwell-Horsfall v West Country Yacht Charters Ltd ('The Annie Hay')* [1968] P 341, 349A–C (Brandon J construing section 3 of the Merchant Shipping (Liability of Shipowners and Others) Act 1958, designed to give effect to the Brussels Convention as to Limitation of Liability of Owners of Sea-going Ships 1957: '[I]f there is any doubt as to the meaning of [an Act intended to give effect to an international convention], then the court is entitled to look at the convention and, in a proper case, to apply [the] presumption [that Parliament intended to fulfil its international obligations].').

9.8.3. **Applying the presumption of compatibility to legislation generally where it addresses the same subject-matter as the unincorporated treaty:**

- *R v Secretary of State for the Home Department, Ex parte Brind* [1991] 1 AC 696 (HL), 747H–748A (Lord Bridge: '[I]t is already well settled that, in construing any provision in domestic legislation which is ambiguous in the sense that it is capable of a meaning which either conforms to or conflicts with the [ECHR], the courts will presume that Parliament intended to legislate in conformity with the Convention, not in conflict with it.'), 760G (Lord Ackner: 'It is well settled that the Convention may be deployed for the purpose of the resolution of an ambiguity in English primary or subordinate legislation.' Citing *R v Chief Immigration Officer, Heathrow Airport, Ex parte Salamat Bibi* [1976] 1 WLR 979, *Fernandes v Secretary of State for the Home Department* [1981] Imm AR 1 and *Chundawadra v Immigration Appeal Tribunal* [1988] Imm AR 161);

Illustration:

- *Salomon v Commissioners of Customs and Excise* [1967] 2 QB 116 (CA), 141F–141H (Lord Denning MR: 'I am confirmed in this view [of the meaning of section 258 of the Customs and Excise Act 1952] by looking at the international convention which preceded the Act of 1952. In 1950 there was a convention between many of the European countries . . . I think we are entitled to look at it, because it is an instrument which is binding in international law: and we ought always to interpret our statutes so as to be in conformity with international law. Our statute does not in terms incorporate the convention, nor refer to it. But that does not matter. We can look at it.').

9.8.4. **The presumption of compatibility applies to policy documents:**

- *Sultan Abid Mirza v Secretary of State for the Home Department* [1996] Imm AR 314 (CA), 318 (Nourse LJ: 'I am certainly prepared to proceed on the footing that there is an analogy between an ambiguity in a policy guidance document and an ambiguity in a statute, and that in either case the court may have resort to the [ECHR].').

9.9. **The presumption of compatibility generally only applies where the statutory provision to be construed is ambiguous or obscure ('the ambiguity requirement') (*cf* [§ 9.3; § 9.14]). However, ambiguity has been defined as being no more than that the provision is capable of a meaning which either conforms to or conflicts with unincorporated treaty obligations.**

9.9.1. **The ambiguity requirement:**

- *R v Lyons* [2002] UKHL 44 [2003] 1 AC 976, [13] (Lord Bingham, referring to the ECHR pre-HRA as: '[Exerting] a persuasive and pervasive influence on judicial decision-making in this country, affecting the interpretation of ambiguous statutory provisions.');
- *R v Secretary of State for the Home Department, Ex parte Brind* [1991] 1 AC 696 (HL), 760D–G (Lord Ackner interpreting the dicta of Lord Diplock in *Garland v British Rail* [1983] 2 AC 751) [**§ 9.9.2**];
- *R v Brown* [1994] 1 AC 212 (HL), 256E–F (Lord Lowry) [**§ 9.8.2**];
- *Attorney-General v Associated Newspapers* [1994] 2 AC 238 (HL), 261H–262B (Lord Lowry: 'The appellants . . . made a positive and emphatic case . . . on the basis that freedom of expression is protected by article 10 of the European Convention for the Protection of Human Rights and Fundamental Freedoms (1953) and that an ambiguous statutory provision must therefore be construed so as to conform with the Convention. The cases show, and the appellants do not deny, that the existence of an ambiguity is requisite for this doctrine to apply in our courts.');

- *JA Pye (Oxford) Ltd v Graham* [2002] UKHL 30 [2003] 1 AC 419, [65] (Lord Browne-Wilkinson: '[It was submitted] that, even under the common law principles of construction applicable before the Human Rights Act 1998 came into effect, the court should seek to apply the law so as to make it consistent with the European Convention for the Protection of Human Rights and Fundamental Freedoms. Any such old principle of construction only applied where there was an ambiguity in the language of a statute.');
- *Quazi v Quazi* [1980] AC 744 (HL), 808D–E (Lord Diplock considering the use of international conventions regarding statutory provisions which are 'ambiguous or vague') [§ **9.11**];
- *R v Chief Immigration Officer, Ex parte Salamat Bibi* [1976] 1 WLR 979 (CA), 984F (Lord Denning MR considering the use of the ECHR pre-HRA regarding ambiguous or uncertain statutory provisions) [§ **9.11**].

Illustrations:

- *R v Secretary of State for the Home Department, Ex parte François* [1999] 1 AC 43 (HL) 51A–E (Lord Slynn, rejecting an argument that the effect of a change in category (from being a short-term prisoner to a long-term prisoner) was a violation of Article 7, pre-HRA: 'That article is of course not yet part of domestic law but it is said that it should be applied by analogy and that since domestic legislation in section 33 and section 51(2) of the [Criminal Justice Act 1991] is ambiguous it should be construed in a way which conforms with the Convention since that must have been Parliament's intention.');
- *Kuwait Government v Sir Frederick Snow* [1984] AC 426 (HL), 435G–436C (Lord Brandon, construing section 7 of the Arbitration Act 1975: 'It has long been established that, if a provision in a domestic Act giving effect to the adherence by the United Kingdom to an international convention is ambiguous, a United Kingdom court is entitled to refer to the text of the Convention concerned in order to obtain assistance, if it can, in resolving the ambiguity. In the present case I do not consider . . . that the definition of "Convention award" contained in section 7(1) of the Act of 1975 is ambiguous. If that is wrong, however, and the definition is ambiguous, it is permissible to refer to the text of the New York Convention on the Recognition and Enforcement of Foreign Arbitral Awards (1958) (Cmnd. 6419) in order to obtain assistance in resolving that ambiguity.');
- *Macdonald v Ministry of Defence* [2003] UKHL 34 [2003] ICR 937, [54] (Lord Hope: 'We can, of course, have regard to the treaty obligations of the United Kingdom in seeking to resolve an ambiguity in the meaning of the statute . . . But the precise way in which the [Sex Discrimination Act 1975] is framed leaves very little room for judicial reform and development.');

- *R (Mullen) v Secretary of State for the Home Department* [2004] UKHL 18 [2005] 1 AC 1, [9(1)] (Lord Bingham using Article 14(6), International Covenant on Civil and Political Rights, given effect by section 133, Criminal Justice Act 1988, to construe 'miscarriage of justice' which has 'no settled meaning'), see similarly [35–54] (Lord Steyn interpreting section 133 by reference to the International Covenant on Civil and Political Rights and related aids to construction);
- *R v Kelly* [2000] 1 QB 198 (CA), 210C (Lord Bingham CJ: 'Recourse to the [ECHR] as an aid to construction of domestic legislation is still permissible only in cases of ambiguity; we find no ambiguity at all in section 2 [of the Crime (Sentences) Act 1997].');
- *Re P (Children Act: Diplomatic Immunity)* [1998] 1 FLR 624 (Fam), 629B (Stuart White J declaring provisions of the unincorporated ECHR and the UN Convention on the Rights of the Child 'of no assistance to the court in construing provisions of the Diplomatic Privileges Act which are clear and unambiguous.');
- *In re Lonrho plc and other* [1990] 2 AC 154 (HL), 208G–H (Lord Bridge, Lord Goff and Lord Jauncey considering the decision of the ECtHR in *The Sunday Times v United Kingdom* (1979) 2 EHRR 245: 'Since the European Convention for the Protection of Human Rights is no part of our municipal law, we cannot resort to the decision of the European Court of Human Rights as direct authority, but the [Contempt of Court Act 1981], on any point on which any doubt arises as to its construction, may be presumed to have been intended to avoid future conflicts between the law of contempt of court in the United Kingdom and the obligations of the United Kingdom under the [ECHR].');
- *Winfat v Attorney-General* [1985] 1 AC 733 (PC) (no ambiguity in the Crown Lands Resumption Ordinance, and therefore no ground for construing it in the light of a bilateral treaty between the UK and China by recourse to the principles of *Salomon v Commissioners of Custom and Excise* [1967] 2 QB 116);
- *Attorney-General v BBC* [1981] AC 303 (HL), 352 (Lord Fraser considering that regard could be had to the ECHR where domestic law is 'not firmly settled.');
- *R v Crown Court at Manchester, Ex parte H* [2000] 1 WLR 760 (DC), 771C (Forbes J stating that the 'arguable ambiguity' in the Supreme Court Act 1981, section 29(3), should 'arguably be construed so as to conform with article 6 [ECHR].');
- *Customs & Excise Commission v Air Canada* [1991] 2 QB 446 (CA), 465A–467G (Purchas LJ explaining counsel's invocation of the presumption of compatibility in interpreting section 141 of the Customs and Excise Management Act 1979 by reference to Article 6, ECHR and Article 1 of the First Protocol but con-

cluding, that: 'The wording of section 141 is, in my view, clear and unambiguous and does not permit of any implication or construction' (at 467G));

- *Post Office v Estuary Radio Ltd* [1968] 2 QB 740 (CA), 754D (Diplock LJ: '[T]he Territorial Waters Order in Council, 1964 . . . was promulgated to give effect to the [Convention on the Territorial Sea and Contiguous Zone, 1958].' At 757C–D: 'But there is a presumption that the Crown did not intend to break an international treaty . . . and if there is any ambiguity in the Order in Council, it should be resolved so as to accord with the provisions of the Convention in so far as that is a plausible meaning of the express words of the order.');
- *Warwick Film Productions v Eisinger* [1969] 1 Ch 508, 521F (Plowman J considering that since section 20(4) of the Copyright Act 1956 was unambiguous 'it is not permissible to refer to the Brussels Convention [1948].').

9.9.2. **The ambiguity requirement defined:**

- *R v Secretary of State for the Home Department, Ex parte Brind* [1991] 1 AC 696 (HL), 747H–748A (Lord Bridge defining an ambiguous provision as being 'capable of a meaning which either conforms to or conflicts with the Convention' [§ **9.8.4**]), 760D–G (Lord Ackner considering that in stating 'it is a principle of construction of United Kingdom statutes, now too well established to call for citation of authority, that the words of a statute passed after the Treaty has been signed and dealing with the subject matter of the international obligation of the United Kingdom, are to be construed, if they are reasonably capable of bearing such a meaning, as intended to carry out the obligation, and not to be inconsistent with it' (*Garland v British Rail* [1983] 2 AC 751 (HL), 771A–C [§ **9.8.2**]), Lord Diplock was not detracting from or modifying what he said in *Salomon v Commissioners of Customs and Excise* [1967] 2 QB 116 ('If the terms of the legislation are clear and unambiguous, they must be given effect to, whether or not they carry out Her Majesty's treaty obligations' (at 143).);
- *Salomon v Commissioners of Customs and Excise* [1967] 2 QB 116 (CA), 143D–H (Diplock LJ: 'If the terms of legislation are clear and unambiguous, they must be given effect to, whether or not they carry out Her Majesty's treaty obligations, for the sovereign power of the Queen in Parliament extends to breaking treaties . . . and any remedy for such a breach of an international obligation lies in a forum other than Her Majesty's own courts. But if the terms of the legislation are not clear but are reasonably capable of more than one meaning, the treaty itself becomes relevant, for there is a prima facie presumption that Parliament does not intend to act in breach of international law, including therein specific treaty obligations; and if one of the meanings which can

reasonably be ascribed to the legislation is consonant with the treaty obligations and another or others are not, the meaning which is consonant is to be preferred.');

- *Pan-American World Airways Inc. v Department of Trade* [1976] 1 Lloyd's Rep 257 (CA), 261 (Scarman LJ after considering that statutes referring expressly, or by inference, to international conventions should be construed in the light of the convention [§ **9.14.1**]: 'There is one other situation in which, in my opinion, it is proper for our Courts to take note of an international convention. It arises when two courses are reasonably open to the Court: but one would lead to a decision inconsistent with Her Majesty's international obligations under the convention while the other would lead to a result consistent with those obligations. If statutory words have to be construed or a legal principle formulated in an area of the law where Her Majesty has accepted international obligations, our Courts—who, of course, take notice of the acts of Her Majesty done in the exercise of her sovereign power—will have regard to the convention as part of the full content or background of the law. Such a convention, especially a multilateral one, should then be considered by Courts even though no statute expressly or impliedly incorporates it into our law.' This was considered to be 'somewhat too widely expressed' in *R v Chief Immigration Officer, Ex parte Salamat Bibi* [1976] 1 WLR 979 (CA), 986B–F (Roskill LJ));
- *Boyce v The Queen* [2004] UKPC 32 [2005] 1 AC 400, [25–26] (Lord Hoffmann) [§ **9.8.1**];
- *Guilfoyle v Home Office* [1981] QB 309 (CA), 320G–321A (Sir John Megaw: '[Counsel] submitted that, if there were two possible interpretations [of Rule 37A(1) of the Prison Rules 1964], one of which was consistent with the provisions of the Human Rights Convention and the other of which was in conflict with those provisions, the court should be disposed to prefer the interpretation which was consistent with this country's treaty obligations, as contained in the Convention. That, if the facts had justified it, would have been a powerful argument and could be said to have involved a question of some importance as a matter of principle in the sphere of human rights.').

9.10. **The presumption of compatibility may extend to permitting the use of unincorporated treaties to complete omissions in statutory provisions, in addition to resolving ambiguities and obscurities (see also [§ 9.14]).**

- *R v Secretary of State for the Home Department, Ex parte Phansopkar* [1976] QB 606 (CA), 626C–G (Scarman LJ, construing the Immigration Act 1971 which did not provide how spouses abroad were to acquire certificates of partiality: 'Delay of this order [in providing certificates of patriality] appears to me to infringe at least two human rights recognised, and therefore protected, by English law . . . in my judgment it is the duty of the courts, so long as they do not defy or disregard clear unequivocal provision, to construe statutes in a manner which promotes, not endangers, those rights. Problems of ambiguity or omission, if they arise under the language of an Act, should be resolved so as to give effect to, or at the very least so as not to derogate from the rights recognised by Magna Carta and the European Convention [on Human Rights].' See also *R v Chief Immigration Officer, Ex parte Salamat Bibi* [1976] 1 WLR 979 (CA), 986B–F (Roskill LJ noting that this dictum was obiter and 'I venture to think it is somewhat too wide and may call for reconsideration hereafter.').

9.11. **The presumption of compatibility requires that after the unincorporated treaty has been considered, the interpretation of the legislation that should be favoured is that which gives effect to the United Kingdom's unincorporated treaty obligations.**

- *R v Secretary of State for the Home Department, Ex parte Brind* [1991] 1 AC 696 (HL), 747H–748A (Lord Bridge stating that ambiguous legislation will be construed by courts on the assumption that Parliament intended to legislate in conformity with unincorporated treaty obligations) [§ **9.8.4**], 760D–G (Lord Ackner) [§ **9.9.2**];
- *Garland v British Rail* [1983] 2 AC 751 (HL), 771A–C (Lord Diplock) [§ **9.8.2**];
- *Salomon v Commissioners of Customs and Excise* [1967] 2 QB 116 (CA) [§ **9.8.3**; § **9.8.4**; § **9.9.2**];
- *JA Pye (Oxford) Ltd v Graham* [2002] UKHL 30 [2003] 1 AC 619, [65] (Lord Browne-Wilkinson) [§ **9.9.1**];
- *Quazi v Quazi* [1980] AC 744 (HL), 808D–F (Lord Diplock: 'Where Parliament passes an Act amending the domestic law of the United Kingdom in order to enable this country to ratify an international treaty and thereby assume towards other states that are parties to the treaty an obligation in international law to observe its terms, it is a legitimate aid to the construction of any provisions of the Act that are ambiguous or vague to have recourse to the terms of a treaty in order to see what was the obligation in international law that Parliament intended that this country should be enabled to assume. The ambiguity or obscurity is to be resolved in favour of that meaning that is consistent with the provisions of the treaty.');
- *Coldwell-Horsfall v West Country Yacht Charters Ltd ('The Annie Hay')* [1968] P 341, 349A–H (Brandon J) [§ **9.8.3**].

Illustrations:

- *R v Chief Immigration Officer, Ex parte Salamat Bibi* [1976] 1 WLR 979 (CA), 984F (Lord Denning MR: 'The position as I understand it is that if there is any ambiguity in our statutes, or uncertainty in our law, then these courts can look to the [ECHR] as an aid to clear up the ambiguity and uncertainty, seeking always to bring them into harmony with it.');
- *Black-Clawson International Ltd v Papierwerke Waldhof-Aschaffenburg AG* [1975] AC 591 (HL), 640H–641B (Lord Diplock (dissenting), construing the Foreign Judgments (Reciprocal Enforcement) Act 1933: 'Where an Act of Parliament is passed to enable or to require United Kingdom courts to give effect to international obligations assumed by Her Majesty's Government under a treaty, it is a well-established rule of construction that any ambiguity in the words of the Act should be resolved in favour of ascribing to them a meaning which would result in the performance of those international obligations—not in their breach.');
- *R v Southwark Crown Court, Ex parte Customs and Excise Commissioners* [1990] 1 QB 650 (DC), 659D–660H (Watkins LJ construing the Drug Trafficking Offences Act 1986 to accord with the Single Convention on Narcotic Drugs 1961);
- *cf Channel Tunnel Group Ltd v Balfour Beatty Construction Ltd* [1993] AC 334 (HL), 354G–H (Lord Mustill, construing section 1 of the Arbitration Act 1975 by reference to the impetus for the legislation, the New York Convention on the Recognition and Enforcement of Foreign Arbitral Awards 1958 (Article II.3) but finding a difference between the two: 'In the light of the history which I have sketched I believe that this [difference] was not an accident of drafting, which might require the Act of 1975 to be interpreted in the same sense as the underlying Convention, but the outcome of a deliberate choice. If so, there is no reason to read section 1(1) as meaning anything other than what it says.').

9.12. **The presumption of compatibility is displaced from application where express statutory provisions make clear parliamentary intention to legislate contrary to the United Kingdom's unincorporated treaty obligations.**

- *Salomon v Commissioners of Customs and Excise* [1967] 2 QB 116 (CA), 143D–E (Lord Diplock: 'If the terms of legislation are clear and unambiguous they must be given effect to, whether or not they carry out Her Majesty's treaty obligations, for the sovereign power of the Queen in Parliament extends to breaking treaties.') [§ **9.9.2**];
- *In re M and H (Minors)(Local Authority: Parental Rights)* [1990] 1 AC 686 (HL), 721G (Lord Brandon noting, pre-HRA: '[W]hile

English courts will strive when they can to interpret statutes as conforming with the obligations of the United Kingdom under the [ECHR], they are nevertheless bound to give effect to statutes which are free from ambiguity in accordance with their terms, even if those statutes may be in conflict with the Convention.');

- *R v Lyons* [2002] UKHL 44 [2003] 1 AC 976, [26–35] (Lord Hoffmann considering that although there is a presumption in favour of interpreting English law in a way which does not place the United Kingdom in breach of the obligations of the Crown under international law, where there is an express and applicable provision of domestic statutory law, courts must apply it even if the effect will be to render the Crown in breach of a treaty);
- *R v Secretary of State for the Home Department, Ex parte Bhajan Singh* [1976] QB 198 (CA) (illegal entrant detained with a view to his deportation and removal asserted an Article 12, ECHR, right to marry), 207D–H (Lord Denning MR: 'What is the position of the Convention in our law? I would not depart in the least from what I said in the recent case of *Birdi v Seretary of State for Home Affairs*, February 11, 1975, Bar Library Transcript No.67B . . . I would, however, like to correct one sentence in my judgment in *Birdi's* case. I said that if an Act of Parliament did not conform to the Convention, I might be inclined to hold that it was invalid (p.9 of transcript). That was a very tentative statement, but it went too far. There are many cases in which it has been said, as plainly as can be, that a treaty does not become a part of our English law except and in so far as it is made so by Parliament. If an Act of Parliament contained any provisions contrary to the Convention, the Act of Parliament must prevail. But I hope that no Act ever will be contrary to the Convention.');
- *Cheney v Conn (Inspector of Taxes)* [1968] 1 WLR 242 (ChD), 245F (Ungoed-Thomas J: '[C]onventions which are ratified but not by an Act of Parliament . . . cannot prevail against a statute in unambiguous terms.').

Illustrations:

- *A v Secretary of State for the Home Department* [2004] EWCA Civ 1123 [2005] 1 WLR 414, [133] (Pill LJ describing Article 15 of the Torture Convention as: '[N]ot part of domestic law. In so far as its application would require an analysis of sources before a reasonable belief or suspicion could be formed, it would be directly contrary to the statutory intention in Part 4 of the Anti-Terrorism, Crime and Security Act 2004.');
- *R (Pepushi) v CPS* [2004] EWHC 798 (Admin) [2004] All ER (D) 129 (May), [30] (Thomas LJ: '[W]e are clearly bound by the decisions to which we have referred [*Tin Council* [1990] 2 AC 418 and *Lyons* [2003] 1 AC 976] to apply the provisions of s.31 [of the Immigration and Asylum Act 1999], if we cannot

interpret them in such a way as to be consistent with the [Refugee] Convention. Where it is clear that, however generous a construction we can give to the language chosen by Parliament to try and make the provision of the Act consistent with the Convention Parliament has chosen to legislate in terms that differ from that of Article 31, we must, on present authority, apply the terms of s.31.' At [31]: '[W]e are bound to apply the narrower provisions of s.31, even if in so doing it has the consequence that the UK is in breach of international obligations under a human rights treaty.' But noting at [34] that, 'neither the view of the Executive nor the terms of s.31 alter the meaning of Article 31 as declared by this court [in *Adimi* [2001] QB 667] for the purposes of the international obligations of the UK.').

9.13. **The presumption of compatibility has a more limited application to judgments of international courts and tribunals established under unincorporated treaties. The rationale of the presumption is that Parliament cannot have intended to legislate contrary to its international obligations [§ 9.5]. It may be supposed that Parliament's understanding of its international obligations under an unincorporated treaty corresponds to the authoritative interpretations of that treaty by the court established thereunder. Accordingly, it is arguable that the presumption of compatibility should apply to judgments of international courts set up under unincorporated treaties; although the presumption could, of course, be displaced by express statutory provisions [§ 8.8.7]. Such judgments have an important role to play, for example, in confirming the proper approach to the construction of legislation [§§ 9.18.10–9.18.11] and in aiding the development of the common law [§ 10.5].**

- *R v Lyons* [2002] UKHL 44 [2003] 1 AC 976, [33] (Lord Hoffman stating that it is open to courts to ensure conformity with judgments of an international tribunal (here the ECtHR) even where that judgment relates to the United Kingdom's international obligations under an unincorporated treaty in relation to 'a judge-made rule of common law or a judicial implication in a statute which did not expressly address the question.' See generally [26–35] on the effect of ECtHR rulings in domestic law);
- *R v Khan* [1997] AC 558 (HL), 581E (Lord Nolan, pre-HRA: '[I]n any event we are not concerned with the view which the European Court of Human Rights might have taken of the facts of the present case. Its decision is no more part of our law than the Convention itself.');

- *R v Staines* [1997] 2 Cr App R 426 (CA) 442–444 (Lord Bingham CJ) [§ **8.8.7**].

9.14. **There are two variations to the presumption of compatibility which depart from strict adherence to the ambiguity requirement [§ 9.9]. First, there is no ambiguity requirement regarding statutes in the express reference or the evidential nexus groups [§ 9.1]. In these cases, the presumption that Parliament intended to legislate compatibly with the United Kingdom's unincorporated treaty obligations is replaced with factual certainty that this is so; either from the face of the statute or from other evidence. Secondly, there is authority suggesting that the presumption of compatibility, absent the ambiguity requirement, may even apply to statutes in the general relevance group with the effect that general words in statutes should be construed compatibly with unincorporated treaty obligations which relate to the same underlying issues or principles as the statute.**

9.14.1. No ambiguity requirement when construing statutes in the express reference or evidential nexus group:

- *Garland v British Rail* [1983] 2 AC 751 (HL), 771A–C (Lord Diplock) [§ **9.8.2**];
- *Pan-American World Airways Inc v Department of Trade* [1976] 1 Lloyd's Rep 257 (CA), 261 (Scarman LJ: 'There is also a well known rule . . . that international conventions may be looked at when Parliament expressly requires it or when it is a proper inference that Parliament, even though no express words have been used, requires the Courts to do so. In such circumstances as for instance in *Salomon v Commissioners of Customs and Excise* [1967] 2 QB 116, it does become the duty of our Courts to look at the international convention and to interpret the law or the words of the statute under consideration in the light of the convention.' See also *R v Chief Immigration Officer, Ex parte Salamat Bibi* [1976] 1 WLR 979 (CA), 986B–F (Roskill LJ noting, in relation to Scarman LJ's opinion, that the 'matter is somewhat too widely expressed.');
- *R (Al-Skeini) v Secretary of State for Defence* [2004] EWHC 2911 Admin [2005] 2 WLR 1401, [301] (Rix LJ referring to 'the presumption that a domestic statute enacting international treaty obligations will be compatible with those obligations.');
- *Cartwright v Superintendent of Her Majesty's Prison* [2004] UKPC 10 [2004] 1 WLR 902, [15] (Lord Steyn quoting from *The Antonis P Lemos* [1985] AC 711, 731: '[I]t is a well-settled principle "that a domestic statute designed to give effect to an international convention should, in general, be given a broad and liberal interpretation".').

Illustrations:

- *R (Mullen) v Secretary of State for the Home Department* [2004] UKHL 18 [2005] 1 AC 1, [5] (Lord Bingham referring to the general need to interpret domestic legislation in the light of the underlying unincorporated treaty: 'It is common ground that section 133 of the Criminal Justice Act 1988 was enacted to give effect to [Article 14(6), International Covenant on Civil and Political Rights] . . . The task of the House in this appeal is to interpret section 133. But both parties are rightly agreed that the key to interpretation of section 133 is a correct understanding of article 14(6).' Later, at [9(1)], referring to 'miscarriage of justice' in section 133 which is 'drawn directly from the English language text of article 14(6)' as being 'although very familiar, is not a legal term of art and has no settled meaning.') [**§ 9.1.2**];
- *R (Pepushi) v CPS* [2004] EWHC 798 (Admin) [2004] All ER (D) 129 (May), [30] (Thomas LJ construing section 31 of the Immigration and Asylum Act 1999 giving effect to Article 31 of the Refugee Convention: '[I]n construing the terms of s.31, we would if at all possible strive to give it the meaning that is consistent with the meaning of the Convention.');
- *R v Bow Street Magistrate, Ex parte Pinochet (No 3)* [2000] 1 AC 147 (HL), 200B (Lord Browne-Wilkinson considering that the meaning of 'official' for the purposes of the Torture Convention, 1984, and section 134 of the Criminal Justice Act 1988 'must be the same.') [**§ 9.1.2**];
- *R v Brown* [1996] AC 543 (HL), 555C–D (Lord Griffiths, without identifying an express ambiguity or obscurity: 'The [Data Protection Act] 1984 was enacted to implement the obligations that this country accepted as a signatory to the Convention for the Protection of Individuals with regard to Automatic Processing of Personal Data (1981) (Cmnd. 8341). The Act should therefore be construed so far as permissible to accord with the Convention.'), 557B–E, 560C–E and 562B–D (Lord Hoffmann, construing the Data Protection Act 1984 by reference to the Convention);
- *Holland v Lampen-Wolfe* [2000] 1 WLR 1573 (HL) 1584E–1585B (Lord Millett, construing section 16(2) of the State Immunity Act 1978 by reference to article 31 of the European Convention on State Immunity 1972);
- *JH Rayner (Mincing Lane) Ltd v Department of Trade and Industry* [1990] 2 AC 418 (HL), 502E–G (Lord Oliver noting that under the Sixth International Tin Agreement and the Headquarters Agreement (unincorporated treaties to which the United Kingdom was party) the International Tin Council was to have legal personality: 'Such was the obligation assumed by Her Majesty's Government and it was to give effect to this obligation that the Order in Council [the International Tin Council (Immunities and Privileges Order 1972] was made. To construe

it so as to produce the effect that no legal personality was conferred has the result that the United Kingdom is and has ever since 1972 been in breach of its treaty obligations. That, of course, is not an impossible conclusion if the court is compulsively driven to reach it, but it is not one which should be embraced with any enthusiasm if a contrary construction is open.'), see also *JH Rayner (Mincing Lane) Ltd v Department of Trade and Industry* [1989] Ch 72 (CA), 230G (Ralph Gibson LJ);

- *Camelot Group plc v Centaur Communications Ltd* [1999] QB 124 (CA) (considering whether section 10 of the Contempt of Court Act 1981, in the absence of any express ambiguity or obscurity, barred delivery up of certain documents by reference to Article 10, ECHR, and case law of the ECtHR where section 10 of the 1981 Act 'was passed in order that our domestic law might reflect article 10' (128H (Schiemann LJ)); 'was enacted to bring domestic law into line with the requirements of the [ECHR]' (132H (Schiemann LJ)); and 'there is no material difference of principle underlying section 10 of the Contempt of Court Act 1981 as applied by the courts of this jurisdiction and article 10 of the [ECHR] as applied by the [ECtHR]' (138G (Thorpe LJ)).

9.14.2. **No ambiguity requirement when construing statutes in the general relevance group:**

- *Attorney-General v BBC* [1981] AC 303 (HL), 354D–F (Lord Scarman referring to the 'presumption, albeit rebuttable, that our municipal law will be consistent with our international obligations' and 'If the issue should ultimately be . . . a question of legal policy, we must have regard to the country's international obligation to observe the [ECHR] as interpreted by the Court of Human Rights.');
- *Garland v British Rail* [1983] 2 AC 751 (HL), 771A–C (Lord Diplock) [§ **9.8.2**] (*cf* the interpretation of *Garland* in *Brind*) [§ **9.8.2**];
- *R v Secretary of State for the Home Department, Ex parte Simms* [2000] 2 AC 115 (HL), 131G–132C (Lord Hoffmann on section 3, HRA, as expressly enacting the principle of legality. See also 131E–G [§ **9.15.4**]);
- *Ghaidan v Godin-Mendoza* [2004] UKHL 30 [2004] 2 AC 557, [60] (Lord Millett: 'Ordinary principles of statutory construction include a presumption that Parliament does not intend to legislate in a way which would put the United Kingdom in breach of its international obligations. This presumption will often be sufficient to enable the court to interpret the statute in a way which will make it compatible with the [ECHR] without recourse to section 3 [of the HRA].')
- *R v Lyons* [2002] UKHL 44 [2003] 1 AC 976, [27] (Lord Hoffmann: 'Of course there is a strong presumption in favour of

interpreting English law (whether common law or statute) in a way which does not place the United Kingdom in breach of an international obligation.');

- *Higgs v Minister of National Security* [2000] 2 AC 228 (PC), 241E (Lord Hoffmann: '[Unincorporated treaties] may have an indirect effect upon the construction of statutes as a result of the presumption that Parliament does not intend to pass legislation which would put the Crown in breach of its international obligations.');
- *A v Secretary of State for the Home Department* [2004] EWCA Civ 1123 [2005] 1 WLR 414, [126] (Pill LJ: 'If free to do so, the court should interpret the law in accordance with United Kingdom obligations under of the Crown under international instruments. These include the obligations under the [ECHR] and [Convention Against Torture] . . . and obligations placed on the United Kingdom by Security Council resolution 1373.'), [266] (Laws LJ: '[T]here is a strong presumption that our law, judge-made or statutory, should be interpreted so as not to place the United Kingdom in breach of an international obligation'). At [267] noting that this presumption cannot be used to defeat the principle of no direct effect [§§ **8.8–8.9**]);
- *Smith v East Elloe District Council* [1956] AC 736 (HL), 765B–F (Lord Reid (dissenting) considering that general words in statutes 'are limited so as not to conflict with international law.') [§ **9.15.7**];
- *Matadeen v Pointu* [1999] 1 AC 98 (PC), 114G–H (Lord Hoffmann on the International Covenant on Civil and Political Rights: 'It is a well recognised canon on construction that domestic legislation, including the Constitution [of Mauritius], should if possible be construed so as to conform to such international instruments.');
- *Saad, Diriye and Osorio v Secretary of State for the Home Department* [2001] EWCA Civ 2008 (2002) ACD 59, [15–16] (Lord Phillips MR, construing section 8 of the Immigration Appeals Act 1993 without referring to an ambiguity or obscurity: 'We approach this case on the basis set out in Bennion on "*Statutory Interpretation*" (3rd ed) p 630 that: "It is a principle of legal policy that the municipal law should conform to public international law. The court, when considering, in relation to the facts of the instant case, which of the opposing constructions of the enactment would give effect to the legislative intention, should presume that the legislator intended to observe this principle." It follows that, absent a clear Parliamentary indication to the contrary, we would expect our primary and delegated legislation to provide a system whereby claimants may have it determined whether they are refugees. It is only that determination which gives them access to Convention rights. We therefore approach questions of construction on that basis.' At [72(iv)–(v)]: 'It is to be inferred that the United Kingdom does

not intend to act in breach of its international obligations, especially since . . . Lord Keith said in this context in *R v Secretary of State for the Home Department ex parte Sivakumaran* [1988] AC 958 [at 990] . . . that the provisions of the Convention "have for all practical purposes been incorporated into United Kingdom law". In these circumstances the 1993 Act should be construed, so far as possible, on the basis that the United Kingdom intended to comply with its international obligations under the Convention and thus to ensure that those who are refugees within the meaning of Article 1A are entitled to enjoy their Convention rights.');

- *R v Broadcasting Complaints Commission, Ex parte BBC* (1995) 7 Admin LR 575, 589B (Brooke J considering 'the long established canon of construction that Parliament must have intended that this country should comply with its international obligations unless the converse is clearly shown.').

Illustrations:

- *R v Secretary of State for the Home Department, Ex parte Venables* [1998] AC 407 (HL), 499B–F (Lord Browne-Wilkinson considering the Secretary of State's 1993 policy (applying the tariff principle to mandatory life imprisonment), which was extended to child murderers, and the factors relevant to the exercise of the discretion conferred on the Secretary of State in relation to children detained during Her Majesty's pleasure (under the Criminal Justice Act 1991): 'In the face of that clear statutory provision [section 44(1) of the Children and Young Persons Act 1933] it seems to me inescapable that, in adopting a sentence of detention during Her Majesty's pleasure, the legislature have in mind a flexible approach to child murderers which, whilst requiring regard to be had to punishment, deterrence and risk, adds an additional factor which has to be taken into account, the welfare of the child. This conclusion is reinforced by the fact that the United Kingdom (together with 186 other countries) is a party to the United Nations Convention on the Rights of the Child (Treaty Series No.44 of 1992) (Cm. 1976) . . . The Convention has not been incorporated into English law. But it is legitimate in considering the nature of detention during Her Majesty's pleasure . . . to assume that Parliament has not maintained on the statute book a power capable of being exercised in a manner inconsistent with the treaty obligations of this country.') [§ **11.9.1**];
- *R v Secretary of State for the Environment, Transport and the Regions, Ex parte Spath Holme* [2001] 2 AC 349 (HL), 383–384 (Lord Bingham construing section 31 of the Landlord and Tenant Act 1985 and although 'not persuaded by [counsel] that section 31 is ambiguous or unclear' (384D) construing it compatibly with Article 1 of the First Protocol of the ECHR: 'Any measure restricting rents, or prices or charges of any kind, must have the effect of

depriving the recipient of what he would otherwise receive but the European Court of Human Rights has respected the need for national authorities to strike a balance between the rights of individuals and the general interest of the community. This would appear to be such an instance' (at 383G).);

- *Alcom Ltd v Republic of Colombia* [1984] AC 580 (HL), 600A–C (Lord Diplock construing the State Immunity Act 1978 by reference to customary international law and the Vienna Convention on Diplomatic Relations 1961, and concluding that given the position under these aspects of public international law: 'It makes it highly unlikely that Parliament intended to require United Kingdom courts to act contrary to international law unless the clear language of the statute compels such a conclusion; but it does not do more than this.') [**§ 13.16**];
- *Waddington v Miah* [1974] 1 WLR 683 (HL), 695C (Lord Reid determining whether the clear, unambiguous penal provisions of the Immigration Act 1971 were retrospective by referring to the prohibition against retrospectivity in Article 7, ECHR and Article 11(2), Universal Declaration on Human Rights: 'I can see nothing retrospective in section 34(1).' At 695E: 'I cannot see how section 34(1)(a) can be construed as having any reference to what any entrant may have done in this country before the Act came into force. At 695H: 'This is a very clear case.' Noting, at 694E, 'it is hardly credible that any government department would promote [such legislation] or that Parliament would pass [it].' See also in the CA: *R v Miah* [1974] 1 WLR 683, 690H–691A (Stephenson LJ referring to the same articles);
- *Ahmad v ILEA* [1978] QB 36 (CA), 48C–F (Scarman LJ (dissenting) construing section 30 of the Education Act 1944: 'Since 1944 the United Kingdom has accepted international obligations designed to protect human rights and freedoms and has enacted a series of statutes designed for the same purpose in certain critical areas of our society. These major statutes include the Trade Union and Labour Relations Act 1974, the Employment Protection Act 1975, the Sex Discrimination Act 1975, and the race relations legislation. They were enacted after the United Kingdom had ratified the European Convention on Human Rights . . . and in the light of our obligations under the Charter of the United Nations. Today, therefore, we have to construe and apply section 30 . . . in a multi-racial society which has accepted international obligations and enacted statutes designed to eliminate discrimination on grounds of race, religion, colour or sex. Further, it is no longer possible to argue that because the international treaty obligations of the United Kingdom do not become law unless enacted by Parliament our courts pay no regard to international obligations. They pay very serious regard to them: in particular they will interpret statutory language and apply common law principles, wherever possible, so as to reach

a conclusion consistent with our international obligations.' At 50E, rejecting a narrow construction of section 30: 'In modern British society, with its elaborate statutory protection of the individual from discrimination arising from race, colour, religion or sex and against the background of the European Convention, this is unacceptable, inconsistent with the policy of modern statute law, and almost certainly a breach of our international obligations.' Concluding that the language of section 30 does not force the adoption of a narrow construction and advocating a broad construction). *cf* 41D–E (Lord Denning MR considering that Article 9, ECHR, did not require a broad construction of section 30 and did not entitle an employee to absent himself from work in breach of his contract of employment for religious worship. At 41D: 'The convention is not part of our English law, but, as I have often said, we will always have regard to it. We will do our best to see that our decisions are in conformity with it.'), see similarly 45E–F (Orr LJ);

- *Rantzen v Mirror Group Newspapers* [1994] QB 670 (CA) 692C (Neill LJ pre-HRA: 'How then should the Court of Appeal interpret its power to order a new trial on the ground that damages awarded by the jury were excessive? How is the word "excessive" in section 8(1) of the [Courts and Legal Services Act 1990] to be interpreted? After careful consideration we have come to the conclusion that we must interpret our power so as to give proper weight to the guidance given by the House of Lords and by the European Court of Human Rights. In particular we should take account of the following passage of Lord Goff's speech in *Attorney-General v Guardian Newspapers Ltd (No.2)* [1990] 1 AC 109, 283–284: "The exercise of the right to freedom of expression under article 10 [ECHR] may be subject to restrictions (as are prescribed by law and are necessary in a democratic society) in relation to certain prescribed matters . . . It is established in the jurisprudence of the European Court of Human Rights that the word 'necessary' in this context implies the existence of a pressing social need, and that interference with freedom of expression should be no more than is proportionate to the legitimate aim pursued. I have no reason to believe that English common law, as applied in the courts, leads to any different conclusion".');
- *R v Secretary of State for the Home Department, Ex parte Bhajan Singh* [1976] QB 198 (CA) (illegal entrant detained with a view to his deportation and removal asserted an Article 12, ECHR, right to marry), 207D–H (Lord Denning MR, pre-HRA: 'What is the position of the Convention in our law? I would not depart in the least from what I said in the recent case of *Birdi v Secretary of State for Home Affairs*, February 11, 1975, Bar Library Transcript No.67B. The court can and should take the Convention into account. They should take it into account

whenever interpreting a statute which affects the rights and liberties of the individual. It is to be assumed that the Crown, in taking its part in legislation, would do nothing which was in conflict with treaties. So the court should construe the Immigration Act 1971 so as to be in conformity with the legislation and not against it.') (Lord Denning MR subsequently revisited other parts of his judgment in *Bhajan Singh* in *R v Chief Immigration Officer, Ex parte Salamat Bibi* [1976] 1 WLR 979 (CA), 984F–H: [**§ 11.4.2**]).

(3) The Principle of Legality

9.15. **The principle of legality, also known as the 'presumption against implicit alteration of law' is a canon of statutory interpretation. It requires general words in primary and subordinate legislation to be construed compatibly with fundamental rights on the basis that Parliament cannot have intended, by using general words, to override such rights [§ 9.5]. Whilst the rights in question must already be a part of domestic law, their nature and scope may be affected by customary international law (rules of which have been incorporated into domestic law [chapter 13]) or by unincorporated treaties (which affect the development of the common law [chapter 10]). Unlike the presumption of compatibility, the principle of legality is not parasitic on ambiguities or obscurities in the legislation. Like the presumption of compatibility, it will be displaced where express statutory provisions make clear Parliament's intention to legislate contrary to fundamental rights.**

9.15.1. **Terminology:**

- *R v Secretary of State for the Home Department, Ex parte Pierson* [1998] AC 539 (HL), 587H (Lord Steyn borrowing 'principle of legality' from *Halsbury's Laws of England*);
- *Mixnam's Properties Ltd v Chertsey Urban District Council* [1964] 1 QB 214 (CA), 233E–H (Danckwerts LJ, quoting from *Maxwell on Interpretation of Statutes*, 11th edn (1962), pp 78–9; principle of legality also known as the 'presumption against implicit alteration of law').

9.15.2. **History of the principle of legality:**

- *R (Morgan Grenfell & Co. Ltd) v Special Commissioner of Income Tax* [2002] UKHL 21 [2003] 1 AC 563, [8] (Lord Hoffmann noting that the principle of legality is traceable to *Stradling v Morgan* (1560) 1 Pl 199);

- *R v Secretary of State for the Home Department, Ex parte Pierson* [1998] AC 539 (HL), 587E (Lord Steyn, citing *Minet v Leman* (1855) 20 Beav 269 at 278: 'In 1855, Sir John Romilly MR observed: "the general words of the Act are not to be so construed as to alter the previous policy of the law unless no sense or meaning can be applied to those words consistently with the intention of preserving the existing policy untouched". ').

9.15.3. **Modern explanation of the principle of legality:**

- *Cross, Statutory Interpretation* (3rd edn, pp 165–166), (quoted in *R v Secretary of State for the Home Department, Ex parte Pierson* [1998] AC 539 (HL), 588B–E (Lord Steyn)): 'Statutes often go into considerable detail, but even so allowance must be made for the fact that they are not enacted in a vacuum. A great deal inevitably remains unsaid. Legislators and drafters assume that the courts will continue to act in accordance with well-recognised rules . . . Long-standing principles of constitutional and administrative law are likewise taken for granted, or assumed by the courts to have been taken for granted, by Parliament. Examples are the principles that discretionary powers conferred in apparently absolute terms must be exercised reasonably, and that administrative tribunals and other such bodies must act in accordance with the principles of natural justice. One function of the word "presumption" in the context of statutory interpretation is to state the result of this legislative reliance (real or assumed) on firmly established legal principles . . . These presumptions apply although there is no question of linguistic ambiguity in the statutory wording under construction, and they may be described as "presumptions of general application" . . . These presumptions of general application not only supplement the text, they also operate at a higher level as expressions of fundamental principles governing both civil liberties and the relations between Parliament, the executive and the courts. They operate here as constitutional principles which are not easily displaced by statutory text.');
- *B (A Minor) v DPP* [2000] 2 AC 428 (HL), 470G–H (Lord Steyn: 'In other words, in the absence of express words or a truly necessary implication, Parliament must be presumed to legislate on the assumption that the principle of legality will supplement the text.').

9.15.4. **The rationale of the principle of legality:**

- *R v Secretary of State for the Home Department, Ex parte Simms* [2000] 2 AC 115 (HL), 131E–G (Lord Hoffmann: 'Parliamentary sovereignty means that Parliament can, if it chooses, legislate contrary to fundamental principles of human rights. The Human Rights Act will not detract from this power. The constraints upon its exercise by Parliament are ultimately political, not legal. But the principle of legality means that Parliament must squarely confront what it is doing and accept the political cost. Fundamental rights cannot be overridden by general or ambiguous words. This is because there is too great a risk that the full implications of their unqualified meaning may have passed unnoticed in the democratic process. In this way the courts of the United Kingdom, though acknowledging the sovereignty of Parliament, apply principles of constitutionality little different from those which exist in countries where the power of the legislature is expressly limited by a constitutional document.' See also 131G–132C, on the HRA and the principle of legality [§ **7.9.3**]);

- *B (A Minor) v DPP* [2000] 2 AC 428 (HL), 470D–F (Lord Steyn, quoting Lord Hoffmann in *Simms* (see above): 'This passage admirably captures, if I may say so, the rationale of the principle of legality.');
- *R (International Transport Roth GmbH) v Secretary of State for the Home Department* [2002] EWCA Civ 158 [2003] QB 728, [73–75] (Laws LJ considering one of the ways in which courts seek to resolve the tension between legislative sovereignty and the vindication of fundamental rights: '[w]here it is suggested that a statute has effected or authorised what would undoubtedly amount to a violation of a fundamental or constitutional right. Here the courts protect the right in question, while acknowledging the legislative supremacy of Parliament, by means of a rule of construction. The rule is that while the legislature possesses the power to override fundamental rights, general words will not suffice. It can only be done by express, or at any rate specific, provision . . . The rule of construction, that only express or at least specific words will suffice to effect such a result, is a brightline rule whose edge is sharp.').

9.15.5. **The principle of legality applies to both statutes and subordinate legislation:**

- *R v Secretary of State for the Home Department, Ex parte Simms* [2000] 2 AC 115 (HL), 132C (Lord Hoffmann: 'What this case decides is that the principle of legality applies to subordinate legislation as much as to Acts of Parliament.');
- *R v Secretary of State for the Home Department, Ex parte Leech* [1994] QB 198 (CA), 209D–E (Steyn LJ: '[I]n relation to rule-making powers alleged to arise by necessary implication, it can fairly be said that the more fundamental the right interfered with, and the more drastic the interference, the more difficult becomes the implication.' At 209H: 'There is a presumption against statutory interference with vested common law rights. That must entail a presumption against a statute authorising interference with vested common law rights by subordinate legislation.');

- *Mixnam's Properties Ltd v Chertsey Urban District Council* [1964] 1 QB 214 (CA), 237D–F (Diplock LJ: 'This general rule of construction [the principle of legality] has a particular application to clauses in statutes by which Parliament authorises other persons or authorities to exercise powers of subordinate legislation, whether directly by means of by-laws or . . . indirectly by subjecting what would otherwise be lawful activities of citizens to conditions, the breach of which gives rise to penal sanctions. Parliament can make whatever changes it likes in the law, but subordinate legislative authorities can make only such changes in the law as Parliament has expressly empowered them to make.').

9.15.6. **The principle of legality applies to statutory conferrals of executive power:**

- *R v Secretary of State for the Home Department, Ex parte Pierson* [1998] AC 539 (HL) (Secretary of State had no general power to increase a sentence fixed and communicated to a prisoner), 575D–E (Lord Browne-Wilkinson: 'A power conferred by Parliament in general terms is not to be taken to authorise the doing of acts by the donee of the power which adversely affect the legal rights of the citizen or the basic principles on which the law of the United Kingdom is based unless the statute conferring the power makes it clear that such was the intention of Parliament.');
- *Mixnam's Properties Ltd v Chertsey Urban District Council* [1964] 1 QB 214 (CA), 237D–F (Diplock LJ) [§ **9.15.5**].

9.15.7. **The principle of legality applies even in the absence of ambiguity:**

- *B (A Minor) v DPP* [2000] 2 AC 428 (HL), 470E–F (Lord Steyn referring to the explanation given by Sir Rupert Cross regarding the principle of legality [§ **9.15.3**] and that 'such presumptions [mens reas] are of general application and are not dependent on finding an ambiguity in the text.');
- *Smith v East Elloe District Council* [1956] AC 736 (HL), 765B–F (Lord Reid (dissenting): 'There are many cases where general words in a statute are given a limited meaning. That is done, not only where there is something in the statute itself which requires it, but also where to give general words their apparent meaning would lead to conflict with some fundamental principle. Where there is ample scope for the words to operate without any such conflict it may very well be that the draftsman did not have in mind and Parliament did not realise that the words were so wide that in some few cases they could operate to subvert a fundamental principle. In general, of course, the intention of Parliament can only be inferred from the words of the statute, but it appears to me to be well established in certain cases that, without some specific indication of an intention to do so, the mere generality of words used will not be regarded as sufficient

to show an intention to depart from fundamental principles. So, general words by themselves do not bind the Crown, they are limited so as not to conflict with international law, they are commonly read so as to avoid retrospective infringement of rights, and it appears to me that they can equally well be read so as not to deprive the court of jurisdiction where bad faith is involved.'), see also 772F–H (Lord Somervell (dissenting) stating that general words in a statute should not be construed as depriving the victim of fraud of all right of resort to the courts), *cf* 769D–G (Lord Radcliffe: 'Merely to say that Parliament cannot be presumed to have intended to bring about a consequence which many people might think to be unjust is not, in my opinion, a principle of construction for this purpose. In point of fact, whatever innocence of view might have been available to the lawyers of the eighteenth and nineteenth centuries, the twentieth century lawyer is entitled to few assumptions in this field. It is not open to him to ignore the fact that the legislature has often shown indifference to the assertion of rights which courts of law have been accustomed to recognise and enforce.').

9.15.8. **The principle of legality can apply only where there is a pre-existing fundamental right in domestic law:**
Illustrations:

- *R (European Roma Rights Centre) v Immigration Officer at Prague Airport* [2004] UKHL 55 [2005] 2 WLR 1, [29] (Lord Bingham, rejecting a reliance on the principle of legality where there was no underlying right in domestic law to have the merits of an asylum application considered abroad);
- *R v Secretary of State for the Home Department, Ex parte Stafford* [1999] 2 AC 38 (HL), 49F (Lord Steyn considering that the principle of legality did not apply in construing section 35(2) of the Criminal Justice Act 1991 because of the absence of the 'necessary contextual backcloth' of a relevant and applicable principle of common law).

9.15.9. **The principle of legality protects fundamental procedural rights:**
Illustrations:

- *R v Secretary of State for the Home Department, Ex parte Daly* [2001] UKHL 26 [2001] 2 AC 532 (HL), [5] (Lord Bingham considering that a person sentenced to a custodial order retained the right of access to a court, the right of access to legal advice and the right to communicate confidentially with a legal adviser and that such rights could be curtailed only by clear and express words, and then only to the extent necessary to meet the ends which justify the curtailment), [30–31] (Lord Cooke) [**§ 10.8.1**];
- *Boddington v British Transport Police* [1999] 2 AC 143 (HL), 161C–F (Lord Irvine, LC: '[I]n approaching the issue of statutory construction the courts proceed from a strong appreciation

that ours is a country subject to the rule of law. This means that it is well recognised to be important for the maintenance of the rule of law and the preservation of liberty that individuals affected by legal measures promulgated by executive public bodies should have a fair opportunity to challenge these measures and to vindicate their rights in court proceedings. There is a strong presumption that Parliament will not legislate to prevent individuals from doing so.');

- *R v Cain* [1985] AC 46 (HL), 55H–56B (Lord Scarman: 'It is a reasonable inference not to be gainsaid save by specific statutory provision that where Parliament prohibits an appeal against sentence it is dealing with the discretionary power of the court to make the order and not addressing its prohibition to orders defective in law. In the absence of express indication to the contrary, it would be unthinkable that Parliament could intend to deprive the subject of his right to appeal against a sentence which the court had no power to pass.');
- *R v Lord Chancellor, Ex parte Witham* [1998] QB 575, (DC), 585–586 (Laws J considering that the right of access to the courts was a common law right which could only be abrogated by specific statutory provision);
- *R v Secretary of State for the Home Department, Ex parte Doody* [1994] 1 AC 531 (HL) (statutory rights not intended to exclude the common law principle of procedural fairness);
- *Raymond v Honey* [1983] 1 AC 1 (HL) (an apparently broad power, in section 47(1) of the Prison Act 1952 construed narrowly on the basis that Parliament cannot have intended to confer power to interfere unreasonably with fundamental civil rights), 10G (Lord Wilberforce: '[U]nder English law, a convicted prisoner, in spite of his imprisonment, retains all civil rights which are not taken away expressly or by necessary implication.' At 12H–13B 'In my opinion there is nothing in the Prison Act 1952 that confers power to make regulations which would deny, or interfere with, the right of the respondent, as a prisoner, to have unimpeded access to a court. Section 47 . . . is quite insufficient to authorise hindrance or interference with so basic a right. The regulations themselves must be interpreted accordingly, otherwise they would be ultra vires.');
- *R v Secretary of State for the Home Department, Ex parte Anderson* [1984] QB 778 (DC), 792 and 793C–794C (Robert Goff LJ considering that a prisoner had right to unimpeded access to court; access to a legal adviser to receive advice and guidance in connection with future possible civil proceedings was an inseparable part of that right; therefore standing orders prohibiting the visit of a legal adviser to advise on prisoners' complaints about prison treatment and restricting their correspondence with legal advisers on such matters unless a complaint had been lodged with prison authorities first, were ultra vires).

9.15.10. **The principle of legality protects fundamental substantive rights:** ***Illustrations:***

- *R v Secretary of State for the Environment, Transport and the Regions, Ex parte Spath Holme Ltd* [2001] 2 AC 349 (HL), 383E (Lord Bingham construing section 31 of the Landlord and Tenant Act 1985: 'I have no doubt that clear and unambiguous words should be used if the citizen is to be deprived of his property without compensation and any reasonable doubt should be resolved in his favour.');
- *R (Morgan Grenfell & Co. Ltd) v Special Commissioner of Income Tax* [2001] UKHL 21 [2003] 1 AC 563 (legal professional privilege was not excluded by the express words of the Taxes Management Act 1970 or by necessary implication from the structure of the 1970 Act: see especially [9], [20], [36] (Lord Hoffmann));
- *B (A Minor) v DPP* [2000] 2 AC 428 (HL) 460F–461A (Lord Nicholls), 470A–H (Lord Steyn) (both construing section 1(1) of the Indecency with Children Act 1960 in the context of the presumption that *mens rea* is required for statutory crimes);
- *R v Secretary of State for the Home Department, Ex parte Leech* [1994] QB 198, 212C–D (Steyn LJ considering that a fundamental right such as the common law right to legal professional privilege would very rarely be held to be abolished by necessary implication. See also 216D–217A considering *Raymond v Honey* [1983] 1 AC 1 (HL) [§ **9.15.9**]);
- *Marcel v Commissioner of Police of the Metropolis* [1992] Ch 225, 234C–H (Lord Browne-Wilkinson, V-C interpreting the Police and Criminal Evidence Act 1984 on the basis that in the absence of express words Parliament could not be assumed to have interfered with the individual 'fundamental human rights' of property and privacy.);
- *R v Secretary of State for the Home Department, Ex parte Khawaja* [1984] AC 74 (HL), 111E–F (Lord Scarman: 'If Parliament intends to exclude effective judicial review of the exercise of a power in restraint of liberty, it must make its meaning crystal clear.')
- *Wheeler v Leicester CC* [1985] AC 1054 (HL), 1063D–E and 1064H–1065E (Lord Browne-Wilkinson considering that express statutory provision is needed to interfere with the right of individuals to hold and express their own views).

9.16. **The principle of legality has prima facie force. Therefore, it will be displaced where the legislation being interpreted, either expressly or by necessary implication, excludes the construction to which the principle of legality leads.**

9.16.1. **Prima facie force:**

- *R v Secretary of State for the Home Department, Ex parte Simms* [2000] 2 AC 115 (HL), 131E–G (Lord Hoffmann: 'Fundamental rights cannot be overridden by general or ambiguous words. This is because there is too great a risk that the full implications of their unqualified meaning may have passed unnoticed in the democratic process. In the absence of express language or necessary implication to the contrary, the courts therefore presume that even the most general words were intended to be subject to the basic rights of the individual.').

9.16.2. **Displacement by express provision:**

- *R v Secretary of State for the Home Department, Ex parte Pierson* [1998] AC 539 (HL) (the principle of legality can be displaced where 'the statute conferring the power makes it clear that such was the intention of Parliament' (575D, Lord Browne-Wilkinson), i.e. where there is a 'clear and specific provision to the contrary'(587D, Lord Steyn)).

Illustration:

- *R v Rezvi* [2002] UKHL 1 & 2 [2003] 1 AC 1099, [19] (Lord Steyn considering that there was no scope for the application of the principle of legality to the Criminal Justice Act 1988 because 'the legislation is explicit in its terms and represents a fair balance between the interests of the individual and those of the community.').

9.16.3. **Displacement by necessary implication:**

- *R v Lord Chancellor, Ex parte Lightfoot* [2000] QB 597 (CA), 625 (Simon Brown LJ distinguishing *R v Lord Chancellor, Ex parte Witham* [1998] QB 575 (DC) which held that 'only specific provisions (express words) in the primary legislation, can abrogate constitutional rights' by referring to Lord Browne-Wilkinson's observations in *R v Secretary of State for the Home Department, Ex parte Pierson* (see below) and *Westminster Bank Ltd v Beverley Borough Council* [1971] AC 508 (HL), 529 (Lord Reid));
- *R v Secretary of State for the Home Department, Ex parte Pierson* [1998] AC 539 (HL) (in enacting section 35(2) of the Criminal Justice Act 1991 ('the Secretary of State may, after consultation with the Lord Chief Justice together with the trial judge if available, release on licence a life prisoner who is not a discretionary life prisoner') Parliament had left untouched the fundamental principle that a sentence lawfully passed should not be retrospectively increased), 573H (Lord Browne-Wilkinson stating that Parliament is presumed not to have intended to change the common law unless it has clearly indicated such intention either expressly or by necessary implication. At 575A–B, commenting on *R v Lord Chancellor, Ex parte Witham* [1998] QB 575 (DC): 'I must not be taken as agreeing with everything said in the

judgment in that case (in particular whether basic rights can be overridden by necessary implication as opposed to express provision).');

- *R (Morgan Grenfell & Co Ltd) v Special Commissioner of Income Tax* [2002] UKHL 21 [2003] 1 AC 563, [45] (Lord Hobhouse: 'A necessary implication is not the same as a reasonable implication as was pointed out by Lord Hutton in *B (A Minor) v Director of Public Prosecutions* [2000] 2 AC 428, 481. A *necessary* implication is one which necessarily follows from the express provisions of the statute construed in their context. It distinguishes between what it would have been sensible or reasonable for Parliament to have included or what Parliament would, if it had thought about it, probably have included and what it is clear that the express language of the statute shows that the statute must have included. A necessary implication is a matter of express language and logic not interpretation.');
- *B v Auckland District Law Society* [2003] UKPC 38 [2003] 2 AC 736, [58] (Lord Millett citing Lord Hobhouse in *Morgan Grenfell* (see above) as authority for the meaning of 'by necessary implication').

9.17. **There is a real question, in the context of the principle of legality, of the extent to which the fundamental rights relied upon are already part of the common law rather than owing their existence, in considerable part, to declaratory judicial decision-making stimulated by the normative force of fundamental rights in unincorporated treaties. The notion that certain fundamental rights are often creatures of declaratory judicial decision-making rather than embedded in the common law is bolstered by the many examples of courts pre-HRA, post-ECHR ratification, declaring the common law to be the same as the ECHR [§§ 10.7–10.8]. As Lord Browne-Wilkinson observed, writing extra-judicially in 1991:**

> 'If it were to be held that general statutory powers were presumed not to interfere with human rights unless Parliament expressly or by necessary implication has so authorised, for most practical purposes the common law would provide protection to the individual at least equal to that provided by the ECHR . . . If the ECHR fulfils no other purpose, it has already served and will continue to serve this purpose by bringing home to the judicial mind that there are wider principles, more fundamental than the merits of a particular case, and that ultimately our freedom depends on defending these principles, come what may.' 'The Infiltration of a Bill of Rights' [1992] PL 397, 408–410.

(4) Miscellaneous Use of Unincorporated Treaties

9.18. **If the nucleus of the relationship between unincorporated treaties and domestic legislation consists of the presumption of compatibility [§§ 9.7–9.14] and the principle of legality [§§ 9.15–9.17] then it is surrounded by a fluid, shifting penumbra. Here, the edges are elusive and defy rigid description; the domestic approach to unincorporated treaties is marked with both creativity and common sense. Thus, without going so far as to read legislation compatibly with unincorporated treaty obligations, these obligations have been used in various ways: as aids in construing legislation, as guiding the proper approach to interpreting legislation, as illuminating the object and background of the legislation and as points of comparison or analogy. This use of unincorporated treaties as soft law is similar to the use of comparative material from other jurisdictions. The examples below illustrate the general enthusiasm with which courts have carved unincorporated treaties into the lexicon of domestic law.**

9.18.1. Unincorporated treaties as aids in construing legislation:
Illustrations:

- *R (Mullen) v Secretary of State for the Home Department* [2004] UKHL 18 [2005] 1 AC 1, [9(4)] (Lord Bingham using Article 3 of the Seventh Protocol to the ECHR to interpret section 133, Criminal Justice Act 1988 (giving effect to Article 14(6), International Covenant on Civil and Political Rights));
- *A v Secretary of State for the Home Department* [2004] UKHL 56 [2005] 2 WLR 87 (Lord Bingham, in determining the validity of the derogation from Article 5, ECHR, in the Human Rights Act 1998 (Designated Derogation) Order 2001 (SI 2001/3644) and the compatibility of part 4 of the Anti-terrorism, Crime and Security Act 2001 with Article 5, ECHR considered the following: [19] (the similarity between Article 4(1), International Covenant on Civil and Political Rights, and Article 15(1), ECHR and the promulgations, under the International Covenant on Civil and Political Rights of 'The Siracusa Principles of the Limitation and Derogation Provisions in the International Covenant on Civil and Political Rights' (1985) 7 HRQ 3), [22] (General Comment No 29 on Article 4, International Covenant on Civil and Political Rights, of 24 July 2001 of the UN Human Rights Committee), [23] (Resolution 1271 of the Parliamentary Assembly of the Council of Europe, adopted on 24 January 2002 and the Opinion 1/2002 of the Council of Europe Commissioner for Human Rights (Comm DH (2002) 7, 28

August 2002) (and also at [34],[57]), [57] (the 'Guidelines on human rights and the fight against terrorism' adopted by the Committee of Ministers of the Council of Europe on 11 July 2002 and the General Policy Recommendations of 8 June 2004, of the European Commission against Racism and Intolerance (a Council of Europe Body)), [58] (the Universal Declaration on Human Rights and the UN General Assembly's Declaration on the Human Rights of Individuals who are not Nationals of the Country in which They Live, of 13 December 1985), [59] (the UN Human Rights Committee's General Comment No 15, adopted in 1986), [60] (Article 4, International Covenant on Civil and Political Rights), [61] (UN Security Council Resolution 1456 of 20 January 2003 and a Report of the UN Commission on Human Rights of 26 May 2003), [62] (the International Convention on the Elimination of All Forms of Racial Discrimination, General Recommendations XI and 14 (of 1993) and 30 (of 2004) of the Committee and the Committee's Concluding Observations on the United Kingdom (10 December 2003, CERD/C/63/CO/11)), [63] (the International Law Association's 'Paris Minimum Standards of Human Rights Norms in a State of Emergency' (1985) 79 AJIL 1072). At [63]: 'The materials I have cited are not legally binding on the United Kingdom . . . [but then concluding] These materials are inimical to the submission that a state may lawfully discriminate against foreign nationals by detaining them but not nationals presenting the same threat in a time of public emergency.');

- *ID v Home Office* [2005] EWCA Civ 38 [2005] INLR 278 [36], [113] and [122] (Brooke LJ considering that the detention of a family was not disproportionate or unlawful under Article 5, ECHR and the HRA, in the light of Article 37(6) of the UN Convention on the Rights of the Child) [**§ 5.16.2**];
- *R (Roszkowski) v Special Adjudicator* (unreported) CO/2609/1999 (Admin) (31 October 2000), [47–48] (Keene J, after noting the similarities between the Criminal Justice Act 1988, section 134 and Article 1(1) of the UN Torture Convention 1984 ([22–23]) considering, obiter, that 'torture' in the Asylum and Immigration Appeals Act 1993, Schedule 2, paragraph 5(5) (relating to appeals against certification by the Secretary of State where the evidence adduced in support of the claim establishes 'a reasonable likelihood that the appellant has been tortured in the country or territory to which he is to be sent') 'must be torture related to the substantive claim for asylum and not something extraneous to it' and that, had it been necessary to decide the issue, he would have held that 'torture' in paragraph 5(5) 'must share the characteristic of persecution' even though the definition of torture in the Convention and section 134(1) 'are not precisely on all fours with such an interpretation of torture.') (CA is at [2001] EWCA Civ 650);

- *R (A and B) v East Sussex CC* [2003] EWHC 167 (Admin) (2003) LGR 529, [93] (Munby J) [§ **5.17.1**];
- *R (Spink) v Wandsworth LBC* [2004] EWHC 2314 (Admin) [2005] 1 WLR 258, [60] (Richards J) [§ **5.16.2**];
- *In re Westinghouse Uranium Contract* [1978] AC 547 (HL), 608B–C (Lord Wilberforce construing the Evidence (Proceedings in Other Jurisdictions) Act 1975 by reference to the Hague Convention on the Taking of Evidence Abroad in Civil and Commercial Matters of 1970 (Cmnd 3991, 6727)), see similarly 617G–618D (Viscount Dilhorne);
- *In re Norway's Application (Nos 1 & 2)* [1990] AC 723 (HL) 794G, 796B–F and 798F–799B (Lord Goff, considering whether proceedings in a Norwegian court were civil proceedings within section 1(b) of the Evidence (Proceedings in Other Jurisdictions) Act 1975 by reference to the Convention on the Taking of Evidence Abroad in Civil and Commercial Matters 1970);
- *Secretary of State for the Home Department v Rehman* [2001] UKHL 47 [2003] 1 AC 153 (in construing 'conducive to the public good' and 'national security' in sections 3(5)(b) and 15(3) of the Immigration Act 1971 (respectively), counsel defined 'national security' by reference to phrases in international conventions and the Johannesburg Principles on National Security, Freedom of Expression and Access to Information; see [14]);
- *The Antonis P Lemos* [1985] AC 711 (HL) (using the Convention for the Unification of Certain Rules relating to the Arrest of Seagoing Ships 1952, in construing the nature and scope of the Admiralty jurisdiction in section 20(2)(h) of the Supreme Court Act 1981. See, for example, 725H (Lord Brandon));
- *Guilfoyle v Home Office* [1981] QB 309 (CA), 321A–D (Sir John Megaw considering whether rule 37A(1) of the Prison Rules 1964 infringed Article 25, ECHR; interpreting the scope of Article 25 by reference to the European Agreement relating to Persons participating in Proceedings of the European Commission and the Court of Human Rights 1969.);
- *Allgemeine Gold-und Silberscheideanstalt v Customs and Excise Commissioners* [1980] QB 390 (CA), 403G–H (Lord Denning MR considering, pre-HRA, counsel's submission that forfeiture of coins under section 44 of the Customs and Excise Act 1952 would be contrary to the ECHR, Article 1 of the First Protocol: 'It is not part of our English law yet. But we do pay attention to the Convention even as it stands.' Concluding, however, at 404B, that in view of the exceptions to the right in article 1 of the First Protocol: '[I]t is quite clear that there is nothing which impairs the right of a state to forfeit property which has been brought into the country in breach of its customs law.').

9.18.2. **Unincorporated treaties as aids to construction regarding incorporated treaties:** [§ **5.16**]

9.18.3. **Legislatives objectives reflected in objectives of unincorporated treaties:**

Illustrations:

- *McIntosh v HM Advocate* [2001] UKPC D1 [2003] 1 AC 1078, [4] (Lord Bingham, considering the premises underlying the Misuse of Drugs Act 1971 and the Proceeds of Crime (Scotland) Act 1995: 'These premises are reflected in the United Nations Convention against Illicit Traffic in Narcotic Drugs and Psychotropic Substances (1992)(Cm 1927) adopted in Vienna on 19 December 1988, which the United Kingdom ratified in June 1991, and in the experience and practice of very many states all over the world.');
- *R v Rezvi* [2002] UKHL 1 & 2 [2003] 1 AC 1099, [14] (Lord Steyn, considering the objectives underlying the Criminal Justice Act 1988: 'These objectives reflect not only national but also international policy. The United Kingdom has undertaken, by signing and ratifying treaties agreed under the auspices of the United Nations and the Council of Europe, to take measures necessary to ensure that the profits of those engaged in drug trafficking or other crimes are confiscated: see the United Nations Convention against Illicit Traffic in Narcotic Drugs and Psychotropic Substances (19 December 1988); Council of Europe Convention on Laundering, Search, Seizure and Confiscation of the Proceeds from Crime, Strasbourg, 8 November 1990. These Conventions are in operation and have been ratified by the United Kingdom.');
- *R (Saifi) v Governor of Brixton Prison* [2001] 1 WLR 1134 (DC), [60] (Rose LJ reviewing a magistrate's ruling regarding the exclusion of evidence under section 78 of the Police and Criminal Evidence Act 1978 where the magistrate referred to Article 15 of the Torture Convention: 'In our judgment reference to the Torture Convention adds nothing to the case. The intent of article 15 has been ensured in our law, by the common law and statute.').

9.18.4. **Unincorporated treaties guiding the proper approach to interpreting legislation:**

Illustration:

- *R (Carson) v Secretary of State for the Home Department* [2005] UKHL 37 [2005] 2 WLR 1369, [18] (Lord Hoffmann construing social security legislation: 'Social security benefits are part of an intricate and interlocking system of social welfare which exists to ensure certain minimum standards of living for the people of this country. They are an expression of what has been called social solidarity or fraternité; the duty of any community to help those of its members who are in need. But that duty is generally recognised to be national in character. It does not extend to the inhabitants of foreign countries. That is recognised in treaties such as the ILO Social Security (Minimum Standards) Convention 1952 (article 69) and the European Code of Social Security 1961.');

- *Lancashire CC v B* [2000] 2 AC 147 (HL), 170F–H (Lord Clyde construing the Children Act 1989, pre-HRA: 'The granting of a care order will only be done by the court after consideration of the matters detailed in section 1 and in particular the requirement in section 1(5) that the order is only to be made if the making of it would be better for the child than the making of no order at all. The need for caution and restraint is underlined by the provisions of article 8 of the European Convention for the Protection of Human Rights and Fundamental Freedoms.'), 168B–C (Lord Nicholls considering acts of the local authority in the context of Article 8, ECHR).

9.18.5. **Unincorporated treaties as providing a point of comparison:**
Illustration:

- *O'Hara v Chief Constable of the Royal Ulster Constabulary* [1997] AC 286 (HL), 292C–F (Lord Steyn, considering section 12(1) of the Prevention of Terrorism (Temporary Provisions) Act 1984, pre-HRA: 'It is clear from the drafting technique employed in article 5(1)(c) [of the ECHR], and in particular the use of the passive tense, that it contemplates a broader test of whether reasonable suspicion exists and does not confine it to matters present in the mind of the arresting officer . . . But section 12(1), and similar provisions, cannot be approached in this way: they categorise as reasonable grounds for suspicion only matters present in the mind of the constable.');
- *R (Mullen) v Secretary of State for the Home Department* [2004] UKHL 18 [2005] 1 AC 1, [6] (Lord Bingham noting that 'despite difference of wording and substance' Article 14(6) International Covenant on Civil and Political Rights 'matches' Article 6, ECHR; section 11, Canadian Charter of Rights and Freedoms; sections 24 and 25, New Zealand Bill of Rights; section 35(3), Bill of Rights, incorporated in the Constitution of South Africa. At [7] noting that Article 5(5), ECHR is 'reflected in article 9(5)' of the International Covenant on Civil and Political Rights);
- *Secretary of State for Defence v Guardian Newspapers* [1985] AC 339 (HL), 361E–F (Lord Scarman on section 10 of the Contempt of Court Act 1981: 'The section, it is important to note in this connection, bears a striking structural resemblance to the way in which many of the articles of the European Convention for the Protection of Human Rights and Fundamental Freedoms (1953) (Cmd 8969) which formulate the fundamental rights and freedoms protected by that Convention are framed: namely, a general rule subject to carefully drawn and limited exceptions which require to be established, in case of dispute, to the satisfaction of the European Court of Human Rights.').

9.18.6. **Unincorporated treaties as providing new vocabulary:**
Illustration:

- *Council of Civil Service Unions v Minister for Civil Service* [1985] AC 374 (HL), 410C (Lord Diplock: 'Adopting the phraseology used in the European Convention on Human Rights 1953 (Convention for the Protection of Human Rights and Fundamental Freedoms) (1953) (Cmd. 8969) to which the United Kingdom is a party it has now become usual in statutes to refer to [the defence of the realm against potential enemies] as "national security".').

9.18.7. **Unincorporated treaties providing a spur to legislative action:**
Illustration:

- *Malone v Metropolitan Police Commissioner* [1979] Ch 344, 380H (Megarry V-C, commenting, pre-HRA, in the context of no legislative or common law regulation of telephone tapping: '[t]elephone tapping is a subject which cries out for legislation . . . the requirements of the [ECHR] should provide a spur to action, even if belated.').

9.18.8. **Unincorporated treaties as background:**
Illustrations:

- *R v Secretary of State for the Home Department, Ex parte Venables* [1998] AC 407 (HL), 484F–H (Lord Goff interpreting part II of the Criminal Justice Act 1991 (pre-HRA): 'Finally, I must refer to the decision of the European Court of Human Rights in *Thynne v United Kingdom* (1990) 13 EHRR 666, in which it was held that, in the case of discretionary life sentence prisoners the penal element in whose sentences has expired, their continued detention should be subject to judicial control by virtue of article 5(4) of the Convention for the Protection of Human Rights and Fundamental Freedoms (1953) (Cmd. 8968). It is against this background [reference was also made to the policy applied by successive Home Secretaries in relation to release on licence] that the effect of Part II of the Act of 1991 can be understood. Section 34 of the Act is concerned with the release of discretionary life prisoners, and it is plain that this section has been drafted to give effect to the decision of the European Court in *Thynne's* case'.), 493B–F and 501C–F (Lord Browne-Wilkinson), 505C–F (Lord Lloyd), 533G–534A (Lord Hope) (all referring to the ECHR and the case law of the ECtHR);
- *Wainwright v Home Office* [2001] EWCA Civ 2081 [2002] QB 1334, [40] (Lord Woolf, rejecting the application of section 3, HRA, to rule 86 of the Prison Rules 1964 made pursuant to the Prison Act 1952 so as to apply it to events pre-HRA: 'The European Convention on Human Rights . . . is only relevant here as background against which the appeal is to be decided.');

- *In re L (A Minor)(Police Investigation: Privilege)* [1997] AC 16 (HL), 32H (Lord Nicholls, considering the extent to which legal professional privilege and the privilege against self-incrimination applied in care proceedings under the Children Act 1989, pre- HRA: 'I can see no reason why parties to family proceedings should not be as much entitled to a fair hearing having these features and safeguards as are parties to other court proceedings. Indeed, it must be doubtful whether a parent who is denied the opportunity to obtain legal advice in confidence is accorded the fair hearing to which he is entitled under article 6(1), read in conjunction with article 8, of the European Convention for the Protection of Human Rights and Fundamental Freedoms (1953) (Cmnd. 8969).').

9.18.9. **Unincorporated treaties as providing evidence of fundamental human rights:**

Illustration:

- *R (Mullen) v Secretary of State for the Home Department* [2004] UKHL 18 [2005] 1 AC 1, [26] (Lord Steyn: 'Gradually a fundamental human right to compensation for miscarriages of justice evolved. The Universal Declaration of Human Rights (1948) made no provision for such a fundamental right. The European Convention for the Protection of Human Rights and Fundamental Freedoms (1950) in its original form also did not contain such a provision. The American Convention on Human Rights (1969) contained in article 10 a weak provision which left it to states to make suitable provision for compensation in accordance with law. The breakthrough came with the International Covenant on Civil and Political Rights.').

9.18.10. **Using ECtHR case law (pre-HRA) as providing confirmation of approach:**

Illustrations:

- *Fitzpatrick v Sterling Housing Association* [2001] 1 AC 27 (HL), 53F (Lord Clyde comparing his conclusion that the same-sex partner of a tenant was to be recognised as capable of constituting a member of the tenant's family under the Rent Act 1977 schedule 1 paragraph 3(1) with jurisprudence of the ECtHR: 'Nor does the decision which I have reached conflict with the jurisprudence of the . . . European Court of Human Rights.');
- *R v Secretary of State for the Home Department, Ex parte Leech* [1994] QB 198 (CA), 217E–F (Steyn LJ: 'The important point is that the decision [in *Campbell v United Kingdom* (1992) 15 EHRR 137], although not directly binding in England, reinforces a conclusion that we have arrived at in the light of the principles of our domestic jurisprudence,' and noting '[W]hen considering the common law and statutory discretionary powers under English law the jurisprudence on article 6 can have a

valuable role to play. English law relating to the ingredients of a fair trial is highly developed. But every system of law stands to benefit by an awareness of the answers given by other courts and tribunals to similar problems.');

- *R v Khan* [1997] AC 558 (HL), 583B–D (Lord Nicholls referring to a decision of the ECtHR, *Schenk v Switzerland* 13 EHRR 242 as confirming the proper approach to be taken;
- *Raymond v Honey* [1983] 1 AC 1 (HL), 10F (Lord Wilberforce, construing section 47(1) of the Prison Act 1952, and noting that the principle that any act which is calculated to obstruct or interfere with the due course of justice, or the lawful process of the courts, is a contempt of court had been 'strongly affirmed' by the ECtHR in *Golder v United Kingdom* (1975) 1 EHRR 524) [§ **9.15.9**];
- *O'Hara v Chief Constable of the Royal Ulster Constabulary* [1997] AC 286 (HL), 302B (Lord Hope: 'I should add that I see no conflict in principle between the approach which has been taken in these cases [on the exercise of statutory powers by police constables] and the judgment of the European Court of Human Rights in *Fox, Campbell & Hartley v United Kingdom* (1990) 13 EHRR 157.');
- *R v Secretary of State for the Home Department, Ex parte Anderson* [1984] QB 778 (DC) 793F (Robert Goff LJ using *Golder v UK* (1975) EHRR 524 to consider the right of access to courts).

9.18.11. **Using ECtHR case law (pre-HRA) where the ECHR underpinned the legislation to be construed:**

Illustrations:

- *Reid v Secretary of State for Scotland* [1999] 2 AC 512 (HL), 538D (Lord Clyde, construing the Mental Health (Scotland) Act 1984: '[I]t was in light of this decision [*X v United Kingdom* (1981) 4 EHRR 188] that Parliament introduced the mechanism of appeal to the sheriff [in sections 63–67 of the 1984 Act].), 549G (Lord Hutton: 'Section 64(1)(a) and section 72(1)(b) were passed to give effect to that ruling of the European Court of Human Rights [in *X v United Kingdom,* 4 EHRR 188].'), see similarly 523 (Lord Lloyd);
- *R v Canons Park Mental Health Review Tribunal, Ex parte A* [1995] QB 60 (CA), 77G–78B (Roch LJ (dissenting) referring to *X v United Kingdom* (1981) 4 EHRR 188 in rejecting a construction of section 72(1)(b) of the Mental Health Act 1983; with whom Lord Hutton agreed in *Reid v Secretary of State for Scotland* [1999] 2 AC 512 (HL), 549H (see above));
- *R v Secretary of State for the Home Department, Ex parte Doody* [1994] 1 AC 531 (HL), 554F–555B (Lord Mustill interpreting the Criminal Justice Act 1967 and considering the effect of *Thynne, Wilson and Gunnell v United Kingdom* (1990) 13 EHRR 666 on domestic law);

- *R v Secretary of State for the Home Department, Ex parte Venables* [1998] AC 407 (HL), 408F–H (Lord Goff (dissenting)), 493B–F and 501C–F (Lord Browne-Wilkinson) (both interpreting part II of the Criminal Justice Act 1991 by reference to *Thynne, Wilson and Gunnell v United Kingdom* (1990) 13 EHRR 666);
- *R v Preston* [1994] 2 AC 130 (HL), 142D–E (Lord Jauncey: 'It is common ground that the [Interception of Communication Act 1985] was passed as a result of the decision of the European Court of Human Rights in *Malone v United Kingdom* (1984) 7 EHRR 14. That case decided that there had been a violation of article 8 of the European Convention on Human Rights inasmuch as the law of England and Wales did "not indicate with reasonable clarity the scope and manner of exercise of the relevant discretion conferred on the public authorities." The mischief which the Act was intended to deal with was accordingly the lack of a clear statutory framework within which telephone tapping could take place and the lack of any form of redress for someone claiming that his telephone had been wrongly tapped.') [§ **9.18.7**].

(5) Unincorporated Treaties in a Written Constitution

9.19. **The international case law of the Privy Council provides informative examples on the use of unincorporated treaties in jurisdictions with written constitutions and important guidance on how to interpret constitutional provisions. This case law has been used, in a domestic context, when interpreting both incorporated treaties and incorporating statutes [§ 5.11.1]. It also provides helpful parallels with our own use of unincorporated treaties (although it should be used cautiously, because of the differing constitutional contexts). For example, the case law recognises that unincorporated treaties have no direct effect in municipal law but that there are canons of interpretation, the presumption of compatibility and the presumption of constitutionality, which permit the use of such treaties when construing constitutional provisions. Unincorporated treaties are also used more generally, particularly where they have a role as constitutional precedents, for example the ECHR.**

9.19.1. No direct effect of unincorporated treaties in constitutional systems:

- *Matthew v State of Trinidad and Tobago* [2004] UKPC 33 [2005] 1 AC 433, [55] (Lord Bingham, Lord Nicholls, Lord Steyn and

Lord Walker (dissenting), interpreting the Constitution of Trinidad and Tobago: 'It is common ground between the parties to this appeal that an obligation binding on a state in international law but not forming part of its domestic law cannot override or even influence the construction and application of a clear and unambiguous provision of domestic law. It is also common ground that if a provision of a state's domestic law is ambiguous and permits of two interpretations, one of which will accord with the state's international obligations and the other of which will involve a violation of those obligations, a court will so far as possible adopt that interpretation which will accord with the state's international obligations. We accept both propositions . . . [They] apply to constitutions as to other domestic law, and apply even if the international obligations were undertaken after the date of the constitution.');

- *Higgs v Minister of National Security* [2000] 2 AC 228 (PC), 241C–G (Lord Hoffmann: '[T]reaties form no part of domestic law unless enacted by the legislature. This has two consequences. The first is that domestic courts have no jurisdiction to construe or apply a treaty . . . The second consequence is that unincorporated treaties cannot change the law of the land. They have no effect upon the rights and duties of citizens in common law or statute law.').

9.19.2. **The presumption of compatibility applied to constitutional provisions:**

- *Boyce v The Queen* [2004] UKPC 32 [2005] 1 AC 400, [25–26] (Lord Hoffmann applying the presumption of compatibility to provisions of the Constitution of Barbados) [**§ 9.8.1**].

Illustration:

- *Matthew v State of Trinidad and Tobago* [2004] UKPC 33 [2005] 1 AC 433, [57–59] (Lord Bingham, Lord Nicholls, Lord Steyn and Lord Walker (dissenting) using the Universal Declaration on Human Rights, the International Covenant on Civil and Political Rights, the American Declaration and the American Convention on Human Rights to interpret the Constitution of Trinidad and Tobago and concluding: '[T]he effect of reversing *Roodal* [which resulted from the majority decision in *Matthew* [**§§ 5.11.2–5.11.7**]] is to put the State in breach of its international obligations under the Universal Declaration, the ICCPR, the American Declaration and the American Constitution.' (at [59])).

9.19.3. **The presumption of constitutionality:**

- *de Freitas v Ministry of Agriculture* [1999] 1 AC 69 (PC), 75F (Lord Clyde: 'It is . . . accepted that in the construction of statutory provisions which contravene human rights and fundamental freedoms there is a presumption of constitutionality

(*Attorney-General of the Gambia v Momodou Jobe* [1984] AC 689).' At 77H–78B: 'While it may be justifiable on occasion to imply words into a statute where there is an ambiguity or an omission and the implied words are necessary to remedy such a defect, in the present case sub-section 10(2)(a) is perfectly clear and entire, free from any ambiguity or omission.');

- *Attorney-General v Momodou Jobe* [1984] AC 689 (PC), 702B–F (Lord Diplock, construing provisions of the Special Criminal Court Act 1979 in the context of the Constitution of the Gambia: '[The presumption of constitutionality] is but a particular application of the canon of construction embodied in the Latin maxim magis est ut res valeat quam pereat which is an aid to the resolution of any ambiguities or obscurities in the actual words used in any document that is manifestly intended by its makers to create legal rights or obligations . . . Where, as in the instant case, omissions by the draftsman of the law to state in express words what, from the subject matter of the law and legal nature of the processes or institutions with which it deals, can be inferred to have been Parliament's intention, a court charged with the judicial duty of giving effect to Parliament's intention, as that intention has been stated in the law that Parliament has passed, ought to construe the law as incorporating, by necessary implication, words which would give effect to such inferred intention, wherever to do so does not contradict the words actually set out in the law itself and to fail to do so would defeat Parliament's intention by depriving the law of all legal effect.').

Illustration:

- *Durity v Attorney-General of Trinidad and Tobago* [2002] UKPC 20 [2003] 1 AC 405, [30] (Lord Nicholls: 'At the forefront of the Constitution [of Trinidad and Tobago] is a resounding declaration of fundamental human rights and freedoms. It is axiomatic that these rights and freedoms, expressly declared, are not to be cut down by other provisions in the Constitution save by language of commensurate clarity. The Constitution itself so declares . . . The court should therefore be very slow indeed to hold that by a side wind the initiation of constitutional proceedings is subject to a rigid and short time bar. The very clearest language is needed before a court could properly so conclude. Such language is noticeably absent in the present case.').

9.19.4. **Using unincorporated treaties despite the principle of no direct effect:**

Illustrations:

- *Thomas v Baptiste* [2000] 2 AC 1 (PC) (construing the due process clause in section 4(a) of the Constitution of Trinidad and Tobago as giving the Crown power to accept the jurisdiction of an international tribunal as part of the domestic criminal system), 22B–C (Lord Millett: '[Section 4(a)] employs different language from that found in the corresponding provisions of the Universal Declaration of Human Rights and the European Convention on Human Rights. They speak merely of "the sentence of a court of competent jurisdiction." . . . [Due process of law] invokes the concept of the rule of law itself and the universally accepted standards of justice observed by civilised nations which observe the rule of law.' At 23E, after recognising the constitutional importance of the principle that an unincorporated treaty cannot alter domestic law: 'The applicants are not seeking to enforce the terms of an unincorporated treaty, but a domestic provision of the law of Trinidad and Tobago . . . By ratifying an international treaty which provides for individual access to an international body, the government made that process for the time being part of the domestic criminal justice system and thereby temporarily at least extended the scope of [section 4(a) of the Constitution].'). *cf* the dissenting judgments of Lord Goff and Lord Hobhouse and, to similar effect, *Fisher v Minister of Public Safety (No 2)*[2000] 1 AC 434 (PC), followed in *Higgs v Minister of National Security* [2000] 2 AC 228 (PC) (see, especially, 245G–246C on the difference between *Thomas v Baptiste* and *Fisher (No 2)*);

- *Briggs v Baptiste* [2000] 2 AC 40 (PC), 54A–C (Lord Millett considering that *Thomas v Baptiste*, 'did not overturn the constitutional principle that international conventions do not alter domestic law except to the extent that they are incorporated into domestic law by legislation. It did not decide that the recommendations of the commission (which are not binding even in international law) or the orders of the Inter-American Court are directly enforceable in domestic law. It mediated the proceedings before the Inter-American system through the due-process clause in the Constitution.'), 55F–G (Lord Nicholls (dissenting) regarding Trinidad and Tobago's refusal to order a stay of execution pursuant to an order for the provisional measure of preserving the applicant's life pending a final decision from the Inter-American Court of Human Rights: 'I am not prepared to accept that the law of Trinidad and Tobago is so foreshortened that the courts of Trinidad and Tobago must stand by, powerless to act, while Briggs is executed. By acceding to the [American Convention on Human Rights, 1969] Trinidad and Tobago intended to confer benefits on its citizens. The benefits were intended to be real not illusory. The Inter-American system of human rights was not intended to be a hollow sham or, for those under sentence of death, a cruel charade.');
- *Lewis v Attorney-General of Jamaica* [2001] 2 AC 50 (PC), 78E–F, 79B–C and 80C (Lord Slynn considering that the exercise of the Governor General's prerogative of mercy in death sentence cases, although not amenable to judicial review on the merits, should, in the light of the state's international obligations, be

exercised by procedures which were fair, proper and amenable to judicial review; and noting that in considering the requirements of natural justice, it is relevant to have regard to international human rights norms set out in unincorporated treaties. At 85B–C stating that the right to the protection of the law in section 13(a) of the Jamaican Constitution and at common law was effectively equivalent to due process of law; that although ratified but unincorporated treaties did not usually create rights for individuals enforceable in domestic courts, when the state acceded to such treaties and allowed individuals to petition human rights bodies thereunder, the protection of the law conferred by section 13(a) of the Jamaican Constitution entitled an individual to complete that procedure and obtain the report of the international body for consideration by the Jamaican Privy Council before determination of an application for mercy in death penalty cases and entitled individuals to the staying of execution until those reports were received and considered), *cf* 88G–89A (Lord Hoffmann (dissenting): '[T]he majority have found in the ancient concept of due process of law a philosopher's stone undetected by generations of judges which can convert the base metal of executive action into the gold of legislative power. It does not however explain how the trick is done . . . [T]here is no explanation of how, in the domestic law of Jamaica, the proceedings before the [Inter-American] commission constitute a legal process (as opposed to the proceedings of any other non-governmental body) which must be duly completed.').

9.19.5. **Using unincorporated treaties as aids to construing constitutional provisions:**

Illustrations:

- *Hinds v Attorney-General of Barbados* [2001] UKPC 56 [2002] 1 AC 854 (PC), [15] (Lord Bingham: 'If sections 18(1), 18(2)(a), 18(2)(b), 18(2)(c), 18(2)(e) and 18(2)(f) [of the Constitution of Barbados] are compared with articles 6(1), 6(2), 6(3)(a), 6(3)(b), 6(3)(d) and 6(3)(e) respectively of the European Convention for the Protection of Human Rights and Fundamental Freedoms (1953) (Cmnd 8969), a close correspondence will be found, often extending to the use of identical language. But there is a striking contrast between section 18(2)(d) and article 6(3)(c). Section 18(2)(d) . . . provides: "Every person who is charged with a criminal offence . . . shall be permitted to defend himself before the court in person or by a legal representative of his own choice." This is indistinguishable in effect from the opening words of article 6(3)(c): "Everyone charged with a criminal offence has the following minimum rights . . . to defend himself in person or through legal assistance of his own choosing." But article 6(3)(c) continues "or, if he has not sufficient means to pay for legal assistance, to be given it free when the interests of justice so require." These words were omitted, plainly deliberately, from section 18(2)(d), and section 18(12) leaves no room for doubt about the reason for the omission.');

- *Reyes v The Queen* [2002] UKPC 11 [2002] 2 AC 235, [17–23] (Lord Bingham, in considering the constitutionality of a mandatory death sentence under the Constitution of Belize, first noted the adoption of a series of international instruments in Belize to protect human rights: the Universal Declaration of Human Rights 1948, the American Declaration of the Rights and Duties of Man 1948, the ECHR 1950, the International Covenant on Civil and Political Rights 1977 and the American Convention on Human Rights 1969. Then, at [27–28]: 'In considering what norms have been accepted by Belize as consistent with the fundamental standards of humanity, it is relevant to take account of the international instruments incorporating such norms to which Belize has subscribed . . . This does not mean that in interpreting the Constitution of Belize effect need be given to treaties not incorporated into the domestic law of Belize or non-binding recommendations or opinions made or given by foreign courts or human right bodies.');
- *Pinder v The Queen* [2002] UKPC 46 [2003] 1 AC 620, [45] (Lord Nicholls and Lord Hope (dissenting), considering the reintroduction of flogging in the Bahamas: 'The Bahamas is a member of the Organisation of American States and has been so since 1982. Although not a party to the American Convention on Human Rights (1969), by becoming a member of the Organisation of American States The Bahamas proclaimed its adherence to the rights expressed in the American Declaration of the Rights and Duties of Man (1948). One of these rights is the right not to receive cruel, infamous or unusual punishment (article xxvi).');
- *Fisher v Minister of Public Safety and Immigration* [1998] AC 673 (PC), 688D–689F (Lord Steyn (dissenting) referring to three principles emerging from the jurisprudence of the ECtHR which had 'important implications' for the construction of Article 17(1) in the Constitution of the Bahamas (the prohibition on torture, inhuman and degrading punishment clause);
- *Pratt v Attorney-General for Jamaica* [1994] 2 AC 1 (PC) (considering the ECHR and ECtHR case law in deciding that a delay of execution of nearly 14 years since sentence infringed section 17(1) of the Constitution of Jamaica (prohibiting torture or inhuman or degrading treatment));
- *Minister of Home Affairs v Fisher* [1980] AC 319 (PC), 330C–E (Lord Wilberforce, construing the Constitution of Bermuda: 'This [construction] would be fully in line with article 8 of the European Convention on Human Rights and Fundamental Freedoms (respect for family life), decisions on which have

recognised the family unit and the right to protection of illegitimate children. Moreover the draftsman of the Constitution must have had in mind (a) the United Nations' Declaration of the Rights of the Child adopted by resolution (1386 (xiv)) on November 29, 1959 . . . and (b) article 24 of the International Covenant on Civil and Political Rights 1966 . . . Though these instruments at the date of the Constitution had no legal force, they can certainly not be disregarded as influences upon legislative policy.').

9.19.6. **Unincorporated treaties as constitutional antecedents:**

- *Minister of Home Affairs v Fisher* [1980] AC 319 (PC), 328G–H (Lord Wilberforce: 'It is known that [Chapter I in the Constitution of Bermuda relating to fundamental rights and freedoms], as similar portions of other constitutional instruments drafted in the post-colonial period, starting with the Constitution of Nigeria, and including the Constitutions of most Caribbean territories, was greatly influenced by the [ECHR]. That Convention was signed and ratified by the United Kingdom and applied to dependent territories including Bermuda. It was in turn influenced by the United Nations' Universal Declaration of Human Rights of 1948. These antecedents, and the form of Chapter I itself, call for generous interpretation avoiding what has been called "the austerity of tabulated legalism", suitable to give individuals the full measure of the fundamental rights and freedoms referred to.');
- *Matthew v State of Trinidad and Tobago* [2004] UKPC 33 [2005] 1 AC 433, [37] (Lord Bingham, Lord Nicholls, Lord Steyn and Lord Walker (dissenting) noting that the Constitution of Trinidad and Tobago is based on the Canadian Bill of Rights and that it drew its inspiration from the ECHR and the Universal Declaration of Human Rights);
- *Matadeen v Pointu* [1999] 1 AC 98 (PC), 114A–B (Lord Hoffmann, using the Declaration of the Rights of Man adopted by Mauritius in 1794, in interpreting the Constitution: 'Although the Declaration of the Rights of Man is a seminal document in the history of human rights, it is however a statement of principles or, perhaps more accurately, aspirations. It does not in itself mean that compliance with such principles by the legislature or executive was in every case to be justiciable in the courts.').

10

Unincorporated Treaties and the Common Law

(1) Introduction

10.1. Unincorporated treaties have informed the content and development of the common law despite the principles of non-justiciability [§§ 8.5–8.7] and no direct effect [§§ 8.8–8.9]. A principle of legal policy, that domestic law should conform to international law, has led to the application of a presumption of compatibility [§ 10.3], similar to the one in the statutory context [§ 9.5] which compels the interpretation of the common law in a way which does not place the United Kingdom in breach of its international law obligations. This presumption permits the use of unincorporated treaties both for the resolution of uncertainties but also, more importantly, for developing the common law in new directions [§ 10.4]. The presumption cannot, however, be invoked in a way which would abrogate the principle of no direct effect [§§ 10.3–10.5]. There are also other, residual, uses of unincorporated treaties, for example, where unincorporated treaties trigger a reappraisal of the common law, are used to confirm a particular approach or interpretation of the common law, or are used as background to the common law [§ 10.6].

10.2. Human rights are a special part of the relationship between unincorporated treaties and common law. Here the use of unincorporated treaties in the common law context overlaps with the statutory context and the principle of legality [§§ 9.15–9.17]. Thus, before the principle of legality can be applied it is necessary to identify pre-existing fundamental rights recognisable at common law. Although the common law is already rich in its recognition of

such rights, the use of unincorporated treaties may provide an important resource in both recognising such rights and strengthening the protection afforded to them by the common law [§§ 10.7–10.8].

(2) The Common Law Presumption of Compatibility

10.3. **In addition to its role in the legislative context, applying to both unincorporated treaty obligations [§§ 9.7–9.14] and customary international law [§ 13.16]) the presumption of compatibility also operates as a rule of construction in the common law [§ 10.4]. Here it operates fairly freely, unconstrained by the need to identify ambiguities or obscurities upon which the traditional statutory presumption of compatibility is based [§ 9.9; *cf* § 9.14].**

10.4. **There is a strong presumption in favour of interpreting the common law so as not to place the United Kingdom in breach of its international law obligations. That includes unincorporated treaty obligations. This clearly applies where the common law is uncertain or developing so that courts will seek to define and/or develop it in accordance with unincorporated treaty obligations. Development of the common law in the light of unincorporated treaties must be cautiously undertaken, to ensure that it does not conflict with express statutory provisions but also to ensure that it does not merely seek to replicate, in the common law, something already provided for by statute. The extent to which the common law presumption of compatibility applies beyond these instances is unclear but it cannot be applied so as to override the principle of no direct effect [§§ 8.8–8.9].**

10.4.1. General presumption of compatibility and the common law:

- *R v Lyons* [2002] UKHL 44 [2003] 1 AC 976, [27] (Lord Hoffmann: 'Of course there is a strong presumption in favour of interpreting English law (whether common law or statute) in a way which does not place the United Kingdom in breach of an international obligation.');
- *A v Secretary of State for the Home Department* [2004] EWCA Civ 1123 [2005] 1 WLR 414, [266] (Laws LJ: '(1) An unincorporated treaty confers no rights directly enforceable in our courts. But (2) there is a strong presumption that our law, judge-made or statutory should be interpreted so as not to place the United Kingdom in breach of an international obligation. These two propositions

are elementary.' At [267]: '[T]he mistake in [counsel's] position, in relation to the common law, is in truth . . . to deploy proposition (2) so as to contradict proposition (1). He seeks in effect to subject the common law to a particular rule requiring compliance with the [Convention Against Torture] article 15 on the back of the general rule (proposition (2)) that our law should be read consistently with our international obligations. The argument proves too much. It would justify the incorporation into domestic law, without a validating statute, of any rule of international law in relation to any subject-matter clearly common to both.');

- *Attorney-General v BBC* [1981] AC 303, 354 (Lord Scarman) [§ **9.14.2**];
- *Westland Helicopters Ltd v AOI* [1995] QB 282, 307G–308A (Colman J: '[T]here is, in my judgment, every reason in principle why the approach of the common law should be consistent with that of public international law unless there is some controlling common law principle to the contrary.');
- *cf Malone v Metropolitan Police Commissioner* [1979] Ch 344, 379B–C (Sir Robert Megarry V-C) [§ **10.4.4**];
- *cf Wainwright v Home Office* [2001] EWCA Civ 2081 [2002] QB 1334 (CA), [91] (Buxton LJ: '[The judge's reasoning was that], by analogy with the approach to legislative construction that was adopted in *R v Secretary of State for the Home Department, Ex p Brind* [1991] 1 AC 696, the common law should be read as being "in conformity with the Convention" even before the passing of the Human Rights Act 1998. While courts before the Human Rights Act 1998 were alert to the importance of the United Kingdom's treaty obligations, there was never any suggestion of an approach as broad as that of the judge, and positive authority against it, specifically in the context of privacy, in the judgment of Sir Robert Megarry V-C in *Malone v Metropolitan Police Comr* [1979] Ch 344.').

10.4.2. **Using unincorporated treaties where the common law is uncertain: *Illustrations:***

- Laws LJ writing extra-judicially in 1993: 'Where the common law is uncertain, the question for the court is not at all what is the meaning *as a matter of language* of previous texts; it is, rather, which way the common law should go. In accepting that where such uncertainty exists, the ECHR may be resorted to, the courts may be said to have assented to the very proposition which I am seeking to advance, that the Convention jurisprudence is a legitimate aid to establish what the policy of the common law should be; but they have done so by a process of intellectual legerdemain: they have likened the use of the ECHR to elucidate the common law to its use for the purpose of elucidating an ambiguous statute, and in doing so have made the process seem conventional and ordinary. In reality there is no such likeness, and what the courts are really about, as they should be, is the development of the common law's substantive principles with the aid of the Convention.' 'Is the High Court the Guardian of Fundamental Human Rights?' [1993] PL 59, 66–67.

- *Derbyshire CC v Times Newspapers* [1992] QB 770 (CA), 812D (Balcombe LJ, pre-HRA: 'Article 10 may be used when the common law (by which I include the doctrines of equity) is uncertain.' At 813B: '[W]here the law is uncertain, it must be right for the court to approach the issue before it with a predilection to ensure that our law should not involve a breach of article 10.' At 813G–818E, considering the effect of Article 10 on an uncertain area of law: whether a civil action for defamation lies at the suit of a corporate public authority), 829D (Butler-Sloss LJ: 'I am driven to the conclusion that in the present [uncertain] state of the law, article 10 of the [ECHR], and equally article 19 of the [International Covenant on Civil and Political Rights] (to similar effect) do apply.' At 830A–C: 'Adopting, as I respectfully do, that approach to the Convention, the principles governing the duty of the English court to take account of article 10 appear to be as follows: where the law is clear and unambiguous, either stated as the common law or enacted by Parliament, recourse to article 10 is unnecessary and inappropriate . . . But where there is an ambiguity, or the law is otherwise unclear or so far undeclared by an appellate court, the English court is not only entitled but, in my judgment, obliged to consider the implications of article 10.' See also 835B–E considering the judge below to have been wrong partly for failing to apply Article 10), 819B–C and 822E (Ralph Gibson LJ considering Article 10 in deciding whether the Council had the right to sue in libel for alleged injury to its reputation) (HL is at [1993] AC 534; reaching the same conclusion as the CA 'upon the common law of England without finding any need to rely upon the European Convention,' at 551F, Lord Keith, with whom the other Law Lords agreed);
- *DPP v Jones* [1999] 2 AC 240 (HL), 265D–F (Lord Slynn: 'It is desirable to look at the [ECHR] for guidance even at the present time [pre-HRA], but this is not a case in my opinion where there is any statutory ambiguity to be resolved or any doubt as to what the common law is.'), 267B, 277E–278F (Lord Hope noting the possibility of using the ECHR but rejecting it on the basis that: 'I do not think that there is any need to have resort to the Convention as an aid to statutory interpretation, as there is no ambiguity in the statutory provisions which are relevant to this case. Nor do I think that there is any uncertainty as to the test which must be applied under the common law relating to the use which the public may make of a highway in the exercise of the public's right to access.' (at 277E–F));
- *R v Secretary of State for the Home Department, Ex parte Hargreaves* [1997] 1 WLR 906 (CA), 921F (Hirst LJ accepting that

'although not part of English domestic law the provisions of the [ECHR] can assist in the elucidation of common law.') [§ **11.9.2**].

10.4.3. **Even where the common law is certain it may be important to consider whether the United Kingdom is in breach of its unincorporated treaty obligations:**

- *Derbyshire CC v Times Newspapers* [1992] QB 770 (CA), 812E (Balcombe LJ pre-HRA: 'Even if the common law is certain the courts will still, when appropriate, consider whether the United Kingdom is in breach of article 10 [ECHR].');
- *R v Chief Metropolitan Stipendiary Magistrate, Ex parte Choudhury* [1991] 1 QB 429 (DC), 449F–G (Watkins LJ, considering whether the common law offence of blasphemy was restricted to Christianity: '[Counsel] accepted that the obligations imposed on the United Kingdom by the [ECHR] are relevant sources of public policy where the common law is uncertain. But, he maintained, the common law of blasphemy is, without doubt, certain. Accordingly, it is not necessary to pay any regard to the Convention. Nevertheless, he thought it necessary, and we agree, in the context of this case, to attempt to satisfy us that the United Kingdom is not in any event in breach of the Convention.' Concluding at 452B–C: '[Counsel] has persuaded us convincingly that the Convention does not demand within any of those articles the creation of a law of blasphemy for the protection of Islam so that as signatory to the Convention the United Kingdom be in conformity with it.');
- *R v Wells Street Stipendiary Magistrate, Ex parte Deakin* [1980] AC 477 (HL), 482G–484C (Lord Diplock analysing the criminal offence of defamatory libel by reference to Article 10, ECHR, and recommending law reform to avoid the United Kingdom being in breach of its international obligations (pre-HRA)).

10.4.4. **Using unincorporated treaties to develop the common law:**

- See the development of fundamental rights in the common law [§§ **10.7–10.8**] and the principle of legality: [§ **9.17**]
- *R v Lyons* [2002] UKHL 44 [2003] 1 AC 976, [13] (Lord Bingham: 'Even before the Human Rights Act 1998, the [ECHR] exerted a persuasive and pervasive influence on judicial decision-making in this country . . . [and] bearing on the development of the common law.');
- *Reynolds v Times Newspapers Ltd* [2001] 2 AC 127 (HL), 223B–D (Lord Cooke: 'International human rights law, whenever relevant, should have an important part to play in developments of the common law. For United Kingdom courts, particular importance must attach to the European Convention for the Protection of Human Rights and Fundamental Freedoms . . . The [HRA] is not yet in force, but naturally the appeal was argued on the

footing that regard should be had to it.' At 223F–224C, on section 12 of the HRA);

- *R v Secretary of State for the Home Department, Ex parte Launder* [1997] 1 WLR 839 (HL), 867C (Lord Hope, pre-HRA: 'It is often said that, while the [ECHR] may influence the common law, it does not bind the executive.');
- *McCartan Turkington Breen v Times Newspapers Ltd* [2001] 2 AC 277 (HL), 300A–C (Lord Cooke referring to the opinions in *Reynolds* (see above) as seeking to harmonise the common law 'with human rights jurisprudence in general and with the European Convention on Human Rights in particular' and applying this to the Defamation Act (Northern Ireland) 1955);
- *R v Secretary of State for the Home Department, Ex parte McQuillan* [1995] 4 All ER 400 (QBD), 421 (Sedley J, pre-HRA: 'Once it is accepted that the standards articulated in the [ECHR] are standards which both march with those of the common law and inform the jurisprudence of the European Union, it becomes unreal and potentially unjust to continue to develop English public law without reference to them.') [**§ 11.6**];
- *cf Malone v Metropolitan Police Commissioner* [1979] Ch 344, 379B–C (Sir Robert Megarry V-C, in response to the submission that the ECHR should be applied as a guide in interpreting and applying English law in so far as it is ambiguous or lacking in clarity and where there was no statutory or common law regulation of telephone tapping: 'I readily accept that if the question before me were one of construing a statute enacted with the purpose of giving effect to obligations imposed by the [ECHR], the court would readily seek to construe the legislation in a way that would effectuate the [ECHR] rather that frustrate it. However, no relevant legislation of that sort is in existence. It seems to me that where Parliament has abstained from legislating on a point that is plainly suitable for legislation, it is indeed difficult for the court to lay down new rules of common law or equity that will carry out the Crown's treaty obligation, or to discover for the first time that such rules have always existed.').

Illustrations:

- *DPP v Jones* [1999] 2 AC 240 (HL), 259B–G (Lord Irvine, LC, pre-HRA: 'If, contrary to my judgment, the common law of trespass is not as clear as I have held it to be, then at least it is uncertain and developing, so that regard should be had to the Convention for the Protection of Human Rights and Fundamental Freedoms in resolving uncertainty and in determining how it should develop . . . Article 11 confers a "right to freedom of peaceful assembly" and then entitles the state to impose restrictions on that right . . . Unless the common law recognises that assembly on the public highway *may* be lawful, the right contained in article 11(1) of the Convention is denied. Of course the right may be subject to restrictions . . . But in my judgment our law will not comply with the Convention unless its *starting-point* is that assembly on the highway will not necessarily be unlawful . . . The fact that the letter of the law may not in practice always be invoked is irrelevant: mere toleration does not secure a fundamental right. Thus, if necessary I would invoke article 11 to clarify or develop the common law in the terms which I have held it to be; but for the reasons I have given I do not find it necessary to do so.');

- *Hunter v Canary Wharf Ltd* [1997] AC 655 (HL), 713H–714D (Lord Cooke (dissenting), considering the right to sue in nuisance cases: 'The United Nations Convention on the Rights of the Child, ratified by the United Kingdom in 1991 and the most widely ratified human rights treaty in history, acknowledges children as fully-fledged beneficiaries of human rights. Article 16 declares, inter alia, that no child shall be subjected to unlawful interference with his or her home and that the child has the right to the protection of law against such interference. International standards such as this may be taken into account in shaping the common law. The point just mentioned can be taken further. . . . [Article 16, UN Convention on the Rights of the Child, Article 12, Universal Declaration on Human Rights and Article 8, ECHR] are aimed, in part, at protecting the home and are construed to give protection against nuisances . . . The protection is regarded as going beyond possession or property rights . . . Again I think that this is a legitimate consideration in support of treating residence as an acceptable basis of standing at common law in the present class of case.');
- *Gleaves v Deakin* [1980] AC 477 (HL), 482G–484B (Lord Diplock considering the difficulties of reconciling the criminal offence of defamatory libel with Article 10, ECHR, pre-HRA. Concluding, at 484B–D: 'The law of defamation, civil as well as criminal, has proved an intractable subject for radical reform. There is, however, one relatively simple step that could be taken which would at least avoid the risk of our failing to comply with our international obligations under the European Convention for the Protection of Human Rights and Fundamental Freedoms. That step is to require the consent of the Attorney-General to be obtained for the institution of any prosecution for criminal libel. In deciding whether to grant his consent in the particular case, the Attorney-General could then consider whether the prosecution was necessary on any of the grounds specified in article 10.2 of the Convention and unless satisfied that it was, he should refuse his consent.');
- *R v Mid-Glamorgan Family Health Services, Ex parte Martin* [1995] 1 WLR 110 (CA), 118H (Evans LJ: 'The fact that the [ECHR] does not form part of English law does not mean that its provisions cannot be referred to and relied on as persuasive authority as to what the common law is, or should be.').

10.4.5. **Customary international law may impact the extent to which unincorporated treaties may develop common law [chapter 13]:**

- *Re McKerr* [2004] UKHL 12 [2004] 1 WLR 807, [52] (Lord Steyn noting that customary international law may have a direct role in determining the extent to which unincorporated treaties can develop the common law. At [51] referring to counsel's submission that the common law should be developed to recognise a substantive right to life and noting: 'The fact that there is no authority for such a development is not in itself fatal.').

10.4.6. **Developing common law by using unincorporated treaties must be cautiously undertaken:**

- *R v Chief Constable of the Royal Ulster Constabulary, Ex parte Begley* [1997] 1 WLR 1475 (HL), 1480H (Lord Browne-Wilkinson: 'It is true that the House has a power to develop the law. But it is a limited power. And it can be exercised only in the gaps left by Parliament. It is impermissible for the House to develop the law in a direction which is contrary to the will of Parliament.');
- *Re McKerr* [2004] UKHL 12 [2004] 1 WLR 807, [51] (Lord Steyn: 'It must be sound principle for a supreme court to develop the law only when it has been demonstrated that the just disposal of cases compellingly requires it. Given that the right to life is comprehensively protected under article 2 of the Convention as incorporated in our law by the 1998 Act, why is there now a need to create a parallel right under the common law?').

10.4.7. **Unincorporated treaties considered but common law not developed:**

Illustrations:

- *R v Chief Constable of the Royal Ulster Constabulary, Ex parte Begley* [1997] 1 WLR 1475 (HL) (Article 6, ECHR, as interpreted by the ECtHR in *Murray v UK* (1996) 22 EHRR 29 used in an unsuccessful attempt to show that every accused person has a common law right to have a solicitor present during police interviews regardless of the offence. See especially 1480B (Lord Browne-Wilkinson));
- *Porter v Freudenberg* [1915] 1 KB 857 (CA), 874G–875B, 877B–878G (Lord Reading CJ concluding that the common law rule, where an alien enemy's rights to sue are suspended during war, were not abrogated by the Hague Convention of 1907 upon the Laws and Customs of War on Land, Article 23 (h) of chapter 1 of section 2 of the Annex entitled 'Regulations respecting the Laws and Customs of War on Land').

10.4.8. **Unincorporated treaties will not be used to develop the common law where there is a pre-existing (incorporated treaty) right:**

- *Re McKerr* [2004] UKHL 12 [2004] 1 WLR 807, [30] (Lord Nicholls), [71] (Lord Hoffmann) (both noting that where there exists a right under an incorporated treaty, the courts will be slow to develop the common law so as to recognise an equivalent, free-standing, common law right. This is based on the reluctance to develop the common law by entering, or re-entering, a field regulated by legislation).

10.5. **Judgments of international courts or tribunals established under the auspices of unincorporated treaties may be used as guidance in developing the common law.**

Illustrations:

- *In re KD (A Minor) (Ward: Termination of Access)* [1988] AC 806 (HL), 823D–E (Lord Oliver considering an argument based on Articles 6 and 8, ECHR, and a judgment of the European Court of Human Rights: 'Although this is not binding upon your Lordships, the United Kingdom is, of course, a party to the Convention . . . and it is urged that it is at least desirable that the domestic law of the United Kingdom should accord with the decisions of the European Court of Human Rights under the Convention.' Concluding at 828H that he did not, 'think that *R v United Kingdom* [the ECtHR judgment] calls for any alteration in the basic approach [in domestic law] in order to conform with the Convention.');
- *R v Lyons* [2002] UKHL 447 [2003] 1 AC 976 (HL), [33] (Lord Hoffmann stating that it is open to courts to ensure conformity with judgments of an international tribunal (here the ECtHR) even where that judgment relates to the United Kingdom's international obligations under an unincorporated treaty in relation to 'a judge-made rule of common law or a judicial implication in a statute which did not expressly address the question.') [§ **9.13**];
- *Darker v Chief Constable of West Midlands* [2001] 1 AC 435 (HL), 455G–H (Lord Cooke, pre-HRA: 'Some support may be gained also, I think, from *Osman v United Kingdom* (1998) 29 EHRR 245. This decision of the European Court of Human Rights seems to be somewhat controversial in England, and its facts are remote from those of the present case. It has some relevance, nevertheless, in its rejection of blanket immunities for the police. The United Kingdom courts can undoubtedly take it into account in developing the common law in grey areas: and this will be obligatory when the Human Rights Act 1998 is brought into full force.');
- *Reynolds v Times Newspapers Ltd* [2001] 2 AC 127 (HL), 210H–211B (Lord Steyn, in considering whether to develop the common law on defamation, pre-HRA: '[A] test expressed in terms of a category of cases, such as political speech, is at variance with the jurisprudence of the European Court of Human Rights which in cases of competing rights and interests requires a

balancing exercise in the light of the concrete facts of each case. While there is as yet no decision directly in point . . . Our inclination ought to be towards the approach that prevails in the jurisprudence on the Convention.' See also 206H–208B [§ **10.8.3**]);

- *R (P) v Secretary of State for the Home Department* [2001] EWCA Civ 1151 [2001] 1 WLR 2002, [67] (Lord Phillips MR noting that the English common law, 'was enriched by the effects of Strasbourg jurisprudence long before the Human Rights Act 1998 came into force.');
- *Lord Advocate v The Scotsman* [1990] 1 AC 812 (HL), 826B–D (Lord Templeman considering ECtHR jurisprudence in deciding whether to grant an interdict (injunction) against the publication of a book of memoirs regarding service with MI5) [**§ 11.12**].

(3) Miscellaneous Use

10.6. The flexibility of the presumption of compatibility in common law enables it to cover much of the interaction between unincorporated treaties and common law. However, unincorporated treaties have also been used without reference to the presumption: for example they have triggered reappraisals of the common law, been used to confirm a particular view or interpretation of the law and provided background for a consideration of the relevant common law.

10.6.1. **Unincorporated treaties prompting a reappraisal of common law: *Illustration:***

- *R v G* [2003] UKHL 50 [2004] 1 AC 1034, [53] (Lord Steyn, considering the common law of recklessness in analysing section 1 of the Criminal Damage Act 1971: 'Ignoring the special position of children in the criminal justice system is not acceptable in a modern civil society . . . [quoting Article 40(1) of the UN Convention on the Rights of the Child 1990] . . . it is contrary to article 40(1) to ignore in a crime punishable by life imprisonment, or detention during Her Majesty's pleasure, the age of a child in judging whether the mental element has been satisfied. It is true that the Convention became binding on the United Kingdom after *R v Caldwell* was decided [in [1982] AC 341]. But the House cannot ignore the norm created by the Convention. This factor on its own justified a reappraisal of *R v Caldwell*.').

10.6.2. **Unincorporated treaties as providing confirmation of approach:**

- *R v Governor of Brockhill Prison, Ex parte Evans (No 2)* [2001] 2 AC 19 (HL), 29D–F (Lord Steyn, noting pre-HRA, that Article 5,

ECHR, 'reinforced' the common law view that the applicant was entitled to recover compensation on the ground of false imprisonment where the executive could no longer support the lawfulness of the detention), 37F–39G (Lord Hope), 46H (Lord Hobhouse: 'Article 5 of the [ECHR] is inconsistent with the Solicitor General's arguments and corresponds to the existing English law. It is therefore highly persuasive against accepting the Solicitor General's arguments or introducing the new rule he contends for into English law.');

- *R (Howard League for Penal Reform) v Secretary of State for the Home Department* [2002] EWHC 2497 (Admin) [2003] 1 FLR 484, [51] (Munby J: 'Neither the UN Convention [on the Rights of the Child] nor the European Charter [on Fundamental Rights] is at present legally binding in our domestic law and they are . . . not sources of law in the strict sense. But both can, in my judgment, properly be consulted in so far as they proclaim, reaffirm or elucidate the content of those human rights that are generally recognised throughout the European family of nations, in particular the nature and scope of those fundamental rights that are guaranteed by the [ECHR].');
- *R (Kenny) v Leeds Magistrate Court* [2003] EWHC 2963 (Admin) [2004] 1 All ER 1333, [41] (Owen J) [§ **5.16.2**];
- *Brannigan v Davison* [1997] AC 238 (PC), 249D (Lord Nicholls on the common law privilege against self-incrimination: 'This aspiration is so basic that it has been incorporated as a right into many charters enshrining fundamental rights and liberties, such as the International Covenant on Civil and Political Rights, article 14(3)(g), the Fifth Amendment to the United States Constitution, and the New Zealand Bill of Rights Act 1990, sections 23(3) and 25(d).');
- *A v Secretary of State for the Home Department* [2004] EWCA Civ 1123 [2005] 1 WLR 414 (Torture Convention used to consider the question of admissibility of evidence obtained by torture);
- *Osman v Elasha* [2000] Fam 62 (CA), 70 (Thorpe LJ: 'The welfare principle as paramount has been the cornerstone of the family justice system in this jurisdiction for many years. We regard it as a touchstone in measuring the quality of other family justice systems. Article 3 of the UN Convention on the Rights of the Child (1989)(Cm 1976) requires no less.');
- *Cambridge Water Co v Eastern Counties Leather plc* [1994] 2 AC 264 (HL), 307C–D (Lord Goff, considering nuisance: 'I wish to add that the present case may be regarded as one of what is nowadays called historic pollution . . . and it appears that, under the current philosophy, it is not envisaged that statutory liability should be imposed for historic pollution (see, e.g. the Council of Europe's Draft Convention on Civil Liability for Damage Resulting from Activities Dangerous to the Environment (Strasbourg 26 January 1993) article 5.1 and paragraph 48 of the

Explanatory Report). If so, it would be strange if liability for such pollution were to arise under a principle of common law.');

- *In re D (Minors)(Adoption Reports: Confidentiality)* [1996] AC 593 (HL), 613H–614A (Lord Mustill, considering disclosure in contested adoption proceedings pre-HRA: 'Next, I must refer to certain decisions of the European Commission and Court of Human Rights, and of the Committee of Ministers, namely *Hendriks v The Netherlands* (1982) 5 EHRR 223, *W v United Kingdom* (1987) 10 EHRR 29, and *McMichael v United Kingdom* (1995) 20 EHRR 205. On the view which I have formed of English law there is no need to engage the important general question which would have arisen if the conclusions impelled by the English legislation and decided cases had differed in important respects from the jurisprudence of the European tribunals. The language of the European Convention on Human Rights naturally causes the discussion to be couched in terms of rights, whilst I would prefer a different vocabulary, but in substance the principles to be derived from that jurisprudence are entirely consistent with those which I propose.').

10.6.3. **Unincorporated treaties as background to the common law:** ***Illustration:***

- *Kingdom of Spain v Christie, Manson & Woods Ltd & another* [1986] 1 WLR 1120 (ChD), 1123G (Sir Nicholas Browne-Wilkinson V-C referring to the International Convention relating to the exporting of works of art 'by way of background' in determining whether the Kingdom of Spain could obtain a declaration to protect property).

10.7. **Unincorporated treaty provisions regarding fundamental human rights may already be duplicated in the common law, reflected in the common law or extrapolated into the common law by declaratory judicial decision-making. This was true for much of the ECHR before it was indirectly incorporated by the HRA [§ 9.17].**

> '[T]he common law has come to recognise and endorse the notion of constitutional, or fundamental rights. These are broadly the rights given expression in the Convention for the Protection of Human Rights and Fundamental Freedoms.' (*R (International Transport Roth GmbH) v Secretary of State for the Home Department* [2002] EWCA Civ [2003] QB 728, [71] (Laws LJ))

10.8. **Thus, unincorporated treaties may contribute to developing the common law by strengthening the protection afforded by common law to fundamental rights. The existence of fundamental rights as**

part of the common law does not render meaningless their domestic incorporation by reference to treaties, for example the HRA in relation to the ECHR. This is because, first, the scope and depth of the common law right may be narrower and shallower than the treaty right. Secondly, because the statutory status of the right provides it with a more secure position and emphasises its normative force.

10.8.1. **Similarities between pre-HRA common law and the ECHR:**
Illustrations of Article 2:

- *Airedale NHS Trust v Bland* [1993] AC 789 (HL), 863H–864B (Lord Goff: '[T]he fundamental principle is the principle of the sanctity of human life—a principle long recognised not only in our own society but also in most, if not all, civilised societies throughout the modern world, as is indeed evidenced by its recognition both in article 2 of the European Convention for the Protection of Human Rights and Fundamental Freedoms (1953) (Cmd. 8969), and in article 6 of the International Covenant on Civil and Political Rights 1966.');
- *In re A (Children) (Conjoined Twins: Surgical Separation)* [2001] Fam 147 (CA), 204 (Ward LJ considering the right to life in the context of a conjoined twins case where the court held that the children should be separated to save the life of the stronger twin, and finding that there was 'nothing in the forthcoming Human Rights Act 1998 which calls for a different answer to the problem to the one I have already given.'), 212 (Brooke LJ considering the similarity between English law and Article 2, ECHR), 257 (Robert Walker LJ considering that 'the incorporation of the Convention into domestic law is a very important event but in this case its effect is to confirm and not to alter pre-existing law.');
- *Bugdaycay v Secretary of State for the Home Department* [1987] AC 514 (HL), 531G (Lord Bridge: 'The most fundamental of all human rights is the individual's right to life and when an administrative decision under challenge is said to be one which may put the applicant's life at risk, the basis of the decision must surely call for the most anxious scrutiny.');
- *R v Secretary of State for the Home Department, Ex p McQuillan* [1995] 4 All ER 400 (QBD), 408 (Sedley J: 'The common law has historically recognised the priority of the right to life.').

Illustrations of Article 5:

- *A v Secretary of State for the Home Department* [2004] UKHL 56 [2005] 2 WLR 87, [36] (Lord Bingham: 'In urging the fundamental importance of the right to personal freedom . . . the appellants were able to draw on the long libertarian tradition of English law, dating back to chapter 39 of Magna Carta 1215, given effect in the ancient remedy of habeas corpus, declared in the Petition of Right 1628, upheld in a series of landmark decisions down the centuries and embodied in the substance and procedure of the law to our own day.'), [88] (Lord Hoffmann considering indefinite detention without trial by reference to Article 15, ECHR: 'I would not like anyone to think that we are concerned with some special doctrine of European law. Freedom from arbitrary arrest and detention is a quintessentially British liberty, enjoyed by the inhabitants of this country when most of the population of Europe could be thrown into prison at the whim of their rulers. It was incorporated into the European Convention in order to entrench the same liberty in countries which had recently been under Nazi occupation. The United Kingdom subscribed to the Convention because it set out the rights which British subjects enjoyed under the common law.'), [222] (Baroness Hale: '[N]either the common law, from which so much of the European Convention is derived, nor international human rights law allows indefinite detention at the behest of the executive, however well-intentioned.');

- *R v Governor of Brockhill Prison, Ex parte Evans (No 2)* [2001] 2 AC 19 (HL), 42B–E (Lord Hobhouse noting the similarity between Article 5, ECHR and common law);
- *ID v Home Office* [2005] EWCA Civ 38 [2005] INLR 278, [69] (Brooke LJ: 'Long before the [HRA] came into force English law attached particular importance to the right of liberty.' Citing *Eshugbayi Eleko v Governor of Nigeria* [1931] AC 662 (HL), 670 (Lord Atkin); *Liversidge v Anderson* [1942] AC 206, 245 (Lord Atkin) and *Murray v Ministry of Defence* [1988] 1 WLR 692, 703 (Lord Griffiths)).

Illustrations of Article 6:

- *Hamilton v Naviede (In re Arrows) (No 4)* [1995] 2 AC 75 (HL), 95F (Lord Browne-Wilkinson noting that 'one of the basic freedoms secured by English law', the privilege against self-incrimination is also protected by Article 6, ECHR);
- *R v Secretary of State for the Home Department, Ex parte Daly* [2001] UKHL 26 [2001] 2 AC 532 (HL), [30–31] (Lord Cooke: '[w]hile this case has arisen in a jurisdiction where the European Convention for the Protection of Human Rights and Fundamental Freedoms applies, and while the case is one in which the Convention and the common law produce the same result, it is of great importance, in my opinion, that the common law by itself is being recognised as a sufficient source of the fundamental right to confidential communication with a legal adviser for the purpose of obtaining legal advice. Rights similar to those in the Convention are of course to be found in constitutional documents and other formal affirmations of rights elsewhere. The truth is, I think, that some rights are inherent and fundamental to democratic civilised society. Conventions, constitutions, bills of rights and the like respond by recognising rather than creating them . . . The point that I am emphasising is that the common law goes so deep.');

- *R v DPP, Ex parte Kebilene* [2000] 2 AC 326 (HL), 377B–C (Lord Hope: 'As a statement of fundamental principle [Article 6(2)] is wholly consistent with the common law of both England and Scotland.'), 342D–E (Lord Bingham in the Divisional Court on the right to a fair trial and the presumption of innocence);
- *R v A (No 2)* [2001] UKHL 25 [2002] 1 AC 45, [51] (Lord Hope: '[T]he principles enshrined in [Article 6(1), ECHR] have for long been part of our common law.');
- *R v Lord Chancellor, Ex parte Witham* [1998] QB 575 (DC), 585D–E (Laws J: 'As regards the . . . [ECHR] jurisprudence I will say only that, as it seems to me, the common law provides no lesser protection of the right of access to the Queen's courts than might be vindicated in Strasbourg. That is, if I may say so, unsurprising. The House of Lords has held the same to be true in relation to the right of freedom of expression . . . I cannot think that the right of access to justice is in some way a lesser right than that of free expression.');
- *Science Research Council v Nassé* [1980] AC 1028 (HL), 1068E–F (Lord Wilberforce: 'Article 6(1) of the [ECHR] guarantees the right to a fair hearing: the appellant . . . relies on this as requiring total disclosure of all information relevant to the case, confidential or not. But this is a fallacy, because the whole aim and object of those carefully worked out provisions of English law which regulate the right to discovery and inspection of documents is precisely to achieve a fair hearing. That is the standard of our law and it is unnecessary to have resort to the convention to establish it.').

Illustrations of Article 8:

- *R (Morgan Grenfell & Co Ltd) v Special Commissioner of Income Tax* [2002] UKHL 21 [2003] 1 AC 563 (HL), [7] (Lord Hoffmann: '[Legal professional privilege] is a fundamental human right long established in the common law . . . It has been held by the European Court of Human Rights to be part of the right of privacy guaranteed by article 8 of the Convention (*Campbell v United Kingdom* (1992) 15 EHRR 137; *Foxley v United Kingdom* (2000) 31 EHRR 637) and held by the European Court of Justice to be part of Community law: *A M & S Europe Ltd v Commission of the European Communities (Case 155/79)* [1983] QB 878.');
- *In re KD (A Minor) (Ward: Termination of Access)* [1988] AC 806 (HL), 811H (Lord Templeman: 'English common law and statute require that in all matters concerning the upbringing of an infant the welfare of the child shall be the first and paramount consideration . . . [referring to Article 8, ECHR] The English rule was evolved against an historical background of conflict between parents over the upbringing of their children. The Convention rule was evolved against an historical background of claims by the state to control the private lives of individuals . . . In my opinion

there is no inconsistency of principle or application between the English rule and the Convention rule.').

Illustrations of Article 10:

- *Attorney-General v Guardian Newspapers Ltd (No 2)* [1990] 1 AC 109 (HL), 256G–H (Lord Keith: 'The general rule is that anyone is entitled to communicate anything he pleases to anyone else, by speech or in writing or in any other way. That rule is limited by the law of defamation and other restrictions similar to [those] mentioned in article 10 of the [ECHR].'), 273C–D (Lord Griffiths: 'Article 10 of the [ECHR] identifies "the interests of national security" and "preventing the disclosure of information received in confidence" as separate grounds upon which the right to freedom of expression may, in some circumstances, have to be restricted. I see no reason why our law should take a different approach.'), 283E–G (Lord Goff: 'Finally, I wish to observe that I can see no inconsistency between English law on this subject and article 10 of the European Convention on Human Rights. This is scarcely surprising, since we may pride ourselves on the fact that freedom of speech has existed in this country perhaps as long as, if not longer than, it has existed in any other country in the world.');
- *Derbyshire CC v Times Newspapers* [1993] AC 534 (HL) 551F (Lord Keith agreeing with Lord Goff in *Attorney-Guardian v Guardian Newspapers* (see above) that there is no difference in principle between article 10, ECHR and the English common law);
- *Reynolds v Times Newspapers Ltd* [2001] 2 AC 127 (HL), 193B (Lord Nicholls: 'The freedom of expression protected by this defence [of comment on a matter of public interest] has long been regarded by the common law as a basic right long before the emergence of human rights conventions.' At 203H: 'The common law approach accords with the present state of the human rights jurisprudence.'), 206H–208B (Lord Steyn considering why Lord Goff, in *Attorney-General v Guardian Newspapers Ltd (No 2)* [1990] 1 AC 109, 283–284, and Lord Keith, in *Derbyshire CC v Times Newspapers Ltd* [1993] AC 534, 551G (see above), could confidently assert that the law of England and article 10 of the Convention are the same [§ **10.8.3**]), 234D (Lord Hope noting the 'powerful dicta to the effect that there is no inconsistency between article 10 . . . and the English common law on freedom of speech.');
- *McCartan Turkington Breen v Times Newspapers Ltd* [2001] 2 AC 277 (HL), 298B (Lord Steyn: 'Freedom of expression is a basic norm of our constitution');
- *R v Khan* [1997] AC 558 (HL), 580D–F (Lord Nolan considering that principles in the ECHR embody familiar principles of domestic law and concepts of justice).

Illustration of Article 11:

- *UKAPE v ACAS* [1979] 1 WLR 570 (CA) 582H–583C (Lord Denning MR recognising that Article 11, ECHR, effectively states a basic principle of English common law).

10.8.2. **Potential weakness of common law protection compared to incorporated treaty rights:**

- *Attorney-General v Guardian Newspapers* [1987] 1 WLR 1248 (HL), 1286B–G (Lord Bridge (dissenting) commenting on the majority view in favour of maintaining injunctions regarding the book, *Spycatcher*: 'Having no written constitution, we have no equivalent in our law to the First Amendment to the Constitution of the United States of America. Some think that puts freedom of speech on too lofty a pedestal. Perhaps they are right. We have not adopted as part of our law the European Convention for the Protection of Human Rights and Fundamental Freedoms to which this country is a signatory. Many think that we should. I have hitherto not been of that persuasion, in large part because I have had confidence in the capacity of the common law to safeguard the fundamental freedoms essential to a free society including the right to freedom of speech which is specifically safeguarded by article 10 of the Convention. My confidence is seriously undermined by Your Lordships' decision . . . Freedom of speech is always the first casualty under a totalitarian regime . . .. The present attempt to insulate the public in this country from information which is freely available elsewhere is a significant step down a very dangerous road. . . . If the Government are determined to fight to maintain the ban to the end, they will face inevitable condemnation and humiliation by the European Court of Human Rights in Strasbourg. Long before that they will have been condemned at the bar of public opinion in the free world.');
- *R v Secretary of State for the Home Department, Ex parte Daly* [2001] UKHL 26 [2001] 2 AC 532, [23] (Lord Bingham: 'I have reached the conclusion so far expressed on an orthodox application of common law principles derived from the authorities and an orthodox domestic approach to judicial review. But the same result is achieved by reliance on the European Convention. Article 8(1) gives Mr Daly a right to respect for his correspondence. While interference with that right by a public authority may be permitted if in accordance with the law and necessary in a democratic society . . . the policy interferes with Mr Daly's exercise of his right under article 8(1) to an extent much greater than necessity requires. In this instance, therefore, the common law and the Convention yield the same result. But this need not always be so.').

10.8.3. **The importance of incorporation:**

- *Reynolds v Times Newspapers Ltd* [2001] 2 AC 127 (HL), 207G–208B (Lord Steyn: 'It is worth considering why Lord Goff [in *Attorney-General v Guardian Newspapers Ltd (No 2)* [1990] 1 AC 109, 283–284] and Lord Keith [in *Derbyshire CC v Times Newspapers Ltd* [1993] AC 534, 551G] could so confidently assert that the law of England and article 10 of the Convention are the same. In my judgment the reasons are twofold. First, there is the principle of liberty . . . Secondly, there is a constitutional right to freedom of expression in England . . . By categorising this basic and fundamental right as a constitutional right its higher normative force is emphasised . . . Now the Human Rights Act 1998, which will incorporate the Convention into our legal order, is on the statute book. And the Government has announced that it will come into force on 2 October 2000. The constitutional dimension of freedom of expression is enforced. This is the backcloth against which the present appeal must be considered. It is common ground that in considering the issues before the House, and the development of the common law, the House can and should act on the reality that the Human Rights Act 1998 will soon be in force. The new landscape is of great importance inasmuch as it provides the taxonomy against which the question before the House must be considered. The starting point is now the right of freedom of expression, a right based on a constitutional or higher legal order foundation.');

- *R v Secretary of State for the Home Department, Ex parte Simms* [2000] 2 AC 115 (HL), 131G–132B (Lord Hoffmann) [§ **7.9.3**].

11

Unincorporated Treaties, Discretion and Legitimate Expectations

(1) Introduction

11.1. General statutory conferrals of executive discretion or power have traditionally been excluded from applications of the presumption of compatibility [§§ 9.8–9.14; § 10.4], on the basis that this would constitute incorporation through the back door.

11.2. This view has been considerably modified by general developments in public law, particularly as a result of concepts based on fundamental rights and often rooted in unincorporated treaty provisions (for example the ECHR, pre-HRA). These modifications have added safeguards where executive discretion relates to fundamental rights [§§ 11.5–11.8]. The common law developed its own interpretative obligation regarding fundamental rights, reading down general and statutory language: the principle of legality [§§ 9.15–9.17]. Beyond the human rights context, there is now a wider use of unincorporated treaties when assessing exercises of executive discretion [§ 11.9]. Another tool which has been used to curb executive discretion in the light of unincorporated treaty obligations, albeit with little success, is legitimate expectation [§§ 11.10–11.11].

11.3. The traditional reticence of courts to invoke unincorporated treaty obligations in the analysis of proper use of executive power contrasts sharply with a clear and consistent practice favouring the exercise of judicial discretion so as to be compatible with these obligations [§ 11.12].

(2) The Orthodoxy: Unincorporated Treaties and Discretion

11.4. **The greatest judicial ambivalence regarding the use of the presumption of compatibility [§§ 9.8–9.14; § 10.4] has been where general statutory provisions confer executive power (as distinct from those instances where statutory provisions require executive power to be exercised compatibly with unincorporated treaty obligations [§ 9.1]). In such cases, the orthodox position has been to deny that such power must be exercised compatibly with unincorporated treaty obligations on the basis that this would constitute incorporation by the 'back door'. Similarly, executive decision-makers were not required to consider unincorporated treaty obligations and a decision could not be impugned simply for failing to take account of such obligations.**

11.4.1. **The orthodoxy: the presumption of compatibility does not apply to statutory conferrals of executive power:**

- *R v Secretary of State for the Home Department, Ex parte Brind* [1991] 1 AC 696 (HL), 748A–F (Lord Bridge: '[Counsel] submitted, when a statute confers upon an administrative authority a discretion capable of being exercised in a way which infringes any basic human right protected by the [ECHR], it may . . . be presumed that the legislative intention was that the discretion should be exercised within the limitations which the Convention imposes. I confess that I found considerable persuasive force in this submission. But in the end I have been convinced that the logic of it is flawed. When confronted with a simple choice between two possible interpretations of some specific statutory provision, the presumption whereby the courts prefer that which avoids conflict between our domestic legislation and our international treaty obligations is a mere canon of construction which involves no importation of international law into the domestic field. But where Parliament has conferred on the executive an administrative discretion without indicating the precise limits within which it must be exercised, to presume that it must be exercised within Convention limits would be to go far beyond the resolution of an ambiguity. It would be to impute to Parliament an intention not only that the executive should exercise the discretion in conformity with the Convention, but also that the domestic courts should enforce that conformity by the importation into domestic administrative law of the text of the Convention and the jurisprudence of the European Court of Human Rights in the interpretation and application of it . . . When Parliament has been content for so long to leave those who complain that their Convention rights have been infringed to seek their remedy in Strasbourg, it would be surprising suddenly to find that the judiciary had, without Parliament's aid, the means to incorporate the Convention into such an important area of domestic law and I cannot escape the conclusion that this would be a judicial usurpation of the legislative function.'). *cf* [§ **11.5**].

11.4.2. **There is no duty to take account of unincorporated treaty obligations when exercising executive discretion:**

- *R v Chief Immigration Officer, Ex parte Salamat Bibi* [1976] 1 WLR 979 (CA), 984H–985C (Lord Denning MR revisting his comments in *R v Secretary of State for the Home Department, Ex parte Bhajan Singh* [1976] QB 198 (CA), 207D–H (in that case Lord Denning had stated that: '[T]he immigration officers and the Secretary of State in exercising their duties ought to bear in mind the principles stated in the [ECHR]. They ought consciously or subconsciously, to have regard to the principles in it—because, after all, the principles stated in the Convention are only a statement of the principles of fair dealing: and it is their duty to act fairly.'): 'I think that would be asking too much of the immigration officers. They cannot be expected to know or to apply the Convention. They must go simply by the immigration rules laid down by the Secretary of State, and not by the Convention . . . it is much better for us to stick to our own statutes and principles, and only look to the Convention for guidance in cases of doubt.');
- *Fernandes v Secretary of State for the Home Department* [1981] Imm AR 1 (CA), 5–6 (Waller LJ, dismissing an appeal against the Secretary of State's decision to deport the appellant: 'What I have said is on the assumption that it is right to take into account the provisions of the Convention on Human Rights, but there is in my view another good ground on which this appeal should be dismissed, namely, that the Secretary of State was not under any such legal obligation [quoting from *Ex parte Salamat Bibi* (see above)] . . . In my judgment there was no legal obligation on the Secretary of State to consider whether or not this was a contravention of the Articles of the Convention.'), 6–7 (Ackner LJ citing *Salamat Bibi* (see above) with approval).

Illustrations:

- *Chundawadra v IAT* [1988] Imm AR 161 (CA), 167–168 (Glidewell LJ agreeing with Taylor J at first instance who stated that there was no obligation on the Secretary of State, when deciding whether to deport individuals under section 3(5)(b) of the Immigration Act 1971, to take into account Article 8, ECHR);
- *R v Secretary of State for the Home Department, Ex parte Kirkwood* [1984] 1 WLR 913 (Mann J rejecting the submission

that the Secretary of State was obliged to consider Article 3, ECHR, when exercising his discretion to extradite prisoners);

- *R v Secretary of State for the Home Department, Ex parte NALGO* (1993) 5 Admin LR 785 (CA), 798A–B (Neill LJ: 'It is not necessary for the Minister when exercising an administrative discretion conferred on him by Parliament to exercise that discretion in accordance with Article 10. Nor will a court when reviewing the decision of the Minister interfere with it on the ground that he did not have regard to the provisions of Article 10.').

11.4.3. **Failure to take account of unincorporated treaty obligations does not, of itself, impugn an executive decision:**

- *R v Ministry of Defence, Ex parte Smith* [1996] QB 517 (CA), 558E (Sir Thomas Bingham MR: 'The relevance of the [ECHR] in the present context is as background to the complaint of irrationality. The fact that a decision-maker failed to take account of Convention obligations when exercising an administrative discretion is not of itself a ground for impugning that exercise of discretion.');
- *R v Secretary of State for the Home Department, Ex parte Binbasi* [1989] Imm AR 601–602 (Kennedy J considering that the Secretary of State's refusal to grant asylum to the applicant was not unreasonable for failing to take into account Article 8, ECHR considerations, particularly where it was not clear whether Article 8 would be breached by returning the applicant to Northern Cyprus).

(3) Unincorporated Treaties: Aids in Developing Public Law

11.5. **The orthodox position regarding the legal relevance of unincorporated treaties where statutory provisions confer executive power has undergone a shift in recent years as part of the general development of public law [§§ 11.8–11.9]. The catalyst for this shift has been the notion of fundamental rights and unincorporated treaty obligations expressing such rights. The role of fundamental rights in developing public law concepts was forcefully presented by Laws J, writing extra-judicially, in 1993:**

> 'What is therefore needed is a preparedness to hold that a decision which overrides a fundamental right without sufficient objective justification will, as a matter of law, necessarily be disproportionate to the aim in view . . . [T]he courts have insisted that statutory power may not be used save for the purpose for which it was con-

> ferred, of which purpose they are the judge. Given this foundation, we would erect no more than a modest structure upon it by presuming that a statute's purpose cannot include or permit any interference with fundamental rights; and that to justify such interference, and to rebut this presumption of construction, the respondent would have to show that there is only one possible interpretation of the statute, and that on that interpretation the policy of the Act is to permit the interference.' ('Is the High Court the Guardian of Fundamental Human Rights?' [1993] PL 59, 74 and 76)

11.6. **This was later developed, judicially, by Sedley J:**

> 'Once it is accepted that the standards articulated in the [ECHR] are standards which both march with those of the common law and inform the jurisprudence of the European Union, it becomes unreal and potentially unjust to continue to develop English public law without reference to them. Accordingly, and without in any way departing from the ratio decidendi of *Brind*, the legal standards by which the decisions of public bodies are supervised can and should differentiate between those rights which are recognised as fundamental and those which, though known to the law, do not enjoy such a pre-eminent status. Once this point is reached the standard of justification of infringements of rights and freedoms by executive decision must vary in proportion to the significance of the right which is at issue. Such an approach is indeed already enjoined by *Ex p Bugdaycay* in relation to a predominant value of the common law—the right to life—which, as it happens, the convention reflects.'(*R v Secretary of State for the Home Department, Ex parte McQuillan* [1995] 4 All ER 400 (QBD), 421–422).

11.7. **The practical effect of such analyses, of the potential to develop public law against the backdrop of fundamental rights found in unincorporated treaties, can be seen in a series of modifications to the traditional concepts of judicial review. These interrelated modifications have recognised additional safeguards where the exercise of executive power concerns fundamental human rights. Despite the modifications, the role of courts has remained unequivocally supervisory. One modification is that judicial scrutiny of administrative decisions is heightened in accordance with the gravity of the subject-matter. Thus, the exercise of executive discretion impacting fundamental rights is subjected to anxious scrutiny. Secondly, where the executive imposes restrictions on fundamental rights, these must be justified by, at least,**

an important competing public interest. Thirdly, when assessing irrationality challenges, consideration may be given to whether a decision-maker took into account unincorporated treaty obligations, especially where the decision-maker claims to have included them in his deliberations as relevant considerations.

11.8. **Much of this development, insofar as it relates to fundamental rights, has been superseded by the incorporation of the ECHR into domestic law. Under the HRA, section 6, public authorities are required to act compatibly with Convention rights [§ 7.6]. This, of course, includes exercises of executive discretion. Nevertheless, judicial review concepts continue to provide a useful analytical framework for exercises of executive discretion under the HRA. They also have an abiding importance regarding fundamental rights in unincorporated treaties, especially beyond the limits of the ECHR.**

11.8.1. **Exercises of executive discretion impacting fundamental rights will be anxiously scrutinised:**

- *R v Secretary of State for the Home Department, Ex parte Bugdaycay* [1987] 1 AC 514 (HL), 531F–G (Lord Bridge: 'Within [the limitations on the court's power of review] the court must, I think, be entitled to subject an administrative decision to the more rigorous examination to ensure that it is no way flawed, according to the gravity of the issue which the decision determines. The most fundamental of all human rights is the individual's right to life and when an administrative decision under challenge is said to be one which may put the applicant's life at risk, the basis of that decision must surely call for the most anxious scrutiny.');
- *R v Secretary of State for the Home Department, Ex parte Launder* [1997] 1 WLR 839 (HL), 867 (Lord Hope observing that although unincorporated treaties may not bind the executive, where the whole context of the discretion being exercised relates to an individual's fundamental rights then that, in itself, is a ground for subjecting the decisions to the most anxious scrutiny; citing *Bugdaycay* and *Ex parte Smith*) [§ **11.8.2**].

11.8.2. **Executive restrictions on fundamental rights must be justified by an important competing public interest**

- *R v Secretary of State for the Home Department, Ex parte Brind* [1991] 1 AC 696 (HL), 748F–G (Lord Bridge: 'I do not accept . . . that the courts are powerless to prevent the exercise by the executive of administrative discretions, even when conferred, as in the instant case, in terms which are on their face unlimited, in a way which infringes fundamental human rights.' At

748H–749B, considering that courts are entitled to start from the premise that any restriction on fundamental human rights requires to be justified and that nothing less than an important competing public interest will be sufficient to justify it), see also 751E–F (Lord Templeman), 757C and 761H–762B (Lord Ackner), 766H (Lord Lowry);

- *R v Ministry of Defence, Ex parte Smith* [1996] QB 517 (CA), 554E (Sir Thomas Bingham MR describing as 'an accurate distillation of the principles laid down in *Ex parte Bugdaycay* and *Ex parte Brind* (see above) the following approach: 'The court may not interfere with the exercise of an administrative discretion on substantive grounds save where the court is satisfied that the decision is unreasonable in the sense that it is beyond the range of responses open to a reasonable decision-maker. But in judging whether the decision-maker has exceeded this margin of appreciation the human rights context is important. The more substantial the interference with human rights, the more the court will require by way of justification before it is satisfied that the decision is reasonable in the sense outlined above.');
- *R v Lord Saville of Newdigate, Ex parte A* [2000] 1 WLR 1855 (CA), [34] (Lord Woolf MR upholding the test of irrationality, as set out in *Ex parte Smith* (see above) where, by the exercise of executive discretion, fundamental human rights are restricted. At [36], approving in the Divisional Court *Ex parte Smith* [1996] QB 517, 538C (Simon Brown LJ): ' "[T]he minister on judicial review will need to show that there is an important competing interest which he could reasonably judge sufficient to justify the restriction and he must expect his reasons to be closely scrutinised".' At [37]: '[W]hen a fundamental right . . . is engaged, the options available to a reasonable decision-maker are curtailed. They are curtailed because it is unreasonable to reach a decision which contravenes or could contravene human rights unless there are sufficiently significant countervailing considerations. In other words it is not open to the decision-maker to risk interfering with fundamental rights in the absence of compelling justification. Even the broadest discretion is constrained by the need for there to be countervailing circumstances justifying interference with human rights. The courts will anxiously scrutinise the strength of the countervailing circumstances and the degree of the interference with the human right involved and then apply the [test of irrationality accepted by Sir Thomas Bingham MR in *Ex parte Smith*].');
- *R (Mahmood) v Secretary of State for the Home Department* [2001] 1 WLR 840 (CA), [18] (Laws LJ, in the context of an immigration decision of the Secretary of State, made pre-HRA: '[It] has become a settled principle of the common law, one which is entirely independent of our incorporation of the

Convention by the Human Rights Act 1998 . . . that the intensity of review in a public law case will depend on the subject matter in hand; and so in particular any interference by the action of a public body with a fundamental right will require a substantial objective justification.' (citing *Ex parte Smith, Lord Saville of Newdigate* and *Ex parte Launder* (see above)). At [19]: '[T]he approach [that where a fundamental right is engaged a decision-maker will have to demonstrate that his proposed action does not interfere with that right or, if it does, that there exist substantive objective justifications for the interference] and the basic *Wednesbury* rule are by no means hermetically sealed one from the other. There is, rather, what may be called a sliding scale of review; the graver the impact of the decision in question upon the individual affected by it, the more substantial the justification that will be required. It is in the nature of the human condition that cases where, objectively, the individual is most gravely affected will be those where what we have come to call his fundamental rights are or are said to be put in jeopardy.'), [37] (Lord Phillips MR: 'These [*Ex parte Smith, Lord Saville of Newdigate, Ex parte A and Ex parte Launder*] all addressed the question of the approach to reviews of executive discretion in circumstances where human rights were at stake but where the minister was not required as a matter of domestic law to comply with the [ECHR]. They support the application of three principles to that situation. (1) Even where human rights were at stake, the role of the court was supervisory. The court would only intervene where the decision fell outside the range of responses open to a reasonable decision-maker. (2) In conducting a review of a decision affecting human rights, the court would subject the decision to the most anxious scrutiny. (3) Where the decision interfered with human rights, the court would require substantial justification for the interference in order to be satisfied that the response fell within the range of responses open to a reasonable decision-maker. The more substantial the interference, the more was required to justify it.' At [40]: 'When anxiously scrutinising an executive decision that interferes with human rights, the court will ask the question, applying an objective test, whether the decision-maker could reasonably have concluded that the interference was necessary to achieve one or more of the legitimate aims recognised by the [ECHR].');

- *R v Secretary of State for the Home Department, Ex parte Daly* [2001] UKHL 26 [2001] 2 AC 532, [28] (Lord Steyn considering 'the general tenor of the observations' in *Mahmood* (see above) 'correct'), see also [35] (Lord Hutton) and [36] (Lord Scott (both agreeing with Lord Steyn));
- *R v Secretary of State for the Home Department, Ex parte Simms* [2000] 2 AC 115 (HL), 125G–131D (Lord Steyn explaining

that the more substantial the interference with fundamental rights, here the freedom of expression, the more the court would require by way of justification before it could be satisfied that the interference was reasonable in a public law sense).

Illustrations:

- *R v Secretary of State for Transport, Ex parte Richmond-Upon-Thames LBC (No 4)* [1996] 1 WLR 1460 (CA), 1481A–D (Brooke LJ, considering the Secretary of State's exercise of power to control aircraft noise at night, pursuant to section 78(3) of the Civil Aviation Act 1982, applying the test in *Ex parte Smith* (see above): '[The right to respect for one's home and family life] is a right of the type which the courts are increasingly willing to recognise as worthy of specific attention within the framework of the approach now helpfully identified in *Ex parte Smith.* Using this approach, I am satisfied that the minister furnished sufficient justification for his decision, albeit that it impinges on the rights of people to enjoy nights undisturbed by unreasonable nuisance from noise, particularly from 6 am onwards, and that his decision cannot be impugned on this ground.');
- *R v Secretary of State for the Home Department, Ex parte NALGO* (1993) 5 Admin LR 785 (CA), 798A–D (Neill LJ stating, pre-HRA, that although a minister need not take Article 10, ECHR, into account when exercising his discretion where the discretion restricted fundamental rights then that would need to be justified by reference to an important competing public interest);
- *R (Isiko) v Secretary of State for the Home Department* [2000] UKHRR 385, [31(2)] (Schiemann LJ: 'Where, as here, a fundamental right is engaged, the court will, applying the law as it was established prior to the coming into force of the Human Rights Act 1998, insist that this fact be respected by the decision maker who is required to demonstrate either that his proposed action does not in truth interfere with the right, or if it does, that there exist considerations which may reasonably be accepted as amounting to a substantial objective justification for the interference.');
- *R (Lika) v Secretary of State for the Home Department* [2002] EWCA Civ 1855 [2002] All ER (D) 230 (Dec), [31] (Lawrence Collins J commenting on Lord Hope's opinion in *Launder* (see above): 'Like the cases on legitimate expectation, what he said represents a development in the relaxation of the basic rule of United Kingdom constitutional law that an unincorporated treaty cannot confer rights or impose duties in domestic law. Indeed, it may be that those developments may yet lead to the creation of an estoppel against the Crown in favour of individuals in the case of unincorporated treaties dealing with human rights which are plainly intended to benefit individuals.').

11.8.3. **Where unincorporated treaty obligations are voluntarily taken into account in exercising executive discretion that self-direction or advice may be reviewed:**

- *R v Secretary of State for the Home Department, Ex parte Launder* [1997] 1 WLR 839 (HL), 867F (Lord Hope: 'If the applicant is to have an effective remedy against a decision which is flawed because the decision-maker has misdirected himself on the Convention which he himself says he took into account, it must surely be right to examine the substance of the argument').
- *R v DPP, Ex parte Kebilene* [2000] 2 AC 326 (HL), 367D–368A (Lord Steyn considering that where in the exercise of executive discretion the compatibility of proposed action with unincorporated treaty obligations is considered by the decision-maker, the resulting decision is amenable to judicial review on the basis that the consideration of the compatibility with unincorporated treaty obligations was erroneous; noting the consistency of this approach with that set out by Lord Hope in *Launder* (see above)), see similarly 375F–376A (Lord Hope);
- *R (CND) v The Prime Minister* [2002] EWHC 2777 (Admin) [2002] All ER (D) 245 (Dec), [61 (iv)] (Richards J: 'A further exception can arise [where national courts have to adjudicate upon the interpretation of unincorporated treaties] where a decision-maker has expressly taken into account an international treaty and the court thinks it appropriate to examine the correctness of the self-direction or advice on which the decision is based: see [citing *Kebilene* and *Launder* (see above)], both of them cases where the court was willing to have regard to the European Convention on Human Rights prior to the Human Rights Act 1998 coming into force.').

Illustrations:

- *Gangadeen v Secretary of State for the Home Department* [1989] Imm AR 106 (CA), 117–119 (Hirst LJ considering that the Secretary of State was properly guided by Article 8 considerations where the Home Office Deportation Guidance Policy was expressly stated as taking into account Article 8, ECHR);
- *R v Secretary of State for the Home Department, Ex parte Johnson* [1999] QB 1174 (DC), 1191G (Bell J considering, in the context of an extradition decision, that the Secretary of State approached the provisions of Article 6(3)(c), ECHR, correctly where it was argued (at 1188F) that the Secretary of State had wrongly asked himself whether the applicant's extradition would contravene Article 6(3)(c) whereas he 'should have asked whether there was a significant risk that the applicant would, upon his return, be subject to treatment by the requesting state [Australia] which was in breach of article 6(3)(c).');
- *R v Secretary of State for the Home Department, Ex parte Arman Ali* [2000] Imm AR 134, 143 (Collins J considering that

Launder (see above) was not limited to extradition and deportation cases and that the Secretary of State's conclusions on the ECHR could be considered: 'An assertion that a Convention obligation has been taken into account in reaching a decision will entitle a court to strike down that decision as irrational if the decision-maker has misinterpreted the relevant Convention obligation.').

11.9. **Alongside the development of public law by reference to fundamental rights, as embodied in unincorporated human rights treaties and international instruments, there has been a parallel, perhaps parasitic, move towards a more broadly articulated principle. That broader approach supports a greater use of unincorporated treaties in general when considering exercises of executive discretion.**

11.9.1. **Presumption that exercises of executive discretion will comply with unincorporated treaty obligations:**
Illustration:

- *R v Secretary of State for the Home Department, Ex parte Venables* [1998] AC 407 (HL), 499B–F (Lord Browne-Wilkinson considering the Secretary of State's 1993 policy (applying the tariff principle to mandatory life imprisonment), which was extended to child murderers, and the factors relevant to the exercise of the discretion conferred on the Secretary of State in relation to children detained during Her Majesty's pleasure (under the Criminal Justice Act 1991) including the UN Convention on the Rights of the Child: 'The Convention has not been incorporated into English law. But it is legitimate in considering the nature of detention during Her Majesty's pleasure . . . to assume that Parliament has not maintained on the statute book a power capable of being exercised in a manner inconsistent with the treaty obligations of this country.') [§ **9.14.2**].

11.9.2. **Unincorporated treaty obligations as a general guide to the exercise of executive discretion:**
Illustrations:

- *R v Lyons* [2002] UKHL 44 [2003] 1 AC 976, [13] (Lord Bingham: 'Even before the Human Rights Act 1998 the [ECHR] exerted a persuasive and pervasive influence on judicial decision-making in this country . . . guiding the exercise of discretions..');
- *R v Khan* [1997] AC 558 (HL), 580D–F, (Lord Nolan, considering that even absent statutory ambiguity, the principles reflected in the ECHR were not irrelevant to the exercise of the power under section 78 of the Police and Criminal Evidence

Act 1984: 'They could hardly be irrelevant, because they embody so many of the familiar principles of our own law and of our concept of justice.' At 582A–582C noting, inter alia: '[I]f the behaviour of the police in the particular case amounts to an apparent or probable breach of some relevant law or convention, common sense dictates that this is a consideration which may be taken into account for what it is worth.');

- *Karanakaran v Secretary of State for the Home Department* [2000] 3 All ER 449 (CA), 469 (Brooke LJ on the correct mode and standard of proof in asylum cases, falling under the Refugee Convention: 'In the present public law context, where this country's compliance with an international convention is in issue, the decision-maker is, in my judgment, not constrained by the rules of evidence that have been adopted in civil litigation, and is bound to take into account all material considerations when making its assessment about the future.');
- *R (Howard League for Penal Reform) v Secretary of State for the Home Department* [2002] EWHC 2497 (Admin) [2003] 1 FLR 484 [**§ 5.16.2**] [**§ 10.6.2**];
- *R (Kenny) v Leeds Magistrates Court* [2003] EWHC 2963 (Admin) [2004] 1 All ER 1333, [41] (Owen J) [**§ 5.16.2**];
- *R v Secretary of State for the Home Department, Ex parte Rosa Maria Moreno Lopez* [1999] Imm AR 11 (CA), 15 (Dyson J: 'When the Secretary of State exercises his discretion and his powers, he is required to have regard to the [ECHR].');
- *R v Secretary of State for the Home Department, Ex parte Hargreaves* [1997] 1 WLR 906 (CA), 921F–922C (Hirst LJ considering that the Secretary of State's decision, changing the home leave arrangements of prisoners from those which they had previously received notification of, did not infringe the principles contained in Article 8, ECHR, and considering Article 8 on the basis that: 'I am prepared to accept . . . that although not part of English domestic law the provisions of the [ECHR] can assist in the elucidation of common law or in the interpretation of a statute.');
- *R v Secretary of State for the Home Department, Ex parte Norney* (1995) Admin LR 861, 871 (Dyson J: 'I do not consider that *ex p Brind* requires me to ignore the [ECHR] when considering the lawfulness of the exercise of the discretion. I accept that, as a general rule, the lawfulness of the exercise of executive discretion is not measured by asking whether it involves an infringement of Convention rights. But where it is clear that the statutory provision which creates the discretion was passed in order to bring the domestic law into line with the Convention, it would, in my judgment be perverse to hold that, when considering the lawfulness of the exercise of the discretion, the court must ignore the relevant provisions of the Convention.');

- *R v Secretary of State for the Home Department, Ex parte Engin Ozminnos* [1994] Imm AR 287 (CA), 293 (Auld LJ: 'Articles of the [ECHR] have at least [here] some role as relevant factors in the taking of a decision.');
- *M v Secretary of State for the Home Department* [1996] 1 WLR 507 (CA), 514G–H (Millett LJ: 'I should make it clear that it is not the policy of the Secretary of State to expel or return to his country of origin a person who can satisfy him that there are substantial reasons for believing that he would be in danger of torture, loss of life or inhuman or degrading treatment, even though not for a [Refugee] Convention reason. To do so would be in breach of the United Kingdom's international obligations under articles 2 and 3 of the European Convention for the Protection of Human Rights and Fundamental Freedoms (1953)(Cmnd 8969) and article 3 of the UN Convention against Torture and Other Cruel, Inhuman or Degrading Treatment or Punishment (1985) (Cmd 9593). The Secretary of State has informed Parliament that a person who is not recognised as a refugee entitled to asylum will nevertheless be considered for the grant of exceptional leave to remain in the UK if there are compelling humanitarian reasons for not returning him to his country of origin.').

(4) Unincorporated Treaties and Legitimate Expectations

11.10. **The law on whether unincorporated treaties may give rise to legitimate expectation has had a troubled development. On the basis of Australian authority, *Teoh* [§ 11.10.1], domestic courts have found, on two key occasions, in *Ahmed* and *Adimi* [§ 11.10.1], that the ratification of an unincorporated treaty could give rise to a representation on which members of the public could rely as creating a legitimate expectation that future executive decision-making would be compatible with the unincorporated treaty obligations. Not only do these decisions stand beside prior conflicting case law, *Chundawadra* and *Behluli* [§ 11.10.2], but they have also been more recently doubted. This, domestic, doubt, is reflected in the concerns cast on *Teoh* in Australia [§ 11.10.2].**

11.10.1. Ratifying an unincorporated treaty may give rise to a legitimate expectation:

- *Minister for Immigration and Ethnic Affairs v Teoh* (1995) 183 CLR 273 (High Court of Australia) (Ratification of the UN Convention on the Rights of the Child by the executive held to give rise to a legitimate expectation that the minister would act in conformity with it by treating the best interests of a convicted drug offender's children as the primary consideration in deciding whether to order the removal of the drug offender from Australia—even though the Convention was not incorporated into Australian law and even though neither the drug offender nor his children knew of the Convention or its ratification), 291 (Gummow CJ and Deane J: '[R]atification by Australia of an international convention is not to be dismissed as a merely platitudinous or ineffectual act, particularly when the instrument evidences internationally accepted standards to be applied by courts and administrative authorities in dealing with basic human rights affecting the family and children. Rather, ratification of a convention is a positive statement by the executive government of this country to the world and to the Australian people that the executive government and its agencies will act in accordance with the [convention]. That positive statement is an adequate foundation for a legitimate expectation, absent statutory or executive indications to the contrary, that administrative decision-makers will act in conformity with the [convention].'), 301 (Toohey J: '[I]t is not necessary for a person in the position of [the applicant] to show that he was aware of the ratification; legitimate expectation in this context does not depend on the knowledge and state of mind of the individual concerned. The matter is to be assessed objectively, in terms of what expectation might reasonably be engendered by any undertaking that the authority in question has given, whether itself or, as in the present case, by the government of which it is a part.');

- *Tavita v Minister of Immigration* [1994] 2 NZLR 257, 266 (New Zealand Court of Appeal considering the submission that the Minister and the New Zealand Immigration Service are entitled to ignore international instruments: 'That is an unattractive argument, apparently implying that New Zealand's adherence to the international instruments has been at least partly window-dressing. Although . . . a final decision on the argument is neither necessary nor desirable, there must at least be some hesitation about accepting it.');
- *R v Secretary of State for the Home Department, Ex parte Ahmed and Patel* [1999] Imm AR 22 (CA), 36 (Lord Woolf MR, dismissing appeals where appellants claimed they had a legitimate expectation that the Secretary of State's powers to make extra-statutory concessions would be exercised in accordance with the ECHR because of the clear statements of policy explaining the Secretary of State's approach, but accepting, 'that the entering into a treaty by the Secretary of State could give rise to a legitimate expectation on which the public in general are entitled to rely. Subject to an indication to the contrary, it

could be a representation that the Secretary of State would act in accordance with any obligations which he accepted under the Treaty. This legitimate expectation could give rise to a right to relief, as well as additional obligations of fairness, if the Secretary of State, without reason, acted inconsistently with the obligations which this country had undertaken. This is very much the approach adopted by the High Court of Australia in the immigration case of *Minister of State for Immigration and Ethnic Affairs v Teoh* [1995] 183 CLR 273.' (see above)), 40 (Hobhouse LJ: 'If there was no statement of executive policy other than the executive's ratification of a treaty, it might be possible to say that there was a legitimate expectation that the executive's treatment and decision of matters falling within the ambit of such a treaty would be dealt with in accordance with that treaty. But that is not the present case. Here there are specific statements of executive policy . . . Under these circumstances the legitimate expectation has to be based upon that statement of executive policy.');

- *R v Uxbridge Magistrates' Court, Ex parte Adimi* [2001] QB 667 (DC), 686B–E (Simon Brown LJ considering whether Article 31 of the Refugee Convention could be enforced in domestic law where only Article 33 of the Convention has been formally incorporated: '[T]he applicants contend that the United Kingdom's ratification of the Convention itself created a legitimate expectation that its provisions would be followed. In this connection they pray in aid the Court of Appeal's decision in *R v Secretary of State for the Home Department, Ex parte Ahmed* [1998] INLR 570, 583 . . . [where Lord Woolf accepted that the act of entering into a treaty by the Secretary of State could give rise to a legitimate expectation on which the public may rely (see above)] . . . I would accept this argument.'), 690E–G (Newman J, referring to the judgment in *Ex parte Ahmed*: 'The conclusion has not been doubted. It received the unanimous approach of the Privy Council in *Thomas v Baptiste* [2000] 2 AC 1 and I take it to be firmly established that treaty obligations assumed by the executive are capable of giving rise to legitimate expectations which the executive will not under municipal law be at liberty to disregard.' At 696D–E: 'A legitimate expectation that the executive will consider whether to afford protection requires no request from the refugee for the duty upon the Secretary of State to consider the position to arise. He should do so whenever the facts disclosed to him give rise to an arguable case for consideration.').

11.10.2. **Doubtful whether ratifying an unincorporated treaty gives rise to a legitimate expectation:**

- *R (European Roma Rights Centre) v Immigration Officer at Prague Airport* [2003] EWCA Civ 666 [2004] QB 811, [51] (Simon

Brown LJ considering that his views in *Adimi* [**§ 11.10.1**] were his conclusion on legitimate expectation were to be regarded as 'at best, superficial' and his conclusion on legitimate expectation was 'suspect' partly because it overlooked *Chundawadra* and *Behluli* (see below)), [100] (Laws LJ regarding *Ahmed* and *Adimi* [**§ 11.10.1**] with 'unease' and stating 'we must not be seduced by humanitarian claims to a spurious acceptance of a false source of law.') (HL is at [2004] UKHL 55 [2005] 2 WLR 1; the judgment does not comment on this issue);

- *Re Minister for Immigration and Multicultural Affairs, Ex parte Lam* (2003) 195 CLR 502 (High Court of Australia), [95] (McHugh and Gummow JJ, comparing the majority judgment in *Teoh* [**§ 11.10.1**] with other Australian case law on legitimate expectation: 'It is one thing for a court in an application for judicial review to form a view as to the expectations of Australians presenting themselves at the gates of football grounds and racecourses. It is quite another to take ratification of any convention as a "positive statement" made to "the Australian people" that the executive government will act in accordance with the convention and to treat the question of the extent to which such matters impinge upon the popular consciousness as beside the point.' At [101–102]: '[I]n the case law a line has been drawn which limits the normative effect of what are unenacted international obligations upon discretionary decision-making under powers conferred by statute and without specification of those obligations. The judgments in *Teoh* accepted the established doctrine that such obligations are not mandatory relevant considerations attracting judicial review for jurisdictional error. The curiosity is that, nevertheless, such matters are to be treated, if *Teoh* be taken as establishing any general proposition in this area, as mandatory relevant considerations for that species of judicial review concerned with procedural fairness. The reasoning which as a matter of principle would sustain such an erratic application of "invocation" doctrine remains for analysis and decision. Basic questions of the interaction between the three branches of government are involved.'), [147] (Callinan J expressing further reservations on *Teoh*);
- *R v DPP, Ex parte Kebilene* [2000] 2 AC 326, 338D (DC) (Lord Bingham CJ after referring to *Teoh* and *Ahmed* [**§ 11.10.1**]: '[Counsel] acknowledges, rightly, the difficulty of basing any legitimate expectation on the ratification by this country of the [ECHR]. This took place nearly half a century ago. It was generally assumed at the time that ratification would have no practical effect on British law or practice, as proved for many years to be the case. It cannot plausibly be said that ratification of the Convention so long ago gives rise to any legitimate expectation today.')(HL is also at [2000] 2 AC 326; see [**§ 11.10.3; §11.11.2**]);

- *Chundawadra v IAT* [1988] Imm AR 161 (CA), 173–174 (Glidewell LJ, in response to the submission that every citizen has a legitimate expectation that, if the ECHR is relevant to a matter under executive consideration, the Minister will take it in account: '[S]ince there is no entitlement to look to the Convention where there is no ambiguity, there can be no question of legitimate expectation and there is nothing from which the expectation can arise. I accept that, if a Minister makes a clear statement of Government policy as to how some matter is to be dealt with in the future, that in itself, while not giving rise to any legal rights, may give rise in particular circumstances to an expectation that, until the policy is altered and announced to be altered, it will be followed. But that is a wholly different situation from that which arises here . . . Here there is an international treaty; the Government of the United Kingdom has acceded to it but it is not embodied in our domestic legislation, and indeed, whether it should be is the subject of a good deal of discussion. But it is not and because it is not it may not be looked at or prayed in aid in relation to matters in these courts save when a question of ambiguity in a statute or other legal text arises. That not being the case here, it may not be looked at all and no expectation that it can be followed can arise. [Counsel] put it in these graphic terms: it is not appropriate to introduce the Convention into the law of England by the back door of legitimate expectation when the front door is firmly barred. I respectfully agree.'), 175–176 (Slade LJ agreeing with Glidewell LJ);
- *Behluli v Secretary of State for the Home Department* [1998] Imm AR 407 (CA), 415 (Beldam LJ, rejecting the submission that three letters written by the Asylum Directorate to bodies responsible for the interests of asylum seekers in the United Kingdom gave rise to a legitimate expectation that after the Dublin Convention on the State Responsible for Examining Applications for Asylum Lodged in one of the Member States of the European Communities came into force, asylum applications falling within the scope of the Convention would be dealt with according to its terms; dismissing *Teoh* [**§ 11.10.1**] as incompatible with *R v Secretary of State for the Home Department, Ex parte Brind* [1991] 1 AC 696 at 762 and: '[T]hat is not the law in this country . . . The extent to which statements can found [a legitimate] expectation must depend on the circumstances in which they are made, whether reasonably construed they can be taken as propounding a policy or are merely statements applicable to particular cases or classes of case, and moreover the background against which they are made, and if made against the background of a statutory provision, the terms of the Act and the relevant rules must be taken into account.').

11.10.3. **No legitimate expectation arises from the ratification of an unincorporated treaty where such an expectation would conflict with a clear statutory intention:**

- *R v DPP, Ex parte Kebilene* [2000] 2 AC 326 (HL) [§ **11.11.2**];
- *R (Pepushi) v CPS* [2004] EWHC 798 (Admin) [2004] All ER (D) 129 (May), [37–38] (Thomas LJ construing section 31 of the Immigration and Asylum Act 1999: 'Where Parliament has enacted in words specifically chosen the scope of an international obligation in relation to criminal law, there is no room for a legitimate expectation to protection other than that which Parliament has provided. To acknowledge that an international treaty [here the Refugee Convention] gives rights to legitimate expectations under our domestic law would in effect be indirectly circumventing the scope of our domestic law as set out in statute in a way that was bound to give rise to very considerable confusion and uncertainty. Furthermore, the CPS must, as a prosecution service independent of the Executive apply the domestic law of the England and Wales where Parliament has enacted the provisions of an international Convention; there can be no legitimate expectation that the CPS could do otherwise.').

11.11. **There are broader difficulties with the view that the ratification of an unincorporated treaty may give rise to a legitimate expectation. For example, even supposing that the constituent elements of legitimate expectation could be satisfactorily proved in an unincorporated treaty case, whilst such an expectation might give rise to procedural protection it could not, unless supported by other constitutional safeguards, give substantive protection, for this would constitute indirect enforcement of the treaty. Further, since a legitimate expectation does not create binding rules of law the government can depart from the expected course of conduct, for example (a) on one approach, where it gives notice of its intention to do so and gives the affected individuals an opportunity to make representations; (b) on another approach, where it can justify the departure on the basis of an overriding public interest. Difficulties such as these significantly undermine the practical utility of legitimate expectation in relation to unincorporated treaties.**

11.11.1. **Legitimate expectation does not create binding rules of law:**

- *Fisher v Minister of Public Safety (No 2)* [2000] 1 AC 434 (PC) (the argument that, under *Teoh* [§ **11.10.1**], the appellant had a legitimate expectation that he would not be executed whilst his petition to the Inter-American Commission on Human Rights was outstanding, was rejected on the basis that even if the appellant had such a legitimate expectation, it could not survive the government's letters to the appellant's solicitors informing them that it could wait no longer than a certain date before carrying out the execution), 447A–C (Lord Lloyd: '[L]egitimate expectations do not create binding rules of law. As Mason CJ made clear [in *Teoh*], at p.291 a decision-maker can act inconsistently with a legitimate expectation which he has created provided he gives adequate notice of his intention to do so, and provided he gives those who are affected an opportunity to state their case. Procedural fairness requires of him no more than that.');

- *Higgs v Minister of National Security* [2000] 2 AC 228 (PC), 241E–G (Lord Hoffmann: '[T]he existence of [an unincorporated] treaty may give rise to a legitimate expectation on the part of citizens that the government, in its acts affecting them, will observe the terms of the treaty [citing *Teoh*] . . . the legal effect of creating such a legitimate expectation is purely procedural. The executive cannot depart from the expected course of conduct unless it has given notice that [it] intends to do so and has given the person affected an opportunity to make representations.');
- *Thomas v Baptiste* [2000] 2 AC 1 (PC) (any legitimate expectation the applicants might have had, that their execution would be delayed pending resolution of their petitions, could not have survived the publication, by the government, of instructions establishing time-limits after which executions would not be postponed);
- *R (Lika) v Secretary of State for the Home Department* [2002] EWCA Civ 1855 [2002] All ER (D) 230 (Dec), [26] (Latham LJ rejecting reliance on legitimate expectation on the basis of 'two insuperable difficulties': 'The first and most fundamental one is that the Dublin Convention . . . is not concerned directly with the provision of rights or entitlements to individual asylum seekers . . . It seems to me difficult to say, in those circumstances, that the Dublin Convention in itself could give rise to a legitimate expectation upon which an individual asylum seeker could rely. But even if that hurdle could be overcome, the policy of the Secretary of State is clearly set out in paragraph 345 of HC 395 . . . this will override any expectation generated by the Convention.');
- *Ex parte Shefki Gashi; Ex parte Artan Gjoka* (15 June 2000) (unreported: CO/3559/1999 and CO/4506/1999), [11] (Collins J assuming, on the authority of *R v Secretary of State for the Home Department, Ex parte Ahmed and Patel* [1998] INLR 570 [§ **11.10.1**], that the ratification by the government of a treaty may create a legitimate expectation but: 'That will only be if there is nothing else to show how the Government will act and no statement of policy.');

- *R v North and East Devonshire Health Authority, Ex parte Coughlan* [2001] QB 213 (CA) (a public authority may resile from a substantive legitimate expectation where there is an overriding public interest).

11.11.2. **Legitimate expectation and incorporating statutes:**

- *R v DPP, Ex parte Kebilene* [2000] 2 AC 326 (HL), 368D–E (Lord Steyn concluding that there can be no legitimate expectation in the period between the enactment and commencement of an incorporating statute where there is a clear statutory intent to postpone the coming into effect of central provisions of the Act; referring to the reasoning of the Divisional Court in which Lord Bingham stated (at 337G–H): 'The applicants seek to rely on a legitimate expectation entertained by them that the Director will exercise his prosecutorial discretion in accordance with the Convention following enactment of the Human Rights Act 1998 and pending the bringing into force of its central provisions. Such expectation is said to derive from the ratification of the Convention by the United Kingdom; from enactment of the Human Rights Act, and in particular section 22(4) of that Act; and from public statements made by ministers since the passing of the Act.' At 339C–D: 'In my judgment, such an expectation is contradicted by the express terms of the Act. Parliament has thought it right, for readily understandable reasons, to stipulate that central provisions of the Act shall not come into force on the passing of the Act but on a later date to be appointed by the Secretary of State. If Parliament had intended the whole Act to take effect upon its receiving the royal assent, it would have so provided. It did not do so. It would in my view fly in the face of the clear legislative intention of Parliament if the central provisions of the Act were to be treated, in a case such as the present, as having immediate effect when the Act itself provides that they shall not.').

(5) Unincorporated Treaties and Judicial Discretion

11.12. **The exercise of discretion by courts is characterised by a consistent recognition of, and respect for, upholding the United Kingdom's treaty obligations, including those that are unincorporated as a matter of domestic law. This is seen particularly clearly where judicial discretion is exercised regarding the grant or maintenance of injunctions and interim injunctions. One ready explanation for this consistency is that, as one of three**

organs of the state, courts consider themselves bound to give effect to the international obligations of the United Kingdom whenever they can do so without undermining the principles of non-justiciability [§§ 8.5–8.7] and no direct effect [§§ 8.8–8.9].

Illustrations:

- *R v Khan* [1997] AC 558 (HL), 571H (Lord Slynn pre-HRA: '[T]he question has also been raised as to whether in exercising his discretion under section 78 of the Police and Criminal Evidence Act 1984 as to whether the evidence should be admitted a judge can have regard to articles 6 and 8 of the European Convention on Human Rights and their application by the Court of Human Rights. In my view he can even if the Convention is not binding on him as a matter of domestic law.' Applied in *Nottingham City Council v Amin* [2000] 1 WLR 1071 (DC), 1077E (Lord Bingham CJ));
- *In re M (Petition to European Court of Human Rights)* [1997] 1 FLR 755, 757D–E (Johnson J: '[W]here an English court has to exercise a discretion, that is to say, it can act in one way or another, one or more of which violates the [ECHR] and another of which does not, the court will seek to act in a way which does not violate the Convention. That really is a matter of common sense. However, that rule is not invariable and the interests of justice . . . may require a decision in seeming violation of the Convention.');
- *Attorney-General v Guardian Newspapers* [1987] 1 WLR 1248 (HL), 1296E–1297F (Lord Templeman, considering the principles upon which the court should act in exercising a discretion, ie the grant of injunctions against various newspapers regarding the publication of allegations about the British security service, MI5, in *Spycatcher*: 'My Lords, this appeal involves a conflict between the right of the public to be protected by the Security Service and the right of the public to be supplied with full information by the press. This appeal therefore involves consideration of the Convention for the Protection of Human Rights and Fundamental Freedoms (1953)(Cmd. 8969) . . . to which the British Government adheres. . . . [considering *The Sunday Times v United Kingdom* [1979] 2 EHRR 245] The question is therefore whether the interference with freedom of expression constituted by the . . . injunctions was, on 30 July 1987 when they were continued by this House, necessary in a democratic society in the interests of national security, for protecting the reputation or rights of others, for preventing the disclosure of information received in confidence or for maintaining the authority and impartiality of the judiciary having regard to the facts and circumstances prevailing on the 30 July 1987 and in the light of the events which had happened.' See

also 1299B, E–F considering the ECHR), 1288A–C (Lord Brandon: 'The public right to freedom of expression cannot, even in a democratic country such as the United Kingdom, be absolute. It is necessarily subject to certain exceptions of which the protection of national security is one. This is expressly recognised in article 10(2) of the Convention for the Protection of Human Rights and Fundamental Freedoms to which the United Kingdom has adhered although its provisions have not been incorporated into our domestic law.'), 1307B–E (Lord Ackner adopting the observations and conclusion of Lord Templeman);

- *Lord Advocate v The Scotsman* [1990] 1 AC 812 (HL), 823C–G (Lord Templeman in deciding whether to grant an interdict (injunction) against the publication of a book of memoirs regarding service with MI5, called *Inside Intelligence*: 'Any such restraint is an interference with the right of expression safeguarded by [Article 10, ECHR] . . . The question therefore is whether the restraint sought to be imposed on the respondents is "necessary in a democratic society in the interests of national security" . . . In my opinion, it is for Parliament to determine the restraints on freedom of expression which are necessary in a democratic society. The courts of this country should follow any guidance contained in a statute. If that guidance is inconsistent with the requirements of the [ECHR] then that will be a matter for the Convention authorities and for the United Kingdom. It will not be a matter for the courts.' After considering the guidance of Parliament in the Official Secrets Act 1989, at 826B–D: 'If the Crown had asserted that future publications by "The Scotsman" would be likely to damage the work of the Security Services, then difficult questions might have arisen as to the nature of the damage feared, as to whether an injunction was necessary within the meaning attributed to that expression by the European Court of Human Rights and as to whether the restriction on freedom of expression constituted by the injunction sought was "proportionate to the legitimate aim pursued" as required by the European Court in *Handyside v United Kingdom* (1976) 1 EHRR 737 and *The Sunday Times v United Kingdom* (1979) 2 EHRR 245.');
- *Venables v Newsgroup Newspapers Ltd* [2001] Fam 430, 452–453 (Dame Butler Sloss P granting an injunction to protect individuals' rights under Articles 2 and 3, ECHR, pre-HRA);
- *Kelly v BBC* [2001] Fam 59, 68–70 and 85 (Munby J considering Article 10, ECHR, pre-HRA in determining whether to vary or discharge an injunction against the BBC restraining the broadcast of an interview with a ward of the court. At 84H considering the observations of Neill LJ in *In re W (A Minor) (Wardship: Restrictions on Publication)* (see below): 'It will be observed that Neill LJ makes explicit reference to article 10. In

my judgment it is clear that the Court of Appeal in that case was intending to give effect to the Convention jurisprudence to which I have already referred.');

- *Rantzen v Mirror Group Newspapers* [1994] QB 670 (CA) [§ **9.14.2**];
- *In re H-S (Minors)* [1994] 1 WLR 1141 (CA), 1148 (CA exercising judicial discretion on whether to maintain an injunction by reference to Articles 8 and 10, ECHR, pre-HRA);
- *R v Central Independent TV* [1994] 3 WLR 20 (CA), 30D (Hoffmann LJ considering an injunction in the light of Article 10, ECHR, and the importance of free speech, pre-HRA);
- *In re W (A Minor) (Wardship: Restrictions on Publication)* [1992] 1 WLR 100 (CA), 102H–103C (Neill LJ in deciding whether to maintain an injunction, pre-HRA: 'Media interest surrounding children who are wards of the court raises difficult issues . . . [extracting from case law the following guidelines] (1) The court will attach great importance to safeguarding the freedom of the press . . . (2) The court will also take account of article 10 of the Convention for the Protection of Human Rights and Fundamental Freedoms (1953) (Cmd 8969).');
- *R v Advertising Standards Authority, Ex parte Vernons Organisation* [1992] 1 WLR 1289 (QBD), 1293A–B (Laws J refusing to grant an interim injunction, pre-HRA, restraining the publication of the ASA report by considering a 'general principle in our law that the expression of opinion and the conveyance of information will not be restrained by the courts save on pressing grounds' because freedom of expression is 'as much a sinew of the common law as it is of the [ECHR].') See also *R (Matthias Rath BV) v ASA Ltd* [2001] HRLR 436;
- *In re S (A Child) (Identification: Restrictions on Publication)* [2003] EWCA Civ 963 [2004] Fam 43, [18–40] (Hale LJ (dissenting, but whose detailed analysis of the law was adopted by the other members of the court) reviewing case law on the exercise of the Court's inherent jurisdiction to protect children from publicity and concluding, at [40]: 'These cases all preceded the implementation of the Human Rights Act 1998. Now that the Human Rights Act 1998 is in force, the relevance of the jurisdiction may simply be to provide the vehicle which enables the court to conduct the necessary balancing exercise between the competing rights of the child under article 8 and the media under article 10.');
- *R v Horseferry Road Magistrates' Court, Ex p Bennett* [1994] 1 AC 42 (HL) (judicial discretion in exercising jurisdiction to prevent abuse of process applied in an extradition context by considering human rights and international law), 61H–62A (Lord Griffiths: 'If the court is to have the power to interfere with the prosecution in the present circumstances [where an

accused was brought to the United Kingdom from South Africa without following the proper extradition procedures] it must be because the judiciary accept a responsibility for the maintenance of the rule of law that embraces a willingness to oversee executive actions and to refuse to countenance behaviour that threatens either basic human rights or the rule of law.'), 76E–F (Lord Lowry: 'The implications for international law, as represented by extradition treaties, are significant . . . If British officialdom at any level has participated in or encouraged the kidnapping it seems to represent a grave contravention of international law, the comity of nations and the rule of law generally if our courts allow themselves to be used by the executive to try an offence which the courts would not be dealing with if the rule of law had prevailed.' At 78B: 'It has been suggested that, since the executive conduct complained of invades the rights of other countries and of persons under their protection and detracts from international comity, the remedy lies not with the courts but in the field of diplomacy. I would answer that the court must jealously protect its own process from misuse *by the executive*.').

PART IV

Judicial Restraint, Act of State and Customary International Law

12

Judicial Restraint and Act of State

(1) Judicial Restraint

12.1. **Courts have generally avoided adjudicating on matters arising from transactions of foreign states or inter-state issues. This policy of avoidance has become known as the principle of judicial restraint. A modern description of the principle of judicial restraint has been given by Lord Wilberforce:**

> '[T]he essential question is whether . . . there exists in English law a more general principle that the courts will not adjudicate upon the transactions of foreign sovereign states. Though I would prefer to avoid argument on terminology, it seems desirable to consider this principle, if existing, not as a variety of "act of state" but one for judicial restraint or abstention . . . In my opinion there is, and for long has been, such a general principle, starting in English law, adopted and generalised in the law of the United States of America which is effective and compelling in English courts. This principle is not one of discretion, but is inherent in the very nature of the judicial process.'(*Buttes Gas and Oil Co. v Hammer (No 3)* [1982] AC 888 (HL), 931F–932B)

12.2. **The operation of judicial restraint is triggered by facts relating to 'transactions of foreign states' or 'inter-state issues' [§ 12.2.1], for example the interpretation of or adjudication upon treaties which are unincorporated in domestic law [§§ 8.6–8.7]. Judicial restraint requires a court to exercise its discretion on whether it is competent to decide the issues raised and withdraw from adjudication where it determines that it is not. Withdrawal will generally occur where the issues are incapable of being judged by 'judicial or manageable standards' [§ 12.2.1] (*cf* where there is an alleged violation of fundamental human rights or a breach of a clearly established rule of international law [§§ 12.5–12.9]). The exercise of restraint**

is prompted by concern to avoid embarrassment in the United Kingdom's foreign relations or breaches of comity; 'transactions of foreign states' and 'inter-state issues' being part of the executive, rather than judicial, domain. The exercise of judicial restraint overlaps, in practice, with the doctrine of sovereign or state immunity, by virtue of which domestic courts lack jurisdiction over foreign states and their officials (unless the immunity is waived by the entity in which it vests).

12.2.1. **Domestic courts exercise judicial restraint regarding 'transactions of foreign states' and 'inter-state issues':**

- *The Charkieh* (1873) LR 4 A&E 59, 97 (Sir Robert Phillimore: 'The object of international law, in this as in other matters, is not to work injustice, not to prevent the enforcement of a just demand, but to substitute negotiations between governments, though they may be dilatory and the issue distant and uncertain, for the ordinary use of courts of justice in cases where such use would lessen the dignity or embarrass the functions of the representatives of a foreign State.') (quoted in *Rahimtoola v Nizam of Hyderabad* [1958] AC 379 (HL), 409A–B (Lord Cohen));
- *Buttes Gas and Oil Co v Hammer (No 3)* [1982] AC 888 (HL), 931F–932B (Lord Wilberforce: [§ **12.1**]. At 938B–C noting that English courts will not consider the content of 'inter state issues and/or the issues of international law' where the issues are such that the court has 'no judicial or manageable standards by which to judge [the] issues' or where the court would be in a 'judicial no-man's land.');
- *Cook v Sprigg* [1899] AC 572 (JC), 578D–E (Lord Halsbury, LC: 'It is a well-established principle of law that the transactions of independent States between each other are governed by other laws than those which municipal courts administer.');
- *R v Bow Street Magistrate, Ex parte Pinochet* [2000] 1 AC 61 (HL), 104C (Lord Lloyd (dissenting) describing the 'whole thrust' of Lord Wilberforce's speech in *Buttes Gas* [§ **12.1**] as being that 'non-justiciability is a flexible principle');
- *R v Secretary of State, Ex parte British Council of Turkish Cypriot Associations* 112 ILR 735, 740 (Sedley J on the role of comity).

Illustrations:

- *R (Abbasi) v Secretary of State for Foreign and Commonwealth Affairs* [2002] EWCA Civ 1598 [2003] UKHRR 76, [67] (Lord Phillips MR, considering the acts of the United States Government arbitrarily detaining a British citizen in Guantanamo Bay: 'It is clear that there can be no direct remedy in this court. The United States Government is not before the court, and no order of this court would be binding upon it.');
- *R v Bow Street Magistrate, Ex parte Pinochet* [2000] 1 AC 61 (HL), 103C–F (Lord Lloyd (dissenting): 'If we quash the second provi-

sional warrant, Senator Pinochet will return to Chile, and Spain will complain that we have failed to comply with our international obligations under the European Convention on Extradition. If we do not quash the second provisional warrant, Chile will complain that the Senator has been arrested in defiance of Chile's claim for immunity, and in breach of our obligations under customary international law. In these circumstances, quite apart from any embarrassment in our foreign relations, or potential breach of comity, and quite apart from any fear that, by assuming jurisdiction, we would only serve to "imperil the amicable relations between governments and vex the peace of nations" (see *Oetjen v Central Leather Co.*, 246 US 297, 304) we would be entering a field in which we are simply not competent to adjudicate. We apply customary international law as part of the common law, and we give effect to our international obligations so far as they are incorporated in our statute law; but we are not an international court . . . In my view this is a case in which . . . we should exercise judicial restraint by declining jurisdiction.') (*cf* [§ **12.4**] for the majority view);

- *R v Secretary of State for the Home Department, Ex parte Launder* [1997] 1 WLR 839 (HL), 854G and 857AD (Lord Hope commenting that the Secretary of State, and not courts, was competent to decide whether the People's Republic of China could be trusted, in the implementation of its treaty obligations with the United Kingdom, to respect fundamental human rights);
- *Westland Helicopters v AOI* [1995] QB 282, 294C (Colman J considering that it would be 'quite contrary to the principle of non-justiciability' to adjudicate on whether there had been a breach of treaty obligations by foreign states);
- *R v Governor of Brixton Prison, Ex parte Kotronis* [1971] AC 250 (HL), 278–279 (Lord Reid noting the impossibility for domestic courts to assume that a foreign government with the British Government has diplomatic relations may act in a clear breach of faith of its treaty obligations).

12.2.2. **Withdrawing from adjudication:**

- *R v Bow Street Magistrate, Ex parte Pinochet* [2000] 1 AC 61 (HL), 90B–D (Lord Lloyd (dissenting): '[A]ct of state is a confusing term. It is used in different senses in many different contexts. So it is better to refer to non-justiciability. The principles of sovereign immunity and non-justiciability overlap in practice. But in legal theory they are separate. State immunity . . . is a principle of public international law. It creates a procedural bar to the jurisdiction of the court. Logically therefore it comes first. Non-justiciability is a principle of private international law. It goes to the substance of the issues to be decided. It requires the court to withdraw from adjudication on the grounds that the issues are such as the court is not competent to decide. State immunity, being a procedural bar to the jurisdiction of the court, can be waived by the state. Non-justiciability, being a substantive bar to adjudication, cannot.');

12.2.3. **Where the Crown has declared a position in its conduct of foreign affairs, courts should speak with the same voice:**
Illustrations:

- *In re Westinghouse Electric Corporation Uranium Contract Litigation MDL Docket No 235 (Nos 1 and 2)* [1978] AC 547 (HL), 617D (Lord Wilberforce considering that where the policy of Her Majesty's Government had been against recognising the United States' extraterritorial investigative jurisdiction against United Kingdom companies then 'the courts should in such matters speak with the same voice as the executive'), see similarly 650–651 (Lord Fraser) (cited in *British Airways v Laker Airways* [1984] QB 142 (CA), 193D (Sir John Donaldson MR));
- *Adams v Adams* [1971] P 188, 198C–D (Sir Jocelyn Simon P: '"Our state cannot speak with two voices . . . the judiciary saying one thing, the executive another" said Lord Atkin in *The Arantzazu Mendi* [1939] AC 256, 264. (Though Lord Atkin was speaking of recognition of foreign sovereignty, his observation seems to me, in common sense, to be of general application in a unitary state in cases such as the instant one) of course, if clear law is expressly based on considerations of public policy the executive must accept it and them unless the law is changed by The Queen in Parliament. But where the law is doubtful or the considerations of public policy may be in dispute, the view of the executive may be of value to the courts—if only in indicating that this may be a matter better left for the direct determination of the constitutional sovereign, The Queen in Parliament.');
- *Lonrho Exports Ltd v Export Credits Guarantee Department* [1999] Ch 158, 179D–E (Lightman J: 'The interpretation of treaties not by statute incorporated into municipal law and the decision whether or not they have been complied with are matters exclusively for the Crown in its conduct of foreign relations. The court must speak with the same voice as the executive and accordingly seek and follow the interpretation adopted by the Crown, and not venture its own interpretation (let alone its own interpretation if at variance with that of the Crown). Nor may it seek to determine whether the parties have implemented its provisions in good faith as required by international law.').

(2) Act of State

12.3. **The act of state doctrine, a rule of domestic not international law, gives effect to judicial restraint [§ 12.1]. The terminology 'act of**

state' is remains the most convenient shorthand expression in this context to describe the non-justiciability in domestic courts of acts of a *foreign* state which occur in the territory of a foreign state, or exceptionally, outside it. The phrase is sometimes (but not here) confusingly used to describe a separate doctrine, relating to the non-justiciability of *domestic* acts of state, for example, making war and peace and entering into treaties [§ 8.5].

12.3.1. Act of state is a principle of domestic law:

- *R v Bow Street Magistrate, Ex parte Pinochet* [2000] 1 AC 61 (HL), 106G (Lord Nicholls: 'Nineteenth century dicta (for example, in *Duke of Brunswick v King of Hanover,* 2 H.L.Cas. 1. . . .) suggested that [the act of state doctrine] reflected a rule of international law. The modern view is that the principle is one of domestic law.').

12.3.2. Act of state gives effect to judicial restraint:

- *Kuwait Airways Corp v Iraqi Airways Co (Nos 4 and 5)* [2002] 2 AC 883 (HL), [135] (Lord Hope: 'The rule [act of state] gives effect to a policy of "judicial restraint or abstention" ').

12.3.3. Act of state applies to the acts of a foreign state within its territory:

- *Buttes Gas and Oil Co v Hammer (No 3)* [1982] AC 888 (HL), 934B (Lord Wilberforce describing the 'normal meaning' of act of state: 'action taken by a foreign sovereign state within its own territory.');
- *Kuwait Airways Corp v Iraqi Airways Co (Nos 4 and 5)* [2002] UKHL 19 [2002] 2 AC 883, [135] (Lord Hope: 'There is no doubt as to the general effect of the rule which is known as the act of state rule. It applies to the legislative or other governmental acts of a recognised foreign state or government within the limits of its own territory. The English courts will not adjudicate upon, or call into question, any such acts.');
- *Jones v The Ministry of the Interior Al-Mamlaka Al-Arabiya* [2004] EWCA Civ 1394 [2005] UKHRR 57, [10] (Mance LJ noting that authorities on state immunity require that courts 'should respect, and not interfere in, a foreign sovereign state's conduct of its affairs, particularly within its territorial jurisdiction' and that this consideration is at the root of different principles falling under the headings of act of state and justiciability.);
- *Luther v Sagor* [1921] 3 KB 532 (CA), 548F–H (Warrington LJ: 'It is well settled that the validity of the acts of an independent sovereign government in relation to property and persons within its jurisdiction cannot be questioned in the Courts of this country.');
- *Princess Paley Olga v Weisz* [1929] 1 KB 718 (CA), 725 (Scrutton LJ considering that: '[O]ur Courts are bound to give effect to the laws and acts of [the Russian Government] so far as they relate to property within that jurisdiction when it was affected by those laws and acts.'), see similarly 736D–E (Russell LJ);

- *Williams and Humbert Ltd v W & H Trade Marks (Jersey) Ltd* [1986] AC 368 (HL), 431C (Lord Templeman after referring to *Luther v Sagor* and *Princess Paley Olga* (see above): 'These authorities illustrate the principle that an English court will recognise the compulsory acquisition law of a foreign state and will recognise the change of title to property which has come under the control of the foreign state and will recognise the consequences of that change of title.');
- *Buck v Attorney-General* [1965] Ch 745 (CA), 770 (Diplock LJ: 'As a member of the family of nations, the Government of the United Kingdom (of which this court forms part of the judicial branch) observes the rules of comity, videlicet, the accepted rules of mutual conduct as between state and state which each state adopts in relation to other states and expects other states to adopt in relation to itself. One of those rules is that it does not purport to exercise jurisdiction over the internal affairs of any other independent state, or to apply measures of coercion to it or to its property, except in accordance with rules of public international law.'), see similarly 768 (Harman LJ).

Illustrations:

- *R v Secretary of State for the Home Department, Ex parte Johnson* [1999] QB 1174 (DC), 1186F (Bell J: 'Once the Secretary of State has material which he is entitled to treat as consent to re-extradition for the purposes of article 15 [of the European Convention on Extradition] the court cannot, in my view, inquire into the quality of that consent without transgressing the principle which prevents assessment of the validity of the act of a sovereign state [here, Austria] done abroad by sovereign authority.');
- *Salaman v Secretary of State in Council of India* [1906] 1 KB 613 (CA) (the East India Company, representing the Crown, annexed the territory of a native State (Lahore), confiscated State property, granted a pension for life to the Maharajah of the State (then an infant), assumed custody over the Maharajah during his minority and took his private property. The Court of Appeal held that these acts were done in the exercise of supreme power as acts of state; the validity of which could not be challenged in the municipal courts and regarding which no action was maintainable).

12.3.4. **Act of state may exceptionally include the acts of a foreign state outside its territory:**

- *R v Bow Street Magistrate, Ex parte Pinochet* [2000] 1 AC 61 (HL), 106F (Lord Nicholls: 'The act of state doctrine is a common law principle of uncertain application which prevents the English court from examining the legality of certain acts performed in the exercise of sovereign authority within a foreign country or, occasionally outside it.');
- *Banca Carige v Banco Nacional de Cuba* [2001] 3 All ER 923 (ChD), [29] (Lightman J: 'Distinct from the doctrine of sovereign

immunity, there is a rule of law requiring municipal courts to exercise judicial restraint in the exercise of jurisdiction in respect of sovereign acts of a state or a separate entity of a state within a state's own territory or outside it and which leads to a form of immunity "rationae materiae" i.e. by reason of the subject-matter . . . It is far from being a principle of overwhelming applicability and is sensitive to the issues in a given case.').

12.3.5. **Act of state applies to de jure and de facto foreign states:**

- *Luther v Sagor* [1921] 3 KB 532 (CA), 551A–C (Warrington LJ: '[I]n my opinion there is no difference for the present purpose between a government recognised as such de jure and one recognised de facto. In the latter case, as well as in the former, the government in question acquires the right to be treated by the recognising state as an independent sovereign state.');
- *Adams v Adams* [1971] P 188, 211E (Sir Jocelyn Simon P: 'Where one has a sovereign legislature continuously in session, it seems to me in every way preferable to leave it to The Queen in Parliament to decide how far recognition should be accorded to executive, judicial or legislative acts of organs of government which are non de jure.');
- *Mighell v Sultan of Johore* [1894] 1 QB 149 (CA), 158 (Lord Esher MR: 'When once there is the authoritative certificate of the Queen through her minister of state as to the status of another sovereign, that in the Courts of this country is decisive.') (cited in *Luther v Sagor* [1921] 3 KB 532 (CA), 556D (Scrutton LJ)).

12.3.6. **The terminology of 'act of state':**

- *R v Bow Street Magistrate, Ex parte Pinochet (No 3)* [2000] 1 AC 147 (HL), 269H (Lord Millett considering the difference between state immunity and act of state: 'As I understand the difference between them, state immunity is a creature of international law and operates as a plea in bar to the jurisdiction of the national court, whereas the act of state doctrine is a rule of domestic law which holds the national court incompetent to adjudicate upon the lawfulness of sovereign acts of a foreign state.');
- *Attorney-General v Nissan* [1970] AC 179 (HL), 211G–212B (Lord Reid: 'I think that a good deal of trouble has been caused by using the loose phrase "act of state" without making clear what is meant. Sometimes it seems to be used to denote any act of sovereign power or high policy or any act done in the execution of a treaty. That is a possible definition, but then it must be observed that there are many such acts which can be the subject of an action in court if they infringe the rights of British subjects. Sometimes it seems to be used to denote acts which cannot be made the subject of inquiry in a British court. But that does not tell us how to distinguish such acts: it is only a name for a class which has still to be defined.' At 212F: 'I think we must say either that all acts of the

executive are acts of state, or that acts of the executive should only be called acts of state in cases where the court will not inquire into them or give relief in respect of them, but should not be called acts of state when the court's jurisdiction is not ousted.'), 237F–238A (Lord Pearson considering the definition of acts of state and their nature).

12.3.7 **Non-justiciable acts of the domestic executive** [§ **8.5**]:

- *Council of Civil Service Unions v Minster for the Civil Service* [1985] AC 374 (HL), 398 (Lord Fraser), 407 (Lord Scarman), 411 (Lord Diplock) (all considering that the subject-matter of executive power and not its source determines justiciability) [§ **8.5.2**];
- *R v Secretary of State for Foreign and Commonwealth Affairs, Ex parte Ferhut Butt* (1999) 116 ILR 607, 615 (Lightman J in the High Court, at [12], on the rule that courts should not interfere in the executive's conduct of foreign relations: 'This extends to decisions whether or not to seek to persuade a foreign government of any international obligation (e.g. to respect human rights) which it has assumed. What if any approach should be made to the Yemeni authorities in regard to the conduct of the trial of these terrorist charges must be a matter for delicate diplomacy and the considered and informed judgment of the FCO. In such matters the courts have no supervisory role.'), 622 (Henry LJ in the CA: 'Whether and when to seek to interfere or to put pressure on in relation to the legal process, if ever it is a sensible and a right thing to do, must be a matter for the Executive and no one else, with their access to information and to local knowledge. It is clearly not a matter for the courts. It is clearly a high policy decision of a government in relation to its foreign relations and is not justiciable by way of judicial review.');
- *R (Abbasi) v Secretary of State for Foreign and Commonwealth Affairs* [2002] EWCA Civ 1598 [2003] UKHRR 76, [28–36] (Lord Phillips MR considering the justiciability of executive action in the conduct of foreign affairs);
- *R v Secretary of State for Foreign and Commonwealth Affairs, Ex parte Pirbhai* (1985) 107 ILR 462 (CA), 479 (Sir John Donaldson MR: '[I]n the context of a situation with serious implications for the conduct of international relations, the courts should act with a high degree of circumspection in the interests of all concerned. It can rarely, if ever, be for judges to intervene where diplomats fear to tread.');
- *Lewis v Attorney-General of Jamaica* [2001] 2 AC 50 (PC), 77B (Lord Slynn: 'Although in some areas the exercise of the prerogative may be beyond review, such as treaty-making and declaring war, there are many areas in which the exercise of the prerogative is subject to judicial review.');
- *West Rand Central Gold Mining Co Ltd v The King* [1905] 2 KB 391 (DC), 408–409 (Lord Alverstone CJ: 'There is a series of

authorities from the year 1763 down to the present time holding that matters which fall properly to be determined by the Crown by treaty or as an act of State are not subject to the jurisdiction of the municipal Courts, and that rights supposed to be acquired thereunder cannot be enforced by such Courts').

Illustrations:

- *R v Foreign Secretary, Ex parte Everett* [1989] 1 QB 811 (CA), 820 (Taylor LJ, discussing *Council of Civil Service Unions v Minster for the Civil Service* (see above): 'The majority of their Lordships indicated that whether judicial review of the exercise of a prerogative power is open depends upon the subject matter and in particular upon whether it is justiciable. At the top of the scale of executive functions under the prerogative are matters of high policy, of which examples were given by their Lordships; making treaties, making war, dissolving Parliament, mobilising the armed forces. Clearly those matters, and no doubt a number of others are not justiciable. But the grant or refusal of a passport is in quite a different category. It is a matter of administrative decision affecting the rights of individuals and their freedom of travel. It raises issues which are just as justiciable as, for example, the issues arising in immigration cases.');
- *Jones & Milling, Olditch & Pritchard v Gloucestershire CPS* [2004] EWCA Crim 1981 [2004] 3 WLR 1362, [13–14] (Latham LJ distinguishing the non-justiciability finding regarding the legality of the Iraq war in *CND v The Prime Minister* [2002] EWHC 2777 (Admin) on the basis, in part, that no declaratory judgment was sought in the present case and that the defendants were seeking to obtain the court's ruling on a matter which affected their rights and duties under domestic law. The issue of non-justiciability did not require to be dealt with substantively because of the court's findings in other parts of the case. In the Bristol Crown Court 12 May 2004 (unreported) (Grigson J considered that the issue of the legality of the Iraq war was not justiciable in domestic courts because the United Kingdom Government was exercising its prerogative powers in relation to foreign policy and the deployment of armed forces into which the court would not inquire. *Jones* applied in *Ayliffe v Director of Public Prosecutions* [2005] EWHC 684 (Admin)[2005] 3 All ER 330.);
- *Coverdale v Tony Blair PM* [2003] EWCA Civ 436, [7] (Buxton LJ pointing out two 'insuperable difficulties' in claims that a war on Iraq by military force would be illegal and that the activities of the United Kingdom and United States in the 'No Fly Zones' in Iraq were illegal: 'First, the foreign relations of this country, and in particular decisions about the waging of war, are an act of the prerogative of a kind the courts have never interfered with and do not see themselves as having jurisdiction to address. Secondly, our courts will not interpret or give rulings under instruments of international law unless there is a question of domestic law

directly involved.' Citing as authority, at [9], *CND v The Prime Minister* [2002] EWHC 2777 (Admin), [37] [§ **8.7.1**]).

12.4. **Act of state does not prevent domestic courts from simply taking cognisance of a foreign act of state where there is no need to investigate or pass judgment on it.**

Illustrations:

- *Salaman v Secretary of State in Council of India* [1906] 1 KB 613 (CA), 639C–640B (Fletcher Moulton LJ: 'An act of State is essentially an exercise of sovereign power, and hence cannot be challenged, controlled, or interfered with by municipal Courts. Its sanction is not that of the law but of sovereign power, and, whatever it be, municipal Courts must accept it, as it is, without question. But it may, and often must, be part of their duty to take cognizance of it. For instance, if an act is relied upon as being an act of State, and as thus affording an answer to claims made by a subject, the Courts must decide whether it was in truth an act of State, and what was its nature and extent . . . But in such an inquiry the Court must confine itself to ascertaining what the act of State in fact was, and not what in its opinion it ought to have been. In like manner municipal Courts may have to consider the results of acts of State, i.e., their effects on the rights of individuals, and even of the Government itself. Acts of State are not all of one kind; their nature and consequences may differ in an infinite variety of ways, and these differences may profoundly affect the position of municipal Courts with regard to them . . . [The] intention and effect [of an act of State] may be to modify and create rights between the Government and individuals, who are, or who are about to become, subjects of the Government. In such cases the rights accruing therefrom may have to be adjudicated upon by municipal Courts.');
- *R v Bow Street Magistrate, Ex parte Pinochet* [2000] 1 AC 61 (HL), 117B (Lord Steyn considering that the act of state doctrine was inapplicable because 'the House is not being asked to investigate, or pass judgment on, the facts . . . The task of the House is simply to take note of the allegations and to consider and decide the legal issues of immunity and act of state.'), *cf* 103H (Lord Lloyd (dissenting): '[I]t is said that by allowing the extradition request to proceed, we will not be adjudicating ourselves . . . But we will be taking an essential step towards allowing the trial to take place.') *cf* [§ **12.12.1**].

(3) Execeptions to the Act of State Doctrine

12.5. **There are three well-recognised exceptions to the act of state doctrine which result in its displacement and make acts of a foreign state amenable to adjudication by domestic courts. First, act of state will not generally defeat a claim which arises out of the alleged violation of fundamental human rights ('the human rights exception').**

- *Jones v The Ministry of the Interior Al-Mamlaka Al-Arabiya* [2004] EWCA Civ 1394 [2005] UKHRR 57, [90] (Mance LJ: '[W]hile the courts of one state should not lightly adjudicate upon the internal affairs of another state, there are many circumstances, particularly in the context of human rights, when national courts do have to consider and form a view on the position in or conduct of foreign states. There are also further and different principles (the doctrine of act of state in particular) which require courts to refrain from adjudication in which no manageable standards exist to enable such adjudication . . . But allegations of systematic torture are by themselves unlikely to raise such considerations.');
- *R (Abbasi) v Secretary of State for Foreign and Commonwealth Affairs* [2002] EWCA Civ 1598 [2003] UKHRR 76, [57] (Lord Phillips, considering that Lord Cross's speech in *Oppenheimer v Cattermole* [1976] AC 249 (at 277G) supports the view that a domestic court does not need a statutory context in order to be free to express a view in relation to what it conceives to be a clear breach of international law, particularly in the context of human rights. At [58–67] taking cognisance of the acts of the United States executive detaining the claimant without trial in Guantanamo Bay and at [64] finding that those acts are, 'in apparent contravention of fundamental principles recognised by both [British and American] jurisdictions and by international law, Mr Abbasi is at present arbitrarily detained in a "legal black hole".');
- *R v Bow Street Magistrate, Ex parte Pinochet* [2000] 1 AC 61 (HL), 117B (Lord Steyn: '[T]he issue of act of state must be approached on the basis that the intent of Parliament was not to give statutory immunity to a former head of state in respect of the systematic torture and killing of his fellow citizens. The ground of this conclusion is that such high crimes are not official acts committed in the exercise of the functions of a head of state. In those circumstances it cannot be right for the House to enunciate an enlarged act of state doctrine, stretching far beyond anything said in the *Buttes Gas* case.' At 117F–H: 'I would endorse the observation in *American Law Institute, Restatement of the Law, The Foreign Relations Law of the United States,* 3d (1986), vol.1, section 443,

p.370, to the effect that: "A claim arising out of an alleged violation of fundamental human rights—for instance, a claim on behalf of a victim of torture or genocide—would (if otherwise sustainable) probably not be defeated by the act of state doctrine, since the accepted international law of human rights is well established and contemplates external scrutiny of such acts." But in adopting this formulation I would remove the word "probably" and substitute "generally".').

12.6. **Secondly, act of state will be displaced where Parliament has made a particular issue justiciable ('the statutory exception').**

- *R v Bow Street Magistrate, Ex parte Pinochet* [2000] 1 AC 61 (HL), 107B–C (Lord Nicholls: '[T]here can be no doubt that [the act of state doctrine] yields to a contrary intention shown by Parliament. Where Parliament has shown that a particular issue is to be justiciable in the English courts, there can be no place for courts to apply this self-denying principle.' At 107C–D giving the example of the definition of torture in section 134 of the Criminal Justice Act 1988, which makes it clear that the prosecution will require an investigation into the conduct of officials acting in an official capacity in foreign countries. It follows that Parliament did not intend the act of state rule to apply in such circumstances), 117D (Lord Steyn: '[A]ny act of state doctrine is displaced by section 134(1) of the Criminal Justice Act 1988 in relation to torture and section 1(1) of the Taking of Hostages Act 1982. Both Acts provide for the taking of jurisdiction over foreign governmental acts.').

12.7. **Thirdly, and overlapping with the first, human rights, exception, domestic courts may disregard foreign legislation where it is contrary to English public policy ('the public policy exception'). The circumstances in which domestic courts are required to consider foreign legislation are fairly restricted (for example in conflict of laws cases where the foreign municipal law is the applicable law). Within this limited ambit, the operation of the public policy exception is, itself, narrow.**

- *Buttes Gas and Oil Co v Hammer (No 3)* [1982] AC 888 (HL), 931D (Lord Wilberforce: 'It is one thing to assert that effect will not be given to a foreign municipal law or executive act if it is contrary to public policy, or to international law . . . and quite another to claim that the courts may examine the validity, under international law, of some doctrine of public policy, of an act or acts operating in the area of transactions between states'.);
- *Kuwait Airways Corp v Iraqi Airways Co (Nos 4 and 5)* [2002] UKHL 19 [2002] 2 AC 883, [138] (Lord Hope: 'It is clear that very

narrow limits must be placed on any exception to the act of state rule . . . a judge should be slow to refuse to give effect to the legislation of a foreign state in any sphere in which, according to accepted principles of international law, the foreign state has jurisdiction. Among these accepted principles is that which is founded on the comity of nations . . . A judge should be slow to depart from these principles. He may have an inadequate understanding of the circumstances in which the legislation was passed. His refusal to recognise it may be embarrassing to the executive, whose function is so far as possible to maintain friendly relations with foreign states.' At [140], considering the golden rule, that the public policy exception must not be applied: 'beyond the true limits of the principle. These limits demand that, where there is any room for doubt, judicial restraint must be exercised. But restraint is what is needed, not abstention.'), [114] (Lord Steyn considering the limited notion of public policy);

- *Vervaeke v Smith* [1983] 1 AC 145 (HL), 164C–E (Lord Simon determining that a Belgian decree of nullity should not be recognised on the basis that upholding the status of marriage was a doctrine of English public policy even where the marriage was entered into for extraneous purposes: 'There is abundant authority that an English court will decline to recognise or apply what would otherwise be the appropriate foreign rule of law when to do so would be against English public policy; although the court will be even slower to invoke public policy in the field of conflict of laws than where a purely municipal legal issue is involved. There is little authority for refusing, on the ground of public policy, to recognise an otherwise conclusive foreign judgment . . . interest reipublicae ut sit finis litium, the "commonwealth" in conflict of laws extending to the whole international community. Nevertheless, there is some judicial authority that the English court will in an appropriate case refuse on ground of public policy to accord recognition to the judgment of a foreign court of competent jurisdiction.').

Illustrations:

- *Luther v Sagor* [1921] 3 KB 532 (CA) (agents of the Soviet Republic seized the plaintiff's sawmill and stock of wood, pursuant to a 1918 decree confiscating sawmills, and sold it to the defendant who imported it into England. The plaintiff sought a declaration that it was entitled to this stock, the 1918 decree being so immoral and contrary to the English principles of justice that English courts should disregard it. The Court of Appeal held that since the British Government recognised the Soviet Government as the de facto government prior to the 1918 decree, neither the decree nor the sale of wood could be impugned in English courts), 558–559 (Scrutton LJ: 'But it appears a serious breach of international comity, if a state is recognised as a sovereign independent state, to postulate that its legislation is "contrary to essential principles of justice and morality." Such an allegation might well with a susceptible foreign government become a casus belli; and should in my view be the action of the Sovereign through his ministers, and not of the judges in reference to a state which their Sovereign has recognised.');

- *In re Claim by Helbert Wagg & Co Ltd* [1956] Ch 323, 349A–D (Upjohn J: 'In my judgment the true limits of the principle that the courts of this country will afford recognition to legislation of foreign States in so far as it affects title to movables in that State at the time of the legislation or contracts governed by the law of that State rests in considerations of international law, or in the scarcely less difficult considerations of public policy as understood in these courts. Ultimately I believe the latter is the governing consideration. But, whatever be the true view, the authorities I have reviewed do show that these courts have not on either ground recognised any principle that confiscation without adequate compensation is per se a ground for refusing recognition to foreign legislation.').

12.8. **In deciding whether or not foreign legislation is contrary to public policy courts should not embark on an independent and unfettered appraisal of what constitutes public policy.**

> 'Courts are concerned with public policy only in so far as it has been manifested by parliamentary sanction or embodied in rules of law having binding judicial force. As to such rules of law your Lordships have the same power to declare, to bind and to loose as in regard to any other judicial precedent. Rules of law expressing principles of public policy therefore fall to be treated with the same respect and circumspection, the same common sense and regard to changing circumstances, as any other rules of law.' (*Blathwayt v Cawley* [1976] AC 397 (HL), 427F–H (Lord Simon))

12.9. **Whether or not provisions of a foreign law are to be disregarded as contrary to English public policy is assessed by reference to contemporary standards, commensurate with the idea that public policy should move with the times. Widely accepted treaties and statutes may indicate the course in which such conceptions ought to move. Public policy includes the safeguarding of human rights and of giving effect to clearly established rules of international law, thus the overlap between the public policy exception and the human rights exception [§ 12.5]. Not all breaches of international law will fall within the public policy exception. It must be possible, for example, for courts to assess the issues by reference to judicial and manageable standards.**

12.9.1. **Public policy as a contemporary standard:**

- *Blathwayt v Cawley* [1976] AC 397 (HL), 426A–B (Lord Wilberforce considering the changing nature of public policy and that widely accepted treaties and statutes may guide its development);
- *Fender v St John-Mildmay* [1938] 1 AC 1 (HL), 23 (Lord Thankerton: '[T]he proper function of the courts in questions of public policy . . . is to expound, and not to expand, such policy. That does not mean that they are precluded from applying an existing principle of public policy to a new set of circumstances, where such circumstances are clearly within the scope of the policy.').

12.9.2. **Human rights as part of public policy:**

- *Oppenheimer v Cattermole* [1976] AC 249 (HL), 263E–F (Lord Hailsham considering that English law may not give a single and unequivocal answer to the problems raised by the unjust and discriminatory legislation of a foreign country and referring to the examples of: *Luther v Sagor* [1921] 3 KB 532; *Princess Paley Olga v Weisz* [1929] 1 KB 718; *Frankfurter v W L Exner Ltd* [1947] Ch 629 and *Novello & Co Ltd v Hinrichsen Edition Ltd* [1951] Ch 595), 278C (Lord Cross: '[A] law of this sort [which takes away property from citizens on a racial basis, without compensation, and deprives them of their citizenship] constitutes so grave an infringement of human rights that the courts of this country ought to refuse to recognise it as a law at all.') [§ **12.9.3**], 282E–283F (Lord Salmon comparing the facts in *Oppenheimer* and *Luther v Sagor*).

12.9.3. **Clearly established rules of international law are part of public policy:**

- *Oppenheimer v Cattermole* [1976] AC 249 (HL), 265D (Lord Hodson: 'The courts of this country are not . . . obliged to shut their eyes to the shocking nature of such legislation as the 1941 decree if and when it falls for consideration'), 277H–278A (Lord Cross agreeing with Upjohn J in *In re Claim by Helbert Wagg & Co. Ltd* [1956] Ch 323, 334: 'that it is part of the public policy of this country that our courts should give effect to clearly established rules of international law. Of course on some points it may be by no means clear what the rule of international law is . . . But what we are concerned with here is legislation which takes away without compensation from a section of the citizen body singled out on racial grounds all their property on which the state passing the legislation can lay its hands and, in addition, deprives them of their citizenship. To my mind a law of this sort constitutes so grave an infringement of human rights that the courts of this country ought to refuse to recognise it as a law at all.' At 278A–B: '[I]t is part of the public policy of this country that our courts should give effect to clearly established rules of international law'.);

- *Kuwait Airways Corp v Iraqi Ariways Co (Nos 4 and 5)* [2002] UKHL 19 [2002] 2 AC 883, [28] (Lord Nicholls, referring to Lord Cross's statement in *Oppenheimer v Cattermole* [1976] AC 249 (HL), 278A–B (see above), that the courts of this country should give effect to clearly established rules of international law: 'This is increasingly true today. As nations become ever more interdependent, the need to recognise and adhere to standards of conduct set by international law becomes ever more important.' At [24–26] rejecting the submission that the public policy exception is limited to infringements of human rights and stating that in appropriate circumstances English courts may consider the content of international law in deciding whether to disregard a foreign law), [114] (Lord Steyn considering that in assessing whether or not a foreign law is contrary to domestic policy, a relevant factor may be that recognising the foreign law not only violates public international law but will put the United Kingdom in breach of its international obligations);
- *Buttes Gas and Oil Co v Hammer (No 3)* [1982] AC 888 (HL), 931D (Lord Wilberforce) [**§ 12.7**];

Illustration:

- *Kuwait Airways Corp v Iraqi Airways Co (Nos 4 and 5)* [2002] UKHL 19 [2002] 2 AC 883 (after Iraq invaded and occupied Kuwait in 1990 the defendant, IAC, was directed by the Iraqi Government to fly 10 of KAC's aircraft out of Iraq. The Iraqi Government later passed RCC Resolution 369, purporting to dissolve KAC and transfer its assets to IAC. Subsequently, IAC treated the aircraft as its own. In military action by the UN against Iraq, four of KAC's aircraft were destroyed. The other six aircraft were evacuated to Iran where they were impounded and, in 1992, returned to KAC on payment to Iran of US$20m. KAC sought damages from IAC under section 3 of the Torts (Interference with Goods) Act 1977 and at common law. The House of Lords held that RCC Resolution 369 was to be disregarded as contrary to English public policy. This case arose on 'highly unusual' facts where there was a 'flagrant' and acknowledged breach of international law ([135], [148–149] (Lord Hope)). The 'standard applied by the court [was] clear and manageable, and the outcome not in doubt'; there was 'nothing precarious or delicate, and nothing subject to diplomacy, which judicial adjudication might threaten', nor did the court need to defer to the foreign state because it had an inadequate understanding of the circumstances in which the foreign law was passed ([26] (Lord Nicholls), [146–147] (Lord Hope)), [29] (Lord Nicholls: 'A breach of international law of this seriousness is a matter of deep concern to the worldwide community of nations . . . Such a fundamental breach of international law can properly cause the courts of this country to say that . . . a law depriving those whose property has been plundered of the ownership of their property in favour of the aggressor's own citizens will not be enforced or recognised in proceedings in this country. Enforcement or recognition of this law would be manifestly contrary to the public policy of English law. For good measure, enforcement or recognition would also be contrary to this country's obligations under the UN Charter.')

12.9.4. **Judicial or manageable standards needed when assessing international law issues:**

- *Buttes Gas and Oil Co v Hammer (No 3)* [1982] AC 888 (HL), 938B–C (Lord Wilberforce) [§ **12.2.1**];
- *Kuwait Airways Corp v Iraqi Airways Co (Nos 4 and 5)* [2002] UKHL 19 [2002] 2 AC 883, [114] (Lord Steyn stating that not every breach of public international law will trigger the public policy exception to act of state), [26] (Lord Nicholls) [§ **12.9.3**], [146–147] (Lord Hope) [§ **12.9.3**].

13

Customary International Law

(1) Introduction

13.1. **Established rules of customary international law [§§ 2.13–2.16] are welcomed into the corpus of domestic law. This reservoir, of an ever-expanding nature, is an important source of law. As Viscount Sankey, LC, observed, more than a half century ago:**

> 'International law . . . is a living and expanding code. In his treatise on international law, the English text-book writer Hall (1835–94) . . . says . . . : "Looking back over the last couple of centuries we see international law at the close of each fifty years in a more solid position than that which it occupied at the beginning of the period. Progressively it has taken firmer hold, it has extended its sphere of operation, it has ceased to trouble itself about trivial formalities, it has more and more dared to grapple in detail with the fundamental facts in the relations of States. The area within which it reigns beyond dispute has in that time been infinitely enlarged, and it has been greatly enlarged within the memory of living man".' (*In re Piracy Jure Gentium* [1934] AC 586 (PC), 592G–593C).

13.2. **The nature of customary international law, and the corresponding difficulties of proof to which it may give rise, are pivotal to**

understanding the extent and the manner in which it may be used domestically [§§ 2.13–2.16]:

- *West Rand Central Gold Mining Co Ltd v The King* [1905] 2 KB 391 (DC), 401 (Lord Alverstone CJ: 'There is an essential difference, as to certainty and definiteness, between municipal law and a system or body of rules in regard to international conduct, which, so far as it exists at all (and its existence is assumed by the phrase "international law"), rests upon a consensus of civilised States, not expressed in any code or pact, nor possessing, in case of dispute, any authorised or authoritative interpreter; and capable, indeed, of proof, in the absence of some express international agreement, only by evidence of usage to be obtained from the action of nations in similar cases in the course of their history.');
- *Compania Naviera Vascongado v SS Cristina* [1938] AC 485 (HL), 497F–H (Lord Macmillan: 'Now it is a recognised prerequisite of the adoption in our municipal law of a doctrine of public international law that it shall have attained the position of general acceptance by civilised nations as a rule of international conduct, evidenced by international treaties and conventions, authoritative textbooks, practice and judicial decisions. It is manifestly of the highest importance that the Courts of this country before they give the force of law within this realm to any doctrine of international law should be satisfied that it has the hallmarks of general assent and reciprocity.');
- *R v Keyn* (1876) 2 Ex D 63, 153–154 (Lord Coleridge CJ: 'Strictly speaking, international law is an inexact expression, and it is apt to mislead if its inexactness is not kept in mind. Law implies a law-giver, and a tribunal capable of enforcing it and coercing its transgressors. But there is no common law-giver to sovereign states; and no tribunal has the power to bind them by decrees or coerce them if they transgress. The law of nations is that collection of usages which civilised nations have agreed to observe in their dealings with one another. What these usages are, whether a particular one has or has not been agreed to, must be [a] matter of evidence. Treaties and acts of state are but evidence of the agreement of nations, and do not in this country at least per se bind the tribunals. Neither, certainly, does a consensus of jurists; but it is evidence of the agreement of nations on international points; and on such points, when they arise, the English Courts give effect, as part of English law, to such agreement.');
- *Re Mckerr* [2004] UKHL 12 [2004] 1 WLR 807, [52] (Lord Steyn: 'The impact of evolving customary international law on our domestic legal system is a subject of increasing importance.').

(2) Customary International Law as Part of Domestic Law

13.3. **Theories about how customary international law becomes part of domestic law may be reduced to two key competing doctrines: the doctrine of incorporation (according to which customary international law is automatically received into domestic law unless it is inconsistent with express statutory provisions) and the doctrine of transformation (according to which customary international law only becomes part of domestic law upon formal adoption in statute, case law or custom).**

13.3.1. **The doctrine of incorporation:**

- *Trendtex Trading Corp v Central Bank of Nigeria* [1977] QB 529 (CA), 553 (Lord Denning: '[The doctrine of incorporation] says that the rules of international law are incorporated into English law automatically and considered to be part of English law unless they are in conflict with an Act of Parliament . . . The doctrine of incorporation goes back to 1737 in *Buvot v Barbut* (1736) 3 Burr 1481; 4 Burr 2016; sub nom *Barbuit's Case in Chancery* (1737) Forr 280, in which Lord Talbot LC . . . made a declaration which was taken down by young William Murray (who was of counsel in the case) and adopted by him in 1764 when he was Lord Mansfield CJ in *Triquet v Bath* (1764) 3 Burr 1478: "Lord Talbot declared a clear opinion—'That the law of nations in its full extent was part of the law of England . . . that the law of nations was to be collected from the practice of different nations and the authority of writers'." . . . That doctrine was accepted, not only by Lord Mansfield himself, but also by Sir William Blackstone, and other great names, too numerous to mention. In 1853 Lord Lyndhurst in the House of Lords, with the concurrence of all his colleagues there, declared that . . . "the law of nations, according to the decision of our greatest judges, is part of the law of England"'.).

Illustrations:

- *Emperor of Austria v Day and Kossuth* (1863) De G F & J 217, 251 (Turner LJ considering that the coining of money for use in Hungary without the consent of the Hungarian Government, 'was and is by the law of England, was and is by the law of nations, wrongful, is, I think, manifest, though whether by the law of England or the law of nations criminal as well as wrongful I think a question not for any present purposes material.');
- *De Wutz v Hendricks* (1824) 2 Bing 314, 315–316 (Best CJ: 'It occurred to me at the trial that it was contrary to the law of nations (which in all cases of international law is adopted into

the municipal code of every civilised country), for persons in England to enter into engagements to raise money to support the subjects of government in amity with our own, in hostilities against their government, and that no right of action could arise out of such a transaction.');

- *Novello v Toogood* (1823) 1 B & C 554, 562 (Abbott CJ: '[The Act of Parliament] must, therefore, be construed according to the common law, of which the law of nations must be deemed a part.');
- *Heathfield v Chilton* (1764) 4 Burr 2015, 2016 (Lord Mansfield: 'The privileges of public ministers and their retinue depend upon the law of nations; which is part of the common law of England. And the Act of Parliament of 7 Ann c.12, did not intend to alter, nor can alter the law of nations . . . The law of nations will be carried as far in England as any where.');
- *Triquet v Bath* (1764) 3 Burr 1478, 1481 (Lord Mansfield: 'I remember in a case before Lord Talbot, of *Buvot v Barbut* . . . Lord Talbot declared a clear opinion—"That the law of nations, in its full extent was part of the law of England"—"That the Act of Parliament was declaratory; and occasioned by a particular incident"—"That the law of nations was to be collected from the practice of different nations, and the authority of writers".');
- *Buvot v Barbut (sub nom. Barbuit's Case)* (1737) Cas Temp Talb 281 (Lord Talbot, LC considering that the 'privilege of a public minister . . . to have his person sacred and free from arrests . . . The question is whether the defendant [a consul] is such a person as *7 Anne, cap.*10 describes, which is only declaratory of the antient universal *jus gentium* . . .' and 'It is the opinion of *Barbeyrac, Wincquefort* and others, that a consul is not intitled to the *Jus Gentium* belonging to ambassadors.').

13.3.2. **The doctrine of transformation:**

- *Trendtex Trading Corp v Central Bank of Nigeria* [1977] QB 529 (CA), 553 (Lord Denning describing the doctrine of transformation: 'It says that the rules of international law are not to be considered as part of English law except in so far as they have been already adopted and made part of our law by the decisions of the judges, or by an Act of Parliament, or long established custom.');
- *Thai-Europe Tapioca Service Ltd v Government of Pakistan* [1975] 1 WLR 1485 (CA), 1495E–F (Scarman LJ: 'I think it is important to realise that a rule of international law, once incorporated into our law by decisions of a competent court, is not an inference of fact but a rule of law. It therefore becomes part of our municipal law and the doctrine of stare decisis applies as much to that as to a rule of law with a strictly munic-

ipal provenance. This has been stated again and again . . . and it is to be found I think by necessary implication in the speech of Lord Macmillan in *The Cristina* [1938] AC 485, 497 [see below] . . . I think therefore that it is not open to this court to apply a new rule or view developing in the international field if it be inconsistent with a rule already incorporated into our law by a decision of the Court of Appeal or the House of Lords.');

- *R v Secretary of State for the Home Department, Ex parte Thakrar* [1974] QB 684 (CA), 701F–G (Lord Denning MR, on the statement that the law of nations is 'part of the law of the land' (William Blackstone, *Commentaries*, 17th edn (1830), Book IV, p 67; Lord Mansfield in *Heathfield v Chilton* (1767) 4 Burr. 2016): '[T]hey were speaking of the law of nations, and then only of that part of it which was universally accepted and known for certain, such as the immunity of ambassadors. They were not speaking of rules which were not universally accepted or known for certain. In my opinion, the rules of international law only become part of our law in so far as they are accepted and adopted by us.');
- *Chung Chi Cheung v The King* [1939] AC 160 (JC), 167H–168C (Lord Atkin: 'It must always be remembered that, so far, at any rate, as the Courts of this country are concerned, international law has no validity save in so far as its principles are accepted and adopted by our own domestic law. There is no external power that imposes its rules upon our own code of substantive law or procedure. The Courts acknowledge the existence of a body of rules which nations accept among themselves. On any judicial issue they seek to ascertain what the relevant rule is, and having found it, they will treat it as incorporated into the domestic law, so far as it is not inconsistent with rules enacted by statutes or finally declared by their tribunals.');
- *Compania Naviera Vascongado v SS Cristina* [1938] AC 485 (HL), 497D–H (Lord Macmillan: '"It is a trite observation that there is no such thing as a standard of international law extraneous to the domestic law of a kingdom, to which appeal may be made. International law, so far as this Court is concerned, is the body of doctrine regarding the international rights and duties of states which has been adopted and made part of the law of Scotland." These are the well chosen words of Lord Dunedin, when Lord President of the Court of Session in Scotland, in a case which raised important issues of international law: *Mortensen v Peters* [(1906) 8 F (JC) 93, 101].');
- *Commercial and Estates Co of Egypt v The Board of Trade* [1925] 1 KB 271 (CA), 295F–G (Atkin LJ: 'International law as such can confer no rights cognizable in the municipal Courts. It is only in so far as the rules of international law are recognized as included in the rules of the municipal law that they are allowed

in the municipal Courts to give rise to rights or obligations.'), 283A–F (Bankes LJ);

- *West Rand Central Gold Mining Co Ltd v The King* [1905] 2 KB 391 (DC), 406–407 (Lord Alverstone CJ) [§ **2.13**];
- *R v Keyn* (1876) 2 Ex D 63, 202–203 (Cockburn CJ: 'For writers on international law, however valuable their labours may be in elucidating and ascertaining the principles and rules of law, cannot make the law. To be binding, the law must have received the assent of nations who are to be bound by it . . . Nor, in my opinion, would the clearest proof of unanimous assent on the part of other nations be sufficient to authorize the tribunals of this country to apply, without an Act of Parliament, what would practically amount to a new law. In so doing, we should be unjustifiably usurping the province of the legislature.').

13.4. **Practical considerations make the doctrine of incorporation preferable to the doctrine of transformation. Suppose that a rule of customary international law is proved and accepted into domestic law. Once it is part of domestic law, the doctrine of transformation subjects it to the usual domestic rules of stare decisis, ie the rule of customary international law must continue to be applied by lower courts until overruled or changed by a court at the same/higher level than the one initially accepting it into domestic law. By comparison, the doctrine of incorporation does not subject rules of customary international law accepted as part of domestic law to the rules of precedent. It permits changes in international law to be reflected in domestic law without first requiring the previous law to be overruled. This flexibility commends the doctrine of incorporation and is the principal reason that it has prevailed as the accepted route for customary international law into domestic law since the 1970s.**

13.4.1. **Comparing the doctrines of incorporation and transformation:**

- *Trendtex Trading Corp v Central Bank of Nigeria* [1977] QB 529 (CA), 553 (Lord Denning: 'The difference is vital when you are faced with a change in the rules of international law. Under the doctrine of incorporation, when the rules of international law change, our English law changes with them. But, under the doctrine of transformation, the English law does not change. It is bound by precedent. It is bound down to those rules of international law which have been accepted and adopted in the past. It cannot develop as international law develops.'), 569 (Stephenson LJ: '[A passage from Lord Alverstone in *West Rand Central Gold Mining Co. Ltd v The King* [1905] 2 KB 391 at 406–408] suggests that the differences between the two schools of thought are more apparent than real . . . for it is the nature of international law and the special problems of ascertaining it which create the difficulty in the way of adopting, or incorporating, or recognising as already incorporated, a new rule of international law . . . rules of international law, whether they be part of our law or a source of our law, must be in some sense "proved," and they are not proved in English courts by expert evidence like foreign law: they are "proved" by taking judicial notice of "international treaties and conventions, authoritative textbooks, practice and judicial decisions" of other courts in other countries which show that they have "attained the position of general acceptance by civilised nations": *The Cristina* [1938] AC 485, 497 per Lord Macmillan: and those sources come seldom if ever from every civilised nation or agree upon a universal rule; they move from one generally accepted rule towards another.');

- *West Rand Central Gold Mining Co Ltd v The King* [1905] 2 KB 391 (DC), 406–407 (Lord Alverstone) [§ **2.13**];
- *Thai-Europe Tapioca Service Ltd v Government of Pakistan* [1975] 1 WLR 1485 (CA), 1495E–F (Scarman LJ) [§ **13.3.2**].

13.4.2. **The prevailing view: the doctrine of incorporation:**

- *Trendtex Trading Corp v Central Bank of Nigeria* [1977] QB 529 (CA), 554 (Lord Denning: 'As between these two schools of thought, I now believe that the doctrine of incorporation is correct. Otherwise I do not see that our courts could ever recognise a change in the rules of international law . . . International law does change: and the courts have applied the changes without the aid of any Act of Parliament . . . it follows to my mind inexorably that the rules of international law, as existing from time to time, do form part of our English law. It follows, too, that a decision of this court—as to what was the rule of international law 50 or 60 years ago—is not binding on this court today. International law knows no rule of stare decisis.'), 578–579 (Shaw LJ, after considering the inadequacies of the doctrine of transformation: 'May it not be that the true principle as to the application of international law is that the English courts must at any given time discover what the prevailing international rule is and apply that rule? . . . What *is* immutable is the principle of English law that the law of nations (not what was the law of nations) must be applied in the courts of England. The rule of stare decisis operates to preclude a court from overriding a decision which binds it in regard to a particular rule of (international) law, it does not prevent a court from applying a rule which did not exist when the earlier decision was made if the new rule has had the effect in international law of extinguishing the old rule.');

- *JH Rayner (Mincing Lane) Ltd v Department of Trade and Industry* [1989] Ch 72 (CA), 207B–E (Nourse LJ: 'For up to two and a half centuries it has been generally accepted amongst English judges and jurists that international law forms part of the law of this country, at all events if it can be shown that there is an established rule which, first, is derived from one or more of the recognised sources of international law and, secondly, has already been carried into English law by statute, judicial decision or ancient custom . . . Beyond this common ground there was formerly a significant difference of opinion. The doctrine of transformation had a rival in the doctrine of incorporation . . . That rivalry was resolved in favour of incorporation by the decision of this court . . . *Trendtex Trading Corporation v Central Bank of Nigeria* [1977] QB 529.'). Nb. the second requirement, regarding rules of customary international law, considered by Nourse LJ has been regarded as 'doubtful' on the basis that: 'Whilst clearly its recognition by statute will ipso facto give it effect, in so far as it is suggested that there must be either a previous judicial decision or ancient custom, in other words, in effect, some clear acceptance by the court of the existence of the rule as part of English law, that would emasculate the principle. It would in effect prevent any clearly established rule of international law from becoming part of English law other than by statute.' (*Jones & Milling, Olditch & Pritchard v Gloucestershire CPS* [2004] EWCA Crim 1981 [2004] 3 WLR 1362, [24] (Latham LJ));
- *Jones & Milling, Olditch & Pritchard v Gloucestershire CPS* [2004] EWCA Crim 1981 [2004] 3 WLR 1362, [24] (Latham LJ, after citing *Blackstone's Commentaries on the Law of England,* Lord Alverstone CJ in *West Rand* (see above), Lord Denning in *Trendtex* (see above), and Nourse LJ in *JH Rayner* (see above)*:* 'There is no doubt, therefore, that a rule of international law is capable of being incorporated into English law if it is an established rule derived from one or more of the recognised sources, that [there] is a clear consensus, evidenced by the writings of scholars or otherwise, or by treaty . . . In our view, the question as to whether or not a rule of international law forms part of English law is governed by the principle of certainty.');
- *cf I Congreso del Partido* [1983] 1 AC 244 (HL), 261H–262A (Lord Wilberforce after referring to *Trendtex* (see above) as authority favouring the restrictive theory of sovereign immunity: 'The case was not appealed to this House, and since there may be appeals in analogous cases it is perhaps right to avoid commitment to more of the admired judgment of Lord Denning MR than is necessary.').

13.5. **Before a rule of customary international law can be accepted as part of domestic law it must be shown to be in existence as at the date of the claim. This is proved by courts taking judicial notice of state practice and *opinio juris* [§§ 2.13–2.16]. To be accepted as part of domestic law the rule of customary international law cannot be inconsistent with express statutory provisions.**

13.5.1. **There must be an established rule of international law:**

- *JH Rayner (Mincing Lane) Ltd v Department of Trade and Industry* [1990] 2 AC 418 (HL), 513B–C (Lord Oliver: 'A rule of international law becomes a rule—whether accepted into domestic law or not—only when it is certain and is accepted generally by the body of civilised nations; and it is for those who assert the rule to demonstrate it, if necessary before the International Court of Justice. It is certainly not for a domestic tribunal in effect to legislate a rule into existence for the purposes of domestic law and on the basis of material that is wholly indeterminate.');
- *Compania Naviera Vascongado v SS Cristina* [1938] AC 485 (HL), 497 (Lord Macmillan considering that before a rule of customary international law can become part of domestic law it must 'have attained the position of general acceptance by civilised nations.') [§ **13.2**];
- *Trendtex Trading Corp v Central Bank of Nigeria* [1977] QB 529 (CA), 569 (Stephenson LJ on the need to prove international law: [§ **13.4.1**]), *cf* 552–553 (Lord Denning on the notion that rules of international law arise out of a consensus of nations) [§ **2.14.3**];
- *cf JH Rayner (Mincing Lane) Ltd v Department of Trade and Industry* [1989] Ch 72 (CA), 207F–208A (Nourse LJ: 'The proposition that international law can only form part of English law if there is an established rule in point is supported by the views of several respected judges, their authority being by no means diminished by the fact that some of them were expressed in support of the doctrine of transformation.' At 220B–E considering an uncertain question of international law: 'Nowadays it is most unusual, if not unknown, for an English court which must decide a question of principle to be confronted with a freedom from authority not generally experienced since the times of Lord Hardwicke and Lord Mansfield. Like every freedom, it carries with it great responsibilities. We must not shirk the decision and, where it may govern a law which is the property of all civilised nations, we must be self-effacing as to our own. Above all, there being no clear and definite consensus amongst the sources which we may consult, we ought to welcome an opportunity of supplementing them with reason and justice . . . It cannot have been for nothing that

Grotius taught us: "The law obliges us to do what is proper, not simply what is just".' See also 208A–210B).

13.5.2. **Customary international law excluded where inconsistent with statute:**

- *R v Secretary of State for the Home Department, Ex parte Thakrar* [1974] QB 684 (CA), 708A–E (Orr LJ: '[A] rule of international law cannot be treated as incorporated into English municipal law where to do so would be inconsistent with the provisions of a statute . . . if it had been intended to preserve any rule of international law not embraced in the [comprehensive] code [the Immigration Act 1971], it is in my judgment clear that express reference would have been made to the rule in question.' Concluding that, from section 3(1) and the long title of the Immigration Act 1971, it was clear that it could not be construed as preserving a duty in international law for the United Kingdom to receive any of its nationals, expelled by another state).

13.5.3. **Customary international law to be considered as at date of claim:**

- *Littrell v United States of America (No 2)* [1995] 1 WLR 82 (CA), 89C–D (Rose LJ: '[I]n the absence of statutory enactment, it is the common law including the incorporated rules of customary international law, which identifies and defines the extent of sovereign immunity. And in my judgment it is the common law at the time when the claim is made which is determinative. I am unable to accept that the viability of the plaintiff's claim should be determined by the state of customary international law as reflected in the common law 40 years ago.').

13.6. Rules of customary international law may become part of domestic law by being embodied in statutes.

13.6.1. **Statutes may embody rules of customary international law:**
Illustrations:

- *R v Bow Street Magistrate, Ex parte Pinochet* [2000] 1 AC 61 (HL), 110B–C (Lord Nicholls) and *R v Bow Street Magistrate, Ex p Pinochet (No 3)* [2000] 1 AC 147 (HL), 268H–269A (Lord Millett) (both noting that section 20 of the State Immunity Act 1978 reflects the rule of customary international law that a current head of state is immune from criminal process);
- *Compania Naviera Vascongado v SS Cristina* [1938] AC 485 (HL), 516B–D (Lord Maugham, in the context of sovereign immunity: 'This immunity, be it noted, has been admitted in all civilised countries on similar principles and with nearly the

same limits. It has been by implication admitted in this country by the statute 7 Anne, c.12, passed in consequence of the taking of the Russian Ambassador from his coach and his imprisonment under the old law by a private suitor. The statute has always been regarded as merely declaratory of the common law.').

13.6.2. **Statutes embodying rules of customary international law do not provide evidence of those rules:**

- *I Congreso del Partido* [1983] 1 AC 244 (HL), 260B–E (Lord Wilberforce, considering whether various transactions were protected by sovereign immunity in the context of the State Immunity Act 1978: '[T]o argue from the terms of the statute to establish what international law provides is to stand the accepted argument on its head. In the particular case, it is clear that international law, in a general way, in 1978, gave support to a "restrictive" theory of state immunity, we do not need the statute to make this good. On the other hand, the precise limits of the doctrine were, as the voluminous material placed at our disposal well shows, still in course of development and in many respects uncertain. If one state chooses to lay down by enactment certain limits, that is by itself no evidence that those limits are generally to be accepted by states. And particularly enacted limits may be (or presumed to be) not inconsistent with general international law—the latter being in a state of uncertainty—without affording evidence what that law is.').

(3) Applying Customary International Law in Domestic Courts

A. Customary International Law as the Applicable Law

13.7. **Where the use of a rule of customary international law is contemplated, and prior to determining the existence of a relevant rule, it must be ascertained whether customary international law, as opposed to the national law of a given state, is the applicable law. It is only if it is, indeed, the applicable law that it becomes necessary to examine the existence and scope of the relevant rule.**

Illustration:

- *R v Bow Street Magistrate, Ex parte Pinochet* [2000] 1 AC 61 (HL), 115F–H (Lord Steyn: 'Is [the] question [what should be regarded as official acts performed in the exercise of functions of a head of state] to be considered from the vantage point of the municipal law of Chile, where most of the acts were committed, or in the light of the principles of customary international law? Municipal law cannot be decisive as to where the line is to be drawn . . . [T]he distinction between official acts performed in the exercise of functions as a head of state [and covered by state immunity] and acts not satisfying these requirements must depend on the rules of international law . . . Given [the] state of international law [condemning genocide, torture, hostage-taking and crimes against humanity], it seems to me difficult to maintain that the commission of such high crimes may amount to acts performed in the exercise of the functions of a head of state.').

B. *Domestic Approach to Identifying Customary International Law*

13.8. **Where courts are required to determine the existence of a rule of customary international law, the range of source material which may be consulted and the weight to be accorded to it are matters for judicial discretion. Examples of sources which have been used are: international instruments and treaties, decisions of foreign and domestic courts, academic writings and research papers.**

- *In re Piracy Jure Gentium* [1934] AC 586 (PC), 588F–589B (Viscount Sankey LC: 'In considering such a question [whether there is a particular rule of customary international law], the Board is permitted to consult and act upon a wider range of authority than that which it examines when the question for determination is one of municipal law only. The sources from which international law is derived include treaties between various States, State papers, municipal Acts of Parliament and the decisions of municipal Courts and last, but not least, opinions of jurisconsults or text-book writers. It is a process of inductive reasoning. It must be remembered that in the strict sense international law still has no legislature, no executive and no judiciary, though in a certain sense there is now an international judiciary in the Hague Tribunal and attempts are being made by the League of Nations to draw up codes of international law. Speaking generally, in embarking upon international law, their Lordships are to a great extent in the realm of opinion, and in estimating the value of opinion it is permissible not only to seek a consensus of views, but to select what appear to be the better views upon the question.');
- *Compania Naviera Vascongado v Steamship 'Cristina'* [1938] AC 485 (HL), 497 (Lord Macmillan giving examples of sources of international law) [§ **13.2**];
- *R v Keyn* (1876) 2 Ex D 63 [§ **13.2**].

Illustrations:

- *R v Bow Street Magistrate, Ex parte Pinochet (No 3)* [2000] 1 AC 147 (HL), 281H–284G (Lord Phillips considering the scope of immunity *rationae personae* by reference to: custom, judicial decisions, academic writings and general principles of law recognised by all civilised nations);

- *A v Secretary of State for the Home Department* [2004] UKHL 56 [2005] 2 WLR 87, [69] (Lord Bingham determining whether international law sanctions the detention of aliens in time of war or public emergency, by considering the Geneva Convention Relative to the Protection of Civilian Persons in Time of War 1949, the Geneva Convention Relating to the Status of Refugees 1951 (and interpretative material: Robinson, *Convention Relating to the Status of Refugees: Its History, Contents and Interpretation* (1953), Grahl-Madsen, *Commentary on the Refugee Convention 1951* (republished by UNHCR 1997), UNHCR Executive Committee Conclusion 44 in the Report of the 37th Session (1986): 'Detention of Refugees and Asylum Seekers', UNHCR Revised Guidelines on 'Applicable Criteria and Standards Relating to the Detention of Asylum Seekers' (February 1999), Goodwin-Gill, *The Refugee in International Law* (1996)), the Convention on the Status of Stateless Persons 1954, the International Covenant on Civil and Political Rights (including interpretative material: Joseph, Schultz and Castan, *The International Covenant on Civil and Political Rights: Cases, Materials and Commentary* (2004)), the UN Economic and Social Council, Commission on Human Rights Eighth Session Report (10 May 1952)), the UN Declaration on the Human Rights of Individuals who are not Nationals of the Country in which they Live 1985, the EC Treaty, the ECHR and American authorities);
- *R (European Roma Rights Centre) v Immigration Officer at Prague Airport* [2004] UKHL 55 [2005] 2 WLR 1, [46] (Lord Steyn, determining the development of the rule of customary international law of non-discrimination by considering the Universal Declaration of Human Rights, its 'direct descendants': the ECHR and Refugee Convention, the development of comprehensive and strong legal norms against discrimination in international treaties post-1965, case law of the ICJ and writings of jurists), [103] (Baroness Hale, in considering the development of the same rule referring to UN General Assembly Resolutions 57/195 (adopted 18 December 2002) and 58/160 (adopted 22 December 2003));
- *Sepet v Secretary of State for the Home Department* [2003] UKHL 15 [2003] 1 WLR 856, [9–20] (Lord Bingham considering whether there is a right to refuse to undertake military service on grounds of conscience by analysing leading human rights instruments, the UNHCR Handbook on the Refugee Convention, General Comment No 22 of the UN Human Rights Committee, the Joint Position of the Council of Europe on the harmonised application of Article 1 of the Refugee

Convention, the Charter of Fundamental Rights of the EU and a draft directive of the Council of the EU), [39–52] (Lord Hoffmann, for the same reason, examining leading human rights instruments (including the intentions of the framers), material illustrating the movement of international opinion since the major relevant instruments were adopted (eg General Comments of the UN Human Rights Committee), case law, and the opinions of jurists. State practice was not fully considered because of the lack of uniformity of practice.);

- *R v Bow Street Magistrate, Ex parte Pinochet (No 3)* [2000] 1 AC 147 (HL), 258A–260A and 263F–265B (Lord Hutton considering whether certain crimes are so grave that they constitute crimes under international law by considering international instruments, statutes setting up international tribunals (eg the Statute of the International Criminal Court), a directive of the UN General Assembly, a report of the International Law Commission, and draft codes of the International Law Commission);
- *R v Bow Street Magistrate, Ex parte Pinochet* [2000] 1 AC 61 (HL), 97B–98H (Lord Lloyd (dissenting) identifying whether there was a distinction between torture and other crimes in state practice, by considering case law, the adoption of amnesties (for those who have committed crimes against humanity, including torture), the existence of special international tribunals for the trial of those accused of crimes against humanity and international conventions);
- *Krotov v Secretary of State for the Home Department* [2004] EWCA Civ 69 [2004] 1 WLR 1825, [30–38] (Potter LJ holding that persecution under Article 1A(2) of the Refugee Convention could be established by the existence of punishment for a genuine, conscientious refusal to participate in a conflict where combatants would be required to act in breach of basic human rules of conduct by considering the 'core of humanitarian norms' prohibiting, inter alia, genocide, rape and torture, recognised by the international community as illustrated by: the four Geneva Conventions on the Law of Armed Conflict (1949), Additional Protocol II to the General Conventions relating to the Protection of Victims of Non-International Armed Conflicts (1977), case law of the ICJ, and a Joint Position statement from the Council of Europe (of 4 March 1996));
- *In re Piracy Jure Gentium* [1934] AC 586 (PC) (in considering whether actual robbery is an essential element of the crime of piracy *jure gentium*, regard was had to Acts of Parliament, opinions of jurisconsults and text book writers (Coke, Molloy, Casaregis, Moore, Hale, Hawkins, Blackstone, East, Hume, Alison, Archbold, Wheaton, Ortolan, Bluntschli, Calvo, Phillimore, Hall and Kenny), decided cases, the proceedings of

a sub-committee of the League of Nations, and the *Oxford English Dictionary*);

- *West Rand Central Gold Mining Company Limited v The King* [1905] 2 KB 391 (DC) (considering the proposition (that by international law a conquering country is bound to fulfil the obligations of the conquered) as a matter of principle, and by reference to the writings of jurists (Grotius, Barbeyrac, Hall, Halleck, Wheaton, Calvo, Heffter, Huber, and Westlake) and decisions of the English courts), 402 (Lord Alverstone CJ: 'The reference which [learned writers on international law] not infrequently make to stipulations in particular treaties as acceptable evidence of international law is as little convincing as the attempt . . . to establish a trade custom which is binding without being stated, by adducing evidence of express stipulations to be found in a number of particular contracts.').

C. *Customary International Law and Treaties*

13.9. **The relationship between customary international law and treaties is important in several respects in international law. For example, treaties may embody rules of customary international law [§ 2.7], they may provide guidance when considering whether a rule of customary international law exists [§ 13.8] or has changed [§ 13.14.2], and treaties may be interpreted by considering customary international law (Vienna Convention on the Law of Treaties, Article 31(3)(c): [§ 4.4; § 4.12]). Despite this cross-fertilisation, it is important, as a matter of domestic law, to maintain a distinction between these sources of international law because they are treated differently in domestic law. Therefore, for example, it is necessary, when seeking to rely on international law to show that it exists as an independent rule of customary international law rather than being ancillary to, or arising out of, an unincorporated treaty obligation (because it will then be exposed to the restraining effect of the principles of non-justiciability and no direct effect [chapter 8]).**

Illustrations:

- *R v Lyons* [2002] UKHL 44 [2003] 1 AC 976, [39] (Lord Hoffmann, pre-HRA, responding to the argument that although the ECHR was not part of English law, effect should be given to the judgments of the ECtHR in relation to these particular appellants because the United Kingdom was bound by Article 46, ECHR, to abide by the judgment and there was a rule of customary international law which required a state responsible for an internationally wrongful act to make restitution by restoring the *status quo ante*: 'My Lords, I cannot but admire the resourcefulness with which [counsel] has painstakingly built this elaborate forensic structure. But I think that its foundations rest upon sand. In the end it comes to nothing more than an attempt to give direct domestic effect to an international treaty . . . The obligation to make restitution may, as [counsel] says, be a developing or even established feature of customary international law. But it is in the present case ancillary to a treaty obligation. It is infringement of the treaty obligation to secure Convention rights to everyone within the jurisdiction that is said to give rise to the obligation to make restitution. [Counsel] himself described it as a secondary obligation in the sense used by Lord Diplock in *Photo Production Ltd v Securicor Transport Ltd* [1980] AC 827 at 848–849. But if there is no enforceable primary obligation, how can its breach give rise to an enforceable secondary obligation?');

- *R (CND) v The Prime Minister* [2002] EWHC 2777 (Admin) [2002] All ER (D) 245 (Dec), [61] (Simon Brown LJ: '[Counsel for the Applicant] sought to avoid the application of that rule [that international treaties do not form part of domestic law] by contending first that this case involves a principle of customary international law (indeed, a principle having the status of "jus cogens") prohibiting the unauthorised use of force and that customary international law forms part of domestic law. It seems to me, however, that recourse to customary international law cannot assist the claimant since what is directly in issue is not a principle of customary international law but the meaning and effect of Resolution 1441, an international instrument not forming part of customary international law.').

(4) Domestically Recognised Rules of Customary International Law

13.10. Diverse rules of customary international law have been identified and applied as part of domestic law, as demonstrated by the illustrations below.

13.10.1. **Need for precision in formulating rules of customary international law:**

- *Hutchinson v Newbury Magistrates' Court* (2000) ILR 499, [11] (Buxton LJ noting the need for: '[P]recision that is required in formulating any alleged rule of customary law, and the degree of certainty with which it must be established. That is because the rules contended for are indeed rules: not merely principles or aspirations or general understandings, but statements that are sufficiently precise and mandatory to form part of the lex lata of an individual state.' At [23] and [28] concluding that no rule of customary international law was discernible from the ICJ's Advisory Opinion on the Legality of the Threat or Use of Nuclear Weapons.)

13.10.2. **Sovereign immunity:**
Illustrations:

- *I Congreso del Partido* [1983] 1 AC 244 (HL), 261A–F (Lord Wilberforce: 'Until 1975 it would have been true to say that England, almost alone of influential trading nations . . . continued to adhere to a pure, absolute, doctrine of state immunity in all cases.' After reviewing the development of a restrictive theory of sovereign immunity, at 267B–D: 'The conclusion which emerges is that in considering, under the "restrictive" theory whether state immunity should be granted or not, the court must consider the whole context in which the claim against the state is made, with a view to deciding whether the relevant acts(s) upon which the claim is based, should, in that context, be considered as fairly within an area of activity, trading or commercial, or otherwise of a private law character, in which the state has chosen to engage, or whether the relevant act(s) should be considered as having been done outside that area, and within the sphere of governmental or sovereign authority.');
- *R v Bow Street Magistrate, Ex parte Pinochet* [2000] 1 AC 61 (HL), 110B (Lord Nicholls expressing 'no doubt' that a current head of state is immune from criminal process under customary international law), 113D (Lord Steyn considering that current heads of state are immune from civil and criminal process in English courts (immunity *rationae personae*)). See also *R v Bow Street Magistrate, Ex parte Pinochet (No 3)* [2000] 1 AC 147 (HL), 201G (Lord Browne-Wilkinson), 265F (Lord Saville), 268G–269C (Lord Millet);
- *Holland v Lampen-Wolfe* [2000] 1 WLR 1573 (HL), 1583E–F (Lord Millett considering that it is an established rule of customary international law that one state cannot be sued in the courts of another for acts performed *jure imperii*; that this is confirmed by the European Convention on State Immunity (1972)(Cmnd 5081); and that these international obligations are given effect in the United Kingdom by the State Immunity Act 1978 and the common law.);
- *Jones v The Ministry of the Interior Al-Mamlaka Al-Arabiya* [2004] EWCA Civ 1394 [2005] UKHRR 57, [104–106] (Lord Phillips, MR summarising the nature of sovereign immunity);
- *Rahimtoola v Nizam of Hyderabad* [1958] AC 379 (HL) (setting aside writ against Rahimtoola, being an agent for the Sovereign State of Pakistan);
- *Thai-Europe Tapioca Service Ltd v Government of Pakistan* [1975] 1 WLR 1485 (CA) (sovereign immunity upheld

where none of the incidents of a transaction, shipment of fertiliser from Poland to Pakistan, took place within the jurisdiction).

13.10.3. **Jurisdiction:**
Illustrations:

- *R v Bow Street Magistrate, Ex parte Pinochet (No 3)* [2000] 1 AC 147 (HL), 288H–289A (Lord Phillips: '[I]t is still an open question whether international law recognises universal jurisdiction in respect of international crimes—that is the right, under international law, of the courts of any state to prosecute for such crimes wherever they occur.'), 276A–B (Lord Millett: 'Every state has jurisdiction under customary international law to exercise extraterritorial jurisdiction in respect of international crimes which satisfy the relevant criteria . . . The jurisdiction of the English criminal court is usually statutory, but it is supplemented by the common law. Customary international law is part of the common law, and accordingly I consider that the English courts have and always have had extraterritorial criminal jurisdiction in respect of crimes of universal jurisdiction under customary international law.');
- *R v Keyn* (1876) 2 Ex D 63, 161 (Cockburn CJ: 'On board a foreign ship on the high seas, the foreigner is liable to the law of the foreign ship only. It is only when a foreign ship comes into the ports or waters of another state that the ship and those on board become subject to the local law. These are the established rules of the law of nations. They have been adopted into our own municipal law, and must be taken to form a part of it.' This was later modified by the Territorial Waters Jurisdiction Act 1878: see *Pianka v The Queen* [1979] AC 107 (PC) 118D–120H and 128D–129D);
- *Chung Chi Cheung v The King* [1939] AC 160 (JC), 167E–G (Lord Atkin considering the jurisdictional immunities of a public ship in foreign waters).

13.10.4. **Right to refuse entry to aliens:**
Illustrations:

- *Attorney-General for Canada v Cain* [1906] AC 542 (JC), 546B–D (Lord Atkinson: 'One of the rights possessed by the supreme power in every State is the right to refuse to permit an alien to enter that State, to annex what conditions it pleases to the permission to enter it, and to expel or deport from the State, at pleasure, even a friendly alien, especially if it considers his presence in the State opposed to its peace, order and good government, or to its social or material interests . . . by the law of nations the supreme power in every State has the right to make laws for the exclusion of expulsion of aliens, and to enforce those laws.');

- *R (European Roma Rights Centre) v Immigration Officer at Prague Airport* [2004] UKHL 55 [2005] 2 WLR 1, [11] (Lord Bingham: 'The power to admit, exclude and expel aliens was among the earliest and most widely recognised powers of the sovereign state.' See also [12–13] considering further that 'those fleeing from persecution have had no right to be admitted and no right of asylum.');
- *A v Secretary of State for the Home Department* [2004] UKHL 56 [2005] 2 WLR 87, [69] (Lord Bingham: 'The first step in this argument was to assert the historic right of sovereign states over aliens entering or residing in their territory. Historically this was the position . . . But a sovereign state may by international treaty restrict its absolute power over aliens within or seeking to enter its territory, and in recent years states have increasingly done so.'), [103] (Lord Hope: 'The right of the state to control immigration has, of course, long been recognised in international law.' See similarly [134]);
- *ID v Home Office* [2005] EWCA Civ 38 [2005] INLR 278, [71] (Brooke LJ noting that the power of a state to control immigration is 'well-recognised in international law').

13.10.5. **Torture** [§ **2.16.2**]:
Illustrations:

- *R v Bow Street Magistrate, Ex parte Pinochet (No 3)* [2000] 1 AC 147 (HL), 198B–G (Lord Browne-Wilkinson considering that the prohibition on torture has the character of *jus cogens* or a peremptory norm; it became an international crime in the highest sense before the Torture Convention of 1984, and the *jus cogens* nature of torture justifies states taking universal jurisdiction over torture wherever committed.);
- *Jones v The Ministry of the Interior Al-Mamlaka Al-Arabiya* [2004] EWCA Civ 1394 [2005] UKHRR 57, [31] (Mance LJ: 'It is common ground . . . That systematic torture would, if established, constitute a high international crime contrary to *jus cogens*—or peremptory international law.'), [108] (Lord Phillips MR: 'The crime of torture has acquired a special status under international law. It is an international crime or a breach of *jus cogens*. That status is reflected by the International Convention against Torture and other Cruel, Inhuman or Degrading Treatment or Punishment 1984.').

13.10.6. **Detention:**
Illustrations:

- *R (Abbasi) v Secretary of State for Foreign and Commonwealth Affairs* [2002] EWCA Civ 1598 [2003] UKHRR 76, [63–64] (Lord Phillips recognising as a 'fundamental part of human rights law' the principle that every imprisonment is prima facie unlawful and requires to be justified as being a legal measure);

- *A v Secretary of State for the Home Department* [2002] EWCA Civ 1502 [2004] QB 335, [130] (Brooke LJ: '[B]oth customary international law and the international treaties by which this country is bound expressly reserve the power of a state in time of war or similar public emergency to detain aliens on grounds of national security when it would not necessarily detain its own nationals on those grounds.') (HL is at [2004] UKHL 56 [2005] 2 WLR 87).

13.10.7. **Use of force:**
Illustration:
- *Kuwait Ariways Corp v Iraqi Airways Co* [2002] UKHL 19 [2002] 2 AC 883, [22] (Lord Nicholls: 'Article 2(4) of the United Nations Charter provides that in their international relations all members shall refrain from the use of force against the territorial integrity of any state. This is also a principle of customary international law binding on states independently of the provisions of the Charter.'), [114] (Lord Steyn: 'It is generally accepted that the principles of the United Nations Charter prohibiting the use of force have the character of jus cogens, i.e. is part of peremptory public international law, permitting no derogation.').

13.10.8. **Payment of debt:**
Illustration:
- *JH Rayner (Mincing Lane) Ltd v Department of Trade and Industry* [1989] Ch 72 (CA), 206F (Nourse LJ (dissenting): '[N]obody would suggest that it is not a principle of international law, conformable with the laws of every civilised nation from time immemorial, that a debtor shall be liable to pay his debts so far as he has the wherewithal to do so').

13.10.9. **Piracy:**
Illustration:
- *In re Piracy Jure Gentium* [1934] AC 586 (PC), 588E (Viscount Sankey LC: 'Actual robbery is not an essential element in the crime of piracy jure gentium. A frustrated attempt to commit a piratical robbery is equally piracy jure gentium.').

13.11. **The difficulties inherent in proving that there exists a particular rule of customary international law are illustrated by the examples below, where such attempts have failed.**

13.11.1. **Sovereign immunity:**
Illustrations:
- *R v Bow Street Magistrate, Ex parte Pinochet (No 3)* [2000] 1 AC 147 (HL), 242F (Lord Hope considering that there is no rule of

customary international law that high crimes, regarded as *jus cogens* under customary international law, are outside the immunity accorded to former heads of state);

- *Jones v The Ministry of the Interior Al-Mamlaka Al-Arabiya* [2004] EWCA Civ 1394 [2005] UKHRR 57, [96] (Mance LJ: '[A] foreign state cannot possess (either under international law or under English common law and the United Kingdom's [State Immunity Act 1978]) any absolute right to claim immunity in respect of civil claims against its officials for systematic torture, even committed outside the country of suit.').

13.11.2. **Conscientious objection:**
Illustration:

- *Sepet v Secretary of State for the Home Department* [2003] UKHL 15 [2003] 1 WLR 856 (there is no internationally recognised right to refuse to undertake military service on grounds of conscience).

13.11.3. **Diplomatic intervention:**
Illustration:

- *R (Abbasi) v Secretary Of State For Foreign & Commonwealth Affairs* [2002] EWCA Civ 1598 [2003] UKHRR 76, [69] (Lord Phillips MR: 'It is clear that international law has not yet recognised that a State is under a duty to intervene by diplomatic or other means to protect a citizen who is suffering or threatened with injury in a foreign State.').

13.11.4. **Right to asylum:**
Illustration:

- *T v Immigration Officer* [1996] AC 742 (HL), 754, 758 (Lord Mustill observing that there is no right to asylum in international law).

13.11.5. **Nuclear weapons:**
Illustrations:

- *Marchiori v The Environment Agency* [2002] EWCA Civ 3 [2002] EuLR 225, [46] (Laws LJ considering that the ICJ's *Advisory Opinion on the Legality of the Threat or Use of Nuclear Weapons* [§ **2.18**] did not disclose that the maintenance of nuclear weapons as a deterrent was contrary to humanitarian principles of international law);
- *Hutchinson v Newbury Magistrates' Court* (2000) ILR 499, [23], [28] (Buxton LJ concluding that no rule of customary international law was discernible from the ICJ's *Advisory Opinion on the Legality of the Threat or Use of Nuclear Weapons* [§ **2.18**]).

13.11.6. **War of aggression:**

Illustration:

- *R (Manson) v Workman* [2003] EWHC 2720 (Admin), [4] (Silber J expressing no opinion on whether there is an international crime of planning, preparing and initiating a war of aggression but concluding that it had not been incorporated 'in any way' into English criminal law).

13.12. **Where no relevant rule of customary international law is discernible from state practice and *opinio juris* [§§ 2.13–2.16], treaties may provide an alternative source of guidance.**

Illustration:

- *R v Bow Street Magistrate, Ex parte Pinochet* [2000] 1 AC 61 (HL), 81D–G (Lord Slynn (dissenting): '[I]t is necessary to consider what is needed [in the absence of both a rule of customary international law and a general international convention] to define or limit the former head of state immunity in particular cases. In my opinion, it is necessary to find provision in an international convention to which the state asserting, and the state being asked to refuse, the immunity of a former head of state for an official act is a party; the convention must clearly define a crime against international law and require or empower a state to prevent or prosecute the crime, whether or not committed in its jurisdiction and whether or not committed by one of its nationals; it must make it clear that a national court has jurisdiction to try a crime alleged against a former head of state, or that having been head of state is no defence and that expressly or impliedly the immunity is not to apply so as to bar proceedings against him. The convention must be given the force of law in the national courts of the state; in a dualist country like the United Kingdom that means by legislation, so that with the necessary procedures and machinery the crime may be prosecuted there in accordance with the conditions to be found in the convention.');
- *R v Bow Street Magistrate, Ex parte Pinochet (No 3)* [2000] 1 AC 147 (HL), 242G–243E (Lord Hope endorsing Lord Slynn's approach in *R v Bow Street Magistrate, Ex parte Pinochet* [2000] 1 AC 61 (HL), 81D–G (see above)).

(5) Changes in Customary International Law

13.13. **Claims that a rule of customary international law has changed must be investigated by considering whether there is sufficient evidence indicative of such a change. The investigation must be cautiously undertaken given the slow, incremental development**

of customary international law and the difficulty in assessing when, as well as whether, a shifting change has crystallised into a new development.

13.13.1. **Measuring change in rules of customary international law:**

- *Trendtex Trading Corp v Central Bank of Nigeria* [1977] QB 529 (CA), 556 (Lord Denning considering that in order to assess change in rules of customary international law one must ask: is there sufficient evidence to show that the rule of international law has changed? If so, domestic courts should give effect to the change). (Relied upon in *R v Bow Street Magistrate, Ex parte Pinochet* [2000] 1 AC 61 (HL), 77D–E (Lord Slynn (dissenting)).

13.13.2. **Need for caution when considering changes in customary international law:**

- *R v Bow Street Magistrate, Ex parte Pinochet* [2000] 1 AC 61 (HL), 80D–F (Lord Slynn (dissenting) asking whether customary international law on sovereign immunity had changed: '[I]t is a difficult question. It is difficult partly because changes in international law take place slowly as states modify existing principles. It is difficult because in many aspects of this problem the appropriate principles of international law have not crystallised. There is still much debate and it seems to me still much uncertainty so that a national judge should proceed carefully. He may have to say that the position as to state practice has not reached the stage when he can identify a positive rule at the particular time when he has to consider the position.').

13.13.3. **Changes in customary international law may be given effect without legislation:**

- *The Phillipine Admiral* [1977] AC 373 (PC), 403A–C (Lord Cross: 'So counsel for the appellant could and did argue with force that granted that the restrictive theory [of sovereign immunity] was to be preferred, the courts should leave it to the government to ratify the 1926 and 1972 Conventions [the Brussels Convention for the Unification of Certain Rules concerning the Immunity of State-owned Ships and the European Convention on State Immunity] and to introduce the legislation necessary to make them part of our law and should not tamper with the law as so far declared in England by applying the restrictive theory to actions in rem. But their Lordships—while recognising that there is force in that argument—are not prepared to accept it. Thinking as they do that the restrictive theory is more consonant with justice they do not think that they should be deterred from applying it so far as they can by the thought that the resulting position may be somewhat anomalous.').

13.13.4. **Potential for growth of rules of customary international law:**

- *Jones v The Ministry of the Interior Al-Mamlaka Al-Arabiya* [2004] EWCA Civ 1394 [2005] UKHRR 57, [80] (Mance LJ: '[I]nternational thinking and jurisprudence have over the last half century moved beyond the narrow view that international law is solely concerned with or enforceable by states. The United Nations Charter of Fundamental Rights and Freedoms, the European Convention on Human Rights, the reasoning of United States courts from the landmark case in *Fiiartiga* onwards and the Torture Convention demonstrate a shift of institutional attention towards the protection of individual human rights.');
- *R v Bow Street Magistrate, Ex parte Pinochet* [2000] 1 AC 61 (HL), 110C–F (Lord Nicholls making observations on state immunity: 'A broad principle of international law, according former public officials a degree of personal immunity against prosecution in other states, would be consistent with the rationale underlying [section 20 of the State Immunity Act 1978]. It would also be consistent with changes in the way countries are governed . . . The conduct of affairs of state is often in the hands of government ministers, with the head of state having a largely ceremonial role. With this change in the identity of those who act for the state, it would be attractive for personal immunity to be available to all former public officials, including a former head of state, in respect of acts which are properly attributable to the state itself. One might expect international law to develop along these lines, although the personal immunity such a principle affords would be largely covered also by the act of state doctrine.').

13.14. A wide range of sources is available when assessing whether rules of customary international law have changed.

Illustrations:

- *Sepet v Secretary of State for the Home Department* [2003] UKHL 15 [2003] 1 WLR 856 (in determining whether there was a right to refuse to undertake military service on grounds of conscience reference was made to the UNHCR Handbook (1979), a Decision of the UN Human Rights Committee (*LTK v Finland* (1985) 94 ILR 396), General Comment No 22 of the UN Human Rights Committee (30 July 1993), the Joint Position adopted by the Council of the European Union on the harmonised application of the term 'refugee' in Article 1, Refugee Convention (4 March 1996), the Charter of Fundamental Rights of the European Union (18 December 2000), and a draft directive of the Council of the European Union on minimum standards for the qualification of third country nationals as refugees (28 November 2002): see [9–16] (Lord Bingham), [48–52] (Lord Hoffmann));

- *R v Bow Street Magistrate, Ex parte Pinochet* [2000] 1 AC 61 (HL), 77E– 78C (Lord Slynn (dissenting), examining whether customary international law on state immunity had changed in the light of developments in international crimes, considering: the Convention against the Taking of Hostages 1979 and the Convention on the Prevention and Suppression of the Crime of Genocide 1948. At 78C–H referring to the Nuremberg Charter: Charter of International Military Tribunal (1945), the Tokyo Convention: Charter of the International Military Tribunal for the trial of the major war criminals in the Far East (1946), Statute of the International Tribunal for the Former Yugoslavia (1993), Statute of the International Tribunal for Rwanda (1994) and Rome Statute of the International Criminal Court (1998). At 79B, using reports of the International Law Commission, Resolutions of the UN General Assembly and academic writings).

13.14.1. **Using state practice to assess change:**
Illustration:

- *The Phillipine Admiral* [1977] AC 373 (PC), 400A–B (Lord Cross: 'According to a list compiled by reference to the various textbooks on international law and put before their Lordships by agreement between the parties there are now comparatively few countries outside the Commonwealth which can be counted adherents of the absolute theory [of sovereign immunity].').

13.14.2. **Using international conventions and conferences to assess change:**
Illustrations:

- *R v Bow Street Magistrate, Ex parte Pinochet* [2000] 1 AC 61 (HL), 77E– 78C (Lord Slynn (dissenting)) [§ **13.14**];
- *Sepet v Secretary of State for the Home Department* [2003] 1 WLR 856 (HL) [§ **13.14**];
- *Jones v The Ministry of the Interior Al-Mamlaka Al-Arabiya* [2004] EWCA Civ 1394 [2005] UKHRR 57, [18–21] (Mance LJ, using Articles 4, 5 and 14(1) of the Torture Convention in considering whether customary international law rules on sovereign immunity had changed);
- *The Phillipine Admiral* [1977] AC 373 (PC), 394H–395C and 401D–H (Lord Cross, referring to the Brussels Convention for the Unification of Certain Rules concerning the Immunity of State-owned Ships (1926) and the European Convention on State Immunity (1972) (together with its explanatory report) in considering the limits of sovereign immunity);
- *Compania Naviera Vascongado v SS Cristina* [1938] AC 485 (HL), 512E–513B (Lord Wright considering the immunity of

public ships by reference to the International Convention for the Unification of Certain Rules concerning the Immunity of State-owned ships, of 10 April 1926), 522C–E (Lord Maugham referring to 'various resolutions of the Conference of London of 1922, of the Conference of Gothenburg of 1923 and of the Genoa Conference of 1925. Three Conferences not being deemed sufficient there was yet another in Brussels in the year 1926.').

13.14.3. **Using charters and statutes creating international tribunals to assess change:**
Illustration:

- *R v Bow Street Magistrate, Ex parte Pinochet* [2000] 1 AC 61 (HL), 78C–H (Lord Slynn (dissenting)) [§ **13.14**];

13.14.4. **Using decisions of domestic courts to assess change:**
Illustrations:

- *Jones v The Ministry of the Interior Al-Mamlaka Al-Arabiya* [2004] EWCA Civ 1394 [2005] UKHRR 57, [32–43] (Mance LJ, considering domestic case law in determining the scope of sovereign immunity).
- *The Phillipine Admiral* [1977] AC 373 (PC), 391F–397G (Lord Cross considering whether the theory of absolute immunity was applicable to an action in rem against a ship by reviewing domestic case law);
- *R v Bow Street Magistrate, Ex parte Pinochet* [2000] 1 AC 61 (HL), 79B (Lord Slynn (dissenting): 'Movement towards recognition of crimes against international law is to be seen also in the decisions of national courts, in the resolution of the General Assembly of the Untied Nations . . . in the reports of the International Law Commission and in the writings of distinguished international jurists.') [§ **13.14**].

13.14.5. **Using foreign case law and statutory law to assess change:**
Illustrations:

- *Jones v The Ministry of the Interior Al-Mamlaka Al-Arabiya* [2004] EWCA Civ 1394 [2005] UKHRR 57, [32–43] and [58–68] (Mance LJ, considering American, Canadian and Irish case law in determining the scope of sovereign immunity.)
- *I Congreso del Partido* [1983] 1 AC 244 (HL), 263, 265E–267D (Lord Wilberforce, considering developments in sovereign immunity by reference to American, Swiss, Austrian, German and Italian case law);
- *The Phillipine Admiral* [1977] AC 373 (PC), 397H–401D (Lord Cross, considering American and Canadian case law on sovereign immunity);
- *Trendtex Trading Corp v Central Bank of Nigeria* [1977] QB 529 (CA), 555, 558–559 (Lord Denning, considering sovereign

immunity by reference to decisions of courts in Belgium, Holland, the German Federal Republic and the United States. At 557 considering sovereign immunity by reference to a US statute, the Foreign Sovereign Immunities Act 1976).

13.14.6. **Using writings of distinguished international jurists to assess change:**

Illustrations:

- *R v Bow Street Magistrate, Ex parte Pinochet* [2000] 1 AC 61 (HL), 79B (Lord Slynn (dissenting)); [§ **13.14.4**]
- *Trendtex Trading Corp v Central Bank of Nigeria* [1977] QB 529 (CA), 555 (Lord Denning referring to the writings of Sir Hersch Lauterpacht in relation to changes in sovereign immunity), 563 (Stephenson LJ considering the writings of Professor Lauterpacht and Dr F A Mann);

13.14.7. **Using commercial reality to assess change:**

Illustration:

- *Trendtex Trading Corp. v Central Bank of Nigeria* [1977] QB 529 (CA), 555 (Lord Denning: 'In the last 50 years there has been a complete transformation in the functions of a sovereign state. Nearly every country now engages in commercial activities. It has its departments of state—or creates its own legal entities—which go into the market places of the world. They charter ships. They buy commodities. They issue letters of credit. This transformation has changed the rules of international law relating to sovereign immunity.').

13.14.8. **Using policy developments to assess change:**

Illustration:

- *The Phillipine Admiral* [1977] AC 373 (PC), 398F–399E (Lord Cross, considering developments in the doctrine of sovereign immunity: 'The next landmark in the shift of opinion . . . is a letter—the so-called "Tate letter"—addressed on May 19, 1952, by J.B. Tate, the acting legal adviser of the State Department, to the then acting Attorney-General of the United States notifying him of a change in the policy of the Department of State with regard to the granting of sovereign immunity to foreign governments. The letter first refers to what it describes as two conflicting concepts of sovereign immunity . . . The letter goes on to list those countries whose courts accept the absolute or restrictive theory respectively—including in the former class the United States itself and the British Commonwealth—pointing out that in many of the countries whose courts still applied the absolute theory academic writers tended to support the restrictive theory and that a number of those countries were in fact parties to and had ratified the Brussels Convention of 1926. It refers to the fact that the United States itself does not claim immunity from suit in foreign courts where it would not be entitled to do so according to the restrictive theory, and says that it will hereafter be the policy of the State Department to follow the restrictive theory of sovereign immunity when considering the claims of foreign governments for the grant of such immunity . . . It was not suggested by counsel on either side that their Lordships should seek the help of the Foreign and Commonwealth Office in deciding this appeal by ascertaining which theory of sovereign immunity it favours. But it is perhaps not wholly irrelevant to observe that the later American case of *Rich v Naviera Vacuba SA* (1961) 197 F Supp 710 suggests that if the courts consult the executive on such questions what may begin by guidance as to the principles to be applied may end in cases being decided irrespective of any principle in accordance with the view of the executive as to what is politically expedient.').

(6) Characterising Customary International Law

13.15. **Once it is determined that customary international law is the applicable law [§ 13.7] and that there exists a relevant rule of customary international law [§ 13.5; § 13.8] then it becomes necessary to consider how the rule should be applied and characterised as part of domestic law. The characterisation of applicable rules of customary international law is analogous to the characterisation of foreign law in private international law. Thus, the sorts of questions to be considered include: is the rule of customary international law to be characterised as a procedural or substantive rule? If the latter, what sort of law does it relate to—is it to be characterised as, for example, a rule of contract/criminal/property/tort law? The answers to these questions will assist in determining the scope of application of the customary international law and may be determinative of the case itself.**

13.15.1. **Need to characterise customary international law:**

- *Hutchinson v Newbury Magistrates' Court* (2000) ILR 499, [36–38] (Buxton LJ: 'It is agreed that a rule of international customary law, if it is sufficiently agreed in international law to be such, is translated automatically into English domestic law. The question however is how it should be characterised once it arrives here. [Counsel] contended after some hesitation, that the rule he had formulated [the threat or use of nuclear weapons for deterrent purposes is contrary to customary international law unless pursuant to a clearly-declared policy of envisaged use which is consistent with international law] was in English law a rule of substantive criminal law, making conduct by the Crown or British Government in contravention of it a criminal act. That is a very striking submission in view of contents of the rule and its terms . . . I hold . . . that [counsel] is wrong on this point, and that the unlawfulness of the United Kingdom Government's conduct that is established in English law by the transformation of the rule of international law is unlawfulness of a more elusive nature than is to be found in the substantive criminal law. What exactly that nature is was never satisfactorily explained to us.');

- *Jones & Milling, Olditch & Pritchard v Gloucestershire CPS* [2004] EWCA Crim 1981 [2004] 3 WLR 1362, [42] (Latham LJ, after referring to *Hutchinson v Newbury Magistrates' Court* (see above): 'The question that we have to determine is whether or not the relevant rules [of customary international law] have effect so as to create a crime of aggression in English law. That requires us to consider the extent to which the rule or rules in question can be said to have been recognised in such a way as to give rise to criminal liability in circumstances such as the present. In determining that question, it seems to us that we have to have regard to the way in which the international community has approached the issue in the context of an individual's responsibility for breaches of such rules and his or her amenability to criminal sanctions.' At [43] concluding, on the basis of a working group's paper on the definition and elements of the crime of aggression (Annex II to the Report of the Second Session of the Assembly of States Parties to the International Criminal Court) that section 3 of the Criminal Law Act 1967 did not include a crime of aggression: 'It is difficult to see . . . how it can be said that there is, accordingly, a firmly established rule of international law which establishes a crime of aggression which can be translated into domestic law as a crime in domestic law, where there is no consensus as to an essential element of the crime.').

13.15.2. **Characterising the applicable rule of customary international law as the putative *lex loci contractus*:**

Illustration:

- *Kawasaki Kisen Kabushiki Kaisha of Kobe v Bantham Steamship Co Ltd* [1939] 2 KB 544 (CA), 556B–F (Sir Wilfrid Greene MR, construing a charterparty by giving 'war' its ordinary common sense meaning: '[Counsel] said with regard to the phrase "if war breaks out involving Japan" that the word "war" had not a loose or popular meaning, but a technical meaning, and that technical meaning, he said, is to be found in the principles of international law. Where these principles of international law for this purpose are to be found I must confess that I remain in complete doubt, since the only source of these principles suggested to us was the writings of various writers on international law. It is to be observed, as indeed it was to be expected, that these writers do not speak with one voice, and it is possible to extract from their pages definitions of "war" which not only differ from one another, but which are inconsistent with one another in important respects. I asked for any authority in which for the purpose of the municipal law of this country "war" is in any way defined. No such authority could be suggested . . . to say that English law recognises some technical and ascertainable description of what is meant by "war" appears to me to be a quite impossible proposition.').

13.15.3. **Characterising the applicable rule of customary international law as a domestically punishable crime:**
Illustrations:

- *In re Piracy Jure Gentium* [1934] AC 586 (PC), 589B (Viscount Sankey LC, where charges of piracy brought against Chinese nationals were treated as charges relating to the international law of piracy: 'With regard to crimes as defined by international law, that law has no means of trying or punishing them. The recognition of them as constituting crimes, and the trial and punishment of criminals, are left open to the municipal law of each country.');
- *Jones & Milling, Olditch & Pritchard v Gloucestershire CPS* [2004] EWCA Crim 1981 [2004] 3 WLR 1362, [30] (Latham LJ, commenting on *In re Piracy Jure Gentium* (see above): 'We accept that this case is authority for the proposition that a rule of international law is capable of being incorporated into domestic law so as to found an indictment which, if proved, can result in punishment. To that extent we accept the submission that international law is capable of being incorporated into English law so as to create a crime punishable in law.' At [24], in deciding whether a defendant in criminal proceedings could challenge the legality of the use of force by the United Kingdom Government and others against Iraq: '[T]he question as to whether or not [a rule of customary international law] constitutes a crime depends on an analysis of whether or not a breach of the rule can properly result in penal consequences. The mere fact that an act can clearly be established to be proscribed by international law, and is described as "a crime" does not necessarily of itself determine its character in domestic law unless its characteristics are such that it can be translated into domestic law in a way which would entitle domestic courts to impose punishment.' See also [42] [§ **13.15.1**]).

(7) Customary International Law and Statutory Interpretation

13.16. **Customary international law may be invoked in two ways when interpreting legislation. First, and most importantly, there is a presumption of compatibility that words in statutes should, so far as possible, be construed to comply with customary international law. This is part of the general presumption, based on legal policy, of which the statutory and common law presumptions of compatibility are a part [chapters 9; 10]. The presumption will be displaced where express statutory provisions make clear Parliament's intention to legislate contrary to international law. Secondly, customary international law may provide the background against which statutory interpretation takes place.**

13.16.1. Customary international law and the presumption of compatibility:

- *Salomon v Customs and Excise Commissioners* [1967] 2 QB 116 (CA), 143H (Diplock LJ: '[T]here is a prima facie presumption that Parliament does not intend to act in breach of [public] international law, including therein specific treaty obligations; and if one of the meanings which can reasonably be ascribed to the legislation is consonant with the treaty obligations and another or others are not, the meaning which is consonant is to be preferred.');
- *Smith v East Elloe District Council* [1956] AC 736 (HL), 765B–F (Lord Reid (dissenting): 'There are many cases where general words in a statute are given a limited meaning . . . they are limited so as not to conflict with international law.');
- *Saad, Diriye and Osorio v Secretary of State for the Home Department* [2001] EWCA Civ 2008 (2002) ACD 59, [15–16] (Lord Phillips MR, construing section 8 of the Immigration Appeals Act 1993: 'We approach this case on the basis set out in Bennion on "*Statutory Interpretation*" (3rd ed) p 630 that: "It is a principle of legal policy that the municipal law should conform to public international law. The court, when considering, in relation to the facts of the instant case, which of the opposing constructions of the enactment would give effect to the legislative intention, should presume that the legislator intended to observe this principle." It follows that, absent a clear Parliamentary indication to the contrary, we would expect our primary and delegated legislation to provide a system whereby claimants may have it determined whether they are refugees. It is only that determination which gives them access to [Refugee] Convention rights. We therefore approach questions of construction on that basis.' At [72(iv)–(v)]: 'It is

to be inferred that the United Kingdom does not intend to act in breach of its international obligations . . . the 1993 Act should be construed, so far as possible, on the basis that the United Kingdom intended to comply with its international obligations under the Convention.');

- *R v Keyn* (1876) 2 Ex D 63, 85 (Sir Robert Phillimore: '[I]t is an established principle as to the construction of a statute that it should be construed, if the words will permit, so as to be in accordance with the principles of international law.');
- *Pianka v The Queen* [1979] AC 107 (PC), 123D (Lord Wilberforce, after citing *R v Keyn* (see above): 'Their Lordships agree with the principle of construction, but are of the opinion that there is no principle of international law . . . which impinges on this situation.').

Illustrations:

- *Alcom Ltd v Republic of Colombia* [1984] AC 580 (HL), 600A–C (Lord Diplock, construing the State Immunity Act 1978: 'Of itself, however, the fact that under public international law, including the Vienna Convention [on Diplomatic Relations (1961) (Cmnd 1368)] to which the United Kingdom is a party, the bank account of the Colombian diplomatic mission that the respondents sought to make the subject of garnishee proceedings would have been entitled to immunity from attachment, at the date of the passing of the State Immunity Act 1978, is not sufficient to answer the question with which your Lordships are confronted in the instant appeal [viz, whether, under the Act the English High Court has jurisdiction in garnishee proceedings to order the attachment of the whole or part of the balance standing to the credit of a foreign state in a current account, in order to satisfy a judgment for a sum of money that has been validly obtained against that state by a judgment creditor]. It makes it highly unlikely that Parliament intended to require United Kingdom courts to act contrary to international law unless the clear language of the statute compels such a conclusion; but it does not do more than this.');
- *Commercial and Estates Co of Egypt v The Board of Trade* [1925] 1 KB 271 (CA), 293H–294B (Atkin LJ, construing the Indemnity Act 1920: 'At present I only refer to the right of angary with its accompanying obligation to make compensation, as an indication that where there is a well recognised conditional power to seize the property of neutrals agreeable to international usage, it would be wrong, unless no other construction is possible, to construe general words in domestic legislation, so as to confer a similar power over the goods of neutrals absolved from the condition of paying compensation, and on that ground not consonant with international usage.');
- *R v Kent Justices, Ex parte Lye* [1967] 2 QB 153 (DC), 179D–G (Salmon LJ, construing 'territorial waters' in the Wireless

Telegraphy Act 1949 by reference to the meaning, in both international and municipal law, in 1949), 189B–191E (Blain J construing 'territorial waters' in the Wireless Telegraphy Act 1949 by reference to the meaning in 1949 (waters regarded as territorial by contemporary international usage, in so far as such usage is recognised from time to time in this country) and then confirming that this remained unchanged by reference to the Convention on the Territorial Sea and the Contiguous Zone (ratified by the United Kingdom on 14 March 1960)).

13.16.2. **Presumption of compatibility regarding customary international law yields to express statutory provisions:**

- *Cheney v Conn (Inspector of Taxes)* [1968] 1 WLR 242 (ChD), 245D–E (Ungoed-Thomas J: 'International law is part of the law of the land, but it yields to statute. . . [quoting Maxwell on the Interpretation of Statutes, 10th edn (1953) at p 148]: "But if the statute is unambiguous, its provisions must be followed even if they are contrary to international law".');
- *Allgemeine Gold- und Silberscheideanstalt v Customs and Excise Commissioners* [1980] QB 390 (CA), 404B–D (Lord Denning MR in the context of the forfeiture of coins under section 44 of the Customs and Excise Act 1952: '[Counsel] went on to rely on the general international law. He suggested that private property was not to be confiscated without compensation: that its forfeiture might be an infringement of the general principles of international law. I believe that the general body of opinion in international law is that you should not confiscate the property of an alien by nationalisation except on due compensation. Nevertheless it is clear to my mind that that provision of international law has no application whatever to a case of this kind. This is property which is smuggled into a country contrary to its own laws for the protection of its customs duties and other duties. No ruling of international law invalidates legislation such as we have here in the Customs and Excise Act 1952.'), see similarly 406D–E (Bridge LJ) and 406G–407C (Sir David Cairns).

13.16.3. **Customary international law as background:**

- *Alcom Ltd v Republic of Colombia* [1984] AC 580 (HL), 597G–H (Lord Diplock: 'The [State Immunity Act 1978], as its short title indicates, deals primarily with relations between sovereign states, though its provisions are capable of extension by Order in Council to relations between the United Kingdom and the constituent territories of federal states. Accordingly its provisions fall to be construed against the background of those principles of public international law as are generally recognised by the family of nations.');

- *R v Bow Street Magistrate, Ex parte Pinochet* [2000] 1 AC 61 (HL), 74G–H (Lord Slynn (dissenting): 'The provisions of the [State Immunity Act 1978] "fall to be construed against the background of those principles of public international law as are generally recognised by the family of nations" . . . [citing *Alcom* (see above)]. So also as I see it must the [Vienna Convention on Diplomatic Relations] be interpreted.'), see similarly 99B (Lord Lloyd (dissenting));
- *R v Bow Street Magistrate, Ex parte Pinochet (No 3)* [2000] 1 AC 147 (HL), 203E (Lord Browne-Wilkinson interpreting section 20 of the State Immunity Act 1978: 'Parliament cannot have intended to give heads of state and former heads of state greater rights than they already enjoyed under international law.'), 210C (Lord Goff (dissenting): '[T]here seems to be no reason why the immunity of a head of state under the Act should not be construed as far as possible to accord with his immunity at customary international law, which provides the background against which this statute is set.' Citing *Alcom* (see above)).

Index

www.ingramcontent.com/pod-product-compliance
Lightning Source LLC
LaVergne TN
LVHW020413220926
848484LV00017B/2562/J